Geohell: Imagining History in the Contemporary World

by Matthew Kenner

What follows resulted from a simulation of what it might look like if someone attempted to explain this world from a historical perspective. In reality, you can't explain this world from a historical perspective. History requires the truth, and everything in this world is a lie. In that sense the exercise called for and relied upon a science of imaginary solutions: a science that can only exist in a version of this world where the one difference is the truth can be sufficiently known. If it were real, I would call the science 'pathology'. But it doesn't need a name. It is not really a science; this was just a simulation.

"At length the life of fools is made into a hell on Earth." – Lucretius, Roman poet, 99-55 B.C.E.[i]

Table of Contents

Table of Contents (cont'd.)

...

Part 1:

World at the End of a Wrong Path

Introduction to the Introduction: Some Initial Thoughts on
Conceptualizing History

Humans experience life through many combined mental/physical worlds. They
perceive their worlds via phenomena – items of meaning. '*The* world' is the combined
continuous appearance all at once of every thing within Earth's domain: specifically, this
defines "the *whole* world", or "everything". Items of "the physical world", those that
appear primarily in visual space, which is to say, "outside" of the human mind, are
always manifested as structures and parts of structures, however simple they may

superficially seem. In other words, every thing, by which I mean every structure, is naturally complex. Most significantly, this leads to a situation where no thing – in this case, no phenomenon – on Earth can be truly understood without having been explained. But if it can be successfully explained, by definition it will be understood.[ii]

For humans, everything (the whole world) must be explained and hence understood primarily in terms of its relation to the planet Earth: Earth is the supreme area of relevance – it's the all-encompassing setting for the whole living system that's ultimately humanity's sole experienced context. Earth is the theater where events are staged. The universe is the all-encompassing setting for Earth; the latter mediates the former to human beings.

Although Earth and the universe are one, enormous differences arise in the human imagination between how each context, in-and-of-itself, can be perceived. For one thing, the universe is perpetually expanding, as well as infinitely diverse in far too many ways that humans aren't used to; so we can't properly imagine it as a whole. In turn, constructed histories of its happenings aren't possible. But human beings live on/in Earth, so they can realistically imagine specific circumstances happening within the planet from perspectives like those of first-hand observers without their having lived those particular circumstances personally. This is because they can understand what has been most significant to the working of Earth *as a whole*, from a certain perspective – the perspective of humanity – and in turn constructed histories of the planet's happenings are possible.

Every latest moment of an individual's life is the most recent moment in human history – this only changes in relation to an individual's life after he or she is dead – so human history is always in one sense final, namely in terms of all such history *until* any given 'present' moment. Generally, the "until this moment" expanse is known as 'the past'. Therefore, on Earth, for humans, there's always a present, and hence always some imaginable past; in turn, on Earth, there's always *'history'* that humans can potentially find. The universe, by comparison, appears as a perpetual future, since (as was said) its nature is to constantly expand. So far as we know, the universe sets its own rules, meaning the rules for everything within its scope. Earth's rules are ultimately set by a "higher power", if only in the sense that it's a physically finite locale within a physically infinite universe. Not only is there always *some* ongoing history on planet Earth, then, but also, besides that, there is in the largest sense always a *single* planetary history (whatever it might entail). In turn, for any phenomenon on Earth, there's always a single history of that phenomenon. Always, a phenomenon is what's historically unique.

A 'human world', that uniquely total, distinctly cultural sphere, is most comparable to a (the) universe, in that, on one level, it sets its own rules and boundaries. But in a much larger, more determinative sense, we know any human world can only work within the constraints set by the Earth as a whole. Thus, the types of conclusions we're able to reach about humanity make it far easier for human beings to understand the human world than the universe at large, because we can know *precisely* (experientially) what bounds the human world. To elaborate, humans, aside from having the same common, broadest physical constraints as everything else on Earth, and aside from having their own physical constraints, just like everything else does on Earth, are most unique insofar as they have *'human psychological'* constraints. Every animal has its own "species' psychology" too, but what I mean here is something different: what I'm referring to is the human *mind*, unlike anything else known to human beings in the universe and so all the more unique in relation to Earth. Above all, the human mind's uniqueness lies in its theoretically limitless potential for attaining knowledge, fostered by the immeasurably vast and ever-increasing stockpile of recorded symbolic communication. Since the human is by definition the only being with first-hand access to observation of the human psyche and relatedly the only one able to employ human intellectual tools, no thing is theoretically in a better position to be explained at the present point in time than the holistic human world.[iii]

However, we've only reached this point where human beings have the potential to understand sufficiently the concept of a holistic human world owing to the history of the "human universe" itself. Human beings today have the potential to know virtually infinitely greater quantities of information than humans from all past eras combined: yet we only have this potential because of everything already accomplished throughout thousands and thousands and thousands of years of cultural evolution, largely achieved via the lives of human beings we're indoctrinated to look at as "backward". As it has happened, the more culturally complex are the worlds humans create, the more conscious in general, and conscious of itself, in particular, humanity can *potentially* become. Generally, though, because of *the kind* of complexity humanity has developed in its culturally most complex environments, namely cultural complexity built on expansive war systems, the practical effect has been essentially the opposite. Certainly this appears to be the case in the most strikingly complex cultural context, the contemporary world – the more culturally complex is the world humans inhabit, the more intrinsically confused are the inhabitants, and confused about themselves, both culturally and individually, most of all.[iv]

While nothing can be understood unless it can be explained, throughout history the whole world has generally "worked" without anyone understanding it completely. This was long true not only about the world as a predominately organic entity – the living Earth itself, in particular during that vast majority of the planet's natural history prior to the development of agriculture – but also about the other world, which has only "just recently" (from an all-historical perspective) started vying for dominance in the same broadest context: the human-created, cultural world. Even and in fact especially at its historically most complex stages, it has indeed "worked" (shortly I'll begin to explain what the exact nature of this "working" entails) with the vast majority of individuals not understanding it at all.

I've constructed the present text because humanity has for some time been rapidly hurtling toward a point where, unless a substantial number of individuals gain sufficient consciousness of what exactly the world *is* as a whole, the making of any working cultural world will be completely unfeasible. That is, unless a significant portion of humanity undergoes a rapid wholesale transformation in its understanding, *there can ultimately be no future humanity*.[v] The present text is the only way I know how of attempting to aid that transformation, which I believe must start with the intersection of three kinds of knowledge: philosophical, social-scientific, and historical.[vi] Additionally, I believe the original subject of study needing to be addressed is naturally the contemporary world, as a whole – specifically, the whole contemporary world insofar as it represents the long historical culmination of what can only be considered, from any perspective, the singularly consequential change in human history. This change was humanity's initially gradual but ultimately, irrepressibly total transition to life in cities:

more broadly, the transformation has entailed humanity's *life in civilizations*. While I'm not sure if humanity can survive even if enough individuals learn about the contemporary world and its emergence out of the long (but certainly not too long, when compared to the planet as a whole) evolution of civilizations, I'm unwavering in my conviction that, *if* humanity is able to avoid total self-destruction, such an understanding must be the first step.

Trying to contribute to so monumental a shift may seem like an all too sweeping and "overly ambitious", possibly even hubristic goal. But, for whatever my own judgment of myself is worth to the reader, I don't believe that hubris drives me here: I attempt such a contribution, rather, insofar as it's the only goal I consider morally worth striving for amidst human history's unprecedentedly urgent present phase. With such a concrete, pressing objective in mind, I'd nonetheless like to start off by mentioning something quite abstract and seemingly, mundane – systems.

All phenomena are entangled within *'systemic webs'*.[vii] In fact, I believe a phenomenon is *only* a phenomenon insofar as it's part of some system. In one sense, a world's systems serve to reproduce that world, and thus in that sense can be considered *"prior to"* the world. But in the larger sense, the systems clearly can't exist without the world. The notion of *re*production itself already indicates that the systems still exist primarily *for* the world: since the world is at least unintentionally the most consequential thing the systems reproduce, and the systems exist precisely on account of their role as "reproducers", the systems exist for re-creation of the world. Thus, simultaneously, the world makes systems and is made by them. That is, a system may, most specifically, exist for itself. However, since its very existence is inconceivable without the world, *reproducing itself also means reproducing the world*. The world must be reproduced to reproduce the system. If the world can't be reproduced, neither can any of the systems it contains. Systems don't have a choice in the matter.

But what's the nature of the world the systems reproduce? Similarly: what's the nature of the systems? And what *are* systems? In the most general way, we can say that systems are *'units of patterned reproducible spatiotemporal interactions between phenomena'*. The definition alone already amply implies the sheer ubiquity of systems. Concerning its explanatory function, though, the apparent uncertainty of such a broad definition may actually contribute to the usefulness of the concept of "a system".[viii] For conceptualizing phenomena in terms of systems can potentially allow one to accomplish no less a task than unification of the theoretical and the practical; the abstract and the concrete – the unconscious and the conscious. It can potentially allow one to see surprising, deep similarities between what are, superficially, completely "unrelated" phenomena. Potentially, such similarities enable one to construct successful metaphors, which are successful insofar as they're *'real'*. The potential depends upon the systems one is able to discover.

In the research project for the present text, I found two main imaginatively separable systems. One of the systems can best be understood in terms of a history of humanity. The other system I discovered, which *in reality*, from my own perspective, is inseparable from the first, is a way of looking at that history. This history and my way of looking at it are the ultimate sources of all my thinking, both on the nature of the contemporary holistic system, as well as, inseparably, the nature of the world the system is largely responsible for reproducing. In the act of writing, I've tried to combine the two systems (my own and humanity's) as effectively as my abilities allow: the result is a third system, which is the present text.

*   *   *

The World is Always All History's Product

What people almost universally seem to underestimate in their thought processes, if they don't simply ignore the matter altogether, is the sheer extent to which the contemporary world is, like all human worlds, shaped and constantly reshaped by history. *All* history: the totality of past events on Earth in their incomprehensibly enormous accumulation. Perhaps the seeming (merely seeming) ability of electronic tool-complexes to wipe completely clean cultural slates many-thousands of years long obfuscates the omnipotent role that the only apparently invisible hand of historical process plays in shaping current events. "Only apparently" because historical process – really, concerning humans, *socio*historical process – totally surrounds us: most tangibly, in everything humanity has thus far done that has destroyed and is destroying and will, if allowed to continue, completely destroy the planet's existing life. If we can find in the presence of the existent world the processes whereby humanity has evolved in its ability to cause such utter destruction to everything around it, we could find the real "touch" of historical process in the world, and most specifically, our contemporary world itself. It might even be the most important human history of all – even as it's just one history – embodying the most important social structure's evolution.

When I began this project, my ideas were very general – in many cases, vague. But I knew essentially what entities I wanted to focus on: civilizations and States. I also knew I wanted to focus on civilizations and States specifically insofar as they seem to have destroyed the planet Earth, concerning what the planet was for literally almost all of its temporal existence.[ix] And methodologically, I knew I wanted mainly to develop and utilize the vital, constantly-in-mutual-reflection interconnections between philosophy, the social sciences, and history present in the construction of all knowledge concerning humanity. From the beginning to the end in this project I've maintained an unbreakable belief in the necessity, if one wants to reconstruct human reality, to always view such reality, both in terms of *what* you're reflecting upon and *how* you reflect upon it, primarily *as a whole*. Specifically, reality for humanity is always most properly viewed in the first instance in terms of holistic cultural worlds, which have all had to carve out their existences within the very particular context of planet Earth. Now that I'm at the end of the project, I can add that, in my thinking, I adhere to this belief above all others because it seems to serve me well in adding to and refining my understanding of the present, which is to say my understanding of how history has shaped the present.

There are two major real-world corollaries interconnected with my underlying adherence to a holist perspective, which have only emerged in their approximately final manifestation after a process of arduous refining, in the form of the research and writing done for the present text. The first corollary states that, in viewing the contemporary world, the broadest *material* (instead of *imaginary*) perspective of human reality one can usefully adopt is one viewing humanity in terms of its cultural dependence on civilizations and States – two entities which can only truly be separated analytically; in reality, they're inseparable – a cultural dependence that exists only insofar as it thrives within the broadest, ultimately most decisive ecological context, planet Earth. In their full real-world manifestations, civilizations and States on planet Earth exist as what I've termed *'civilization-State-complexes'*. The second corollary states that Earth-bound civilization-State-complexes are entities best understood through the tools provided by three general and interconnected forms of scholarship, *all revolving around the central subject of human history*: philosophy, the social sciences, and of course, history, i.e., historiography. Therefore, concerning the most relevant "whole worlds" I'll be explicitly or implicitly referring to throughout this text, they'll always be referenced as in some way relating to my understanding of the long historical existence of civilizations and States. And every whole world will always be viewed from a metaphysical perspective that considers humanity, by which I mean, in its broadest definition, 'the totality of human beings on Earth at a given time', foremost as a manifestly *'cultural but thereby also sociohistorical phenomenon'*.

Essentially, I view 'the social' as 'the cultural manifestation of humanity's predominately politicoeconomic aspect', and 'the historical' as 'the cultural manifestation of humanity's predominately chronological-geographic aspect'. Hence the most important thing about my view (in that it's what most greatly characterizes its presence throughout the text) is what I've tried to imply by using "compound" labels ('politicoeconomic', 'chronological-geographic', and 'sociohistorical').[x] That is, the view as embodied in the text as a whole emphasizes how for any human culture, it's in reality impossible to separate the political from the economic, or the chronological from the geographical; and even more broadly, it's impossible to separate the politicoeconomic from the chronological-geographic. Cultures are the *'human populations inhabiting and inhabited by holistic artifactual environments'* – environments simultaneously both physical and metaphysical – and so *most* broadly, cultures can't be separated from their politicoeconomic/chronological-geographic surroundings, i.e., their *'sociohistorical contexts'*,[xi] just as, in parallel, human populations can't be separated from their cultures.

How I view humanity, then, is in a practical sense inseparable from what I perceive it to be. I perceive humanity to be an entity whose definition is completely dependent upon the environment within which it emerges, and I perceive this environment to be definitively cultural – so long as it's kept in mind that every cultural phenomenon wholly depends upon and intertwines with whatever sociohistorical context it emerges through. This perception, as it evolved, with all of its implications, determined the basic intellectual tool-sets I would rely upon to construct the text, just as the intellectual tool-sets would reciprocally determine the evolving perception.

Then naturally, I'd use the kinds of tools individuals use when they want to know about cultural phenomena, social phenomena, and historical phenomena. I make this sound much simpler than it was in practice. At the present late date, humans have long-since amassed innumerable "specialized" knowledge bases, in their totality aiming to answer the most wide-ranging assortment of "scholarly problems". Theoretically, this should be the greatest-ever boon to the pursuit of knowledge and understanding. In practice, for the most part, the disciplines interact with each other either poorly or not at all. Not only that, but mainstream contemporary scholarship mainly frowns upon individuals who try to move freely across the supposed intellectual "boundaries", implicitly scoffing at the notion that anyone could possibly know anything about more than one individual thing, even in cases when such things have only been artificially individualized by the conventions of contemporary scholarship.

Already at the project's start I intuited that this general confinement of scholars to such limited perspectives purely stemmed from the most general sociohistorical processes: it wasn't primarily the result of something inherently necessary to scholarship. In other words, I felt it wasn't something attributable mainly to contemporary academia itself that was to blame for the claustrophobic degree of its specialized pigeonholes; there could only be an explanation steeped in the deepest cultural realities. For, in the contemporary dominant culture, more or less every profession is specialized to the most outrageous degree imaginable. This is so expected in the contemporary latest stage of endlessly intricate total politicoeconomic relations that pointing it out at first seems almost meaningless.

Yet precisely because it's so pervasive – so pervasive that when first mentioned it seems near meaningless – it surely must have consequences practically everyone underestimates and/or overlooks. When we examine in-depth those facts (and 'facts' on Earth are always historically determined; 'human cultural facts' are always *socio*historically determined) that seem most unsurprising, progressively we find more and more surprises in places where, in the very first instance, we'd never have thought to look. Often, these surprises result from the discovery of unexpected connections. The discovery of many such connections can potentially lead to discovering systems. The discovery of the right systems can potentially lead one to conclude that every thing is connected to everything else.

No thing is specialized simply on its own. Things *become* specialized, as the result of processes. If the purpose of specialization in academia wasn't primarily a purpose related to scholarly learning – if specialization didn't happen primarily on account of necessities stemming from the goal of improving formal knowledge – what was the true purpose? (And if the purpose wasn't to improve humanity's attainment of such knowledge, then couldn't there be more effective practices for improvement than those exemplified by contemporary academia?)

The purpose is the same purpose we ultimately find when we look beyond the surface of *all* contemporary 'hyperspecialization': the perpetuation of the contemporary social structure, which in turn represents the core basis stabilizing the contemporary dominant culture. Here's a perfect opportunity to realize concretely what I mean when I say that looking at phenomena in terms of their entanglements within systems might be the crucial step towards uniting the theoretical with the practical. So before we look at what the politicoeconomic phenomenon of hyperspecialization accomplishes culturally in the contemporary world – why it "works", which is to say *what it works for* – I'll contextualize the specific question within the most general framework.

When I look at human systems in the world, I'm using the idea of "systems" in order to determine how it is that key phenomena existing in the present world exist *at the same time*. This is of unparalleled significance because as I said, there's only one, finite planet Earth, so at any given time, there must be a finite quantity of possibilities in terms of the particular nature of the everything in human existence. Actually, when we consider what history must empirically constitute for there to be something real we can rightly call history – and, as the present text in full is meant to attest, I think what we can rightly call history is the realest "thing" there is – not only is there a finite number of possibilities; in reality there's only one: that possibility embodying all those things which have really happened and are really happening.

On Earth, in relation to human beings (in relation to anything, but what we're discussing is human beings) in the largest (longest) sense there was (/is) only one historical process, whether or not human beings can ever honestly figure out in full what it entailed. Obviously human beings can't figure out what the history has been in *literal* comprehensive fashion. But anyway, discerning humanity's history literally comprehensively is not what's important about knowing there's a singular long historical process called "human beings living on planet Earth". The important thing about the fact is that it's the all-important boundary for our imagination when conceptualizing any possible example of human history. Everything happened within that widest framework. We're now able to think about human history with the most realistic broadest imaginary context in mind: human history is in this sense 'the one totally accumulated existence of human beings on planet Earth'. Even the most open-ended imagination regarding human history, if it's to be practically useful, has to be situated in real facts. We have to use the knowledge of facts to guide but not restrain our imaginations.

Since from the grand perspective there's only one human history, it means that all shorter human histories, which is to say all human histories shorter than the process of the human animal's natural evolution, are commonly circumscribed within a single finite set of imaginary boundaries, however "large" an area those boundaries might ultimately enclose. Therefore, that there are connections between any two different human histories is *always* a possibility, no matter the amount of investigation one might have to undertake in order to demonstrate those connections, concerning most individual cases. Moreover, in the present text, I'm not primarily concerned with individual cases involving the entirety of human history, but only individual cases substantially related to the total historical emergence of civilizations and States, and most specifically individual cases concerning the history of civilizations and States that seem to me most qualitatively relevant to the history of the contemporary world. It might not seem like it yet, but from the outset this narrows our focus considerably.

The real point of importance here is that, because there's only this one planet with its one human history, we should expect a greater proliferation of *literal* human connections within and between every significant sphere of human life, the more spatiotemporally compressed is any given whole world in relation to the totality of its human beings. If I can successfully explain in sociohistorical terms the progressive, intertwined growth and spatiotemporal compression of the whole world in relation to its human beings culminating at last in the total growth and *'total spatiotemporal compression'* achieved by the late contemporary world (1995 –?), I should thereby be able to establish the proper basis for demonstrating the most general connections welding together our contemporary world's greatest problems. (I do this in part 2 to set the stage for the philosophy-history in part 3.)

The next vital imaginary boundary for studying human history concerns the material (biological) definition of 'human beings' ('anatomically modern *Homo sapiens*'): from this perspective, human beings have existed for about the last 200,000 years of planet Earth's existence, which has lasted so far for about 4 billion years. The universe is roughly 13.8 billion years old – around 3.5 times older than the planet Earth, which has been around for about 20,000 times longer than human beings. The juxtaposition of these quantities has a characteristically qualitative impact, in the mind of the human observer: instantly we can see that while no span of time is intrinsically 'long' or 'short', spans of time are truly long and short when considered in relation to other such spans. From the points-of-view of human beings, spans of time can be looked at as indicating 'histories', which measure 'existences', the actualized presences of phenomena. So when a history is short in relation to another history, it means one existence is short in relation to another existence. History has to be history *of* something.

Human history as a whole is the longest history directly relevant to the study of human culture, but it's still just part of a much, much longer historical process of "the existence of planet Earth", in its turn part of an even longer historical process, "the existence of the universe". By the same token, but from the inverse perspective, no matter how long is the existence of any individual human culture, it'll always be much shorter than the existence of human beings in general. Therefore, no matter what, we know that whenever we're studying individual human cultures we're studying entities that have appeared very briefly in comparison with all other broad environmental contexts relevant to human life. And in turn we know that, in this sense, when studying *a* human culture we're studying something of the most extreme particularity, certainly compared to the rest of the universe and the planet and even compared to the study of human culture as a whole.[xii]

This is at the same time as, in another sense, human cultures are so uniquely long and general. That other sense – to now adopt a further inverse perspective – is the individual human life. The human culture is thus the most significant link between individual human lives and all human history, and from there all prior natural history. I assert as well that we should *study* both human culture and the histories of individual human cultures precisely in this light. In other words, the human culture is the empirically proper "unit" for historical scholarship.

Quantitative phenomena with qualitative consequences, such as spans of time that humans make 'long' or 'short' when imagining them in juxtaposition with other spans of time, are of the utmost significance to the study of human history. Moreover, inextricably, they're equally indispensable to the study of general human social structures. In terms of what I'm thinking of at any given time, for instance, I don't really care what the U.S.'s exact GDP is in relation to the GDP of every other nation (a cultural problem that must be studied both socially and historically). Indeed, I fully recognize that GDP is in-and-of-itself a completely arbitrary measure more representative of a self-fulfilling prophecy than anything else. Yet, having acknowledged this, I still care about the fact that, on a planet with finite resources, which at this point in history is controlled by an essentially perfectly singularized global politicoeconomic system, the U.S.'s GDP is so disproportionately large in relation to that of every other nation, literally every living individual is coerced into a direct interest in the specific policies of the United States. Two things are important here: an establishment-approved fact always mean *something*, even as it (almost certainly) doesn't mean what the establishment-promoted mindset suggests; and a "qualitative" perspective always necessitates to some extent the study of "quantitative" measures.

To complete the narrowing of our broadest focus, we have one last indispensable boundary for imagining human history: the greatest transformations, by which I mean the cultural changes that are both most rapid and most complete in human history,[xiii] have occurred mainly within the span since the earliest origins of agriculture until today. In total, this includes only about the past 13,000 years.[xiv] Moreover, even within this span, the most concentrated period of great transformations has occurred within about the past 5,000 years. Additionally, within the latter "temporal zone", the past 500-or-so years have been especially event-full. Finally, the most extremely concentrated period of all has taken place within only the last 116-or-so years, specifically that span I refer to as "contemporary history".

So there appears, upon the most cursory glance, some true justification for setting aside the period of civilizations and States, as well as that period immediately before and immediately responsible for it, as something remarkable in terms of its being an object of study. If there's any semblance of a legitimate (non-chauvinistic) reason why, when typical contemporary human beings refer to "History", they invariably seem to mean the period wherein civilizations and States have reigned (they call the time before "Prehistory"), even though this period encompasses only about 3% of the total past temporal existence of anatomically-modern *Homo sapiens*, surely this fact must have something to do with it. It just seems that individuals only rarely approach this exact problem – the sheer uniqueness of history in civilizations and States – in quite the right way.

*   *   *

States Do Specific Things; They're the most Consequential Things for Everyone Else

For instance, it's interesting that, in studying the State, every contemporary individual who did so didn't start with the trifecta of most distinct qualities characterizing all contemporary States, the three things States are permitted to do and, at least nominally, no other entities are. I say it's interesting, but it's not surprising. I'll get to why it's not surprising in a moment. First let me name the things: the State can raise and maintain militaries, the State can enforce general ("macro-") economic policies for entire national populations, and the State can administer "justice". These three extraordinary "rights" present themselves most crucially in – respectively – the State's use of mass organized deadly force, the State's taxation of its populations, and the State's incarceration of those individuals found in violation of its criminal codes. In the specific sociohistorical context of the contemporary world, if you live under State rule – and at the present date, you invariably do, which I must add is a positively aberrant phenomenon in human history[xv] – you live in what's called, from a contemporary perspective, a national State, by which I mean, to be completely specific, a national *'State-ruled polity'*. Most generally, it's supposedly only the nation that makes war (we'll eventually get to why "supposedly"), the nation that taxes, and the nation that puts people who "break the law" in prison.

Again, I must reiterate that these functions are *nominally* under the greatest purview of national States in the contemporary world. In the world as it presently exists, that it's the national State with the lone ability to pursue and accomplish these most unique tasks is, certainly from a global perspective, merely the ideal; I realize the reality diverges from this ideal strikingly. But it's nonetheless the ideal in itself which we need to use as our point of departure – namely, to begin to try to understand why on Earth it's the "ideal" in the first place, and why so often it seems to "fail" in practice.

In terms of what national States intend to accomplish by their domination via these three exceptional abilities, the ideal has long been put into practice successfully by what are considered the world's "leading" nations. Indeed, this does much to explain, while also simultaneously being much explained by, the favorable global positions of those nations. The central nexus of Earth's current leading nations, which have been the leading nations all throughout the contemporary era (even long before that in some cases, but here I'm exclusively concerned with contemporary history) are primarily situated in a category commonly referred to, ever since the Cold War, as the "First World". In terms of its origins, aside from Japan, the "First World" originated exclusively in what's known as "Western civilization".

At the same time as these national States have been the dominant entities all throughout contemporary history (which I define as having started in its earliest manifestation in 1898, see below), what exactly a national State entails has been a constantly shifting process. Whether or not they ever were, throughout contemporary history national States have definitely never been anything like "independent" entities. The critical variable has been the exact degree of extreme interdependence shaping the relationships between the planet's nations. Although people seem to mean many different things by it, I view the present politicoeconomic system on Earth – there's a single dominant politicoeconomic system for the entire planet, which is the most unique thing about this latest phase, and makes it the most unique period in human history – more or less in terms of the 'globalization' paradigm.[xvi] Rather than being a just recently emerged phenomenon though, I think globalization explicitly started with the U.S. and British wars of 1898 and 1899 (we'll get to these in part 3).[xvii]

What I mean by globalization can't be fully known to the reader until the text in its entirety has been read. However, since it's so central to our whole journey, I must explain here what I mean by it most briefly. Simply, I consider 'globalization' to be the planet's singular, contemporary dominant cultural form, held in place by what is, in absolute terms, the largest politicoeconomic system in human history: even more importantly, I argue, it's the largest* politicoeconomic system that *can ever* exist in human history. And this is precisely because it's the perfect culmination of all prior human cultural growth.

Not only is it the largest, but it's also the most *politically centralized* human culture that can ever exist. Almost universally, scholars seem to miss this point about the existent world – the world embodying globalization – including scholars who otherwise know well about globalization.[xviii] I believe the explanation for this has to do mainly with the improper conflation of politics and economics in some instances, and the inability to

---

* By "largest" I'm referring both to "total population living under the regime" and "total resources used by the regime".

see the ultimately total interconnection between the two spheres, in others.[xix] In the end, one can't shake the strong sense that, however many people there might be who know quite precisely about individual microscopic political or economic phenomena, very few individuals in the present world have clear ideas about what politics and economics *are*, to begin with.

That's essentially why it's not surprising, how every individual who has studied the contemporary State hasn't started with its most notable, most unusual characteristics – characteristics which can only fairly be called 'powers', instead of 'rights'. It's not even surprising how *almost no one at all* has started with these powers. For how can you understand the quintessential context where politics and economics converge in reality – the State – if you don't understand the two main interacting phenomena themselves? How would you know if you'd found what you were looking for, if you didn't know beforehand with at least some substantial degree of accuracy what it looked like?

But does that mean no one in the contemporary world, specifically this current, latest phase of the contemporary world, has said anything useful at all about politics and economics in general, and about the State in particular? No – though interestingly, scholars have largely only been able to avoid *complete* irrelevance on account of hyperspecialization. Scholarly commentators for the most part limit themselves to such tiny intellectual niches, that a great deal have at least some valuable things to say for more broadly encompassing researches, albeit things said within totally over-determined frames-of-reference.

The compulsion towards viewing knowledge as inherently specialized ensures the preclusion of one's developing a useful broadened perspective (philosophical outlook). Contemporary scholars are generally inept at conceptualizing the State *as a general entity* because the hyperspecialization in contemporary scholarship is really hyper*compartmentalization*. Looking at phenomena through artificially specific lenses, if not properly complemented with a coequal, constantly interacting process of cultivating a general point-of-view, leads to disciplinary results that are basically only "good for" employing specialists within particular subdisciplines. Indeed, absent from the existence of hyperspecialized knowledge, and especially hyperspecialized knowledge related to the study of humanity, is any sense at all that pursuing knowledge *should* be inherently useful to general human understanding if it's to be worthy of our energy and time. Hyperspecialized disciplines are disciplines under the unreflective sway of market logic, not the pursuit of knowledge, so "usefulness" is typically measured purely in terms of money-morality (see part 3, *BOOK TWO*), not human understanding. This is why we can't really say that the hyperspecialization in contemporary academia mainly has to do with academia itself – academia is sadly in the end just like any other contemporary occupation. The whole situation seems just a little bit worse though, because it seems like scholarship should acknowledge a greater duty to favor truth over money than should the typical profession.

Academia thus has become hyperspecialized just like everything else, which has somehow still allowed scholars to say some useful things about a world hardly anyone seems to understand – a world that as a whole seems to be most unique insofar as it's characteristically incomprehensible – at the same time that such hyperspecialization represents contemporary academia's worst flaw. The solution of completely unhindered interdisciplinarity/non-disciplinarity within "humanity studies" is then ideal: it allows us to salvage the useful contributions of contemporary mainstream humanities and social scholarship, while in the same motion it can also destroy one of the greatest obstacles to the advancement of knowledge. The useful contributions may be a relatively tiny proportion, but within such a uniquely enormous pool that proportion represents quite a considerable sum. However, the potential usefulness of these contributions can only be substantially realized *if* thinkers embrace continuous interaction between, on the one hand, strictly disciplinary approaches, and, on the other, broader outlooks.

The typical understanding of highly "disciplined" contemporary scholars allows them to get by when they stay in their cages: when they never try to study history itself as a whole (even just to see whether such a thing truly exists), but, for instance, "20th-century American labor history"; when they ignore any possibility of scientifically studying social structures in general, setting out instead to study, say, "environmental sociology of the postmodern world". The problems seem to set in when scholars try to talk about "bigger" things. I'm not even talking about a situation where the "20th-century American labor historian", for example, largely avoids discussing how her or his subject relates to history in general. I'm not expecting everyone (or anyone) to know about every thing. What I mean is, "the scholarly community" as a whole, nowadays, seems to be rather unwilling to accept the notion that *anyone* can successfully cultivate anything resembling a broader perspective.

In other words, how can I possibly claim to know about politics and economics both, and to such an extent that I claim there are always at least indirect connections between the two, *and* that the combined politicoeconomic system is, further, inextricable from the human culture relying upon it?

The most important thing I'm claiming here, in fact, isn't that I know about politics, economics, and culture (etc.), but rather that you can't truly *understand* any of these things individually unless, when you study them, your underlying approach constantly remains in tacit acknowledgement of their overall inseparability. Demonstrating my knowledge of these phenomena is the necessary byproduct of achieving the primary goal, which is to conceptualize the phenomenological interconnections as thoroughly as possible. Whether the demonstration accomplishes what I'm setting out to accomplish in sum is ultimately subject solely to the reader's judgment. What I'm seeking to accomplish is something simple, difficult, and, I believe, potentially most beneficial: the provocation of truly independent, practically valuable thought concerning humanity's present existence.

Metaphysics of the 'Peak Globalization' Culture

i

For the rest of part 1, what I'm concerned with is the broadest cultural atmosphere of what I called in the preceding section the *existent* world – and I think I'll stick with this label to discern between the latest, most acute phase (established 1995) and the rest of the contemporary world (conceived 1898; officially born 1947).

In embarking upon our discussion of the contemporary dominant culture, I'm not departing from, but rather can only continue, my exposition of the contemporary State. For, our contemporary world (the world of fully-fledged globalization) is a civilization; civilizations are most uniquely defined insofar as they're *'conquest-imposed cultures'*, and a civilization's conquest function is fulfilled most centrally by the State. Few people approach the study of civilizations as such in the right way because almost everyone fails to recognize that civilizations themselves are distinct entities insofar as they're the cultures resulting from the greatest historical acts ('meta-event-clusters', see second section of part 2) of human intergroup conquest.

The great repressed fact of the contemporary civilization – at this point in history, there's only one (something completely unique to two civilizations in history, the first one and the present one) – the culmination of a tradition passed down for over 500 decades worth of human beings, is that civilizations are cultural worlds literally fueled by conquest. Meaning the world is being fueled *right now* by conquest: studying civilizations then is in no uncertain terms an urgent matter, a matter of life and death. Since this fact is repressed above all others, it's essentially impossible for the typical individual inhabiting the contemporary dominant culture to fully psychologically assimilate the notion that the State, in its most functionally "efficient" form, is a machine for violent conquest.

Scholars, being foremost typical individuals inhabiting the contemporary world, find it no less difficult to see the State for its true cultural role than those in any other of the conquest culture's sectors. Hence, beyond the hyperspecialization of contemporary academia, we have the much deeper reason why almost no one studying the State starts by focusing on how the leading contemporary States have such tools in their arsenals as monopolies over national militaries, monopolies over national economic policies, and monopolies over national criminal justice apparatuses. Such a small number of individuals see the State this way because it rarely occurs to anyone that in terms of their real-world institutional presences, these most distinct functions hold significance primarily insofar as they're inextricably interconnected machines utilized towards the end of long-term conquest-perpetuation.

Perhaps individuals think, "What other than a State *could* perform those most serious tasks?" In other words, how could I possibly even question the State's – for instance, the U.S. Government's – "right" to rule? "Surely it's just *a certain kind* of State you're calling into question." But this would prove precisely my point: inhabiting the existent dominant culture makes it virtually impossible to see any use whatsoever in even asking a most necessary question (no matter what your eventual answer might be) like, why is it the State, and not some other entity, which has such decisive power over life and death, over personal economic livelihood, and over the incarceration of individuals' persons? In existent America, for instance, merely asking these questions almost automatically leads a political observer to be identified as "Libertarian", a word sadly defiled within the context of the contemporary U.S., now somehow indicative of a most logically inconsistent form of reactionary.

Although here I'm concerned with the question of the State from an explicitly cultural (rather than an explicitly political) perspective, it may immediately expel what would be a ridiculous characterization of me as a reactionary if I anticipate the text's later portions. I consistently argue, as a matter of theory/principle as well as in terms of practical real-world manifestations, that the State is nothing but a fictive catchall – an *'imaginary legal shield'* – serving to agglomerate the major intergroup activity sustaining humanity's most *Powerful* vested interests. That is, politically, *the State* epitomizes what's most reactionary in a civilization: the State exists solely as the quintessential vehicle for neutralizing struggle against the status quo emanating both from external and internal (external and internal to the State) politicoeconomic sectors. Many scholars would refer to it as "class struggle"; but that's not really what it is. However, it nonetheless has everything to do with what can be conceived of theoretically as class struggle. I can best start explaining why it's not class struggle by asserting the overriding conclusion one will have to reach, after I actually undertake the explanation: "If class struggle had truly been the main thing going on, the exploited classes would've won by now." The exploitative classes couldn't win an honest class struggle. The main reason it's not class struggle is because, if we consider the contemporary culture, for instance, from a hypothetical class perspective, only one of its sectors can be rightly said to act like anything resembling a unified group.[xx] If we view the present reality from a class perspective, only within the ranks of the exploitative sectors do we find cases of what could be honestly called collective ("class") action.

This isn't coincidental, but is perhaps the most clearly apprehensible direct result of what the struggle actually entails. The struggle itself actually exists to ensure that nothing constituting a true "class struggle" – the violent competition of antagonistic economic forces – can come into existence. It stops real class struggle before it can start. More than any other kind of State-formation in human history, the type of State uniformly found all throughout the existent world has fulfilled this task, and has more importantly been deliberately designed to fulfill this task. Indeed, the existent State actually *preempts* class struggle, by aggressively fostering what are most properly called 'ideological (rather than politicoeconomic) divisions' amongst the populations under its control.[xxi] Since there isn't an actual class struggle going on, we need an alternative, appropriate analytic framework with which to confront reality.

It's really in the first place a cultural struggle – a struggle between different "subcultures" within the largest, holistic framework. This takes on the characteristic appearance of a psychological conflict, whereas a class struggle would be in the first place a physical conflict. By "in the first place", I mean, "regarding what the type of struggle most intentionally serves to accomplish". Cultural struggle is for a context wherein the "middle class" is the mass element most significant to the social structure. Participants in a class struggle would strive to change fundamentally politicoeconomic (physical) relationships, whereas participants in the cultural struggle strive to change fundamentally cultural (ideological) relationships. Earnest participants in each usually fail to see the vital interconnections bonding the most significant politicoeconomic to the most significant cultural factors shaping human life. Tragically, failing to acknowledge such interconnections continuously leads to multiple repetitions of past mistakes for individuals sincerely interested in changing the world. It seems sensible then to try to determine what those interconnections are.

Everything within the human domain is cultural, because humans *make* everything cultural. Most notably, everything is cultural in this sense because language is cultural.[xxii] Culture is the clothing that chronological-geographic (historical) entities wear; language is the main fabric comprising the clothes. Humans can do nothing without ideas, and, once they've become fluent in a language, they can't help but experience all ideas as linguistic, and thus cultural. We experience past cultures only as ideas, so '*a culture*' is the proper designation for any past humanity as-a-whole, and hence also for the whole humanity constituting the central subject of "history in the present" at a given time in one's own life.

Culture is of course not merely "cause" in relation to politicoeconomic systems, but equally, and simultaneously, "effect". This is indeed what "interconnection" most manifestly implies: two phenomena have entered into a relationship of reciprocal cause-and-effect (what's known as a "feedback loop"). Reciprocality is of indispensable importance to all study of complex adaptive systems. As culture is the clothing and chronology/geography is the flesh and skeleton, the politicoeconomic system is the soul animating the clothed individual. By the time in a culture's history when a politicoeconomic system is in such a state that we can rightly consider it to be its individuated "self", the holistic culture's more explicitly cultural (ideologically-based) characteristics have been reciprocally related to the culture's intertwined political and economic framework for so long, the two spheres have become inseparable. Basically, the later it is in any culture's "life-span", the more inextricable and hence indefinable is that culture's historical existence from the much more mundane but no less necessary social structure holding it together. The social structure is, in turn, equally codependent upon the culture's psychological existence.[xxiii]

The main tangible interconnection between the two spheres is stored energy. This was true for the entire history of humanity, ever since human beings first became recognizably cultural "agents". But it has been especially true since the initial innovation of settlements and agriculture, even truer during the history of agriculturally-sustained civilizations and States, and it has been truest of all, within this latter stage, in the span of time leading up to and including the contemporary world.[xxiv]

The crudest explanation for that last point lies in the ever-increasingly globalized dominance of *industrialization*. This unprecedented form of combined politicoeconomic/cultural system continuously spiraled out of control from the space-time of its first emergence unto the present point, where it has gone so far past the threshold of over-saturating the planet's entirety that prospects of the most spectacular and terrible collapse, rather than being absurd prophecies dreamed up by lunatics, have long seemed all but completely unavoidable if nothing drastically alters the present course. The soberest scholarly voices profess as much.[xxv] Hence our worst politicoeconomic "problems" – megacrises is what they are – are also and even more pressingly our worst cultural problems/crises. Of course, industrialization isn't the full explanation for such interconnection between cultural and politicoeconomic systems in the contemporary world, but it is what I consider the only appropriate starting point.

Industrialization only ever happened historically as the ultimate long-term result of the originary state-of-affairs shaping the earliest emergent settlements and agricultural systems, which would ultimately catapult humanity into its most complex cultural format, that of civilizations and States. At the same time, industrialization can and in the present text should be considered a full-scale cultural innovation comparable in its magnitude to the earlier one, which, leaving aside for now the also very significant phenomenon of cultural diffusion, emerged independently in several places across the globe within a span of about 5,000 years, beginning around 8500 BCE. Including those two, the major cultural innovations subsequent to the interglacial transition were as follows: (1) as noted, the emergence of settlements and agriculture, civilizations and States (peak earliest emergence about 4000-1500 BCE); (2) the widespread emergence of phonetic script (starting around 1000 BCE) and of cash (starting around 600 BCE); (3) the emergence of Christianity and Islam (peak earliest emergence between 100 CE and 632 CE); (4) the Ottoman conquest of Constantinople, the printing press's spread throughout the West, and the Western "discovery" of the "New World" (1450-1492 CE)[xxvi]; (5) "Revolutions" and (again, as noted) industrialization (between 1689 and 1865); (6) the advent of nuclear weaponry and introduction of TV as mass medium (1945 and 1950s); and (7) the mass commercialized global emergence of digital communication devices, especially the World Wide Web and cellular phones, in conjunction with the official establishment of a single global market (1995).

The striking thing about this list, aside from the seemingly diverse nature of the developments, is that although all the developments would, if not immediately, at least eventually have global consequences, they also all initially emanated from civilizations originally of the same general chronological-geographic (historical) "lineage". From the broadest perspective, the civilizations whose earliest origins lay in the southwest Asian/northeast African/southeast European nexus were directly involved in all of them – if not solely, then at least largely. Starting at the time of the first civilizations in Mesopotamia and Egypt and lasting until Columbus (5,000-or-so years), this "quadrant"[xxvii] repeatedly provided the basis for the planet's most consequential examples of that entity I've labeled the *'intercivilizational structure'*.

Certainly, the Western-oriented approach to explaining all of history is one of the worst pathologies plaguing contemporary academia. But an even worse scenario for understanding our present world arises when individuals rightly try to correct this ethnocentric tendency by wrongly avoiding whatever central role the West *has* actually played in shaping the history of the whole planet: because the West's central role really has had the greatest consequences for everyone and everything else – these consequences have just been eminently disastrous.[xxviii] Again, understanding industrialization is the first key to understanding this. Through the present, all of human history has pivoted on industrialization.

Yet in the middle and late periods of the contemporary world, i.e., the span of history since the Cold War, there has been something greater than industrialization shaping history, even as – just like the relationship between industrialization and agriculture – it only happened as industrialization's quintessential result. Obviously, I'm referring to the industry of atomic energy, which most prominently includes the production of nuclear and thermonuclear arms.

Admittedly, it might seem strange to consider a single class of weaponry so supremely definitive of humanity. But leaving all other history aside for a moment, when one thoroughly considers the total holistic effect of nuclear and even worse thermonuclear weaponry on what I refer to as contemporary history's middle (1947-1991) and late (1995-?) periods, it no longer seems so strange. For instance, during these most peculiar years in humanity's history, there has been no greater factor than the "nuclear turn" in determining the whole existence of all the world's dominant military apparatuses.

More broadly, whether or not we can do anything more than vaguely know what's meant to begin with, it's nonetheless impossible to deny that this temporal span containing the global civilization has had more "total history" condensed within it than did any other comparable quantity of time in human history. In other words, in terms of the history of civilizations and States, history has been happening far more rapidly in the contemporary world than it ever had at any other point in the previous span of 5,000-or-so years.[xxix] In general, human history has been sped-up to the extreme as a result of the emergence of civilization-State-complexes; thus, 1947-? is, from a historical (chronological-geographic) perspective, literally the most extreme ever portion of humanity's existence. And nothing's more centrally significant for explaining our anomalous history than the emergence of nuclear and thermonuclear weapons systems.[xxx] Other interdependent facts are also indispensable to understanding this collectively lived extreme, but no single fact sits higher in its relationship to everything else. So from the grand perspective there's something quite unique indeed about humanity's nuclear transformation, which can't be paralleled by anything else in the history of civilizations. It can only be compared to an innovation like settlements and agriculture, which *gave rise to* civilizations and thus by definition preceded them; or one like language, which gave rise to all culture and hence is what's most responsible for making *Homo sapiens* truly "human", in the first place.

If the emergence of language is considered a development of pure creation and that of agriculture is an essentially equal mixture of creation and destruction, it should then be clear where on the spectrum the development of nuclear weaponry lies.

So is it possible to say that as history proceeded and eventually got faster and faster, "things got worse"? It's really what I just said: the general human potential to *destroy* has proliferated since the origins of civilizations and States, and the general human potential to *create* has plummeted. What's "better" or "worse" in a sociohistorical context depends completely upon the judgment brought to bear on reality by the individual human mind. But in this respect it may be worth mentioning here, that as a matter of "principle" the contemporary dominant culture ruthlessly militates against the individual's ability to make decisions based on his or her own individual judgments.

In fact, before we move forward, please set aside all your existing notions of "better or worse". They're most likely extremely unhelpful – not notions of "better or worse" themselves, but specifically the ones most likely shaping how you think right now. Concerning the way such notions are installed into the contemporary mass individual by the dominant culture, they serve only to confine individuals within a single tiny box or one of its similarly tiny opponents. We don't have time for tiny things. We must view our contemporary world differently – holistically. We must start over.

*   *   *

ii

All civilizations collapse.

That is, concerning all the civilizations prior to the presently existing, globally singularized one, whose ultimate fate is still not sealed (but I'll make a fairly safe prediction – it will collapse), all of history's earlier civilizations have collapsed.[xxxi] There's truly good reason, then, for the way so many historians choose to title their works: civilizations really do, definitively, "rise and fall". Far from an empty cliché, I find this phrase to be an exquisitely succinct representation of what it's like to live in civilizations; what it's like for human beings to live in conquest-imposed cultures dependent upon massive intercity systems, insofar as these are unlike all other types of human cultural formation. But the representation only shines most strikingly when one considers an additional fact: all civilizations collapse, *and at the same time*, throughout history, relatively very few individuals living in civilizations have ever realized it (in terms of histories preceding those acute phases immediately leading up to collapse).

Thus, individuals inhabiting dominant cultures, just like they largely repress the certain inevitability of their own deaths, do the same regarding the practical inevitability of the holistic culture's death. Or rather, inherent in the nature of a conquest-imposed culture is this very repression; individuals living in such cultures then absorb it naturally and from there, to varying extents, contribute to its perpetuation. "Repressed" doesn't have to indicate an active agent intentionally implementing the repression – such an individual would more specifically be engaged in "*sup*pression" – but can simply mean that facts affecting an individual or a group of individuals are someway in sight yet remain undiscovered by individuals' overt consciousnesses. The facts don't "register" on the conscious level. Once the fact has been explicitly discovered (verbalized, for instance), one can no longer say it's completely repressed, at least not in relation to the consciousness or consciousnesses that have made the discovery.

So in general, conquest-imposed cultures have, in the past as well as the present, somehow succeeded at concealing their utter mortality – the quintessentially temporally limited quality determining all those cultures' existences – from their inhabitants. Moreover, right away we know that, if it ever was, this concealment still couldn't *always* have been a state-of-affairs brought about intentionally, because civilizations existed for around 2,000-or-so years before the first one (if one is viewing Sumer as the first civilization "on record") collapsed.[xxxii] Therefore, during that span of time at the very least, the repression of the civilization's definitively finite life span *couldn't* have been deliberate, because literally no one could've possibly known that civilizations are, from a long-term perspective, inherently temporary.

This is a perfect example of how the individual's ability to know history is, in the first place, constrained by the history that has happened up to and including the individual's lifetime. For the most part, individuals' consciousnesses cannot greatly exceed the precise historical contexts those individuals are situated within. To be sure, in every cultural context, there may be individuals who intellectually "anticipate" future happenings. I'm not referring to prophecy (not that prophecy is necessarily impossible,

I'm just presently unconcerned with it), but simply to those skills of discerning perception humans bring to bear upon phenomena they *'know'*, referring here to the phenomenon of human knowledge explicitly as such. Anticipation is a most significant manifestation of knowledge, wherein the human being feels a definite sense of presence concerning things that are as yet not present, though they are "about to be" – you walk into a room that you've been in many times before (a room you 'know'), and before you walk in you have clear expectations of where certain things will be. When I say "definite" ("a definite sense of presence"), I essentially mean that a human being experiencing the sense can accurately verbalize it, although not necessarily that he or she can explain it, because being able to explain it would more precisely indicate *'understanding'* rather than knowledge.

Anticipation is externally manifested, albeit "after the fact", when humans are presented with frames-of-reference and they point out certain characteristics assertively, typically either objects themselves or aspects of objects. When they can't anticipate certain frames-of-reference and are consciously presented with them, they're likely to point out those characteristics interrogatively rather than assertively. Now, when human beings can verbalize things – because they know them – to the extent that they can, with some significant degree of accuracy, predict certain relevant occurrences in advance of their occurring, *this* is what I mean by "individuals anticipating future happenings", and this is what can, for instance, sometimes give off a sophisticated illusion of prophecy. Whether or not the explanation is successful at giving off such an illusion depends first of all upon what the explainer's intentions are, and also, just as more importantly, upon the nature of the audience. The nature of the audience is directly interrelated with individuals' consciousnesses, and thereby is also primarily linked with historical context.[xxxiii]

Thus, we can see what I mean when I say, "For the most part, individuals' consciousnesses cannot greatly exceed the precise historical contexts those individuals are situated within." In terms of "exceeding" an historical context, the individual still has to start out by understanding and explaining things *within* his or her context, even if by doing so he or she ends up "going beyond" that context, via systematic anticipation. The most successful thinkers of any given historical context, then, still must start from within the context. And, more particularly, concerning the different constraints imposed upon populations living in civilizations by contrast those living in all other types of cultural formation, the special nature of these constraints always leaves the vast majority of individuals living in civilizations deprived of the tools enabling the most successful thinkers to achieve success.[xxxiv] Such constraints are ideal embodiments of that aspect of human historical context that really makes it, more specifically, *socio*historical context. The greatest constraint of all is the scale of politicoeconomic stratification uniquely endemic to civilizations, which as a rule only *deliberately* aids the wealthy few in their potential to truly "think freely", in the exact sense I intend here by this phrasing: to think without the physical (life-support) obstacles holding back the vast majority of "civilized" human beings. Obviously, from an absolute perspective, there are many individuals who stray from the norm – but *not* many, proportional to civilizational populations-as-wholes. And proportionality is what's relevant here: that which is defined by the most general and thereby most broadly consequential social-structural patterns brought about through the holistic presence of civilizational environments, concerning how they've existed throughout their entire history. I consider the stratified distribution of "socially-legitimate" education to be among the few key determinants of the nature of every civilization's audience, and inextricably, every civilization's sociohistorical context.[xxxv]

The general pattern is what's important because, if we consider what attributes are systemically inherent to any kind of culture, these are the most likely ones to be the result of deliberate – *planned* – actions, whether directly or indirectly (we'll certainly delve into this more and more extensively as the text unfolds). In other words, even concerning developments that take hold which aren't explicitly the result of some plan, if those kinds of developments still always seem to happen in civilizations, then it's likely they're still the *unintended* consequences of some other developments which prove upon the examination of history to typically occur as the result of planning.

Since civilizations are conquest-imposed cultures, the conquerors' interests are naturally always the primary interests served by a civilization's very existence. To put it slightly differently, civilizations exist in the first place because conquerors have interests: wealth-stratification isn't endemic to civilizations so much as civilizations are endemic to wealth-stratification. So if we're considering an individual civilization, even if we don't know for a fact that its politicoeconomically influential members intentionally plan on using restricted access to formal education as a primary means of perpetuating wealth stratification, we should nonetheless still suspect in the first place that the two things might turn out to be closely related. Perpetuation of wealth-stratification is the most significant force driving the holistic structural activities of all civilizations generally, and the completely unequal distribution of institutionalized education is definitive of every civilization (while always varying in its exact degree).

Notice how I said we should expect the perpetuation of stratified wealth structures *"might"* be closely related to unequal access to the formal means of education. I didn't say we should automatically assume there's a demonstrable connection. But I think we *would* be foolish to consider such a connection impossible. However small this assertion might sound, it's nonetheless the first step towards the truth, whatever that might be.[xxxvi] I've already said what I think "the truth" is: civilizations are environments of extreme wealth-stratification primarily reinforced by roughly parallel structures of knowledge-stratification, with the interlocked stratifications held in place by intrinsically and extrinsically hierarchical cultures of violent conquest. Yet this is something I can't properly illustrate with a few paragraphs – it's in fact the overarching task I aim to accomplish through the text as a whole.

Moreover, specifically regarding our immediate concerns, if a significant connection between wealth-stratification and knowledge-stratification exists, the connection may also have something to do with how all civilizations collapse, and how simultaneously almost no individuals in civilizations realize they're living in inherently temporary environments. I must reiterate here: while I point out that "*all* civilizations collapse", this truly concerns me in the end mainly insofar as it relates to the contemporary civilization (which, as a *globally singular civilization* is sociohistorically unprecedented). My direct interest in the contemporary world is what causes me to reflect upon the crucial history that ultimately led to our global culmination. Starting to determine the relationship between the twin stratifications, and from there the intertwinement of stratification and collapse, will bring us finally back to the question of the contemporary national State and its three extraordinary powers, which will also serve as the immediate transition into part 2.

Somehow, although based on originary acts of conquest constituting occasions of violence on basically unimaginable scales – thereby seeming to be most unstable entities – the cultural orders embodying civilizations come into being and stick around until they're (1) conquered by other civilizations or (2) grow until some ultimate limit and collapse according to their own momentum. All civilizations preceding the current global civilization fell either the first or second way, or else some combination of the two. How do we explain such extreme regularity shaping the destinies of these historically most unusual cultural formations? Referring at least to our central touchstone of the existent world, the present order has been able to continuously operate as it has, most of all, because it has actively maintained the *'legitimacy'* allowing it to do so.

Legitimacy is a difficult thing to define with precision, since it's a phenomenon definitively associated with morality. That is, for some reason the mass of individuals embodying the contemporary dominant culture's audience tacitly consider the existing order to be a *morally acceptable order*. Considering how our civilization, through its primary functionary, the State, is perpetuated on the most amoral of grounds, certainly the contemporary dominant public's conferral of such outstanding moral legitimacy on the State is at least interesting, even if it's not surprising. I must of course ask then: why does an order that denies its obligation to act morally – however much it may camouflage this denial – enjoy such uniquely consequential moral favor?

Mainly, I believe the existing order has legitimacy for the most absurdly simple reason. The existing order has legitimacy predominately because it exists (the State "wasn't born yesterday"): other, alternative orders don't exist; hence the present one, *at all times*, automatically has a tremendous "head start", an incalculable advantage over any potential (imagined) contenders.[xxxvii] At the same time as it has legitimacy because it exists, it exists because it had legitimacy. How can this seeming tautology truly explain anything, let alone the very capabilities sustaining the most determinative phenomenon in the contemporary world, in turn the most broadly determinative phenomenon in the history of humanity, the dominant culture of globalization?

First, it's not really a tautology: the order's existence and the public's attribution of legitimacy to the order comprise a feedback loop, with each side of the loop happening in a different state-of-affairs, which attain cultural interconnectivity via sociohistorical process. One state-of-affairs is from the past and has bled into the present, and the other is a state-of-affairs in the present that bleeds into the future. At any given moment in any given locale of humanity's history in civilizations, some form of civilizational existence bled out of the past into the present, allowing a civilization to have moral legitimacy; and some form of legitimacy bleeds from the present into the future, allowing for the civilization's continued existence.

As I've said, my view of "contemporary history" locates its earliest explicit origins in the U.S. and British wars that started in 1898-99, at the same time as its implicit origins were cumulatively building for thousands and thousands of years of human cultural evolution. These at first glance seemingly unimportant wars in fact achieved nothing less than the beginning of the culmination to the Western vision of global dominance initially established by the Columbian conquest,[xxxviii] which was itself the culmination of something implicitly strived-for in practically the entire history of civilizations and States prior to 1492 – *Power* over everything. In the later culmination, we start to see in the clearest imaginable way the true underlying purpose behind the existence of civilizations and States.

In the end, the purpose is nothing more than to service miniscule groups – *'elite factions'* – struggling against one another for mastery over humanity's systems of war and trade, two supremely conflict-centered activities which are so inherently interconnected with one another that they constitute what I call a singular *'war-trade competition'*. When I refer to the contemporary world, then, I'm referring in the first place to a historically distinct cultural arena in the form of a vast geographically-defined symptomology: the contemporary *'war-trade environment'*, an environment evolved across thousands of years of systematized human violence in service of organized wealth storage, transportation, and exchange. The unprecedentedly individuated, planet-swallowing cultural environment comprising the global civilization has grown with absolute interdependence upon the growth of the global war-trade competition.[xxxix] Most notably, *literally comprehensive* singularization is what the 'conquest-imposed culture' entails in the specific sociohistorical context of the existent world. The war-trade competition is totally singularized, and so the culture it fuels is totally singularized.[xl]

Let's compare the contemporary world during two different manifestations of its existence, in order to see in practice what I mean by existence that bled out of the past into the present and legitimacy that bleeds from the present into the future. The existent world actually offers the best environment for inquiries concerning cultural change, and not merely because it's still (as of this writing) here. Equally it's because cultural change happens so quickly in the present phase of history (what I call period seven), so we can track the largest of transformations in the briefest of instances. This is the most striking result we could expect by observing the acceleration of the sociohistorical process I previously mentioned. Further, it relates to what I mentioned about the primary constraints on our historical consciousnesses following from the history that has happened up to and including our respective lifetimes.

In the first place, let's consider the phenomenon people would've commonly designated as "human history" at the time of the first Gulf War (in 1991). Secondly, let's consider the same phenomenon at the moment immediately before the events of September 11th, 2001. The first moment will serve as our representation of 'the past', and the second will serve as our representation of 'the present'. The existence of the U.S.-epitomized global dominant culture at the "moment" of the Gulf War bled into the time immediately preceding the September 11th, 2001 attacks. Thus, when the latter attacks happened, it was the existent United States ("America") as a nebulously conceived *'imaginary entity of group unifying self-perception'* – a holistic culture – that would be in position to receive the lion's share of moral legitimacy on account of those attacks. The legitimacy attributed to the U.S. by the contemporary dominant public as a result of what's ubiquitously called just "Nine Eleven" bleeds into "the future", by which I mean our literal present time.

In this present time, the U.S. military has only recently ended (sort of) a nearly decade-long occupation of Iraq and continues its occupation of another national population in Afghanistan, a conflict the U.S. started almost two years before the one in Iraq. Besides these more ostentatious states-of-affairs, the U.S. military's three branches of course also keep bases in nations all over the planet, while myriad "Intelligence Agencies" occupy the world "covertly". Past contemporary wars served as the original main justifications for these latter two aspects. (We'll get to them in part 3.) In terms of the present, the U.S. Government and all the many parts inseparably attached to it have done/are doing all of these things largely on account of the moral legitimacy garnered by the destruction of the World Trade Center and attack on the Pentagon. Specifically concerning Iraq and Afghanistan, the only thing truly involved in permitting these occupations – aside from sheer logistical capacity, which is the other major aspect we'll ultimately deal with – is the moral legitimacy emanating from the public, which certainly exists in some substantial albeit as yet indefinable way. Based on tradition, the other relevant potential justifications would be legal and/or military. There's no formal legal justification for Iraq and, while I suppose one can debate the technicalities of the legal justification for the occupation of Afghanistan, there's unequivocally no formal military justification for the particular kind of occupation exercised by the U.S. and its menagerie of colleagues.[xli]

Thus, even if we can't explain it completely yet, we can already strongly perceive that "moral legitimacy" has little or nothing to do with whether or not actions made possible by such legitimacy are truly, in any conceivable sense, moral. Although hardly anyone ever asserts it quite this blatantly, actions having to do with interstate relations have long been seen by conventionally sanctioned "Experts" on the subject to be fully outside all normal questions of moral obligation.[xlii] The existent State, like all its predecessors, is by definition an amoral entity: an entity existing outside the realm of morality. Nevertheless, and again like all of its predecessors, it's in the peculiar position of always having to make its actions *appear* moral, in the eyes of its relevant public – its audience.[xliii]

The contemporary world's individuals seem rather generally to be in consensus that it stands in direct defiance of morality for a State to make war just because it can, solely toward a calculated benefit. Personally, I completely agree. In fact, I think it's the very height of amorality when States make aggressive war.[xliv] But that's because I'm opposed to war in all forms, as a matter of ideological perspective – a perspective I work hard to base wholly on my understanding of history. Logically *I* would agree with the notion that war-purely-for-profit represents the epitome of amoral behavior. What's positively bizarre is that so many individuals in the existent dominant culture seem to think they agree with this idea, too.

It's bizarre, but yet again, it's not surprising. The vast majority of individuals inhabiting the existent dominant culture don't really understand anything of true political significance, let alone something as uniquely important as war. The culture itself ensures it. If there had been perfect means available to successfully spread practically valuable information to the masses, such means would've rather quickly destroyed the system – and the system remains intact. Indeed, if even the *possibility* of such means existed, the system, directly or indirectly, would've exterminated every trace of that possibility.[xlv] This presents a great problem for anyone wishing that the planet's current life wouldn't be completely destroyed once and for all.

The public – the contemporary civilizational audience – destroys the planet with its ignorance: as the planet burns alive, all the time other things consume the masses. How else do you make sense of the fact that the flimsiest conceivable excuses, presented in the silliest ways, serve as perfectly workable justifications for the occupation of entire regions? The regime can barely hide its conquest-lusting pathologies at all anymore, and yet the people acquiesce on every major issue; or at least they don't make trouble. Existent masses don't even deem that an option. Thus the regime successfully portrays itself to its subjects as if there's nothing else besides what's immediately in front of them – nothing besides what's staring right back in the public's face saying, "Nothing to see here!"

Anyway, there's much to see/do within the security of the culture itself: the people are never lacking in possibilities for sensory stimulation. Indeed that's pretty much all there is. It's an endless cycle of instant gratification, whirling through the population like a circulatory system. People never knew they had so many desires! But there they all are, impatiently waiting for satiation. There's always new wants to indulge and ingest until one can no longer move. The regime, in the meantime, continues churning – resources go in one end, death comes out the other. The public remains preoccupied with its toys. No one questions anything. Everyone unconsciously understands that nothing is to be questioned if one wishes to live in relative "comfort".

The stratification of knowledge is voraciously at play here, perhaps in more than any other possible context. Not "stratification of knowledge" in any simple sense; rather it permeates every sector of the contemporary dominant culture, and changes (in the form of shape-shifting) along with every sector. Culture in the global civilization is completely interchangeable with the stratification of knowledge.

The division of labor, which as we know is hyperspecialized in the existent world, manifests at the holistic cultural level as a million[xlvi] different subcultures, all turning inward and not understanding any of the others, or at best, hardly understanding a couple of the others. This means that, although the world is still divided most broadly along "class" (caste) lines, there are also innumerable other subdivisions beyond, which seem innocuous until you realize the whole state-of-affairs yields a global scenario wherein no one really understands what anyone else is talking about, unless the someone else comes from an identical or extremely similar atomistic social – occupational – milieu. Resultantly, those common frames-of-reference in the contemporary dominant culture that aren't largely or entirely determined by the intimidating arsenal of electronic media screens at the masses' collective disposal, are comprised of very small pockets of individuals.[xlvii] Since these screens are most typically utilized for activities that, if abused, make people dumber, the vast majority of individuals inhabiting the contemporary dominant culture constantly albeit unwittingly contribute to the collective perpetuation of their own stupidity.

The screens don't "have to" be used for purposes that detrimentally impact the user's overall intelligence, but in practice, they're almost universally used that way. What do I mean by "activities that make people dumber"? Just think of what pretty much everyone does with the majority of time they spend on "the Internet" (World Wide Web). Mostly, they're either (1) absorbing corporate-sanctioned "news" (largely composed of gossip); (2) "posting" about the sort of routine daily happenings in their own lives that have no conceivable justification for being documented, and witnessing the same sort of documentation purveyed by others; or (3) engaging in the watching of pornography. To be sure, none of these things is *inherently* so harmful (perhaps with the exception of number 2). However, the human beings fully inhabiting the dominant culture, which at this point in history is a globally totalized enterprise, seem to have lost all control of themselves, and the worst sinners of all are the ones who live in the nations supposedly "in control" of the world. Moreover, it's especially the ones in the "well-to-do" politicoeconomic sectors of the population who are the very worst sinners, which is significant above all insofar as these individuals are thought to be *most* "in control" of the "in control" nations. This indicates that we have to change our minds, not just about who really is "in control", but even more so about what "control" really entails.

It's not only the content; equally it's the form of the existent electronic media screens, which provides the grounds for individuals' self-imposed stupidity.[xlviii] This stupidity is above all a crisis of *historical perspective*. For almost all of history in civilizations and States, there was only the public square. With the invention of television – referring here not to the tool itself, but to the cultural medium the tool facilitates – easily the greatest cultural hallmark of the early Cold War (the first phase of what I call period six), there was, for the first time ever in history, an audiovisually-stimulating *'private square'*: in other words, a stage for mass ritual participation located in virtually every individual's own domicile. Not only that, but individuals could soon enough access the rituals any time they desired. There's no way to quantify the potential for cultural transformation inherent in this monumental logistical shift.[xlix] Only a fundamentally qualitative assessment allows one to truly grasp the meaning of the change; and I can't imagine a "method" for expressing the qualitative dimensions more effective than metaphor. Humans can create *'real metaphors'*, by viewing phenomena through the lenses of archetypes. The only archetype for the television is the public square, the primary center where inhabitants of civilization-State-complexes met for thousands of years prior to the 1950s (the television was technologically existent in the late '20s but not until the '50s did it see wide commercial proliferation) in order to gaze *en masse* upon their respective culture's official rituals – the quintessential bathhouse for getting lathered in coercive group-feeling.

The switch from a public square to a private square wasn't the only thing that happened in the explicit lifetime (from the "official birth", onwards) of the global civilization: the most pronounced single change in humanity's history was still to come, with the commercial popularization of the Internet in the form of the World Wide Web. This would very quickly result in the practical universalization, from the first decade of the 21st-century continuing on through right now in the second one, of an exponentially proliferating "special case" of the private square: what's best considered, when juxtaposed with the others, the *'personal square'*. Especially, the universalization of the personal square was the direct consequence of the extreme miniaturization of laptops in size and weight, with the machines' being ultimately translated into pocket proportions with the anthropomorphically named "smart phone". Individuals no longer merely stare at the screen – now they interact with the screen; *they're in the screen*; they go fully under, and if they so desire they never have to come out. The screen is on them – they're on the screen – at all times.

If at first it seems like it technically necessitates more exertion than does the fish stare one must assume when watching television, humans adapted quickly enough to whatever minimal motion is involved in personal square usage, and so, for the typical mass individual of the existent dominant culture, the act proves to be what you might call "absolute watching". For the user, it creates the sensation of something like a full-being fish stare. The popular language alludes to the true reality well, if unintentionally, when it proclaims the imaginary biosphere created by digital media instruments to be nothing less than a "virtual world". Yet, from the standpoint of reflective consciousness, it's clear that few individuals inhabiting the culture are in any way prepared to accept how true the phrasing is, with all of its literally worldwide implications. Because it seems indisputable that the virtual world really exists – that it's not "just a name" – surprisingly, something not nearly so nebulous as popular ideas usually are. But which world is the virtual world?

With the virtual world, the totalized nature of the inextricable relationship between the culture and the politicoeconomic fuel machine comes full circle, as the system of globalization creates a truly full *sphere*: it encloses the entire planet in a single grasp, creating an authentically artificial worldwide web, entangling everything. The complex agricultural cultures that, starting six-millennia-or-so ago, gradually created the first social structures we can rightfully view as statist, finally evolved into the first social structure to be near-instantaneously transformed into a full-blown culture, when the global regime whose birth was iconically indexed with the World Trade Organization (WTO) produced the global idea environment of the WWW. Stratification of knowledge is at its most absurd possible extreme at the present point in time, wherein every individual lives in his or her "own world" mentally, even as humanity has achieved a singularization so complete as to have been nothing short of physically impossible amidst any phase in history prior to our currently unfolding (and unraveling) period.

Of course, humanity has reached such extremely divided proportions precisely *because of* the singularization. The hyper-atomization is nothing but the cultural (ideological) aspect of what's manifested as singularity at the level of the social. Such an unsurpassable lived contradiction is, most of all, made possible by the endless instant gratification loop oozing from personal square devices, which with its rapid-fire assault on the individual's audiovisual space completely rules out any potential for the individual's coming to possess a consciousness of actual sociohistorical context. An individual like this hereby becomes politically neutralized.

Returning to the content: the main rituals presented on personal square devices are especially peculiar because, once more in a manner absolutely unique throughout history, they seem to be trying to ritualize nothing besides "life itself". Everyone acts like everyone else, because everyone can always see how everyone else acts all the time: it's a completely new type of content, which although it can only exist because of the precise technological nature of the device screening it, takes on a life of its own; it becomes the real world, one separated from all conceivable context not of its own making.[1] It takes what used to be the mundane, the simply enjoyable living part of life that once was definitively fleeting, and brands it with virtual permanence in a "communal" space – a kind of seal of officialdom. What used to be the frontier of non-ritualized human behavior has become ritual's main vehicle of expression. Nothing remains outside the realm of mass collectivized automation. In turn, Earth itself becomes the virtual world – bodies going through motions, but motions that never had real-world existences – body machines. How dare we think that anyone would recognize it at this point, if "the machines took over"?

What's more immediately relevant here: how would anyone really know what's a plausible case for a "moral war", and what's not? As I've already suggested with my drawing attention to the three main things people typically use the personal square for – gossip-style news, simulated "social networks", and porn – most existent dominant individuals are informed about such serious things as war on the exact same stage where they view, for instance, the most recent photographic documentation of peers acting drunkenly. They simply approach the former with much less serious concern than they do the latter. Moreover, because they're so marked in their tendencies to act exactly like everyone else, it's almost impossible for them to consider adopting any viewpoints that seem to stray from the comprehensively-defined norms established in full by the ubiquity of the square's content. Being someone who's "against the war", for instance, in any way that goes beyond the superficialities of mere group-identification is almost invariably out of the question, if only because it seems right away to require too much work; "too much trouble". What's perceived in the square makes this abundantly clear. But there's so much other stuff, blissfully easy stuff, to experience in the square: no one needs to even think about – and thereby, they don't "need to know" about – anything else.

This distraction in the personal square is the most sought-after commodity in our world.[li] I'm not surprised, because as I've already suggested by pointing out the historically unprecedented degree of amorality coloring the two major "wars" (occupations) undertaken by the contemporary dominant culture's metonymic State since the second year of the 21st-century, the existent dominant culture has been "up to no good" in the new millennium, to say the least. As I always view humanity from a long historical perspective first, this is probably the least surprising thing of all, in the whole sequence of unsurprising developments I've mentioned thus far. Dominant cultures are always up to no good, to some substantial extent; how else do you think they remain dominant? It's only the mechanisms of distraction that have changed, and the overall level of geostrategic compartmentalization determining the distribution of State violence. Western civilization, the direct precursor to the global civilization, always trended towards this ultimate extreme – we're just finally at the point where the ultimate extreme is being materialized in real time.

Nevertheless, precisely because of the global civilization's deepest historical roots, there's still always something like an element of surprise to be found in observing just how great is the tendency for cultural environments to stick to detailed scripts written by thousands of years of sociohistorical evolution. Particularly as the existent culture's implicit destruction of all historical context in everything it exudes makes one unconsciously prone to thinking about the world as if the whole slate of prior history had been erased; *tabula rasa.* But not only is the existent culture the product of all prior history: *it is, in its entirety, nothing besides the vast organismic symptomology of all of humanity's worst aspects throughout history manifesting at once.* This is nothing besides Hell.

Hell is the last stage in the evolution of *Power*. After it, *Power* becomes extinct. At history's present moment, it appears that what human beings choose to do is ultimately going to determine whether everything else becomes extinct along with it.

*   *   *

iii

The existent State, then, is "merely" the quintessential symptom of Hell. Concerning both sides of one contemporary form of politico-ideological model, the "top" on the one hand and the "down" on the other in a "top-down" formula, which, when transferred to a specifically cultural plane is actually one of the best explanatory devices we have for all civilizations, the State is the mediating function between the two that acts on behalf of the top. State history is clearly not the only history constituting the existence of civilizations; but all history in civilizations *revolves around* the State.[lii] The top-down formula is the best representation of the explicitly cultural (ideological) side of life in civilizations, but the best historical (chronological-geographical) representation is a solar system: the civilization is always shaped, at any given time, by an *'orbital dynamic'*, wherein all less *Powerful* cultural entities revolve around the most *Powerful* cultural entity, which, because the top-down framework mainly appears in the form of a pyramid, I call an 'apex'.

So regarding the civilization as a whole, on the primarily cultural level (the ideological level) a civilization is a pyramid; and on the primarily historical level (the chronological-geographical level) it's a solar system. We have the "mind" and the "body": how about "the soul"? Recall I said earlier in this section that the soul is what manifests at the level of the social structure (the politicoeconomically-based level). This is the soul because it's invisible in relation to the other two things – but at the same time, drives all of their actions; while it thus can't perceptibly exist to human beings on its own, it's nonetheless completely visible via everything manifestly happening in a human culture. And it's the soul because it's where we find the ultimate shapers of any civilization's morality, at any given time and in any given place where the culture exists.

The soul also interlinks and thereby synchronizes the mind with the body – the cultural with the historical. If the State is the quintessential social/politicoeconomic domain of a civilization, isn't it then also the epitome of a civilization's soul? Indeed, whether or not the State itself always directly shapes a culture's morality, we always, as I phrased it, find the ultimate shapers working there in some capacity. At the very least, the State is always the primary instrument utilized to shape the morality of populations living in civilizations.

Considering our own civilization, for instance, tracing its earliest tangible roots to the explicit origins of Western civilization, the key formative molder of Western morality was the Roman (Catholic) Church. Already this seems to contradict what I said about the State and its role in constructing morality. However, during most of its initial reign in what I designate the third intercivilizational period (632-1492), the Catholic Church was the most State-like entity in Western civilization.[liii] Every civilization starts out with an organized religion (or something approximating it) as its central *'cultural repository'* (originary institution). And as such, in civilizations, religions or their equivalents are always the first entities to resort to the use of institutionalized violence for the maintenance of *Power*. To the extent that institutionalized violence starts to be employed, a fully-fledged State starts developing, thus explicitly creating the civilization and the State simultaneously, which is to begin with why, in terms of how such things exist on Earth, there's no scenario where civilizations exist independently from States – there are only civilization-State-complexes and the larger systems encompassing agglomerations of these entities (whole civilizations and intercivilizational structures).

When I refer to a repository, I'm referring to an institution beyond all other institutional levels, which in its "beyond-ness" allows other institutions to emerge and persist. A repository is a metainstitution. Civilizations never emerged out of nowhere, in history, but quite contrarily only arose under already highly-evolved, extremely distinct sociohistorical conditions. To begin, it's argued by many archaeologists that civilizations arose independently (or "pristinely") – that is, in places where the civilizational conditions hadn't been "spread", but arose relatively organically – only six times throughout history: in (modern-day) southern Iraq, in Egypt, in China, in India, in Mesoamerica (the Olmecs), and in South America (the Chavin).[liv] One can make a strong argument for the independent emergence of Minoan Crete, as well, but whether the exact number is six or seven, it's clear that civilizations are, in the first place, functions of the chronological shaping of a certain kind of geography. In an agricultural environment (remember that all civilizations necessitate agricultural environments), this further implies a directly corresponding politicoeconomic aspect, as agricultural environments strive to maintain airtight interconnections between the chronological-geographic and the politicoeconomic.

All the so-called pristine civilizations originated in areas with unusually high densities of relatively long-standing, relatively complex agricultural settlement systems, in geographical landscapes that, while no doubt extremely diverse overall from one civilization to the next, still conveyed, in certain of their notable features, remarkable similarities across civilizational bounds. For instance, as has long been well-known, all the pristine civilizations arose surrounding river valleys. Of even greater primacy than the enormous advantage in communications and transportation promised by the successful development of a riverine navigation system, the life-support benefits accruing from the proximity to water and mastery of alluvial agriculture must've first drawn then more importantly *sustained* the populations of the earliest civilizations.

Even compared to population levels starting with the advent of human food production, the original civilizational populations were huge; when compared to anything preceding agriculture, they were gargantuan. Thus, pristine civilizations only emerged in places where constantly increasing quantities of stored metabolic energy (food/fuel) could be produced, which were nestled within crude networks of regional trade, at chronological junctures when humanity's organizing (logistical) capabilities had long-since reached what we can call, on account of our present historical vantage point, the precivilizational level. In its earliest form, the precivilizational level was the crudest phase wherein multiple simple settlement systems had been combined into new singularized systems. In other words, it was defined by being one level more complex than the original, simplest settlement systems.[lv]

In places where civilizational conditions had been more or less deliberately "spread" rather than arisen largely from localized circumstances, civilizations emerged because of extensions in the "spreading" civilization's war-trade network. That is, a culture of conquest was adding to its existing domain. Civilizations didn't spread deliberately in other ways: they spread through war and/or trade – and trade includes the missionary work of religious organizations, at least when such occurs in a context of colonization.

Finally, when civilizations arose in settings where there had been a civilization previously – when a civilization collapsed, and sometime in the future a new civilization emerged where that old civilization's territory had been – they did so insofar as new institutional forms were arising to consolidate the social relations centering the latest emergent system of economic growth.[lvi] Always in history, the definitive originary institutions in these circumstances took the general form or otherwise fulfilled the general functions of what we in the contemporary world call "organized religion". This was perfectly natural, as human beings in civilizations are, for the most part, fundamentally religious animals: when there's a cultural atmosphere of "no religion", for people who are not only used to it but are in fact socially dependent upon it (such as when the prior civilization and hence the prior culture has collapsed), human beings, consciously or unconsciously, tend to seek out new religions. In a given territory where the effects of a prior collapse are still ostensibly being felt, the evolution of cultural complexity is in a sort of stasis, desperately itching to resume if only some institution can find a way to cultivate the unique orderliness indispensable to maintaining socially controlled human populations.

The Catholic Church spread throughout Europe in this fashion during the medieval period, and the same is true about what's called today the Eastern Orthodox Church, in its respective geographical domain.[lvii] In fact, even though still very few scholars in the contemporary West appreciate the connection, the medieval period (as I specifically define it, 632-1492) began with the emergence of Islam, which of course explains why I mark this third intercivilizational period as having started in 632, the year of Mohammed's death.[lviii] Within literally the identical sociohistorical context (for I define sociohistorical contexts regarding the "Old World"-originated civilizations in terms of distinct periods of unique intercivilizational relationships), the three civilizations emergent out of the collapse of the Western Roman Empire all began as *monotheistic* institutionalized religions that were either States themselves or else were entirely State-like in their behavior. Surely this suggests enough of a "common ground" to provide a sound basis for establishing what exactly civilizations and civilization-State-complexes are.

We'll get to that in part 2 of our journey. Here I want to focus on two things: (1) the order of greatest baseline complexity for the three civilizations emerging from the ashes of Rome ran as follows – the Arabic (or Islamic) civilization, the Byzantine (or Orthodox) civilization, and Western civilization. And (2) their being civilizations had everything to do, foremost, with the practical inextricability of the new religions and the new States, ensured by the *'dynamic of interformation'* between these two institutional forms. So that both parties could attain the common goal of least possible social instability, originary religious hierarchies and originary military hierarchies combined, which is to say they "joined forces", at least in those arenas where it was mutually beneficial. An arrangement of this sort, or any arrangement achieving the identical purpose, has surrounded the origins of every civilization.

Concerning our civilization of greatest interest, the global civilization: since it's at once the first true globally singular civilization *and* the last manifestation of Western civilization, its deepest sociohistorical and cultural roots lie nowhere besides the medieval world. Having already established that when all three civilizations surrounding what was at the time by far the world's greatest naval theater – the Mediterranean Sea[lix] – first emerged, they all did so as religious organizations that were, directly and/or indirectly, militarized, I'll now assert that the differences lay in the particular layout characterizing the combination of central institutional structures found in each civilization.

The most intrinsically synchronized layout was the one in the Byzantine civilization, both reflecting and reflected by Byzantium's role as the archetype for the other two civilizations within the intercivilizational structure. Before the fall of Western Rome, of course, what's today known as the Byzantine Empire constituted the Eastern Roman Empire, and therefore Byzantium embodied a direct link between the second and third intercivilizational periods: between what's typically labeled the 'Classical world' (ca. 900 BCE to ca. 378 CE) and the medieval world. Epitomizing the intrinsic synchronization was the figure of the Byzantine Emperor, who was nominal head of both Church and State. Such perfectly realized inter-organizational unification was indeed "the ideal" to aim for, from each other civilization's perspective.

There was another direct link between the Classical world and the medieval world, realized at essentially the exact moment of Islam's full emergence. The Arabic civilization, unquestionably the wealthiest and most complex civilization throughout the entire medieval period, was largely able to rise to such great heights so quickly because it conquered what was one of the most complex dominant cultures in the Classical world, the Sassanian Empire. This was a direct representation of the preindustrial nature of civilizational evolution. Before industrialization, an aberration that, within the history of civilizations, can't be paralleled by anything else besides the origin of civilizations itself, the last civilization to rise during a given period always provided the conditions for what would end up the most complex at the start of the next period.[lx] It's very simple why that was: by the time the last civilization in a period rose, the earliest civilizations had already long-since reached some fundamental limit to the complexity sustainable by their own natural resource bases, a state-of-affairs which, in its earliest manifestation, constituted one of the main reasons why the intercivilizational war-trade network was reaching out to a spot where a new civilization could arise, in the first place.

In the Classical world, the Greek city-States altogether constituted one of the archetypal civilizations (the other being the Phoenician civilization), sitting within the same general niche in the intercivilizational structure at the beginning of the period as Byzantium would at the beginning of the medieval period. Relatedly, if we can compare the overall composition of Classical Greek (or Phoenician) civilization to that of any other prior civilization, it's Sumer, one of the archetypes for the first intercivilizational period, which I designate rather conventionally as the 'ancient period'. Early on in the medieval period, the Italian city-States collectively had the same sort of general makeup; by the end, it would largely prevail throughout the West as a whole. So between the beginning of the history of multiple interrelated civilizations (ca. 3100 BCE) and 1492, around 4600 years, the civilizations our study takes most direct interest in – the ones happening in the intercivilizational zone centrally responsible for catalyzing the evermore-rapid evolution of *Power* – went through three periods of distinct structural relations, the first one starting in a dense cluster of warring city-States and the last one ending in a dense cluster of warring city-States-cum-national States. In order, the periods lasted around 2000 years, around 1300 years, and around 850 years, displaying overall an unequivocal pattern of "accelerating acceleration".

As abstract as it might sound, what the Columbian conquest concretely accomplished was the beginning of the geographical "inversion" of the intercivilizational long historical process. Once this beginning was accomplished, industrialization completed what the earliest Great Powers had started. There's a definite parallel between the initial process of agricultural diffusion during the earliest history of the intercivilizational zone and what happened with the incomprehensibly violent European conquest of the Americas. It's like the history of "Old World" agriculture began all over again in a new environment, except this time following a much narrower path, as determined by two indispensable qualifiers: (1) human beings were now starting the process of diffusion with outright *intentionality*; and (2) agriculture in general and civilizations in particular now already existed in many places all over the planet, including the first regions where Europeans experimented with total all-encompassing conquest.

Further, largely because of and best signified by the conditions created via Columbus's conquest on behalf of the Spanish Crown, the intercivilizational structure's westernmost points were evermore rapidly, once and for all, determining its fate. Civilization-State-complexes now thrived throughout the entire key intercivilizational zone, which consequently, in terms of its existence by the start of the 16th-century, had probably never displayed such equally distributed complexity throughout its domain.[lxi] (Although this common level of complexity would essentially be over by the end of the 17th-century.)

Above all, it was the rapid rise of the new overseas Empires that spurred the new situation. This started with Spain and Portugal, as I said, but already by the beginning of the 17th-century the locus of geostrategic control was finally shifting to the "Old World's" most northwestern extremes: France, the Low Countries, and England. Of course, the greatest extreme – England – would end up the most *Powerful* of all, a Power which itself "gave birth" to the most enormous, westernmost Power in the history of the planet, the United States of America. So if we consider the original, "Old World" intercivilizational zone as a unit, in the span from its precivilizational beginnings until 1492, the spread of agriculturally based complexity started out the span in the southeastern-most point and ended up in the northwestern-most. At the beginning of the next unit the process would be starting out in a new hemisphere; but it would nonetheless still be geostrategically dominated by the old hemisphere's northwestern-most point. Once industrialization started, this process became truly irreversible: resultantly, a situation arose wherein the originating Powers would remain the most *Powerful*. All competition now took place largely *within* the scope of the originary Powers, although there was still a prominent theme of conquest's continuing to evolve unto its westernmost bounds; only, as I said, the movement now followed along a path almost entirely predetermined by the initiating conquerors. This is why I say the Columbian conquest began the inversion of the long historical process, and industrialization ultimately completed it.

Clearly, since human culture was already so complex before civilizations even emerged, every institution in every civilization has necessarily formed in a world where other institutions already existed. Even – no, especially – the most *Powerful* institutions never exist as individual entities, but on the contrary always have to "make deals" with other *Powerful* institutions, a process that never stops during the entire life-span of any civilization. Since it's such an important word in the present text: what do I mean by 'institution'?

Once more, this is something only the whole text will tell; for our purposes here, two points must be made. First of all, an organization isn't necessarily an institution. However, certain organizations can become institutions, and every institution has some strong organizational aspect – some attribute or attributes requiring humans to at least occasionally organize – even if it's mostly distinguishable from any individuated organization. Secondly, as I hinted at earlier, some institutions can become cultural repositories. In other words, some rare institutions, because of the precise sociohistorical contexts within which they emerge, become 'originary' institutions; they become the foundational entities for entire new cultures. The three monotheistic religious institutions that came to *Power* in the wake of Rome's collapse are probably the most striking examples of cultural repositories in the history of civilizations. Indeed, the three civilizations surrounding the Mediterranean for the entire medieval period were, ideologically, practically synonymous with these repositories. Even today, when religious institutions have been completely de-contextualized from their original purposes, precluding contemporary individuals from properly understanding what religions *were* to earlier human beings, it's nonetheless impossible to conceive of Western civilization without Christianity. And regarding the regions where the two other religions initially formed, one can't understand either region in its present cultural existence without acknowledgment of the deep sociohistorical context framing its dominant religion's emergence.

I certainly don't intend to argue that the only significance of religions lies in their being employed as institutional *Power*-centers. Actually, the major reason why they are and always have been so successfully employed as such is precisely because religions have unparalleled significance in many other ways, both tangible and intangible.[lxii] Thus, in the first three intercivilizational periods, when complexity started drastically rising for the first time in any given locale on account of reciprocally-related explosions in agricultural production and human population levels, it was always the religious bodies that *Powerful* interests, those singularly ambitious drivers of every civilization's sociohistorical process, turned to in order to legitimize their own efforts to reap the largest/fastest wealth-subsidies possible, by going to war against other *Powerful* interests. At a time of heightened conquest consolidation in a civilization due to its first great dual growth spurt of life-support and human population, the religion properly so-called is, from the standpoint of conquerors looking for an exploitable official ideology, the "only game in town".

The religious *central hierarchy*, though, as considered separately from the religion as a holistic entity, is by no means some hapless patsy in its dynamic of interformation with its chosen military allies. The papacy itself actively cultivated the original, most shockingly barbaric breed of European nobles, epitomized by the innumerable petty warlords catalyzed into overdrive as a result of the Carolingian

Empire's logistical failure at consolidating rule. Further, when this situation soon enough proved governmentally untenable, the papacy favored its best State clients with recognition as "Monarchies", unanswerable to anything but the Holy See.[lxiii]

Although the Vatican no doubt saw Columbus's opening to the "New World" as its key to perpetual Earthly dominance, it wasn't long after the Spanish "discovery" when some formidable contenders rose their heads. To start, there were Luther and Calvin, spiritually splitting Christendom with their monumental instigation of the "Reformation", which tellingly began well short of a century into the era of the printing press in the West. Less than two decades after that, the English monarch Henry VIII declared that he was answerable to no one besides God, i.e., even Rome itself couldn't constrain him. This didn't only have to do with the best-known story about Henry's needing a divorce in order to procure a new wife who could produce for him a male heir. It also involved England's desire to claim a stake in the "New World", which territory Pope Clement in 1494 had declared the preserve of Portugal and Spain; and also involved the alliance of England with the newly Protestant States in Europe's religious wars, which plagued the continental front during the long 16th-century while the conquistadores and disease from European livestock plagued the overseas front. In 1534, Henry officially separated England from the jurisdiction of the Roman Catholic Church, creating the Church of England. Henry was now the head of State and Church both.

Thus, while Byzantium started the medieval period (established ca. 632 CE) as the most internally coherent civilization, and the Arabic civilization was relatively quite coherent at first, the West wouldn't even begin to reach anything remotely approaching such intrinsic unity until the 16th-century, and it must be stressed doubly that this was still just a beginning. Such both reflected and was reflected by the essentially never-ending warfare going on between all the petty warlords (nobles), and, in the later centuries of the medieval period, the similar but perhaps even more troublesome warfare between Italian city-States. Yet in the period of "unity" – precisely on account of this initial medieval background – the problem of never-ending warfare worsened, as European States found they could, at the later point, only achieve *internal* unity through spreading *external* division. The new, eventually national Western Powers that really started to take off throughout the 17th-century found their solution in exporting conflict, which in turn would become Western civilization's greatest cultural legacy to the rest of the world.lxiv

　　We're gradually starting to see why when studying history it's so important not to view as separate the cultural, the politicoeconomic, and the chronological-geographic: these aspects have never been separate *in reality*. How could you possibly separate the West's overall politicoeconomic (socio-) system of mercantilist-imperial monarchies from its chronological-geographic (historical) niche as the westernmost point in the intercivilizational structure? If we periodize as I suggest, for the reasons I suggest, the relationship between period three and period four (medieval and early modern) reveals itself to be much the same as the relationship between period one and period two (ancient and Classical) but on a much larger scale. Foremost, the commonalities lay in the intercivilizational structures. Compared to all other types of cultural form in human history besides the universal civilization (the form of the Roman Empire and the global civilization), the intercivilizational structure clearly facilitated the broadest-sweeping holistic consequences in the three interrelated cultural categories – cultural (ideological), social (politicoeconomic), and historical (chronological-geographic) – and did so multiple times in a rather homogeneous fashion. All this doesn't mean, "history repeats itself". It means the most stable force in the history of urbanized humanity prior to industrialization was the "Old World" central intercivilizational zone, which fostered periodic spurts of dynamic but wholly well-patterned expansion.

　　Through the sociohistorical process it sustained, the zone was eventually totally conquered by the most extreme ever manifestation of its *Power*-building capacity. That manifestation used this point of departure to ultimately fully industrialize, thereby essentially conquering the planet (Western civilization, period five – 1865-1945). Finally, the state of crude planetary conquest was intentionally consolidated into a global civilization (periods six – 1945-1991 and seven – 1995-?), representing a Western-dominated intercivilizational structure taken beyond itself to its own logical extreme, which within the all-supreme context planet Earth means a total planetary (global) industrial civilization.

　　The whole time, *Power* evolved amid the never-ending deal- and warmaking evermore-consequentially undertaken by elite factions, those largely unofficial yet most rigidly hierarchical regiments composed of the weightiest interests in distinct but strategically interlocking fields. Groups of these diverse mutually interrelated conquest sectors face off against other such groups; our existent world is the penultimate symptomology of their long historical conflict. "Penultimate" because it's the last possible existence on Earth of this precise type of cultural formation – the civilization, which in its last phase is the global civilization – before it destroys the potential for so much of the planet's life. The longer we allow the world to remain this way, the closer we get to the inevitable absolute catastrophe: hand-in-hand into a suicide mission.

No single conceptual representation can on its own properly account for the totalitarian nature of the crisis we're collectively repressing. It's not only externally all-encompassing; internally it possesses endless intricacy. Hyperspecialization, which defines not only all contemporary knowledge, but even more broadly all contemporary thought, is a most prominent part of the latest phase of divide and conquer. And in its worst sense, this particular aspect isn't something that needs to be implemented very deliberately, at least not at the present late point in time. What's far more daunting, indeed, is how it's built into the entirety of the system simply from sociohistorical process's sheer momentum. At the same time as our physical planet has never seen greater singularization, due to an identical sort of counterpart process animating our human imaginary world-within-the-planet (culture) wherein all humans are *unconsciously* more "the same" than at any time prior, the perverse necessities inherent in the mere continuation of the very same system's existence make it so that human beings appear to be more divided than ever before. My holism aims to combat this by seeking to reclaim the truest identity of every human being: every human being is, most fundamentally, a part of Earth. Shouldn't the parts be concerned with the well-being of the whole? No representation on its own displays the true magnitude of our meta-/megacrisis, but I believe everything else can be best conceived within the singular *context* of a tragically sick and dying planet, a planet that we're killing simply by our living. At the present point in time, there's nothing to understand that's more important than "how humans systematically annihilated the only habitat they ever knew". Everything telling this story has the most tangible urgency.[lxv]

We can now get back to where we started, this time approaching our question with the appropriate sociohistorical contextualization as a direct preparation for part 2. First we must ask the right question, which means asking our original question the right way: why, at this point in history, is the same entity that was historically responsible for waging war-for-profit on behalf of Western civilization's expansion[lxvi] also responsible for decisively determining both overall economic relations (through comprehensive public policy) as well as the culture's collective moral framework (through the criminal justice system)? In other words, since the world wasn't always "like this" – quite contrarily, the full monopolistic extent of today's global circumstances are for the most part completely unique to the contemporary world, and in so many astonishing ways completely unique to the existent world – *what happened in history that made it like this*?

Hyperspecialized scholarship can't provide answers to such questions. It shouldn't be expected to: like I've said, the primary purpose of hyperspecialization in academia is to employ hyperspecialized academics, not to explore brutally challenging problems that affect the whole living planet. If any way of looking at the world has the potential to answer a question like the one we're forced to ask, it's a view of humanity's history as the story of a holistically evolving cultural atmosphere – and in the most critical stage, from my own perspective, as the process of humanity's urbanization – implicitly and/or explicitly touching every conceivable field in the humanities, the human sciences, and the social sciences.

The culture of hyperspecialization simultaneously leads to and exemplifies those conceptualizations of reality wherein every thing is neatly, obsessively compartmentalized – every individual phenomenon stored in its own jurisdiction and presented as existentially unaffiliated with everything else. Nothing in the world actually exists this way, and so hyperspecialization as a rule creates completely distorted perceptions of reality. This isn't to say that there are any completely *un*distorted perceptions of reality: however, I believe individuals can certainly learn to minimize certain distortions if they work continuously at it, and in this vein I think it would be better for humanity's understanding of its own history if individuals tended more towards trying to minimize distortions, as opposed to frantically cultivating them in an unreflective frenzy.

When studying humanity, there's nothing that isn't fully within the purview of human history. If something involving actual human beings happened – if some such thing *existed* – it happened, it existed, in human history; just like if any "natural" phenomenon happened, it happened in natural history. And of course, human history in the broadest sense is, itself, a part of natural history.[lxvii] This is why, although in practice (in history) it has led to great confusion, I don't see it as inherently a problem that people use the word 'history', referring to the history of humanity or anything else, in so many different ways: it's in fact potentially beneficial to our understanding of history to have so many different perspectives on such an unimaginably vast and dense "subject". (Really, every thing is the subject of history.)

Context, of course, is as always the important factor. And in the present text, the relevant broadest contexts in which one might use the word are manageably limited. I've narrowed them down to three, and they can simply be considered the three main emphases of my interdisciplinary/non-disciplinary approach: there's history in a philosophical context; history in a human-/social-scientific context; and history in a historiographical context. Moreover, all three of the perspectives are, at least from my own point-of-view, inextricable with each other.

Since every thing that happened did so in history, all three of these "field types", and any others I'm not explicitly considering that would have valuable light to shed, have legitimate claims to study history, and I feel the study of history would be much better served if each only recognized those rights of the others. When scholars think too much about who is *allowed* to study what, they're unconsciously setting up hegemonies of knowledge – the "accepted ways" of doing scholarship – in the very act of thinking along those lines.[lxviii] If one adheres too strictly to this way of thinking, it doesn't accomplish anything besides the preemptive restraint of one's imagination, and hence so often has positively detrimental effects on the creation of knowledge. Inversely I find it quite helpful, when studying human history, to consider the distinctions between each most general way of thinking, i.e. philosophical, scientific, and historical, in terms of which particular emphasis is most useful in a given context, while the whole time acknowledging from the holistic perspective that *the world studied is always in the grand scheme one world*. Everything that could possibly be studied in direct relation to humanity had to happen in that world, which is at once cultural, social, and of course historical.

"What goes where" can only be determined after the process of inquiring into history has already begun. It can only be realized after one has already done "enough" studying – whenever that may be – which histories are important to know about in order to discover a solution to a human problem, and which connections are really relevant to the understanding of certain histories. I wanted to find out the important histories to know regarding the complete domination of everything on Earth by the globalized version of Western civilization, and more specifically I was trying to determine how the State on a globalized scale has played a role in this total dominance. At the beginning of the research/writing project, I already intuited that the greatest singular symptom of the unmatched devastation characterizing the existent world's most routine processes is globalization's status as the long historical culmination to Western civilization's evolution – even if I couldn't verbalize the intuition with the same specificity as I can now. The critical point is that intuitions can set highly effective boundaries from the outset of intellectual journeys, so long as one is always willing to be sufficiently flexible. To reflect on my own studies, as I started, by simply following my intuition instead of adhering rigidly to some body of "the literature", truly *every thing* was up for consideration in my researching and writing processes, so long as it seemed like there was a possibility that thing might've played a substantial role in the unprecedented crisis existent humanity finds itself in as a result of Western civilization's globalization.

Schematically, I knew I needed a model for translating such a monumental crisis into a monumental representation of the crisis. I suppose this is why I thought of Dante immediately; but whatever the reason, I thought of Dante immediately. Homer's not the Homer of Western civilization, but of Classical civilization – Dante's the Homer of Western civilization. And he's the West's Homer because of one work, or more precisely, one work comprised of three works: *The Divine Comedy*, made up of *Inferno*, *Paradiso*, and *Purgatorio*.

The definitive tropological character of each narrative as well as the overall metanarrative is *progression* – a purposeful journey. Specifically, a journey through humanity's most amoral tendencies, with the ultimate goal not only of denouncing those tendencies but also, and even more loftily, *deliberately cultivating our most moral ones.* A psychologically transformative journey: a philosophy narrativized. Spiritual alteration doesn't end with knowledge, but I believe Dante was right to say it begins there.[lxix]

At first I just wanted to use the mythological structure of *Inferno* as the model for my own present textual structure – I was just interested in 'the form', in the form as a primary example for how I might organize my ideas mnemonically. But the more I thought about the work itself, the stranger it seemed, and in turn I became more and more interested in 'the content'. Most simply, I couldn't stop thinking about why Dante would choose to express such prosaic concerns in such a definitively poetic format. In the most distinctively Catholic culture in history, Europe during the late medieval period, wouldn't placement of a real historical person in Hell be the most radical criticism you could make? What was it about the world he lived in that made Dante so willing to be so overtly critical (at least in this one respect)? Cultural criticism wasn't something I would've immediately thought to associate with that particular sociohistorical context.

With such a seemingly abstract, distant – literally otherworldly – context as the afterlife, why did Dante use mostly "real-world" characters, especially in the *Inferno*? After all, we know that in at least one other major instance, Dante chose to write about his more obviously worldly interests in prose.[lxx] Dante's non-poetic work during the same period shows that he was more concerned with politics than just about anything else, almost certainly because this was at the beginning of his politically-motivated exile from Florence, on account of which he would die without ever setting foot again in his native city.

Dante's exile had to do with something very ordinary within the sociohistorical context of early 14th-century Florence: the ouster from *Power* of the Guelph faction he was implicitly aligned with. The Guelphs and the Ghibellines carried on a perpetual blood feud with one another in late medieval Italy, representing the papacy and the Holy Roman Emperor, respectively; not only that, but there were, further, splits within each broader grouping, as well. The Guelphs were divided into two sides, the "Black" Guelphs and the "White" Guelphs,[lxxi] embodying in name one of the earliest examples of what already was and would continue forever after to be the typical Western State's main pathology – the division of absolutely every part of the world into necessarily opposed groups, groups culturally conditioned to go for the other groups' throats.

In his exile, Dante grew to resent not solely the Black Guelphs, but factionalism in general (even if he didn't refer to it explicitly as 'factionalism'), therein displaying an unusually sophisticated understanding of political factors for a European writer of his time. That this was Dante's main focus is especially enlightening when one considers the exact Florence serving as Dante's immediate sociohistorical background. I never thought about it until long after I started using Dante's text as a model for my own, but Florence was by no means "just anywhere" within the context of Western civilization at the time. Indeed, to the extent that there was something we can rightly call "Western civilization" in the early 14th-century, the Italian city-States epitomized it. At the exact moment when Dante was writing, further, Florence itself was the West's veritable epicenter. When it was finally overtaken, it was overtaken because the newest Powers of Western civilization filled more efficiently the precise sociohistorical niche Florence had been so instrumental in evolving.

Relatedly, and even more strikingly, though "strikingly" because it displays such a typically static component of civilizational history, we can directly account for certain politicoeconomic conditions that Dante was at least tacitly criticizing from his moralistic perspective. For we must wonder *why* Florence was the late medieval epicenter of Western civilization – what did that status entail, precisely? If we can answer this, we can truly begin to understand what civilizations are, what our civilization is, and most importantly from a metaphysical perspective why, when studying humanity, we must always view cultural, social, and historical phenomena as being wholly interrelated. In parallel, we will have also truly begun to understand the question linking part 1 to part 2, concerning why, in the existent world, the same entity determines univocally our global culture's greatest issues of violence, human livelihood, and morality.

It may be one of the most clichéd bits of information in the history of historical analysis, but it's no less true, in one significant sense, that Western civilization begat our contemporary version of capitalism: however, if this is to be a useful conceptualization in relation to understanding contemporary history, we must be absolutely clear about what we mean by "Western civilization begat our contemporary version of capitalism". As you can already see, to begin, it's only valuable as a starting point if we make sure to acknowledge that it's specifically *our* contemporary version of capitalism, in other words, the capitalism of globalization, which Western civilization was ultimately responsible for creating. As usual, much of the difficulties in understanding why this distinction matters stem from lack of general clarity concerning what exactly capitalism *is*.

Personally, just like I view globalization as the long-term culmination of capitalism's evolution, I view capitalism itself, from an even longer-term sense, as the culmination of the evolution of civilizations. Therefore, I view globalization as *the ultimate culmination of civilizational evolution*. Globalization is in turn, in one sense, the culmination of history, meaning the history that has happened up to now, which to reiterate is the only history of which human beings can be conscious.

Why did civilizations eventually evolve into a Hell on Earth – a real-life global inferno?

As distinguished from my historical (chronological-geographical) periodization of the genealogy of civilizations originating surrounding the southwest Asian/northeast African/southeast European intercivilizational zone, my cultural periodization of civilizations (dependent upon the same zone as its main contextualizer) sorts civilizations in relation to the evolution of capitalism. Expectedly, my design of the historical periodization and my design of the cultural periodization are mutually interrelated, because the aspects of history they describe are realistically inextricable. I view the history of civilizations in terms of precapitalist, protocapitalist, and properly capitalist epochs: roughly, i.e. with some definite overlap, the ancient and Classical periods are precapitalist, the medieval period is protocapitalist, and everything subsequent is properly capitalist. Within the properly capitalist phase, additionally, I view this history as internally divided into three smaller eras: (1) mercantilism, (2) industrialism, and (3) globalism.

Three things are intuitively clear about "Old World" civilizations when viewed from a long historical perspective, which render this periodization a most useful approach. First of all, by the height of the Classical period, i.e., starting the last several centuries or so before Christ, all the "Old World" civilizations were organized in ways such that the essential "primordial ingredients" of capitalism were there, especially in the areas closest to the epicenters of the Classical world. Nonetheless, secondly, what we can call "proper capitalism" – capitalism as the distinctly modern cultural form – didn't start to emerge until the late medieval period, and didn't emerge in anything like a fully recognizable form until the post-Columbian order was well-established, say around the middle of the 16th-century.

The third thing is the most important, not least of all because it's probably what causes the greatest confusion about the real world in terms of common understandings of capitalism, including most prominently common *scholarly* understandings of capitalism. Capitalism in its fully-fledged manifestation in no way emerged from a single civilization, and more importantly it couldn't have emerged in such a manner. To begin, although a cash economy in itself isn't enough to explain capitalism, recognizable capitalism certainly can't exist without a mainly cash economy. And there were *no* economies on the planet at all that were based on cash to any substantial extent until well into the Classical period, say around 600 BCE at the very earliest, when they started to emerge with an astonishing similarity across a wide terrain, from Greece to China.[lxxii]

Again, the most essential of capitalism's primordial elements were present for a long time prior to capitalism's earliest explicit emergence: which, I argue, was embodied in the first flickering of a truly worldwide war-trade competition, epitomized by the West's simultaneous direct politicoeconomic interlinking with both the "New World" and China, which occurred as it did primarily according to preconditions effected by the post-Columbian conquest. Indeed, I don't see how capitalism could've finally burst forth as it did except through wide-reaching long-term evolution, especially considering the long-term global evolution capitalism itself has caused to happen at an ever-faster rate. With that in mind, all the various elements in all their disparate locations finally seemed to materialize into an individuated (holistic) capitalist cultural form with the full emergence of a post-Columbian order, bringing us to our other best clue towards understanding what capitalism properly is, in addition to the first clue, the presence of an emphatically cash-based economy.

Capitalism as the guiding principle for a holistic culture was what happened when companies finally emerged as Powers on a level similar to that of the States that originally created them. This came very late in the history of civilizations from a temporal standpoint, but at the same time happened much earlier than is usually recognized by most contemporary scholars. I suspect much error comes from thinking what constitutes 'a company' primarily in terms of the modern corporation. Certainly, the modern corporation is the direct descendant of the original early modern companies; but as this already suggests, the history of companies didn't start with the modern corporation. And it still remains to be explained what the modern corporation's status as descendant entails.

As is well attested in the contemporary body of historical scholarship, the modern company explicitly starts with the European trading company: *it starts with the precise sociohistorical niche of Columbus*, in the sense that trading companies represented the institutionalization at the State level of conquistador-facilitated trader imperialism, the beginning of which Columbus certainly symbolizes. The trading company was the quintessential embodiment of "what Columbus did" insofar this originary form of company became the basis for the characteristic early modern Western overseas imperial system. England finally emerged as the archetypal State for industrialization, and hence constitutes globalization's primordial State, because it turned out to be that mercantilist government with the greatest potential for constant growth, i.e., the constant increase of additional energy supplies per capita for its domestic population.

Mercantilism,[lxxiii] "the first capitalism", was in turn an outgrowth of the quintessential protocapitalist model, the one developed through the system comprised principally of the late medieval Italian city-States, and, at the latest and most complex phase of the period, Florence. Hence, there's a demonstrable genealogy linking the culture from the latest part of the protocapitalist phase – what we can consider the end of capitalism's "gestation" – to our existent phase of capitalism, the final peak of its globalization. In other words, there's a demonstrable genealogical connection between Dante's Hell and our own. The link is the prevailing symptom of Western civilization: its most profoundly definitive empirical aspect.

Inferno exceeds the usual model. It stands as a comprehensive indexical icon[lxxiv] of our present metacrisis's true beginnings, which metacrisis results from the original manifestation of a Western history of upward-spiraling potential for mass catastrophe. By "indexical icon" I mean that it not only portrays symbolically, as a work of art, the nature of the lethal environment we make collectively (this is the "iconic" aspect); as a primary document, it actually constitutes a real part of this environment's historical origins (this is the "indexical" aspect). Maybe the connections Dante's work displays between our time and his are all "accidental" – maybe he had absolutely no idea what was going on in the social structure he was referencing – but that would only make the connections even more striking, in fact, because it would mean that without any intentional agenda he somehow stumbled across the most consequential problems of moral practice recurring throughout the history of Western civilization.

However, I think many of the essential connections aren't accidental: that is, I think he was deliberately making a type of criticism that an analyzer of existent capitalism could make; only, as we should expect, he did so almost completely unreflectively and relatedly, in the parlance unique to his own sociohistorical era – because he was naturally capable of employing no other. Most notably, he was criticizing money's unfettered domination of all human life. This is one half of the reason why he referred to his capital of Hell as the city of Dis – "Dis" was the Latin name for the god that in Greek was called Pluto, viewed here in his aspect as the god of wealth – the other half of the reason being that he was also the god of the underworld; I believe Dante clearly intended to exploit the double meaning.[lxxv] In one sense, this should make many of the problems Dante pointed out less surprising, but in the other, deeper sense, it makes his criticism far more shocking, because it shows with an unmatchable documentary succinctness the very worst problem of all. The problem is that in the long run, in relation to civilizations, and regarding our own civilization, most of all, *nothing essential ever changes* – underlying structures simply get transposed onto ever larger scales at an ever faster rate, always adding new functions but never really getting rid of the most significant old ones so much as reinterpreting them.

In other words, my point in referencing Dante is not at all something like "look at how wise people used to be, compared to nowadays". Rather, it's much more something like "look at how completely futile it is to try to truly change the world (the culture) by continuing to work within the framework of the civilization-State-complex, as is clear when studying evidence even from the very lowest stages of our own civilization's complexity". The civilization-State-complex is always a framework of maintaining conquest, so when civilization-State-complexes grow, it's in the first place because conquest grows, and not primarily for any other reason. Changes that arise are changes in formats of conquest – the most important ones being transfers from internal conquest to external conquest, or from external conquest to new forms of internal conquest – which happen because a state of conquest, like anything else, has to adapt in order to survive.

Sometimes adaptations lead to increased opportunities for much more than mere survival, at which point the rate of evolution increases for the civilization. This is what happens when civilizations "grow". Most basically, civilizations achieve growth either when they find better methods for utilizing the energy resources that they protect, exploit, and otherwise generally control through their States, or when they acquire new supplies of such resources. Particularly enormous examples of such growth have led in the past to what contemporary people usually call "Democracies" and/or "Republics", which were achieved by the wealthiest civilization-State-complexes in history, wealthiest precisely because they had control over the greatest shares of energy resources in the relevant sociohistorical contexts. There *is* progress in history – and it's the progress of conquest, a process largely coextensive with the evolution of *Power*. But since it's dependent on a finite planet this progress/evolution of conquest can't happen at an actually infinitely increasing rate.[lxxvi] There must eventually be a stopping point.[lxxvii]

We live in an afterlife of the evolution of *Power*. The system that once started out as Western civilization in medieval Europe is still in place; however, at the present point it seems to have lost its potential for overall growth.[lxxviii] Thus, we're in the strange situation where we definitely know the system must collapse at some point soon – "soon" from a long historical perspective, which could still mean years, though I would guess not many years – and yet it's still there, trying so hard to convince us it's perfectly normal.

In one sense, it *is* normal – it's normal because it's a culture of perpetual conquest, which is what every civilization is. But when we think of what most contemporary dominant individuals usually associate with "normal", it's the most absurd thing there could be. When most human beings in our contemporary dominant culture think of "normal" things, they don't think in reference to a world embodying a culture of conquest at its most evolved possible point – though this is what really defines our culture.

Nothing else in civilizations works like *Power*, and yet ultimately *Power* is what shapes everything else in civilizations. Here is the epicenter of the stratification of knowledge, the most daunting force of inequality of all, the greatest possible separator of those who know from those who don't. It's also the best start towards explaining why, in the contemporary dominant culture, the national State is considered the quintessentially legitimate force for controlling the use of organized violence in relation to the culture's inhabitants, for determining their economic relations, and for shaping their collective morality. The "need to know" basis in civilizations, taken to its logical extreme, is what leads the contemporary dominant culture's inhabitants to look at State-enabled corporate monopolization over all life as something completely normal.

What happened in history that gave the dominant national State and thereby all of its controllers such truly superhuman abilities was indeed the corporate takeover of all human life. At the same time, of course, corporate *Power* in turn never could've been magnified to its now fatally over-inflated stature without the concomitant constant maintenance of the national State's total domination. Therefore, to truly understand globalization we can't look at the totally-dominant national State as a relic of the past, but rather as an irremovable formative part of the global capitalist system, which was simply given a new niche in a globally transformed evolutionary context. The change to the national State inherent in the earliest institutionalization of globalization, explicitly brought on by the creation of the U.S.-dominated global system through the catalyst of World War Two and as an international phenomenon originally mainly symbolized by the UN and all its accessory institutions, was a change to a format where there was now *'officially'* "one level higher" than the national State's *Power* prevalent across the planet. While it took some time for this system to attain through sociohistorical process its fully individuated persona, the system nonetheless did so soon enough, at which point the national State truly became just machinery in an entirely globalized environment.[lxxix]

We must be careful to keep foremost in mind that the globalization of the cultural environment isn't a real globalization for anyone outside the ruling class and its immediate recipients of largesse (individuals who live "First World" lifestyles). Or, it's not the same sort of globalization for the very many as it is for the very few. Globalization for the richest overall planetary sector, the "First World" within the "First World", so to speak, really is deterritorialization, denationalization, and all the rest. But to think globalization means the same thing to all people overlooks the most characteristic, most consequential aspect of globalization – the very thing epitomizing globalization as a whole – which is the perpetual re-rigidifying of *the greatest disparity between the world's richest and its poorest that has ever existed*. This necessitates that the globe's poorest become evermore fettered by their immediate territory, even as the fetters are administered by a warden with no roots but a global jurisdiction.

Actually, to return to the previous point, it's the greatest disparity between the world's richest and its poorest that *can ever* potentially exist, since growth has reached its very peak. The notion of an "economic downturn", which is indeed one aspect of reality, nonetheless hides what is in the long-term the much more critical fact: even as there's a recession, the human world is still organized such that its most natural tendency is the total production of total resources, in other words total production of total planetary wealth. So then what's happening? How can there still be total growth yet less wealth to go around? I thought everyone already knew:

We're running out of resources.

That is, there's a certain quantity of people on the planet, and there's a certain quantity of vital resources. Also, there's a system in place for producing, distributing, and exploiting those resources. But the quantity of resources necessary to sustain the current number of human beings at current growth levels, within the context of the current system, is insufficient. Realistically, at some point soon, there won't be enough energy material to fuel the operations of all the machines used to live our lives. You, I, we all used too much, not least of all in our endless destruction of "consumer goods". For such a supposedly advanced culture, the silliest of problems is the final herald of our downfall. Perhaps this has always really been the case: what if it was primarily the bread and circuses and not the barbarians that in the end explicitly sealed Rome's fate?

*   *   *

iv

It's interesting that we associate Dante so singularly with the "Middle Ages". Interesting since in the contemporary mainstream mindset, this almost always, at least superficially and immediately, brings to mind the *Dark* Ages: feudalism – thus, ruralism – and the supposed general ignorance inculcated by religion. Personally, I still see feudalism as a completely useful framework within which to view the European kings and nobles that emerged in the medieval world. However, one greatly misunderstands medieval history, especially in its status as holistic archetype for all later Western history, if one looks at the kingdoms and nobilities as medieval Europe's greatest "invention". For particularly concerning "late" medieval history, by which I mean the span between ca. 1000 and ca. 1492, the most notable European *innovations* were the towns and in some places, cities, springing up all throughout the rapidly-growing Western civilization.

Western civilization was a very late bloomer in this respect. Much of western Europe really was "barbaric" – ruled by peoples the Classical dominant cultures called "barbarians"[lxxx] – when the medieval period started, by contrast to the original, central components of the West's overarching intercivilizational structure, which were for almost the entire period quite fully "civilized". To begin with, only Western civilization had real "room to spread out", and it had lots of it.[lxxxi] Contemporary dominant scholars almost universally overlook this face (as usual, except for certain individuals in relevant specialties), since the contemporary dominant culture trains the masses, and most of all, the masses in its "homelands", to look at the West as if it invented "civilization" (there's no such thing as "civilization" in my view, rather there *are* civilizations). It rarely occurs even to most historical scholars, let alone anyone among the West's mass inhabitants, that there could've been more complex ("more advanced") civilizations than the West during the medieval period – the formative period for the emergence of the modern world, and hence ultimately for the contemporary world, as well. In fact, every civilization in the "Old World" was more complex than the West for essentially the entire medieval period, and the ones in the "New World" arguably were, too, although it's much more difficult to compare "New World" to "Old World" civilizations than it is to compare different civilizations within the same "World".[lxxxii] Since, before the unprecedentedly bloody era of the conquistadores, the two worlds never had substantial interaction (so far as we know), and had indeed barely ever interacted at all, there were enormous differences between the general kinds of economy possible in each hemisphere.

As we in the existent dominant culture are in general so far-removed from the true basis of all civilizational economies, it occurs to almost no one that, throughout all of history before industrialization, in civilizations as well as in all less materially complex cultures, the indisputable basis for all *actual wealth* – that is, energy-material or stored energy – was food itself. Being the basis for all actual wealth, food was hence also the basis for all economies. In turn, further, it was, in a context of settlement, the basis for all *politico*economic systems. Finally, as the basis for all politicoeconomic systems it was therefore the basis for all settled human cultures.

Even in a world of industrialization food plays one of the few most central roles in creating actual wealth. It has merely been taken to one level removed in terms of its value as a resource, on account of the contemporary world's utter dependence for all of its food production on fossil fuels, at every level of production and distribution.[lxxxiii] Differences relating to humanity's provision of its own sustenance, then, have always necessarily led to the most broad-sweeping effects on all other areas of human life. Ultimately, nothing else can rival it in its primacy.

Surprisingly enough, then, of all the possible points of differentiation between the "Old World" and the "New World", no singular aspect was more fateful for Western conquest than pack animal domestication. Before Western conquest, there was only one place in the Americas with domesticated pack animals: in the western lands of what's today called South America, the Inca kept alpacas and llamas. Throughout the entire Western hemisphere, there were no domesticated cows, no domesticated pigs, no domesticated sheep or goats, and no domesticated horses. This alone could've been enough to ensure Western conquest of the "New World". Of course, it was far from the only contributing factor.[lxxxiv]

More specifically to the discussion of the rise of Western cities, the biggest point of differentiation ensuring long-term Western conquest of the "New World" involved the wholesale Western switch to an economy wherein cash crops were the quintessential wealth input. This was also the most significant real-world transformation signaling what eventually became the *conclusive* Western dual institutional shift to a cash-ruled economy and companies as Powers. Not only did the mass advent of cash crops mean a long historical shift in terms of the way agricultural land was used; just as consequentially, it meant the slave trade, epitomized in its early modern manifestation by the singularly ghastly Atlantic passage, which marked the explosive start to the West's never-ending destruction of the African continent and all its people. The central players in the slave trade were the top elites of the original European bourgeoisie, the business sector that dominated practically all late-medieval towns and cities. Even at the very beginning of the modern world, in the early 16th-century when domination of the "New World" was just getting going, the bourgeoisie had already been on the rise for quite some time.[lxxxv]

Why did the slave trade in Europe reemerge exactly when and how it did? It had almost totally disappeared in Roman Catholic Europe with the collapse of the Roman Empire. In fact, the institution of slavery was pretty much the one form of violent oppression medieval European peasants simply wouldn't accept under any circumstances, even as the rule of lords was so miserable in practically every other aspect. The peasant refused to be utter property, in the medieval world and beyond. That was a step too far.[lxxxvi]

So, amidst the conquest-of-all-conquests, with the perpetual genocide of "New World" subjugation having all but totally destroyed indigenous populations throughout the entire hemisphere – proportions of death that, so far as we know, are wholly unique in human history – the conquerors found themselves without any substantial labor population comprised of commoditized human beings: without the "necessary" supply of explicit slaves. *'Explicit slavery'*, as opposed to *'wage slavery'*, and *'debt slavery'*, is the form of slavery first exemplified in the civilizational economies of the Classical world. Such slavery is unique insofar as it operates through plain and simple exchange of cash (or the equivalent of cash) for human beings. That's why I refer to a labor population comprised of *commoditized* human beings. The distinction is necessary because it's not the only form of slavery, but it's generally agreed upon to be the most strikingly inhumane kind.

It's usually known as "chattel slavery".[lxxxvii] However, I prefer 'explicit slavery': most people immediately think of this form of slavery when they think of "slavery" because it's responsible for creating human beings who are *explicitly considered* "slaves". Immediate mental association of slavery in general with explicit slavery unconsciously acknowledges the special form of cultural depravity necessary to think that it's justifiable, or even morally righteous, to relegate to certain human beings the status of purchasable objects. At the same time as it does this though, and because it does this, it also makes seem relatively benign all types of slavery not considered "slavery" as such.[lxxxviii]

In some sense, one can "rank" examples of amorality: considering all the things that can possibly be considered amoral, certain things are clearly worse than certain other things. But how do we determine that, and how does it help us to understand morality? And especially, how does it help us solve the problems caused by amorality? Before you write these off as hopelessly subjective concerns, unanswerable from any analytical perspective, I must point out what should be obvious: amorality clearly has the most "objective" (physically verifiable) of consequences. Basically all of the current megacrises in our world are primarily attributable to people feeling no responsibility whatsoever to think about how their behavior might affect other individuals and the holistic surrounding environment.

All of the current megacrises shaping our metacrisis are such because they're not only institutional, but are also systemic. By this I mean, they're not only inherent to certain key social structures; the megacrises are, additionally, inherent to the holistic politicoeconomic system itself – to *the* social structure, as a whole. It's a cultural crisis, something wrong with the way in which the contemporary dominant culture "naturally" leads human beings to live their lives.

Explicit slavery, for instance, indeed probably was one of the few worst things that human beings have ever done. But *why* was it one of the worst things – in other words, what does that status mean? And can we fix it? The West certainly didn't fix it simply by abolishing the explicit legal framework of slavery within its own domestic territories.[lxxxix] If only sociohistorical process were so easily remedied!

In particular, sociohistorical process spreads most rapidly and thus has the widest and longest-term impact through the totally-encompassing actions of dominant cultures based in intercity systems, or civilizations. The worst thing about the modern revival of slavery, then, is that it didn't "just" destroy the individuals it directly affected – also, it was perhaps the most instrumental factor in consolidating the initiating process of a dominant culture that would eventually spread over the entire planet, ultimately threatening to destroy it altogether. When dominant cultures spread they spread eco-psychological *'conquest syndromes'*, which affect everyone who inhabits them, as well as every *thing* within such a culture's inhabited domain: everything within the purview of the culture becomes dominated one way or another. To be dominated is to live on the receiving end of an act of domination. So, what is the nature of behavior that dominates, and how does the civilization "give domination" to such a total extent?

First of all, the city gives domination to the landscape. This is true not just in terms of the city's immediate jurisdiction, but is equally true regarding the city's surrounding territory, the hinterland. Throughout the historical existence of cities, no city has ever had everything it has needed strictly within its own geographical limits, which for almost all of civilizational history were in most places visibly marked off by city walls. On the contrary, a city can only emerge and continue to exist when there are readily available, sufficiently transportable, steady supplies of strategic resources in areas outside of the city's actual domain. Again for almost all of history, because of logistical necessity, the most important of such resource-supplies had to be extremely close-by in relation to the city – "close-by" judging from the standards we're used to in the contemporary era of globalization.

The most significant strategic resources were always water and staple-foods in all history before the contemporary era, our era being so anomalous in this specific sense primarily because of the unparalleled role of petroleum-as-food in the global civilization.[xc] Thus, the necessary supplies of food and water for urban populations always had to be readily available within a distance that could be regularly traversed by the given sociohistorical context's existing transport systems, which in all preindustrial contexts meant nothing faster than sail and a bit later, horse. For almost all of history in civilizations, then, cities and their immediate hinterlands were so bound up with one another in comparison to everything else, this latter entity representing "the outside world" to those fully "inside" the city, the two areas were in every case more or less inseparable.

This is the primary reason why, to properly study both civilizations and States in terms of their existences as real historical phenomena, we must study what I call civilization-State-complexes. Even in the contemporary world, where that particular form of direct linkage between cities and States in specific locales has been wholly replaced by a globally-arranged (conquest-imposed) resource extraction and distribution system, the pattern still obviously stays much the same, since the "national capital" – a perfectly-updated imaginary embodiment of the inseparable bond between civilizations and States – is the global civilization's quintessential geopolitical subunit. Indeed, the only reason there has been a separation breaking the direct link between all cities and their *immediately surrounding* hinterlands is because, on a much broader, global level, the originally dominant form of urbanization has long-since so totally conquered everything on the planet that the overall scenario has ultimately evolved into what's essentially a single, globalized city and its single, globalized hinterland. Nowadays, the relationship is mainly represented not as a directly discernible geographic phenomenon, but as an indirectly discernible, supply-and-demand phenomenon. All physically-based cities are merely administrative subunits in a larger psychologically-based globalized city, dominating its subordinate psychologically-based hinterland on the basis of the most purely articulated capitalist deployment of resources one could imagine, preeminently including hydrocarbon-juiced human beings used as automated tools of gigantic technocratic occupational hierarchies.

Bringing us to the second reason for domination by the city: because of its domination of the landscape, the city is easily – almost automatically – able to culturally dominate the human inhabitants of its landscape. To begin, most obviously, the individuals who cross the city's boundaries and enter into the city's limits must play by the city's rules. The authority of the government *ruling over* the city is the singular flashpoint for symbolization of "the rules" needing to be adhered to by human beings interacting within the city's sphere, and this authority is signified above all in the figures of the leading public officials. As the concept of signification implies, such authority doesn't truly lie within any individual human being, but within the institution the individual human being represents, always centrally represented in civilizations in the form of sacred (monumental) architecture ("the capital buildings").

This is the greatest difference separating all State or State-like forms of government from all less complex forms: with the advent of its characteristic form of State, a sociohistorically specific manifestation of *Power* officially becomes more a function of institutions than individuals. Indeed, the coming-into-being of the original States can rightly be called the first full institutionalization of *Power*, a processual landmark always channeled whenever the State came to any locale for the first time, or simply when a new State formation was consolidated in an area where State rule already existed. Therein lies the perpetually replenished source of any State's unique advantage – the advantage, no matter what, of having always been "there first" in the field of organized violence, concerning the area of its dominion and the inhabitants in its dominion.

A civilization, then, can't take full advantage of its potential to dominate its inhabitants – it can't most ideally actualize its position as a civilization – until it becomes fully entangled with the characteristic form of State sustaining it, as the State's emergence forces the civilization to be the main tangible phenomenon shaping the popular mindset. (Actually, this is the only way anything resembling a "popular" mindset can even materialize in the contexts wherein States emerge.) When the civilizational population observes a human being adorned with the State regalia, the honorably-clad human being suddenly becomes "something more than" a human being. The vast majority of the population can't explain exactly what confers such status on the State official, but that doesn't make the general effect of such status any less real. Unconsciously, the population is definitely on the right track. There's something more than just a "regular" human being there: but it's nothing mysterious – even if it's mystifying; it's simply the inimitable social strength of official *Power*.

Once the entanglement of a city and a State, or many cities and a State, already exists, it's merely a matter of reconsolidating those original conditions, since, concerning human history dating from the emergence of civilizations, the combination of city and State has been the most *internally* stabilizing social force. As we've seen, the most literal manifestation of this, the city-State, was the main subunit of all civilizations for thousands of years. And that only changed with the nationalization of Europe which had its earliest observable origins in the rise of absolute "Monarchies" around the time of Columbus, but which would really begin in earnest towards the end of the 17th-century with the English "Glorious Revolution", and towards the end of the 18th-century with the "Revolutions" that would officially give birth to late modern France and the United States.

The most *externally* stabilizing social force in the history of civilizations – that is, the force most responsible for providing the city as a whole with stability within the larger civilizational and intercivilizational environments – has always been the war-trade competition. Violent conflict over the wealth provided by war and trade at the broadest, civilizational or intercivilizational level is ultimately what keeps civilization-State-complexes "in business", or alternatively, puts them out of it. Geostrategic factors, then, always primarily determine the nature of a civilization-State-complex. Throughout the history of civilizations and States, the geostrategic is the sociohistorical in its realest sense.

A city-State is a fundamentally complete geostrategic unit, blatantly in preparation by the very fact of its existence to compete with other similar units, or any other possible serious enemy of the city-State, over the resources necessary for fueling the relevant conquest syndrome. When a civilization successfully adapts and thereby evolves, it simply means that the civilization experiences an innovation in response to its environmental circumstances that will allow the civilization to continue existing. Above all, the key to understanding what civilizational evolution in the "Old World"-originated civilizations entailed isn't so much an understanding of any individual civilization in-and-of-itself, but rather, an understanding of the given civilization that views it as the fulfillment of a particular niche within a broader intercivilizational environment. To understand the latter, of course, it's equally necessary to understand the intercivilizational environment's own place within the all-supreme context for humanity, the planet Earth.

As I've already suggested by associating the evolutionary process of the civilization-State-complex with a fundamentally geostrategic purpose from the outset, civilization-State-complexes, starting in the "Old World" in the archetypal city-States of the ancient and Classical periods, are always most characteristically militarized entities.

This best accounts for the nature of the unbreakable bond that exists between the civilization-State-complex's internal and external sources of order: at base, the individuals within the city limits adhere to the city's rules because the ruler is the symbol of the State's unique ability to make war, which somehow (we'll get to this) translates into the population's unconscious as an utter dependence on the State for *protection*.[xci] Civilizational individuals typically lose conscious sight of this in the midst of their daily living, particularly so the closer to the epicenter of *Power* an individual's own politicoeconomic milieu is, and so inhabitants of such dominant cultures come to associate the State's *Power* with other, "nobler" elements common to States. This is especially easy to do in the most complex civilizations, and hence easiest of all in the existent world, wherein the State has taken on so many other functions seeming to be outside the explicitly military sphere. But the very fact that these functions are located directly within *the State*, and not some other entity, by itself indicates that such functions probably exist mainly because of their complementarity to the military, and primarily not for any other reason.

Let's once and for all get back to our question of why, in the existent world, the same old core social structure, that of the Western national State, still seems to have such abnormally concentrated influence on all planetary affairs, through decisive control over wars, economic relations, and morality. Rather than a question made obsolete by the phenomenon of globalization, globalization actually makes it all the more urgent for us to center our focus on the national State. We have to ask why, if national borders appear so completely irrelevant in so many significant ways, they nonetheless still provide the basis for such utter omnipotence in so many others, namely, those ways most overwhelmingly detrimental to the lives of the world's poorest, most culturally defeated individuals – the individuals forgotten or stomped on by globalization?

Even in the age of globalization – or especially in the age of globalization – economic relations and moralities are indeed still organized substantially around national militaries. The most significant thing to know for understanding globalization, however, is what these national militaries themselves are organized around. All of our answers, about the possibility of solving problems of amorality and everything else, will ultimately be developed in reference to this question. It may seem overly specific for such avowedly broad concerns, but in reality it's simply the minimal amount of empirical grounding necessary in order to properly address all those concerns.

Somehow, not just in the most metaphorical cultural terms but also in the most tangible politicoeconomic terms, our path towards understanding starts exactly where Dante's did, in late medieval Florence amidst the cataclysmic peak of the earliest stages of Western urbanization. Amidst the cataclysmic peak of the latest stages of Western urbanization, we find our only possibility for moving forward in looking back: the remedy for the lethal psychological sickness of the fully evolved capitalist conquest syndrome is historical medicine.

Part 2:

How the Path Was Selected: Theorizing

Sociohistorical Process

It appears to me that all my ideas in the present text have sprung from and revolve around one common question: what if there really are examples of "progress" to be found throughout history as a whole? That is, what if some kinds of institutions don't just come and go according to completely random factors? What if there is, in some sense, continuity – well-patterned emergences and recurring processual transformations from period to period centered around and centering the broad-scale social structures and cultural systems found throughout history?

Remember though, before even hypothetically approaching what seems at first glance to be an irreparably outdated concept – progress – that we already have some provisional idea of what the present world *is*. In other words, based on part 1, I'm clearly not going to try and argue for one second that the progression of history "makes things better". But anyway, why does 'progress' have to inevitably imply overall *improvement*? I believe the problem of *what it is that progresses* stands as the truly important thing to discover.

As I've maintained from our very first foray into Hell proper, one can't dispute that humanity's holistic ability to destroy has, on the longest-term scale, continuously and evermore-rapidly improved, from the beginning of civilizational history through the present. Now, regarding the idea that progress has to imply overall improvement: in the case of continuously improving human-caused destruction, at least, we find an example of an entity that has unequivocally progressed throughout history, which in fact prevents overall human improvement precisely to the extent that it progresses. There's only one question worthy of our attention in this respect – what has been the particular sociohistorical nature of the relationship, if any, between civilizations and the progression of destruction?

Amidst the first part of our journey I hinted at the main ideas interwoven throughout the present part. But such ideas, insofar as they reference a distinctly sociohistorical nature, can *only* be hinted at until one explains the structural processes shaping the existence in the world of what those ideas indicate. And the ideas are rather useless for the purposes of historical analysis if the processes outlined have no actual resonance with reality. Eventually, in order to most properly explore my conceptualization, I'll need to construct a perspective on contemporary history; that is, a narrativized conceptualization of the contemporary world in full, beyond the surface constituted in part 1.

Before I can do that, however, I need to explore the longest-term processes behind the key systems and subsystems shaping the overall environment of our contemporary world, which is the world of fully-fledged globalization. I need to do this, first of all, in order to demonstrate empirically the basis for my general assertions about the genealogy running from Dante's world to our own, and where this genealogy fits in with the broader one outlining the whole history of civilizations. Secondly, in turn, this will ultimately provide me with the most relevant point of departure to serve as a backdrop for explaining the processual aspect of that broader genealogy; its *evolutionary* aspect – in other words, the aspect dealing with "what it is that progresses" in human history. This theoretical explanation of my concept of sociohistorical process on a long-term scale will set the stage for explaining it, relationally, on a short-term scale, specifically referring to that short-term scale of the civilizational context immediately prior to our own: that of the West in the late modern period, defined by the full emergence of industrialized national States, which would soon enough lead to the simultaneous gestation of the contemporary world.

Thus, to sum up in order for us to move fully onward to our ultimate goal of constructing the narrative, I first need to exhaustively explore my periodization of the history of civilizations prior to the global one, the necessary preparation for properly appreciating what is, at once, our own world's aberrant absurdity and utter conformity, detailed in part 3.

Geonomics: A Medieval Introduction to Intercivilizational Structures

I

Dante's central model for Hell was the city he was born and raised in:[xcii] where he lived until he was exiled in 1302, having spent more than half of his life there. Florence, in the specific historical context of Dante's life (1265-1324), was among the five largest cities in all of Europe, perhaps the largest. Monetarily, it was probably the wealthiest; moreover, the source of its monetary wealth was largely money, itself. In other words, Florence was a banking capital – one of western Europe's first international banking capitals; and, I argue, the one most singularly consequential for the emergence of all the others. Contemporary scholars have called the florin, Florence's eponymous gold coin, "the dollar of the middle ages".[xciii]

Essentially no other information is even necessary for us to see what great value may potentially lie in bringing Dante's world and our own into direct metaphorical relation. What more significant connection could there be, within a long-term cultural context whose unrivaled sociohistorical individuation is owed precisely to its inextricability from the rise and fall of international banking capitals? The exact sociohistorical process preeminently defining all other Western dominance over human history originated in Dante's world, and is only finally collapsing in our own. Throughout all the time lying in between, what would ultimately become our Hell – an environment under the absolute sway of a form of *Power* nothing can control – most turbulently evolved unto its ultimately unsurpassable, totally globalized heights. The only step left is literally "the final step". Either the system will be destroyed because human beings born in civilizations, for the first time ever, will find some way to succeed *en masse* at acting like true human beings, or the system will be destroyed when absolutely everything, i.e., the planet Earth under its uniquely characteristic life-supporting aspect, has been destroyed – destroyed by all the implications of humanity's ever-refining ability to create systematized destruction. I'm not exaggerating the scale; we've just spent far too long avoiding the undeniably fatal severity of everything our world does as a matter of routine.

Why did the primordial stage of absolute dominance by Western international banking begin at Florence in the 13th-century, and why did its afterlife stage end up on "Wall Street" in the 21st? Before we even begin to answer the twofold question, we need to properly frame it, laying out the precise sociohistorical context.

First of all, it's clearly in one sense a serious misnomer to refer to a phenomenon of "*international* banking" in any context predating the early modern world. Even in the latest part of the medieval world, the 14th- and 15th-centuries, there were as yet no real "nations" in the West – and in fact no real "nations" in the rest of the world, if we're using the common modern definition of "a nation", in which case we're referring to an entity that at most has existed for less than five centuries.[xciv] Yet if we broaden our perspective concerning what "international" can rightly mean, it's not so incorrect after all to speak of what was, in the latest part of the medieval period in the West, something of a primordial "international field" that anticipated the one in the modern world (out of which grew ours in the contemporary world).

Instead of "nations", there were practically innumerable institutional structures whose identities were largely indistinguishable from their respective geographies, constituting the outgrowths of three major kinds of cultural repositories. The three major institutional groupings were: (1) religious, falling mainly under the general umbrella of the Catholic Church; (2) political, most notably embodied by the nobilities spread all over the European hinterlands; and (3) commercial, involving the merchants, those definitive representatives of that most characteristic innovation in late medieval Europe, the commune, who were largely running the as yet relatively "informal" operating systems related to non-agricultural commodity production and trade.[xcv] As this explicitly mercantile portion of the commercial sector was by necessity most concerned with the regular transport and interchange of goods between faraway locales, the premodern Western prototype for a general European international field would specifically emerge, above all, out of the operational requirements associated with the sheer existence of wide-reaching trade networks. At the same time, while late medieval Europe's merchants comprised the greatest direct impetus for the emergence of what would eventually become the modern and finally the contemporary international field, these merchants themselves were absolutely dependent for their collective existence on the other two major forms of network, the one primarily religious and the other primarily related to agriculture/landowning. Thus, the international field emerged in the way it did most of all on account of the direct impetus of the mercantile sphere, but specifically insofar as that sphere was *situated within* the broadest contexts shaping Western social relations.

I don't think you can understand the history of civilizations in general, and you certainly can't understand contemporary history's global civilization, unless you generally understand what happened throughout the medieval sociohistorical development of civilizations. You can't understand our civilization's most characteristic aspects solely by considering the formational processes driving the medieval world – but only in this way can you *start* to understand those aspects. Especially, you need to consider such formation as it happened amid the relevant intercivilizational zone, the one centered around the geographic nexus connecting southwest Asia, northeast Africa, and southeast Europe.[xcvi] One already starts to gauge its significance by focusing on how the first three intercivilizational periods, ancient, Classical, and medieval, originated and subsequently evolved as they did precisely because of this nexus's broadest economic implications.[xcvii]

As I mentioned in part 1, and as is a cliché of historical knowledge, the medieval world's emergence was more or less the holistic consequence of the Western Roman Empire's collapse. Quite literally, then, the birth of the medieval period resulted from the Classical period's death: a novel hierarchy of dominance could now be established in relation to the intercivilizational zone. To reiterate, the Eastern Roman Empire, which in terms of its medieval history has come to be known as the Byzantine Empire, was left standing after the fall of the Roman West. From the perspective I'm constructing here, however, the demise of Rome proper wasn't in itself enough to constitute the beginning of a new intercivilizational structure. Rather, it merely constituted the end of an old one. It's precisely when we look at such threshold moments of change – destruction and creation – that we see most clearly what an intercivilizational structure is, and why the intercivilizational structures traversing this particular geographical crossroads collectively played such an extraordinary role in shaping humanity's life in civilizations.

As the very label *inter*civilizational structure already suggests by implying the presence of interaction between at least two civilizations, subsequent to Rome's collapse, the emergence of a new such structure in our relevant zone could only occur upon the establishment of some fully new civilization. The collapse of Western Rome yielded essentially the entirety of Europe without a civilization, and in the aftermath the vast majority of western European territory didn't have the kind of cultural residue necessary for "immediately" (from a long-historical perspective) rebuilding one. From the opposite direction, on the other hand, geostrategic constraints existing in this exact historical context yielded a situation wherein a unique civilization – meaning, around its moment of emergence, a *new* civilization – could come to inhabit northeast Africa and the Levant. First of all, aside from having some of the longest civilizational histories of any Roman possessions, these two areas had also been probably the most valuable foreign territories the Roman Empire held; the collapse of the latter left much complexity and hence a serious *Power*-vacuum in its wake. Secondly, the Byzantine and Persian civilizations, the only civilizations in the central intercivilizational zone that still existed, weren't capable of decisively conquering the Levant and northeast Africa in the long-term, although Byzantium remained the nominal occupying Power of these two connected, immensely crucial subregions.

Combining these facts with the relatively most simple level of overall interregional military technology at the time – "relatively most simple" precisely because this was the very beginning of a wholly new period of military complexity – circumstances existed that were far more favorable for a unique political center near the Levant and Egypt than for the extension of an existing political center to the Levant and Egypt. Concerning the Levant in particular: only much later would there be a civilization (industrial Western civilization) capable, like the Romans had been, of successfully maintaining long-term conquest in the Levant without its having originated in southwest Asia. The clear difficulties present in the one possible counterexample, the West's brief conquest during the Crusades, only help to illustrate the point. The Arabic civilization's emergence, then, symbolized by the death of Muhammad/birth of Islam, signified the true beginning of the medieval intercivilizational structure. Resultant of its unbelievably rapid expansion, the other two civilizations we're concerned with would eventually be led to set their grandest designs on what was, in the context, *the* supremely valuable geostrategic "prize"; the war-trade wealth of the Levant.[xcviii]

To be most accurate, the beginning of the medieval structure was originally manifested in the general institutionalization of a distinct long-term war-trade relationship between the Byzantine Empire (representing Orthodox civilization) and the Islamic caliphate (representing Arabic civilization), with all the countless fractions comprising the nascent Western civilization only gradually but at a certain point (around 1000 CE) increasingly quickly becoming incorporated into the framework. "Long-term" shouldn't imply non-fluctuating. Referring to a war-trade relationship, and considering it at the level of the intercivilizational structure – in the present case, for instance – long-term means that, so long as there was the holistic cultural form of a medieval-era Byzantine civilization, embodied empirically above all in the Byzantine Empire's hegemony over the seat of *Power* at Constantinople, any civilization forming in the Byzantines' general vicinity would have to create its "Constantinople policy" with this precise reality in mind. And once that first new civilization – Arabic/Islamic civilization – was established, thereby establishing a new intercivilizational structure, a competing group from any other civilization in the structure would also have to create its "Levant policy", its "North Africa policy", and its "al-Andalus policy", in reference to the reality of all such Islamic Powers.[xcix]

Thus, how significant the geostrategic locale of Constantinople was to the overall war-trade system at any given point of time in period three would determine exactly what 'long-term' ultimately meant. To generalize, the flow of events at the seat of *Power* in Constantinople was consistently among the most significant factors shaping/reflecting the whole intercivilizational structure that medieval Byzantium was so instrumental in setting off.[c] To hint at its significance for both the destruction and creation of intercivilizational structures, even after many centuries of decline the Empire's true, ultimate ending was still held off until 1453. At this point, Constantinople was finally conquered by the Ottoman Turks, who were of course Islamic, at once signaling and directly providing the greatest impetus for the medieval intercivilizational structure's end, which finally came in 1492 (although it would then take some years after that for the reality to substantially hit the individuals who were to begin with unknowingly living it).

The latter both reflected and was reflected by two extremely well-known mega "events" (really, event-cluster-sequences; see later in the present subsection), whose real relationships to the broader history of Western civilization aren't quite so widely acknowledged. I'm speaking of the very first European terror spree in the "New World", undertaken by Columbus, with the blessings (before the fact) of the Spanish crown and (after the fact) of the Pope, as well as the Spanish monarchy's somewhat earlier but near-simultaneous domestic terror spree associated with the Inquisition, which mainly targeted what had long been unequivocally the most civilized culture on the European subcontinent – the Islamic kingdom of Granada (home to "the Moors"). So I can hopefully avoid any perception that I'm equating "civilized" with "morally superior", by saying Moorish Spain was the "most civilized" culture in Europe, I merely intend to emphasize that from a material perspective, it had generally been comprised of the most culturally advanced civilization-State-complexes for its specific chronological-geographical (historical) context.

To now refer to morality as a separate issue from "being civilized", the Arabic civilization was also certainly far more moral than Western civilization – concerning how the medieval period unfolded, it couldn't have been otherwise, basing this statement on purely sociohistorical criteria. It was far more moral in the simplest, most functional sense: the Arabic civilization had *a far greater concern for communal morality* than Western civilization did, at least within the timeframe we're considering now. This was "by necessity", which is to say, for a Western civilization to emerge how/when/where it did, there needed to be far greater opportunity for individuals to act amorally on the civilization's behalf. I'm again taking the simplest definition here, defining 'amoral' as 'in no way concerned with communal morality'.

Communal morality is obviously something that can only emerge amidst a community already in existence. In 1492, the countless, mostly quite tiny communities now evermore rapidly solidifying as Western civilization had existed in something remotely resembling their fully-emerged form for not more than a few centuries, and during these few centuries the West was still seeing substantial, almost constant growth, aside from the fifty-year dip on account of the Black Death in the second half of the 14th-century. The Arabic civilization, on the other hand, had existed for over 700 years, and had seen by far its greatest period of expansion during the second century of its existence. Thus, however much communal morality there was at the level of local communities throughout the territory the West occupied, at the level of the West as a whole – the newest civilization in the intercivilizational structure – the communal morality was, by sociohistorical definition, in its lowest possible state, though essentially always growing.

Viewing the medieval world as the literal pivot point between ancient and modern times, we can see what almost every scholar of history in the contemporary dominant hyperspecialized culture overlooks: the West emerged to achieve such a historically unparalleled status because it was the least civilized dominant culture in its formative context, not the most. Aside from the scholars, this surely must also ring as the utmost of heresies to the existent mass mindset, or else it must seem utterly confusing, or just irrelevant. But in these cases it would be the conventional understandings of history that deserve indictment, not my own. For it's not only in the medieval period where we find the greatest politicoeconomic advantages accruing to institutional formations that "start late"; it happened in one way or another in every intercivilizational or civilizational period, in all times both before and after the medieval period, and within every different sort of politicoeconomic system.

Concerning the central intercivilizational zone during the Middle Ages, moreover, the advantage for latecomers manifested in a way that tightly paralleled its manifestations during both the ancient and Classical periods. In both the ancient and Classical worlds, civilization-State-complexes first emerged in what the Western-dominated existent world calls the "Middle East" – what's somewhat less ethnocentrically called "southwest Asia" – and then sprung up subsequently in northern Africa and southern Europe. In the ancient world, no civilization emerged west of Egypt until Minoan Crete, which according to historians appeared sometime around 2000 BCE or so[ci] – around 1200 years after the earliest outburst of Sumerian civilization[cii] and approximately 950 years after the rise of pharaonic Egypt.[ciii] Although the preconditions for civilizations a little further north and west were in place at the end of the ancient world, with the emergence of wealthy but crude seaports in Greece and Anatolia, there was no individuated civilization west of Crete until about 1200 years after the Minoan culture's explicit establishment, at which later point Hellenic civilization emerged in the form of the first Greek city-States, signaling the full beginning of the Classical period. Finally, civilizations emerged farther west of this densely clustered locale, in the eastern Mediterranean just west of the Levant, when the Carthaginian (northern African) and Latin (southern European) civilizations emerged, which would be most heavily influenced by the Phoenicians and the Greeks, respectively.[civ]

Therefore, in the 3,000-or-so years of civilizational history prior to the emergence of Christianity, we can for our present purposes break down the intercivilizational zone's history into three "sub-periods" of fairly comparable lengths. The first sub-period, of riverine navigation, lasted from around 3000 BCE to around 2000 BCE, and as the name suggests was built predominately upon evolving civilizational exploitation of human and goods transport systems surrounding rivers, which in the presently relevant cases happened to be some of the world's largest. Most important here, of course, were the Euphrates and the Tigris that shaped Sumerian civilization and the Nile that shaped Egyptian civilization. Second, there was the sub-period between around 2000 BCE and around 1174 BCE, when there was a very gradual though no less momentous initial expansion of the intercivilizational structure north and west, most notably bringing the first predominately maritime civilization in history (Minoan Crete) into the network. However, this structure was still so dominated by the originary, southwest Asian and northeast African civilizations, we can't speak of a new intercivilizational structure, but instead of the expansion of the same structure to new territory. This isn't to say that the original civilizations "spread" (diffused) to Crete: rather, we should say that Crete's until then precivilizational existence reached a truly civilizational level of complexity on account of its entry into what had started out as a southwest Asian/northeast African war-trade structure.[cv] Finally, the third sub-period, between around 1000 BCE and around 27 BCE, witnessed the earliest example of the Mediterranean Sea's full incorporation into – and eventually its total domination of – the intercivilizational structure. The timeframe marks on its earliest side the beginning of the Classical period through the reemergence of a Phoenician-led maritime trading network following almost 200 years of dark ages, with the start to these dark ages having been most visibly symbolized by the invasions of the "sea peoples" that destroyed so many of the cities in the eastern Mediterranean.[cvi] On its latest side, it marks the official establishment of the Roman Empire, the beginning of the end for both Rome and the Classical world.

Leaving aside for now any specifics regarding the era of the Roman Empire, we can restart our consideration of the medieval period as a holistic process, incorporating now our understanding of the clearly-defined pattern comprising the first two intercivilizational periods. Resultantly, the medieval world's overall economic pattern is clearly revealed as a kind of admixture between those of the ancient and Classical worlds, but achieved in a far shorter length of time. To elaborate, let's primarily consider the pre-Columbian versions of the central intercivilizational structure to be economic mechanisms for sustaining interconnected civilizations across all three subcontinents converging around the Mediterranean – thus, on the pre-Columbian planet, any such structure served as essentially the sole *explicit* conduit of interaction for civilizations from all three continents. Also, summing up what I noted in the previous paragraph, let's take the first two intercivilizational periods as a whole, and the medieval period as another whole, strictly for the purposes of showing where *Power* started and ended up in each whole. From the beginning of the ancient period to the end of the Classical period, the center of *Power* shifted from the southeastern-most portion of the intercivilizational structure to the northwestern-most portion of the intercivilizational structure. From the beginning of the medieval period to the end of the medieval period, the intercivilizational structure, likewise, started in the southeastern-most subregion and finished in the northwestern-most one.

In the latter case, the end of the medieval period: the first explicit index of this ending, a real-world indication both of one era's completion and of the next one's primordial origin, was the aforementioned combination of two terror sprees undertaken by the Spanish crown in 1492, one domestic and one foreign. In each case, all of the innumerable associated happenings subsumed by the whole episode combined with one another, within a sociohistorically common system, to form what I refer to as an *'event-cluster'*, which I define as exactly what's implied by referring to "events that combine within a sociohistorically common system". In other words, to constitute an event-cluster, there must be at least two events that happen in such close historical proximity, within a system shared by both events – a system strictly defined in terms of interrelated politicoeconomic and chronological-geographical boundaries – that all the separate events are perceived together, as a function of the same systemic behavior: in the cultural imaginary, the events cluster together.

Moreover, while Columbus's setting off the spark of monumental conquest and the Crown's elimination of Islamic *Power* from Western territory were about as closely related in sociohistorical context as two event-clusters could be, they were still different event-clusters, insofar as they were separate operationally; this makes the combination between the two event-clusters an *'event-cluster sequence'*, or lived narrative. These in particular were all the more striking because they were so notably impactive from a long-term perspective. They comprised, in actuality, a *meta*-event-cluster sequence: an explicit part of the lived metanarrative. (See the next section.)

It might be argued that this sequence only indicated the beginning of a final shift of *Power* generally to the farthest western part of the intercivilizational structure, not yet more specifically the farthest *north*western part. But such an argument would overlook the main reason why the Spanish monarchy possessed such a unique geostrategic advantage in the intercivilizational structure during this exact timeframe. And it would also overlook the ultimate shift once and for all to the northwestern-most part of the "Old World"-portion of the early modern war-trade system that was about to rapidly take off already very early on in the 16th-century, starting in the Low Countries, moving by the end of the century just as rapidly to France and England. Considering the "New World"-integrated intercivilizational structure Spain so consequentially set off with its events of 1492, by sparking the process this State was also simultaneously ensuring the inevitability that it would lose its status as the leading Power: the highest geostrategic advantage in the emergent post-Columbian Great Power system would soon enough be found in Amsterdam, London, and Paris – not Madrid.cvii

Of course, this wasn't the beginning of the dominant process shaping the late medieval West – it was the very end. The process, the rise of Western protocapitalism, ended, logically, when protocapitalism started evolving into capitalism, which is the main reason, from the perspective I'm constructing, why Columbus and Inquisition together comprise such a uniquely iconic index of the early modern West's emergence: early Western capitalism would be wholly dependent upon the *Power*-structure first explicitly signaled by the event-cluster sequence starting in 1492. The establishment of Western protocapitalism had started in other places during the late Middle Ages; "the" (there wasn't really just one) key original "center" was in the Italian city-States, and the most culturally characteristic place of all turned out to be Florence, specifically regarding the manner in which it existed starting ca. 1250, just over a decade before Dante's birth.[cviii]

Like all other phenomena, international banking capitals – by which I mean cities that serve as "home bases" for international banking networks, not places where the bankers running those networks meet with international bankers from all over to perform international banking operations – have specific characteristics. An international banking capital is likely to emerge in one kind of politicoeconomic (socio-)/chronological-geographical (historical) context, and not in other kinds. Most importantly, such capitals typically need to be located within the cities that are the controllers, in any given sociohistorical context, of the greatest quantities of precious metals. Above all, these cities, and more specifically their public mints, need gold and/or silver.

After Florence's gold florin was minted in 1252, it would take less than half a century for it to become the *de facto* international monetary gold standard for western Europe[cix] – probably the very first of its kind in the history of Western civilization, and certainly the very first to achieve such a notable level of universality. Its historically-significant status had everything to do with precisely when Florence burst onto the scene as a notable force in Europe's nascent international field. The West's entire stretch between around 1000 and around 1348, the time of the Black Death, was a period of enormous growth in practically all areas of civilizational life, with all the growth ultimately revolving around two main interrelated expansions, in population and economic resources. Florence, which hadn't become anything we can rightly call "urbanized" (even within the quite limited scope of the medieval West) until about 1200, hit its greatest growth spurt between ca. 1250 and 1348, the peak of Western civilization's own first great growth spurt.

Though the West as a whole would of course see what were historically more impressive and "visibly" more striking periods of expansion in later centuries, this initial period set the stage for all later periods, and thus it has a place of special significance all its own. Moreover, Florence itself would never be nearly as large, at any later point –

especially in a proportional sense, though also in an absolute sense – as it was immediately before the Black Death. Considering the city in its precise context as one of the most integral components of Western civilization at the end of the latter's earliest stage of growth, Florence was, for the time-place, something of an urban colossus, with over 100,000 inhabitants by 1300[cx] (just a couple of years before Dante's exile).

The frequency of examples of dramatic urban growth across late-medieval Europe was incomparable to anything happening anywhere else throughout the "Old World" at the time. Two interrelated factors seem to account for this: (1) western Europe, which was, at the beginning of the medieval world, almost entirely either sheer wilderness or else at least non-urbanized, was (as already mentioned) by far the last territory within the intercivilizational structure to develop a new civilization; and (2) European territory had a natural potential for cultural expansion simply impossible within the internal scope of the other general territories. Owing to the first factor, western Europe's late start, the European cities that emerged in the relevant timeframe (1000-1348) could form in the matter of what was from a long historical perspective a moment's notice, since all they had to do was plug into a highly sophisticated intercivilizational trade network, not create one largely on their own. The primary driving purpose of this intercivilizational trade network sustaining the medieval world was the logistical connection of the Levant trade to the territories immediately to the Levant's west.[cxi] This had been so ever since the beginnings of the medieval structure in the 7th- and 8th-centuries, and the underlying purpose only became more and more vital throughout the later medieval period, with the ever-greater incorporation of territories ever-farther west (and north) into the workings of the whole structure.

Most importantly, the central intercivilizational structure in the medieval world fully incorporated the products of China and India; indeed, the overland "silk route" across the steppes, which connected southwest Asia to central Asia and central Asia to southeast Asia, was originally and perpetually one of the structure's most vital elements. Thus, the Levant was significant as a marketplace not due foremost to its "domestically" produced goods, but rather because it was, by geostrategic necessity, the supreme international emporium connecting the "Old World" west to the east. The luxury goods whose primary redistribution point was the eastern Mediterranean coast – as mentioned, silks, and just as importantly, spices – were the most sought-after "items of consumption" for the most *Powerful* elites all across the intercivilizational structure. As such, the trade in these items that largely derived from south-central and southeast Asia, on the one end – where the mightiest but relatively most isolated Powers of the early medieval world could be found (the European Powers weren't the most isolated because they didn't exist yet) – and northwest/north-central Africa on the other, was the key engine for all other "international" commercial activity in the sociohistorical context. All mercantile locales that emerged surrounding the western Mediterranean during our relevant timeframe (ca. 700-1100), then, including both those associated with Arabic civilization, mostly in the southwest (aside from al-Andalus), and later on, those associated with Western civilization (and al-Andalus) in the northwest, first came into existence primarily dependent upon the coastal trade of Asian and African luxury goods to the inland political elites on that farthest-west side of the intercivilizational structure.[cxii]

Collectively, those particular goods would constitute the main link connecting every place throughout the structure during the medieval period, and the state-of-affairs didn't much change until such an only-one-time-in-history transformation as the Spanish conquest of the "New World" created the first ever war-trade network spanning both the Western and Eastern hemispheres. Before that later development could happen though, the all-important preconditions had to be put into place via western Europe's urbanization. Again, the impressive thing about this episode wasn't the growth of cities and towns in an absolute sense. As we should expect considering the widely divergent levels of complexity when comparing the West to the East in this historical context, no European city came remotely close to matching the largest cities in Asia either in terms of population numbers or in terms of overall economic development.[cxiii]

To truly appreciate the growth of the West at the time, you must view the matter from a perspective that individuals inhabiting the contemporary dominant culture have traditionally been constitutionally incapable of adopting. What was impressive about Western civilization's initial period of growth was something I've already mentioned: how, in the matter of about five centuries, the West transformed from being truly barbaric, as well as a wilderness, to exhibiting the first phases of a civilization eventually capable of conquering everything on the planet. What was interesting about the rise of the

West in the late medieval period was the *proportional* level of growth, in comparison to what had been in Western territory immediately before. To an extent unparalleled by any other "Old World" civilization of the age, cities and towns were springing up in places for the very first time, creating originary urban populations almost in real time and to a substantial extent, out of peasants who had been at some point displaced for one (often violent) reason or another. Throughout the vast majority of northern Europe, the last place where a civilization emerged in the pre-Columbian "Old World"-dominant intercivilizational structure, there were hence no thousands of years of civilizational evolution for the mass populations to ideologically absorb, as there were in so many places across southern Asia. Ruling elites shifted from the archetype of Viking and Gothic raiders to the archetype of "nobles" within the span of a couple of centuries, an absolutely remarkable transformation – and one which had nothing primarily to do with the nobles' personal qualities and everything primarily to do with the fortune determined by longest-term, widest-spread sociohistorical process.

Every locale in the burgeoning Western civilization during the few centuries before the year 1000 reflected essentially the same minimal though slowly growing level of cultural complexity, but the overall pattern appeared in degrees that varied from place to place. Much earlier than in most other places, for instance, some locales in Italy (especially northern Italy) strikingly defied the *total* monopoly of *Power* by the earliest, most barbaric castes of nobles – although please note with extra care that they were only able to avoid such a monopoly in its sheer totality; they weren't able to avoid it altogether, nor were they even able to mostly avoid it. Rather, since, as I've said, in the earliest part of the medieval period the nobles themselves were almost the only customers of individuals involved in European international commerce, the commercial classes in this initial phase were still at base inextricably intertwined with the nobility, however consciously or unconsciously the mutuality of interests may have been manifested in any given locale. Whether or not alliances were always *deliberately* cultivated between merchants and nobles, their respective interests were always aligned in a most substantial way. Again, this wasn't at all something unique to western Europe geographically in the medieval world, nor was it unique to the medieval world chronologically. It was the pattern found in every civilization in the "Old World" during the medieval period, which itself recapitulated the archetypal *Power*-structure that had evolved out of almost four millennia of intercivilizational structures.[cxiv]

    As I mentioned earlier, that wasn't all. There was one more caste of characters: the preeminent one at the time for funneling Western intellectual culture into politico-military elites, which was then forced by those elites onto their subjects. The Roman Church, like the Byzantine Empire, was a carry-over from the Classical world. Before the establishment of the medieval structure, in the relative no-man's land between the Roman Empire's fall and the rise of new Powers, this had allowed the papacy to project itself as the natural original conduit for very slowly re-spreading civilizational knowledge across barbaric northern Europe, thereby starting to add a glossy veneer of ritualized legitimacy to the bloodthirsty prototypical *Power*-relations of the warlord nobilities. This explains why I call the Catholic Church the original cultural repository for all of Western civilization. Thus, the inextricable alliance of interests tacitly formed between nobles and merchants was, more accurately, an inextricable alliance of interests tacitly existing between nobles, merchants, and clergy.

    Many if not most of the individual facts comprising the basis for my account are well-known – some of which to the point of seeming cliché. But they're not less true because of that, and in their truth they've had unusually enormous consequences for all subsequent history. How did these three medieval institutional groupings, represented by Roman Christianity (Catholicism), land-holding nobility, and "international" commerce, have such a collectively dominant influence on all other Western history, in turn eventually affecting all global history? This question has both long-term and short-term aspects: the aspect of all civilizational history in the first instance, and the aspect of each relevant sociohistorical period in the second. In the next two sections, I'll discuss the long-term aspects and the short-term aspects of the other periods (besides the medieval one), and in particular the theoretical bases for both long and short perspectives. Here, in addressing the more specific, short-term aspects of the medieval world, we're best served by viewing details within the overall framework of "how the system that ultimately shaped Western civilization as a whole was dominated in its crudest beginnings by the late medieval Italian city-States". Since the system is characterized above all by Western civilization's sociohistorical status as the central field for an ever-increasing and ever-increasingly totalized *Power*-structure run by international banking, we'll also be at the same time starting to address the question, "Why did the primordial stage of absolute dominance by Western international banking begin at Florence in the 13th-century, and why did its afterlife stage end up on "Wall Street" in the 21st?"

II

After the Western Roman Empire's collapse, the Arabic civilization was able to become the first new civilization in the old intercivilizational structure's territory mainly because the Levant, which the Arabs quickly came to control, was the central territory facilitating the Mediterranean's access to the China and India trade. Since this is the most important geostrategic reason explaining the Arabic civilization's emergence, it's the most important reason of all, because all civilizations, along with their indispensable real-world counterparts, States, are quintessentially geostrategic entities, which is to say they "live or die" based on geostrategic trends of events. The word 'geostrategy', in terms of how I'm employing it all throughout this text, means nothing so much as "the art of mastery over the war-trade competition".

If we consider the civilization, uniquely, to be the intercity cultural environment in its comprehensive, reciprocally related mental and physical aspects, and the State to be the singularly legitimized vehicle for initiating and instituting conquest over locales within a civilization, we can see exactly what I mean when I say that the civilization-State-complex is fundamentally a geostrategic unit, for which the city-State was the original prototype. The elite factions who ultimately rule over all civilization-State-complexes, and the most *Powerful* of these, who rule over intercivilizational structures (or other entities that fulfill the same purpose), are elite because they're the individuals who dominate the war-trade competition. All civilizations appear externally ("on the surface") as cultural hierarchies, which are internally comprised of long-evolving politicoeconomic hierarchies, and the intercivilizational elite factions – those comprised of the elites who deal with the top elites from other civilizations – are by the nature of the war-trade competition always at the very top (apex) of any civilizational hierarchy. Already, this puts into clearest perspective the unrivaled role in influencing all subsequent Western civilization played by the inherently interlocking relationship between the Catholic Church, the noble warlords, and the wealthiest international merchants.[cxv]

There wasn't enough Western demand for intercivilizational trade to the point where western (especially northwestern) Europe could be brought into the structure on any sort of substantial scale until sometime well into the 10th-century, at which point the Byzantine and Arabic trade connected to China and India had been going on for about four centuries.[cxvi] Thus, since the system was already so well-established, the strategic advantage for successful cities and hence for any successful merchant States in western Europe would go, at first, to the places most immediately ready to be sustained by involvement in a far-flung trade network: that is, besides the initial overarching geographic determination of proximity to the coastline, namely that of the Mediterranean and (a bit later) the Atlantic. So at first, in medieval western Europe, the ideal locales for successfully entering into the intercivilizational trade structure and hence, for sparking the creation of a truly urbanized holistic environment, were those with the best access to the seas which also had the relatively highest level of cultural complexity at the time when demand returned.

Originally, concerning those preconditions, Venice was without question the ideal geostrategic location for dominating western Europe's participation in the medieval trade structure, such as that participation was before the 11th-century. For about the first 200 years or so of its existence (750-950), Venice was in fact one of western Europe's only links to the structure, at all. Moreover, owing to its position in Italy's northeastern-most corner, Venetian elites were able to establish privileged trading relations with the Byzantine Empire quite early on, and in the late medieval period city notables always maintained a strong presence abroad in Constantinople. Indeed, for a long time Venice displayed much closer cultural associations with Byzantine civilization than it did with the rest of what would eventually become Western civilization. Thus, Venice would be the most significant locale linking western Europe to the Levant trade when western Europe's incorporation into the trade started in full force right before the year 1000.

Likewise, on the directly opposite side of the Italian peninsula, Genoa became one of the first new seaports whose establishment signaled the explicit beginning of the West's "commercial revolution".[cxvii] To put things a bit differently, Genoa's emergence as a sea Power was a direct indication of the fact that now, for the first time, there was room in the Western trade system for a competitor in that part of the game Venice originated (and which it thereby originally dominated). Finally, we ultimately can't separate any of these developments from the parallel shifts in the contemporaneous Western (land) war system: in the late medieval world, the most definitive aspect of competition in each military sub-sphere – land on the one hand and sea on the other – was that success, to an ever-increasing degree, became dependent on one competitor's ability to fruitfully coordinate his own strategies with those of some competitor in the other sub-sphere.

Within whatever tool-complex constraints prevail throughout any given time-place, a human transportation system can traffic just about anything in the scope of the consciousnesses of those human beings utilizing the system. Among the things not precluded by physical limitations, on the other hand, what gets transported is, to begin with, typically a matter of what's already being profitably produced in the same cultural/sociohistorical context. But once there is in place a system to profitably transport the first item(s), the definition of what has the potential to be profitably transported wholly transforms – items whose trade hadn't been profitable when nothing else was being transported can suddenly gain that potential once a continuous transportation system has been successfully opened up. In this way, in a polity mainly involved in the transit trade, the controlling profit share tends initially to go to those who were the first to monopolize the polity's involvement in trafficking: in the cases of the relevant medieval polities, such monopolists became the bases for marine-mercantile/naval States.

Therefore, once one agglomeration of human beings opens up a transit system, and these people profit from it – as they must for their enterprise to continue – other agglomerations will follow. At some point, after a great many additional individuals have taken to using the system, certain sectors will emerge that seek out whatever else can possibly be transported for a profit. Of course, too, it's not only the transporters themselves who depend on the transportation system for their livelihoods: in fact, many more times the amount of individuals existing within the transport and mercantile sectors proper now need the system for their very survival, because their gainful employment is at the crudest, most crucial level contingent on the fact that goods are regularly transported from this place to that place.

Even without the transporters finding new things to traffic, then, the quantity of people and objects traveling via the system still naturally rises with the mere continuation of the system, moving as trade cargo only the bare necessities of life and a minimal amount of foreign luxury goods – the system's staples. Moreover, transporters and traders obviously can't live at sea in perpetuity, especially concerning the logistical circumstances characterizing all contexts preceding the unprecedented transit speed and gargantuan storage capacities of mass industrialization. In other words, the individuals who were making their living on the transportation system itself, merchants in the truest sense, needed places to stop for general sustenance. This was really the main purpose for the emergence of most ports in the first place, rather than their use as trade emporiums. Such places to stop, to have been worthy of stopping at them, needed full-time inhabitants who could manage the mechanisms for survival the transit trade sector relied upon to fulfill its functions. Thus, in-and-of-itself, regardless of any growth within the category of "things transported for a profit", the transportation system sustaining an emergent civilization continually reproduces the underlying conditions for its own existence, in turn perpetuating the civilization's future potential.

But lack of expansion within the commercial sphere proper clearly isn't a very long-lasting scenario either, particularly so when the sociohistorical context is the beginning of a phase of great commercial growth such as that experienced by the West in its medieval commercial revolution (950-1350). Western civilization's rapid adjustment to an existence based largely on seafaring trade in goods both reflected and was subsequently reflected by the vastly improved nautical capacity for transporting cargo in comparison with previous ages, a phenomenon prevalent all across the medieval world's coastal portions. Success in the naval sphere was thus almost entirely a matter of cultural diffusion to the West from other sources, at least during this earliest phase of Western complexity's initial boom.[cxviii] That without much effort, western Europeans were practically immediately able to profit from technology only developed by other civilizations through centuries of expense and struggle, does much to explain the West's commercial revolution, which after all was only a "revolution" insofar as it brought the relatively quite primitive West closer to, but still not yet at, the general level of complexity prevailing across the other civilizations comprising the structure.

Again, the greatest geostrategic advantage typically goes to the civilization-State-complexes that start late – after the earliest, formative stage of an intercivilizational period, wherein the advantage goes to the civilization-State-complexes that start first. In other words, the seat of *Power* in an intercivilizational period starts in what's initially the most complex portion on the map, and ends in what was initially the least complex,[cxix] and indeed this state-of-affairs is a mandatory reference point for any notion of "starting" and "ending" in relation to intercivilizational periods. Here's why:

Obviously every intercivilizational structure must originate *at one geographic point*: surrounding the civilization-State-complexes that emerge first, amongst which one of them must be the very first. From there, as it grows, the overall system sustaining the originally most complex locale must spread ever-farther geographically in some general direction, touching points with potential geostrategic significance at fairly evenly spread intervals along the way, until it reaches its point of final expansion. If, as I'm arguing in this text, there are such things as intercivilizational structures, and since such structures, if real, must ultimately be dependent on planet Earth, intercivilizational structures can in reality only spread in such a geographically-determined way. The only partial exception to this rule is the contemporary globalized world. As by definition, it has evolved beyond the stage of the intercivilizational structure, those particular geographical determinations no longer apply to the global civilization. However, this is only the case due to around five millennia of intercivilizational evolution along precisely geographical, and even more precisely geo*strategic* lines, and so this feature is in fact all the more relevant in the contemporary world on account of its having been so successful that it ultimately put itself out of existence (naturally this happened when the Westernmost Power, the "end of the line" for the geostrategic evolution of civilizations, conquered all human existence).

The most striking examples of this trend throughout history involved all the civilizations most directly "related to" the southwest Asia/northeast Africa/southeast Europe nexus, insofar as these civilizations saw the most rapid and hence most volatile phases of growth in history. Specifically, I'm referring to what we've been focused on all along in this section, concerning the expansion of the structure from the southeast to the northwest in the first three intercivilizational periods. To be sure, I don't focus on these civilizations so exclusively in the present text because I think they're in some way inherently "better" (the most obvious clue being the title of the work in which they're discussed so extensively). I focus on them because their overall original geostrategic "fortune" in being born so densely clustered to one another has had such uniquely profound consequences for the history of humanity. Nothing less than the evolution of humanity's ability to systematically destroy the planet saw its greatest impetus from the collision of so much civilizational tension surrounding such a naturally interconnected, wealthy environment.[cxx]

By sheer geographical necessity, keeping in mind the technological capabilities available at the chronological juncture, in order for Arabic commerce surrounding the medieval Mediterranean to expand (a task which Arabic merchants, according to the politicoeconomic nature of civilizations, tried to accomplish to the fullest extent), one of the most natural possibilities, and the most fateful possibility they indeed chose was to open up markets scattered across the northern Mediterranean coast (southwestern to south-central Europe). Over the long-term, their conquest didn't really extend to more than a handful of key footholds, although some of these locales, most namely those in Spain, left a remarkably sophisticated urban culture in their wake.[cxxi] The greatest sociohistorical effect of the Arabic civilization's extension into western Europe, though, was the impetus it gave to the return of western Europe's high commerce *by providing the earliest hopefuls in the intercivilizational trade network's Western zone a tangible aim for conquest*, which made for a relatively much easier task than would've been the forging of completely new *Power*-relations. Not only that, but the position of conquering a network already in existence tends to have a much higher ceiling for growth than the position of being the first to set up any network at all, because the conqueror of the existing network starts from a high level of complexity while having invested nothing in it personally. Therefore, the expansion of the Arabic civilization into western Europe – Islam's westernmost frontier, a frontier which in this logistical context never could've been adequately controlled and protected by a southwest Asian or northeast African center – led to an ultimately tragic result for the civilization, and indeed for humanity as a whole.

A notable increase in population density is probably the best single symptom of cultural complexity[cxxii] that's either about to expand, already expanding, or perhaps most typically, a combination of both. This last scenario occurred in the main territory of what was still only just turning into the entity we can rightly call "Western civilization", in the years just before, at the beginning of, and during its commercial revolution. So population density was, in the first place, increasing surrounding the centers of this overall expansion of complexity in the nascent Western economic system; and once the process of expanding complexity revved up further, population density increased evermore rapidly, still, hovering about these same centers. At that point a clear, potent feedback loop had been established between the growth of commercial centers and the growth of population density, each causing the other to constantly increase until some limitation, whether initial or final, was reached. Western growth was as uncontrollable and violent to those that experienced it – and yet also as well-patterned, from the outside looking in – as any mass growth process in the ostensibly more "natural" world, revealing a quite characteristic example of those well-defined patterns in systemic behavior that humans in the contemporary age like to think of themselves as being impervious to, because of the human freedom to choose supposedly inherent in "more civilized" cultures.

The real-world manifestation of the pattern was simple: where material wealth already was, humans went too.[cxxiii] And the complementary pattern, forming the interconnection with this first one: the more humans there were who went to those *'wealth-centers'*, the wealthier, in an absolute sense, the centers tended to become. In turn, the centers attracted yet more human beings, making every such case an example of what's called an autocatalytic process: due to its relationship with the other end of the feedback loop, a phenomenon's growth in the present more or less automatically leads to its own new growth, often even greater growth, in the future.[cxxiv] In such scenarios, true outright control – as in "*social* control" – can never be achieved. Instead, those supposedly "in control" of whatever human system is experiencing growth are simply trying to achieve, *within the constraints of the existing system*, the bare minimum of general order – which should really be considered, more accurately, the maximum amount of general *dis*order the underlying system can tolerate while still continuing to function. The bare minimum of order/maximum amount of general disorder in a civilization is best represented by what's simply called, in the contemporary world, "the law".

Here we'll use a quite broad definition of "the law" within the context of any civilization-State-complex: 'the total set of policies State governments use to regulate the behavior of the human beings subject to their rule'. I'm by no means intending to say that laws of this sort have their origins exclusively in civilizational central governments, i.e., States; this is just the sole context I'm presently concerned with. Specifically, I'm concerned with what kinds of laws are created in particular kinds of States as opposed to other kinds, what correspondent kinds of institutions pass and implement the kinds of laws, and what characterizes the chronological contexts that see the emergence of certain forms of law-making bodies.

What's always true, but what almost no one outside of a handful of scholars in certain hyperspecialized sociological fields appears to adequately appreciate – not even with the seemingly infinite amount of scholarship produced in the contemporary world – is that new States, or new State-forms that are so different from their predecessors that they essentially constitute new States, typically come into existence as the direct results of mechanisms for economic growth that are already well-established.[cxxv] The determinate form of a State arises in defense of those already-established *Power*-relations commanding the growth-mechanisms: accordingly, we can say that the State always institutionalizes a hierarchy that precedes the State itself. Thus, historically, new central law-making bodies (central *governments*) come into existence according to the broadest patterns of politicoeconomic growth. Consequently, old forms fall out of existence according to reverse sides of the same patterns. The broader and hence more consequential the trend is in long historical terms, the more "revolutionary" the State-governmental transformation tends to be. The State is always the greatest effect of a *Power*-structure already in place outside and above the State, before it becomes, additionally, an end-unto-itself.

This explains why, as is much better known, the form of State government corresponds above all to the State's primary form of wealth-production. Thus, concerning the medieval world, as has been pointed out by Charles Tilly among others, there were, most generally, merchant States, such as the ones that emerged in western Europe through a process entirely interdependent with the commercial revolution; these were communal "Republics". Also, there were agricultural States – "Kingdoms"/ "Principalities" – which had started to emerge in western Europe much earlier as a result of three interconnected factors: the collapse of Rome, the fleeing of urban populations to the countryside, and the invasions of barbarian warlords from north-central Europe, Scandinavia, and the steppes of Eurasia. The interconnection between these three elements largely explains the rise of warlord "nobilities" all over western Europe after the collapse of Rome, and thereby also explains the essentially never-ending petty warfare of the medieval period all throughout what would ultimately become Western civilization. So it's also the primordial sociohistorical explanation for why there arose the Great Power "Monarchies" and "Republics" that existed as perpetual-motion military machines in the subsequent intercivilizational period (period four, 1521-1776; 'early modern period').[cxxvi]

We'll get to those last-mentioned States in a later section. Regarding the original merchant States of the late medieval world now, considering them as a group, the policy regimes of all these States, and in turn the kinds of governmental bodies sustaining those regimes, were necessarily most complementary with the day-to-day operations of the relevant occupational hierarchies participating in international trafficking (textile manufacturing, banking, etc.), within the more general contexts of the civilizational and intercivilizational economies. Because of everything I've already said about geography and the trade-dependent movement of the intercivilizational structure, the best real-world entry point for detailing the phenomenon in the archetypal, late medieval period is the agglomeration of northern Italian city-States generally, and among those, Florence in particular.

Overall, in the late medieval period, the growth of the city-States in northern Italy reflected more strikingly than that in any other subregion, what would be the distinctive nature of the intercivilizational structure's (eventually total) western shift. More specifically to the "internal" sphere of Western civilization, Florence in the latest part of the medieval period before the Black Death of 1348 was as in-line with the intercivilizational/civilizational growth trends as any other locale in the West. As I've said, during the last half-century peak in this first phase of Western growth before the Black Death (ca. 1300 – 1348), the city was one of only five cities in Western civilization with over 100,000 inhabitants. Three of the other cities were in the territory of modern-day Italy, but of these Italian cities Florence was the only one with a predominately "provincial" attitude, even as it made its living largely via the international sphere.[cxxvii] Florence, then (besides Paris of the non-Italian cities), gives us the perfect example from the context of what would be the dominant characteristic of all most *Powerful* Western civilization-State-complexes for the rest of Western history: the use of profits from internationally-oriented economic exploitation to fund domestically-oriented conquest cultures. Florence gives us a perfect example, in the uniquely crucial primordial phase, of what would eventually become Western civilization's most characteristic social structural innovation, the national State.

The metaphor is only useful, though, if we pay closest attention to the word 'innovation', particularly insofar as its definition contrasts to that of 'invention'. By using the former as opposed to the latter, I mean to connote the West's most definitive position in the late medieval world, which was its position as a subsystem filling a niche in a systemic context much larger than that represented by just the West itself. If we don't view the evolution of *every* civilization from such a primarily intercivilizational perspective (or something else similarly broad), it's quite likely that we'll make the grave error of thinking that the most significant developments shaping a civilization happen mainly on account of factors that civilizations can themselves control – we're liable to attribute one civilization's "success" mainly or even solely to that civilization alone, and to attribute another civilization's "failure" to similarly self-determined causes. Since the planet Earth is a fundamentally finite environment, and since civilizations are such uniquely enormous entities for what they most generally constitute – human cultures – no cultures on Earth are more strikingly dependent upon the broadest context in which human beings in general reside: the organic planet (the singular setting for all events important to the world humans live in). That is, every civilization must initially emerge and then be formatively shaped by nothing besides the ultimate constraints of the living Earth, and on a far greater scale than all other types of human culture.

Moreover, what might have seemed baffling at first to many readers, but what hopefully has started to appear much less strange: more than any other civilization in history before the global civilization, without question, the West was shaped by its broadest context, made up of the two inseparable components of the planet Earth and the Earth-bound intercivilizational structure. Western dominance was, from the very beginning, dominance via systems it didn't originally make, and couldn't have originally made, on its own. Indeed, the ability to invest initially and for so long after its emergence almost solely on outright dominance, which it was able to do because it inherited practically all of its more intellectually-driven cultural traits, was mainly what allowed a Western-originated monopoly on conquest to become the ultimate global historical reality.

Movement towards the formation of the national State epitomized this process of investment in outright dominance over everything else made by the West's main constituent parts. I'm defining 'outright dominance' as the activity represented by a culture's military means, and when I refer to the West's 'main constituent parts', or when I refer to any civilization's main constituent parts, I'm referring to its civilization-State-complexes. Civilizations are comprised of civilization-State-complexes just as intercivilizational structures are comprised of civilizations. The West eventually achieved complete dominance over the total planetary intercivilizational structure – which Western civilization itself was most explicitly responsible for creating, as such a structure only started to become a distinct realistic possibility with the Spanish conquest of the "New World" – owing in the first place to the Western national States that emerged and evolved evermore rapidly throughout the early modern world (1492-1776). Paralleling the city-State's status as the singularly-effective mechanism for perpetuation of *Power* in the pre-Columbian, "Old World"-dominant history of civilizations, the national State would be the singularly-effective mechanism for perpetuation of *Power* in the post-Columbian, pre-industrialization, "New World"-dominant history of civilizations.

Thus, tying everything together, there were three wholly interlocking short historical processes slowly starting to develop all over the late medieval world and in scattered areas across Western civilization, which would become ever-increasingly refined as the subsequent, early modern world progressed: (1) mass cash monetization of civilizational economic systems; (2) westward-movement of the intercivilizational structure; (3) domestically-oriented, internationally-dominant cultures within Western civilization.[cxxviii] All of these processes in their systemic entanglement eventually resulted in the national State's place as the insuperable form of civilization-State-complex by the end of the early modern period (1776), leading at last to the industrialized Western national State as the international juggernaut in the late modern/early contemporary period (1865–1945). This latter development, in turn, led to the international blocs run by nuclear national State empires in period six, the first period of the global civilization (1947-1991). And that state-of-affairs, finally, led to the national State's last, virtualized act, in the second period of the global civilization (1995 -?), where all the national States on the planet – a planet that had at some point been more or less completely divided into national States – formed amongst themselves, at an even higher, *globalized* level, a literal if "unofficial" global State. Essentially, at our final stage, we have, from one perspective, globalized federalism, under the auspices of the entire complex of global capitalist governing institutions; from another, deeper perspective, we have late medieval Europe all over again, in a setting of innumerable corporate fiefdoms,[cxxix] with all of them clearly interconnected somehow but in a way that's overtly clear to no one.

The rise of Florence, especially in its century-long phase of proportionally greatest *Power* within Western civilization, between 1252 and 1348, was the best encapsulation in a single civilization-State-complex of the late medieval gestation – represented by the three interlocking long historical processes mentioned in the preceding paragraph – of the long-term capitalist culmination to *Power's* evolution. This is why I say Florence gives us a perfect example of the late medieval origins to the West's eventually total planetary dominance, a dominance that pivoted politically on the national State (just like it pivoted economically on industrialization). Florence prospered because it was the most efficient existing "package", in the precise sociohistorical context, of the intertwined main evolutionary currents of mass cash monetization, westward intercivilizational expansion, and the use of international dominance to sustain domestic prosperity. These processes taken together as one overall systemic movement answer the question, "What niche did Florence fulfill by coming into existence when it did, which allowed it, at least at first, to attain such striking success?"

The waning of Florence's florescence with such relative quickness doesn't negate the validity of my overall argument that Western total dominance started, not solely in Florence, but in Florence most characteristically of all amongst other most characteristic places. This city in its original, late medieval manifestation matters to us now as an iconic index of the birth of late medieval (protocapitalist) Western civilization: it was a holistic subunit of the holistic Western subunit within the medieval intercivilizational structure, which wasn't only uniquely definitive of its own particular combination of broadest sociohistorical contexts (locales within Western civilization, during the late medieval world). It also did much to produce the long-term perpetuation of those overall conditions throughout later history. As such, because its significance lies in its role as a starting point, the fact that Florence's success was so great that it led to the city's "putting itself out of business" – the city's failure to sustain its great heights in the early modern world – doesn't hurt my argument at all. Depending on whatever particular aspect or aspects made Florence fade into history while other locales in Western civilization took the lead in planetary conquest, it potentially even provides more evidence in the argument's favor.

III

The national State evolved into its individuated self as the quintessential middleman for the earliest stage of capitalism proper. Here's why the archetypal national States, which appeared in this phase – most namely Britain, France, and Spain, not coincidentally the three Great Powers to achieve the greatest dominance in the "New World" – *would become* the archetypal national States; the ultimate structural models for all other national States that emerged around the globe, mainly during periods five and six (1861-1945; 1947-1991). It also explains why, concerning their respective importance to the formation of the model for all subsequent national States, those three Western States should be listed in the order I've just listed them in. Starting with the early modern world's inception, they would control (to differing extents at different times) with equal parts organized morality, organized violent force, and organized monetary wealth the incomparable potential for *Power* inherent in the most vital geostrategic access-ways between worldwide supply and demand. Basically, you couldn't dominate international trade in the "New World"-dominant era of civilizations without dominating these geographic nodes.

Florence wasn't in an ideal geographical location for internationally dominant middleman status in the chronological context of the early modern period. However, considering the geographical distribution of complexity specific to the immediately preceding, late medieval world, Florence's location was ideal enough to allow the city to become the first true capital for "international" merchant bankers in Western history. Florence's geography precluded it from being an international emporium, and kept it even from seeing much traffic at all in individuals on the way to other international emporiums – but as counterintuitive as it may seem, these were at the time geographical advantages, not disadvantages, for the establishment of an international banking capital. Moreover, in their capital city Florentine merchants had a home base that easily allowed them to reach Venice and Genoa, respectively the greatest and one of the greatest international emporiums in all of Europe during the medieval period. Thus, Florence had all of the benefits the banking sector itself needed in order to insert itself in the middle of intercivilizational and international transit-trades, without having to invest much at all in the infrastructural wealth sustaining such traffic; quite a large asset considering the level of wealth one had to invest in military means in order to sustain a notable trade emporium. Of course, a substantial naval fleet was the most costly investment of all that Florentine merchant bankers could "outsource" to foreign Italian cities: therefore, it was the investment those merchant bankers gained from most in the short run by their being able to avoid making it themselves. In the long run, the city of Florence, in terms of its existence as a civilization-State-complex, would be eminently ill-served in its Great Power potential by lack of a State navy that could compete internationally.

At any rate, the major northern Italian city-States composing the heartland of the Italian Renaissance formed amongst themselves something of a flexibly incorporated precursor to the national State. By 'Italian Renaissance', I simply mean the era in northern Italy starting around the end of the 14th-century and finishing about the middle of the 16th, which represented a pronounced sociohistorical transition between the late medieval and the early modern worlds. No singular official hierarchy claimed to encompass the cities' total systemic interactions, and in turn they didn't combine to create a decidedly *individuated* system: this is why I say their collective interactions constituted a "precursor" to the national State. Yet all of the component parts were still there, waiting to be pieced together somewhere, someday, into a deliberately singularized machine, provided that the necessary resources could be acquired and continuously preserved by a single institutional complex, within a juridically-bounded space.cxxx

Among the main component parts of Italy's northern urban region at the time – Florence, Genoa, Milan, and Venice – the first-named city was the most fit for prefiguring the national State: not the nation, but the nation's State, which is something different. The national State is at the apex of a nationally-defined hierarchy; although in being such an apex, by definition it doesn't constitute a nation. Nations are polities, which are human-occupied territories defined by some form of juridical boundaries, while States are dominant cultures, which are material institutional manifestations of the broadest social relations shaping urbanized spaces. Specifically, the State is the dominant culture for enforcing the highest official level of political centralization within a given finite territory. Most uniquely, this makes the State the utmost command center for the use of large-scale, officially-sanctioned organized violence (military means), towards the end of exercising decisive control over the economic system of a juridically-defined territory within a civilization.

I've just given a definition of the State, which I feel must seem so overly complicated to the reader that I have to actually point out I've just given a definition of the State. However, in my own defense, the State is a necessarily complicated entity. Mostly, this has to do with what I find myself endlessly reiterating, that States can't exist in their truest forms without existing in civilizations, just like civilizations can't exist in their truest forms without existing surrounding States. So many preconditions have to align for an actual State to emerge in a sociohistorical context, that you simply can't define the State in general without reference to the common preconditions sustaining all States. But this doesn't make the State a purely hypothetical entity, an artificial schema only useful for intellectually grouping together many somewhat similar but ultimately very different things. Rather, every State is defined precisely insofar as it is, *empirically*, the necessary imaginary representation of the realest set of politicoeconomic relations within any given civilizational territory – those relations involving officially-imposed life and death, a function of the State's control over its subject territory's food supply and its control over its subject territory's military and police forces.

Besides the fact that a State only persists continuously in a civilization, a State only survives through decisive influence over the management of a territory's food supply, a factor wholly interdependent with the State's decisive influence over the territory's militarized "protection". These are wholly interdependent for the simplest and most consequential reason: the level of control over a civilizational population's food supply necessary to sustain a State can only be physically achieved through a complementary level of control over the same population's military, which reciprocally can only be reliably maintained with the adequate regular supply of food ("armies move on their stomachs"). Florence, which had such a large population and such a relatively inadequate supply of food in its immediate hinterland, from the earliest stages of its growth could only hope to feed itself by importing agricultural commodities, mainly grains, from foreign territories, especially in southern Italy (above all Naples), Sicily, and North Africa, all intercivilizational and thereby international flashpoints. Therefore, even compared to inhabitants of all other contemporaneous city-States, Florentines were particularly dependent upon their State as an assurance of a regular food supply, since only the State could ensure reliable access to international trade on a sufficient scale.

Florence's absolute dependence on imported grains only changed in the era starting somewhat after the Black Death, around 1375, and ending around the middle of the 16th-century, running almost exactly concurrently with the Italian Renaissance of which Florence was the *de facto* center. It's no coincidence at all that this cultural era happened when it did, in the phase of unprecedented per capita economic growth following the plague. While the plague hit Florence with unusual severity – around 50% of the population; Florence would subsequently never come close to recovering its pre-plague status as a proportion of the overall Western population[cxxxi] – the economy in Florence, as in many other European commercial cities, only seemed to improve once the immediate shock of horrifying death in unimaginable quantities began to subside.[cxxxii]

The city moved into a position in the Western economy beyond the new areas of growth – which its own early success had played no small role in catalyzing – assuming a role much like that of the most advanced "boutique" economies in our contemporary globalized economy. This boutique niche was the defining symptom of how those aspects of the Renaissance that were more explicitly cultural manifested themselves at the economic level, with Florence's artisans becoming the envy of monarchies and aristocracies all across Europe in the late medieval era: such courtly figures became the best international customers of Florentine-produced luxury goods.[cxxxiii]

Moreover, Florence, which had already had a booming textile industry in the century or so before the Black Death, perpetuated and intensified its status as one of the leading "industrial" centers in the preindustrial Western economy. More than its production of luxuries, the international trade in woolen goods was still the heart of the domestic Florentine social structure. Yet further on into the Renaissance era, in the middle and late 15th-century, luxuries started to assume an evermore-significant place in the textile sector as well, when Florence became one of the centers of the burgeoning Italian silk industry, and also stepped up its production of high-grade wool products.[cxxxiv] This movement towards the large-scale Italian production of silks was one of the best possible real-world indicators of the westward movement in the intercivilizational structure, as silks were among those items indispensable for sustaining the medieval overland route between China and India and southwest Asia ("the silk road"). The West wasn't yet surpassing any of these civilizations in overall complexity, by any means. But such "import substitution" certainly signaled that the long-term process of growth in Western complexity was certainly starting to approach parity with the civilizations to its east in some crucial respects.[cxxxv]

Almost constant growth of home industries doesn't make the label of "middleman" any less applicable to Florence: middlemen can't reach their optimal levels of success unless they can provide access to goods and/or resources that can only be found on turf to which they're guaranteed primary access. Florence, in fact, emerged as it did, as the first substantial base-of-operations for an international banking network in Western civilization, precisely because of the earlier and, once Florentine banking came into existence, simultaneous further growth of the international wool firms that had rapidly constructed the widest-spanning, densest commercial network throughout the West by about 1300. By this time, only a couple of years before Dante's political exile (ostensibly the most significant personal experience catalyzing his authorship of the *Comedy*), Florence was among a handful of the largest, monetarily wealthiest cities in Europe, which constituted amongst themselves the foundation for the original experiment of Western civilization. As I've said, out of all of these centers, the most insular at the time were Florence and Paris, and the former most of all, as it didn't lie along any important trade routes – intercivilizational, international, interregional, or regional. It seems that it truly emerged as a force in nascent European international politics for no other reason than that it provided an ideally secluded geographic locale for the establishment of a home base for international merchants and merchant-bankers. It was located between the western and eastern Italian coastal ports, and closest to Rome of any of Italy's northern cities, yet not easily accessible by foreign armies and/or navies: a place where all the gold the prosperous Florentines brought home to their mint could be safe, and where commerce and industry could in turn comfortably thrive.

Resultant of its thriving commercial atmosphere, the most important development to take place in Florence – where it happened as early as in any other place in the West – was the innovation of the medieval, primordial version of the trading company, which in its earliest form there appeared not yet as a full-fledged company in the sense of a completely individuated legal personality, but as a highly informal pooling of resources undertaken between individuals who each brought complementary assets to the operation. Whenever individuals who had the knowledge and/or money to do so wanted to engage in their own commercial enterprise of any kind, whether it was in banking, manufacturing, or the international transit trade, they would draw up articles of association with each other. These documents defined commercial partnerships called *compagnie*, and interestingly, at least around the earliest time for which their documentation still survives – the early 14th-century – they were simply privately written notes of mutually agreed-upon terms of operation, not even requiring the minimal legal sanction of a notary.[cxxxvi]

These weren't like modern companies in the sense that they were fully private organizations with no real institutional structure outside of the one embodied in the work of the individuals performing the organization's operations. In other words, there was no corporate "body" separate from the partners, and in this vein the partnerships were written up for finite, fairly brief periods of time, usually only for increments lasting between three and five years.[cxxxvii] However, it often happened, and presumably, concerning the most successful partnerships, usually happened, that the partners would renew the articles of association.[cxxxviii] Mostly, *compagnie* involved at least two individuals. Sometimes a single individual would form a "partnership", using all of his own capital, both material and mental; but here I'm directly concerned with the phenomenon of multiple individuals joining their experience and money together to create and manage from the top-down a profit-producing enterprise, as this was what made the Florentine partnership stand among the most significant precursors to early modern overseas trading companies.

The partnership's almost totally unofficial status, best signified by the already-mentioned fact that individuals didn't even need recourse to a notary to start one, just a certain substantial body of information made accessible by the right social connections and start-up money, was the other thing making the Florentine partnership such a notable precursor to the earliest modern companies. Protocapitalism was different from, and prior to, the capitalist system it spawned precisely insofar as there weren't yet individuated 'companies' (in the simplest sense, 'legally-sanctioned private business organizations') on the same level of *Power* as the "international" European land-based Powers. It can be said that a truly capitalist system started to appear alongside the emergence of the post-Columbian order, when trading companies legally sanctioned by the greatest European States became the first "feet in the door" for those States' new overseas Empires. The historically unprecedented wealth unleashed into the now interhemispheric war-trade structure – wealth both actual and monetary, primarily in the forms of plantations and bullion, respectively – would in the end make companies that were just as *Powerful* as the States they supposedly served.

But that level could only be reached precisely because, in the few centuries or so leading up to Columbus, private *Power* had been rapidly asserting itself in the new Western cities sparked by (and reciprocally sparking) the commercial revolution. And the *most* private *Power* of all had accrued in places like Florence. The phenomenon of a wholly private sphere of economic exploitation may not have started in this locale alone, but this was where it was best documented during the initial stage's most complex portion,[cxxxix] strongly suggesting along with all the other geographical and economic factors I've mentioned that Florence was one of the earliest places to exhibit such independent *Power* in civilizationally-significant economic matters. By "independent *Power*" and "a wholly private sphere", I'm specifically referring to independence and privacy from Church and State, meaning, in the former instance, the Catholic Church, and in the latter instance referring both to any concerned nobilities as well as to the communal governments of the medieval European merchant States. Institutional independence from the traditional *Power*-centers on such a significant level as this had essentially never happened before. Therefore, the private organization-building made possible by the model of the partnership – at first a pure logistical middleman existing solely to coordinate the operations of many other, subordinate operations; to essentially pull its own value out of the air – became so successful that it would eventually give rise to a brand-new form of cultural repository: the company, properly so-called.

Only later, once it became a full-fledged company, did the conceptualized partnership itself come to "own" things; in turn it finally took on a corporate 'body', a "life of its own". In short, it became the individuated modern company. For instance, there were the first companies in the Americas that came to own their own land and thereby their own plantations, via Portugal and Spain, then Britain and France; and the company in India that for a time owned essentially the whole sub-continent (the British East India Company). Those small, seemingly innocuous and "free" Dutch "Republics" had all kinds of company-owned, State-sanctioned colonies like these – indeed, the company-owned colony may very well have had its earliest explicit origins in what's today the Netherlands – where the unwritten "rules of the game" essentially guaranteed that Europeans would leave genocides and annihilated natural environments in their wake wherever they ended up. As it turned out, the company, not the priesthood or the nobility, was the principal metainstitution, the key *cultural repository*, in all the places that fell victim to Western overseas politicoeconomic expansion. In the post-Columbian world, companies constituted the central gateways between Western dominant culture and its targets of conquest.

At the same time, to be sure, the companies never could've reached such unparalleled levels of success without their necessary alliances with the various Churches and States in their respective western European locales of origin. Remember, medieval merchants emerged within a context where nobles and Christian high clergy already existed as the most *Powerful* elements in the culture's domain. Thus, the merchants rose to their own unique level of *Power* at a later point in history, and did so precisely on account of the kind of "independence" from existing dominant institutions that great commercial wealth alone was able to afford. Yet they still only ultimately rose to such prominence and stayed there long enough to eventually dominate everything because of an absolute dependence upon the civilizational conditions held in place by elite factions from the other spheres.

Here, in reflecting on everything we've seen thus far, we realize in such striking fashion why a basic understanding of the medieval world is so valuable for understanding all civilizations; why it's especially valuable for understanding our contemporary global civilization; and what's inextricable from both, why we can only truly understand any history if we view all history as a whole. Through the present, the phenomenon most consequential to humanity's existence has been the total domination of the planet by a comprehensive urban cultural environment of western European origins: what I call the capitalist culmination to the long historical evolution of *Power*, a culmination which has itself culminated in globalization, the ultimate merger of long and short historical processes. This has been the most consequential phenomenon in the history of humanity for the very simple reason that it has completely destroyed the planet's ante-civilizational existence. However, this historical phenomenon, which has been centered so uniquely upon the West, at the same time never had anything to do with the West as an "isolated" phenomenon, as if anything on Earth could truly be removed from its context and then understood, let alone a civilization, let alone the civilization that led to the culmination of all civilizations. Indeed, considering the exact manner in which Western civilization came to highest *Power* and stayed there for the remainder of its evolution – especially concerning the processes directly leading up to and directly leading from industrialization – no historical phenomenon requires more thorough contextualization in order to be properly explained/understood.

Complexity and Speed: Cultural Evolution Since the Origins of Agriculture and Settlements

I

On Works Cited

Every source I consulted in order to write the present text is related in some way to history, but the sources are of many different kinds. The different kinds are related to history in many different ways. At first, and for awhile, I couldn't really explain exactly why I chose to do research like this; it just continued to seem to be what I needed in order to deepen my understanding of humanity. Now I've come to realize what I was doing: when I studied history how I did in order to construct my journey that I'm reconstructing for you here, I was simply trying to look at as many unique appearances of human cultures as I could, in as many different sociohistorical contexts. Naturally, given the present text's particular subject, I ended up looking most of all at those cultures that were civilizations.

Primarily relevant here for explaining what I mean by "why I chose to do research like this", is *what* I studied in reference to history, and also *how* I studied it. Additionally, then, besides looking at as many different historical appearances as I could of civilizations and other cultures, I looked at these histories from as many different angles as I could conceive might be helpful, meaning, in the terms of contemporary scholarship, from the perspectives of as many different "subdisciplines". Every subdiscipline is nothing besides one kind of tool for viewing its subject matter. When the subject matter is generally related to human history, as is anything studied by the human sciences, social sciences, or humanities, everything relevant involves some aspect of the finite planet humans live in. Therefore, just as every individual matter related to human history can potentially shed light on all other matters related to human history, every *way of looking at* human history can potentially shed light on all other ways. Limiting ourselves to one way of viewing history – allowing ourselves to use just a single tool – is equally as big an error as limiting ourselves to one overly specific sociohistorical context. Both errors are rampant in basically all existent (hyperspecialized) fields of human cultural, social, and historical scholarship, depicting a structural problem inherent throughout the whole of existent academia.

What purpose could there be in self-imposing such highly restrictive boundaries? As I said early on in part 1, the main issue is that the operation of everything within the globalization system – which has long-since become more or less every thing on the planet – is dictated solely by the most perverse form of market logic. As a matter of course, scholarship too has been swept up by the onslaught of hyperspecialization. But in any case, the significant thing is that there's certainly no purpose anyone might discover which would have anything to do with the understanding of history *per se*, except concerning the minimal (occupational) level of understanding necessary for the production of more officially-sanctioned "Historians". Since our purpose here, on the other hand, is the understanding of history, and as much understanding as is possible, we can't afford to limit our possibilities arbitrarily. We must instead find out how to understand history holistically, which surely can't just involve the highly particular methods of one artificially hyperspecialized subdiscipline, nor even the general kinds of methods utilized by just one artificially specialized group of subdisciplines, i.e., anthropology, sociology, or history (historiography).

Substantial numbers of human beings must come to properly understand history: strangely enough, I believe this will be indispensable, if humanity is to avoid complete self-destruction, and I think at this point it's clear that one can only reach such an understanding through constant incorporation of multiple dimensions of historical perspective. As I mentioned already at the very beginning of this text, my way of fulfilling this necessity is, first of all, to view every known human phenomenon as part of some world, with all the phenomena together ultimately embodying part of *one* whole world. Secondly, and in turn, I'm fulfilling it by viewing all such phenomena from "a metaphysical perspective that considers humanity, by which I most broadly mean 'the totality of human beings on Earth at a given time', foremost as a manifestly *cultural but thereby also sociohistorical phenomenon*."

For better or worse, those two sentences encapsulate my attempt to look at human history from a multidimensional perspective: the way of looking and the specific object of vision must forever be in constant adaptive interaction with each other, throughout every instance of study. Carrying this out in our intellectual actions, I believe, is how we successfully build up our intuition (in this case, specifically as it relates to human history). In the sense of the word I intend here, the main problem 'intuition' aims to solve is summed up with the question, *"What do I need to know about what I need to know?"* To put it another way, intuition is the understanding we bring to a phenomenon we're immediately presented with before we really know anything about it in particular.

Thus, while "every individual matter related to human history can potentially shed light on all other matters related to human history", and "every way of looking at human history can potentially shed light on all other ways", are, by themselves, far too general to help in really narrowing down our perspective, they nonetheless become eminently valuable when combined with a well-honed sociohistorical intuition. The better we are at grasping human history as a whole, the more immediately we can recognize the most significant "individual matters related to human history" when we're confronted with them in specific cases, no matter the particular context. The more accurate is our recognition of the most significant sociohistorical elements in particular cases, the more our overall understanding subsequently improves again.

Mainly, so long as one carefully defines one's research goals and chooses one's sources accordingly, the individual can hone her or his sociohistorical intuition through a most conventional method: reading works of historical scholarship. Since, in order to be empirically useful, any piece of historical information must at minimum reference something that really happened, the historical investigator adds to her or his overall historical experience in the first place by reading what are traditionally called "histories", or "historical narratives". However, this is *truly* only in the first place, and even this phase of research isn't nearly as simple as it sounds, as it will shape the intellectual boundaries for the whole investigation. In this vein, one should keep in mind that all historical researches are inherently limited by the relevant studies accessible to the investigator. Clearly, one can use raw data in addition to secondary sources, but the latter have far more direct impact on the expansion of historical understanding as opposed to "only" the expansion of historical knowledge. The better* the general selection of secondary sources on human history available to the researcher – referring both to the quantity of works available on the research topic(s) and to the qualitative value of those works – the broader a view the researcher can potentially attain. Once something already exists, which in this case means once a successful history has actually been constructed concerning a certain sociohistorical phenomenon, individuals experiencing the existent then have the opportunity to "go beyond it". Concerning the raw materials used to make the secondary source, when there are only the primary sources related to a phenomenon, no history of that phenomenon yet exists, specifically meaning "historical narrative" with this use of the word 'history'. (On the other hand, of course, the production of secondary sources is to begin with inherently limited by the availability of primary sources.)

"Going beyond" is the fundamental premise behind all research in pursuit of understanding, not just human historical research. Going beyond is utilizing what other researchers have bestowed on us with their hard-fought efforts, in order to somehow gain an even deeper grasp than those researchers of whatever subject it is that's being studied: not towards the end of success in competition between researchers, but rather towards the end of furthering human knowledge and understanding. Yet the investigator can only ultimately go beyond what other researchers have accomplished if he or she incorporates the phenomenon being studied into a broader context, such as the one I started to put Western history into in the previous section, and the even broader one I will develop in the present section. In the case of historical investigation, then, the more histories the investigator is acquainted with, and the wider the variety of histories he or she is acquainted with, the broader the context that can potentially be brought to bear on any individual historical phenomenon.

The bodies of reasoned out empirical data the investigator confronts in the form of secondary source histories, as well as the raw empirical data of primary sources, represent the main constituents of the 'what' in relation to historical knowledge, in terms of "what I studied" to write the present text. But in terms of the 'how', if the investigator hopes to understand the history he or she is studying as fully as possible – here, 'history'

---

* The reader can consult the bibliography of the present work to see what I think constitutes a "good selection" of secondary sources for a historical study.

as in the process itself, not the written works about the process – the combination of histories and raw data in-and-of-itself is insufficient. For instance, unless one is referring to human history before humans employed anything remotely resembling language, which according to some current researchers almost certainly must've been more than 40,000 years ago,[cxl] all human history that has ever happened has involved humans existing as quintessentially cultural beings. From my perspective, it's so completely outside the verbal human's understanding to imagine what it was like to live as an ante-verbal human being, there was truly nothing we can reasonably call "human history", explicitly meaning 'the history of humanity', before the development of language. Thus, humanity began with language – in other words, human culture began with language; thereby, *properly human* history began with language. To know about human history, then, in addition to the empirical sequence of event-clusters textually epitomized by the narrative, you must possess theoretical knowledge about human culture and therefore human culture*s*, subjects that in the tradition of contemporary scholarship have been primarily within the purview of anthropology.

In order to understand human culture, though, you can't just know about things conventionally considered "cultural", like language, art, and religion. Equally, you must know about social structures – that is, the prime objects shaping "political economies", what I refer to generically as politicoeconomic systems. The reader may have noticed that I never use the word 'society' or 'societies', when referring to aggregations of human population. This is because there's no such thing as "*a* society", at least concerning how all modern scholars typically mean it: they commonly use this phrase when what they're really referring to is "a culture". "What difference does it make?" you might think.

If the phenomenological basis for one's sociological perspective is "the society" – a voluntarily-joined organization – as the universal model for collective human formation, like it is for almost all contemporary sociologists, then one's starting point for sociological analysis is in a holistic sense already on shaky ground. One might be able to understand texts strictly within the sociological sector in this way, but viewing "society" as the underlying entity centering human population implicitly divorces one's understanding from the fact that the culture – the material-psychological idea environment – is, on the surface, the entity that tangibly shapes mass human behavior at all times. To the extent that one is studying something real when one studies sociology, this real thing is the *social structure*, the invisible though no less determinative framework for all group-centered interhuman behavior within cultural environments, fundamentally guided by the broadest politicoeconomic activities.

In other words, cultures shape human behavior directly, but every culture is socially structured, and this structuring in turn shapes mass human behavior relatively *in*directly. Neither the culture nor the social structure can exist in any way independently of the other, while the notion of "a society", considered in-and-of-itself, presumes something decidedly autonomous; as if, for instance, there really were things called "nations" separately from the existence such entities enjoy within the human psychological domain. In the same way, from the inverse perspective, to analyze civilizations without concomitant politicoeconomic analysis is to act like such cultures aren't wholly trapped from within by those entrenched social hierarchies physically permitting their continuation.

Our focus has already been made much more specific than it was at the start, by the contextualization of Western civilization within the central intercivilizational structure during the late medieval era. Why bother bringing up such general problems now? It's when we're already in the midst of such sociohistorically-conditioned contexts that we can most effectively continue our more explicitly philosophical inquiries.

I admit it's impossible for me personally to think of a philosophical question that doesn't have to do with humanity in some way. But even if it can't be agreed upon that the questions of philosophy are unimaginable separate from humanity, then at the very least, one must agree that, concerning all philosophical questions unequivocally related to humanity, every question we ask will need to be answered by referencing a human reality that's definitively historical,[cxli] and from my own perspective, sociohistorical (which is also to say, cultural). With this in mind, how can we ever begin answering the most vital questions if we don't transgress all existent disciplinary boundaries in our pursuit after knowledge – while at the same time acknowledging that the entities conventionally considered "disciplines" have in so many cases facilitated the development of indispensable methods for discovering and producing knowledge? From the other perspective though: how *do* we maintain a delicate balance? My attempt is embodied in the method employed for constructing the present text. Yet it remains to be addressed: are there any assumptive principles involved in this method, or is it entirely experimental – "trial and error"?

I started out with what you might call intuitive principles, or put another way, intuitive boundaries, ultimately leading to a regular system of research that can rightly be called 'a method', which I now understand, insofar as I can coherently verbalize (explain) it. In the first place, the utilization of certain aspects of multiple existent, relevant subdisciplines as a means to construct "non-disciplinary" historical knowledge can only be based on an underlying assumption that there must be, in some sense, a single entity identifiable *as history* – whatever one happens to think this word means. That is, just like anything else, for something called "history" to be studied successfully it must be real, and if it's real it can only be one thing, no matter what disciplinary methodologies one utilizes. There can be no real singular 'history' properly studied by different disciplines if, for instance, history is allowed to mean one thing to sociologists, a completely unrelated thing to anthropologists or to philosophers, and yet something else again to historians. Rather, there must be one thing similar to all the disciplines that can nonetheless be observed through its different aspects, with each discipline focusing on an aspect of history that's distinct from but ultimately interrelated to the others.

So I intuited from the beginning of my research that while each discipline might use its own unique language, all the disciplines are unconsciously talking about the same phenomenon. Each discipline simply focuses on different "features" of history, and often, because of the great proliferation of subdisciplines, there's much variation as to what features are discussed within supposedly singular fields. Just as often, too, there are great similarities between scholars from supposedly different disciplines. Ostensibly it's all very confusing. But if nothing else I was, through time and continuous research, still able to understand more and more history than I had understood when I started, and more pertinently my understanding was increasingly amenable to expression in a holistic fashion, referencing the same phenomenon from varying perspectives. However, none of these perspectives was interchangeable with any existent subdiscipline, even though at some level all the subdisciplines I drew my sources from had contributed to the overall approach. What was the relationship, then? *If* I was able to strike a balance, what did it entail?

For one thing, it entails recognizing that as much as anything else, and in the contemporary context, perhaps more than anything else, conventional scholarship is primarily a symptom of the world it inhabits. Therefore, it's quite natural that we find extreme overproduction for its own sake: a preponderance of waste, but with many incredibly valuable items scattered throughout. Again, we're faced with simply accepting that while disciplines are on the one hand artificially contrived traditions acting as social dictates concerning how to "appropriately" view phenomena humans experience in their worlds, on the other hand scholars working within well-defined disciplines in the contemporary world have discovered and transmitted enormous quantities of valuable knowledge. What we must always keep in mind, if we're to see everything in the proper overall perspective: *proportionally*, does the knowledge discovered seem to be "worth the trouble"? With all the human effort and wealth expended on conventional scholarship, what has been accomplished?

Certainly, human beings as a whole aren't more understanding, something we already explored in part 1. Considering the general conditions of private and personal squares, i.e. television and digital media devices, and what "information" is most commonly accessed on these tools, it seems like it would've been impossible for conventional scholarship, of all things, to have changed the broad outcomes in any substantial way. Referring in particular to the individuals within the academic sector, though, it's not at all clear that even this small percentage of the population is any more understanding than its counterparts in past ages, and there are many valid reasons for arguing that scholars in the existent world are less understanding than scholars from many other civilizational worlds (most relevant since "scholar" specifically is an archetype originating solely in civilizations), even if they have better knowledge.

Of course, this is to say nothing of how "well-informed" individual scholars in the current world are. Information isn't the same thing as knowledge and understanding. The latter refer to the products of actions humans undertake with regards to information, a relationship much the same as that between understanding and knowledge, and indeed part of the same exact process, the process of human learning. Information is therefore *preliminary to* knowledge, in the same way that knowledge is preliminary to understanding. (And in another, reciprocal sense, understanding is preliminary to both.)

Scholars in the contemporary world rarely seem to get past the very threshold of understanding: a scholar may perfectly understand something extremely specific about the topic studied in his subdiscipline, but since he typically doesn't study anything outside of his hyperspecialized niche within the subdiscipline, he can't really go beyond it in his thought processes. In turn, the typical scholar in the contemporary world is largely incapable of explaining how his or her knowledge is related to the world as a whole. Thus, such knowledge can't be practically useful to the world as a whole, and only will be if some framework is developed for incorporating that knowledge into a holistic perspective of the world, this latter thing being what's commonly called "a philosophy". Since most current scholars outside philosophy, which anyway has somehow long-since been fractured into hyperspecialized subdisciplines itself, wouldn't be concerned with this kind of problem, the vast quantities of knowledge and infinite splinters of information accreted in the contemporary world remain for the most part practically useless.

But there are still many individual scholars in the contemporary world, albeit not many proportionally – always, in the end, the most important thing – who have made the hyperspecialized knowledge practically useful. Indeed, I certainly never would've noticed the inadequacies of hyperspecialization as such if nothing in the world existed for comparison. And such individual scholars are always "interdisciplinary", or, even better, non-disciplinary, thinkers, who nonetheless use the results of conventional scholarship to go beyond it.

I'm not surprised by the state of contemporary scholarship, wherein it seems not to have made us more understanding – not even scholars – especially when one considers the much greater quantity of available information and scholarly production in comparison to all periods prior to the contemporary world. Even though this might seem like the worst outcome that could be expected in terms of a return on humanity's investment, and thus quite a harsh indictment on my part, my intention in pointing it out has nothing to do with that. Instead, I'm far more concerned with the fact that we should've never expected contemporary scholarship to produce different results to begin with: it was never the primary purpose of all the many different disciplines comprising the lineage of Western conventional scholarship, which ultimately gave rise to the conventional scholarship in the contemporary world, to increase humanity's overall understanding. The primary purpose was always something else. To be sure, though, we can only discover what this something else was by viewing history outside the myopic lens of any subdiscipline.

The Holistic World-Shaping Nexus: Three Interconnected Cultural Spheres

In the Western tradition, just like in the traditions of all civilizations that came before it as well as all the civilizations contemporary to its archetypal form in the late medieval world, officially-sanctioned scholarship was always employed as the primary institutional means for intellectually servicing the *Power*-structure.[cxlii] Since such a state-of-affairs was so prevalent, there must be some explanation common to every context wherein it arose, which would explain for us its emergence in one form or another in every civilization, throughout every part of the world, in every era of civilizational history.[cxliii] From my own perspective, officially-sanctioned scholarship is one irreplaceable aspect of any conquest syndrome – perhaps ultimately the most significant aspect of all. It's thereby an ideal analytical entry-point for getting to the heart of the intercivilizational structure.

Utilizing the progression of intercivilizational history as our core chronology provides us with the most proper framework for judging civilizational evolution. An intercivilizational period, as I see it, is an individuated entity insofar as it embodies the unfolding of a historically distinct level of holistic cultural complexity sustained by the broadest politicoeconomic relationships connecting different civilizations. Thus, individual civilizations "occur" as functions of the evolution of complexity on the intercivilizational scale, at the same time that the intercivilizational structure reciprocally evolves as a function of what occurs at the level of each civilization. Concerning civilizations that share a common intercivilizational structure, the civilizations and the intercivilizational structure are only conceivable as interwoven entities: even as the intercivilizational structure forms the broadest cultural environment within which the civilizations it houses are primarily shaped, the larger structure obviously can't exist without the smaller structures it's composed of. And of course, while a civilizational population may see itself as largely cut off from the rest of reality, the breakdown of the existing intercivilizational structure will greatly if not wholly transform the same population.

More simply put, both the civilization and the intercivilizational structure it's situated within are simultaneously evolutionary systems and evolutionary environments. The civilization is at once an evolving system shaped by the environmental context of the intercivilizational structure, as well as a part of an overall environmental context shaping the latter structure's own evolution. Most broadly, civilizations and intercivilizational structures share this feature with all other interrelated evolutionary systems/environments on the planet – a situation the planet itself brings into being, as the living system constituting the planet's biosphere shapes and is in turn shaped by all the innumerable living systems that depend on it for existence.[cxliv] While individual civilizations are comparable to solar systems in miniature, the intercivilizational structure that is the combination of these units is comparable to the living Earth: every civilization in an intercivilizational structure is like a cultural solar system fitted for a niche determined by the intertwined existence of two living Earths, the primarily natural one and the primarily human-made one mirroring it.

But the civilization is a sociohistorically fluid solar system, where the "sun" – the center – fluctuates along with the narrower intermittent structural fluctuations of all the locales surrounding the center, as well as the broader structural fluctuations of the intercivilizational totality. Almost always, after a sun in an intercivilizational period is initially established, one of the locales – one of the planets orbiting the center – will eventually take the sun's place. The process continues, adding new planets, and shifting to new suns at moments that resultantly mark and are marked by the beginnings of geostrategically transformative intervals, typically until the solar system reaches its maximum level of expansion. Once this happens, the last point of expansion remains the sun until the solar system collapses, which occurs when it's no longer profitable at all for the solar system's inhabitants to continue investing in its central mechanism of growth.[cxlv] The collapse of the intercivilizational structure is usually the best signal of this breakdown, since the war-trade environment on the broadest scale is in the end most responsible for sustaining the gargantuan levels of growth reached by civilizations. Otherwise, in special cases like the Roman Empire or the global civilization, the overall collapse is best signified by the collapse of the central State, which serves as the same sort of organizing principle as the intercivilizational structure in scenarios where the latter has been superseded.

All of this, and everything I relate to my concept of intercivilizational history as the indispensable chronological framework for humanity's civilizations stage, is primarily intended to solve the unavoidable problem that arises when you try to view human history *as a whole* – when you try to view it metaphysically: why does the evolution of cultural complexity seem to happen at such different rates in different historical periods? We'll get to the specific reasons behind this later on in the section. First, we must understand why the singularly relevant means of comparison in relation to this problem is found in the chronological unfolding of the intercivilizational structure's evolution. Interestingly, the chronology, which I was solely concerned with devising at the beginning as a means of framing the history of civilizations that reflected as closely as possible the intercivilizational structure's unique role as a cultural evolutionary environment/system, turned out also to be extremely similar to the most conventional recent scholarly chronologies of "world history", a similarity which I think serves as further confirmation of the schema's usefulness.[cxlvi]

In other words, the chronology works just as well in terms of its use for synthesizing a typical contemporary scholarly conceptualization of civilizational history as it does for explaining the idea of a long-historically evolving intercivilizational structure, a concept I've constructed. When I realized this, I was at first embarrassed that I'd been so unoriginal; however, soon enough it just ended up decisively solidifying my sense that the intercivilizational structure really does have a special relationship with the long-term cultural evolution of humans in civilizations. But I finally came to that conclusion only because I could explain the evolution structurally, by which I mean, in this case, from a *social*-scientific perspective. Moreover, the explanation is quite simple.

Cultural evolution in civilizations, a process described overall by the intercivilizational chronology, starts with the fact that, more than anything else, humans in civilizations, just like humans from every type of culture, need water, food, and shelter to survive. No matter what kind of culture human beings live in, the process of mass fulfillment of water-food-shelter provisions shapes the culture's geographical boundaries, and from there shapes its overall evolution and hence also determines its core chronology. This complex of needs constitutes what's called in ecology a 'limiting factor': the ultimate limiting factor for human cultural environments. To singularize into one idea the three interrelated indispensable necessities for human beings, I refer to the material means fulfilling those necessities collectively as *'life-support resources'*.

But the geographically dependent supply of life-support isn't the only essential factor when it comes to humanity's provision of its own survival. Concerning properly human history, i.e., the history of human beings since the almost entirely incomparable innovation of language and thereby also culture, *technological* means have grown ever-increasingly determinative in their influence on humanity's success at achieving its own sustenance. Language is the original technology, without which there could be no other technology. Technology, in fact, is a quintessentially linguistic phenomenon. Despite the mass understanding of the word in the contemporary world, I believe the word 'technology' shouldn't refer generally to 'artifacts utilized in practiced ways to routinely accomplish specific desired results' – instead, this definition is what I refer to with the word 'tools'. Separately, but inextricably, 'technology' should refer to the 'human knowledge and understanding related to the production and use of a given tool'. Here we see what culture truly is in its purest form, as the counterpart relationship between tool and technology runs precisely parallel to the dynamic between culture's dual manifestations, one material (tool) and one psychological (technology). I believe this particular "two sides of the same coin" relationship between tools and technology – spoken words on the one hand, the knowledge and understanding to create and use speech on the other – first gave birth to the basic reality of culture.

Thus, in addition to the material means impacting on any human culture's self-sustenance, there are the interconnected technological means. To appreciate the significance of this connection in practical terms, consider humanity's existence during the history spanning between the earliest emergence of language and the "big bang" (around 40,000-32,000 BCE in various places), at which later point human beings went through what was perhaps the first great cultural advancement following the innovation of language, proportionally one of the greatest-ever historical advances in cultural complexity.[cxlvii] In the transition between what was by chronological definition humanity's simplest cultural era and the subsequent stage, what more consequential material purpose could there have possibly been for the increased and refined employment of language/technology, than humanity's collective improvement at directly providing its own sustenance?

(Here it must be stressed that whenever I talk about cultural complexity, I'm always referring to phenomena on a specifically material (structural) level; I'm not referring to spiritual "complexity". I put complexity in quotation marks precisely because, in an intellectual sense, primarily mental phenomena are only "complex" insofar as they're trapped within physical entities. Intellectual "complexity" therefore doesn't and can't manifest itself in the same way as material complexity. On the other hand, it's also true that the material aspect manifested as cultural complexity always has its corresponding mental component.)

What I mean can be immediately understood by my mentioning how some scholars have rightly pointed to the "invention" (innovation) of language as the greatest *biological* evolutionary adaptation in the history of the planet, citing the life-support advantage I've referenced here.[cxlviii] So language surely must also be the greatest *cultural* evolutionary adaptation in history – if only because it's the one that started it all ("In the beginning, there was the Word"). Biologically, evolution most crudely involves the individual's sheer survival and reproduction amongst other similarly-structured individuals. How could cultural evolution, at its very beginning – when humanity's explicitly cultural aspect must've revealed a more immediate concern with material provision of survival than it would at any other time in humanity's existence – have been any different? At base, cultural evolution is a most special case of biological evolution: the form of biological evolution achievable by humanity alone. The cultural aspect only became an end-unto-itself at a much later and very different phase of complexity (the agricultural epoch); this was precisely when *Power* started to grow.

As language, the archetypal technology, is so singularly definitive of human beings as cultural agents, we can rightly say that human beings, cultural animals, are, interchangeably, technological animals. At the same time, because they're technological animals, human beings are also institutional animals, deliberately using the word 'institution' here to refer to institutionalized organizations. A concept I've found essential for explaining human cultural evolution, which so far I've already used in the text quite frequently, is the *'primordial manifestation'*: entity A exists before entity B; though the former, by way of a sociohistorical process, in large part ultimately becomes the latter. Entity A in this case represents the primordial manifestation. This sums up, for one, the ontological nature of the repository in relation to the civilization. But from a long historical perspective, there's a still much earlier entity that's relevant here – the primordial manifestation of the institution itself: the *family*, the original cultural "organization" in the history of humanity, which was for tens of thousands of years essentially the sole organizational means serving to reproduce all the human methods for capturing and exploiting resources (technologies).

Resources, technologies, and the primordial form of institutions couldn't help but get caught in holistically manifesting feedback loops with each other wherever and whenever they appeared in history, since the very beginning of culture/language. I believe these entities in all their different possible combinations as structural foundations for human cultural systems are, most centrally, what drive sociohistorical process. In other words, they're predominantly responsible for driving the long-term material evolution of all human environments. In the civilizations stage in particular, the institutions are the most determinative elements: especially, (1) those related to the organized fulfillment of the water-food-shelter (life-support) complex of needs, as I've already mentioned; (2) those related to the organized storing, spreading, and receiving of information (above all through language); and (3) those related to organized killing.

In our seeking to understand this unusually consequential phenomenon, we'll refer throughout the rest of our journey to the *'three interconnected cultural spheres'*: we'll refer to the life-support sphere, the communications sphere, and the military sphere. While we must distinguish between the three for analytical purposes, I must ask the reader to always keep somewhere in mind: "interconnected" is the most important part of the term. None of the spheres ever exist in the world autonomously; rather, each always exists in interdependent combination with the others, all of them forming a whole, just like every institution forms a whole with its correspondent resources and technologies, etc. Within the largest whole – composed of all three spheres with all their components, forming a single complex – at any given time in the history of civilizations, in any given civilization, there's always contained at the highest level the core management for the historical sun, which, simultaneously, ideologically represents the apex of the all-mighty cultural pyramid. This tiny elite syndicate is responsible for exercising hegemony, or attempting to, over the other, lesser (at least for the moment) Powers in the civilization ("the planets").

Each cultural sphere ultimately becomes one primary arena in which the major groupings of elite factions constantly organize and reorganize, with each sphere, at certain of its vital points, overlapping indistinguishably with the other two in personnel and purpose. In sum, regardless of the particular sphere's main wealth-producing activity, *managers of major cultural institutions utilize their characteristic technologies to control resources and engage in conflict with other institutions and therefore other humans over those resources.* In such fashion the war-trade competition connects everything that it's imposed upon: at the highest levels hierarchies translate across sectoral bounds. And resultantly, the war-trade environment, which, in most of the cases relevant to the present text, manifests at its broadest level in the form of the intercivilizational structure, provides as an external context the minimal level of constant stability ("order") necessary for systemic continuation, while remaining quite variable internally. No matter the particular *Power*-building activity, elite factionalism represents the key object of sociohistorical study – the key human phenomenon for understanding how the cultural spheres are so instrumental towards constructing civilizational worlds: as a collective sector, a "ruling class", as a potential or actual momentary core of the historical sun, elite factions are most tangibly responsible for manifesting the invisible but structurally-formative hierarchical realities on the external, cultural level. All elites find themselves amongst the tiniest politicoeconomic sliver in relation to their culture's whole population. Socially, maintaining their high status requires that they constantly interact solely amongst themselves, with all of them, however consciously or unconsciously, adhering to the same general order. They can only choose to adhere or not adhere to the order; once it's in place, individuals acting as individuals can't change the order, they can only consent to or reject the collective working towards the order's continuation.

Spheres control the transformative processes of history via their capabilities for maintaining relative order – which in turn maintains *the* order – in the midst of great economic shifts. No changes are more significant for the catalysis of all other such processes than those explicitly involving humanity's ability to sustain its own life; and of course, the life-support sphere's greatest-ever transformation occurred through the emergence of agriculture. The first agricultural settlements, starting around 8500 BCE, were located all throughout southwest Asia – this is why that portion stretching from the Levant to northern Syria to modern-day northwestern Iran is called the "Fertile Crescent" – and very shortly after, agriculture also developed (it wasn't "invented") independently in southeast Asia (around 7500 BCE). Agriculture then appeared gradually but steadily across northeast Africa, southeast Europe, and south-central Asia (leaving the "New World" aside for now).[cxlix] It matters to us that it emerged not in the form of an invention, but instead in the form of gradual development – what we'll also refer to in the present text as "innovation" – because we need to understand, foremost, how slow and in most ways unintentional a process the emergence of agriculture was at first for the human beings experiencing it, as well as the general form it took: evolutionary. For the initial few thousand years, the earliest agricultural populations couldn't possibly survive solely on the product of farming, but had to combine it with what they got from hunting and foraging,[cl] which of course had been humanity's only methods of acquiring food for the first 40,000-plus years of its history.

To sociohistorically contextualize the problem, as we must in order to continue our inquiry into the intercivilizational structure, before all else we need to ask: what was different? Why did humans start to farm in these places, at these times, and not in other places, at other times? If you want to properly understand the (evolutionary) history of civilizations, this is among the few indispensable questions to be explored.

In part 1 I asserted that stored usable energy is the singularly significant interconnection between a culture's imaginary, explicitly cultural side and its structural, explicitly politicoeconomic side. Most fundamentally, this interconnection embodies the life-support resources' unsurpassable vitality. Now, by definition, only farming cultures, whether we're referring to civilizations or other smaller-scale farming cultures such as "chiefdoms", can produce their own food resources. Thus, aside from very atypical instances that may have occurred from time to time in the past for brief stretches, the farming culture is the only kind of culture in history that has ever even had the potential to acquire constantly increasing supplies of consumable energy – i.e., in all cases besides wood, fossil fuels, etc., food.

This means farming cultures are essentially the sole cultures in history that have ever confronted a holistic environmental reality of wealth surpluses. Even if there were incidental surpluses in hunter-gatherer environments at anomalous points in humanity's history, it's extremely unlikely, almost inconceivable, that there were surpluses in any hunter-gatherer environment to the point where the environment's general cultural reality led to its humans' becoming accustomed to constant surpluses. Moreover, considering the slow, piecemeal nature of the process that brought farming into existence, it's hard to imagine that, for at least the first few thousand years in the history of farming, even a single culture experienced substantial energy surpluses. Certainly, the earliest appearance of regular energy surpluses, in the form of excess food production, must've been the greatest conceivable effect of agriculture leading to the emergence of civilizations, marking the pivotal moment between (1) humanity's original transition to an agricultural way of life and (2) humanity's original transition to urbanization. But surpluses still can't explain (1), for the very reason that, during all the time when it was such an uncertain process, agriculture couldn't possibly have seemed like a better option than hunting/gathering for the achievement even of "mere" subsistence – let alone the production of surpluses, which no one would've been thinking about anyhow.

In fact, it's not just farming to acquire surpluses that couldn't have been the main original purpose catalyzing the eventual emergence of agricultural settlements – the original purpose couldn't have been farming, at all: in the earliest locales wherein farming ended up being developed, settlement came first, long before agriculture; though not because hunter-gatherers were incapable of understanding the processes of agriculture. It has often been remarked upon in contemporary scholarship that hunter-gatherers must've known, long before agriculture came into existence, how vegetation grows from seeds planted and germinated in soil.[cli] The unwarranted assumption of hunter-gatherers' ignorance stems from modern individuals' unconscious (and often also quite conscious) presumptions of the inherent superiority of civilizational and hence agricultural lifestyles, presumptions which encourage the notion that all human beings, if they'd been given the "option", would've naturally "chosen" to farm.

The assumption stems from a belief in one kind of culture being "better than" another kind largely on the basis of each kind's "choices": totally overlooking how inadequate it is to think of things in terms of "choice" in this case, or in so many other cases of large-scale sociohistorical process, especially such transformative ones as the development of settlements and agriculture. This development wasn't based primarily on choice for the human beings who partook in originating it but on a complex combination of necessities and possibilities, which themselves were in the first instances based on geographical factors out of the control of any individual human being, or even any individual group of human beings.[clii] Additionally, the factors involved were just as much chronological as they were geographical: as always, human lives on planet Earth were simultaneously both space and time sensitive. So when we ask why settlements and farming emerged when and where they did, we're asking a fundamentally chronological-geographical (historical) question about a quintessentially politicoeconomic (social) phenomenon. In fact, we're asking precisely about the primordial sociohistorical context for the history of civilizations.

The primordial sociohistorical context for civilizations was *monumental crisis*: this is how the beginning of the interglacial period must've been perceived by the individuals most directly affected by it, in the southwest Asian "Fertile Crescent" and its immediately adjacent locales. It must've been such a perception that set the stage for the emergence of settlements, which in turn would create the preconditions favorable for the development of agriculture. The most affected locales of all were in the southwest Asian/northeast African/southeast European zone, which as I argue ended up being the original breeding ground for the intercivilizational structure.[cliii] As we'll see, the general crisis – the most recent planetary transition to an interglacial period, or what's more commonly referred to as "the end of the last Ice Age", and which started around 12 000 BCE – shared the most intimate processual interconnection with the trans-regional establishment of the intercivilizational structure. Moreover, this interconnection wasn't only historical: it was also ontological. In the beginnings, of settlement and civilizations, clusters of events completely out of the control of all human cultures (let alone individual human beings) almost exclusively shaped mass human action, i.e. the constantly moving total social behavior of human systems.

The events related to the initial transition, however, were "natural events" in the strictest sense – although, I'm not so much interested in classifying what "kinds of events" there are; I'm interested, rather, in viewing things from the perspective of an all-historical 'continuum of event-*causes*', with "natural" on one end and "cultural" on the other. A comprehensive theory of history needs to make some attempt not only to describe, but also to account for the precise ways in which events constitute the "material" of history, seeing how the event has always been what has characterized historical study most distinctly. I believe study of the event and events holds the most promise for addressing the different rates of change in complexity found in different examples of the intercivilizational structure. For instance, one can see most clearly the long-term evolution of cultural complexity by focusing on how the speed of events both reflects and is reflected by culture's increasing ability, over space/throughout time, to "drown out" the events caused entirely or mainly by the prevailing natural ecology.

What do I mean by "the speed of events"? Essentially I'm referring to the quantity of major occurrences that happen on Earth in a given quantity of time in a given sociohistorical setting, which are "major" to the extent that, when they happen, they drastically alter or annihilate the courses of human lives. I assert that at a given time, in a given locale, the more that events in general tend to cluster towards the cultural end of the spectrum, the faster major occurrences tend to happen in relation to the human beings inhabiting the locale. Resultantly, in a given span of time, *more* events tend to happen in the locale than did previously in an identical length of time. At least, this is how things have always been, up to the present point in history, starting from some certain yet unknown point in the human past. That is, not only have human beings created crisis after crisis, with each crisis distributing its devastation with evermore velocity than the last, but also, and because of this first condition, there has been a tendency for greater numbers of such events to happen in a similar quantity of time, when comparing a certain type of locale with its cultural/historical predecessors.

The appropriate next question to ask, then, is "What causes events to generally cluster near the cultural end of the spectrum, in a certain place during a particular chronological context?" To begin, it must be said that the continuum always exists on two different but interdependent fronts: long-historical and short-historical. From the long-historical perspective, we're concerned with differences and similarities of complexity/event-speed *between* intercivilizational periods, or between intercivilizational periods and precivilizational cultural epochs. From the short historical perspective, we're concerned with differences and similarities of complexity/event-speed *within* intercivilizational periods: between different contemporaneous civilizations, as well as within a single civilization, contrasting two different points of its existence. So when I say events were clustered near the cultural end of the spectrum in a specific sociohistorical setting, depending upon the context it can mean, on the one hand, that the culture in which the events happened was close to the cultural end of the spectrum for its epoch. Or, whether or not the culture was close to the cultural end of the spectrum for its epoch, it could mean the culture was in an epoch that was closer to the cultural end of the spectrum in comparison to other epochs.

In either case, there are many factors that must simultaneously contribute in order to bring about the cultural state-of-affairs, which are invariably sociohistorical in nature. As might be obvious, the more complex the overall state-of-affairs – the highest overall levels being found in the most complex periods at their most complex phases – the more factors there are that contribute to the overall conditions. However, as might also be obvious, all the individual factors aren't equally determinative. The greatest factors of all for judging cultural complexity and thus the speed of events, both between and within periods, are those most involved with the three interconnected spheres.

The cultural complexity/speed of events in a culture therefore shift as a result of the evolution of the *'central world-shaping nexus'*: the whole sphere of interconnections between a culture's life-support, communications, and military activities, involving the feedback loops between resources, technologies, and institutions in all three of what are, from the broadest perspective, subsystems. The more complex the central nexus, the more complex is the culture as a holistic entity. In a civilization, the *most* central nexus is whatever happens to be the epicenter of *Power* at a given moment. Everything revolves – and evolves – around the historical sun.

The sun can maintain this unique *Power* because it has the decisive individual share of control over the distribution of energy supplies throughout the civilization. Further, a sun falls out of *Power* when a contending Power has gained a greater share of control over energy-supply distribution, or otherwise when the seat-of-*Power* itself collapses, leading the civilization to collapse altogether. Remember, at a given time, every other Power in a civilization is itself a potential possessor of (or close partaker in) the central orbital position, until the civilization has reached its maximum point of expansion, at which point whatever Power is acting as sun remains in that position until both it and the civilization it rules over finally die out.

That last element, whereby every major Power in a civilization can potentially assume the sun position, or can at least directly partake in that position in its own small yet substantial way, sustains an ever-present hierarchical situation within every Power's internal sphere of influence that's directly parallel to the hierarchical situation existing in the civilization-at-large, as well as, in a different way, the most broadly determinative pecking order at the level of the intercivilizational structure. Just as the primarily *historical* metaphor for the civilization is a solar system, the primarily *cultural* metaphor for the civilization is a pyramid (as I also said in part 1). The civilization-State-complex within its civilizational niche, the civilization within its intercivilizational niche, and the intercivilizational niche in its holistic Earth-bound environment, in total constitute nothing so much as a series of pyramids – pyramids within pyramids. In the end, this is the only way to ensure that every man "knows his place" (and then the man, always in these cultures under some form of patriarchic rule himself, teaches the woman "her place") within the world of the intercivilizational period. Along these lines, hierarchical structures became translated across civilizational boundaries in the periods when the intercivilizational structure still existed. In a similar way but along sociohistorically unique lines the same phenomenon exists within the global civilization, across the boundaries of different (sub)cultural niches.

We can now also understand how the same institution seems to stick around from one period to the next, and yet periodically takes on additional sets of functions so novel that it becomes each time essentially a completely different entity: juxtapose the social role of the Catholic Church in the modern world to its role in the contemporary world; contrast both with the Catholic Church's role in the medieval world. Once we know what institutionalized organizations in general are used for in civilizations, it becomes much easier to understand why certain institutions seem to have such remarkable staying *Power*. It becomes much easier to understand why certain organizations are so significant that they represent nothing less than repositories facilitating the preservation and transmission of the eco-psychological conditions necessary for perpetuating civilizations (these conditions-as-whole-sets being what I call conquest syndromes). Institutionalized organizations are simply *Power*-factories churning out culturally prestigious employment opportunities, ultimately for no "higher" reason than to sustain the dynasties sought after and defended by the elite factions that have evolved generation after generation for thousands of years. Since civilizations-as-wholes are literally indefinable without them, repositories are the most successful *Power*-factories of all, a status which both stems from and is reflected by their unique capabilities for adaptation.

For an institution to endure a substantial portion of an intercivilizational period, let alone the entire period or even multiple periods, the tangible goals of the institution necessarily must change over time. But in terms of the broadest possible goal for the institution, this never really changes no matter how long it lasts: the goal is nothing more than the institution's own continued existence. In other words, institutions fight to "stay alive". And such institutions ultimately stay alive in no other way except by making a profit, either directly or indirectly: either a given institution makes the profit itself, or its existence allows an associated higher-up institution to profit. Repositories have the greatest profit-making potential of all institutions because by definition they encompass the domains of entire civilizations, or at least entire States. Naturally, then, humans have throughout history fought over repositories to a far greater extent than all other institutions, and relatedly, repositories have had the greatest proportion of weight "thrown behind them" in terms of the resources human beings devote towards keeping institutions alive.

As the last sentence indicates, since institutionalized human organizations are of course not primarily physically-based individual material entities but imaginatively-based individuated agglomerations of human and material entities, intellectually coordinated from the top-down by some tiny group ("the leadership"), such institutions survive only insofar as the hierarchically-facilitated labor of human beings allows them to survive. Once a profit-making institution is successfully created, some or another group of human beings will typically see to it that the institution continues running until (1) events destroy the institution's ability to exist, or (2) the institution simply "runs out of steam". The reason that its being a civilization- or State-wide phenomenon allows the repository to have the highest profit-making potential isn't just because such breadth allows the repository to employ the greatest quantity of people. Insofar as it *is* a literally civilization- or State-wide (and in some cases intercivilizational) phenomenon, the repository actually *imbues meaning onto* the lives of the greatest quantity of people, and so, in a way that no other institutions can rival, repositories are difficult or impossible to destroy. This is truly what it means when institutions are considered 'sacred': they can't be destroyed unless the culture they're keeping together is destroyed, which won't happen so long as a sufficient number of individuals feel they owe their very "personhood" to the culture.

Herein we find the real secret weapon behind the perpetuation of the war-trade competition: *its* leading institutions become "our" leading institutions. Or really, human beings in civilizations belong to the war-trade competition's leading institutions, not the other way around. These institutions, the repositories, are responsible for nothing less than *making a humanity* out of a population of humans: since a concept of 'humanity' is truly unimaginable without culture, human beings as individuals are unimaginable without the cultures that mold them into livable existence. Events pass, but civilizations live on so long as repositories withstand events, ready to ensure that human populations *en masse* will repeatedly enact future versions of past mistakes, putting all their "stock" in institutionalized organizations – and this is where the ever-expanding tragedy dominating the long history of civilizations has always resided.

II

Narrativized Hypothesis of The Emergence of Civilizations, States, and the First Intercivilizational Structure

The more complex a culture is, and hence the faster is the speed of events that happen in its environment, the greater is the potential for crises to arise in the culture. Or, more precisely, as a culture continually diminishes the potential for a certain category of crises – a category that would encompass primarily "naturally-caused" crises – it tends at the same time to increase the potential for primarily "culturally-caused" crises. Few examples are more meaningful in this regard than the case of those earliest human settlements to become successful mainly or solely as agricultural settlements, subsequent to original emergence of agriculture that started around 8500 BCE in the Fertile Crescent. Thus, we're talking about human beings most likely living between around 6500 and 6000 BCE.[cliv]

Their cultural ancestors, so far as we know among the very first human settlers in the planet's history, had been shocked into action by the wholesale drastic environmental change brought on by a once-in-100,000-years transition to an interglacial period: a warmer climate and its different weather patterns, floods, extinctions of food supplies. All of the places where original "farmers" – again, they weren't yet actual farmers, but rather had transitioned imperceptibly from hunter-gatherers to hunter-gatherers who also grew some crops and kept some animals, a process that itself had taken at least two thousand years – successfully settled for extended periods of time were, naturally, environments that had offered the surest promise of stability for their lifestyles. In southwest Asia, the earliest partial-agricultural settlements that survived for substantial lengths of time were invariably those situated at the ideal geographical crossroads between multiple micro-ecologies, allowing settlers the largest, most diverse possible supply of food within viable reach. So already, even before they became true farmers, any community of originary settlers had been linked to the specific natural (*micro-*) environment of their culture's insular physical domain in the most intimate way possible.[clv]

To be sure, nomadic hunter-gatherer cultures had also always been inextricably connected to their natural environments. The difference was that their environments naturally extended over much greater ranges: the relationship between humans and land was temporally disbursed to the utmost extreme. In "war" involving land-disputes, a nomadic culture would've been defending its ability to use the land's products, not its attachment to the land. Successful settlement entails defending that attachment itself, defending one's insular group-identity insofar as it's actually defined by constant settlement and thus perpetual ideological dependence upon a certain explicitly-defined zone of land, not just by the immediate, comparatively momentary use of the land's resources. The settled culture defends its own ability to continuously exist within its assertively finite territory, illustrating a relationship between humans and their surroundings wholly divergent from the relative open-endedness characteristic of a hunting-gathering lifestyle's perpetual periodic relocation.

The intertwined progression of settlement and agriculture yielded, most significantly, a quantum leap in humanity's capacity to make full-blown war. As humans increasingly shifted to cultural strategies of settlement, they eventually came to rely more and more upon agriculture; the more they relied on agriculture, the more *implicitly* militarized settled humans became. Humanity only became more and more *explicitly* mired by the latter tendency amidst all the cultural complexity that evolved beyond simple agricultural settlements. Settlement, which started out as the most drastic ever response by human beings to a wholly natural crisis, started to become, in less than four thousand years in some places,[clvi] history's primary catalyst of largely cultural crises.

Civilizations happen systematically, which is to say a civilization is a system. Civilizations as systems – somewhat more specifically, *living* systems – emerged in the same way in relation to intercivilizational structures, as, on a narrower scale, nations did in Western civilization, in relation to the international system (concerning our discussion in the last section). In other words, to now restate things in the proper chronological order, the way the primordial Western "international" system sociohistorically preceded the emergence of nations echoed the much earlier process wherein the original intercivilizational structure's primordial manifestation preceded the emergence of civilizations. We can best understand this if we look at an intercivilizational structure not only the actual interactive framework for multiple civilizations, but also, and even more fundamentally, as the holistic set of potential social relations connecting transregional geographical extremes and everywhere in between. While the very earliest form of such a set didn't constitute the first fully-fledged version of an intercivilizational structure, such a structure would at the same time only emerge long after the most basic, localized trade networks were already in place across a transregional expanse. Civilizations, even in their most "primitive" manifestations, don't appear ready-made out of thin air: although, such an assumption would be very much like how the first civilizations themselves thought about history.[clvii]

  This argument, concerning humanity's first intercivilizational structure, attempts to answer one of those questions, and perhaps even *the* question, which can only be answered by empirical consultation of human history as a whole: "How did humanity's first war-trade environment emerge?" Necessarily, we must start by turning our focus towards the long-term background leading up to the earliest "Old World" civilizations that we know of. In the most broadly determinative ways, these civilizations really did start to set the global stage for all the civilizations that would come later. However, we can only put this in its proper perspective if we look at civilizations not as independent actors largely able to choose their own fates, but rather as *'cultural symptomologies'*, growing (as things called cultures generally do) within the adaptive boundaries set by the broadest sociohistorical (politicoeconomic/chronological-geographical) contexts. In parallel, cultured human populations "grow" within the ritually-directed domains of these symptomologies, mainly via the agency of violently-enforced *Power*-structures: the core social structures of dominant cultures.

  This is really the most proper way to view the history of civilizations – the continuous, evolving growth of mass symptomologies/mass populations absorbing those symptomologies – rather than as a story of "free agents" who comprise "societies" that they consciously create themselves and participate in voluntarily. And it must be emphasized that such a characterization doesn't describe solely the earliest civilizations. In fact, to take a long view, humanity's history through the civilizations stage went like this: the more materially complex a culture was overall, the less "free" (from my perspective, able to make up their own minds) human beings inhabiting that culture typically were. This isn't so much because of some detrimental attribute inherent in the phenomenon of complexity; rather, it's because of *how* material complexity expanded via civilizations, as seen both when generally comparing civilizations to less complex forms of culture, and comparing history's most complex civilizations to its least complex ones.

Prior to the origin of agriculture, the military sphere was necessarily the least technologically complex of the three interconnected cultural spheres, owing to the logistical incapacities for making warfare in a truly civilizational sense – two organized sides engaged in lethal combat for a geostrategic "prize" – in the context of the nomadic lifestyles and relatively miniscule population densities characteristic of hunter-gatherer cultures. The military sphere *per se* may even have been non-existent. This isn't at all to say that hunter-gatherers never fought to the death over commonly desired, finite resources; just that they didn't do so, and couldn't have done so, in a way lending itself to ever-evolving military structures, which is the distinguishing aspect of warfare in civilizations. Clearly, murder rates amongst hunter-gatherers before the emergence of settlement must've been quite high – much higher than they are in the contemporary world, and perhaps much higher than in any civilizational context. But there's also an enormous difference between one individual killing another individual due to what are, in the context of definitively most-minimal possible or even nonexistent *Power*-structures, socially uncontrollable desires, and one individual killing another because of orders received from a higher-up in the context of a professional hierarchy, as part of an intentionally-designed, profit-seeking *strategy*.

The first type doesn't have much room for constant escalation, whereas all the latter type seems to do is escalate. War isn't mainly an incident-dependent activity, contingent upon intergroup tensions that can be "settled" short of war; it's primarily an ever-increasing sphere of human *politicoeconomic activity*, and has a purpose all its own aside from what's accomplished, and beyond what's accomplished, by any actual, individual event. Once it came into existence, the purpose rather quickly became the underlying purpose of civilizations, and eventually their overarching purpose, as well: the military sphere became individuated and then ever-increasingly autarkic in relation to absolutely everything else – every single other thing became subject to military autarchy. In the long run, this happened as a direct result of the emergence and long-term evolution of the State, the civilization's quintessential political manifestation. Although to phrase things most accurately, this development didn't take hold "because of" the State; rather, it was a generally prevailing phenomenon that, throughout history, became embodied in the State most of all. That is, the State originally emerged because of the realizable potential for military individuation, and then once that existed the State continuously reconsolidated its military function: now doing so also to perpetuate the State's own existence/increase its own wealth, not simply to "solve" the problem that had originally led to its institutionalization.[clviii]

But what allowed the individuation of the military to occur in the first place? Once again, I'll point out that while humans can and do engage in actually or potentially lethal fighting against other humans for all sorts of reasons, there are relatively very few reasons that tend to lead to hostilities in the context of a warfare system, by which I mean a system wherein militaries are sustained explicitly for the purpose of competition against other militaries. Mainly, this stems from the extreme specificity of the type of context in which militaries thrive.

Historically, true militaries, mass *bodies* of human beings (at first, and in most of the history since, almost always men) organized hierarchically to kill and otherwise do violence to other such bodies of men as well as their associated human populations, don't appear until large numbers of agricultural settlement systems begin to appear, at which point they only start to emerge, in their most primordial forms. Thus, in the days before the first long-term agricultural settlement systems started to become fairly widespread in any subregional locale – up until around 5000 BCE or so at the very earliest (in parts of southwest Asia, the heartland for the contemporary dominant culture's earliest cultural ancestry) – it's hard to imagine that human beings could've ever gone to war in anything remotely resembling the civilizational way of war. This isn't to say that human beings were, as a whole, less "naturally" inclined to go to war, but that technologically, they had less viable means for making war. It seems rather obvious that they weren't naturally (biologically) less likely to go to war than would be human beings in later, more complex cultures, seeing how these human beings transitioning into the original agricultural settlement systems embodied the bases for precisely those cultures that would raise the earliest "militaries" so rapidly after gaining the logistical potential.

That last point, concerning how the earliest "militaries" (bands of raiders) rapidly emerged more or less as soon as the logistical potential arose, is the first great real-world systemic connection between the life-support and military spheres in civilizations. Once more, the existence of a division of labor proves to be the all-important phenomenon, as the connection in its primordial manifestation stemmed from the characteristically most limited options for making a living in the originary agricultural settlements. Such constraints existed by purest necessity, as by definition the first evolutionary stage of complexity for a living system is the simplest; and division of labor is the most significant single index of overall complexity in a settled human culture. At no other point in the history of farming have human beings ever been more reliant on agricultural products as direct "payment" for their labor.

Speaking of payment, this brings up another crucial difference that would forever distinguish humanity's life in civilizations from life in less complex human cultures: overall, agriculturalists were expending far more energy than hunter-gatherers had, in order to accomplish the primary goal of their labor – life-support. And even after human beings in some locales could start to rely mainly on farming for subsistence, between around 6500 and 5500 BCE in southwest Asia, neither the amount nor the nutritional value of the food humanity provided for itself came close to what successful hunter-gatherers had been able to achieve.[clix] I consider this one of the very best pieces of evidence that agriculture arose independently for the first time in broad geographical subregions (such as southwest Asia) *only* insofar as it derived from locales where human beings had long-since lost the ability to feed themselves adequately with the products of hunting-gathering alone. That is, the human cultures that independently developed farming came to rely on it, naturally, only where the development of agriculture was an absolute necessity for survival. Therefore, at first, humans weren't just less competent technologically as farmers than they had been as hunter-gatherers, in a given locale experiencing the typical chronology of humanity's original transition to farming – it's hard to imagine how this wouldn't have been the case, given the tens of thousands of years of experience "built into" hunting and gathering – but even the most skilled farmers were less than adequately fed. All of this amounted to much more work for much less payoff. If farming hadn't been an ecologically indispensable strategy for living in the relevant geographies at the relevant time in history, why would human beings have stuck to it?

At any rate, within the scope of the earliest successful agricultural communities, there emerged two most general ways of feeding oneself: growing crops, in particular grains, and animal husbandry. All the later complexities of the holistic agricultural division of labor would unfold from these humblest origins, which, as unformed as they were in one sense, were in another sense already extremely rigid in their complexity, by comparison with the type of economic systems that preceded successful farming settlements. The only real division of labor existent in prior epochs had been a division between sexes, as, depending on the geography, men mostly hunted and women mostly gathered. But where it existed, this phenomenon would've been attached mainly to established gender roles, not based primarily on politicoeconomic considerations.

Predominately politicoeconomic considerations were now slowly but steadily becoming the most decisive factors shaping who did what jobs: the division of labor became defined for the first time by the establishment of explicitly *occupational* hierarchies.[clx] This is most essentially what *Power* entails, and it's the main reason why I set it apart textually as a unique term. *Power* is the ability some human beings have, under certain environmental conditions and in the midst of certain scenarios, to tell other human beings what work to do; to be "the boss". All of the *Power* that exists now is what has existed since these earliest moments of its evolution, encompassing all cultural growth in between – *Power* is a living text that's always being written.

The division between nomadic hunting and gathering along gendered lines hadn't necessarily entailed an inherent conflict between distinct human cultural groups based on productive land-use. Nomadic hunting took place mainly in different landscapes from nomadic gathering, and hunting and gathering were anyway decidedly complementary rather than antagonistic economic activities relative to one another. In this way, we can consider nomadic hunting-gathering the first form of human economic system. As it initially began to give way to settled hunting-gathering/early farming, and finally to the first fully-fledged settled agricultural economic systems, the division of labor as a whole still must've been unformed, a situation that would've prevailed for as long as human beings still weren't successful enough farmers to feed themselves solely via agriculture. But soon enough, once they were stabilized, some of these early agricultural settlements – which, geographically, were at this earliest stage necessarily all isolated from one another – steadily became more successful, by which I mean they were able to feed more and more humans, more and more sufficiently, over an extended period of time. After this chronological juncture (probably between around 6500 BCE and around 6000 BCE, depending upon the location), once many successful isolated settlements had emerged, events throughout our relevant zone, starting in the original epicenter of southwest Asia, began happening much more quickly: the speed of events saw a long historical escalation.[clxi]

Subsequently, the very first settlement systems started to emerge, a development most strongly associated with the initial instances of settlements' being forged so closely to one another that they had to interact as a matter of politicoeconomic constitution. In other words, at least two settlements were so spatially proximate that a presumption of politicoeconomic interaction got built into the holistic structure of each settlement. This hadn't happened at all in the first phase of settlement[clxii] – the phase ended by the appearance of the very first successful agricultural settlements – which I think is perhaps the best indicator as to why humans in southwest Asia (and elsewhere) had turned to settlement to begin with. In accordance with the most severe communications and military limitations bounding early settlers, settlement systems in their originary incarnations could only come into existence on vast open plains: large enough to facilitate multiple settlements, though small enough that human beings could easily move on foot between locations. However, if the purpose behind the earliest phase of settlement had been, above all, *protection from other human groups*, then open plains clearly would've defeated the purpose.

In the places that had been most immediately, dramatically affected by transition to the interglacial period, namely all the places where agriculture would emerge (relatively) independently, overpopulation and hence depletion of resources must've been almost the sole factor leading to the long-term perpetuation of settlement, and in turn, the emergence of farming. This is the only thing, in the first place, that would've led the earliest settlers to so readily accept such a marked decrease in their "standard-of-living", compared to that of the last truly nomadic hunter-gatherers: the ecological possibility for that higher standard-of-living altogether ceased to exist because there were now far too many human beings competing for far too few resources. When that happened, in these scenarios where absolutely nothing resembling a settled hierarchy yet existed, it had been essentially every clan for itself. At those points in time and space, humans were competing over the barest essentials for survival, and when they had to take other humans' lives to save their own, they must've done so without thinking twice. Moreover, in that phase marking the beginning of the interglacial transition, the situation must've reached a more extreme degree than any similar situation previously experienced by humans: such monumental natural resource scarcity had never happened in a context wherein humanity was, as a whole, so strikingly adept at providing the basis for its own survival. All the individual factors, when thrown together in forming a single sociohistorical context, had resulted in a situation where the critical subregional transformation from well-fed to wide-scale malnourishment occurred – in long historical terms – essentially overnight, leading human beings to murder each other at a faster rate than ever before, which in turn led to the survivors' seeking evermore long-term refuge. Finally, after some thousands of years, nomadism was fading out in many local, isolated spots, and the earliest flickers of agriculture began to appear, as the first truly permanent settlements became established.

What had allowed some locales to achieve consistent agricultural success with such relative speed?* As yet, with still no systematic *cultural* distinctions having emerged, the initial distinctions had to have been primarily *natural*: geographical and ecological. Simply, some geographical locales were particularly well insulated from the rest of the world, and amongst these, some were ecologically more conducive to farming. When settled agriculture had evolved to the point where those features visibly distinguished some settlements from others on the landscape – since the accumulation of human beings in these naturally more successful locales had grown so quickly compared to all other settlements – it can be said that such settlements were reaching agricultural overpopulation for the first time. Certain affected human beings living in these settlements needed to respond in one of two ways: fighting or fleeing. As it was the first time in history wherein human beings faced this new type of *culturally-caused* collective crisis, there were no better-designed plans to turn to.

---

* With this still not happening anywhere until a few thousand years or so into the history of agriculture, at the earliest.

Now we're back at that point concerning which, above, I said "events across our relevant zone" really started to speed up (around 6500 BCE to 6000 BCE). This was the first primarily cultural speeding-up of the long historical process subsequent to the singularly fateful natural speeding-up initiated by the shift to the interglacial period. Its rapidity owed especially to the fact that, until this point, cultural progression had been essentially identical at all similar places throughout southwest Asia. Thus, all of the most successful isolated settlements were reaching the particular chronological phase around the same general time. Here was the first example of human beings in the relevant geographical context turning to the locales originally left unsettled, the open plains – because now there were many human beings who saw no other option.

Once again, we find that the greatest natural advantage went to the human beings who got there first: at least, the ones who could *secure the territory* first, which in the relevant context amounted to the same thing. "Securing the territory" meant ensuring that a settlement could be built and continuously maintained. Only the human beings who were the best at organizing physical violence could do this.[clxiii]

Throughout history, whenever a situation arose wherein multiple unaffiliated human beings wanted to use the same vital, limited resource supply, it was almost guaranteed that at least two human beings would eventually use some form of violence against one another to gain dominance over that supply. In each case, additional key variables determined the overall extent of the violence, the degree of effort required for the victorious party to secure the supply, and the number of individuals jockeying for position. Respectively, the variables are the proportional magnitude of the resource wealth in relation to the overall sociohistorical context, the know-how that interested human beings can bring to bear on their competition, and the organizational capacity of each human being (or group of human beings) who attempt to consolidate their positions. Resources, technology, and institutions.

There's an all-important "secret" to civilizational history, a supremely-ruling ontological fact demanding great respect for the sociohistorical significance of simple facts in general. To understand it, one must first recognize that for preindustrial agriculturalists, there existed no resource more valuable than quality farmland. *The fact*: the great landowners in any given polity were typically the families or descendants of the most recent individuals who had been able to successfully defend the land with violent force. To "defend" the land, however, in this sense, implies that at one point the ancestors or living relatives of the great landowners had overtaken the land, meaning they had committed an originary act of enormous force. "Lords" were always "warlords", in the first instance, before becoming "landlords", and this was how States would eventually form.

It's not literally a secret: for one thing, I'm far from the first individual to point it out.[clxiv] It's a secret, rather, in the sense that it's a *key*, a means towards seeing the history of civilizations from a broad evolutionary perspective (without which it's difficult or impossible to see things holistically); it's a real-world feature that makes translating histories across civilizational contexts not only possible, but in fact absolutely necessary if we're to truly understand what civilizations are. Most significantly, until at least the beginning of the post-Columbian order, when cash crops started to grow exponentially in their significance to the overall intercivilizational politicoeconomic system, the lineages of the great landowners had almost always originated with herders: leaders of animal-packs – in our presently relevant historical context, ancient southwest Asia, particularly sheep.[clxv]

Thus, shepherds were the archetypal "leaders of the pack" for humanity at large amidst the formative sociohistorical context of history's first civilization, in ancient southern Mesopotamia. Whether wrangling sheep or peasants, the shepherd had to be an individual uniquely suited for imposing blunt discipline on unruly animals, implemented by the crook's swift smack.[clxvi] Moreover, even among the shepherds there had to be hierarchies, as well. For these earliest successful shepherds, the necessities of pasture required much more land in a shorter time than did the requirements of crop farming: successful shepherds were thereby put into situations where they competed violently against one another long before successful peasants did, as shepherds were always in search of more land to graze. And to accomplish its intended goal, a mobilized attack had to be undertaken under the direction, however crude, of a single leader – a primordial army general.[clxvii]

To ensure that an open plain could remain secure, a prerequisite for launching one of the original successful settlement systems, the unconsciously ruling herders in a given territory kept the border of the system's settled space patrolled. Certain select herders let their natural wealth graze while waiting for some contending group to try and cross their boundaries, or otherwise just for some poor unwitting migrant to end up where he or she didn't belong. The inevitable result must've been war, individualized murder (under the right circumstances, in the form of public sacrifice), or enslavement. So even if a contending group of herders ended up winning, the system wouldn't – or, in the context, *couldn't* – really change. The victors over the incumbents simply slaughtered all those men presumed capable of future violent resistance, raped those women who were in their child-bearing years, enslaved the rest, then installed their own loyal subordinates to collect tribute. Or, somewhat later, they could just hone in on the settlement system's old leadership, becoming the new top bosses of the subordinate populations after some well-directed and hence beneficially limited show of terror on the local population, to enforce the transfer of *Power*. This last-mentioned scenario must've become more and more frequent once there were contexts wherein the politicoeconomic conditions required one center to maintain conquest over two or more other centers: for one settlement system to rule over at least two other settlement systems (at which point there would emerge the necessity for the next stage of complexity, the city).

In other words, the more culturally complex human settlements became, in this initial transition from individual, isolated settlements to increasingly large settlement systems, the more violence could be and was used in an organized, systematic way, as opposed to being embodied by much less overtly strategized and in this way much less predictable slaughter between inter- and intracultural antagonists. My argument in no way entails an assertion that all human beings are naturally prone to constant violence, and that as a whole they increasingly tend toward violence as history proceeds. In fact, as I'll explain, concerning the violence in social structures, the argument, while acknowledging that such violence has always uncontrollably existed, also necessitates our accepting that the existence of violence in a given *settled* social structure necessitates its domination by a minority of individuals. When left unchecked by external forces, which, when in human form always appear as other, more successfully violent individuals, *this minority of individuals ultimately evolves into the top political leadership of the settlement or settlement system.*

Now, as I alluded to in the paragraph immediately before the last, in the most materially complex settlement systems, with those related to a context shared by multiple intercity environments (multiple civilizations) being from my perspective the most complex in history, it's much more likely than it was in originary agricultural circumstances for competitors over political leadership to just aim for "cutting off the head" when they're performing acts of conquest. By this I mean destroying the old political leadership and replacing it with one's own preferred rulers, while leaving the existing system largely intact. Typically, conquerors don't care about "changing the system", and throughout history, especially at the most complex levels, they couldn't care much about this if they wanted to be successful conquerors, which in the first place requires successful *consolidation* of conquest. Given the most serious logistical challenges involved in mobilizing for audacious acts of war, this (the perpetuation of the status quo) was throughout most of civilizational history a physical requirement for the very coming-into-being of such acts, in accordance with how the evolution of civilizations mainly took place: centralized around the consolidation of conquest. Indeed, to say nothing of the sheer technological capabilities, there was very rarely cultural (ideological) opportunity for completely transforming civilizations at will. In the contemporary world, we seem to completely lose sight of this fact as a result of the apparent effortlessness ("at the push of a button") with which "Technology" can change culture – although of course this itself is only the long-term result of the evolution of conquest.

As the proportion of physically violent individuals in a settled culture gradually decreases, physical violence in general can become even more organized – and in turn the culture can, over the long term, grow still more complex.[clxviii] More specifically relevant to the setting of originary "Old World" civilizations, this process was coterminous with the fact that, in the earliest settlement systems, where there were herders of livestock and settled agriculturalists existing in the same territory, the herders naturally became the dominant practitioners of organized violence. Such farmers, by virtue of the need to stay near their crops, were always at a disadvantage in terms of mobility and hence a disadvantage in terms of speed relative to the transhumant herders. It was thus far more preferable for the crop farmers to pay tribute rather than to fight and surely die, and this must've been the defining political atmosphere surrounding the first successful settlement systems in human history.[clxix] In turn, after this beginning, herders would once again become much more competitive with one another than they were with the growers of grain.

In the context of precivilizational ancient southwest Asia (ca. 5000-4100), settled crop farmers would eventually reach locales where the land wasn't suitable for any domestication at all, herding or farming, without the farmers' controlling some substantial institutional capacity separate from though interdependent with that of the shepherds and cowherds. Resource and technological determinants saw to this institutional development. In certain places in southern Mesopotamia, for instance, farming couldn't be successful without knowledge of irrigation, which surely took many centuries to hone. Thus, at this stage where only the crudest official institutional presence existed in the midst of the lowest technological capabilities, the only individuals who could play leadership roles for directing the geographically indispensable practice of irrigation were individuals who had hands-on experience in that particular "field", i.e., individuals who lived and farmed in areas requiring irrigation.[clxx] Herders would've had a very difficult time consolidating any potential military conquest of these particular territories, and if and when they eventually did successfully consolidate conquest in a given irrigation-dependent locale, it wouldn't be by installing just any farmers, but primarily by aligning with those who had been there before the conquest.

In the southern Mesopotamian sub-region in particular – the land of Uruk, which, so far as we know, was the very first historical sun (epicenter of a civilization) in human history – the results were somewhat different; and this had to do mainly with the lagoon geographies in present-day southern Iraq, most specifically the terrain situated at the cusp of the Euphrates and the Persian Gulf. At the point in history we're now concerned with, the era of the so-called Ubaid culture, as well as the first several centuries or so of its successor, the so-called Uruk culture (ca. 4000-3100), water levels in the Persian Gulf were much higher than they would be at any subsequent point. This gave settlers of the lagoon territories (earliest descendants of the "marsh Arabs") ideal defense mechanisms to protect against herder invasions. Coupling that dynamic with the territory's positioning between a major inland sea and a major river, such lagoon settlements were the perfect geostrategic "safe zones" to collectively form the epicenter of the primordial manifestation of humanity's first intercivilizational trade network.[clxxi] By the end of the Ubaid period, there were successful agricultural settlements throughout southwest Asia, northeast Africa, and southeast Europe (not to mention the areas further east and west). Additionally, there were scattered across those areas gradually increasing numbers of settlement *systems*, growing steadily in size. The more all of the individual processes that altogether made up the larger process intensified, the more the potential increased for the eventual emergence of successful far-reaching trade networks. Most indicative of the overall growth – although located not in Mesopotamia but rather east of the Tigris, in the southwest of modern-day Iran – there was, by the beginning of the Uruk period at the latest, what we can probably rightly consider one of humanity's very first true cities, Susa.[clxxii]

Now, there existed at the same time (1) perhaps the most singularly significant portion of the originary intercivilizational structure's primordial manifestation and (2) the primordial manifestation of one of the first cities, in about as close proximity to each other as they could be without sharing a common sub-region. While the southern Euphrates represented the epicenter of the precursor to the first intercivilizational structure – the system of which the civilization is a subsystem – it's most likely that Susa was the regional prototype for the earliest cities, and hence the primordial manifestation of the civilization-State-complex, the definitive subsystem of a civilization. It was only when not just one but multiple fully-fledged civilizations emerged in a shared context, though, that both of the civilization's two major interdependent entities, the intercivilizational structure and the civilization-State-complex, could start to appear in *their* fully-fledged forms. Thus, the first civilization had to explicitly emerge before the first true civilization-State-complex as well as the first intercivilizational structure. The first civilization naturally emerged once multiple primordial cities had been explicitly combined into an individuated system along the central, Euphratean portion of the primordial intercivilizational structure.

So, a combination of the prototypical city and the Euphratean trade route, geographically relatively independent from one another though spatially quite proximate, existed by around 4000 BCE. Trade between far-reaching regions, if not yet a direct process, could be accomplished indirectly through the myriad smaller networks of localized trading connecting settlements and settlement systems located in between: from, say, the Aegean Sea at the farthest Western side to the Indian Ocean on the farthest Eastern side.[clxxiii] Settlement systems, although not yet so large as to provide impetus for multiple cities within striking distance of each other, were large enough in some cases to support isolated cities scattered across sub-regions.

Before we move further, this is a good place to pause and consider what a city most fundamentally is. What differentiates the city from all units of settled culture that, no matter how complex, still fall below what we might call an "urban threshold"? Why was Susa the first city in history; or if not quite so unique as that, then certainly among the handful of first cities, which, considering its proximity to the relevant geographical context, makes it an ideally representative example of the earliest origins of urbanization? It seems to me that since a city is most fundamentally a type of settlement system, settlement geography provides the most proper methods to employ for beginning to understand the city *as a social structure*. My perspective here has been influenced in the first place by the work of Hans Nissen, among the greatest living scholars studying the origin of civilizations in southern Mesopotamia. Nissen chose the framework of settlement geography as the primary analytical tool for his indispensable overview of the emergence of civilizations in southwest Asia, which I believe itself constitutes no small indicator of the specifically geographical significance characterizing the formation of cities and city systems.[clxxiv]

Right now, in determining the imaginative contours of the city, I'm concerned much more with function than I am with population size. For although, soon enough after their emergence, cities would lead to by far the greatest population densities in the history of humanity – multiplying to even greater heights the already unprecedented population densities that had been reached by long-term agricultural settlements and settlement systems – cities were not originally innovated mainly as means to store more people. Rather, they appeared for another, more primary reason; and this, I argue, is what would ultimately lead to the unprecedented amplification of human population density.

Returning to what I brushed upon above, cities first emerged to fulfill certain *regulatory* necessities[clxxv] that arose when simple settlement systems, having started to encroach upon each other, were then naturally led to conquer their neighboring systems. The abstract politicoeconomic realities of settlement systems would thereby forever afterward manifest themselves concretely on geographical terrain. And in order for such politicoeconomic realities to be grasped by the populations subject to and subjugated by them, the simultaneously geographical/politicoeconomic phenomenon constituting the city needed to be immediately visible on the ideological level – which yielded, additionally, a properly so-called *cultural* phenomenon.[clxxvi] "Center-periphery" describes the total phenomenon (combination sociohistorical and cultural) well enough, so long as we understand what exactly the relationship between a center and its periphery entails. The establishment of a relationship between a center and its periphery always serves as an official hierarchical expression of the relatively more organic hierarchies that exist within occupational sectors, which in its (the expression's) designated centrality serves to regulate the shared existence of *all* the various occupational sectors residing in a single polity: the quintessential tangible expression of the narrow and always-narrowing social stratification endemic to the historical growth of agricultural complexity.

Of course, by the time the city itself emerged, it was only the transposition onto a greater contiguous territory of the original version of such a relationship. That version had existed between the center of the simple settlement system and its periphery settlements – a "two-tier" hierarchy. The city took complexity a step further than the originary center. It was defined by the addition of an extra apex, utilized to control the competing centers – each seated atop a simple system – which had arisen within striking distance of each other. The emergence of the city is in this sense synonymous with the earliest establishment of a "three-tier"[clxxvii] hierarchy: the conquest of one settlement system by another.

All of this makes it much easier to understand the transformation that took place at a constantly increasingly rate throughout the fourth millennium BCE – the outburst of a fully-fledged civilization.[clxxviii] As the potential for more systematic trade had grown with the heightened stability of settlements and settlement systems, and as this process became so regularized that, for the first time, cities emerged, there occurred another primarily natural development affecting our relevant geographical zone: one certainly not as monumental as the prior transition to the interglacial period, but which would nonetheless have a general effect nearly as momentous. This was the point at which a cooler, dryer climate yielded the substantial, fairly rapid reduction in the level of the Persian Gulf, opening up an enormous amount of rich farmland all throughout southern Mesopotamia in areas previously uninhabitable, or else inhabitable only by isolated settlements or simple settlement systems.[clxxix] So vast an expanse opened up that, for the very first time, it was necessary for multiple cities – three-tier settlement systems – to arise within a territory that could be regularly reached by a singular means, referring in this case to the Euphrates.

I say such a development was "necessary" insofar as settlement became so extensive in this particular context of cultural complexity, that *for any of the land at all to be exploited*, there needed to be multiple centers in a common territory, each one regulating the hierarchy of a single settlement system over two or more settlement systems. And there must've been quite a strong perception that this was a necessity for maintaining the socially regulated exploitation of the land (which a great many individuals apparently wanted to do), because from here on out, this process of urbanization – of creating three-tier centers – would become extraordinarily rapid all throughout southern Mesopotamia. It therefore seems most necessary on my part to ask, how do we explain such striking rapidity?

Although the enormous acceleration of the originary urbanization process after about 3800 BCE was, as I've said, catalyzed in the first place by a natural transformation to the environment, everything in response to this natural change was only able to happen so quickly because, by the time the land opened up, humanity's experience in settlement systems had already been evolving for well over a thousand years. What's more, humanity's experience in settlement systems had been evolving most of all in those areas immediately surrounding southern Mesopotamia.[clxxx] In other words, a significant shift to the natural environment facilitated the cultural speeding-up of the long historical process yet again. But this time it occurred much faster than had that prior acceleration involving the overpopulation of the first successful agricultural settlements – precisely *because of* the preceding cultural acceleration: human beings weren't innovating the model of the settlement system for the very first time, but were, rather, "simply" transposing the preexisting concept onto a new landscape. In fact, human beings now settling in southern

Mesopotamia didn't even have to figure out how to consolidate the conquest of one settlement system over another, because the solution of the city already existed. So, throughout the newly-opened expanse, settlement systems emerged virtually immediately (from a long historical perspective). Once settlement systems emerged, just as quickly, cities became established.

In terms of the formation of the first cities in southern Mesopotamia, developments must've occurred in a slightly different way than they already had in Susa, and as they would in most other places where cities later emerged "independently" – and I believe this, above all, will explain how the first explicit civilization (holistic intercity cultural environment) emerged here so quickly after the land gained that potential. Instead of cities having to be constructed "from the ground up", so to speak, the new settlement systems along the southern Euphrates valley simply formed surrounding the existing trade outposts that had for some time already been exploiting the Euphrates' connection to the Persian Gulf. Ultimately, this is why I consider the transitional zone between the Euphrates and the Gulf during this phase to have been the epicenter of the intercivilizational structure's primordial manifestation, connecting the supply coming from every direction outside Mesopotamia to the demand booming on account of the burgeoning civilization itself. Additionally, this would explain the carry-over of the Uruk culture from before the lowering of the sea level to after: the center's existing culture, which, according to the archaeological evidence, seems like it was remarkably homogeneous for the entirety of the Uruk period (ca. 4000-3100), wasn't fundamentally transformed, so much as it was consistently added to.[clxxxi]

What was "added to" this culture? There's one kind of phenomena that can be added to a culture in order to make it see further growth along existing lines: the culture's vital resources. Always, the most vital resources of all are those directly related to life-support, i.e., food, water, and whatever the culture uses to make shelter.[clxxxii] In my definition, shelter must also include clothing, since the latter in its most functional sense is nothing else. (As an aside, it's interesting to note that, from a long-term perspective, it appears that textiles constituted the major category of production initially catalyzing many of the greatest trading Powers in civilizational history.)

Whenever it was that a true civilization emerged for the first time in southern Mesopotamia, the prime impetus must've been the beginning of an unprecedented growth in population density, which the civilization's full establishment would spark further in its turn: only a physical possibility owing to the epochal increase in the total quantity of food produced. And that was permitted primarily by the opening up of so much previously uncultivable agricultural real estate in a specific context wherein neighboring cultural complexity had advanced such that migrants in sufficiently great numbers were capable of exploiting the new opportunities. All these settlers had to do in order to exploit the land was pay tribute to the existing central authorities in their new homelands – tribute in the form of some specified amount of grain, and/or whatever else any given locality produced. Thus, despite all those newly wealthy individuals who were flocking to the open alluvial territories, even at the very beginning the greatest *singular* beneficiaries were still the centers, represented above all by their centrally emblematic official institutions: the geographically-relevant repositories of complexity predating and facilitating the relatively enormous populations of the fully-emergent Mesopotamian cities.

Whether in ancient southwest Asia or the medieval Italian peninsula, civilizations only emerged in history at moments of most extraordinary growth, *and only within contexts of surrounding settlement system evolution that were already well-advanced for their settings* – evolutionary contexts that had long-since surpassed the simplest settlement systems for whatever period one considers.[clxxxiii] This is evidenced most strikingly of all by the general scenarios surrounding the emergence of the earliest civilizations, which, even though by definition they were the least complex civilizations in history, still needed existing bases of what was (even compared to civilizations much later in the precapitalist epoch, for instance) extraordinarily high settlement system complexity before they could be established. In other words, the formative process of civilizations was *always* invariably something largely out of the control of individuals, and in the hands primarily of organizations – to the extent that it was in the hands of anything "worldly", at all. Precisely this is the defining characteristic of all civilizations.

Such organizations, once they were established, always inevitably took on as their *primary* purpose the exploitation of public wealth for amassment of privately-enjoyed *Power*. For thousands and thousands of years, to an ever-increasing and ultimately total extent, humanity has been shaped by this exact dynamic of individuals versus organizations: no matter how many people there have been who've actually viewed things in this particular light. Everything has more or less "worked" (continued to exist) without the vast majority of individuals understanding why. Until very, very recently, it truly seemed to most everyone as if things might go on this way forever.[clxxxiv]

III

The Sacred Consolidation of Civilizations and their Contexts

Now that I've expressed my perspective on the primordial manifestation of the civilization along with its two major intertwining contexts – both internal (the civilization-State-complex) and external (the intercivilizational structure) – we're ready to move on towards understanding civilizations and their contexts in their fully-fledged forms. This is significant not only for determining what we can rightly consider to be historical reality, but equally so in terms of figuring out how to view what humanity commonly takes history to be. As I've said, I would never suggest that anyone should arbitrarily limit the possible meanings attributed to a given word, least of all 'history', given its absolutely unique role in relation to everything else. I believe that history, like any word, needs as many meanings as it has major contexts, and that a context should be considered major when an indispensable relation between the use of the word and the particular context is successfully demonstrated. A successful demonstration entails displaying a necessity for the general understanding to use whatever word in whatever context.

In the same vein, I also clearly wouldn't argue that individual words should have endlessly variable definitions: some contexts are necessarily more determinative than all the others in relation to a topic's whole, and some definitions are necessarily better suited than others for these most determinative contexts. The best definitions in the most determinative contexts is precisely what's figured out by the process of successful demonstration alluded to above. In this sense, although we clearly shouldn't accept the conventional definitions of 'history' – what I'll refer to altogether, for convenience's sake, using the label "History" – as our own, there's nonetheless much insight to be gained by trying to elucidate what the conventional understanding typically means by "History".

First of all, I think we can rightly take "the conventional understanding" in this case primarily to refer to what people think "Historians" study; and by "Historians", I relatedly consider the conventional understanding to mean "professional academics who study human history in civilizations". These are the most useful reference points to consider because they're the ones with the greatest cultural legitimacy: as with any other field of knowledge, it's the norm in the contemporary world to deem as "Experts" those individuals who've been sanctioned by the contemporary dominant culture's official scholarly institutions, to the exclusion of more or less everyone else. So, in the conventional understanding, 'history' above all means the proper area of study for officially-sanctioned "Historians", and thus that meaning is what I designate "History". Since, as I've repeatedly asserted, there's little more guiding what "Historians" study than the purely occupational considerations of hyperspecialization, we can't expect there to be much explicit coherence unifying the mass of "Expert" conceptions of history, at least not much coherence that would be truly useful for a practical understanding of history.

There's not much explicit coherence; but there's a bounty of *implicit* coherence, which is why it's so useful to try and understand what it is that "Historians" study. "Historians" will indeed help us determine what we can consider historical reality, albeit largely as a result of the accident of tradition. At the same time, we also need to excise so much of "History's" accumulated tradition that it'll often seem as if I'm denigrating the thing I myself rely upon most – that I'm "biting the hand that feeds me".

Maybe so, but anyway I'm not primarily interested in preserving the tradition itself: I'm most interested, rather, in extracting whatever useful methods have been maintained by the tradition incidentally. This can obviously be applied to all other conventional disciplines as well – I look to the establishment's scholarly methods because, for the moment, I consider them to generally be the soundest existing methods to use. In turn, I also use much of the facts discovered/constructed by practitioners of those establishment-founded methods, if only because the intellectual establishment is where the greatest quantity of useful facts resides, when it comes to understanding humanity and human history. This itself is only the result of another great tradition – a more general one: the restriction of access to knowledge imposed on every civilizational population, perpetuated above all by elite control over the spread of information.

Elites, who, throughout history, have only existed in civilizations (if we include in our definition of civilizations those primordial cultures paving the way for civilizations), are able to decisively control the spread of information because they're always at least indirectly tied to the military sphere, itself always directly tied to decisive control over agricultural production;[clxxxv] and both are in the end inseparable from the communications sphere. It goes almost wholly unrecognized by the relevant scholars, but for a State to continue existing at all in its juridically-defined territory within a civilization, there needs to ultimately be more or less monopoly control over the civilization-State-complex's strategically indispensable resources. This means that the overall monopoly in each sphere can only be consolidated and reconsolidated because at an even higher level, there's an oligopoly, an unbreakable bond between the elites in all three spheres. This is in accordance with the singular nature of the planet Earth at any given time, and at all given times. Simply by participating in anything within the scope of an Earthly space-time locale's broadest evolutionary context – which during the civilizations stages of humanity has always been the context perpetuated by the all-encompassing politicoeconomic activity that is the war-trade competition – the elite factions in separate spheres, from all the civilization-State-complexes, must at least indirectly be "working together". That is, simply by participating in the war-trade competition at all, however consciously or unconsciously, all the spheres have some roughly equal parts in contributing to the war-trade competition's long historical continuation, and thus each sphere (at least implicitly) comes to rely on the others in all the places where they're manifested, in any historical moment of a total planetary cultural environment, whether intercivilizational or global civilizational.

Now, within a narrower scope, which in contrast to the intercivilizational structure would mean within the scope of a civilization, or a much narrower scope, meaning that of a single civilization-State-complex, we should automatically expect that the explicit dependence by one sphere upon the others becomes far more prevalent, with the prevalence increasing or decreasing depending upon just how narrow or broad is the cultural scope. So if the narrowest cultural scope at a given time in an intercivilizational structure is within the same civilization-State-complex, we should thus expect elite interdependence between the spheres to occur most explicitly of all within the scope of individual civilization-State-complexes. In civilization-State complexes most of all, then, we should expect the cultural spheres to be *mutually reflective*: each sphere in an individual civilization-State-complex must explicitly reflect the others to some significant extent, as the livelihood of each so directly influences the others.

This is another thing that gives the repositories such unique significance for understanding the history of individual civilizations and civilization-State-complexes. Since the nature of *Power* is such that its overall tone is always set by its extremes, the repositories, being the most *Powerful* structures, always control the greatest individual shares of responsibility for setting the tone in civilizations and their subunits, all fundamentally creatures of *Power*-structures. In the narrowest scope, the civilization-State-complex, where each repository exhibits most explicitly its dependence for existence on the others, the *meaning-making* shaping the activities of each repository is in fact only meaningful at all because of its interdependence with the meaning-making shaping the others. Further, since a given history of humanity is the story of a distinct movement in human consciousness, the prime subject of a human history – a human cultural system – can only ultimately construct its own meaning in reference to the meaning-making record of some past holistic culture or cultures, or else one of its own past cultural phases. Because the repositories are most responsible for reproducing the conquest-imposed cultures (civilizations) over which they rule, and each repository is defined most of all insofar as it directly shares a single context with the others, the holistic relationship between the repositories is the most significant single phenomenon we can study in order to understand the history of a civilization.

Incidentally, this gives the subject studied by "Historians" its special significance for understanding *'lived history'*. The methods of "History" are the ideal methods for studying *Power*-structures, and the *Power*-structure's need (and ability) to study itself was in fact precisely what led to the innovation and preservation of any form of historical method in the first place.[clxxxvi] In this way, we can rightly say that a certain kind of lived history was the actual catalyst for the study of history in general, and this certain kind of lived history – the history of *Power*-structures – is what became the ultimate conventional representation of historical study, "History".

This was itself demanded by sociohistorical necessity: for over a thousand years into the history of the originary urban environment, the only existent writings that even came close to resembling the modern conception of historical records were royal inscriptions, which first appeared around 2500 BCE in Sumer.[clxxxvii] Moreover, the initial main technology necessary for writing "History" in the central intercivilizational structure – alphabetic script – wouldn't really exist anywhere in even its crudest form until sometime in the early-to-mid 2nd-millennium BCE,[clxxxviii] and it would be a much longer time still before it existed in a manner non-formulaic enough for an actual historical account to be written. When "History" finally emerged, then, it wasn't because individuals living in one type of civilization-State-complex, the Classical Greek type, were naturally "more philosophical" or "more rational" than individuals elsewhere. In general, this sort of explanation almost invariably fails in accounting for historical developments; it aims for a naturalistic explanation, whereas only a cultural explanation will suffice. It aims to attribute cultural phenomena to primarily biological factors: but in civilizations, cultural phenomena are, as I've just said, based primarily on *Power*-structures. Therefore, they're attributable mainly to politicoeconomic factors.

Of course, politicoeconomic factors ultimately must be explained in reference to biological factors. Indeed, this is my main point in framing politicoeconomic systems as the quintessential civilizational mechanisms related to the human capture and distribution of energy resources, thereby serving as the fundamental material bases for the continuation of human life. However, specifically within the sociohistorical context of civilizations, where the social structures (the proper domains of politicoeconomic systems) themselves play such unrivaled roles in shaping cultural evolution, they're able to do so precisely insofar as they supersede predominately biological factors by emphasizing and encouraging a supreme role for ideological factors in human life.[clxxxix] Politicoeconomic systems are able to accomplish such encouragement on account of their most functionally characteristic behavior, the selective distribution of security and wealth – two phenomena which in the deepest sense amount to the same thing – the preservation or (much more rarely) advancement of some lives, and the destruction or oppression of others, with the latter category always containing the vast majority of individuals in civilizations.

By "feeding" and protecting certain entities via life-support and military structures, and destroying others by withholding life-support and utilizing armed force against targeted enemies, the repository plays the role of a vengeful god, deciding which cultural phenomena survive, and which are annihilated. All the more interesting, then, how repositories and all the lesser institutions they birthed seem to have originated through religious organizations and divine beings, and how, relatedly, repositories always take hold for the first time in any given historical period via institutionalized religion.[cxc] Just as one or another god is imagined to "stand for" and protect the institution, the institution's human managers likewise share that protection with individuals who behave in ways favorable to the institution, and either overtly punish or simply tacitly neglect those human beings defiant of its rule. Such *'official religion'* is always the sociohistorical starting point driving civilizational complexity forward and upward to higher levels. Seemingly this complexity can't move forward beyond the primary level without the sanctification of religious authority.[cxci]

In the long run, three-tier settlement systems became true cities insofar as they successfully cultivated and maintained their positions as sacred centers, sitting at the geographic apices of religious administrative hierarchies.[cxcii] Accordingly, these apices became the initial epicenters of communication in the very earliest State-ruled polities: the first city-States. All subsequent ancient and Classical city-States would originate along these same lines.

In making connections between disparate examples of civilizations – for instance, between the Sumerian civilization on the one hand and the city-States of the early Classical Greek world on the other – it's much less necessary to imagine in detail the actual kinds of processes going on, in the same way as we did regarding the preceding phase. Knowing what we know about the material and ideological cultures that developed in both cases, there's in fact a very limited range of plausible theoretical possibilities concerning what most general kind of process was happening (and in reality of course only one possibility, which is the thing that really happened). Otherwise, if there was nothing common to both cases, 'a civilization' in the way I've described it thus far refers purely to a human-concocted description, not a real kind of entity. At least, not a real kind exemplified in the same way by both Classical Greece and ancient Sumer.

To paraphrase Roy Rappaport, a complex adaptive system is in the end nothing more than the set of relationships held in place – *"bound"* – by its indispensable adaptive mechanisms.[cxciii] Now, by 'intercity system' or 'holistic intercity cultural environment', I mean to indicate a specific kind of *'complex adaptive* system', namely the kind that a civilization, among others, is. The "others" here are of course intercivilizational structures and civilization-State-complexes; but the civilization is the most representative form, since, as I've said, the other two can't exist in their fully individuated manifestations until there's already multiple civilizations that can communicate/interact with one another. This is in the same way, from the inverse perspective, as no civilization can emerge until there's already the primordial manifestation of civilization-State-complexes and an intercivilizational structure within a *'chronologically communicable space'*. By the latter term I refer to the total geographical distance over which certain individuals within the same designated zone are technologically capable of profitably transporting themselves and their goods.

The chronologically communicable space is the most basic premise behind my conceptualizing the civilization and its larger and smaller contexts as complex adaptive systems, because it's the most necessary in order to explain the insurmountable real-world significance of our three vital cultural repositories, the interdependent adaptive mechanisms centrally defining the systems. Each repository is able to survive and thrive insofar as the culture it transmits in part and the subculture it transmits in full is in someway translatable across the entirety of the chronologically communicable space. A specific conquest syndrome can only take hold inside the geographical range throughout which it's capable of spreading at the particular historical juncture. The historically-specific conquest syndrome epitomizes what's expressed in the notion of, for example, the 'medieval world', or what I aim to represent with my narrative of the 'contemporary world'. Thus, the conquest syndrome has intertwining intercivilizational, civilizational, and State aspects. Further, in a given setting, each aspect of the overall conquest syndrome is most greatly emphasized by one of the three major forms of cultural repositories.

Above all, the civilizational aspect of the conquest syndrome is embodied in the religious/ originary communications repository. Rappaport made what is in my mind the definitive case for ritual as *the* "social" act basic to all other "social" behavior, and organized religious hierarchies as the central mechanisms for transmitting rituals throughout affected human populations. The only thing I'd modify concerning the general thrust of his argument is what I've indicated with the quotations in the previous sentence: from the perspective I've been constructing throughout this text, what

Rappaport considers "social" – explicitly related to "societies" – is essentially the same as what I consider "cultural" – explicitly related to "cultures".[cxciv] In our immediate context, the difference is not insignificant, for a few reasons. First of all, I've argued for the cultural sphere as the ultimate overall determinant of humanity's mass behavior. Second, in the relevant long sociohistorical context of humanity's civilizations stage, the entity I've equated with the cultural sphere before all others is the civilization itself. Third and finally I've asserted that, in relation to the total conquest syndromes that emerged periodically across the planet throughout the history of civilizations, the process manifested at the civilizational level was always the one most visibly symptomatic of the syndromes-as-wholes.

Thus, when I assert that institutionalized religion has been the fundamental cultural adaptive mechanism *specifically* during the agricultural epoch, I'm deliberately associating religion with everything I've designated as characteristic of 'cultures' and 'the cultural' throughout the entire text: holistic artifactual environments absorbing and reciprocally absorbed by human populations via ideological enforcement. This is why, out of all the technological spheres, I link religion most closely with communications, at least concerning how civilizations originally existed. So even if contemporary ideologies aren't the exact equivalent of premodern religions, the former certainly are the ultimate historical outcome of the latter. Compared to human beings trying to communicate across civilizational bounds, human beings within the same civilizations are able to communicate – exchange meaning – so successfully with one another precisely because individuals inhabiting the same civilization typically share a common primary ideology.[cxcv] To be sure, civilizational ideologies are never determined solely by religion. However, to the extent that there's an ideology singularly common to a civilization, its development must *start* historically from a religious foundation, which is the explanation for what I said a moment ago, about how every civilization moves forward beyond its primary level of complexity based on the civilization's cultivating acceptance of its own unique version of what Rappaport refers to as a "liturgical order".[cxcvi] Representatives of social structures can only encourage their populations to emphasize ideological factors over biological ones insofar as some existing ideology reproduces, more or less automatically, a coherent culture within the geographical scope of the social structure's rule.

In civilizations, this constitutes the primordial sociohistorical connecting tissue joining the properly cultural (ideological) to the properly politicoeconomic: the central apparatus of cultural transmission (*'religion'*) and the central politicoeconomic system, held in place at the subunit level by the overarching dominant social structure that's epitomized culturally by *'the State'*. What's always being studied above all by "History", whether "Historians" know it or not, is the chronological-geographical process of this dominant ideological transmission at the level of the explicitly cultural, employed primarily to support the politicoeconomic perpetuation at the level of the explicitly social. During every intercivilizational period prior to industrialization, the military aspect of the social structure, ultimately epitomized at the cultural level by the State, typically didn't start off with nearly enough independent wealth production capacity to necessitate or warrant the implementation of its own unique 'official ideology'. The main point psychologically was made to be religion.[cxcvii]

'Official' refers to a phenomenon that only occurs full-blown in civilizations – to the point where it might even be better to say that civilizations only occur full-blown in the realm of 'officialdom'. But as with most other dominant cultural phenomena, the official domain isn't without its precivilizational precursors, and we've already said wherein they primarily lay: those sacred centers constituting foundations for the very first cities. If civilization-State-complexes, civilizations, and intercivilizational structures are all truly subsystems of the same overall complex adaptive system – 'urbanized humanity' – they all must've grown, ultimately, as part of the same unified process; the same evolution. It seems to me once again that this process really isn't described more concisely than it is in the most basic concept of settlement system hierarchies.[cxcviii]

Most basically, the "full-blown civilization" is nothing besides an ideologically institutionalized four-tier settlement hierarchy. Although we still don't know enough about the Uruk culture to know exactly what form its particular holistic cultural expression (its sense of "imagined community") took, we nonetheless know that throughout the middle and late fourth-millennium BCE Uruk must've been the center for a four-tier settlement hierarchy in the sphere of intercity trade, explicitly making the culture it centralized a civilization – almost certainly the very first in human history.[cxcix] It seems to me that this fact is essentially responsible for that conventional view that sees what took place during the fourth-millennium BCE in southern Mesopotamia (among other places) as "the beginning of history".[cc] Really, it was the beginning of "History".

Perhaps the most notable hallmark of "Historians" is that they don't consider 'human history' to be composed of non-written information.[cci] "History" more or less exclusively relies upon written documents, the major constituents of what "Historians" refer to as "primary sources"; a conventional contemporary belief has thereby emerged that history began where and when the most striking immediate precursor to writing began – the Uruk period of southern Mesopotamia. There are certainly many exceptions to the "writing only" rule. But I'm purely interested in what has been the most dominant form of "History" *throughout* history, the most conventional of the conventional understandings. The "History" that's meant when we refer to the tradition of contemporary historical scholarship that runs from the original Classical "Historians" onwards through the medieval chroniclers from every civilization, the early modern humanists that originated in Renaissance Italy, the late modern Western nationalist narrativists, and finally the typical professional academics in the business of "History".

The most conventional "Historians" are all those who have written about human history as if it were explicitly comprised of *Power*-structures, but mainly without recognizing that's what they were doing. In this way, they've accidentally preserved and actually sharply honed the best tool in history for looking at human *Power*-structures, the 'analytic narrative'. But while their empirical methods are exceptional, their metaphysical ones are for the most part tragically neglected, and this is why "Historians" seem unable to know that in framing "History" as the only real human history, they're unconsciously (and inaccurately) equating the record of all human behavior with a form of documentation that has appeared in the most extremely limited range of cases of human cultures.[ccii] This is where hyperspecialized knowledge is most harmful to a useful understanding of human history, and resultantly where it proves to be most destructive of humanity's chances for using knowledge and understanding to solve its metacrisis.

Since in a context of hyperspecialization, archaeological knowledge and historical knowledge are for the most part kept completely separate, the barrier between "History" and "Prehistory", however artificial, nonetheless acts as a formidable obstacle for cultivating a historical understanding that would unify humanity's precivilizational and civilizational existences. And without such an understanding it's impossible to construct a picture at all reflective of humanity's singular Earthly all-historical process of cultural evolution, a process that a general understanding of the history of civilizations through the present intuitively tells us must've always been taking place. The connection between the two leads us back to the connection between the same all-encompassing, always processually totalizing human spectrum – "natural-cultural" – which, as we've seen, defines between its two extremes the broadest range of possibilities for the causes of events affecting human life.

While I introduced this particular spectrum in a previous subsection, it remains to be said why the notion of a spectrum is generally the most proper tool for analysis of specifically *human historical* phenomena, which is to say, as defined in the present text, all phenomena related to what has happened surrounding human cultural existence on Earth. "Has *happened*" is the definition's most important feature: only the things that actually happen can contribute to the process of history on Earth in general and human history in particular. However, this doesn't mean that we need a record of every single event in order to understand how human history happens as a single process, which is the most important element towards understanding holistic history. Indeed, in proportion to the whole we don't need a record of many events at all, in order to understand the definitive qualities of sociohistorical process.

Most of all, this is because, at the present date, we can look back at the temporally short but chronologically long human history that is the unconsciously accepted topic of "History" – the history of *Power*-structures – and as it's so uniquely large and visible "on the surface", and relatedly, so uniquely well-documented, we can see what actual long-term historical change truly looks like from a more or less exhaustive documentary perspective in this one sphere of human history. But since it's true beyond doubt in this one phase, we must accept that humanity throughout the long historical process – human beings viewed primarily as masses of cultural worlds, not primarily as individuals of biological species – has unfolded evolutionarily. For any individualized human collective evolutionary process to be real at all, one of which we know absolutely is (the history of the globalized *Power*-structure, see next paragraph), *all* historical human reality before this must've been evolutionary at a similar most broadly determinative level. Every part of history on Earth is shaped in some way by all the history that came before, and human history presents this phenomenon most strikingly because human beings increase the rate of their own evolution through their primary adaptive mechanism, culture. What's more, this general unfolding of human cultures according to a unified evolutionary process makes it necessary for human beings to understand the all-historical human reality in terms of a narrative. I call this story of humanity's total spatiotemporal reality – as opposed to the stories of humanity's insular group realities – 'the lived *meta*narrative'.[cciii]

Human history has been most accumulative of all in the ecologically most-complex portion of humanity's history, the past 116 years, which has been so ecologically complex because, simultaneously, it's also the culturally most-complex portion of Earth's history. In this way, the sociohistorical nature of *Power*, wherein the longer it exists and the more widespread it grows, the larger and better documented its examples become, allows us to see not simply "one example" of the evolutionary character of human historical process (sociohistorical process) on Earth. In fact, it allows us in the existent world to see the example constituting what has been unequivocally the greatest amount of constant cultural change in the shortest time, giving us the potential for first-hand knowledge of historical reality at the culturally most complex and hence fastest part of the real-world spectrum. Since we know this spectrum applies in the contemporary world, because we can easily compare Earth and its global *Power*-structure in 1898 to Earth and its global *Power*-structure in 2015 (the earliest point in the contemporary world through the most recent point) for the purpose of perceiving the unprecedentedly rapid evolution in cultural complexity, we can thereby expect that spectrum to be pushed back until *Homo sapiens* first emerged as linguistic beings, around 50,000 years ago at the latest. (We expect it to begin with, and then we try to find as much evidence as possible that some other framework is better for explaining reality.)

In other words, the historical spectrum is most fundamentally a measurement of complexity imagined, in the first, most undefined place, as a simple linear expression of the passage of time in years. "Natural" on the one side and "cultural" on the other can hereby be seen, in the crudest way, as baselines generally related to what side a given humanity's total planetary historical context falls closest to: 50,000 BCE or 2015 CE. "In the crudest way" because, as we already know, human history doesn't happen at an identical rate along every point of the temporal line, which is precisely why a chronology in the form of 'periodization' is necessary in order to truly understand the human historical process. So what the spectrum really describes is the *general stage* of humanity's evolution that was typically present on the planet Earth at a given time. We can then label the extremes of the total temporal line with a "least complex" side, of "culture *like that* in 50,000 BCE", and a "most complex" side, of "culture *like that* in 2015 CE".

In fact, this is essentially how an archaeologist chronologically organizes the culture he or she examines (see all archaeological sources cited), except I'm using the paradigm not to look at the evolution of particular cultures, but rather to look at the evolution of culture in its entirety across the whole planet, throughout all of history. But in order to make this a reflection of reality, we have to make one significant modification: we have to say, more specifically, that we're looking at the spectrum as a measurement of the *most* complex cultures on the planet at any given time. The assumption here is that, since cultural complexity is itself utilized functionally as a means to enhance the prospects of continued biological existence for some human group (the adaptive beneficiaries of complexity), the most complex cultures are those with the greatest ability/likelihood to spread and thence evolve, setting the tone in the long-term for all other evolution. Thus, at the broadest level, defined by the central structure of chronological periods, a real lineage exists connecting the most complex cultures of all the successive spans between the least complex and most complex phases.

The first stage, representing the "least complex" side of the spectrum, comprises the stretch between ca. 50,000 BCE and ca. 32,000 BCE. Whatever the actual dates, the critical point is that this side is meant to represent the period after human beings originally gained the ability to construct complex languages and before the beginning of the period sometimes known as the "big bang",[cciv] which I've referred to as the first great cultural explosion subsequent to the original innovation of speech. The "big bang" eventually led to a second stage of complexity, which evolved in greatly varying and fluctuating ways everywhere it was spread and sustained until the beginning of the interglacial period (ca. 13,000 BCE). After this point the concentration of so great a number of human beings – human beings fleeing to the same finite number of commonly-desired spots – employing this level of complexity in such naturally fragile ecosystems, led to the third stage of complexity in the affected locales, that of the earliest human settlements.[ccv]

Earlier in this subsection, we saw how the third stage of complexity, encompassing the development of agriculture, eventually led to what we'll consider the fourth stage of complexity, the original evolution of human settlement systems. This latter stage started at around 6000 BCE, as I've said, with the origin of simple settlement systems, and ended around 3100 BCE, with the end of the first phase of the first fully-fledged civilization, in southern Mesopotamia.[ccvi] It may seem strange that I haven't set aside the start of the Uruk period as a distinct "beginning": but when any civilization first explicitly emerged throughout history, it was *always* a sign of an already well-advanced stage in settlement system evolution, rather than solely or mostly a holistic cultural "explosion". The geographical preconditions necessary for the emergence of an explicit civilization are so complex that civilizations literally can't appear except by a practically organic convergence of already-emergent systems, which must morph into subsystems of a larger whole due to new historical circumstances. These subsystems were nothing besides individual cities, or at least the immediate precursors to cities, which, when they appear in special chronological-geographic circumstances, directly embody the long-term processes individually that their civilizations will embody collectively: we saw this already in relation to the emergence of the earliest civilization, but this aspect of the process is always applicable whenever a new civilization emerges. New civilizations indicate the continuation of existing processes just as much as the beginning of novel ones.

In the same way, ends of civilizations mark the primordial manifestations of new processes. The fifth stage of complexity lasted from about 3100 BCE, with the end of the Uruk period and hence the potential explicit start to the Sumerian civilization, along with early stirrings of the pharaonic civilization that would itself explicitly start around 2950 BCE,[ccvii] until the early 12th-century BCE, with the beginning of the collapse of the Bronze Age civilizations and the commencement of the post-ancient, pre-Classical "Dark Ages".[ccviii] This stage was defined by the evolving existence, for the very first time in human history, of an explicit intercivilizational structure: a sociohistorical context featuring multiple civilizations within a shared chronologically communicable space. Herein lies the main empirical justification for framing the first civilization's emergence as the culmination to the fourth stage of complexity, not the start to the fifth. The real-world link between intercivilizational structures, civilizations, and civilization-State-complexes is the fact that each has historically represented one indispensable interlocking component in the complex adaptive system I'm calling 'urbanized humanity'. Thus, in urbanized humanity's long historical evolution, literally *the* most vital moments – ever, in its entire history – have been those wherein components became individuated.

Once a component became individuated to begin with – once each component made the transfer from "primordial manifestation" to "fully-fledged entity" – the existence of the component would continue, which means it would continue *evolving*, until maintenance of the component became energetically impossible. That is, once an intercivilizational structure was individuated for the first time in the fifth stage of cultural complexity, it would remain in place so long as it could continue to feed its adaptive mechanisms with the vital resources. Putting things in empirical terms, since the "international" traders comprised the most representative repository in relation to the intercivilizational structure, so long as traders could continue to traffic goods for profit from a civilization at one geographical extreme to a civilization at the other extreme, the structure would remain in place, and could adapt to whatever other circumstances presented themselves. It wouldn't matter if today's most *Powerful* traders went out of business tomorrow: as long as someone could be found to replace them, the structure would remain fundamentally in place. And as long as trading itself remained profitable, it was more or less an absolute certainty that someone could be found to replace them.

Though even if the particular empirical example of the component "went out of business", it wouldn't be the end of that evolutionary line unless all direct emulations of the component got extinguished, as well. Historically, this has been essentially impossible in relation to civilizations and civilization-State-complexes, because there was never a point when all civilizations from a period collapsed around the same time. There's always been at least one civilization remaining to "pass the torch". It clearly didn't happen to any substantial extent whatsoever in the wake of the Roman Empire's collapse – as we've seen, the only place left without a unique civilization was that geographical portion of the old intercivilizational structure which would become Western civilization – and it hadn't even happened in the preceding, much more widely-encompassing collapse of the early 1100s BCE.[ccix]

But whenever an intercivilizational structure collapsed in human history, it was truly the end of an old order, since the existence of multiple intercivilizational structures within a single chronologically communicable space was an almost completely unheard-of state-of-affairs. (I argue that it only happened once, when the Islamic land-dominant structure and the Christian sea-dominant structure competed for initial worldwide hegemony in the post-Columbian order, mainly throughout period four). Therefore, at least in this one respect, everything had to be rebuilt following an intercivilizational collapse, as there was no emulative component there to "pick up the pieces" within a meaningfully short timeframe. New intercivilizational structures *mirrored* old ones: but literal continuity between the old and the new was absent at the intercivilizational level.

On the other hand, new intercivilizational structures possessed literal links to the past in the form of those rare but always-present civilizations that were able to transcend intercivilizational periods, which for this reason I call "archetypal civilizations": they're there from the very beginning of an intercivilizational period because they were still there after the last period ended. We truly can't define civilizations without them, as, at the start of every period, they actually defined what it would mean to be "*a* civilization". Of the greatest sociohistorical consequence, and accordingly of the greatest consequence for understanding human history, this is precisely what's entailed by that most characteristic quality of *Power*: nothing else sharing a system where it appears is able to act quite like it, and yet it sets the tone for everything it touches.

At these historical junctures where the archetypes started to spread, it's not simply that we see the ideal empirical examples of how the transmission of conquest syndromes takes place. These ideal examples are in fact "ideal" precisely insofar as they represent *the actual historical origins of the spread of distinct conquest syndromes*. The conquest syndromes that actually happened comprise the only ones that we can possibly refer to, if we're to study human history empirically in any way – as we must, if we're to understand it *as* human history, by any definition. Thus, if we want to understand how the historical transmission of conquest syndromes actually originated, such archetypal examples are literally the only ones we can study if we want to understand reality. When I speak of conquest syndromes, I'm speaking of entities that are singular on the planet for their respective zones of influence at any given time on planet Earth; conquest syndromes are the most *Powerful* entities in their respective zones of influence, and as with any superlative, "most *Powerful*" is by definition a status that can only be attributed to a single entity in a given context. But even in relation to other superlative human historical phenomena, there's something especially interesting about conquest syndromes. Because the existence of each syndrome is ubiquitous on such a spatially gigantic scale, and since each syndrome, once spread, lasts until it's energetically impossible, the total number of actual historical cases ('the ones that really happened') we can study is relatively most miniscule.

I believe this is the essential structural explanation concerning why, when we study "History" – the history of *Power*-structures – we're studying something so distinctly definitive of the human historical process in general. Human history can only be human history insofar as it refers to phenomena *shared* by human beings of a certain setting, and there's no phenomenon in history besides the live planet itself that has actually served as a common context of consciousness for more human beings in a more striking way than the *Power*-structure. *Power*-structures are the singular all-encompassing entities that, in civilizational (including protocivilizational) contexts, wholly transcend cultural, social, and historical boundaries, providing the potential for all other such literal connections to be made. No *Power*-structures are all-encompassing over greater historical distances than those sustained by intercivilizational structures, and this is primarily why I've chosen to periodize history within the civilizations stage of cultural complexity according to their rise and fall.

Therefore, the periodization of civilizational history according to intercivilizational structures is above all meant to reflect as exactly as possible the actual phases of cultural evolution undergone by all historical humanity within the relevant timeframe, in turn providing the simplest (and, I hope, realest) possible basis for unifying the understanding of precivilizational and civilizational historical process. I believe this provides the best means for qualitatively comparing the historical *speed* characterizing different moments of cultural evolution, when those comparisons involve timeframes that, while viscerally wholly disparate as regards speed, also elude simple explanation regarding the same. We can then say, "This kind of cultural change happened in so many years" during period X, with some grounds for contrasting such change to that which happened in a similar quantity of years during period Y.

I'm not interested then in an exact quantitative measurement of sociohistorical speed, as the most significant thing about sociohistorical speed is the most definitively qualitative thing there is: judgment emanating from the single human mind. Like every thing having to do with meaning, the speed of events only has meaning insofar as human observers perceive it: and the speed of events has more to do with human-perceived meaning than anything else, because it's the purest embodiment of how humanity's cultural (self-) consciousness is sociohistorically determined. That is, human beings perceive everything according to they're positions as cultural actors, wedged unconsciously in politicoeconomic systems directly dependent upon chronological-geographic contexts; the speed of events plays the central role in setting the tone for all such human perceptions.[ccx]

Thus, the thing that truly seemed important for me to figure out was exactly what *kinds* of factors – rather than exactly what *amounts* of factors – must've contributed historically to the actual speed of events from the perspectives of individual human observers. From my perspective, it was the kinds that actually shaped whether overall perceptions were comparatively "slower" or "faster". Moreover, although I've said it so many times, I nonetheless must reiterate once again that, because historical reality is comprised ultimately only of the things that have actually happened, we can only truly compare individual events to other individual events that have happened within the one general sequence of humanity's total Earthly existence. Consequently, real *Power*-structure events don't solely have theoretical relationships to all other events that have happened in all parts of the world, throughout all spans of time within the history of *Power*-structures. Potentially, depending most of all upon the historical proximity between the events, it's quite likely that any two events will have a *literal* relationship with one another. Any such relationship must primarily be studied through qualitative means, even if the realities we study are best described as the constantly transforming qualitative effects of constantly transforming quantitative changes: and this is always the signature of the self-conscious movement of humanity as a complex adaptive system.

Resultantly, the present text necessarily studies the relevant phenomena through symbolization at the level of metaphor rather than symbolization at the level of mathematics. *"Metaphor"* in the largest sense: referring to all related linguistic tropes that humanity has always used to define and exploit its surroundings. In this sense, we can see that a conquest syndrome, *in sociohistorical reality*, is always something that only works through some form of metaphorical (linguistic) practice on behalf of the conquering individuals.[ccxi] So when metaphorical analysis is emphasized in the study of humanity – "the cultural world" – theory and practice are as ideally lined up as they are when mathematical analysis is emphasized in the study of "the natural world".

The human being has historically been an individual solely insofar as he or she is part of a group setting. The "civilized" human being in particular, however consciously or unconsciously, defines him- or herself as 'person' primarily insofar as he or she is "a Sumerian" or "a Roman" or "an American". Of course, there are other conceivable ways of transmitting 'cultural personhood' except by conquest syndromes; and these ways comprised the main ones utilized for the vast temporal majority of human history. But qualitatively, in terms of the actual changes that took place in relation to the numerical measure of time – speaking of *chronology* instead of crude temporality – the conquest syndrome was clearly the most successful means (the *fastest* means) in history for transmitting cultural personhood, making "History", the history of *Power*-structures, the natural metonymic form of human history during the civilizations stage. Because this is true, we can realistically extend the historical span of "History" backwards as far back in human history as we can actually trace the evolution of *Power*-structures. I've traced it as far back as immediately following the interglacial transition, this being what I consider the ultimate environmental catalyst for *Power*'s evolution. It was precisely this point when cultural event-causes started to rival natural ones in their influence over human populations, what I consider the definitive state-of-affairs coloring the original explosion of the speed of events, which would eventually lead to its truly exponential explosions in the scope of the late modern and contemporary worlds. From a perspective starting with the interglacial transition, then, the rate-of-change in the speed of events – the acceleration of events – is found to be coterminous long historically with the stages of cultural evolution within the setting of agriculturally-dependent settlements: and thereby coterminous with the evolution of *Power*-structures, as seen through the long-term development of the components of urbanized humanity I've described.

How, in particular, do we use all this to translate "History" into 'history'; to unify our understanding of the precivilizational and civilizational existences of humanity – looking at things most bluntly as humanity's all historical transition from nomadic hunter-gatherers to urbanized agriculturalists? Even if we look at the development of complex languages and the much more complex hunter-gatherer technologies these facilitated as humanity's ultimate act of creation, allowing human beings to thrive in the ecosystems they lived off of while at the same time keeping those ecosystems intact, we can still look at the same development, from another perspective, as the primordial manifestation of humanity's eventually total domination of all of nature. In the end, this primordial manifestation would evolve into the domination of some groups of human beings by other groups, which in turn gradually evolved into the domination of ever-larger agglomerations of human beings by proportionally ever-smaller groups. The latter process continued at a constantly though dynamically increasing rate until an entire planet filled with far and away the most human beings ever alive at one time was ruled by a sector composed of a small fraction of a single percentage of the population.

There we can finally adequately see what we'll now be exploring in our examination of certain lived narratives: the indispensability of understanding the whole history of civilizations in terms of the primordial conquest of relatively much more sedentary, much larger planting populations, by relatively much more mobile, much smaller herding populations. It seems to me that, for them to have had such monumental historical resonance in the human universe, conquest syndrome only could've originated via the cultural transmission of a preceding natural (biological) process – and, I argue, this explains why it's even possible to construct a successful conceptualization of cultural evolution: the total domestication of certain animals eventually led to the domesticating animal's total *self*-domestication.

Perfecting Conquest: The Emergence and Establishment of Modern Western Power-structures

I

The Medieval Structure's Ancient Origins

When an intercivilizational structure collapses, as did that of the ancient world parallel to the invasions of the early 12th-century BCE – the epitome of the general transition to the ancient "Dark Ages" – whatever's "left over" in the collapse's wake will become part of the new "natural" baseline bounding one side of the subsequent period's "natural-cultural" spectrum. In turn, all cultural evolution within the old intercivilizational structure's geographical scope will chronologically proceed from this point forward, *so long as* a new intercivilizational structure emerges along similar lines. This largely explains how, after the new, medieval intercivilizational structure emerged, civilizational evolution picked up its pace so quickly and then continued onward with so much rapidity, in comparison to the ancient and Classical worlds.

No collapse of a conquest syndrome within the spreading culture's geographical context was responsible for leading to the directly following, early modern intercivilizational structure, the structure catalyzed into evolving motion by the monumental genocide forging the post-Columbian order. Instead, the spread of one conquest syndrome (that epitomizing the primordial early modern West) led to the collapse of those already existing in the "New World"; and then a completely new intercivilizational structure was constructed while the original one was still "in business" – with the new one, for the first time in human history, encompassing the Eastern *and* Western hemispheres. The originary meeting of "Old World" and "New World" marked the beginning of the most asymmetrical competition between conquest syndromes in history, which would result in a collapse of "New World" civilizations that was, from a long historical perspective, essentially immediate.[ccxii]

Notably, it was the civilizations in the "New World" that collapsed most quickly, rather than the vast majority of other, less complex cultural units, both nomadic and settled. Thus we see how the fastest way for intercultural destruction to occur is for there to be a similarity in kind between two different cultures, and a disparity in degree. Competition between two different cultures naturally tends to be most ruthless when they're both examples of an identical type of cultural unit, vying for politicoeconomic dominance within an identical historical (chronological-geographical) context. And in actual scenarios within the history of *Power*-structures, the ruthlessness typically emanated most strikingly from the faster culture, which was always the culture with the greater *baseline* complexity. So even though civilizations in the "New World" may've been at more complex phases within their historical processes than Western civilization was in its own, there was an inherent speed to Western civilization that the "New World" civilizations simply couldn't compete with. Such speed exemplified the interrelated facts that Western civilization (1) emerged from what had been up to this point a zone characterized by the greatest cultural complexity in all of history, and (2) its own particular geographical base-of-operations was now allowing it to surpass the most complex period yet in this zone's existence. In sum, the early modern West's baseline complexity was in a completely different stratosphere altogether compared to contemporaneous civilizations in the Americas.

The spheres associated with the relevant Western conquest syndrome had sharpened their knives in a world quite fully saturated with urban complexity and in turn, constant direct intercivilizational competition. But even within that world, Western civilization had become easily the most violently competitive war-trade arena.[ccxiii] Why was this? What was it about the formative modern Western States that made them such naturally potent war-machines relative to all prior States in history? We must find this out if we're to understand the contemporary world, since it was these States that, already at the early modern world's very beginning, were starting to lay the groundwork for the comprehensive transfer of the Western conquest syndrome throughout the Americas.

Individuals in the contemporary world take it for granted that the Western-originated form of State-system is the one prevailing across the globe, as if it's something that "just happened", without any clear explanation – and essentially not requiring one, because what difference does it make anyway, except to "Historians"? But if one truly understands history, and not just "History", it becomes apparent how nothing, in the end, has proven to have a greater effect on more people across larger quantities of space and time than the State. More specifically, nothing has played a more singular role in determining sociohistorical process than *the kind* of State prevailing in a given territory. As such, finally, the kind of State in a given space-time locale reveals itself as the ultimate real-world index, wherever and whenever it exists, of the longest-term sociohistorical process.

This is because, looking back at history from the present point in time, the thing that has *lasted* in civilizational history, the sociohistorical phenomenon that has actually possessed an autonomous ability to sustain true lineages, is conquest: to the extent that something has really spread from one generation to the next for every successive generation through 2015 CE, it has been the dominance spread through conquest. As I've said, from the longest view, the dominance started with language, and what we'll call humanity's *'unconscious dominance of nature'*. It transitioned gradually from that beginning through the earliest part of the interglacial transition, until the radically transforming climate finally caused unprecedentedly chaotic weather patterns in certain locales, compared to anything the affected human beings had ever experienced or heard about in the mythological traditions of their oral cultures. The weather was so chaotic, so disruptive to the ecosystem and so frightening to the human psyche, confluences of more or less simultaneous, mass panic-induced migrations ensued. Since every migration was driven by a search for roughly similar ecotones (probably starting with the highest livable ground), of which there were a great many but still finite number of examples, after a certain amount of time passed – not much time from a long historical perspective, lots from a short historical perspective – human beings had to settle the favored territories permanently or semi-permanently for the first time in human history.[ccxiv] The catalyst for settlement was the vital necessity that the small settled groups of human beings saw in guaranteeing the favored territories for themselves and their kin.

At that moment, the phenomenon called "domestication" started. Not yet domestication of crops or animals: an even earlier domestication – in fact, it was the primordial domestication. By necessity, it was the direct precursor to the subsequent, specifically agricultural domestication, wherever the latter would emerge. This represented humanity's domestication of *itself* through the simultaneous, inextricable domestication of the micro-geographies constituting the bases for the first settlements. Here was the true beginning of *'conscious human-on-human dominance'*, which had to be imposed to begin with via the central mechanism of the material settlement complex itself.

The potential for wholly *'domesticated environments'* emerged first, and thus had primacy; domesticated food sources necessarily emerged derivatively, and thereby later in the relevant chronologies. With the proliferation of settlement and holistic domestication there was concomitantly a tremendous indirect proliferation of the means used by present-day researchers to study lived chronologies – in this case referring most simply to the sequences of how land was permanently or semi-permanently occupied.[ccxv] Thus, not only do such lived chronologies make themselves blatantly apparent as the most basic structures defining the boundaries for the lived narratives of the relevant places. This fact also allows it to become just as clear precisely how the chronology and hence the narrative of the place really sped up as soon as settlement started, increasing parallel to the increase in settlement.

By its very nature, the settlement is a concentration of human energy. To the extent that this concentration of energy itself could grow in terms of population and contiguous space, at the place-times where human beings were first transitioning from nomadic hunting-gathering to settled hunting-gathering, the settled space was already in a position that had never been possible throughout all humanity's existence in nomadic hunter-gatherer cultures. The number of nomadic hunter-gatherers within an arbitrarily designated wide geographical space certainly could've grown, albeit at an extremely gradual rate. Yet the phenomenon of an intensively populated, constantly expanding area inhabited by human beings of a shared culture couldn't have existed in a nomadic hunter-gatherer context. The closest thing to a settlement in the nomadic hunting-gathering cultural universe was the campsite. But the cultured concentration of human energy within the space of such a camp couldn't have literally grown, except in the most anomalous of situations. It absolutely never could've grown *continuously*, from a historical point of view, because from this perspective it was definitively temporary: its primary function was as a staging area for the nearest-term food-procurement operations, rather than as a residential area constantly inhabited in order to secure a long-term food supply.

Therefore, "growth" in reference to a hunter-gatherer camp only could've meant growth in the longest historical sense, and thus we would almost certainly only see real, visible, *structural* change if we compared hunter-gatherer camps from ages very far apart, separated by thousands of years (for instance, between the span of ca. 40,000 BCE – ca. 15,000 BCE). Moreover, even in this limited sense, and symptomatic of it, "growth" of a camp could only mean growth from a total, never from an individual, perspective: it would've been the result of overall human population growth, embodied in the growth of the size of camps in general, not human population growth within the scope of a single camp that "grew itself" (facilitated its own growth). That is, the growth of a hunter-gatherer camp would've been something attributable to the growth of population within an ecologically-unified natural region as opposed to a human-unified cultural region; the growth of the typical camp, not growth that we could specifically assign to the chronological happenings of an individual human culture.

Clearly, then, already at such an early date, the scenario of a settled human culture's growth put humanity in entirely new sociohistorical terrain, figuratively as much as literally. And by "figuratively", I'm referring concretely to the parallel psychological processes that the unprecedented concentration of material cultural change gave rise to. Human beings in the earliest days of settlement and agriculture must've perceived the need for social stability and cultural order in a way so dire that it's basically unimaginable for human beings inhabiting the contemporary dominant culture. The initial semblances of organized religious tendencies, in the form of sacred burial objects that were handed out only rarely – available to primordial elites alone – surrounded settlements and settlement systems from the earliest points in the world's first successful agricultural chronologies that we know of.[ccxvi] However crude, the successful agricultural settlement must be a *Power*-structure even at its most basic level; so apparently, *Power*-

structures require sacred branding to persist. It was from the apex of the primordial *Power*-structure, ultimately, that even greater concentrations of human energy would be steadily brought together during the immediate precursor to the ancient world, always under the aegis of the official religious imagery, enforced by the shepherd's blood-drenched staff.

The sacred center, whether embodied foremost in a single person – a "chief", a "priest", or some combination of the two; or a single place – in a political capital, the officially-sanctioned headquarters of a government – constitutes the focal point for managing cultural complexity within a successful agricultural settlement or settlement system: for controlling the speed of sociohistorical process, to the extent that the latter can be "controlled" at all. "Managing" is really the better way of putting it.

Typically, in all periods prior to mass industrialization – i.e., for all but the past 200-or-so years – human beings weren't able to see exponential rates of politicoeconomic change in real time. The changes in the human capacity for planning resultant from this once-in-history transformation have been so enormous, yet simultaneously, seemingly so invisible to the investigator, they've defied all simple means of measurement. Only a characteristically sociohistorical grasp of holistic cultural transformations can bring such shifts to light.

Albeit with some brief periods of discontinuity in some areas, the major trend in human affairs throughout civilizational history has involved, in the long run, the ever-increasing inextricability between the State and everything else. Beginning at the end of the 18th-century, this trend took a momentous all-historical turn upwards, marked most notably by the "Revolutions" in France and the new United States; it finally went completely vertical with the inception of the 20th-century-beyond era, what we've been framing as contemporary history. In other words, about 200 years ago the most dominant civilization and its States became practically inextricable once and for all: that civilization/those States originating in premodern western Europe, with the most *Powerful* of such Powers having extended themselves since around 1500 to the Western hemisphere and then back over the rest of the world. About 100 years ago, the now globally-dominant civilization and its States had grown *absolutely inextricable*, and in conjunction, what would be in the end the dominant civilization-State-complex of all time – the U.S. – started its journey towards total inextricability from the planet as a whole.

All this short historical process emanated from violence, and essentially from nowhere else. It had evolved out of a long historical process emanating from violence, and essentially from nowhere else. Certainly, the violence isn't the *end*, but the *means* – but it's the most reliable means for achieving the general end, on behalf of those who use it. In a given case, that end is the labor product of a targeted human population. In this way, war was for almost all of civilizational/State history paid for with slavery, often only in order to acquire the "right" to *more* slavery. That is, war was paid for with outright enslavement as well as tribute – taxes – towards the end of "Victory"; and on the grandest scale "Victory" meant that the hypothetical warmaker got to subject the "Vanquished" State's people to his own State, meaning that now, they quite literally "worked for him".

In this sense, war is a perfect example of an autocatalytic process: it always necessitates more war in-and-of-itself, which is why it's such a nightmare that the war system, i.e., the interstate system, started in the first place – once it got up-and-running, it was practically impossible for it to end. More war necessitated more slavery to pay for it; more war created more slaves, which yielded more pay for the winners. This dynamic might be phrased in the abstract, but it roughly describes every successful dominant State in history. Concerning the most *Powerful* State in the ancient world, Rome, it was more or less *literally* what happened: the Romans built an expansive politicoeconomic system almost purely on slavery as early as the "Republic" days, and constant explicit conquest rapidly became an outright necessity just for the system to maintain the status quo. Once conquest reached a fundamental limit in terms of its economic cost/benefit ratio early on in the Common Era, it was essentially inevitable that the Roman State would never recover.[ccxvii]

Again, once the process starts, it's practically impossible for there to be a change of direction until the system destroys itself, because some groups will always be willing to employ the strategy, no matter how detrimental it should prove for humanity as a whole. The process can't be reversed even if most of the *Powerful* individuals want it to be. The State has formed around conquest, so conquest is the only core strategy it can use to keep the system functioning. Eventually, the State collapses sometime after it surpasses its cost-benefit climax; sooner or later some new Power takes its place.

Although this particular manifestation of historical process didn't start in western Europe, that's where it would exist most pervasively, and stemming from what happened there, it would eventually become just as pervasive throughout the rest of the planet. The ultimate reason for this is quite simple: *territory*. Western Europe originally had the planet's most conducive territory for warmaking and thus State-building; and when Westerners finally took the collective step of bringing their warmaking/State-building to the rest of the globe, their motherland proved the best possible *base-of-operations* to support that development. Territory was the original reason why the process overtook western Europe so strikingly in the Classical world, and why the process similarly pervaded premodern western Europe – and western Europe *and* its colonies in the modern world, which would directly pave the way for the contemporary Hell.

As we've seen many times regarding the way agriculture first developed in southwest Asia and its surrounding regions, the most significant point to remember is that initially, not all areas on the planet were equally fit to support the agricultural way of life.[ccxviii] Resultantly, whichever culture happened to have found the best agricultural territory *and* discovered the soundest strategy for defending a socially ordered way of life in that territory "won out". The most successful strategy involved an unwaveringly top-down social command structure, with the chieftain/warrior/herder caste or the priestly/farmer caste at the top. Such a strategy was the most successful strictly in the sense that it was most effective for taking over other territories and reproducing the culture it represented in those new territories. And it could accomplish such feats foremost because it was the most "efficient" at using violence to achieve its desired goals, with those goals, again, altogether amounting to the forcibly-appropriated products of other populations' labor.

Now, all of this gives us an idea of how any such strategy would've emerged in the first place. However, it doesn't necessarily explain why it would've been perpetuated once it was established. Here I must bring into the discussion the well-known sociological theory of 'path-dependent processes', one of the most reliably effective explanatory frameworks for a sociohistorical approach. In fact, throughout our journey we've been tacitly incorporating an adherence to this theory, primarily as the basis for our notion of how long and short historical processes interact. We're specifically concerned here with *self-reinforcing* path-dependent processes: "In these sequences initial steps in a particular direction induce further movement in the same direction such that over time it becomes difficult or impossible to reverse direction."[ccxix] The reader will likely have already noticed that, above, this is precisely how I described the autocatalytic process of war and slavery – a politicoeconomic system becomes dependent on slavery fed by conquest, leading it to rely evermore on slavery to keep the war system going just as it relies evermore on war to keep the slave system going.

A cultural unit – here, we're most concerned with the crudest form of agricultural settlement – doesn't necessarily have to become established in exactly the way I've described: a top-down hierarchy with the chieftain/warrior/herder or priestly/farmer castes at the apex. At first, indeed, it was probably quite a low-percentage of settlements that actually did become established in this way. But again, once the pattern is established, there will always be individuals willing to keep the particular strategy of conquest going for as long as the available resources will allow, since they'll personally see immense benefit from it. Additionally, once the strategic pattern is established, it can be utilized in any locale where the essential elements are reproducible.[ccxx] Europe was the ideal territory for the strategy's extreme proliferation, once it became established in the first place. We in fact have overwhelming evidence to suggest that a primordial version of this strategy of conquest was proliferating in Europe even before the explicit emergence of the first civilizations.

Languages of the Indo-European language family are spoken as native tongues by nearly half of the world's people, making it by far the single largest language family in this regard. Many linguistic scholars believe that when two or more languages share a common 'family', this is an indication that those languages and all the other languages in the family ultimately descend from a single common language. Linguists determine which languages are likely to be "relatives" using (1) phonetic and (2) morphemic methods. Generally, the first involves the study of how speech is formed inside the mouth when humans talk, focusing on the tongue. Every natural language maintains its own peculiar way of making sounds, but a language's phonetic structure exhibits greater similarities to the structures of languages within its own family by comparison with languages across familial boundaries. Morphemic methods most generally involve the study of how languages are structured grammatically and syntactically. Again, the sentence structures and grammar of languages in a common family are far more similar to each other than they are to those outside the family. This possibly (in my opinion, almost certainly) leads to fundamentally different tendencies in the thought processes of two speakers from two different language families.[ccxxi] What all this means in relation to Indo-European speakers is that ultimately, if a significant strain of thought within linguistics is to be believed – and at least in the sense addressed here, I think it definitely should be – our native languages all descend from a common "mother tongue".

A 'Proto-Indo-European language' has long been theorized, and a fragmentary Proto-Indo-European vocabulary has been formulated, with over 1000 common roots shared by all Indo-European languages. The search for the "Proto-Indo-European homeland" has been endlessly pursued, mercilessly derided, and somehow got wrapped up into the ideology of a Nazi occultist sect. Nonetheless, a 2007 book by the archaeologist David W. Anthony, *The Horse, the Wheel, and Language: How Bronze Age Riders from the Eurasian Steppes Shaped the Modern World*, makes a convincing case for the Caspian Steppe in southern Russia and Ukraine as the Proto-Indo-European motherland. Anthony's case is made based on his argument for these central facts: first of all, the Proto-Indo-European language must've been spoken at its height between 4000 BCE and 3000 BCE. Secondly, all the Indo-European languages, starting with the earliest recorded Indo-European languages, have extraordinarily similar roots for many important words related to horses: in turn, thirdly, this strongly suggests that the Proto-Indo-Europeans were the earliest domesticators of horses. Finally, with all this in mind, Anthony argues through research and analysis of many other interconnecting material and ideological dimensions that the Caspian Steppe in southern (modern-day) Russia and the Ukraine is where horses were first domesticated. It's somewhat unfair to summarize this important, extensive work with such brevity, but I only feel confident in summarizing it so concisely because of the strength of the argument as a whole: the research carefully incorporates variables from a wide variety of areas of historical human life, and the analysis represents an impressive synthesis of knowledge from two disciplines – archaeology and linguistics – that typically don't cooperate as fruitfully as they could.[ccxxii]

Not only were the Proto-Indo-Europeans likely the first to domesticate horses: also, they were primarily a herding culture. Moreover, all the ancient and premodern Indo-European cultures were primary exemplars of cultures sharply divided into priestly, warrior/herder, and peasant farmer castes. Also, Anthony has posited that the Proto-Indo-European language was at its height spoken throughout the years between 4000 and 3000 BCE – as a close reader may have noted, the same years that the Sumerian and Egyptian civilizations were in their earliest stages, indicating that similar processes certainly could've been taking place somewhat earlier (with Proto-Afro-Asiatics replacing the Indo-Europeans, and without the horses) in southwest Asia and northeast Africa. Additionally, Anthony posited that at least by the late 4th-millennium BCE, some groups of Proto-Indo-Europeans represented vital overland trade links connecting the earliest burgeoning civilizations.[ccxxiii]

Significantly, if it truly did exist, the Proto-Indo-European culture that Anthony argues for so successfully would've had little to do with race. Rather, "Proto-Indo-European" (that is, whatever the Proto-Indo-Europeans really called themselves) would've been a purely religious/linguistic distinction at the time the culture existed. Would homogeneity in race have become one part of the overall phenomenon after some long period of time spent concentrated in roughly the same zone? Almost certainly; but then this would've been a biological effect of culture, not a cultural effect of biology. Anyway, the Proto-Indo-Europeans conquered – raped, killed, and enslaved – in places scattered everywhere surrounding the steppe; and from those places, eventually, Indo-Europeans would conquer practically everywhere else they went. That is to say, wherever they went, they became assimilated into the local populations, so determining what "race" they were at the beginning seems almost pointless. After a very brief period of time from a long historical perspective, the "Proto-Indo-Europeans" simply became ancient Persian conquerors, ancient Indian conquerors, ancient Greek conquerors, etc.[ccxxiv]

Wherever they went, they were the State in its earliest embryonic form. Whenever civilizations developed in the places where they conquered, their cultural descendants would ultimately become the social focal points of the State proper. They established the original pattern that has been reproducing itself ever since, albeit taking on different particular outward manifestations with changing times and places.

Europe was the ideal place for these conquerors, first of all, because no matter where you went, the geography was almost always perfect for their primary economic activity, herding. Even if farmers had been there first: "Between about 4200 and 3900 BCE more than six hundred tell settlements of the Gumelnita, Karanovo VI, and Varna cultures were burned and abandoned in the lower Danube valley and eastern Bulgaria," Anthony writes. In addition, "People scattered and became much more mobile, depending for their food on herds of sheep and cattle rather than fixed fields of grain." What's more, "Metal objects now were made using new arsenical bronze alloys, and were of new types, *including new weapons, daggers being the most important*" (emphasis my own). Although this may not be the whole explanation, it certainly seems, as Anthony says, "…like the tell towns of Old Europe fell to warfare, and somehow, immigrants from the steppes were involved."[ccxxv]

Again, the argument isn't that this kind of process is what "caused" all chiefdoms, nor even all States. Except in the subregion that's home to modern Peru, where the earliest predecessors to the Incas domesticated llamas, the State *couldn't* have originated in this way anywhere else in the "New World", because all other regions were devoid of domesticated pack animals. Oppenheimer pointed this out in *The State*, and argued that where there were no herders in the presence of farmers, hunters would've assumed the role, although the initiating catalyst for this may not have been as strong.[ccxxvi] If this is the case, I think rather than "disproving" the point, the fact that the State emerged in other ways in other places actually makes an excellent argument for why civilizations and States emerged *so much earlier* than they did anywhere else, in the places where they first existed. It also goes a long way towards explaining why, at the end of the premodern world, the most *Powerful* Europeans started conquering – raping, killing, and enslaving – everything they came into contact with.

II

The Medieval Structure Becoming the Early Modern Structure

During the civilizations stage, the long historical process is most basically comprised of the periods (the largest "units" of short historical process) in their successive waves; short historical process thereby implicitly serves to carry forward or put an end to aspects of long historical process. This is the nature of the interchange between long and short historical process – the short historical process is the story of the "birth, life, and death" of an overall cultural environment human beings have established, which has only been established ultimately as the result of relevant long historical process. In this sense, there are almost always many stories overlapping simultaneously; there are almost always different short historical processes being played out at once.

I say there are "almost always" many stories overlapping simultaneously, because this hasn't really been the case for about 70 years, since the start of the Cold War, which didn't truly end but more precisely changed "Enemies" after the fall of the Soviet Union. This is something completely unique in all of human history. At least since the inception of the World War II-beyond era, the story has been one in which all the human beings on the planet have been increasingly subjected to the circumstances of *a single history*; in this sense, we can say that during this period, long historical process has melded almost indistinguishably into short historical process. We now see the greatest long-term developments on the "World Stage" in literal real time: things have never happened so quickly, and relatedly – and more importantly from the standpoint of sociohistorical perspective – human beings have never had *the potential to perceive* so many things so rapidly, especially concerning those things called "current events". This hasn't necessarily been a good thing. In many ways, actually, in terms of how the state-of-affairs has played out in reality, it's the primary cause of our Hell. When things happen this fast, it seems that human beings have practically no choice but to conform to whatever environment embodies the system. As such, given what we described in part 1, an overwhelming proportion of individuals have been conforming to the most extinctive conceivable system – the most extinctive conceivable *path* – in human history.

But of course, this can't be the only cause for our Hell. After all, humans – contemporary "First World" humans more so than any other humans in history, and as a general group they're the worst sinners of them all – supposedly have freedom to choose what actions they undertake, so they technically didn't really *have to* go down this path. Why did they do so, in the first place?

In relation to the "European experience", what I would more precisely call the "Western experience", Charles Tilly came up with a concise list of sociohistorical elements that shaped modern western European State-building, a process that would ultimately shape the entire global interstate system of the contemporary world. The first element:

> Men who controlled concentrated means of coercion (armies, navies, police forces, weapons, and their equivalent) ordinarily tried to use them to extend the range of population and resources over which they wielded power. When they encountered no one with comparable control of coercion, they conquered; when they met rivals, they made war.[ccxxvii]

(This point is of the same rank as Oppenheimer's definition of the State [see the last section]; it can in fact be seen as a specifically Western "corollary" to Oppenheimer's definition, applicable to all post-Roman Empire, western European State-formations.)

As we've seen, the fall of the Western Roman Empire directly gave rise to the eventual sociohistorical conditions wherein three competing civilizations arose. The first civilization, which can be said to have been in its earliest existence even before the West fell, was originally represented by the Eastern Roman Empire, or Byzantium. Soon, it would become what's best called "Orthodox civilization", organized as it was around the confluence of church and State embodied in the interlocked relationship between the "Eastern" (what's today called the Orthodox) Christian Church and the Byzantine Emperor. The second civilization, which can be said to have been in its earliest existence around the beginning of the 7th-century CE, was the vast totality that we're referring to as "Islamic civilization", which would eventually include at least three States serving as its main *Power* centers. Originally, and for the whole third period, this was, overall, by far the most complex, most sophisticated, and wealthiest of the three civilizations.

The last of the civilizations, "Western civilization", was originally organized around the loosely-fitted relationships between the "Western" Christian Church (what's today called Roman Catholicism) and local rulers scattered across areas that had once either conquered or been conquered by the Romans – the Church's militarized defenders. At first, the relevant areas were mostly clustered along a relatively narrow path turning gradually northwest from Rome, all the way through Britain.[ccxxviii] In terms of short historical process, one could rightly say that during its earliest existence, Western civilization grew more complex as the essential relationships between the Roman Church and all the myriad local rulers became more systematic; and that as the civilization became more complex, the relationships in turn became more systematic again. Epitomizing this interconnection was the original greatest episode encompassing the increase in Western complexity, which actually came quite late in the premodern era, at the very end of the 11th-century CE. This was "the First Crusade".

We need a slightly deeper background before we can properly hone our focus in on this particular historical episode. As I just said, the Islamic civilization, referring collectively to all the relationships going on between the various caliphates and the enormous Islamic intercity system, which spread from Persia all the way across the Mediterranean coasts, was, from the beginning of the 8th-century until at least the 15th-century CE, the most complex, most sophisticated, and wealthiest civilization of the three. Practically anything about the tradition of Western civilization that people usually call "good" – philosophy and science most especially – was originally spread to "the West" via the Islamic and Orthodox civilizations, by way of those ancient knowledge storehouses last in the hands of the Greeks and the Romans.[ccxxix] (The Westerners would just end up being able to fund more research by controlling a higher proportion of plundered wealth.) For quite some time after the fall of the Roman Empire, the "other" two civilizations represented essentially the only cultural entities on the planet carrying on the traditions of learning that had evolved over millennia in the ancient and Classical worlds. Whenever advanced institutionalized education grows unto a substantial scale in any civilization, it's one of the best possible indicators of the highest complexity in any period. More generally, when certain institutional forms arise *en masse* in a system for the first time, it's a sign of some corresponding systemic necessity that's being met by the institution's creation.[ccxxx] Advanced educational institutions, such as the university, the modern "European-style" form of which was immediately preceded by centers for higher education in the Orthodox and Islamic civilizations, only appear when a civilization is already fully established. No system less complex than a fully-fledged civilization has any urgent need for this institutional form, at least not urgent enough to the point where the system produces it on its own.

This is of indispensable significance for illustrating the different growth-rates in systemic complexity taking place at different times amongst the three different civilizations. It's indisputable that an institutionalized advanced education system emerged on a broad scale much later in Western civilization than it had in the other two civilizations. During the entire premodern period, between 632 and 1492, there was an enormous difference between the short historical processes taking place within Western civilization and those taking place within the Orthodox and Islamic civilizations. For starters, as I've already begun to suggest with the example of education, both of the latter two civilizations started from a much higher baseline of complexity than the former, in the period after the fall of Rome. Of course, Byzantium's capital, Constantinople, had been the capital of Rome's Eastern Empire starting in 330 CE when it was given that name by the Roman emperor Constantine, and Constantinople would remain more or less as that particular *Power*-center (with one brief period of Italian rule after the Fourth Crusade,[ccxxxi] which anyhow changed nothing essential) until it fell to the Ottoman Empire in 1453. Thus, Byzantium's growth and decline during this period can basically be seen as synonymous with the growth and decline of Orthodox sovereignty over Constantinople.

Islamic civilization, which rose a few centuries afterwards, also inherited from its very beginning an extremely complex tradition of civilizations; even more complex than that which had been inherited by the Orthodox civilization. Around the very same time that the Western Roman Empire was collapsing, the Sassanian Empire emanating from Persia was flourishing. Indeed, the primary reason the Caliphate was able to establish such a high level of complexity so quickly was because it more or less just conquered an empire that wasn't prepared to defend itself against such an energetic challenger. Islamic civilization controlled a fully-formed base-of-operations from the outset, and its expansion naturally exploded from that starting point, at first without many robust competitors to contest it.

Western civilization, on the other hand, essentially had to start more or less from scratch in the premodern period: it was starting from behind. First of all, Europe was always extremely difficult terrain for any form of wide-scale conquest, namely a single unified empire. This was one of the major underlying factors involved in Rome's downfall, and would also be the central factor associated with the crumbling of Charlemagne's "empire" and its successors, a couple of centuries prior to the Crusades' onset. One of the most enlightening components of Tilly's perspective on modern European State-formation involves this very issue.

In the premodern era, the almost endless natural boundaries spread throughout western Europe's geography, along with the subregion's relative lack of general politicoeconomic development, facilitated the creation of practically innumerable *Power* centers by comparisons with the civilizations in the West's immediate surroundings; all these *Power* centers were able to compete with each other fairly successfully for centuries.[ccxxxii] Europe was a land of outright, completely uninhibited scramble for conquest over an incomparably greater period of time and across an incomparably broader geographic scale relative to everywhere else during the premodern period. Only at the very end of the period did this start to change, and after about 1500 the "nation-States" in their earliest manifestations began emerging. But even then, the burgeoning national States still had to compete directly with each other in their seemingly endless warfare aimed at swallowing up and/or protecting their smaller neighbors, i.e., the buffer zones (And this isn't even to mention the competition for overseas Empire.) A single *Power* center was out of the question; even a single group of *Power* centers wasn't possible during the premodern period. Consolidation of *Power* in premodern Europe was thus an eminently uncertain process, and as a result it occurred far more gradually than in the Orthodox and Islamic civilizations.

What all this means is that the crudest aggressive warfare was a vital element in premodern Western politicoeconomic affairs to an extent that was just never matched by the other two civilizations in terms of its sheer prevalence and inextricability from the system, and certainly not over anything close the same time-scale experienced in the West. This was primarily what led to the "First Crusade", and all the "Crusades" to follow. So: what was a "Crusade"?

A "Crusade" was like a prototypical herder raid on the most complex conceivable scale. It was really just organized long-distance pillage – or as "organized" as pillage can get – which happened to be broadly motivated by its receiving sanctification from the Roman Church. But on account of this very sanctification, it wasn't *just* pillage for pillage's sake; it was undertaken towards the end of cultural conquest. In this way, it constituted quintessential State-building: and insofar as it was the first great premodern catalyst for the modern Western State, it was also the first great premodern catalyst for modern Western civilization. Of course, both Western civilization and the Western States it subsumed had already been forming, coequally, for a long time. But the Crusades tied everything together – they *organized* everything around one central source – on a level that hadn't been previously approached in Western history, thereby driving the Western short historical process forward toward a destination that would end up being the definitively western European, modern national State.

In the West, the mass ritual represented by the Crusades as a whole served the purpose of sewing together all three vital originary repositories: communications (the Church), life-support (the estates and nobles), and military (the noble armies and trader navies), and it did so in the form of constructing a holistic intercity system that bound all the cities of Western civilization into a single cultural environment. Once again, I must reiterate that each of these elements had long been present in western Europe in some primordial, subsystemic form; but the Crusades served the invaluable function of driving all three elements forward into a singularly interconnected systemic package, unto a wholly heightened level of material complexity.

At the time of the Crusades, and since the decline of Charles's empire, which had anyway never been an empire in the same sense as the caliphates and Byzantium, "…the 'Catholic core' had been thrust onto the defensive by a wave of external attacks, some of them, indeed, launched by peoples of the 'Catholic fringe'."[ccxxxiii] The 'Catholic fringe' was comprised of the newly converted lands; at the time of the First Crusade, this mainly meant what's today called "central Europe" as well as some areas in Scandinavia.[ccxxxiv] These areas were especially prone to raids by "pagan" herders pouring into Europe from the steppes; some external attacks also emanated from Muslim settlers in North Africa and southern Italy.[ccxxxv] At the time when they occurred, none of these attacks, whether by "pagans" or Muslims, were due to any sort of overtly religious (in an ideological sense) antagonism. Rather, they occurred because of pure politicoeconomic considerations: the endless jockeying for strategically valuable territory that's desired by many other parties or factions – in other words the main thing that always drives the activities of the *Powerful* in civilizations and States.

Ideology was the indispensable decorative paper wrapping up the brutal politicoeconomic package: the securing of territory. And it was all excellent territory – the territory upon which Western civilization, the most *naturally* (as opposed to monetarily) wealthy civilization in this formative period, would build its initial "domestic" base-of-operations. Throughout the 11th-century, then (up until the First Crusade), Rome's primary goal was to quell "external attacks" in the newly converted lands (the 'Catholic fringe'); to completely lose control in those territories would've meant an unacceptable geostrategic step backwards. Yet not even the 'Catholic core', the label used by medieval historian John France to refer the area "comprising what is now southern England, France, Germany, and much of Italy",[ccxxxvi] i.e., the original central domain of Western civilization, can be said to have appeared anything like a fully structured whole, in the few centuries leading up to the First Crusade.

Quite the contrary: "The savage struggle of the ninth and tenth centuries against external attack was clearly the result of internal dissent as the Carolingian dynasty became divided, and then died out. But these conflicts did not generate another great political authority." In other words, all throughout the 11th-century, any semblance of monarchy in western Europe was still hardly to be found, and the nobles were running rampant: as France writes, the immediately preceding "…leaders of the 'Catholic core', the Carolingian aristocracy, …[had] achieved [articulated dominions] by annexing governmental power to their landholdings, *forming the characteristic institution of lordship*" (emphasis my own). This explains the practically endless, always-increasing supply of lords all across the crude manifestation of Western civilization at this time and for the next couple of centuries afterwards at least, and it's one of the major reasons why *Powerful* "Monarchies" would take so long to fully form, not really doing so to any substantial extent until the very end of the premodern era (around 1500). France describes these new "lords" with utmost succinctness: "They were aggressive, greedy and opportunistic: as early as the tenth century the counts of Flanders were founding castles to encourage the growth of towns and, therefore, taxes."[ccxxxvii]

The founding of castles by warlords – the original, premodern European nobility – to "encourage towns and taxes" constituted the earliest incarnation of what would become the modern European State. This certainly fit the mold of Oppenheimer's axiomatic definition, as well as Tilly's corollary: we find an institutional arrangement originally tied at first exclusively to the land, wherein a dominant group representing an elite minority – the warrior caste – uses violence and the threat of violence, or conquest and consolidation of conquest, to economically exploit the vast majority of individuals, primarily in the form of tribute, or taxes. Not only that, but we even find the specifics that Oppenheimer outlined so brilliantly: "…the economies of the lands within [the 'Catholic core'] were dominated by grain production made possible by a settled peasantry tied to the land. There were major areas of pastoral farming and huge marginal zones, but these were being colonized by a disciplined peasantry in the service of the elites."[ccxxxviii] That is, the warrior/herder class was still in charge, just as in the ancient primitive State; only, by the year 1000 or so, they had gone the extra step and annexed their jobs as herders to some particularly fortunate peasant underlings, so they could focus simply on being aristocrats, which necessarily includes being warriors. But the identical *Power*-relations that Oppenheimer described as having been present during the origins of all "Old World" States were instrumental from the outset.

When we compare each of the first three periods to the other two, we can see that the three medieval civilizations were, from their respective foundations, fulfilling the same roles that earlier civilizations in the central intercivilizational zone had fulfilled when they first emerged, and that this latest opportunity to fill those niches had most immediately arisen on account of the Roman Empire's ending. Uniquely, though, the premodern world represented a set of intercivilizational circumstances wherein the "period-starters" for all three civilizations existed in such close politicoeconomic and chronological-geographic – to use one word that refers to the combination of both, *sociohistorical* – proximity to one another, that the newly-founded intercivilizational relationship itself played more or less the same formative role in all three civilizations, almost at once.

I've said that the underlying "motor" of sociohistorical process in civilizations is the mutually reinforcing link between the three cultural spheres: life-support, communications, and military. But how does this motor manifest itself overtly in reality? The best sociohistorical reference-points for answering this question are found in the contexts where one can explicitly perceive the formation of new civilizations. This is why I've been so focused in our discussion on the moments when new periods start: the start of the first period in our last section, the start of the third period here. What "field" allows us to witness most clearly the beginnings of new periods, which most significantly mean the beginnings of new intercivilizational relationships?

The primary catalyst for new intercivilizational relationships (new periods) lies in what's known in modern terms as *international trade*. Most essentially, this is what connects intercity systems – civilizations – in the first place. It's why civilizations have always led to the creation of evermore-centralized States. And it's why, whenever possible, civilizations have formed structural relationships with other civilizations.

Remember, we've seen from our definition of 'technology' that it's 'understanding applied to *materials*'. The only way for humanity as a whole to maximize its technological capabilities is for a sufficient number of humans to have access to the *materials* allowing them to do so. In civilizations, humans accomplish this most effectively via far-reaching trade networks. You can't "reduce" all of human history in the past 5,000-plus years to this fact. But it has, nonetheless, recurrently served the baseline for all further cultural complexity on the intercivilizational level. Concerning civilizations and States, then, the more complex a system of international trade becomes, the more complex become the civilizations *dependent on* this international trade. The more complex the civilizations become, the more complex become the States protecting those civilizations' wealth. And when the civilization-State-complexes in any system of international trade become more complex, in turn, so too do the structural relationships between different civilizations (intercivilizational structures), beginning the cycle all over again.

Thus, when we look at the periodic shifts affecting civilizations plugged into intercivilizational structures, we're looking at thresholds when the changes in the system of intercivilizational trade are so overwhelming that *holistically* new trade systems emerge. Of course, the first time this happened was through the first example of multiple, necessarily interacting civilizations; thus the era marked by those interactions was/is the first intercivilizational period. The next time it happened, around the start of the Classical era, transregional trade began to explode again (roughly around 1000 BCE) after the passing of the "Dark Ages" that had begun about 1174 BCE. It happened once more after Rome collapsed, when there emerged a new far-reaching trade system originally hovering around southwest Asia – just as it had in the first and second periods, only now its central locus was positioned at this subregion's southwestern-most extreme. The trade system momentously expanded into Europe as well (again, just as it had in the first and second periods), this time so that the Orthodox and Islamic civilizations could tap into Europe's actual wealth, yielding the reciprocal effect of allowing the new elites (lords) in Europe to receive luxury goods from the East in return for the agricultural material that their violently-coerced subordinates produced.

The fourth period started when the Europeans "discovered" the "New World", which would most significantly result in the intercivilizational trade system's center shifting to the Atlantic, creating incalculable new *Power* in its wake. The fifth started around 1865, after the U.S. Civil War provided the final impetus for sparking the beginning of a fully industrialized world. This meta-event-cluster sequence allowed the Industrial Revolution to push forward for its primary supporters on the most advantageous possible political footing, namely on behalf of the British imperial system, and all its various (often tawdry) global connections.[ccxxxix] The sixth period started with the official beginnings of the Cold War in 1947, after the unofficial beginnings in 1945 with the U.S.'s dropping atomic bombs over Japan; this was the first period that started in contemporary history, making it the start of the contemporary world proper. The seventh and last (at least, as yet) period started in 1995 with the U.S. Government's globally-encompassing institutionalization of its self-ascribed role as "lone remaining superpower". – The specifically trade-based aspect of those changes characterizing the last two periods will be honed in on during part 3.

All of these developments embodied such complete changes to the conditions defining those trade structures they affected that we can only consider the changed sets of structural relationships to be markers/makers of holistically new periods. In this way, we can see that it's not so much the general causes that need to follow fundamentally similar patterns – as new periods can be and have been brought into existence owing to many different kinds of factors – so much as the general effects. The 'causes' that create new periods can be practically anything, so long as they bring into being distinct overall patterns of intercivilizational (or global civilizational) trade. Herein lies our explanation concerning the apparently extreme rarity of new periods: massive changes in civilizations-as-wholes, necessarily being such uniquely complex sequences of event-clusters, arise fairly infrequently in-and-of-themselves; how much rarer must it be then when changes arise that similarly affect multiple civilizations at once. But such "moments" did happen a few times in the nexus of regions that produced the contemporary dominant culture's original ancestors, and a few other times afterwards on account of this dominant culture itself and its direct antecedents.

Then again, changes approaching the same scale as that associated with periodic shifts were certainly far rarer at any time prior to humanity's dependence on agriculture: so from this perspective, actually, periodic shifts have been happening quite frequently since then. They've been happening with almost incomprehensible rapidly in the past half-millennium, and especially so concerning the last couple of centuries. We can see that in fact, the intercivilizational periods have been occurring with greatly increased rapidity in each successive period; in other words, the periods have been getting shorter and shorter. Therefore, we can say that the short historical processes, and inseparably, the long historical process, have/has been getting consistently, progressively faster since civilizations and States first emerged. I believe that based on our particular area of interest – the contemporary dominant culture and its ancestors, to which the theory of the intercivilizational periods is most directly applicable – the best explanation for this fact has to do first with humanity's mastery of river transport. Next, building from there, it has to do with humanity's mastery of the Mediterranean; then humanity's mastery of the Atlantic; and then it has to do with turning this same type of mastery back on all the rest of the oceans of the world; and eventually in the skies, as well; finally, in space. And as they happened, all of these changes, in the first place, were coterminous with the evolution of humanity's war-centered trade networks.

Once again, notice how this process, which is the very essence of international trade and ultimately the very essence of capitalism, has certainly had nothing to do with anything we can call "free trade" (define), and really nothing to do with anything one could call "freedom" at all. Well – it had to do with the "freedom" of the most *Powerful* interests. But how can you call something "free" when it has been built, more than anything else, on slavery? It would of course be nice if international trade had evolved entirely – or even partially – through "free" human interactions, unto its contemporary globalized and space-based state. However, it didn't happen that way. As I've repeatedly said, in the history of civilizations and States, particularly civilizations and States in our area of interest, civilizations have always arisen out of wealth built on intercity systems of trade, and States have always been perpetuated – at least in large part – *to protect that wealth,* i.e., that trade. No systemic relationship is more symbiotically profitable for the agents that enact it than the reciprocal bond that always goes on in civilizations between the trader caste and the warrior caste, between merchants and lords. And no relationship has been more destructive to everything else, both to human beings and even more so (whether you care or not) to the planet itself. From a pre-industrial perspective, these two sociohistorical truths never revealed themselves more strikingly than they did in premodern and modern Western civilization. (From an even broader view, these truths have *never* been more evident than they've been in the contemporary global civilization that the West directly spawned.)

Returning our attention specifically to the late medieval West, then: with the growth, starting around 1000 CE, of the new bourgeoisie towns that would go on to define modern western Europe so characteristically, emergent every place in reach of the rapidly heightening international trade – not just in seaports but also, and more especially from an internal civilizational perspective, along inland routes and on rivers – a small but steadily increasing percentage of migrating peasants became solely artisans and/or traders. Just as the nobles grew organically out of the warrior/herder caste, the new burghers grew mainly, and quite naturally, out of the peasant farmer caste.

As we've seen, the era of Charlemagne and his closest successors was defined by circumstances wherein an "empire" existed but there was no centralized apparatus that could sufficiently enforce it, creating the worst of all possible worlds within the period, whereby lordship was concocted as the only means of fulfilling the *Power* pyramid's requirements. And as we've just seen, as well, this *Power* pyramid was starting to reemerge in full force because international trade was spreading again in bits and pieces, something which really only benefited the new lords and the clergy, i.e., the elites, at first (besides its most obvious beneficiaries, the initially very tiny niche of traders). Starting mostly in the 9th and 10th centuries, this general state-of-affairs facilitated the consolidation of locally-ruled States. This did *not* mean locally-ruled polities, which would actually be the most preferable (and is, in civilizations, a totally theoretical) arrangement – it meant locally *State-ruled* polities, which allows for the most overt, unabashed form of official violence imaginable, insofar as it brings the conquered within the closest proximity to their conquerors. The governance of local State-rule under this particular format is more or less synonymous with the phenomenon of warlordism; the earliest European lords were perhaps the most prototypical kind of warlords of any in history. Using little to nothing besides raw terror to dominate their subjects, they did so solely for the purpose of the most basic and harshest kind of economic exploitation, wherein they were literally stealing the food out of peasant mouths. And these murderous thieves comprised the original version of the later (modern) European nobility. That nobility would be largely responsible for making the early modern European State.[ccxl]

As John France writes, beginning in the 10th-century this budding aristocracy established the pattern of building central castles around which their peasant subjects would congregate and pay tribute – taxes. To the extent that they're not used in any way for a redistributive purpose but are based solely on relationships of *Power* instilled by violence, taxes of this kind constitute nothing besides pure profit – and pure *theft*. These taxes, then, are not only employed to maintain rigid *Power*-relations; they actually embody the acting out of such *Power*-relations: the peasant *is* stolen from ("pays tribute"), therefore the peasant *is* subject. This maintains an indispensable ritual (cultural) aspect for the relationship of tribute between the nobles and the subjects of their oppression.[ccxli]

Additionally, the actual wealth consolidated by the nobles in their receiving taxes eventually led to further, more subtle and so in the long-term more successful establishment of *Power*-relations, as it allowed the nobles to build evermore complex material apparatuses around themselves, which ultimately came to include evermore complex systems of largesse, used by the nobles to build support networks resting on selective wealth-distribution. They were, quite literally, purchasing legitimacy. Although a less direct method than building their own official technostructural apparatuses, perhaps the most significant form of such legitimacy purchasing was the growth of towns themselves that followed in the wake of the reemergence of substantial demand for international trade in western Europe. Tragically, European peasants *en masse* escaped the constant torment of living under noble thumbs…only to wind up in the towns where they would make the very material goods so central to furthering the systems from which they fled.

But things surely never would've been expressed explicitly in these terms to the new burghers, and anyway in time the growing towns – and soon enough, full-fledged cities – would be filled with individuals who had largely forgotten their farming ancestry. Indeed, increasing generations of new European town and city folk, on a substantial scale probably by around 1200, in places such as the Italian city-States and select locales scattered farther north throughout western Europe, would've never had any experience farming at all. This growing pattern of booming towns and cities continued until about 1348, the year marking the beginning of a particularly severe outbreak of bubonic plague, likely stemming from a combination of these rapidly expanding urban populations and the absolute filth of basically all Europeans at the time – with both phenomena made especially destructive by the constant movement to and fro between town/city and country. Even while steadily increasing proportions of Europeans in the 'Catholic core' were able to carve out niches for themselves in these premodern, protocapitalist economies, it was by no means the majority: it's not unreasonable to think that, for quite some time, individuals would as often as not end up heading for (or back to) the estates, just as there was always a constant flow of individuals leaving them for the towns and cities. Many human beings in the sociohistorical context must've been truly conflicted about which lifestyle they hated more, that of the countryside or the one in the city. This would be a frequent pattern in European history for at least several more centuries, until the earliest phase of the Industrial Revolution in England at the end of the 1700s. When the pattern changed around this later date the vast majority of individuals could now decide it was clearly the city they hated more than anything else.

At any rate, the growth pattern was suspended for about another century subsequent to 1348, but after that point urban population growth resumed once more. It grew steadily for more than two centuries and then really started booming in England concurrently with the Industrial Revolution, spreading to each polity more or less parallel to mass industrialization. It has then exploded with ever-greater frequency since about the mid-1800s, becoming an evermore-global phenomenon all throughout the 20th-century. It truly can't be overemphasized how remarkable the most recent population growth has been: the planet never held a billion people at one time until about 1830; 184 years later, there's more than 7 billion.[ccxlii] Comparing especially the past 116 years or so to all prior history, there's absolutely nothing comparable in terms of how many human beings have been alive on the planet during any one era.

Concerning this phase of rapid population explosion, if one looks only at the evolution of the most superficial, outward manifestations of juridical forms, and if one adopts only the most conventional general view on human affairs emanating from the contemporary dominant culture, one might reasonably think something like, "Human population and 'freedom' have grown side-by-side." Certainly, in a completely superficial sense, this is true. The entire world is now covered with national States that all appear more or less equal in status – and they are, in a completely superficial sense. The vast majority of these States have governments that are called "Democracies", i.e., there is widespread popular rule – although just in the most superficial sense. Universally, people have their material needs met through a system called "Free Market Capitalism" – but of course, it's only superficially "free".

The primary reason why it has all been completely superficial change – and thus completely superficial freedom – is because there has never been serious alteration to the system's fundamental structural relationships. In fact, they've only exponentially grown from their original bases in the interlocked relationships between elite nobles in the countryside, and their looked-down-upon but highly useful cohorts in the towns and cities, the merchant elites central to harnessing the protocapitalist economies. These structural relationships have grown infinitely more complex, and more people have been (very superficially) allowed to personally benefit from the system; but precisely because it has only grown after starting from these original bases, we can't say that the current politicoeconomic system is ultimately very different from its predecessors. The premodern/early modern system and the late modern/contemporary system may be completely different on their respective surfaces – i.e., *superficially* – but at the innermost core, the whole state-of-affairs has been essentially the same ever since elite lords started terrorizing their "lowly" peasants. And even more so, things have been the same ever since the wealth of the wealthiest traders (who very quickly turned into financiers) in the cities of the 'Catholic core' became so disproportionate to any social benefit trading really had, that the traders' number-one priority became neither trading, nor investing, but the perpetuation of their own *Power*. All else has followed from these starting points.

I must start to illustrate the ways in which the essential structural relationships have remained fundamentally similar, since an understanding of this is going to be absolutely crucial to our account of the contemporary world. To begin, ever since the start of the fourth period – the period whose inception was marked by the earliest Western conquest of the "New World" – the central story of the dominant culture's politicoeconomic history has been one of simply transposing the preexisting underlying Western *Power*-relations over the rest of the planet. As I've said, speaking at least of England and France, the States that would ultimately be the most *Powerful* in the world at the beginning of the fifth period (the period of industrialized national States), these *Power*-relations were above all defined at the highest levels by a relatively balanced intertwining of lord and merchant castes, who profited by subjugating peasants and artisanal laborers, respectively. More or less all the other most *Powerful* European States were closely following this pattern by the beginning of the fourth period; one would be quite right to say that the more closely a State was able to follow this pattern, the more *Powerful* that State had the potential to ultimately become. Since the pattern had been established in some fully formed albeit still crude way by the time Columbus descended upon the Western hemisphere, it was easy for European elites to successfully impose it upon the Americas. And of course, once the European elites had easily, successfully imposed it upon the Americas, it was natural for them to try and impose it upon the rest of the world, an aim they would eventually accomplish throughout the 17th, 18th, and 19th centuries (limiting ourselves now to the period preceding the contemporary world).

It wasn't just "easy" for European elites to impose their *Power*-structure upon the rest of the world: it was, in fact, far easier than it had ever been in Europe. Nowhere was this truer, or more tragic, than in the Americas. Not only did Europeans destroy almost an entire hemisphere of human beings – numbering, perhaps, as many as *100 million individuals* at the time of the earliest conquest, which makes this at once far and away the worst (perpetual) case of plague and the worst (perpetual) act of genocide in history.ccxliii Because their populations were so disease-ridden, and because they had enlisted such genocidal savages to do their dirty work, the European elites almost immediately found themselves without a sufficiently large supply of unpaid labor. Clearly for the most part lacking any consciences whatsoever when it came to "natives" – indeed, in large part feeling utter moral superiority on account of their anti-human behavior, developing an impenetrable ideology that would forever reinforce this feeling – they also had no qualms about beginning what would be another centuries-long pillage of yet one more continent when they started to "buy" human beings *en masse* in Africa. The slave trade that played *the* crucial role in forging the European elites' politicoeconomic success in the Americas represented the most sinister conceivable amalgamation of the lords' and merchants' respective interests.

For all subsequent humanity, the saddest part is – from the elites' perspective it was also the most *successful* conceivable amalgamation of their respective interests.

From the start of the fourth period onwards, the Western dominance system would spread to the rest of the world, and in a far more rigidly hierarchical form even than what had been transpiring in Europe for over 500 years. Mainly because now, at least in the new overseas colonies that were starting to emerge, the "lowest class" European peasants would no longer be playing the collective role as the greatest target for elite domination. Now, there were whole new continents filled with "Others" that were even better at playing that role, because the European conquerors could most successfully act like these "Others" weren't human beings at all. As far as the dominant culture was concerned, these entities – these "Indians" and "Negroes" – were nothing but objects. If one didn't just destroy these objects completely, it was only because using them as labor motors was the far more sensible thing to do from a business perspective. But, sure, for those objects in particular that showed any form of resistance – that is, for those "objects" most obstinate in professing that they were really *human beings* – one could of course destroy them as one wished. In fact, in these particular circumstances, this was also the sensible thing to do from a business perspective: one could simply never fail to illustrate who was "Master" and who was "Slave". Quite quickly, and forever after, everyone received the message loud and clear.

The dominance system never changed its pattern of lord/merchant subjugating peasant/laborer: the dominance system just *exponentially expanded*, with that exact pattern as its point of departure. Throughout time, some more "subtle" gradations were added between the top and the bottom of the *Power* pyramid. But freedom? Freedom was never added to the pattern. What was happening was that there were all the time greater and greater quantities of wealth being pumped into the system – it goes without saying that the vast majority always went to the very top – and gradually, then increasingly quickly, then exponentially during the fifth and sixth periods, the system was growing large enough in absolute terms that the "First World" countries could support increasing numbers of individuals "in the middle". These "middle-class" individuals were seeing enough benefits from the intercivilizational dominance to the point where they tacitly supported the status quo's continuation, then ultimately took active part in supporting it – largely doing so with sheer jubilation[ccxliv] – during the unprecedented growth of the fifth and sixth periods, which saw the rise of the late modern national States (fifth) and the middle contemporary ideological blocs (sixth).

The near-universal abolition of explicit slavery – abolished at least in relation to Africans "traded" in the Americas, although the practice itself would by no means ever be honestly destroyed[ccxlv] – was an important thing, but it didn't happen because humans just spontaneously decided as a collective mass to be "nicer". And that's certainly not how it happened concerning the United States. It's true that the U.S. Federal Government (the U.S. *State*) finally ended up abolishing explicit slavery primarily because of the particular context and outcome of the U.S. Civil War, which of course pitted the North against the South. Both the Northern states and the Southern states, meaning the elites on both sides, had the same basic goal: to extend their own side's particular politicoeconomic system to the territories that had been annexed in the West as a result of the earlier war between Mexico and the United States; and the most precious prize of all was California. In a related but deeper sense, they were trying to impose their own side's *cultural hegemony* on the upcoming Western states. Really, the *Power*-structure on each side was simply doing what the European States had done to found their colonies in the Americas in the first place, with every European *Power*-structure pitted against every other European *Power*-structure, each vying to have its own system be the one that would reign dominant in the "New World". Thus, the U.S. Civil War was just like every other war between Powers in the history of civilizations, except it encompassed a much larger scale than ever before.

But precisely for that reason, we can't say that a desire for "freedom" – specifically in the form of the cultural movement of abolitionism – ever played a major politicoeconomic role in the war between North and South, because neither politicoeconomic system was ever designed to institutionalize human freedom. They were both designed to institutionalize *Power*, so no matter which side won, *un*freedom was going to be the most general outcome. Of course, again, I recognize that the war's outcome did lead to the abolition of explicit slavery: but this was primarily because the abolition of such slavery meant that no matter what, the Southern states couldn't impose *their* existing politicoeconomic system on the Western states, whereas the Northern states could, which meant that they now held the potential for hegemony over the United States as a "nation", since they had sufficiently proven they could back up such hegemony with force.

The silliest contemporary understanding of this outcome – which has of course for this reason become the most widely promoted viewpoint by the contemporary dominant culture – says, "Abraham Lincoln freed the slaves", with the implication being that he *wanted* to do so, that he did so as an abolitionist. Abraham Lincoln was merely a President – a figurehead – and thus couldn't/wouldn't have done anything so significant just because "he wanted to" (we'll get into this general phenomenon much more extensively in part 3). Moreover, concerning this particular case: he wasn't an outright abolitionist, and had no interest in doing anything except for what was politically expedient for himself, which for him translated into "preserving the Union" by any possible means.[ccxlvi] (If he'd wanted to "change the world", he wouldn't have become a politician.) Again, in this sense, he was like virtually every single public official in history. But for that reason – again – *freedom had nothing to do with why the war was fought* – not even the very limited, superficial "freedom" represented by the abolition of black slavery, considering how it (abolition) actually happened.

Going even deeper, I must point out that even if we didn't know it was what *did* actually happen historically, the U.S. abolition of the form of slavery existing approximately through the Civil War still would've been the most expected long-term outcome with respect to the institution. Moreover, this isn't because it had already happened in other similar countries, most notably England, which had abolished this kind of slavery a few decades earlier than the United States (although the specific reason why it happened in those nations is certainly more evidence that proves our point). It's because, first of all, *slavery in a legalistic sense had already done its job on behalf of the elite* – it had consolidated a system with rich landholders at the top and destitute dependents at the bottom. Whatever law the government passed, this essential pattern was already set, so unless there was a holistic change of the culture, *nothing* could really change. In that case, the Government was better off saying the specific institution of slavery was abolished, because that would be better for the long-term perpetuation of the status quo (we'll get into this particular point more extensively throughout our discussion ahead).

We must explain this phenomenon whereby "slavery did its job for the elite" in greater detail. When *Power* pyramids grow, they don't grow equally from the top to the bottom, in absolute terms: for every extra individual that's sitting closer to the top, the pyramid requires that many more individuals be forced into sitting at the bottom. This explains why the form of slavery that the European elites profited from so viciously was such a perfect fit for the preexisting European system of domination in the first place – those millions of innocent African victims weren't even treated like they were at *the bottom* of the pyramid; they were treated like they didn't even qualify for the pyramid, at all. They were treated like the dirt that sits under the weight of the entire pyramid – even the base.

That type of treatment, insofar as it's repeated generation after generation after generation, and especially when there's a constant influx of new individuals entering into the pyramid, becomes all the time a more entrenched component of the system as a whole. In this way, ideologies grow up in parallel to the system*, ideologies that have the sole underlying purpose of justifying the dominant party's subjugation of its victims. You can't fundamentally change the central focus of such an emotionally potent ideology simply with the enactment of a few laws, just like you can't change the system as a whole even with the enactment of a million laws. And especially, you can't change *Power* relations simply by enacting laws, particularly the *Power* relations that are the most entrenched and thereby most vital to the system's workings as a whole.

No *Power* relations are more entrenched – and thus, no *Power*-relations are more vital to the *Power* pyramid's workings as a whole – than the direct domination of the "lowest" group of human beings by the "highest" group, including the attendant ideologies that grow up to justify that domination. The "Master/Slave" relationship is *the* archetypal example of such direct domination. Structural relationships like this simply can't be changed if the entire system itself isn't changed. The system remained as it had in the South; it was just given a new name, and eventually, industrialized. This would only change somewhat substantively in a civil rights sense about 100 years after the Civil War: it would absolutely never change in any essential politicoeconomic sense, just like things essentially never changed and only intensified in the industrial manufacturing/shipping economy, run by international banker elites, that emerged largely from the Northeast.

The point is that the Federal Government could've passed virtually any individual law, or even any set of laws that it wanted, and the fundamental relationships would've stayed the same, and the system would've been perpetuated in the same way it always had been. So when large groups of people – like abolitionists – were finally starting to speak out against an institution as obviously repugnant and inhumane as black slavery, why not just "give the people what they wanted", and say "Slavery is abolished"? Then all the (white upper-class) Americans could congratulate themselves about what a free, "civilized" country they all lived in, and that particular pressure would be removed from

* And then of course the system, in turn, grows further in response to the ideologies.

the system. Meanwhile, blacks would hardly be freer than they were before the Civil War, as the practically identical institution of sharecropping almost immediately sprang up to take slavery's place. Eventually, too, the Southern states came up with some of the most ingeniously cruel methods of oppression in modern history, whereby they simply criminalized all sorts of things – specifically targeting blacks – turned untold numbers of "free" blacks into prisoners, and stole their labor-product that way.[ccxlvii] (In its presently existing form, this is called the "War on Drugs".) Things were just the same as they always were. Except people had lost all empathy for the constant atrocities that were still being committed against blacks – they weren't "slaves" anymore, they were just indigent farmhands and criminals, so who could they blame now besides themselves? Therefore, culturally, this "new" system was much better for business, because now certain sectors of the upper-class whites – the people who actually had some say in what the Federal Government did (the upper-class white males, at least) – wouldn't have to feel any guilt at all.

III

The Familiar Novelty of the Late Modern Structure

Of even greater long historical significance, and from a more purely business perspective, there was another reason, inextricable with the first, why abolition – and interchangeably, the South's downfall – should've been the most expected long-term outcome regarding U.S. slavery: *industrialization*. Here we're just going to focus on the broadest meaning of the term: 'industrialization', most broadly, and limiting its application to the phenomenon that started revving up in England in the 18th-century and then spread elsewhere throughout Western civilization in the 19th-century and everywhere else on the globe in the 20th-century, refers to *all mass production/distribution technological processes that depend upon metal machines powered by fossil fuels*. Lots of other things, of course, characterize industrialization as well, but *most broadly*, "metal machines" – part or all of the metal almost invariably being steel, the most essential non-fuel throughout the Industrial Revolution – "powered by fossil fuels", for the purpose of "mass production/distribution" of commodities, were the most significant elements of change originally responsible for giving rise to and in fact defining the fifth period, that of industrialized national States (c.a. 1861-1945).

Metal machines powered by fossil fuels and operated by human beings can perform exponentially greater quantities of work than can basically any group of human beings working without metal/fossil fuel-powered machines.[ccxlviii] Moreover, ever since human beings started using them for the purposes of industrialization, fossil fuels have been given outrageously low prices in comparison to their *actual value*, even if only determined by the broadest common sense[ccxlix] point-of-view, comparing fossil fuels' scarcity to their significance. For practically the entire stretch of time since the inception of industrialization, the price considerations have been based mostly on the crudest capitalist consideration of, "How much will people pay for it today such that it will produce the greatest immediate monetary profit?" This has yielded a sociohistorical situation wherein materials so priceless in terms of their ability to do work and so generally poisonous to the environment when used constantly at evermore rapid rates have been systematically priced and utilized in such a way as to ensure that people use them as wastefully and with as much ecological destruction as possible.

Therefore, the combination of (1) the potential to do exponentially greater work, and (2) to do so at far cheaper rates than would be necessary if one were to pay human beings to do the same quantities of work, was too irresistible for international capitalists to resist. The cost of fossil fuels, as priced by the international market – with the biggest players in the international marketplace of course acting in conjunction with various Powers,[ccl] represented by the States competing in the international system – was ultimately the factor most responsible for the Northern tide that turned against black slavery. The Northern-style politicoeconomic system of the 19th-century *had* to win out in these circumstances, because slavery, by comparison to industrialized labor, simply wasn't a viable economic strategy in the international marketplace; and the international marketplace has always been the number-one factor shaping the political considerations of the (capitalist) Western States.

Basically what I'm saying is that the abolition movement, solely referring here to its history in the U.S. surrounding the Civil War, wasn't one of the real politicoeconomic factors catalyzing the war, and factors of this sort, above all, truly determined "why the war was fought". On the other hand, the abolitionist movement was of indispensable *cultural* significance insofar as it justified the war morally, both during the lead-up to the war and after the fact, in the eyes of the broad cultural milieu surrounding the victors. The war was going to happen with or without the abolitionists: without them, some other moral justification would've been concocted to permit the decision to go to war. The abolitionists, however, made the war appear utterly indispensable to "the national interest", and in this sense abolitionism had irreplaceable value for allowing the warmakers to go to war at the exact time when they did, in the exact manner in which they did.

In other words, no matter what, the elites who now had the most *Power* in running the U.S. Government, emanating as they did from the rapidly industrializing metropolises in the northeast, would've tried to impose their hegemony on *all places that weren't industrialized*, since industrialization was the politicoeconomic system those elites supported/were supported by financially. Moreover, this economic system in particular could work pretty much anywhere, and typically had the greatest, most surefire financial payoff in locales of new growth. The Southern, plantation-based agricultural economy had a far more limited scope (and would likely take longer to set up in virgin territory). Significantly, though, many of the areas conquered by the U.S. in the war against Mexico fit within that far more limited scope; and California was indisputably the top conquest lusted after by the most *Powerful* factions from the North as well as the South.

Because the most *Powerful* factions from the South no longer represented a much greater capacity for wealth-production, whether actual or monetary, than the most *Powerful* Northern factions, there was no longer justification for the Southern factions to hold much greater *Power* in running the U.S. Government; whereas in the preceding phase the Southern state of Virginia, for instance, once held by far the bulk of the nation's wealthiest/most *Powerful* men. If the South had been able to exercise real control over the U.S. Government in 1861, the Southern states wouldn't have had to secede: since they had little real control of it anymore, the most *Powerful*, slave-holding factions from the South naturally decided to leave the Union and start their own Government, i.e., their own State. Hypothetically, if it had existed for longer than a few years, this State wouldn't necessarily have become a strong, singularly centralized apparatus in exactly the same way as "the Union" eventually would. Most likely, it would've been comprised of *many*, smaller centralized apparatuses – late modern editions of *locally* State-ruled polities – all held together within a loose confederation, somewhat akin to what we described before in relation to the medieval European institution of lordship. However, the "updated" Southern version would've likely had a strong federal police presence.[ccli] As we've said, the locally State-ruled polity is necessarily the most overtly violent stage in State-formation, because it places the oppressor and the victim in the closest daily proximity. Indeed, at its essence, the Southern institution of slavery was practically indistinguishable from the institution of lordship – except for the quite significant fact that in the later context, slaves were explicitly considered the *purchased property* – the "Objects" – of the slaveowners.

So the *Powerful* Southern factions seceded and made their own State; to reiterate, their primary goal in mind was to impose the Southern-style politicoeconomic system on the Western states. In this way, the interstate competition represented by "North versus South" in the U.S. Civil War has given us just about the most ideal possible case study for analyzing what particular direction the most successful international Powers were heading in by the second half of the 19th-century. Subsequent U.S. history reveals that the war's final result was a sociohistorical index pointing unequivocally to what direction such top international Powers ultimately selected, at the expense of all others. I've already been implying what direction the State ultimately decided upon for the nation, all throughout this subsection. The U.S. State, by crushing the Confederate State's attempt to form – in other words, by using "might" – consolidated its ultimate "right" to administer the laws of the entire nation, representing the original major *formal* consolidation of *Power* for the northeast banker/industrial elite in the United States, the collection of factions that, in one form or another, has more or less ruled the world ever since.

This isn't an ideal case study solely in that one sense; more generally, it's an ideal case study for illustrating how the very same processes that originally build State-ruled polities *"internally"* become responsible for driving those States' *Power*-consolidation activities *"externally"*. In fact, the U.S. would repeat essentially the same State-building process that it underwent internally during the Civil War three subsequent times. The main difference was that, these latter three times, the process would reach wholly outside the nation's "domestic" bounds.

There was World War I, the aftermath of which allowed the U.S. and Britain, for the first time, to take up their increasingly formal roles as international mediators. Then, of course, came World War II, the event-cluster-sequence directly responsible for molding the sixth period. World War II saw as its final outcome the U.S. State's taking politicoeconomic control over the entire "First World". Finally, there was the end of the Cold War, which directly catalyzed the beginnings of the current, seventh period, wherein the U.S. State has taken for itself the job of "lone remaining superpower", "forced" to spend all of its energy "combating" "Terrorists" and "Drug Lords".

In each of these three cases, something of a civil war occurred, only on a much larger, much more comprehensive scale than that entailed by a conflict within a single nation, getting both larger and more comprehensive with each subsequent war. World War I represented a civil war between the Western Powers (including the U.S.) for control of the European Empires; World War II represented a civil war started by the Western Powers for control of the burgeoning global system; and the Cold War (World War III) represented (heavy emphasis on represented) a civil war between everyone on Earth, with everyone compelled to divide themselves into two predominate "ideological blocs" aiming for control of the entire planet. Just like in the U.S. Civil War, in all three cases, the victorious side – which always turned out to be the U.S. State, run predominately by a New York-London/Washington financial-energy-political axis, also just like in the U.S. Civil War – gained the "right", through victory in matters of "might", to make and administer law, or devise, implement, and enforce public policy, for the losing side. The only circumstances that differed from case to case had to do with how wide a geopolitical scope the Anglo-American State and its allies gained dominion over. But the rules that always bind together international war and international law – at least in the Western experience, which as we've said many times, yielded the contemporary interstate system – never change: and these rules always emanate from and are paralleled by the "domestic" rules of State-building, which forge the individual members of interstate systems – States – in the first place. At its core, *might always establishes right*, and in the end the two are always completely indistinguishable, in this type of (State-run) system. It's thus fundamentally illustrated that States have only one underlying purpose, and this is revealed most clearly when we look at moments of State-formation, wherein humans make war, and war makes States. And then States make more war – which keeps the States in business.[cclii] Oppenheimer's definition always holds true:

The winners always make the losers their slaves.

Of course, such slavery almost never happens as explicitly as it did in extreme cases like the United States' "Old South". And I believe this primarily explains why the South's system was fated for failure from the very beginning, within a contemporary context: the Southern system was wholly dependent on *Power*-relations that were far too explicitly oppressive. We can see this most vividly if we try to imagine the transposition of explicit slavery to the setting of the late 19th-century United States: if this *had* been attempted in an industrial setting, it would've failed. What I mean is, if someone in the U.S. at the end of the 19th-century had attempted to establish relationships between "bosses and laborers" that were culturally identical to the relationships between "Masters and Slaves", in the specific sense that bosses literally purchased the laborers' persons and then did essentially whatever they wanted with them, the capitalist who attempted to do that would fail as a businessman.

I believe this is true for many significant reasons; here I'll mention only the three that I consider most important. First of all, most simply and crudely: for the precise reason that we mentioned earlier, slaves had become extraordinarily expensive when compared to industrial wage-laborers – human beings operating metal machines powered by fossil fuels produce exponentially more labor per dollar than human beings using only their own muscle-powered energy. Certainly, this is only true because of how artificially low have been the prices assigned to these resources through the industrial capitalist system; but the prices have always been artificially low, so this has always been true.

Therefore, no one employing slave labor alone could've successfully competed with any of the big industrial operations that would already be fixtures in the U.S. economy by the end of the 19th-century. At least, no one could've done so on any large-scale basis; and it would've required some such operation for slavery to exist on an industrial level at all, because otherwise whoever owned the slaves would've been better off using them as labor motors for agricultural production. I know it's quite sickening to have to think of a thing like slavery purely in terms of a rigid economic calculus. But one must imagine things in these terms to truly understand the underlying logic of the late modern/ contemporary financial mindset. We can rightly see the monetary price paid by slaveowners for their slaves, then – in the crudest, most materialistic sense – as *the price of outright subjugation*: to oppress human beings so openly in that exact sociohistorical context had become literally (monetarily) far more expensive than the alternative, which was a much "subtler" and thus much more successful form of oppression.

The second reason why explicit slavery was too openly oppressive for a late modern context has to do with a cultural phenomenon, which I believe explains its greater significance: it's immeasurably more difficult for sheer quantitative "rationality" to change at will the historical direction of cultural (ideological) problems, than it is for the same to change politicoeconomic ones. What I'm referring to is the wave of abolitionism that was increasingly animating the Northeast's intellectual elite in the years preceding the Civil War. The reader may object that I've already said abolitionism had little to do with why the North decided to go to war against the South. But – to begin – "why the North went to war" is a different matter from "why slavery would've failed no matter what".

Additionally, I didn't say that abolitionism had little to do with the war; I said that it wasn't one of the politicoeconomic reasons behind the war, and that war itself is always primarily motivated by politicoeconomic factors. But I also said that abolitionism served as the moral justification for the war (this frames "what kind" of cultural phenomenon we're dealing with). In this sense, then, of course we must say that the two phenomena – abolitionism and the Civil War – became inextricably interconnected sociohistorically: however, the notion that they had to become culturally interconnected via contingent historical events already in itself suggests that they weren't literally indistinguishable in the first place.

Going back to what I just mentioned, then, we must recognize that it's far more difficult to impose cultural changes from the top-down than politicoeconomic changes, especially in all eras preceding electronic mass communications. Or rather, it's far more difficult for "the top", in this instance, the U.S. State, to impose any cultural changes that might be beneficial at any given moment. We've already discussed the significance of this in relation to the late 19th-century South: in most ways, in the long run, it wasn't really important that the specific institution of slavery disappeared, because the Southern dominant culture was determined to subjugate blacks no matter what, and soon enough they would find methods allowing them to do just that. If anything, these methods, epitomized by "Jim Crow laws", ended up being more lastingly "successful" – from the standpoint of the dominant whites, that is – because for a long time they allowed the vast majority of white Americans to feel like they had no responsibility whatsoever to empathize with blacks, even though blacks suffered at least as much as they always had under the institution called slavery. The politicoeconomic relationships could only change in superficial ways because the culture hadn't changed at all. In fact, Southern whites now felt even more justified in subjugating blacks, because the former largely blamed the latter for the wholesale destruction wrought upon the South during the Civil War.

In a different way, the same general principle held true in relation to the Northern culture, insofar as it mainly emanated from the northeastern intellectual elite. To put it most bluntly: unlike the old days when the richest Northern merchants traded in Southern slaves, or at least participated in the same trade system overwhelmingly buttressed by the Southern slave trade,[ccliii] there was nowadays absolutely nothing in it for most Northern politicians if they defended slavery, because slavery had long been seen as largely economically unimportant and potentially even detrimental to the Northern social structure. (Inversely, then, when there had been something in it for Northern politicians, they supported slavery.) On the other hand, there was very much to be gained for a great many Northern politicians who supported abolitionists, both overtly – from a moral perspective – and covertly – from a politicoeconomic perspective.

That last sentence is what it all comes down to: the deep interlocking relationship between overt actions and covert motives that exploded in its importance in human governing structures in the 19th-century, across what eventually became the "First World". It was of particular importance in locales where representative government had become the characteristic institution of the State – most notably including the U.S.; and it represents our third reason why slavery was an institution too openly oppressive to succeed in the late modern context. Moreover, it's essentially the culmination of everything we've already seen.

It may seem that I've been both repeating and contradicting myself in the construction of the argument so far. Our last reason, the "culmination", will illustrate clearly why I haven't really been doing either. What I've really been doing is showing how the same overarching issues had simultaneously become crucial points of contention in a multiplicity of areas in the U.S. surrounding the setting of the Civil War: and such a perspective exemplifies how one should view sociohistorical contexts *holistically*, which in turn is the only way one can ultimately understand what truly characterizes particular historical episodes. If the argument has been repetitive in certain of its aspects, this has been necessary in order for us to look at the same event-clusters and sequences from many different angles. One must acknowledge that all singularized historical event-cluster-sequences, such as the Civil War, or massive sociohistorical processes, such as industrialization, affect many different though interconnected spheres of human life at once. At the same time, one can't simply take for granted *how* these events and spheres are interconnected – such facts need to be demonstrated. So what I've been demonstrating, and what I said above specifically in relation to the interface between the Civil War and abolition, is that events and spheres only become interconnected through contingent historical processes. We may think that slavery could've "only" been abolished via a Northern victory in war against the South, and that very well may be true: but it only happened in reality a single time, so above all we must do whatever we can to explain *why* it happened *how* it did. And essentially, from my perspective, the why-how in this case involves factional grand strategies. This is primarily what I've been attempting to explain: wars are, in the first place, *signs of the strategies selected*.

We've been exploring the two broadest, most relevant phenomena for determining why a war would've taken place between the North and the South in the U.S. at the precise time when it did, between 1861 and 1865. These phenomena are: abolitionism and slavery's downfall. Now, the reader may think, rightly, that these are just two sides of the exact same phenomenon. But the truly critical point is that they're only two sides of the same phenomenon because they *became* that way. This is why I've framed the argument as I have, by looking at abolition from a long-term perspective, in the sense of why it was the most probable long-term outcome; and by looking at slavery from a similarly long-term perspective, in the sense of why slavery's failure, also, was the likeliest long-term outcome. Again, this might seem like the exact same thing phrased in two slightly different ways: but the apparent semantic similarity in the end only serves to highlight the real-world discrepancy. For, if the ultimate failure of slavery had happened first, abolitionism would've been rendered a moot point: if everyone knew that slavery had become a failure in an economic sense, as it absolutely had against a background of industrialization, what moral high-ground could be gained, after it had already failed, by utilizing abolitionism as a rhetorical weapon? Such a scenario – the failure of slavery prior to any success of abolitionism – could've even meant the possible collapse of the whole U.S. State as it existed at the time, instead of "just" that State's monumental transformation.

And at the same time: if slavery's value to the national economy hadn't been plummeting, would abolitionism as a cultural phenomenon really have garnered so much elite support? Indeed, we know it almost certainly wouldn't have, insofar as, in the wake of emancipation, two much more politicoeconomically viable, equally oppressive institutions – sharecropping and the criminalization of blacks towards the end of coercing them into carceral labor – emerged to replace slavery essentially immediately. After that, Northern whites would, for almost 100 years, barely have any interest in white atrocities against blacks, which if anything only proliferated more pervasively in the entire span between post-Reconstruction and Civil Rights.

Here's our key to understanding the relationship between overt actions and covert motives relative to the modern elected officials of representative governments: no matter what their rhetoric says, the elected politicians with "staying power" can only do what *Powerful* interests allow them to do. Notice I didn't say that *all* elected politicians can only do what *Powerful* interests allow them to do. But – in the United States, at least – those politicians who adhere to select *Powerful* interests are almost invariably the only ones allowed repeated incumbency, and are absolutely the only ones allowed to rise to entrenched national prominence. In an American context this most notably describes, each to its own particular extent, the President, the politicians at the highest positions in

Congress, the justices of the Supreme Court, and of course the individuals actually running things day-to-day, those atop all the contemporary administrative and military bureaucracies. When/where there are exceptions, they still serve the same systemic function, providing an illusion of possibility for real dissent within the system's constraints.

Now, by the same necessity, the popular conceptions held by most individuals living in those State-ruled polities that have long been characterized by representative governments – again, referring most namely to the United States, but it's true to differing degrees everywhere else in the "First World" – are quite at odds with what I've just divulged in the above paragraph. Herein lies our primary explanation as to why the politicians comprising such governments must go to so much trouble to synchronize overt actions with covert motives: as a matter of course, the politicians' overt actions are undertaken for completely different reasons than what those actions "say" in public. Such "different reasons" are what we're referring to here as covert motives, and there also exist certain overt motives that are basically in line with the politicians' overt actions: for instance, the crasser motivations of "Party", which are deemed more or less acceptable to the extent that they're seen as the necessary evils required so the politician can stick around and do "the really important things". These overt motives help hide the politicians' covert ones – from the public and often, I imagine, from themselves.

That is, the system operates in such a way that it's not necessary for a politician to frequently think in terms of, "I'm serving such-and-such *Powerful* interest and lying to the public to do so." Rather, I believe it's necessary for a politician to almost never think such things, for the sake of his or her own mental well-being (unless that politician happens to be a true psycho- or sociopath, which is certainly an occasional possibility). Those kinds of thoughts must be reserved only for their darkest moments of inner turmoil, if ever. Just as politicians supported slavery so long as it was (1) economically dominant and (2) they could somehow convincingly justify it to themselves morally, politicians could only decisively turn against it once it was both (1) economically weak and (2) seen as overwhelmingly morally unjustifiable by the relevant constituencies. An elegantly simple point-of-comparison: in the years immediately preceding the Civil War, those states most economically dependent on slavery were also home to the ideological factions supporting it most virulently – and these proslavery factions displayed that virulent support precisely in their uniquely disturbing attempts to come up with intellectual bases for their position. Collectively, such attempts at imbuing black slavery with moral decency acted as one of the greatest catalysts in U.S. history for what's most typically known as 'racism'. If this theory seems too crudely obvious to be accurate, at the time directly preceding the Civil War, the states in between the North and the "deep" South – the so-called "border South" states – had an economic dependence on slavery at a level somewhere in between the practically non-existent dependence of the North and the absolute dependence of the cotton-growing states in the deep South. True to our simple (but for that, no less useful) theory, politicians from these border states were as a group almost perfectly divided between those for and those against slavery. [ccliv]

The reason for all of this was money; specifically, the money that a *Powerful* entity brings in on account of its position in the international market. Long before the Civil War – and mainly before the 19th-century – the most *Powerful* Southern factions had been in a clear position of dominance over the most *Powerful* Northern factions, because the significance of (what became) the United States to the international market was overwhelmingly centered upon its cash crop industry. Cash crops were Southern domain.

About the beginning of the 19th-century – the interperiodic break between periods four and five – this all started to change; it would only change evermore rapidly throughout the 1800s. Cash crops were still Southern domain. But now, something else was primarily driving the United States' role in the international market: industrial manufacturing, pure Northern territory. However, the most important manufactures of all, at first, were textiles, so this meant there was still a role for the South – and a momentarily increased role for slavery, since the main raw material used in textile manufactures was cotton. Cotton was grown and harvested by what, in the early-to-middle 19th-century, had only recently (yet rapidly) become the states that were by far the most dependent of all on slavery. Again, these were the seven deep South states: South Carolina, Georgia, Florida, Alabama, Mississippi, Louisiana, and Texas.[cclv]

Yet, at that very same time when slaves had come to comprise more than half of the populations in these states, there had also started to emerge enormous new manufacturing projects emanating from the northeast: projects that didn't really require cooperation with the South, at all – at least, so long as the factions traditionally aligned with the South could no loner exercise the greatest control over U.S. government. Most notably, those projects included steamships and railroads, and I consider railroads especially significant in this context. The scale of railroad-building was so unprecedented that, essentially for the first time, capitalists were faced with manufacturing and logistical challenges that couldn't possibly be met successfully by any single investor or company, or even any small group of individuals and companies. The project of building the first railroads in the United States required many large groups of investors and companies working within endlessly complex frameworks of cooperation, on levels both national and *inter*national. Although the U.S. economy in the early-to-mid 19th-century had been growing unto heights never before possible, there wasn't enough ready capital in the entire country to service something so vast.[cclvi]

The burgeoning industrial capitalists in the United States turned to Europe. It was an easy choice, because the northeastern elite had already been working for years with bankers from the big European cities, especially London and Paris, before the Revolution. It's probably even more accurate to say, the international bankers in Europe turned to the burgeoning industrial capitalists in the United States. After all, as I've said, industrialization was a fact of existence at a far earlier time in England than anywhere else. And after having grown up for about a century by the time of our focus – the phase starting around 1830, continuing through the Civil War – industrialization was no longer a solely English phenomenon, but had spread to other parts of the West, in the same exact way that Europe's capitalist system had never remained a solely Italian phenomenon, after it began there in its primordial (protocapitalist) phase. Throughout a process continuing long after "Independence", the United States has always been a haven for foreign capital, echoing precisely the manner in which England, and most especially the City of London, had become a haven for all of Europe's foreign capital*ists* in the preceding period.

Despite this plethora of capitalists from all over Europe that hit yet another unparalleled jackpot when they started their industrial (re)colonization of the United States via the nation's northeast corridor, the dominant culture in the United States would nevertheless remain one of English origins, as it had been since about the middle stages of American colonialism (before the territory became the United States): in other words, the Northern elites were "Anglophiles". So were the Southern elites, no doubt, just in a slightly different way. To put it simply, they were more like English lords, whereas Northerners were more like English merchants. For the most part, the coexistence of these two cultural strains had actually worked out quite well in the years leading up to the Revolution, and indeed for a few decades after it. For quite some time before the American War of Independence (a.k.a., the "Revolutionary War"), the most successful Southern "lords" were those who were also merchants, which was a much more natural fit than one might initially suppose, given that the primary commodities grown on their slave-worked estates were cash crops.[cclvii] These Southern merchant-lords not only became the wealthiest individuals in the nation during the 18th-century, but, because of that, they also naturally became the most *Powerful*. An overwhelming proportion of the top leadership for the "Revolutionary" factions in the War of Independence – the "Founding Fathers" – were some of those very same merchant-lords, originating especially from the state of Virginia. This of course led to the emergence of four of the first five U.S. Presidents, including George Washington (the first) and Thomas Jefferson (the third), spanning from 1789 to 1825, out of this merchant-lord milieu. (Incidentally, this is also a perfect example supporting my claim that politicians are fundamentally constrained, foremost, by what their *Powerful* factions allow them to do.)

The *modus operandi* between merchants and merchant-lords started to deteriorate when the merchant elite in the Northeast became a mainly merchant *banking* elite, a trend greatly catalyzed by the beginning of U.S. industrialization, i.e., the era we're now discussing. To make things less confusing when talking about merchants and merchant bankers, we'll use the more usual name they're given in the contemporary United States, investment bankers.

(I feel compelled to make a side note here: it's well known that certain actors within the investment banking community, which is by nature an *international* field of "employment", comprise what seems to be one of the main elements responsible for the great crime against humanity known as "the financial crisis of 2008". Since the financial crisis was at least culturally centered around New York City, I think it's useful to point out here that the investment banking elites we're now concerned with relative to the few decades before the Civil War were the U.S.'s earliest modern antecedents of those criminals. This is perhaps the most crucial factor contributing to the long-term sociohistorical significance of the circumstances I'm outlining in this section.)

Although merchants and bankers must cooperate, if only for the purposes of regular business, the two groups ultimately have contradictory interests. Here's why: *interest*, as in, how bankers make their money: the interest rate, which comes directly out of the merchant-lords' profits.[cclviii] Now, it's not as if merchants or even bankers always think of things in such starkly zero-sum terms. But speaking of the merchants and bankers we're presently focused on – those operating in the late-18th and 19th-century United States – the most *Powerful* among them certainly did. Quite naturally, I might add – the most *Powerful* individuals are always those most acutely aware of why and how they've become so *Powerful*, which quite prominently includes an awareness of what it is that interferes with their *Power*.

Thomas Jefferson, for instance, good political writer and great friend to slave-worked estates, and Alexander Hamilton, idol to all subsequent financial oligarchs, engaged in one of U.S. history's most famous political conflicts mainly on account of this singular issue. Jefferson, representing the merchant-lords, was willing to fight to the death against the implementation of a U.S. central bank (although it was Aaron Burr, not Jefferson, who ultimately killed Hamilton in a duel). Hamilton, representing the investment bankers, seemed to think that instituting a central bank was the whole reason the colonies had fought for their "Independence" in the first place. Hamilton won out in the short-term, although somewhat later the appalling Andrew Jackson, one of the worst scourges on American Indians since the *conquistadores*, succeeded in letting the central bank expire, a task that took up practically all of his time not spent on the gleeful perpetuation of genocide. The end of Jackson's two-term presidency brings us to 1837, or about 25 years before the start of the Civil War. It was around this time when things really started heating up on the U.S. politicoeconomic stage.

Before we go further, I should point out that it's easy to understand why the conflict between merchants and bankers intensified so ferociously when the merchandise in question was cash crops. The clashing interests setting merchants and bankers against each other on account of the latter's profit-by-monetary-debt – usury – becomes most pronounced in situations where the merchant deals in those products that are most highly variable products in terms of supply and demand. This stems from the simple reason that "payday" might never come for the merchant, but the banker *always* expects and demands his profit. Keeping this in mind, there weren't many kinds of systemically-vital products more vulnerable to supply-and-demand fluctuations at the time than agricultural commodities (obviously including cash crops), insofar as these items are most directly dependent upon natural processes. The only other "product" I can think of that would've been in the same league: slaves.

Although the Southern estate-owners weren't "true" nobles, nonetheless, the Southern elite's direct sociohistorical antecedent was the landed gentry of early modern Western, and in particular English, origins.[cclix] Especially in a properly cultural (ideological) sense, we can treat both sectors as parts of the very same lineage. In this vein, racking up enormous quantities of debt has forever been in the nature of the Western aristocratic lifestyle. This may sound strange because we're used to thinking of aristocrats as being so excessively wealthy. It's true that the aristocracy was (until industrialization) the wealthiest *caste*; however, even within the aristocracy, wealth was always disproportionately concentrated: a pyramid within the apex of the pyramid. Additionally, even many of the wealthiest fell into ruin intermittently and had to maul their way out of the "bottom" if they were to have any hope of regaining what they'd lost. What caused this, mainly, was the fact that the aristocratic lifestyle required so much constant wealth just to be maintained; and it *had* to be maintained, for as soon as it wasn't, one would at that moment cease to be truly noble.[cclx] Status may not be everything for all human beings, but it's indisputably everything for all elites, with the gentry of distinctly English origins being perhaps the quintessential modern example.

Moreover, as noted, the gentry, by definition the landed caste, was invariably dependent primarily upon agricultural production for its actual wealth. Therefore, in this sense too, the Southerners weren't different from their European ancestors, but rather were merely invested in a different type of products, which type happened to directly intertwine their interests, on the international politicoeconomic stage, with those of the mercantile factions. To reiterate what I pointed out above, this meant that while the nobility was absolutely dependent on a constant stream of wealth, at the same time, not every noble could realistically expect that his agricultural holdings would always "pay off" sufficiently due to the extreme supply-and-demand fluctuations associated with agricultural products when these constitute monetarily-priced commodities. This goes a long way towards explaining why the nobles were also traditionally the premier warmaking caste: when your livestock had a rough year or your social subordinates had an unexpectedly weak harvest, there were few remedies better suited for providing quick wealth subsidies than making war on someone who had what you wanted.[cclxi] Of course, the nobles who remained steadily wealthy knew this just as well, and so they were perennially concerned with building evermore-capable systems of security.

Once a security complex is built in the first place – that is, once the estate-owner has had to invest in warfare to some substantial extent – no matter what the original purpose was, the estate-owner's urge to use his military *Power* purely for additional gain, rather than simply to protect what he already has, seems to be practically irresistible. If he possesses merchant allies, and the most *Powerful* nobles always do (if they're not in fact also merchants themselves), this strategy becomes equally irresistible for the merchants: nothing has a higher potential payoff for traders than a good war. The interests in making war hence "naturally" combine, and each interest is the better off for it.

So already, long before they were ever an established fact in the United States, we see that there had been, built into the lineage of Southern elites, a distinct, endlessly sharpened complex of mutually reinforcing technological capabilities – communications, i.e., the particular ideological culture the gentry brought with it, embodied in the interlocking religious and educational institutions; life-support, represented by the gentry's coercion-based agricultural labor system; and military, highlighted by the gentry's initial necessity for and, consequently, eventual ever-increasing profit-seeking in organizing for war. For the most *Powerful* Southern elites, like those symbolized by the "Founding Fathers" and the slightly later beneficiaries of the "Cotton Kingdom", this holistic technological complex had translated into so much success so quickly in the "New World" that the gentry must've viewed its reign over the U.S. Government more or less as eternal. Yet the whole situation would start to change during the thirty-or-so years leading up to the Civil War.

That change was first precipitated most dramatically by the panic of 1837, a year that also marked the end of Andrew Jackson's presidency. Besides the sectors that see the greatest negative impact in all financial crises and the recessions/depressions resultant from them – the vast majority of human beings living under financialized regimes, and the totality of those who are most oppressed (whom also always have the least personal responsibility for said crises) – the biggest losers, among the elite in particular, were mainly individuals investing in land, cotton, or slaves. As might be expected, the most negatively affected of all were individuals invested in all three: namely, the gentry in the deep South, the milieu that would serve as the immediate catalyst, at the end of 1860 and the beginning of 1861, for the secession from the U.S. by the majority of the Southern states, starting with South Carolina. In all, seven Southern states would join to form the Confederate States of America, the collective action, of course, that most overtly triggered the Civil War.

The decline in social standing owing to such a spectacular loss of wealth must've been especially humiliating for all the Southern elites that experienced it, and in particular those who were in early adulthood at the time. Again, I emphasize that the blow had much less to do with wealth itself than it had to do with status. For the landed gentry, wealth was only useful insofar as it was a means to such status; with enough accumulated status, wealth will basically take care of itself. In the decade following the panic of 1837, then, there were lots of individuals who weren't yet wealthy, but wanted to be – and culturally, *needed* to be – wealthy more desperately than anything, because they were, as yet, individuals with no status, living in one of the most status-dependent regional cultures in history.

Few splinters of humanity bode more dangerously for the whole than one most urgently desiring to rise in the midst of an economic depression.

I'm not even referring here to the Civil War itself, but rather to the preceding major military conflict, which itself would lead to the exact circumstances wherein the Civil War became inevitable: as I said earlier, the Mexican-American War. The relationship between these two episodes is an excellent illustration of the phenomenon whereby every war practically ensures another one in the future, which also means, from the inverse perspective, that every war is essentially caused by the ones in its past. In this sense, ever since the earliest origins of civilizations and States, the long historical process has been just one autocatalytic cycle of inter- and intrastate warfare. Again, history isn't "reducible" one such cycle: but in State-ruled polities, all other history revolves around it, just like the State revolves around (and is simultaneously revolved around by) the civilizational and intercivilizational structures based mainly on trade. Herein we find the ultimate real-world significance of the three interlocking technologies – communications, life-support, and military.

Throughout the reciprocal evolution and change characterizing sociohistorical processes both long and short, the combined intercivilizational/interstate system has turned out to be nothing besides one long, endlessly bloody competition between elite factions for control over the greatest share of human wealth. The overarching strategies pursued by elite factions who dominate civilization-State-complexes are revealed via the central histories of the systems they create and manage: and the history of a civilization-State-complex is always primarily defined by mutually-profitable ideological alignments between the most *Powerful* interests involved in any such culture's communications, life-support, and military subsystems. Participation between factional groupings in the war-trade competition has been *the* essential organizing principle[cclxii] for this type of cultural entity, with the rules of competition, in the end, invariably rewarding whatever group most successfully consolidates in one holistic "package" its culture's ability to cultivate, maintain, and expand systems of wealth-production. A group accomplishes success in this field insofar as its own particular total social structure is better at controlling resources than other groups' total social structures: it can control more resources, more quickly. Putting everything in this paragraph together, a group's success, specifically in the sense just mentioned, is determined by the group's *grand strategy* relative to competing groups' grand strategies.

Thus we see precisely why the technological behavior of communications, life-support, and military spheres can't be separated *in practice*; they can only be *analytically* distinguished. Earlier, we saw why we can't separate the three spheres in terms of precivilizational and the earliest civilizational human cultural environments; now we see the same is true of all the modern civilization-State-complexes that have descended from those originary worlds – the only difference being that the modern ones constituted far more complex arenas. Above all else, they can't be separated because they're all mutually reinforcing means that, at their most significant levels *within* the context of a whole system, work towards the same overarching purpose – exercising control over resources (military), in order to extract and employ them (life-support), towards the end of perpetuating an ideological culture (communications).

To take as an example the U.S. Civil War-era war-trade competition, there's a definite sense in which the rifle played just as large a role in the ability of the *Powerful* to wield control over communications and food systems, as it did in their ability to wield control over the military system. Certainly, insofar as the industrially-produced rifle was one of the most characteristic artifacts contributing to the activities of the relevant armed force organizations, it primarily represented military technology. But of course *military technologies* are in reality nothing besides the State's primary means of gaining and consolidating political *Power*, just as the *communications technologies* (administrative organization, for instance) that shape the governing system are nothing besides the civilization's primary means of consolidating the *Power* inherent in controlling the *life-support technologies*, which latter, in turn, primarily shape the economic system. Indeed, in reality, since all of these technological systems constitute amongst themselves *sub*systems in their constant structural interchange, creating between them one complex system based upon perpetual (until the system collapses) feedback loops, it works the other ways around, as well. That is, a reliable increase in economic *Power* also can and does become the prerequisite for further communications and/or military *Power*, and so forth, with all the conceivable variations being possibilities. Which particular combination exists in the relationship between the three sub-strategies varies depending on the specific case one considers. In other words, within one system, *any* tool can potentially become a means of communication, life-support, or military technology – or all three – depending on how the strategist chooses to employ the tool.

It may be easier to comprehend this phenomenon, at first, on an individual-to-individual scale. Most relevantly, we can imagine a typical case of armed robbery. The thief accosts his or her victim, presents a gun, and informs the victim what it is that he or she wants. Already, we have interlocking military and communications technologies. The gun represents to the victim the pure potential for gainful violence (military), but the words (communications) represent the victim's potential to avoid that violence by giving the thief what he or she demands. Now, concerning the world as it has been since handguns have existed, specifically in such a "conveniently" purchasable way that a common thief might own one – what is it that the thief demands? Almost invariably, the thief demands cash; but even if it's not cash, the thief will still most certainly demand something that can be exchanged for cash relatively quickly, such as jewelry. But cash is best because it's the easiest method for assuring that there are "no questions asked" when the thief exchanges his or her "take" for actual wealth.

As we've frequently seen, 'actual wealth' is at its roots only based on stored-energy – the most significant example of which is food – and that's why I refer to the totality of methods explicitly related to obtaining stored-energy as *life-support* technologies. If one couldn't exchange cash for stored-energy, then the cash would have no actual value. To phrase the identical concept from the inverse perspective, cash (and money in general) has value *only insofar as one can exchange it for stored-energy*. Thus, one's gun and one's words become indistinguishable from one another in the act of theft, so that both are simultaneously military and communications tools. And the thief gains the victim's stored-energy, so both in turn also become life-support tools, because this is how the thief has chosen to use the gun and the words; that is, this is the overarching *strategy* that the thief has pursued. Strategy is that level of consciousness where all kinds of tools can become interchangeable.

The war-trade system is defined by the exact same phenomenon: the essential differences only lie in the fact that the war-trade system on the one hand, and individual armed robbery on the other, represent respectively the largest and smallest conceivable examples of the single form of structural dynamic. The corollary to "largest and smallest" here is "most complex and simplest". (The individual and the intercivilizational structure are extremes on a single continuum of cultural complexity.) Throughout known human history, the most broadly encompassing and thus most generally consequential trend in human social structures has been a tendency for growth in human population and growth in the complexity of social structures to reciprocally, positively affect one another. In other words: as the one increases, so does the other. But make sure to pay close attention to the word *"reciprocally"*, because it seems to me to be far off the mark to say that one of them in particular is always the cause, the other always the effect. I believe rather that the relationship between the two forms of growth seems to be yet another example of autocatalysis, and as such, it's much better to view the process as one phenomenon – 'growth' – composed of two inextricable parts.

We can see this most clearly in the two most dramatic eras of human population growth in history. These are the two eras that have been our primary focus in part 2: the era of the original agricultural settlements of all kinds, from isolated settlements to civilizations, and the era since the beginnings of industrialization. Not coincidentally, the two eras also saw history's greatest increases in social structural complexity, during the span from immediately before each one until the end. This is of the utmost significance to our underlying theme in this stage of our journey, organized violence, because the reciprocal growth originates from nowhere else but the evolution of the war-trade system.

The character of such growth has everything to do with what we said earlier in relation to explicit slavery: as its prevalence grows, the cultural pyramid – being a pyramid – doesn't expand equally at every level, in an absolute sense. For every additional individual at the top of the pyramid, the system needs ten more (obviously not an exact quantification) individuals at the bottom. And, also since it's a pyramid, the same pattern repeats itself between the very top and the very bottom, but of course in increasingly less extreme ways as you move towards the middle from each end. So the system has the most individuals in the "Middle Class" as a whole, with much fewer individuals in the "Upper Middle Class", obviously, than in the "Lower Middle Class". The point is that there has indeed always been something akin to a "Middle Class" in every civilization-State-complex, but it only ever emerges historically long after the initiating actions that catalyze the social structure upon which the culture is dependent in the first place. These initiating actions are epitomized by the originary state/State of outright robbery: what, owing mainly to Oppenheimer and the archaeologists, we described in the preceding section through the example of the primordial Statemakers, the originary herder-conquerors and farmer-priests who first catalyzed civilization-State-complexes in southwest Asia/northeast Africa/southeast Europe. The same fundamental process happened again, in a new environment, with the emergence of monarchs/merchants/ministers that would ultimately catalyze the early modern European

Empires at the start of the fourth period; and once more with the Northern/Southern factions in the United States, which did so much to anticipate the transition from the fifth to the sixth period. Finally, looking ahead, the general pattern is illustrated just as vividly, albeit cloaked in infinite "Information", by the origins of the sixth and seventh.

Every period is essentially a new phase of intercivilizational (or a similarly broad contextual form) growth characterized by interconnecting higher social complexity and increased population levels in the relevant locales – new stages completely driven by evermore-expansive systems of organized violence seeking ever-greater quantities of wealth. From the early modern world through the contemporary world, the pyramid expanded from its premodern origins in medieval Europe to affect:

- First, whole populations – the indigenous Americans, the humans stolen from Africa and forced into slavery, and the vast majority of other individuals in every other place where European imperialism spread;

- Second, whole continents – the internal spread of the *late modern* European version of the war-trade competition in the fifth period, the circumstances most responsible for the creation of the contemporary international system;

- Third, and finally, the whole planet – the *intensive* growth in the sixth and seventh periods of the system's *extensive* growth in the fourth and fifth periods.

Thus, as the "top of the pyramid" came to be represented by essentially an entire dominant culture, the "bottom of the pyramid", and the "dirt beneath the pyramid" came to be represented by essentially everyone else – and every*thing* else – that existed. This is the precise sociohistorical context of Hell. It's the result of the same thing that always eventually leads civilizations to reveal themselves as having been dead ends from the start. Ultimately, no one ever deliberately creates them and keeps them going but elites, who do so, implicitly and explicitly, with no other method besides the utilization of organized violence towards extracting the greatest share of wealth, which essentially means the greatest ability, at any given moment, to destroy the most resources: i.e., to distribute the most goods for "consumption".[cclxiii] With there always being a finite quantity of resources available at any given time, at some point a system that trends towards ever-expanding use of resources *must* run out of things to destroy.

Part 3:

Pathology; or, the Cataclysmic Path

BOOK ONE – **The Devil is in the Details:** A Brief History of the Introduction of Globalization

Given enough time and energy, everything unconscious has the potential to become conscious. Considering all the energy and time humanity devoted to building *Power*-structures for the entire history of civilizations until about 116 years ago, the Great Power game as it existed in the year humans call 1898 AD/CE should come as no surprise. Yet the way the game had steadily evolved from 1493, when Columbus returned to Spain, unto its form two years before the official turn of the 20th-century, when the U.S. State finally launched its overseas Empire and hence officially became a competing Great Power, is still impressive to contemplate even in retrospect, at this point in the 21st. By 1898, the game was already so consciously realized, and had gone through a century of such rapid expansion, that it's astonishing there could be another era of unprecedented growth coming any time soon for the Great Powers. But the great *Power*-structure not only continued to grow beyond its state at the beginning of contemporary history: it grew so exponentially in its size and (relatedly) complexity, soon enough the planet Earth would only be able to support a single politicoeconomic system.[cclxiv]

By the end of the 20th-century, there was a long-since-established, singular civilization – a single *intercity war-trade environment* – connecting every city on Earth in a unitary network of production and distribution relations. There was a globally singularizing communications technology, which made it at least theoretically possible for a single planetary "community" to emerge. And, most necessary of all to the system as a whole, a single military actor held it all in place; it kept things "orderly". Thus, in other words, in addition to the one intercity system there was essentially one central *State*, managing the most important "public" affairs.[cclxv]

Control over the means of mass organized violence was so thoroughly monopolized by the 1990s that it would be possible to deny the emergence of practically any conceivable threat with potential for challenging the singular Power. Among everything else, the nation's dedication to maintaining its weapons systems was displayed foremost via its military budget, which ate up the majority of the discretionary budget of the wealthiest government in history, and represented a sum greater than the military budgets of the next dozen or so countries combined. Those ostensibly running the Power's governmental apparatus recognized its unparalleled superiority in the military realm, in turn referring to the State as the "last remaining superpower" or the "lone indispensable nation". These descriptions were true enough, regarding the context of the Great Power game. But then, they also begged the question: why did the United States of America still have to be so totally mobilized for war when there was no military left that could compete with it, in the first place?

The explosive turning point of the War of 1898, representing the U.S.'s tacit declaration of its own Great Power status, has rarely been seen in its proper light. For the most part, scholars either say it was the beginning of the United States' history as "an Empire", which is completely wrong; or they rightly recognize that the U.S. has always been fundamentally imperial, yet then proceed to wrongly view 1898 as "merely" the beginning of U.S. overseas expansion. (The beginning of overseas expansion is a singularly significant thing from a Great Power perspective, though 1898 also wasn't really the beginning of U.S. overseas expansion, just the beginning of U.S. overseas *colonization*.[cclxvi]) Somewhat idiosyncratically, I think we need to view it not as a process of transformation from continental to overseas, or from national to international, but instead as a transformation from unconscious to conscious. Also, more concretely, we can't view it as a transformation effected by some purely American entity; rather, we have to view it primarily as the product of a supranational capitalist ruling class, which instrumentalizes the American hegemony over the global civilization as its greatest means of maintaining *Power* and thus, systemic order. In fact, these two assertions, one abstract and one concrete, one theoretical and one practical, are simply coequal counterparts of the exact same phenomenon. The phenomenon is a certain ever-present[*] human sector's desire to act as the supreme god-upon-Earth.[cclxvii] The main premise behind this narrative is that, in the contemporary world, the sector finally came closer than anything ever has or ever will to realizing that dream, with the results being best summed up with the phrase "history's greatest tragedy". Whatever supranational class it is controlling globalization's politicoeconomic affairs represents the conquest syndrome's managers' last greatest failed attempt at playing God.

What is this sector? To what extent is it organized? I can't say, exactly; but then that's its point: it's not supposed to be known by the public. However, this in itself doesn't necessarily rule out proving the sector's existence. Information explicitly concerning the sector's individuated existence is far less important to a discussion of it than the vast totality of information that, when every available bit is combined, points only in one general direction. This body-of-evidence points to the existence of an unofficial, centrally determinative ruling class, which, precisely because of its unofficial nature, has attained such an outrageously disproportionate share of global *Power* as to often appear to have reached all-supreme-deity status. Yet in the end, what exactly constitutes the postulated class's unparalleled *Power* only reveals how far from godliness it truly is.

What information do we have, making "its" existence almost certain, because such an existence appears so logically necessary? First of all, let's try and describe its broadest outlines.[cclxviii] It must literally be the apex of the apex of the global *Power* pyramid, which latter phenomenon can only be looked at, at this point in history – for the first time ever – as a unitary cultural pyramid for the entire planet. We know there's only one because the cultural pyramid is the central "internal" structure of every civilization, and since the sixth period's inception, there has been just one civilization on the entire planet.[*] "Externally", the global pyramid is manifested on its largest scale in the form of the visible *Power*-structure, insofar as the global civilization is organized imperially into

---

[*] In one form or another.
[*] See the next section.

an absolutely rigid hierarchy of "nations", with what we can still basically call the "First World" nations at the top, the most favored vassal nations of the "First World" nations immediately below, etc. The pyramid continues until one reaches the base and immediately underneath the base: the global working poor and then the people who simply don't exist, from the perspective of the system. These latter sectors, of course, are by far the numerically greatest populations on the planet, but they're allowed no input at all concerning the workings of the system, even though almost all the world's nations are nominally "Democracies".

As we've seen, the *Power* of a State, however enormous it might be, doesn't exist primarily on its own account but rather is created and largely gets perpetuated in order to serve "private" interests, embodied at their highest levels of *Power* by elite factions. Here, I assert that the larger the State, the smaller must be the proportion of the hegemonic sector relative to the size of the State's subordinate polity as a whole. A State-ruled polity needs to be orderly to grow, as well as, particularly, to *maintain* its existing level of growth, and can't be orderly unless its actions are tightly regimented: the larger and more complex the polity the tighter the necessary control.

The global *Power*-structure, materialized in the existent world as the core of one global civilization-State-complex, controls the largest population of any "polity" (really, the entire planet) in history. But considered the State itself still doesn't (and can't) have "final say" when it comes to its own actions. These actions can in their most controlled aspects only be effected by a global ruling class, components of which *must* periodically come together, in the appearance of informal groups, to make decisions: therefore, at least at its very highest level, this ruling class must be conscious of itself as a (the) supremely *Powerful* actor in the field of human affairs. And indeed, that perception would be correct: nothing else offers even a remotely fair comparison to the full extent of total human *Power*-consolidation on planet Earth existing in the contemporary world, especially in this latest phase, period seven. *The global hegemonic sector must constitute, proportionally, by far the smallest ruling class ever in existence.* It must exercise almost unbelievable influence in the overall field of human affairs. However, the limits to its *Power* are now being revealed, as the ruling class's *Power* can only exist so long as the fundamental resource supplies are sufficient to support its hegemony. As I've said many times, the fundamental resource supplies on Earth are no longer sufficient to indefinitely support the current hegemony.

Obviously, I don't have the same curious and often pitiful fear of what are always derisively called "conspiracy theories", as do most historical scholars (for instance, see the sources utilized in the next few sections). Many commentators who, otherwise, often purport to feel disdain towards the establishment – defining 'the establishment' most broadly as all the individuals who benefit from the politicoeconomic status quo – seem to actually have the greatest disdain of all for individuals like those they call "conspiracy theorists".[cclxix] Such commentators may or may not realize: no matter what the intentions behind shutting off the specific avenues might be, it's the status quo that always benefits most from blindly cutting off avenues of thought. To completely deny the possibility that conspiratorial behavior is a significant factor shaping the contemporary politicoeconomic system reflects the arbitrary whims of automatically responsive ideological preference, *not* a true understanding of historical process. In fact, until very recently in the contemporary world, conspiracy was a quite conventionally accepted aspect of history, and especially Western history.[cclxx]

However, while I recognize the deep significance of conspiratorial behavior to human governing systems, I also don't think it would be totally accurate to consider every example of such behavior to be part of "a conspiracy", without differentiation. To phrase things as I did in the previous sentence, much or all of the hegemonic sector's behavior might be 'conspiratorial', i.e., characterized by secret planning for committing what are technically illegal, certainly amoral acts. Yet, in the existent world especially, the most significant of such actions will clearly never be prosecuted so long as the current regime is in place. Actually, the problem is even more serious than that: not only will the behavior never be prosecuted; it actually *can't* ever be effectively prosecuted – it can't be stopped – if the system is to continue to exist, because the entire system, which is to say, at the present moment, the entire global civilization-State-complex, depends primarily upon such behavior for its very existence.[cclxxi]

Think about that: the system itself relies on a set of *Power*-relations most notably characterized by the fact that the entities with the greatest *Power* – States – institute "laws". Yet many of the most significant laws are passed primarily for the purpose of allowing those truly in charge to break the laws, themselves. Phrased this way, it sounds absolutely insane. I, for one, think it literally *embodies* insanity (i.e., conquest *syndrome*). However, it doesn't change the fact that civilization-State-complexes have always worked more or less in such fashion.

By definition, every State, Western or otherwise, has eventually had to gain at least some semblance of a monopoly on violence within its designated territory. But never were these monopolies sought after as crucially as they were by Europe's *Powerful* in the period that immediately gave birth to the fifth (the period of 'industrialized national States'), which in turn gave birth to globalization. And always in history, before period four, the monopoly on violence in its most successful forms meant nothing so much as "it's completely legal for the King's or the city's military to kill, and illegal for everyone else (everyone else not sanctioned by the King or the city)".[cclxxii] All period four did was take this underlying structure, nationalize it, and re-create the equation to state "it's completely legal for the national State's military to kill, and illegal for everyone else (everyone else not sanctioned by the national State)". Period five took this reinterpreted formula and pushed it a step further by fully industrializing it: "it's completely legal for the industrialized national State to kill, and illegal for everyone else (everyone else not sanctioned by the industrialized national State)".

Period six took things still a step further. Since things now had to be managed so much more closely than at any time prior, the private interests became formally institutionalized within the State, giving the "deep state"[cclxxiii] an "official" – *conscious* – realization at the level of the public State not yet experienced in history. The financial-corporate Powers were, by the start of the Cold War, in complete control of the publicly visible *Power*-structure. Everything else regarding the global civilization unfolded from there. The equation was now "it's completely legal for the financial-corporate hegemons' paramilitaries" – the "Intelligence Agencies" – "to kill, and completely illegal for everyone else (everyone else not sanctioned by the financial-corporate hegemons)".

Resultant of all the time and energy invested in the underlying *Power*-structure, everything unconscious became conscious: the leading private interests, who had always at least indirectly controlled the most significant things, now formally controlled *every*thing – everything that could be controlled, that is. A system based entirely on planned mass destruction can only control so much of the chaos it intentionally creates. If the class that sees itself as God were truly omnipotent, it wouldn't have any limitation on its ability to control things; there would never be time-energy constraints on its actions.

Even so, while it didn't reach the level of an actual god, this class certainly did exercise extraordinary influence over human affairs in its heyday – the contemporary world – and in the process caused quite a lot of damage. But, to exist, the system needs people to not consciously realize the extent of the damage, because to consciously realize that would reveal how outrageous the system truly is and has always been.[cclxxiv] It obliterates all potential for sufficient moral legitimacy, which the system depends upon to survive. While explicit proof of such a central global authority may not yet be forthcoming, there certainly exists such an overwhelming body of irrefutable evidence suggesting the existence of such an authority, that we can now consciously realize, if not the story of the authority itself, then at least the story of the system only "it" could've created and sustained.

Now, when the 20th-century turned it really was the beginning of something big, building off of a momentum so bottled up that its outburst couldn't even wait for the 1800s to pass. Perhaps this was because the epochal eruption itself arose from a process much larger than the ending of one century: throughout the last half of Western civilization's 19th-century CE – one of the most volatile settings in humanity's history – Europe's Great Powers had, after four-plus centuries of overseas conquest, been rapidly dividing between themselves what little of the planet remained that had yet to fall under their jurisdiction. This very last round of expansion for modern human history's most brutally violent governing system, the formal style of European colonialism symbolized at its birth by the Spanish Crown's terrorism and enslavement of the "New World" indigenous populations via Columbus, started with the so-called "Scramble for Africa" that in its earliest phases was most notably marked by the Berlin Conference of 1884.[cclxxv]

The Berlin Conference was one of the first precursors to what would be, literally, the dominant theme (the theme of dominance) in the history of globalization: meetings where representatives of the Powers, "only the top people", would come together behind closed doors to decide the entire fate of the international community. Of course, top public representatives of modern European States had always done this to varying extents, ever since there were entities that can rightly be called modern European States.[cclxxvi] But almost always, before the late 19th-century, meetings so determinative were only held to decide the fate of the peoples of the West, and typically only after major wars. The Powers had never tried to cooperate so extensively before (and during a general time of supposed "Peace") towards the goal of collectively regulating the overseas Empires. Ever since the bulk of the territory of Europe had been divided up more or less to the important Powers' likings, with endless minor modifications over time resulting from the never-ending marginal shifts to the balance-of-power, the overseas territories had always been the areas of most intense competition between European States.

The ever-fiercer competition between Western Powers waged for the prize of overseas holdings was evidenced, for instance, in the competition between Britain, France, and Spain in the Americas,[cclxxvii] and between Britain and France in China and India. These are only the most striking examples: if there was a single Western Power somewhere, conquering with cannon, commerce, and Christ,[cclxxviii] it's certainly that there would be at least one other Power there too, at some point, looking to get some of the action. Growth in the size of each European Power fueled more conquest, more conquest fueled more growth, and both created still more intense competition, until, by the last few decades of the 19th-century, the West's constantly-expanding overseas war-trade environment left much of sub-Saharan Africa as one of the globe's sole remaining regions outside the chokehold of colonial tentacles.

To be sure, the general lack of formal colonialism in sub-Saharan Africa preceding the late 19th-century didn't signify that there had been a lack of Western *imperialism* there. Historically, even without the constant rapacious occupation of Western colonial settlements, sub-Saharan Africa had still always been one of the most ravaged overseas zones of European conquest, ever since the original rise of Atlantic naval Powers during the 15th-century: the precise context that spawned Columbus, thereby setting the stage for a worldwide imposition of Western State terrorism, dominant in areas across the globe to an ever-increasing extent, in one form or another, for about 500 years. In fact, Portugal, technically the very first European naval Power of the kind that conquered the planet in the post-Columbian world, cut its teeth on the war-trade route established by its merchants along Africa's western coast, which promptly forced much of the sub-Saharan region into the slave trade. Of course, the human beings stolen from their homes and thrown violently into some of the most grueling *Power*-relations imaginable – that is, the ones who weren't killed by the incomprehensibly inhuman conditions definitive of the Atlantic passage – largely served out these cruel unearned sentences in the Americas, coerced for centuries into producing the original wealth which built Western dominance. Naturally, they received none of that wealth themselves.

Nevertheless, so long as an area had been left unvarnished by actual settlement on behalf of the West, it could usually maintain, at least to some extent, its same less miserable existence that characterized basically all pre-colonial settings relative to their successors. Unhappily, in this regard sub-Saharan Africa's time was running out. The latest, industrialized form of Western politicoeconomic domination was proving to have absolutely no end to its voraciousness. Additionally, new and portentous Powers were trying to make their mark in the game of Empire; most especially, this included the recently-founded *singular* German nation, only having been unified in 1871 following Prussia's triumph in its war with France.

Concerning the broadest and hence most consequential sociohistorical context shaping Western civilization, unification of Germany was essentially synonymous with the nation's entry onto the Great Powers stage. Tellingly for the period, the name for the new nation translates into English as the 'German Empire'. In this way, insofar as German unification happened specifically how it did – under the aegis of a Prussian hegemony – the new German national State was primarily meant to serve as a vehicle for Prussian imperial policy. Whatever particular policies were going to be implemented, exactly, was for the moment a matter of far less overall importance than the creation of such conditions as were absolutely necessary if such policies (whatever they would someday be) could have any chance of ultimately being implemented with ideal efficacy. In other words, the British and French displayed the best models for success in the Great Power game at the time, and thus it followed that a successful Power had to be a totally unified national State along the same lines as Britain and France, whatever might've been its qualitatively different makeup in terms of domestic culture. In any State that would follow the dominant Western model during the late 19th-century, international politics was the crucial determinant for domestic organization: to reach the highest levels of success, a State had to have a successful Empire. Moreover, rather than being a relic of the past, this maxim has only continued to become evermore applicable. As usual in the history of civilizations and States, the only major aspect that has transformed is the specific set of rules by which the *Power* game is played.

But changes to the *Power* game's rules are uniquely significant in their determinative effects on humanity as a whole. And owing to the explosive industrialization of England starting at the end of the 18th-century, there was a singularly monumental change to the rules of the Western *Power* game that had started sweeping across all the most affected areas (the centers and burgeoning centers of late modern Western civilization) at an exponentially increasing rate fairly early on in the 19th-century. Most generally, the change entailed the advent of industrialized national politicoeconomic systems approximating that of the English; and because the rules of the *Power* game evolved toward this end with such unprecedented speed and regularity for most of the past couple of centuries, *all* the human systems across the globe would eventually converge, and finally, since the start of the seventh period in 1995, there has been just one central global system of production/distribution, communications, and security.

How did so extraordinary a change (especially one so extraordinarily synchronized) take place? Why was it necessary for a singular planetary structure of intertwined political economy and culture – what I've called a single global civilization – to emerge? What sequence of event-clusters allowed the most *Powerful* conceivable civilization in history to rise in that era we humans call the 20th-century, and why has it already started to fall so early in the 21st?

For me, these are the most important questions that must be addressed in order to construct a perspective on the central lived narrative shaping the contemporary world: not "the history of everything" in the 20th-century-beyond era, but the single history most responsible for shaping everything else. Further, knowing what we already do about the general shape of Western history, I think it's safe to say that if I'm to construct such a perspective successfully, I must explain how the global civilization rose and fell *insofar as* this rise and fall was directly parallel to the evolution of the contemporary Anglo-American hegemony. No matter how one looks at the culture of globalization, it seems rather indisputable that the bases both of its emergence and its full establishment were inextricably linked with an Anglo-American dominance over a globally industrialized politicoeconomic system. Most fundamentally, I argue, the interlocked politicoeconomic and cultural dominance has entailed three main forms: (1) an Anglo-American dominated global system of energy corporations; (2) an Anglo-American dominated global military system; and (3) an Anglo-American dominated global financial system. Insofar as globalization has been defined by an Anglo-American hegemony, the hegemony has been achieved through the holistic recurring incorporation of these three indispensable control mechanisms.

From my perspective, hegemony doesn't have to be "purely" articulated to qualify as hegemony (whatever such idealized "purity" might actually mean). (See certain leading IR scholars.) For a hopeful hegemon to become the dominant actor in an interstate system, which dominance is the principal criterion for dominating in a *civilizational* system, the hopeful "only" needs to conquer and maintain conquest in three major spheres of wealth-exploitation: the three oft-mentioned spheres of life-support, communications, and military. Everything else is secondary. Mainly, this is because – as I've also said, in accompaniment, all throughout this work – the three sub-strategies are always interconnected, concerning how they must manifest themselves in reality (through civilization-State-complexes).

It's more explicitly a philosophical point than an historical one, but I can't make it clearer any other way: reality does not primarily happen divided into spheres; it happens holistically. Reality is then *secondarily* (and analytically), roughly "divided" into spheres, which throughout time never stop reproducing the primary holistic system. It's a constant interchange between the system and the spheres, with events first happening in the system-at-large and the spheres then collectively responding – whether everyone in every sphere is fully conscious of the collectivity of the response, or not. As long as the system maintains its capabilities for amassing and circulating the necessary energy, a continuous cycle between events and responses perpetually persists, with present events being shaped primarily by past events and responses and future responses always affected by present responses and events.

Yet just because, to begin with, the spheres and the responses are secondary to the system and its events, this doesn't necessarily mean the spheres and responses are less significant to the overall process. In the first place, the system and its events take precedence. But in some systems, most relevantly the comprehensive systems comprised by human cultural units, at least considering how civilization-State-complexes, the most *Powerful* of such units in history, have existed in their 5,000-or-so-years, *the spheres and their responses eventually completely overtook the systems and their events.* During the contemporary era, the unitary civilization-State-complex itself came to totally dominate its two largest immediately surrounding systems, the more immediate to itself and second-largest being the planetary civilizational structure, and the less immediate to itself but largest being the holistic planet Earth, the globe. Such domination is what most fundamentally describes the explicit process behind globalization: the definitive cultural expression of a time when a short historical process became evermore-closely entwined with the long historical process, until the two processes ultimately merged completely at the beginning of the seventh period, peak globalization.

Central to this argument is my assertion that, concerning whatever is the most immediate large-scale system a human cultural unit is a part of at any given time and place, *that* system itself is what's most fundamentally responsible for constraining the relevant cultural unit's short historical process. Such short historical process is reflected, for instance, in what certain human populations refer to as, "our nation's history". The truly most significant large-scale systems embody the central nodes of the long historical process's unfolding, which unfolding is something more to be posited and searched for than seen, in terms of how it compares to the short historical process. In other words, the events defining a culture's sociohistorical existence and the context most responsible for shaping those events can only truly be linked through systematic historical investigation.

This means that, in most settings throughout the history of civilizations, and certainly for almost all of the individuals throughout the whole history of civilizations, a dominant culture's inhabitants are in fact largely unable to see the true meaning of their culture's history, which most fatefully precludes them from seeing the full reality of their culture's present. I believe this is what's most definitive of the concept of 'historical consciousness' (more properly, '*socio*historical consciousness'), at its core: any individual can only be conscious of the information (and the *kinds* of information) readily available to him or her at any given time-place.[cclxxix] Beyond that, because of the special, stratified nature so uniquely inherent in civilizations, information and knowledge in these most *Powerful* cultural units has always been literally dominated – made an object of conquest – by the most *Powerful* individuals, i.e., the individuals constituting the apex of the cultural pyramid consists of at any given time. Information and knowledge then has the potential to spread more freely the closer one is to the apex of the pyramid, and is more closely restricted the closer one is to the pyramid's base.

Like everything else crucial to the existence of a civilization, the restriction of information and knowledge is, for much of any civilization's history, more so something inherent simply in the organization of the overall *Power*-structure rather than an explicit strategy whose implementation needs to be consciously undertaken by the *Powerful*. A civilization's sphere of information and knowledge (communications) only grows in its complexity after there has been established a deep foundation of almost constant politicoeconomic violence emanating from the civilization's military sphere. Like all human cultural units, the civilization only maintains and increases its complexity – it only evolves – insofar as it gains the capability to increase its *orderliness* throughout time, over larger quantities of territory and population. Historically, a given civilization gained such a capability, in the first place, by centralizing the legitimate means of violence: that is, by conferring upon a single entity, the State, the sole legal authority to inflict or threaten to inflict death as a punishment or deterrent against what the *Powerful* view as undesirable behavior. Once the civilization reaches a certain level of violence-monopolization, orderliness can be gained to some larger extent by other means, but only so long as the legitimate use of violence continues to be adequately centralized. (Remember, this refers to what has been the historical reality thus far, not what will always necessarily be true.)

Among all civilizations, Western civilization found it uniquely difficult to consolidate the legitimate means of violence in its prime geographical arena, meaning that during the West's formative period, there was, relatively, more constant violence over a much longer period of time than there had ever been anywhere else prior. Such violence lasted for the entire period of Western formation (period three – 632 – 1492

CE). When I say "relatively", I mean it in terms of comparing the West, especially from the time of the first Crusade until Columbus's conquest and the Inquisition, to the other major actors in the West's original intercivilizational structure. Quite simply, Western civilization found it particularly difficult to "civilize".

This context provides a uniquely apt opportunity for making comparisons between separate civilizations, since each key civilizational territorial niche within the intercivilizational structure at the time, which besides the West primarily included the Islamic civilization and the Orthodox civilization, was in its third civilizational period. So each civilization was the heir of cultures, from both of the first two intercivilizational cycles, which fulfilled the same roles in their respective intercivilizational structures, as the period three civilizations would in their medieval intercivilizational structure. The Islamic civilization in its emergence was fulfilling much the same niche in the period three intercivilizational structure that the original civilizations in its approximate zone – namely in southern Mesopotamia and Egypt – had fulfilled in period one (a period in fact initiated by those two earlier civilizations). Additionally, on account of the particular setting of conquest defining Islamic civilization at its inception, not only would it take over the roles fulfilled by Mesopotamia and Egypt in the Classical period (period two); what was more important at the time (632 CE), in fact, was that it also conquered and thereby fulfilled the niche of Persia's Sassanian Empire (of late Classical origins). Thus, Islamic civilization was, at its very foundation, the product of over four-and-a-half millennia of civilizational evolution, including that which had been achieved by the most sophisticated civilization of the latest sociohistorical context.

Although it couldn't claim such a lengthy lineage, the Orthodox civilization centered in Byzantium, nonetheless also directly inherited quite a substantial civilizational history. Orthodox civilization's emergence can be properly viewed with reference to its fulfilling the role originated by Crete and Troy, during the earliest stages of southeastern Europe's incorporation into the intercivilizational structure that began under southern Mesopotamian and Egyptian domination. Of course, this role had eventually passed to what became, in period two, the Greek centers of the Classical world. Therefore, in terms of its politicoeconomic purpose, the Orthodox civilization was fundamentally defined by its position as the central war-trade pivot between the central-to-southwest Asian/northern African overland caravanning route and the northern African/southern European Mediterranean sailing route.[cclxxx] Here's perhaps the perfect example of what it has meant in reality, that the war-trade competition has been the main factor shaping all of the most consequential sociohistorical evolution since the earliest origins of civilizations and States. Because civilization-State-complexes are, definitively, entities formed out of competition in war-trade systems, at any point in history when a far-reaching war-trade system started to form, it was practically inevitable that civilizations would evolve in the system's key locales. In this vein, the complexes *always* initially developed along lines inextricable from their geographical niches in the intercivilizational and civilizational war-trade environments: and initial developments mainly dictated later ones.

Thus, regarding Western civilization: once the Islamic world's development initiated period three of the relevant intercivilizational structure, seeing a new war-trade system emerge with the Islamic and Byzantine civilizations as its leading actors, the general contours of the West's development were basically a foregone conclusion, even though it was as yet largely unformed. Actually, *precisely because* the West was as yet largely unformed, the general contours were a foregone conclusion. First, the West would fulfill the role of agricultural "swing producer" (to borrow a contemporary term) for the already-rich civilizations to its east. Then, once its politicoeconomic development reached sufficient levels owing to its favorable trade balance, Western States would use their strategic geography and greater potential for growth, both things due in large part to the West's position as the relative newcomer, as means for attempting to conquer as much as possible of the traditionally much more complex but for that reason now declining principal actors in the intercivilizational war-trade environment.

That same pattern, more or less, had already emerged in periods one and two: the pattern had merely taken longer to unfold in period two and longest to unfold in period one. In period one it happened when Crete, Troy, and Mycenae entered into the Mesopotamian and Egyptian dominated trade network, and in period two when Rome, the latecomer to the Classical network, quickly came to dominate it – and ultimately tried to conquer everything in its path, with results that rapidly rose and just as rapidly fell. All three times, in periods one, two, and three, trade moved ever farther west, and once it reached a consolidated position in the form of a westernmost Power, war moved as far back east as it could go.

The pattern changed greatly in empirical terms, but in structural terms only barely, with Columbus's conquest of 1492 that began the interperiodic phase separating the end of period three and the beginning of period four (1521-1776): an entirely new intercivilizational dynamic started to form, but it was only different insofar as the old intercivilizational structure was being reproduced in the Western hemisphere. The basis for this lay in the exploitation of a completely different naval "territory" – the Atlantic Ocean – than those that had been dominant in the first three periods. In periods one through three, of course, the dominant naval territories were, in chronological succession, the southwest Asian and northeast African river systems and the major bodies providing connections between these, such as the Red Sea; and then the Mediterranean Sea and its peripheral seas, i.e., the Black Sea, the Aegean, and the Adriatic. Things had been approximately just this way for a fairly substantial length of time, so any fundamental shift to the underlying system would have to result from some quite rare development.

Certainly compared to riverine navigation, but also compared to transport over the coastal Mediterranean, inter-hemispheric open-ocean sailing constituted a completely new way (at least from an intercivilizational perspective) for humanity to exploit planetary wealth – and one completely dependent upon interconnected Western communications, life-support, and military technologies. But one must keep foremost in mind, concerning the 1492 version of what John France refers to so aptly as the 'Catholic core', that the West's strengths in these categories at the time were almost entirely the result of cultural diffusion from the other civilizations in the West's formative intercivilizational structure. The Islamic civilization was important not only because it dispersed to the West its own remarkably advanced cultural achievements, but equally because it was the primary conduit through which the West first encountered those arduously-achieved, long-in-development knowledge bases deriving from so many civilizations both contemporaneous and historical. Orthodox civilization, too, through interaction in the intercivilizational sphere, provided the West with an enormous stock of humanistic and scientific knowledge – the quintessential bases for ultimately developing all the most complex technologies, and especially all the most significant communications technologies – to draw from. Perhaps most notably, it was largely through Byzantium that late medieval Western thinkers initially gained access to the Greek intellectual heritage[cclxxxi] that had been lost to the West long before.

Now we come once more to what's simultaneously the strangest and most familiar aspect of the West's contemporary understanding of its own history, in a certain sense more pervasive now among contemporary scholars than it is among the public at large: the notion that the West advanced to its position over the past 500 years, culminating in continued Western domination during the globalization period, because it was/is simply better than all the other cultures, with "better" above all indicating "higher intelligence". Nothing is more tragic for the rest of the planet and for all of history (nor more characteristic of what the dominant contemporary *Western* mindset became on account of its deepest sociohistorical roots) than a sincere belief in the notion of a contemporary Western superiority naturally inherent in Western individuals themselves.

Throughout part 2 and thus far in part 3, I've tried, as far as my abilities allow, to discursively destroy all possible bases for any belief in natural Western superiority. I consider all such belief to comprise the greatest single factor contributing to the total lack of understanding of Western history most definitively characterizing the contemporary dominant culture. Since the contemporary dominant culture is fundamentally a culture of Western origins, and as we've also seen, above all, an Anglo-American culture, this lack of historical knowledge pervading globalization is then fundamentally *a lack of self-awareness*, especially insofar as the complete dispossession of historical context is manifested at its worst in the global imperial heartland itself, the United States.

One is literally incapable of understanding contemporary history if one continues to harbor any shred of belief in a Western "superiority" that's based on anything besides the outright violent force of military conquest, and the concomitant repressed psychological terror imposed by the constant threat of more force, which imprisons all victims of violence aiming at conquest. On the other hand, once one accepts that, in the end, any concept of Western "superiority" at all correspondent to reality *can only* be, in the end, based entirely on an appreciation of the West's endless employment and threat of violence, most other components comprising a useful understanding of contemporary history can eventually fall into place. The purpose here has nothing to do with castigating the West. It has to do with cultivating an historical understanding unencumbered by the endless supply of misinformation and disinformation built-up from century upon century of church, State, and corporate propaganda, which propaganda always seeks and has always sought to morally justify Western military dominance by insisting upon the inherent moral superiority of Western civilization. It's expected that warring States – and Western States are *always* at war – would succumb to the use of information as a weapon. What's most tragic is that people in the West have actually believed the propaganda: and the scholars were the biggest dupes of all, the one sector that should've been protecting truth but wouldn't, because the herd mentality always wins.

Things weren't always lacking in truth so absolutely. The story of the 20th-century-beyond era tells us how it got so bad. In turn, then, I think it also tells us which things must unequivocally change, if humanity can ever create a culture capable of humane survival. It's not a pleasant story. But – if the lived metanarrative is to continue – it's one that must be told.

I

In Medias Res: The Cold War's Explicit Emergence

The global hegemons, having realized some time ago that they would need a singularly-encompassing global social structure with nationalized corporate-States as its largest subunits, had relatedly also realized that such a structure could only be feasibly consolidated under the aegis of the United States Government. But from a public point-of-view, there couldn't be just one Power in the world, insofar as there also needed to be a sufficiently threatening "Enemy":[cclxxxii] and the only possible "legitimate" choice in the sociohistorical context was the Soviet Union. As ever in the world since the start of the 20th-century, the most significant consideration contributing to this choice was petroleum. Since petroleum is *the* strategic limiting factor constraining all contemporary politicoeconomic and, inextricably, all contemporary military affairs, the only way a global structure consisting of two blocs ever could've successfully emerged was for the two nations with the greatest control over petroleum reserves to act as the definitive "Enemies". At the time when the Cold War was first being planned, this meant the United States and the Soviet Union.

The two "Enemies" had to be separated precisely in this fashion because, being "Enemies", each nation's *sphere of influence* – in other words, the particular State-controlled, internationalized, totally-mobilized marketplace (bloc) each "Superpower" was to be put in charge of – needed to be as *officially* separated as possible from the other's.[cclxxxiii] And since it would've been impossible for anything else to parallel the singular significance represented by petroleum in the contemporary global economy, the blocs had to be divided primarily according to what this resource dictated. Even before World War Two, it was already all too clear to the global hegemons that a contemporary civilization could be ultimately organized on no other grounds besides oil. No later than immediately after World War Two, it became clear that a contemporary civilization could be organized on no other grounds except oil and uranium: adding still further significance to the division maintained between West and East Germany, as the bulk of Soviet uranium supplies and production were located within the boundaries of the latter.[cclxxxiv] Finally, the two blocs had to seem naturally antagonistic from a cultural standpoint in order to provide the broad moral justification for permanent war – hence, the "Capitalist" United States vs. the "Communist" Soviet Union.

Essentially, then, we can see both of the world wars, and especially the second one, as pre-emptive strikes against any potential future challenges to Anglo-American hegemony over the planet's oil.[cclxxxv] Most of all, the world wars were the first pre-emptive strikes against all possible *nationalization* of any territory's oil, always the worst conceivable scenario for the leading contemporary internationally minded interests, i.e., the groups that in their totality comprised the global hegemonic sector. Lack of control over any decisive share of Earth's petroleum reserves would've, in itself, also meant lack of total control over global finance, and nothing less than total control over the most significant strategic mechanisms is required to successfully maintain hegemony over a cultural system. Conveniently, World War Two ended with the interstate combination of the U.K. and the U.S. holding what was the most monopolistic control over the planet's petroleum reserves in the history of the oil industry. Moreover, as mentioned, the Anglo-American alliance had an "informal" agreement with the Soviet Union that split more or less the whole world into two spheres of influence. While this agreement could only be publicly enforced insofar as the two blocs pretended enmity towards one another, the agreement clearly worked much better for the hegemons than, say, an open declaration of diplomatic "friendship" would have, evidenced not least of all by how, during the entire length of the Cold War, no sectors benefited more than the elites in both blocs. In fact, the history of the Cold War shows quite unmistakably how, in *both* blocs, the "conflict" really didn't accomplish anything besides the perpetuation of the global State capitalist social structure.

The hegemons had realized by some point early on during the "interwar" years, that, on a global scale, the potential continuation of the particular system they preferred – an international capitalist system – could be achieved by literally only one thing (along with all of its implications), which was the imposition of a permanent war economy. The simultaneous end of World War Two and start of the Cold War, with the latter conflict, as is now quite well proven, having started well before the former was officially over, can be said to have accomplished nothing at all besides the imposition of permanent war economies on both sides of the "Iron Curtain", which was such an enormously consequential holistic transformation that no other fundamental change was necessary. All the changes that would emerge, emerged surrounding this one, which as it happened was completely inseparable from total financial mobilization of petroleum and uranium supplies within a single cultural system.

Therefore, the world broke up into two "antagonistic" sides, which in reality meant that the United States would – in a variety of ways – buttress its own "Enemy" in its assigned sphere, and call it "Communism"; whereas the Soviet Union would exploit the U.S.'s "Enemy" role as the central premise behind its own totalitarian form, wherein it openly asserted its right to crush ruthlessly any internal dissent, always under the pretext of defending "Socialism".

It was "necessary" for things to be presented in such a manner because tension had to be inflated through public opinion on a constant basis, on both sides of the "divide" – even as the two nations would/could certainly never engage in open warfare against each other. This was the most significant aspect of the strategy as a whole: the respective publics of each superpower had to be kept in perpetual terror of the military might emanating from the opposite side, despite the fact that at the highest levels open warfare would never be an option. (In this sense, the purpose was to dupe a great majority of those working for the State, just as much as the public-at-large.) This would keep the masses nice and supportive of unending military commitments. But if soldiers who truly believed in the cause were ever allowed to actually face off against each other, there's no telling how out of control things might get. Once the blood of a soldier from either polity was spilled, war against whoever spilled that blood would've been a necessity, and hence out of the invisible controllers' hands.[cclxxxvi] As I've said, total control over the global system was the one strategic "principle" guiding every hegemonic action in the post-World War Two context, since it was nothing less than a question of "total control" vs. "no control". The all or nothing climate sustained to one degree or another by every most *Powerful* civilization throughout history had never been so consciously realized. It had never before been necessary – or, interdependently, possible – for any group of hegemons to realize it so consciously.

Interestingly, the best evidence for what had been going on at the highest/deepest levels is actually what occurred at the most public levels: the U.S. State underwent a transformation so fundamental and so rapid, one couldn't rightly say that the government appearing after the change was the same one that had existed before. And yet the transformation was so calculatingly instituted, hardly anyone in the country noticed its true implications for about a decade.[cclxxxvii] I'm of course referring to the complete reorganization of the U.S. Government in the "postwar world" – a particularly ambiguous term, even for the middle and late contemporary world of infinite verbal ambiguity. It's supposed to mean "post-World War Two", though even this isn't very accurate. Let's look at it for a moment as if it really does mean, literally, "postwar", as in, after all wars. Because when people use the phrasing without the original context at their mind's forefront, it's likely that they adopt that perspective to some degree, if only subconsciously. In a way, it would be correct, since, based on how war was always defined, epitomized by the events of World War Two – which remains fully representative of how the contemporary dominant culture still trains the average individual to think about war today – the world since August 1945 has indeed been quite a departure. On the other hand, in another sense the world as it has existed during this time has clearly been a direct culmination of all the thousands of prior years of military evolution: again, epitomized by World War Two. Thus, simultaneously, in the beyond-World War Two portion of the contemporary era, everything has changed, and everything has stayed the same.

In fact, to me, that apparent contradiction, concerning both its abstract sense and the concrete sense in which it's relevantly manifested here, isn't really a contradiction, but is rather the most definitive aspect of civilizational history: everything changes, and everything stays the same. Moreover, this axiom, inherent to the 'physical' makeup of all civilizations, also has an inextricable and reciprocally-related 'psychological' counterpart: *'given enough time and energy, everything unconscious has the potential to become conscious'.*

Typically, everything unconscious remains fundamentally the same, and everything conscious changes. When everything unconscious fundamentally changes, something truly unusual has happened: with the beginning of the contemporary world's full emergence, it happened in the form of everything unconscious becoming conscious.

This isn't significant from a philosophical/psychological perspective alone: it's equally significant from a predominately anthropo-/socio- logical perspective. (Suggesting the deepest interconnection between philosophical/psychological phenomena and anthropo-/socio- logical phenomena.). As a counterpart in the social structure to the philosophical (ontological) conceptualization of the abstract/concrete sides comprising civilizations' physical systems and the unconscious/conscious sides comprising their psychological ones, the politicoeconomic system of a civilization experiences a dually-encompassing process of (1) evolution and (2) change throughout its history, precisely what I've referred to overall as 'sociohistorical process', which occurs at any given moment on two scales, 'long' and 'short'. Further, the primary nexus representing the "center" around which all other historical processes ultimately revolve is what I've referred to as the three interconnected cultural spheres, which serve the purposes of (1) securing life-support materials, (2) storing and transmitting communications, and (3) military organization. Finally, the evolution and change centralized in these three mutually reinforcing spheres can only exist as a pair of reciprocal entities, thus essentially creating one phenomenon; change represents the catalyst for future evolution, while past evolution is the framework within which present change takes hold.

Additionally, I always intend the long scale and the short scale to be thought of purely insofar as they're relative to one another: the long scale always unfolds through short scale "events" and "event-clusters", while the realistic potentialities for these short scale scenarios are ultimately determined by the relevant long scale history. For instance, let's consider as generically as possible the phenomenon of a contemporary national election in the United States. There can be 'short scale' variation in the event-cluster sequence, including variables such as who's running, what "seats" are being sought, what party is likely to win and the likely extent of its victory, what the main "issues" of the moment are, etc. But in terms of the 'long scale', many schematic aspects of any U.S. national election will and must be invariable, and so we can say they play a decisively *determinative* role in their relation to the short scale potential for variation: all of the potential short scale variations are *only* real potentials insofar as they fit within the framework determined by long scale conditions. The very existence of a short scale event-cluster sequence such as a national U.S. election is possible solely because of the long scale process represented by the progression of U.S. government throughout its history.

To imagine our broadest horizon here, consider the natural history of our known universe as the singular overarching process, concerning everything conceivably relevant to humanity's history. No matter how long a chosen process *within* this overarching universal process has been, it can nonetheless always be seen from the perspective of a broader timeline: and, in terms of anything we can speak of, there's always at least one shorter process going on which this first process determines, if only partially. In the context of our example, what I pointed out in the above paragraph as the long scale process would, from an even longer perspective, also be a short scale process in relation to the long scale process called "the progression of Western governments", a history without which anything rightly labeled "United States government" would have no ultimate meaning. In turn, of course, "the progression of Western governments" is itself a short scale process in relation to "government in civilizations", and so on, until there's nothing relevant left which you haven't in some way covered, if not explicitly in a discourse then implicitly, in the line of reasoning behind the discourse.

The style of warfare inherent in civilizations – the longest scale version of the sociohistorical phenomenon most relevant to the present narrative – was evolutionarily epitomized by World War Two, and in being so epitomized, directly gave rise to something completely new, yet completely dependent upon its immediate evolutionary precursor. This perfectly exemplifies the inseparable combination of change and evolution in history. The Cold War, which unofficially started before World War Two ended and officially began less than two years after, was throughout its entire existence the concrete embodiment of those particular philosophical and sociohistorical underpinnings. As I've also said, the contemporary world is most unique insofar as long and short historical processes are indissolubly *melded*, which I consider the fundamental ontological rule of globalization. The grand dreams for total *Power* that always most broadly shaped human affairs in civilizations have been enacted so efficiently in the contemporary world as to have practically no historical parallel, even as these unparalleled circumstances never could've come about without the prior thousands of years of hegemonic conquest, always towards the end of greater *Power* and truly concerned with nothing else.

It should go without saying that the rupture embodying the end of World War Two, interchangeably the critical turning point marking the midway between the Cold War's unofficial and official beginnings, was the U.S.'s use of nuclear weapons in combat against Japan in early August 1945, which was done for no other purpose than to provide the "opening shot" of the Cold War.[cclxxxviii] Such a deliberate strategic turn to nuclear and shortly thereafter, *thermo*nuclear warfare was the most extreme possible expression of all prior long-term evolution in the organization of civilizations around their warfare-making capabilities. Collectively, the latter have comprised the central purpose for the existence of States in the global civilization: all subsequent evolution of the global civilization in other spheres has revolved around these capabilities. Again, civilization-State-complexes are by their nature entities tending towards extremes in the long run: in this way, the nuclear/thermonuclear shift has represented the epitome of civilizational evolution. The global civilization, both in the sixth period (1947-1991), wherein it was a civilization surrounding a single interstate system, and the seventh period (1995-?), in which it's a civilization surrounding just a single State (this is why I've dubbed it the age of "peak globalization"), has embodied nothing less than a civilization in its most *ideally actualized* form.

Fully bearing out the assessment's accuracy, the best evidence suggests that the overarching purpose of the U.S.'s use in combat of nuclear weaponry, specifically concerning the deepest intention behind this use – to represent the opening shot of the Cold War – was to establish the U.S. unequivocally as the hegemon over a totally-singularized global capitalist market.[cclxxxix] In other words, the purpose was nothing less than the extension over the whole planet of a single imperial actor's dominion, articulated in the form of globalized fascism – the politicoeconomic/cultural garb most peculiar to the contemporary world. This has been the same essential regime in charge of human affairs across the globe ever since, with only superficial modifications introduced from time to time.

Such a purpose is about as in line as anything could be with my comprehensive perspective of the war-trade competition as the definitive activity of civilization-State-complexes, which activity shapes and is reciprocally shaped by the cultural pyramid expressed in every civilization's historical fabric. The nuclear bomb is the ultimate representation linking everything preceding it to everything that came after. The history of civilizations exploded over Japan, and all the time we're evermore trapped in the aftermath.

Everything unconscious became conscious.

It was now clear beyond any formidable doubt that humanity's political side – simply, the human desire to wield *Power* over other human beings, particularly encouraged by war-trade environments – was the world's greatest source of evils. Never again would it be reasonable for humans to take seriously any notion that the State, humanity's quintessential political manifestation, existed for any purpose other than the imposition of conquest towards the end of mass economic exploitation. The possibility of "right" having any ability whatsoever to meaningfully restrain "might" within this system of conquest was forever shattered. It had never been very likely to begin with. But all hopes of it could be completely forgotten about once there existed States on the planet Earth possessing thermonuclear weaponry: and a State possessing "mere" nuclear weaponry for the first time was the initial explicit step in that direction.

And yet… at the time when the Cold War's fully-fledged public personae really began (the 1950s), few individuals inhabiting the contemporary dominant culture were aware of these most essential truths; and there were more or less none at all who were allowed to share such ideas in anything remotely resembling a public forum. Moreover, there were plenty of individuals who fervently believed in a wholly-imagined "reality" of ever-imminent warfare, representing more or less the complete opposite of a nuclear world's unavoidable facts. Concerning the world since the start of the interperiodic phase separating periods five and six – that crucial less than two-year-span between the official end of World War Two and the official start of the Cold War – the U.S., sociologically, is most properly understood as the global imperial heartland, rather than anything reflecting in any way the notion of an "independent nation". In this vein, it should simultaneously be considered, during its era of supremacy, the intellectual headquarters for the contemporary dominant culture. Nuclear and soon thermonuclear weapons were the key determinative factors making this a sociohistorical reality: but at the time of its initial emergence, hardly any individuals inhabiting this central core of the contemporary dominant culture even realized that the U.S. Government was now at the apex of a global imperial scheme. It goes without saying, then, that the vast majority of such individuals couldn't understand the indispensable role played by nuclear weapons in the scheme. The hegemons got a lengthy head start, which has proven all too important for the subsequent history of globalization – all too tragically important.

Speaking of the contemporary dominant culture's complete incapacity for acknowledging simple facts, it always astounds me that even today very few people seem to find it peculiar, how rapidly the United States and the Soviet Union turned from wartime allies to "Peacetime" "Enemies". One might be justified in saying it literally happened overnight, if the night in question was the night before August 6th, 1945, when the United States dropped the first atomic bomb on Hiroshima.

I don't even mean I'm surprised at how few people seem to find it "suspicious". For a moment setting aside our quest to view things from a deeper perspective: isn't it just the most striking example of humanity's never-ending, ever-evolving conflict, i.e., the central narrative in the history of civilizations? Even conventional writers of today, albeit mostly academic types (who usually have inherently quite limited possibilities for reaching substantial numbers of the population), acknowledge that the Cold War began before World War Two was over.[ccxc] In other words, the "Enemies" were already "Enemies" before they were done being allies – allies in the most gargantuan war in humanity's history. Shouldn't that be something worth discussing in "public discourse", if public discourse is actually meant to serve any purpose besides confirming everything the contemporary dominant culture believes about itself ("Communism" bad, "Capitalism" good)?

We don't even have to acknowledge that indisputable fact about how World War Three started before World War Two ended. Let's pretend the Cold War didn't begin until what was more or less its official start date – March 12th, 1947, when Truman initiated a long Cold War tradition of rhetorically terrorizing the public as well as much of the Congress with tall tales of "Communist" aggression, a Pavlovian stimulus solely intended to ensure unthinking acquiescence of unending military commitments. Of course, the latter had been planned for years; this was just the hegemons' way of psychologically "conditioning" everyone for what was going to happen. Letting people make up their own minds was far too messy in a global nuclear empire. It simply wouldn't do.

Truman originated the tradition during a "State of the Union" address, giving the call to permanent war a most publicly revered setting for its pronouncement. Even within such an eminently official context, then, the U.S. was already mobilizing again for war barely eighteen months after the "cessation of hostilities" that concluded World War Two. Naturally, the public of the imperial heartland was too war-weary to care much what was going on, and many probably wished the Soviets dead simply for making them think about nuclear bombs when all they wanted to think about was cars and baseball (and soon, TV).

The National Security Act of 1947 was passed several months after Truman's "State of the Union" war dance, and since then the U.S. State has been a fundamentally different creature than ever before, even as the conditions building up to that point for so long had made the final outcome practically inevitable. Truman got everything he asked for, to be sure, although also apparently much that he did not. For instance, the president later claimed that he hadn't intended for CIA to be "a cloak-and-dagger operation", which it would become more or less immediately upon its formation. He even likened it to the "Gestapo", which was unusually sharp for a contemporary U.S. president.[ccxci] Indeed, in my opinion the Nazi secret police seem to have been one of the main archetypal bases for CIA (specifically its ultra-secret covert operations wing, OPC), along with the J.P. Morgan outfit, specifically concerning how the latter existed in the early 20th-century.[ccxcii]

CIA, the first independent spy agency to be institutionalized within the U.S. Government, is perhaps more synonymous with the U.S.'s side of the Cold War than any other phenomenon. CIA's creation was "inevitable", if the war-trade competition was to persist in a nuclear world. Since the perpetuation of the war-trade competition in a nuclear world had been the primary goal of the hegemons' overarching strategy all along, its creation was entirely inevitable.

Most notably, the agency has a definitively "above-the-law" stature, evidenced above all by the particularities of the very language permitting its existence, when contrasted with the agency's standard operating procedure. The "charter" creating the CIA as an amendment to the just-mentioned National Security Act was deliberately worded so as to prevent the *unrestrained* use of the agency as an instrument for covert operations. This theoretical restraint (see NSC 10/2) was immediately broken in practice,[ccxciii] and obviously, the CIA has been used precisely towards its explicitly-forbidden end at an evermore-rapidly-increasing pace throughout its existence,[ccxciv] suggesting that its creation represented the fulfillment of a fairly long-term desire on behalf of some (elite) group. Thus, in its very founding it was, and in its perpetuation it has been, a perfect embodiment of the insoluble problem with State-rule, that States are imposed specifically to "legitimately" evade and/or ignore the major laws everyone else has to obey. The agency and its ilk have saturated humanity with this problematic contradiction throughout the global civilization's entirety.

Over time, CIA predictably gained ever-increasing momentum towards total rule of the U.S. Government, which it ultimately achieved in a strikingly short span. As the U.S. Government, itself, was gaining ever-increasing (strategically predetermined) momentum towards total rule over the global civilization, CIA was thereby moving towards decisive control of the entire planet, as well.

But one must keep in mind here, that in terms of any individual institution, the acquisition of "decisive control of the entire planet" sounds like a much more challenging task, and thus a much more "impressive" achievement than it was, in reality. As it happened, the development was the end of one very long process, even as it was the start of another much shorter one. Between 1898 and 1945, the whole *systemic* tendency of the world's intercivilizational structure had already been moving evermore rapidly towards Western imperial control over the Earth's total surface as well as, in a process beginning early on in this first phase of the contemporary world but truly taking hold with World War Two and its immediate Cold War aftermath, Earth's skies.[ccxcv] The key variable determined by the events of primarily Anglo-American initiated globalized total warfare was the answer to the question, "Who will ultimately take control over the uncontrollably globalizing industrial civilization?"[ccxcvi] Merely posing the question implies the truly important fact to remember, that it was never a question of whether or not Western civilization would finally turn into a fully singularized entity reigning imperially over the planet's entirety. The only questions, rather, were related to what Power would take greatest control over a global imperium, when precisely it would do so, and what precise form the Empire would take.

Even these latter three questions, though, weren't up for much debate, as shown by the history spanning 1898-1945 shows (see next two sections). Once the grand strategy for a fundamentally U.S.-led global capitalist hegemony was forged, all that needed to take place was the strategy's implementation. The minutest particulars related to fulfilling the strategy certainly changed over time, like with any grand strategy, but by 1945 the result was more or less everything Western hegemons had always wanted: a single global *Power*-structure comprised of a meticulously-designed war-trade hierarchy, held in the hands of a stunningly few individuals. The basic logistical structure and all the plans for the global civilization were there; it just required an adequate guiding hand emanating from the pyramid's apex, invisibly linking everything at the highest (deepest) levels to everything subordinate. This was the role assigned to, among other similar institutions, CIA, which, as much as anything else related to the original actualization of Earth's first truly global *Power*-structure, wasn't only a historical departure but was equally so a historical culmination.

Thus, by 1947, three intertwined processes had been well established, and the evolution of their interplay would shape the rest of the contemporary world. In the order of longest scale to shortest, they were: (1) the culmination of Western civilization unto the conditions making the global civilization possible (a system which would now be primed to grow until collapse); (2) the culmination of the United States' Empire unto conditions whereby it was possible to exercise hegemony over the emergent global civilization; and (3) the official institutionalization of a shadow government within the center of the U.S. State. While each of the three processes can be *analytically* distinguished, the defining characteristic of each process *in reality* was its inextricability from the other two in the years following 1947 and the official birth of what's commonly called the 'national security State', via the U.S. Government.

As we can start to see, the global civilization has always been inextricably related to the U.S. State and the transnational shadow government ultimately controlling it. Concerning the global civilization's early years, at least, CIA was in a class by itself in terms of its decisive influence over this "informal" imperial arrangement. It's fair to say the agency played midwife and then nanny to the hegemons' infant planetary dominion.

*   *   *

Barely a few years after the unveiling of the National Security Act of 1947, resultant of which the U.S. started to transform once and for all into a permanent war machine, the machine, naturally, was put into dramatic action: *Power* can only be consolidated insofar as it's exercised, or expressed – or, as U.S. planners like to say, 'projected'. "The world stage", of course, was the proper forum for the machine's introduction of itself. And at this point in history, the world stage was now an almost literally singular entity, epitomized in the United Nations, an organization constructed and maintained strictly under U.S. control, despite the constant American attempts to portray the U.N. as independent from any individual State. Anyway, these attempts were, as always, significant solely concerning their value for 'domestic consumption'. Outside the imperial heartland, the hegemons could do pretty much anything they wanted, so long as they could find some "plausible" way to keep their behavior dissociated from general perceptions of American officialdom.

Truman referred to the Korean War as a "police action", because if he called it a "war" he would've had to involve Congress in the decision, per the U.S. Constitution; and the global shadow government needed to know it could do what it wanted while still maintaining a facade of solemn respect for the Constitution. Nonetheless, there was still some truth to the phrasing, after all: the Korean War marked the first outward step for the global *Power*-structure along what has been its dominant path ever since – U.S.-led *State policing* of human affairs all over the planet. The dominant conventional narrative of the conflict designates it as overt U.S. intervention in a "civil war" between "North" Korea and "South" Korea. Few individuals today, apparently, find it strange that the U.S. should have such hands-on involvement with so serious a matter in the internal affairs of what was supposedly a sovereign polity; perhaps because, at the present, later date, it just seems to be such a normal thing for the United States to do.

In any era of U.S. history but our own, though, that would've indeed seemed a quite peculiar thing for the United States to do. While the idea of 'neutrality' in international affairs suffered a near-fatal blow due to how much rhetorical abuse it suffered in the setting of World War One, there were still at least pretensions of a "return to normalcy" leading up to World War Two. However, just as the U.S. Government illustrated at the beginning of World War One, and throughout the "interwar years", that it would invoke "neutrality" whenever it was beneficial to its own cause,[ccxcvii] the U.S illustrated all the more clearly, via the mechanically managed, deliberate production of a "war" in Korea, that neutrality had no place whatsoever in the new global setting. This would be precisely the point of the Cold War, in fact, as sparked off, most visibly, by the Korean War itself – every nation was ostensibly being forced to choose between "Capitalism" or "Communism".

But the idea of nations actually choosing between "Capitalism" and "Communism" was a moot point, because as we've seen the United States and the Soviet Union already had a basic spheres of influence agreement in place, so no nation was given any real choice in the matter. Regarding whether or not the agreement was a serious one, the U.S. Government certainly violated the Soviet sphere of influence when it desired, but the U.S. did this *covertly*. In terms of actual, open military conflict, although the Soviet Union was invariably portrayed as the puppet-master behind every opponent in all the many conflicts the U.S. involved itself in throughout the Cold War, the fact remains that, at least in the U.S.'s two major "hot" wars of the era (not including the emphatically proxy wars) – in Korea and Vietnam – the Kremlin didn't have *decisive* control over "the Enemy", and the U.S. was mainly responsible for initiating both episodes.[ccxcviii] (Obviously, the Soviets were also spying and undertaking operations in the U.S.'s sphere of influence, including in the domestic U.S. itself, but once more, this was always covert activity, and it was never anything the hegemons couldn't ultimately deal with. It could in fact often be to their benefit.) Again, this is because, on a planet with nuclear and soon thermonuclear weapons, nothing less than *total control at all times* was necessary at *Power*'s highest (deepest) levels in a world, and thus whenever a "hot" war was being fought, one "higher-up" side had to ultimately be managing things for both of the opposing, "lower-down" sides. I realize how ridiculous this sounds to individuals trained to think by the contemporary dominant culture, but it doesn't make it any less true; indeed it has been perhaps the most uniquely significant determinant in the holistic field of human warfare since the start of the sixth period (1947). Such a "necessity" to wield total control over both sides in an armed conflict was probably the single most influential factor catalyzing the exponential rise of "Intelligence Agencies" (official paramilitaries) in the contemporary world.[ccxcix]

Along with the creation of CIA, the establishment of the Department of Defense was among the handful of greatest changes brought on by the post-World War Two reorganization of the U.S. Government. Concerning the real historical results, these were probably the two greatest institutional transformations of all. After Korea, the purpose of which, as far as I'm concerned, was little more than to serve as a test case/establishment of precedent for the new strategy, these three entities – CIA, DoD, and the rest of the U.S. Government – began being woven together evermore tightly, with CIA, true to its nature, playing the role of key "handler" in the process. Just as in all major governmental departments, and eventually in any it might conceivably consider important for any reason whatsoever, CIA set up a "liaison" office between itself and the Department of Defense so as to best facilitate CIA infiltration of the new U.S. military establishment. Responsible for setting up the particular Joint Special Operations unit charged with secretly coordinating covert and overt combat activity for the Air Force was L. Fletcher Prouty, who would write two books about the contemporary shadow government and ran the unit he set up during one of the most critical ten years in contemporary U.S. history, between 1955 and 1964.[ccc] Seeing things from a perspective at the heart of the direct interconnection between the U.S. Government's two greatest organizational transformations, thereby truly witnessing one small portion of the global civilization's rise, the value of Prouty's first-hand knowledge concerning the workings of the global capitalist hegemony can hardly be overstated.

Getting his start as a pilot during World War Two, Prouty was part of the last generation to experience the old War Department form of U.S. military organization. Most notably, the Army and the Navy were totally separate entities, and the air force was simply a specialized division within the former. In other words, there wasn't an official, comprehensive centralization of all decision-making concerning U.S. military affairs. This design, if it had outlasted World War Two, would've made it impossible for all U.S. grand strategy to be implemented covertly by a single group, whether that group was officially "inside" or "outside" the government proper. The U.S. military as a whole was thereby not nearly as effective an instrument towards outright imperial mobilization in the pre-Cold War years, and outright imperial mobilization was of course the major goal and in turn the major consequence of the reconsolidation and streamlining of the U.S. warfare system, the definitive action marking the combined origins of the U.S. national security State and the Cold War. In the "old" style of running things, at least since 1898, only the Navy and its own specialized division, the Marines, had been used primarily as tools for perpetuation of U.S. overseas conquest during times of "Peace".

So, besides this total centralization of all U.S. military affairs, mainly towards the end of ultimately controlling said affairs by CIA – and really, only the relatively tiny, covert operations segment within CIA[ccci] – the other biggest change in U.S. warmaking capabilities directly brought on by the 1947 National Security Act was the creation of an independent Air Force. Once it was created, it quickly became a "first among equals" in relation to the Army and the Navy. Just like CIA's rapid behind-the-scenes rise to governmental dominance, this was another excellent institutional signal regarding what the hegemons were throwing their weight behind in order to get the Cold War machine up-and-running. Additionally, these two elements – CIA and the Air Force – in no way emerged in isolation from one another, but were, rather, established largely in tandem, at least from a deep perspective.

On the surface, the reason for the Air Force's immediately-attained prominence within the U.S.'s shiny new national security State had everything to do with what all emergent Cold War phenomena had everything to do with: the nuclear bomb. Amidst the bureaucratic setting of the U.S. Government at the time when such decisions were being made, each of the three heads of the DoD's new Cerberus tried to make the case that his budding military bureaucracy was best qualified to star in the nuclear grand strategy. In reality, the decision had already been made regardless of any individual argument, because the hegemons were already plotting a U.S. Air Force buildup. No one outside the chosen circle of key decision-makers would be allowed to know it yet, but the U.S. and the S.U. would shortly be in a nuclear and, soon enough, thermonuclear arms race, strictly according to the designs of "the American Century". This was going to require an explosion in airpower most of all, since, in a nuclear arms race, the delivery system for such weapons is the truly crucial thing. And remember, all of these decisions about the direction of U.S. government in the post-World War Two era were being long before the Soviet Union's successfully detonation of its first atomic bomb (which wouldn't happen until 1949), so those individuals in the rarest positions to influence public affairs surely knew there would be another nuclear Power on planet Earth in the very near future. The broadest-sweeping U.S. Government actions were being undertaken as if that were already the case.

Fairly close to the highest levels of "official" (officially unofficial) government even in these days prior to his helping set up one of the critical units connecting U.S. military strategy to CIA "policy" (infiltration), Prouty's writings certainly affirm that enormous strategic positions of the U.S. Government were, in these earliest days of the Cold War, starting to be put into place well in advance of any public discussions related to those positions. That is, at least in certain extremely consequential cases, the public discussions were relevant solely to the extent that they could produce public support for decisions already being implemented. Obviously, I've been arguing this all along, often times simply on the basis of common sense: how else can such an unprecedentedly vast, incomprehensibly complex structure such as the global social structure function on such a constant basis without at any point (yet) completely destroying itself? But rarely has the logical overarching viewpoint been confirmed in as much startling detail as Prouty's uniquely lucid reportage.

I consider it no exaggeration to assert that, if one is lacking a familiarity with the primary sources represented by Prouty's two works, *The Secret Team* (1972) and *JFK* (1990), one can't possibly fully understand the era of 1947-63, the global civilization's first explicit phase and in many ways, its "golden age". And, to an extent only possible in the contemporary world, all subsequent global history has been inextricably dependent on this remarkably eventful time in U.S. history between the passage of the National Security Act (July 26, 1947) and the coup d'etat that replaced John F. Kennedy with Lyndon B. Johnson as the President of the United States (November 22, 1963).

Keeping with this narrative's dominant theme of 'consciousness', it's my belief that, once the politicoeconomic system turned fully nuclear and hence required and received as close to total synchronization around the globe as was possible, cultural consciousness resultantly could (and did) become so globally synchronized that every individual event close to the seat of greatest *Power* took on an exponentially inflated overall significance compared to individual events in pre-nuclear history. If you want something we might call an "imaginary quantification" expressing how greatly inflated events became, compare the force of the atomic bomb to that of the most destructive bomb preceding it, the British 'Grand Slam'. This bomb came from the directly prior sociohistorical context, World War Two, and yet the atomic bomb was over *two thousand times* more potent.[cccii] Thus, if we use the comparison between "most *Powerful* arms available" as a rough leading indicator of how significant any given individual event is surrounding the seat of greatest *Power* – in this case, the U.S. Government – then even compared to similar individual events in the years immediately before, individual events surrounding the seat of *Power* in the world spawned by the nuclear weapons dropped over Hiroshima and Nagasaki can be viewed as over 2,000 times more significant. The inflated *Power* manifests itself firstly in the form of a scramble to manage potential for uncontrollable disorder.

Again, this is meant to serve as metaphor rather than direct quantitative correspondence, so that we can garner some realistic sense of just how much more rapidly history was happening in these years of nuclear and thermonuclear weapons, and mainly on their account. Imagine it in these terms: since the seat of greatest *Power* is by definition so very *Powerful* primarily owing to association with the capacity for organized violence, then every individual action occurring in such a seat of *Power* is distinctly related in some way to the potential for using such violence. In that vein, the closer one gets to the epicenter of organized violence – which, here, would be in the deep shadows behind the executive branch of the U.S. Government – the more apt the comparison becomes.

Thanks to the advent of the nuclear arms race, which became a thermonuclear arms race more or less right away, this *Power* became all the greater still, with each Superpower quickly gaining the capacity to destroy the preponderance of the planet's existing life. Absolutely nothing else in history can be justly compared to this horrifying state-of-affairs in its all-encompassing potential to transform reality, to an extent no one is really prepared to contemplate.[ccciii] Everything else in the global civilization is nonetheless rigidly organized around this incomprehensible potential, and has to be for the system to exist at all, insofar as the system only "works" if the center rigs the game completely, as the center has done to an astonishingly thorough degree ever since the Cold War began. (Aside from its clear success at destruction, though, the *overall* "success" of the system can be gauged by the fact that it has existed for well short of a century and yet it's already breaking down – and has been for many years.) In a context where certain potential paths can lead to the destruction of all life, it's easy to persuade almost everyone, in one way or another, that the masses should be the last people permitted input on important decisions.

The Power in charge is able to ensure such faithful mass acquiescence to its monopoly on organized violence for one reason: in a system where, so long as it exists, humanity's energy use is naturally trending towards infinite expansion, the center is by nature in decisive control of this energy use, or else the system wouldn't be "infinitely" expanding in the first place. Thereby, the center can influence the remainder of the civilization – and in a globally encompassing civilization the "remainder" is the rest of the entire planet – in a way not only unparalleled by all prior civilizations, but in a way that literally *couldn't* have been paralleled by any other system in history. Now, this may make it seem like those responsible for managing the center are truly godly, that they can control absolutely anything at will. But the control represented by the hegemony itself actually implies a *lack* of any true control by the people running it, at least at the level of the individual. The very existence of the system is dependent on the precise manner in which the hegemons perpetuate it; this already confirms that they can't just make any decision they want to. Indeed, they're locked into extremely specific types of decisions –

precisely those types ensuring that the rigged game keeps on running. Prouty's testimony provides an unmatched primary source* illustrating how the game was/is rigged, starting with its earliest Cold War origins.

The predominant theme woven through all of Prouty's writings is the inextricability between individuals in civilizations and the States they're subject to, an interrelationship that I believe is exhibited in its most striking manifestations at the very top and the very bottom of the *Power*-structure. Prouty himself, for instance, who worked as close to the top of the true contemporary *Power*-structure as any other individual to date that has willingly shared his or her firsthand knowledge, shows how a human system's *Power* can be seen as being *exactly proportional to how consequential its actions are in the scope of its overall context*. During the middle and late (1947 -) contemporary periods, the hegemons have ruled over the most *Powerful* conceivable command structure in the most enormous possible civilization in history. Accordingly, the absolute effects of the *Power*-structure's actions illustrate a scale simply incomparable to that of any other sociohistorical context.

Moreover, to an extent not even thinkable in any other era in human history, individuals who have had decisive control over the actions of the contemporary *Power*-structure – above all, the hegemons – can not only achieve but can actually *see* the effects of their own actions on a global scale, and can do so in literal real time. This becomes all the truer once one reaches the beginning of the sixth period (1947), and increases exponentially in truth from that point forward. So, while the actions of individuals surrounding the top of the *Power*-structure produce a greater total impact on the rest of humanity and the planet-at-large, these same actions are simultaneously more immediately, apparently effective than ever before – the intentions behind the actions are more tightly in-line with the results of those actions than ever before. The actions taken by those at the helms of this supreme command post literally affect all of humanity, and indeed all of the rest of the planet, as well: and at a time when there has never been such a great quantity of material making up humanity and the substances of its world. And those commanding can *feel* this *Power* instantaneously.

---

* Really, "primary-secondary" source – see Part 3, *BOOK TWO*.

But even so uniquely dominant a social structure as that holding the global politicoeconomic system in place can by no means exist on its own. It needs to constantly secure the cultivation of a *global culture*, in order to ensure its own continued existence. This provides the primary explanation for the nature of the *Power*-structure's ever-increasing dependence on psychological warfare throughout the contemporary world's history. The necessity for emphasizing uniquely ideological tactics, above all other forms of warfare, emerged mainly on account of two factors working in combination: (1) the need to "subtly" coerce worldwide acceptance of U.S.-led hegemony over a global State-capitalist regime; and (2) the need to create the appearance of a real dire contradiction between the U.S. and its "opponent", the S.U., when only the most imaginary contradictions existed.

Thus, a threefold process emanated from the core of the global hegemony and rapidly exploded across the planet throughout the 1950s: individuals at the top of the *Power*-structure were becoming evermore successful at perpetuating the structure; the structure was becoming evermore *Powerful* in an absolute sense; and the more easily controlled, more *Powerful* structure was ever-increasingly becoming the sole sociohistorical context subsuming everything else on Earth. It ran parallel to the other major threefold process happening at the same time on the more conscious, more 'public' level, whereby the conditions for globalization emerged; the U.S. Empire culminated its long-historical evolution by gaining hegemony over this globalization culture; and the U.S. Government, the empire's heart, silently got hijacked by an officially-instituted shadow government. This sociohistorically enormous compound of interlocked processes was the precise scenario within which individuals like Prouty were embedded.

In the second half of the 20th-century, the process Prouty observed at what was basically its earliest visible point would constitute one of the handful of most significant lived narratives shaping everything else human beings call "*the* world". For CIA was at the center of that exponentially-increasing consolidation of global *Power* animating the heart of U.S. Empire. More specifically, the mechanism of control lay in the Agency's ultra-covert clandestine operations function, which would become the original major flashpoint between CIA and DoD – quite naturally, since clandestine operations are nothing besides military operations, albeit military operations of an extremely specialized kind – the exact area of Prouty's experience. Such explains how CIA took decisive control of the U.S. military at the Cold War's outset, and how it then used this most formidable base-of-operations to garner sway over the entire U.S. Government. It's difficult to think of any institutional nexus in the entire world more critical towards securing the initial formative period of fully-emergent global civilization than this tiny fraction Prouty worked for.

In both of his books, Prouty repeatedly returns to the crucial point that CIA, as he saw it materialize, was almost exclusively the creation of Allen Dulles and his closest associates. Although, this was purely from a "within the government" standpoint: Prouty simultaneously reiterates that, as it happened – and as he so aptly notes, what's implied by the very term 'agent' – Dulles was clearly never primarily representing his own interests in the course of his "public service".[ccciv] Indistinguishable from his "private" job as a Wall Street lawyer, working for a Rockefeller-dominated law firm (Sullivan & Cromwell), Dulles in his government activities was always acting as the subordinate of his financial-corporate controllers, just as the government itself ended up being subordinate largely to Dulles and his brother, the Secretary of State, John Foster Dulles.[cccv]

Not only would Dulles become the longest-serving Director of Central Intelligence (ceremonial head of the original public apex atop the U.S. "intelligence community"), acting in that capacity during Eisenhower's entire presidency and fatefully remaining for about the first year of Kennedy's aborted term; also, he was almost singularly instrumental in drawing up the original plans behind the Agency's charter. When performing this latter-mentioned task, Dulles wasn't even working in government at the time, but was back on the "private" side of U.S. government's revolving door. In its very inception, the CIA as it came to exist was only nominally a creation of the official Government: quite true to form it crept in through back channels.

As the story goes, Truman and Congress had agreed to an agency that would "coordinate the nation's intelligence", and solely agreed to the creation of some hypothetical "central intelligence agency" on that basis. All of the governmental contention surrounding the process leading to the Agency's creation, such as there was, rather surprisingly centered on the truly significant issue: the majority were dead-set against sanctioning an official arm of the U.S. Government with license to carry on unlimited clandestine operations during "Peacetime", and they especially feared the idea that such operations would be based within the same institution responsible for intelligence gathering. Even Truman was apparently worried by the potential for disaster inherent in the very concept of a clandestinely operating paramilitary unit of the U.S. Executive Branch, which is precisely what CIA became.[cccvi] Considering that Truman is the only world leader throughout all of history to authorize the use of nuclear weapons during active combat, I think it says quite a lot when *he* had reservations about something. Naturally unconcerned with the objections of a mere president, Dulles, ever the able attorney, constructed the legislation's language in such a way that later on, when he was finally putting into practice the plan to seamlessly infiltrate the State via his long pre-selected position as DCI, he could – and frequently did – justify all of his actions on the basis of the language of the law. (All this of course raises a very interesting question, if one still takes at face value the overarching worldview inculcated by the contemporary dominant culture: if those officially in charge of the publicly-acknowledged system really have a speck of true control, how could any group completely bypass the President and the U.S. Congress, implement its own grand strategy via the highest levels of the U.S. Government, and never be subjected to any viable checks on its activities? – Unless that group, in fact, was the real governing Power in charge.)

Based on the general texture exhibited by Prouty's main concerns as a writer, we can sum up what was CIA's main objective from the start – whether or not it was ever spoken of in the exact terms I'll use. Its main objective, and hence the main thing sought after by its ultimate controllers, was to assure that the global *Power*-structure would, in any conceivable instance, have at least the potential to violate the sovereignty of practically any nation. It would do so primarily by utilizing what originally seemed to be an endless supply of material means at the disposal of the U.S.'s burgeoning national security State, in a context where the entire planet would soon be divided into national States supposedly subject to nothing besides strict international law. In turn, at the same time, and again considering the very nature of the sociohistorical context during the early Cold War years – both internationally and in the imperial heartland – the other, equally indispensable objective for CIA was to smother its activities in endless informational obfuscation. Notice that it's not completely correct to say that CIA's other main objective was 'secrecy', *per se*; more accurately, it was to keep everyone in as uncertain a state-of-mind as was possible regarding what it, or anything it controlled, was really up to. As history has shown, compared to simple secrecy, the fulfillment of this objective is a far more surefire way for an organization in the contemporary world to successfully hide its true activities, and in turn, its true purpose. In a context of global mass communications and necessarily global interaction between populations, the goal of real secrecy never could've been comprehensively achieved anyway, as has long been well known[cccvii]; and it's simply a mistake to think that the individuals controlling the shield of "Security" have ever been unaware of this fact.

Once again, the hegemons were purely concerned with packaging information in a way suitable for domestic consumption, and exhibited caution regarding very little else.

But then, the core of the real plan had been in the works for years, long before the end of World War Two and, in the most broadly significant ways, long before that war even began; so "public opinion" was really the only variable yet to be dealt with, in order to fulfill the well-laid hegemonic strategy. And the hegemons, of course, were masters of this game above any other: public opinion, although still technically a variable, was nonetheless a variable that had become wholly susceptible to an almost unimaginable degree of influence on behalf of the global system's controllers.

Only apparently coming to his conclusions in their ultimately laid-out form after much reflection, during the aftermath of a career so rare in its documented significance and yet so largely unnoticed, Prouty would at some point realize and assert the centrality of his governmental milieu in furthering a hegemonic grand strategy through the utilization of U.S. military *Power* as one of the few most vital links in a global imperial chain. One gets a strong sense that Prouty's self-realization came with a heavy heart, and the very fact that he wrote his two books with so much apparent honesty is the greatest evidence of that. Most simply, we can concisely sum up his milieu as the underlying, unspeakable nexus coordinating secret operations, the Department of Defense, and the rest of the U.S. Federal administrative bureaucracy. The explosion of this triangle of purest *Power*, starting all throughout the 1950s, would quickly allow the United States to take full control of the post-World War Two order, in an "informal" way that ultimately proved far more effective than the wildest fancies of the most megalomaniacal pre-nuclear imperialist.

Simultaneously, the "unofficial" Powers were finally, fully taking control of this virtually infinite *Power* inherent in the contemporary official State, which the unofficial Powers (the hegemons) had been cultivating for decades, through two world wars and "the Great Depression". Unsurprisingly, I might add – we shouldn't expect that they would've just let all their hard work go to waste. The Cold War was the fruition of their greatest long-term investment: the global civilization.

II

Going Back to the Beginning: Industrialization, Financial Politics, and the Necessity of Empire

It's hard to say precisely when, but certainly by 1898 a plan was in place to inextricably synchronize the global actions of two separate States: the old British Empire and what was among the most newly emergent Great Powers, the United States. Militaries must work, most broadly, according to *grand strategies*, referring to the conscious total distribution of a militarized entity's resources over geographical space, not to *battle strategies*, meaning the overall plans driving individualized acts of warfare. By definition, then, there must also be individuals formulating the strategies, or plans – there must be planners. In 1898 and 1899, the United States' lead planners, its grand strategists, would instigate wars on two fronts, in two different hemispheres, which nonetheless had a single aim in common; this single aim represented a perfect example of what I mean by "grand strategy".

The U.S. Government claimed the aim was to aid in the "liberation" of two Spanish colonies from their imperial mother: Cuba in the Western hemisphere, and the Philippines in the Eastern. "Secretly", but what was nonetheless still quite obvious (even to some observers at the time),[cccviii] the purpose was to officially initiate the U.S. into the Great Power game, which at this point in history was evermore quickly becoming a fully globalized contest. As it turns out, this initiation, more than any other factor, would aid in that globalization's completion. On the British side, true execution of the grand strategy didn't officially start until 1899, when the almighty British Empire instigated a war against the tiny Boer republics in what's today South Africa, so as to ensure that, if ever necessary, British interests would be in position to exercise strategic control over the latest South African discovery of an unprecedented supply in precious minerals, this time in the form of gold. Ultimately the plan belonged to a cabal headed by Cecil Rhodes, who, upon his death in 1902, would become the namesake of Oxford University's much sought-after Rhodes' scholarship. Rhodes had for years spoken of the need to institute tighter management over the British Empire, which he imagined would someday operate in the form of a global confederation of States, managed by an omnipotently maneuvering central organization. Rhodes wanted the latter to be directed from the top by a tiny 'Society of the Elect' – with himself at the head, of course. He referred to this idealized cadre as a "Church for British Empire", envisioning that it should work much like the Jesuits.[cccix]

Why was it necessary for these two monumental episodes, near-simultaneous yet otherwise so seemingly disparate, to be so intimately connected? Primarily, it was already quite clear at the time that both States, the U.K. and the U.S., had one great enemy in common: the rising German Empire. The parties with greatest influence over U.S. governmental policy had come to particularly abhor German penetration into the U.S.'s "sphere of influence" in the Caribbean and Central and South America. Despite the decades-old U.S. wish represented by the Monroe Doctrine, however, U.S. military supremacy over Latin America remained merely a wish – until the War of 1898, when the U.S. ended its four-month participation in the intervention for "Cuban independence" by imposing protectorate status on Cuba, which marked the official start of interference in Cuban government that continues to this day. More generally, too, the U.S. has since then essentially never loosened its imperial grip on Latin America as a whole, despite constant resistance to what has at different times been variously a U.S. Empire or the U.S. head of a broader global empire.

The *Powerful* factions running the U.S. Government, though, knew the plan couldn't be fully executed without the Philippines: nor, further, could combined control over Cuba and the Philippines reach its full potential for sustaining the holistic U.S. politicoeconomic system without the long-rumored, much-troubled attempts to construct a Panama Canal getting on the right track. If a Panama Canal were indeed successfully constructed under U.S. auspices, with a U.S. hegemony dominant over both Cuba in the Caribbean and the Philippines in the Pacific, the control over world trade accruing to whoever was in charge of U.S. affairs would be almost beyond imagination.

Only, someone must've actually imagined that scenario – and not only imagined it, but devised a grand strategy aiming to make it a reality – because that's exactly what happened after the War of 1898, which ended up also becoming the War of 1899 when the U.S. similarly declared war in order to "pacify" the Philippines.[cccx] Just like in Cuba, U.S. policymakers said the nation's soldiers were going to aid the Philippines in "gaining independence", and then in actuality completely annihilated all potential for real Filipino independence. After taking imperial control over Cuba and the Philippines, U.S. interests took control over the Panama Canal by way of the U.S. military in 1903, a campaign spiritually led by the U.S. president, Teddy Roosevelt, who had first become nationally famous by having himself filmed while "participating in combat" amidst the short Spanish-American war (which of course ended up being a very long Cuban-American war).

From there, the Anglo-American hegemons, whose activities in the U.S. were originally centered almost exclusively in the leading financial houses of Wall Street – in particular, the hegemons were reliant upon the incomparably *Powerful* Morgan Company – used their newly-elevated control over the world market to effect the Panic of 1907.[cccxi] This control had intensified not only because of the emergent American hegemony over the Panama Canal route, which added to what was more or less an existing British hegemony over the Suez Canal route, but owing also to the British hegemony gained over South Africa's mineral wealth resultant from the Boer War.

Now, throughout the 19th-century, the direct prelude to the birth of globalization (interchangeably, the gestation of the global civilization), the gold standard was the central organizing mechanism for Western-based international trade. However, throughout the first fourteen years of the 20th-century there was a complete breakdown of the international trade structure, and the predominate reason was the collapse of the gold standard as a realistic means of running national politicoeconomic systems in a world ever-increasingly dependent upon an *inter*national economy.[cccxii] Already in the earliest years of the 1900s, the existing politicoeconomic system, formed not only on an international but also on an intercivilizational level by the dominant Western forces – the Great Powers – was far too large and complex to be monetarily sustained solely by the traditional gold standard.[cccxiii]

If the money supply in a completely monetized economy is directly equivalent to the quantity of gold (or any other fixed commodity) in circulation, then the economy can only grow as fast as the rate of gold-production allows. Whether one thinks this is a laudable trait or an undesirable one, the fact remains that it made the gold standard completely unfeasible for the Western system of the early 20th-century, if the system were to continue growing the way it had been. This system was based on the logic of "infinite" economic growth while at the same time, still trapped within the preindustrial framework of always-expanding interstate conquest. Obviously, infinite growth on a finite planet would prove fairly quickly to be the most unfeasible option of all, especially as it happened to be organized around industrialized warfare. During the early 20th-century, though, people clearly couldn't yet see exactly *how* limited was the growth available to that particular form of Western system, and the ideal of infinite war-based industrial growth would easily win out.

Indeed, the ideal had already won out: whether or not people viewed it in those exact terms, the logic of infinite growth was itself the factor most responsible for the Western industrial system's initial spreading all over the planet. This phenomenon was epitomized empirically by the "Scramble for Africa", but more significantly it was essentially inevitable once the system had spread throughout the West in the first place, as it had starting around the beginning of the 1800s. Historian Thomas Schoonover puts the state-of-affairs most aptly and simply in the context of 'social imperialism', by which he refers to the dominant Western belief at the time, whether the late 19th-century/early 20th-century governmental elites couched it in the language of "empire" or just referred to it as a "civilizing mission", etc., that domestic order could only be lastingly achieved through "exporting disorder" to the desired areas of overseas expansion. The export of disorder could be achieved rather literally by sending elements "troublesome" to home stability across the world, to some "savage" territory – individuals taking this route were known as "colonists" – or, what was becoming the favorite method by the beginning of contemporary history, by forcing upon conquered territories the "surplus" goods produced by domestic production.[cccxiv]

Above all, the desire to keep the gold standard in place reflected the almost total control over the Anglo-American system exercised by international financiers. The economy of Germany, on the other hand, the leading rival of the U.K.-U.S., was based on corporate industrial monopolies, which would eventually come to embody the German cartel system. These monopolies provided the key explanation for how Germany emerged to achieve such imposing Great Power status in such an astonishingly short time. An international financial system run completely on the gold standard and an international production/distribution system run by industrial monopolies couldn't long coexist, because the production/distribution monopolies required perpetually increasing supply-demand relationships for their survival, which as I said couldn't be supported in the long-term by a monetary system based solely on the gold standard. The problem for the Anglo-American hegemons then was that they naturally wanted to keep their unparalleled control over human affairs, but their unparalleled control over human affairs, based on control of the gold standard, had arrived at a moment when the gold standard was clearly being superseded. No matter *how* it "had to happen", Germany and all other similar possible contenders had to be destroyed, giving the hegemons the breathing room to put their new system in place.

To crush Germany, the Anglo-American hegemons needed access to the U.S.'s seemingly unlimited economic potential. The hegemons knew this couldn't be achieved without a U.S. central bank – in the new context of globalization, the first absolutely indispensable monopoly was a money monopoly. A Great Power needed to be able to *totally mobilize* its dominion's wealth, if it were to have any chance of fighting a great war successfully. On the scale of a large, early 20th-century national State like the United States, nothing approaching total mobilization of wealth could be achieved without the singularly centralizing mechanism of a central bank, which would produce a unitarily managed national money supply under the aegis of a private consortium comprising the nation's most politically influential financiers. With a controlling share over the transport logistics of global trade and similarly decisive control over the world gold supply – two inextricable phenomena at the time, both centered in London[cccxv] – combined with incomparable dominance of the U.S. financial system via the Morgan Co. and associates, the Anglo-American hegemons were, fortuitously for Anglo-American hegemony, in prime position to manipulate U.S. markets.

In 1908, stirred on by the public for financial reform, the U.S. Congress passed a resolution to have something called "financial reform" drawn up and made law: the Monetary Reform Commission was brought into existence. Nelson Aldrich, a Senator from Rhode Island, was in charge of the commission. Unsurprisingly, Aldrich was a banker himself, and, as *Powerful* individuals are always wont to do, had married into much greater *Power* via his daughter Abigail, when she betrothed John D. Rockefeller, Jr. The Rockefellers, of course, aside from being fabulously wealthy, were also among the handful of most consequential factors in American politics. They ran Standard Oil and as such had become *the* favored industrial faction of J.P. Morgan, just like J.P. Morgan had become the Rockefellers' favored investment-banking faction. Naturally, the latter had moved rapidly into the financial industry as well, controlling the Chase National Bank and the National City Bank.[cccxvi]

Therefore, after a financial crisis in 1907 with particularly severe economic repercussions affecting the public at large, the person assigned responsibility for coming up with a solution was more or less the direct representative of those individuals most responsible for the crisis.

It shouldn't really be surprising: but even most historians, unless the relevant period and sociohistorical context happens to be their particular area of specialization, rarely seem to recognize how incomprehensibly open in its corruption, compared to today's standards, the U.S. Government was at the beginning of the contemporary world. And the corruption of the government at that time has ultimately produced the most far-reaching consequences for all subsequent history (not just U.S. history, either). Even merely from a common-sense standpoint, though, despite how unprecedentedly rapid the rate of sociohistorical evolution has been, all throughout the 20th-century-beyond-era thus far, I must remind everyone that 116 years is still almost nothing from a long historical perspective. Certainly, 116 years between 1898 and 2014, in many significant ways, is completely different from 114 years at any other point in history; but in other significant ways, it's still exactly the same. Information about the world as it existed at the beginning of this era, then, remains of the utmost relevance to the existent world.

Under certain conditions, it's practically impossible to change the deepest structural foundations underlying a human culture. It seems to me, for instance, that if one truly wanted to change a culture, a good way to do it *wouldn't* be to invest the greatest quantity of energy ever expended into perpetuating the culture's existing set of *Power*-relations. Indeed, I think that would be the worst possible way to fundamentally change a culture, and the best way to send it hurtling evermore-quickly in its same direction. Largely following from what was happening at the very beginning of the 20th-century, the dominant culture has been making precisely this investment all throughout the contemporary era, and the holistic result has been the creation of the most destructive human system that can ever potentially exist: Western civilization taken to its logical extreme.

The contemporary dominant culture accomplished such a feat insofar as it was primarily based on control over the world's non-renewable energy stocks, most namely petroleum, towards the end of supporting an ever-expanding money supply – ever-expanding until the entire system simply collapses – defended by an ever-expanding security machine (again, ever-expanding until the entire system simply collapses). This is precisely what allows a U.S.-inspired global culture to thrive. Insofar as the Anglo-American hegemons, which is to say, the hegemons most responsible for controlling the global civilization *monopolized* by the U.S. social structure, are the leading agents making the system run, the system has ultimately been their creation. But don't miss the critical point: everyone who benefits from globalization has played a role in producing and reproducing the system on a constant basis. The most important reason why the hegemons' story must be told, from my perspective, is to show that – concerning everyone who benefits – this is, ultimately, what they benefit from. This is their doing as well.

Returning to the Monetary Reform Commission, the near unsurpassable conflicts-of-interest inherent in its very existence might not have had such harmful consequences, were it not for two interesting bits of information, one related to why it was created in the first place, the other related to what the commission ultimately produced. Again, the motivation behind creating the commission was instigated by the Panic of 1907, which, while it might've most broadly had structural origins, nonetheless was finally catalyzed in the particular way it was owing to deliberate manipulation of financial markets by the relative handful of men in New York and London who really controlled the American financial system.[cccxvii] Indeed, most generally, panics of the sort we're familiar with in the contemporary world – severe financial crises emerging from "runs" on banks, themselves invariably created by investment bubbles – always emerge initially from structural conditions inherent to market economies, and then are in the end "pushed over the edge" by those leading investment bankers who will benefit from the devastating aftermath.

The reason is so simple that it's truly painful when it passes through your brain: the leading investment bankers are typically the only individuals who have significant opportunity to affect financial markets in real-time. Because they are, definitively, the most up-to-date individuals on the relevant kind of information whose opinions actually matter to the specific type of event-cluster sequence – the contemporary form of financial panic – and thus by definition the individuals whose actions are most consequential to the specific type of sequence, they're typically the only individuals in positions to willfully benefit from financial crises. Moreover, referring especially now to the broad sociohistorical context of the Panic of 1907, such individuals were always the only individuals with enough relevant *Power* to manipulate markets exactly how they wanted them to be manipulated; that is, *the only individuals who could weaponize the market itself.*

But now, something is bound to seem strange about this perspective, related to the Panic of 1907 and the Monetary Reform Commission. Why were the hegemons so eager to tinker with a system that had made them so *Powerful*? The answer is in the "reform" eventually produced: the Federal Reserve Act of 1913, responsible for creating the Federal Reserve System, the U.S. central bank system officially instituted about a year later. Although it's true that the Federal Reserve bill was presented as an alternative to the Aldrich Bill, which was widely and rightly seen as a "Wall Street bill", the nature of the "alternatives" and how the successful one got passed actually prove, as well as any other aspects of the process, who really benefited from the system that ended up being put into place.[cccxviii]

While the bills were essentially identical in their makeup, Wall Street, led behind the scenes by the individuals most responsible for creating both proposals, railed against the Federal Reserve outline in the press. Clearly, the purpose was to sell the public on Wall Street's hatred for the Federal Reserve bill, because the public hated Wall Street, and Wall Street knew it. But Wall Street hated the public just as much: the difference was, the bankers had the means to do something about their hatred. And Wall Street's "opposition" to the Federal Reserve bill was a relatively easy lie to spread. Out of all the individuals at the time who might've possibly gotten to read the bill – members of the U.S. Congress – not very many of them did. (Although not many people understood financial matters anyway, so who knows how much of a difference that would've made?)

In this case, however, Congress's failure to read the bill was less the politicians' own fault than one could usually assume. Immediately preceding the bill's passage, two days before Christmas, 1913, there had been a strangely urgent push to get it done, and it was finally voted on in the affirmative during the wee morning hours.[cccxix] If it had to wait until January, when the public wouldn't be so occupied with the holidays and people had better opportunity to review and compare the two proposals, the bill might not be enacted so smoothly. That was simply unacceptable, to the hegemons: the United States had to have a central bank, and it had to have one as quickly as possible. Thus, everything was put on the line to assure that the Federal Reserve bill would succeed. Those individuals who were most in control of the politicoeconomic system – an absolutely miniscule group of internationally minded financiers and industrialists – were the only ones that could assure the introduction of so monumental a change with such great speed.

This wouldn't be so convincing an explanation as to how the Federal Reserve bill was passed were it not for one thing, which happened only about eight months afterwards: World War One started. What's the relevance, here? The Allies, led originally by Britain, literally couldn't have paid for the war if it weren't for loans arranged by said group of internationally minded financiers and industrialists,[cccxx] who themselves couldn't have arranged the loans without the total mobilization of funds made possible by the U.S. central bank, the Federal Reserve – which would officially become a working institution only a few months after the war began.[cccxxi] And of course, besides U.S. loans – made in actuality through the private banking firm of J.P. Morgan, even as the government would eventually be forced to guarantee them in the war's aftermath – the Allies won the war almost entirely because of how great an advantage they had in the speed and security of their lines-of-supply, thanks to the combination of U.S. naval control over the Panama Canal and British naval control over the Suez Canal.

As we've seen, before the U.S. started to firmly establish its dominance over the Caribbean and Central America via exploitation of the Panama Canal, the greatest threat to the U.S.'s desire to attain hegemony in Latin America had been Germany. The U.S.

only established such dominance, in the first place, resultant from the war on Cuba. As we've also seen, Britain had long viewed Germany as its greatest threat in that other imperial "contest" with uniquely hideous results for everyone besides its tiny group of prime beneficiaries, the "Scramble for Africa". In this vein, at the same time that the U.S. started waging aggressive war on the Philippines (1899), the "Scramble for Africa" was manifesting itself most notably in the aforementioned aggressive war waged by Britain on the Boer republics, which had similar strategic implications for any potential future Anglo-American alliance. Here, U.K. governing elites were afraid of the Boer Republics' apparent wish to try and court the Reich as a means of separating themselves from the British Empire (a potential which could always resurface if Britain's hold over southern Africa wavered at any moment).[cccxxii]

There was enormous crossover between the highest politicoeconomic elites in the U.K. and the U.S. The strategic field of utmost consequence was international finance, the *raison d'etre* of the key hegemonic circles in both nations, and the small group of financiers epitomized by Morgan had personal interests in essentially all major developments affecting anything related to Anglo-American government and industry around the turn of the century. It would've been utterly bizarre, then, if these individuals had nothing to do with their nations' participation in all significant international conflicts between 1898 and 1918; and we know for a fact that they were intimately involved at all the major stops along the way. If my overall perspective is controversial, it's only because I've taken one further step that seems to me, in light of all the facts to be not controversial at all: I've asserted that all of these individual episodes were related, that altogether they contributed to a coherent sequence – not in terms of how they ultimately affected world politics (for that would be indisputable), but in terms of how they were *planned*. Concerning how magnificent was the ultimate reward created by the sequence for the very Anglo-American hegemons in charge of their nations' policies, any other scenario would be completely unrealistic.

My argument isn't that the exact episode of World War One was in the works as the precise goal the whole time, from the War of 1898 and the Boer War to the beginning of August 1914. The argument, instead, is that the potential for an Anglo-American victory over Germany in a major war became all but completely certain as the direct result of a series of event-cluster sequences first catalyzed by Anglo-American success in the wars of 1898 and 1899, continuing through the Panic of 1907, and finalizing with the enactment of the Federal Reserve Act of 1913. The broadest-sweeping strategic goal the whole time then was to institute a central bank in the United States, in order to secure the ultimate war chest for a potential attack on Germany that was expected to happen sooner or later. This was no small goal at all. Rather, concerning a certain cadre representing the vast worldwide interests tied up with the hegemony of the British imperial system – and most notably, those working through the two major Anglo-American *Power*-centers (the governments of the United Kingdom and the United States) – it was the only thing at the time they found truly important.

Thus, right around the turn of the 20th-century, the most *Powerful* interests exercising hegemony over the British imperial system (with these interests being run from the top-down by their respective elite factions) would, from the deepest political levels, invest everything they had in crushing that pesky, explosively rising Great Power stationed in central Europe, the German Empire. The specific aim for each particular interest was somewhat different: yet their collective strategy ended up being so successful precisely because all of their individual goals could be solved, at least for the moment, with a single sweeping set of actions that would move the two States, Britain and the United States, ever-closer together. So just as the individual, 'tactical' goal was to gain the capability for mobilizing the totality of U.S. funds by instituting a central bank, the general, 'strategic' goal this tactical device was primarily servicing was to inextricably interlink the policies of the United States with the policies of the United Kingdom. Since the Anglo-American hegemons were the most *Powerful* individuals in the world at the time, if any group could've accomplished those two main goals, it would've been a group in which all of them were members.

As the goal was literally nothing less than a total reconquest of one of the planet's most enormous polities, filled with individuals who thought they were "Free", who, contrary to history, thought the rule of right took precedence over the rule of might, absolute secrecy had to be the method employed at all times. At this point in history, surrounding the specific epicenter of the Anglo-American hegemony, the propaganda and the reality were becoming so clearly divergent from one another at such a rapidly increasing rate, and in a broad context where the truth would've caused such uncontrollable social tension, that the system conceivably could've imploded immediately following the cession of State secrecy. Therefore, disinformation, an aggressive form of secrecy, was laden throughout and surrounding every major control mechanism of the two leading State components jointly aiming to gain monopoly control over Western civilization. Long before the explicit outbreak of World War One, the Anglo-American hegemons considered themselves at war with Germany and were acting accordingly, albeit necessarily keeping unknown the true intentions behind their actions, and even always trying to keep unknown which actions in particular were theirs'. This is typical behavior during times of war, and the aggressive conflicts of 1898-99 had ensured that the emergent Anglo-American Empire would always be at war with anything exhibiting the audacity to resist its will.

It's easy to see why the aforementioned "single sweeping set of actions" could satisfy all the divergent aims of all the most *Powerful* interests tied up with the British imperial system, when one considers what that single sweeping set of actions entailed. Since, by the start of contemporary history, the Great Power system had long since been spreading at an exponential rate across the entire planet, and as Germany was the only competitor at the time representing a realistic rival to British hegemony, crushing Germany would essentially provide *the potential for a globally-encompassing hegemony* – as complete control as was possible over the politicoeconomic affairs of the whole planet. Really, at the time, what more could the elite factions and their correspondent interests have asked for? What more could any elite factions ask for, at any point in history, in any civilization? What *wouldn't* a hegemonic mindset think up to achieve such a goal?

And, most importantly, if/when it was achieved – what wouldn't the hegemons do to make sure things stayed their way?

*   *   *

Thus, at the time of the Anglo-American global Empire's earliest stirrings, and in the precise milieu causing those stirrings, three things were once and for all becoming inseparably fused: Anglo-American finance and industry, Anglo-American governmental administration, and Anglo-American military might, all working towards one common objective, which was secure establishment of the global Empire, itself. Clearly, in both the U.K. and the U.S., all three of these components, ever since they'd existed in their recognizably late modern forms (essentially since the early 19th-century, regarding the sociohistorical perspective that's relevant here), had been inextricably interrelated. (In part 2, we discussed how the financiers who formed the original, informal alliance between the industrial U.S. and the industrial U.K., via New York and London, respectively, established a Northern hegemony over the entire United States through the North's victory over the South in the U.S. Civil War.)[cccxxiii] But never before had the alliance caused all three areas – finance/industry, government, and military – to be so explicitly synchronized, with such crucial consequences for the affairs of both nations. The allies had never perceived it to be so necessary as they did now, for the alliance and all of its implications to be taken to such drastic extremes.

The allies had never been so frightened of an enemy as they were of Germany. The rise of the German economy was spectacular, and even more importantly, it was swift. Moreover, whereas the Anglo-American mode of operation can largely be characterized as "controlling the government via the industrial system", the German mode, in contrast, should be characterized as "controlling the industrial system via the government". The resulting differences between the overall systems were not primarily ideological, at least concerning what I'm specifically discussing here: I'm not talking about the purely philosophical question of whether it's "better" for the State to be largely separated from economic affairs or largely in control of them. I'm talking about the sole empirical sociohistorical context within which contemporary States emerged – the context of an industrialized system of international imperial warfare, which at the time of our present concern (the turn of the 20th-century) was the dominant factor in Western civilization and from there, the world-at-large.[cccxxiv]

The main reason why the Anglo-American hegemons had undertaken less direct State intervention in the industrial economy until that point, at least in the U.S., was because, since the inception of mass industrialization, the financial systems in both the U.S. and U.K. had always been in indirect yet decisive control of the industrial systems, anyway, and by way of Congress and Parliament, respectively, they'd also been largely in control of the governing systems. There had simply been no *need*, until the rise of a unified Germany – a development that, according to Carroll Quigley, "ended a balance-of-power in Europe which had existed for 250 or even 300 years", the very "balance-of-power" in which England had become so overwhelmingly dominant[cccxxv] – for the State to intervene in large-scale industrial planning so directly. Besides, the financiers who became so synonymous with Anglo-American policymaking by the end of the 19th-century had preferred that the State stay out of such things. They'd preferred to use their central governments as vehicles for promotion of "free trade", basically taken to mean "the most beneficial arrangements possible for Anglo-American merchants wherever they did business"; in other words, favorable trading conditions for Anglo-American elites. "Free trade" in this meaning of the phrase was always merely a euphemism for "terms most favorable at any given time for international merchants", and thereby – even more importantly – for merchant bankers, i.e., the leading financiers.

The balance-of-*Power* had started to change when the Prussian industrialists led the way in successfully forging a unified German nation. In this sense, it's not even entirely appropriate to say that Germany's political system was in control of its economic system, unless one understands what such control actually entailed: in reality it's most appropriate to say, Prussia's industrial elites created a unified German political system, and this politico-industrial system would control the new German economy. One must always keep in mind that the Prussian industrialists were the major factors in control of German politicoeconomic affairs during the several decades before World War One. And the second, economically more audacious half of this era marked the time when the Anglo-Americans really started to consider Germany such a grave threat.[cccxxvi] Thus, the imperial rivalry between the Anglo-Americans and the Germans that sparked the emergence of the contemporary world was most fundamentally a rivalry between financially-controlled industrial and political systems and industrially-controlled political and financial systems. But since both holistic systems were defined most of all by their competitive roles in the same *globalizing* Great Power game, even mentioning this slightest difference in precisely where the levers-of-control lay probably overstates the actual contrast between Anglo-American political economy on the one hand and German political economy on the other.

Both systems, as holistic entities, were of course primarily used, and primarily perpetuated, as *Power*-machines for their controllers; just like all other civilization-State-complexes in history. The critical difference between the systems was that, because the Prussians had such tight, almost uncontestable control over their systems of production and distribution, it would eventually be far easier for the German style of system to dominate militarily than it would be for the Anglo-American style of system, should Germany continue to grow uninhibited as a Great Power. The hegemons knew that dominance of international trade via naval strength was the linchpin of general politicoeconomic control, so thoughts of the kind of navy the new German industrial system could ultimately create were too fearful for the hegemons to bear. By 1898, from the eyes of British financial-industrial controllers, and thus from the eyes of the U.S. financiers-industrialists allied with them, the specter of a rising German Empire on the back of a booming German navy hinted at the strong possibility that British *Power* could someday soon be a mere historical relic.

At least in the modern Western tradition, it's not too much to say that 'Great Power' and 'naval strength' were always more or less synonymous terms. Other factors also mattered in defining a nation's imperial prowess, but no singular element ever conferred a greater long-term effect on all the others than the quality of a State's navy: conquest of the seas (around 70% of the Earth's surface) was the only true gateway to conquest of the planet, a fact which has in the end had uniquely determinative consequences for human history. No sector of humanity ever possessed so clear a vision of this truth as the Anglo-American hegemons at the beginning of the 20th-century, considering how great was the prestige afforded them by the position of global oceanic conquest sustained by England's navy. The British navy had been unequivocally the greatest in history until that point and would remain so even for some time after, until at last the U.S. Navy, rather appropriately, eclipsed it in the midst of World War Two.

The hegemons, then, decided that in terms of overarching U.S. policy, success in a competition with Germany could in the first place really mean just one thing: the U.S. needed to more or less immediately become the planet's ultimate Great Power, i.e., it had to invest in creating the world's strongest navy. Why couldn't Britain defeat Germany single-handedly? F. William Engdahl, an independent researcher, points out that the U.K. was secretly bankrupt immediately before World War One.[cccxxvii] No one else that I've read mentions this, but it certainly isn't surprising, since all throughout the 19th-century the U.K. was run as little more than a headquarters for a global trade empire, not as anything even remotely resembling "self-sufficiency", a characteristic no nation can ever truly possess anyway. At the veritable epicenter (London) of the most unprecedented era of economic growth in human history, almost the whole time without any viable contenders, the British imperial elite had long since grown wholly complacent.[cccxxviii] Resultantly, when they saw everything rapidly dissipating in front of their eyes they became desperate, grasping onto the most promising "Great Power shell" they could find, holding on for dear life.

The American public, for its part, didn't really seem to mind the Great Power game, at least not at first. Americans largely thought empire to be a perfectly acceptable goal, and Cuba and the Philippines, for instance, were widely seen as fine places for war, and military occupation.[cccxxix] And concerning every other territory, in this burgeoning American overseas Empire that was most immediately catalyzed by conquest of these two new locales – the Cuban and Filipino pattern would be followed almost identically. It should be obvious why the public so readily approved of military outposts in such "tropical" regions; but I'll say why, anyway. Ideologically, the American public in the early 1900s perfectly reflected its place amongst one of the most overtly xenophobic, certainly the most overtly racist culture ever in existence, the culture of Western imperialism. Fortuitously for the evolution of *Power* in the late 19th- and early 20th-centuries, these natural targets for hegemonic advances from a geographical and resource perspective also happened to be filled with people whose very physical appearances made them primary focal points for endless ethnocentric hatred.

However, concerning the white Americans who collectively comprised the most prominent base within the emergent 20th-century "Middle Class" (whose "public opinion"[cccxxx] it was that Anglo-American politicos actually felt they had to worry about) – they originally came from Europe. With all the European immigrants pouring into the U.S. throughout the late 19th- and early 20th-centuries, many new Americans still had families there. None of them wanted a European war, and they certainly didn't want Americans to have to participate in a European war. It would be a shame to kill white people. Woodrow Wilson, in fact, won election in 1916 for a second term as U.S. president by using "he kept us out of war" as the central tagline of his campaign.[cccxxxi] Then in the springtime of 1917, right after Wilson had been inaugurated for the second time, the United States entered the war on the Allies' side.

Rightly, the public was outraged. To quell as much indignation as possible, the Wilson administration simply drowned it out by turning the volume way up on the State-glorifying rhetoric, while simultaneously unleashing what was at the time the greatest-ever policing effort in U.S. history aimed at crushing domestic dissent.[cccxxxii] Like all U.S. presidential administrations, the Wilson administration was basically just an empty vessel, there to be filled with the policies preferred by whatever particular group of moneyed factions had most recently put together the winning strategy for gaining the public's confidence. Nonetheless, there was something especially brazen about the way the London-allied U.S. financial-corporate elites employed Wilson, and thus a brief point needs to be made explicitly about him – however, as always, we're primarily concerned with what he *represented*, rather than with him "personally", as an individual. As with all individuals who serve *Power*-structures, he was most significant insofar as he was a symptom.

Wilson was perhaps the most blatant example in history of the contemporary Anglo-American hegemons' direct hand in selecting the contenders for U.S. "high politics", and was also among the earliest. An understanding of the Wilson presidency thus serves to shed invaluable light on the basic pattern shaping American national electoral campaigns all throughout the 20th-century-beyond era. The Wilson administration's pushing the United States into World War One immediately after pledging against it was only the most flagrant instance, and we'll get into it more shortly. Another telling example involves the rate at which Wilson catapulted to the presidency and the occupational road he took to get there, which information can only be viewed as quite astonishing – unless an expectation of the grey eminence's practicing the purest of puppetry is kept foremost in mind, in which case one may clearly recognize said information as being perfectly ordinary. Until 1910, when Wilson became Governor of

New Jersey, the man had never held elective office; he was a longtime political science professor and, at the time of his gubernatorial victory, he had recently become the president of Princeton University. Two years later, he would be elected President of the United States.

Still, none of this is so interesting to us here unless one appreciates the sociohistorical context of contemporary electoral politics in the United States, namely insofar as it was initially shaped by the late 19th-century U.S. electoral politics of the major urban centers, i.e., U.S. electoral politics in the notoriously unabashed-in-its-corruption "Gilded Age". To begin, the most important thing to remember about the general nature of electoral party politics in the recognizably contemporary system – a phenomenon of quintessentially Western origins – is that campaigns cost money: a great deal of money. Clearly, to the extent that any given governmental system fails at providing legal safeguards against the influence of money on the outcome of campaigns for political office, this fact alone has always proven in reality to be the surest possible guarantee of the electoral system *itself* becoming the greatest breeding-ground for political corruption.

The simplest expectation in the world to have, of course, if the influence of money is left completely unchecked, is that the particular policies a politician supports will be largely determined by whatever groups provide him or her with the greatest quantity of campaign funds – the "fuel" propelling electoral political machines. Later in the 20th-century, some of the nations comprising the core of the global civilization, notably some leading western European nations, logically solved this individual problem by leveling the playing field regarding the role of money in electoral campaigns, requiring by law the payment of campaign expenses solely or largely with publicly-allotted funds. By bringing this up, I in no way wish to align myself with the notion that public funding for political campaigns is a miracle cure ensuring the elimination of all possibility for governmental corruption. It absolutely isn't. Rather, I wish to assert how absolutely obvious and well-known is the *certainty* of rampant political corruption in any electoral system where campaign finance is completely uninhibited, to the point where leaving the role of money completely unconstrained is basically a tacit invitation for unending quantities of such corruption. In the precise sociohistorical context responsible for producing Woodrow Wilson, there were essentially no restrictions whatsoever on how individuals could finance campaigns (there were some restrictions on corporate donations). Thus, wealthy individuals, if they were so inclined, could more or less purchase candidates at will, investing whatever it took to get "their man" enough votes to win. Needless to say, by the beginning of the 20th-century's second decade, when Wilson's rapid rise to governorship was to be followed in short order by an even more rapid rise to the presidency, the U.S. national electoral system had, at its very core, long-since become a fundraising arms race between combinations of (transnational) elite factions.

There was only one real limiting factor in this regard – but it was a significant one: the threat of the public's moral censure. And the U.S. public at the time was characteristically prone towards intense moral censure, at least concerning specific issues "the masses" rightly though only vaguely perceived as dangerous to their own interests. Now, contemporary conceptions of "American freedom" indisputably have been completely overwrought and are almost always irreparably tainted with hypocrisy, insofar as they typically ignore how dependent "Free" Americans are for their "Freedom" on the outright violent subjugation and somewhat more indirect economic exploitation of the vast majority of human beings on the planet. Nonetheless, it's still true that, when compared strictly to their European counterparts who comprised "Old World" Western civilization, *"Middle Class" white* Americans were on average, in certain important ways, freer than Europeans of comparable social standing. This was especially true at the point in history of our concern here, the fifth period (1865-1945) – in particular the stretch spanning roughly from 1890 to 1914, approximately the decade before until the decade after globalization's inception.

Most of all, Americans at the time had more freedom than Europeans in that category of things usually called 'civil liberties'. This was less because of the actual design of U.S. government and more because the late 19th-century/early 20th-century U.S. Government simply was, compared to European States, not very strong relative to the total U.S. population. It was generally harder in the U.S. than in Europe, for instance, to jail urban individuals for mere dissent, if only because the sheer number of individuals was so overwhelming for the existing State machinery.[cccxxxiii] In the short term this naturally played a large role in shaping the population's culture, putting the Anglo-American hegemons in a momentary bind. Mainly, I feel the explanation lies in the fact that the U.S. was a much younger State at that point in terms of time but more importantly in terms of complexity, compared to the leading European States; and as we've seen, it had been run for over half a century at that point almost solely by a tiny number of financiers funding seemingly innumerable industrial operations. In the context of the late 19th-century this was terrible for the masses' economic freedoms but had the potential to be good for their political ones: when investors are tied to extremely competitive, constantly shifting markets like the U.S. was during the relevant period, they like to have as much freedom as possible to move their cash around, and big expensive governing machines get in the way of that.

By the end of the 19th-century, however, the leading American financiers and industrialists had grown so *Powerful* that they felt there was a realistic opportunity to monopolize American industry, at a moment when continued competition would only be a hindrance to them. Further potential growth could only be achieved by destroying their competitors: but also, the holistic system itself couldn't be allowed to remain competitive, as that would mean future competitors might someday arise that could destroy the presently reigning companies. They had to destroy their competitors in order to set up the necessary monopolistic conditions, i.e., they had to eliminate even the possibility of serious competition within the critical industrial fields.[cccxxxiv]

Moreover, at this point, the leading American financiers, and the leading American industrialists in the most strategically significant fields – the key constituents of the true American ruling class – were highly concerned with achieving economic "stability": basically, the leading industrial outfits had become so enormous that their planners were constantly facing the need for ever-greater quantities of lead-time to successfully design and execute their businesses' operations. This concern with economic order, by extension, simultaneously made the hegemons highly concerned with achieving political order.[cccxxxv] Resultantly, they became much more proactive in utilizing their decisive influence over the U.S. Government, towards the end of grabbing absolute control over those affairs affecting the nation's whole population. Thus the United States would become an explicitly national entity to an extent never before seen – at the same time that it was becoming more of an explicitly *inter*national entity than ever before. It in fact turned out that these two processes were completely inextricable, not least of all because so many of the same *Powerful* individuals were involved in controlling both processes.

As our leading financiers and industrialists were starting to find out in the first decade of the 20th-century, monopolies or trusts were hard and perhaps even impossible to establish via purely economic means – in other words, solely via the "free market", which at this time in American history was actually about as "free" (lacking regulation by explicit State policymaking) as it had ever been. There was far too much uncontrolled growth in practically every significant industry for any single firm or any single collection of a few firms to unequivocally dominate. For one thing, beyond certain levels of growth, the economies-of-scale in many such industries in the early contemporary American economy didn't necessarily favor the larger companies merely because they were larger. This had the practical effect, in the relevant fields, of allowing far greater success for smaller companies than would eventually be the norm. Thus, in comparison with the present-day economy, there was a much larger pool of important firms and a much smaller pool of *all*-important firms, especially in the most militarily-dependent sectors.[cccxxxvi] To sum up, whenever a hopeful syndicate would come together in order to fix prices, one of the parties privy to the deal would inevitably give in and lower them, undercutting the arrangement.[cccxxxvii] In a period when the Anglo-American hegemons were constantly writhing from largely but not wholly exaggerated fears of a burgeoning German Empire buttressed on the back of the world's largest industrial outfits, possible failure by the U.S. branch – including most representatively the Morgans (financiers) and Rockefellers (industrialists) – to possess a controlling interest over a stabilized national production/distribution system must've seemed like all but begging for German conquest of international markets. Lack of monopolistic control, therefore, was just unacceptable. In turn, as Gabriel Kolko wrote, "Having failed in the realm of economics, the efforts of [big business/big finance] were to be shifted to politics."[cccxxxviii]

The hegemons had turned first to their friend Teddy Roosevelt, of Cuban war and Panama Canal fame, to achieve their goals of "business reform". From the hegemons' perspective, this meant implementing national industrial regulatory apparatuses aiming to establish singular sets of national policy, which would be designed to ensure the most favorable possible legal conditions for the stable emergence of enormous national corporations. One of big business's biggest hatreds throughout the first decade of the new century was that there were as many different sets of regulations in the United States as there were states (provinces). Besides making it extremely difficult to undertake corporate planning on a national scale, big business hated this so much because the local businesses in every state – the greatest domestic competition for the largest companies, which needed to consolidate national positions in order to effect their already-in-the-works, subsequent emergence as *multi*national corporations – naturally used their local state legislatures to adversely affect the profitability of corporations operating out-of-state. In other words, the state legislatures tried to legally deter the creation of such gargantuan companies. As a response, big business characteristically used its own preferred policymaking weapon, which of course had the potential to be much weightier than all of the state legislatures combined: the U.S. (Federal) Government.[cccxxxix] As would be a recurring theme in the sociohistorical process now being sparked, big business, headed from behind by big finance, won.

William Howard Taft, who had been Roosevelt's secretary of war, succeeded "TR" as president, serving from 1909-1913. The Anglo-American hegemons used him to further many of the same goals of national regulation, and were fairly pleased. But there ended up being a huge problem with Taft: his business policies were good enough, but he seemed to be against getting the United States involved in Great Power conflicts – that is, wars between Great Powers, themselves, and not "mere" colonial wars, which pretty much everyone agreed were acceptable, if not essential. Meanwhile, the trajectory of European affairs was already signaling, to some extent even in public, the practical inevitability of the first major Great Power war in nearly 100 years. In private, Britain had been "secretly" maneuvering for years to make military alliances with France and Russia, the Powers to Germany's west and Germany's east, respectively, and unquestionably Germany's greatest acknowledged rivals. What was officially unacknowledged, then, but still well-known by Germany, was that although Britain claimed neutrality in continental affairs, the English had long been gearing up for a showdown against the Germans.[cccxl] Besides, in the war-trade competition, no one even has to expressly announce such things, for the most part: positions of dominance are merely understood by the true contenders, and measures are taken in response. In this case, the tacit understanding between competitors regarding England's jockeying reciprocally sparked a much greater German military buildup than the one already in motion.

The United States had always professed the utmost neutrality with respect to the affairs of Europe, as well. In the coming conflict, however, the American branch of the hegemons had already decided long ago that whenever the next war should come, the U.S. would break its neutrality – in favor of only one side, because as far as they were concerned the fate of the U.S. could only ever lie with the British, since that was where their own fates lay.

Sometime during Taft's term, then, the hegemons decided to turn their attention to the Democratic candidate for the next election, the political science professor and university president Wilson, who had just been elected to his first political office, Governor of New Jersey, when it was decided that he would run for President of the United States. Wilson was a proponent of the "Progressive movement", to the extent that it served primarily as a "grassroots" front vehicle for the leading financial-corporate controllers. This movement simultaneously achieved two goals that were only apparently contradictory: (1) it harnessed a decisive share of popular resentment against the politicoeconomic status quo; (2) it provided an impetus for the particular type of governmental regulation of industry favored by the hegemons, who were themselves of course the very epitome of the politicoeconomic status quo. Obviously, this was a uniquely insidious tactic, but if executed properly it was also uniquely effective, as would be shown most tragically throughout the rest of contemporary history. Giving voice to vague generalities through the medium of someone who was considered a skilled orator and a most worthily chosen statesman, the tactic allowed whoever used it to accomplish precisely what the orator purported to be fiercely critical of, effecting an ideal neutralization of the most threatening public opposition. It was successful so long as the masses remained generally ignorant of the intricate global realities behind all goings-on in contemporary politics.

Even though they'd found a spokesman who came to be respected with such immediacy – and the public always loves the story of a meteoric rise to success – the hegemons needed to be absolutely certain that they'd win the 1912 election. The fate of whether or not there would be a great war depended on it; and there had to be a great war. The hegemons would have to split the Republican vote, which, unlike the Republican vote of today's United States, carried throughout the first half of the 20th-century a significant "isolationist" element, represented most notably by Taft: in the precise context, this basically meant the party was fervently against participation in European wars, although certainly not against the use of military means in general.

It primarily involved respect for an idealized conception of traditional adherence to "neutralism" and "the international law of nations", and typically didn't reflect antiwar or anti-imperial sentiments, *per se*. From what we've seen in retrospect, with the hindsight of all 20th-century and a decade-plus of 21st-century history behind us, it's easy to recognize that no regime of international law ever could've significantly "tamed" the Western war system, considering the exponentially-increasing sociohistorical momentum propelling the leading Western Powers forward by the year 1898, fueled by completely irrational but no less deeply-held goals of eternal infinitely-expanding conquest. As I've shown, throughout a period lasting over a millennium, the Western war system had been gradually, and then ever-increasingly, and finally exponentially pushing towards military occupation of the entire planet, and at the beginning of the 20th-century the goal of total planetary conquest became a truly realistic possibility for the first time, as envisioned under the aegis of an Anglo-American hegemony. No explicitly-defined structure of international law, if superimposed on that system which, so far as the contemporary West was concerned, really might as well have been "how things are" for eternity, could've ever done anything effectively besides legally sanction the existing international regime represented by whatever the state of the Great Power competition was at any given time. Nevertheless, at the beginning of the 20th-century's second decade, gearing up for an election as they always did by trying to decide which candidate they needed to be the winner, the Anglo-American hegemons thought the "isolationists" hinted at enormous potential to make cultural trouble, for anyone who might want the U.S. to make a

European war. The Democrat had to win in 1912. As I've said, the hegemons had apparently even already decided it would be Woodrow Wilson.

Getting Wilson the Democratic nomination was easy enough. Now they needed some opposing candidate they could support, who, if he won, would be able to get them into the war: but of course it would be much better for public opinion if he didn't win, so that the public's feeling of betrayal could be minimized, thus allowing the coming war a workable baseline of moral approval. A healthy mass of perceived national unity buttressed by positive public opinion was always the thing that mattered most, as the "Old World", British branch constantly reiterated.[cccxli] A much more ideal arrangement than pulling a bait-and-switch with a Republic, then, would be to get a war-ready third-party candidate to run – one who could steal enough votes from Taft to make a difference.

The hegemons called upon that old Cuban warmonger and champion of American Indian conquest Teddy Roosevelt, who'd decided not to run for office again in 1908. Ever a patriot for the hegemonic fatherland, though, Roosevelt dutifully came out of retirement, which he'd been spending by killing Africa's wildlife, a passion which made him long to transform the entire continent into a paradise preserve for white men of good stock to go "on safari". Roosevelt, acting quite unselfishly, put on temporary hold his beloved life of leisure and formed a "Progressive Party", ostensibly as an attempt to regain the presidency in favor of sweeping reform, but in reality being nothing more than a ruse to quash the mass following behind Taft. And considering the specific policies Roosevelt claimed to support, the plan had the added, by no means insignificant benefit of absorbing and thereby neutralizing tons of unruly energy irritatingly pestering after substantive governmental change.[cccxlii]

The plan worked splendidly: in Wilson, the public could expect someone who would make reforms, albeit not necessarily reforms quite so "radical" as those pledged in Roosevelt's platform. The hegemons got someone who with enough rhetorical suggestion could make practically anything seem palatable to the masses. This was most crucial, because they were going to be in severe need of a figure who could convincingly appear to support one policy while the ground was simultaneously, surreptitiously being set for the opposite course of action. The most important reason involved the upcoming war to crush Germany, itself: America's participation in the conflict – it had to look like an accident.[cccxliii]

*   *   *

All that's required to make the masses approve of war is to convince them wholeheartedly of a noble purpose. Did you think the Anglo-American hegemons at the time wouldn't have known that? Do you think they don't know it now? Do you think it's not their underlying driving focus at all times, however consciously it's realized by any given individual, to always come up with new "noble purposes" for war?

Indeed, the very concept of a modern Western Empire presupposes a "noble purpose" for conquest – and conquest is basically what war always amounts to in the context of a civilization-State-complex, or at least, what it's always aiming for, on behalf of those parties who choose to make war. Obviously, then, there's nothing fundamentally new about that aspect of contemporary history. My argument can only be considered radical insofar as it asserts that the process of imperial conquest is nothing "old", either: in other words, the *same* process never stopped, it continued, and it continues to this day (though for how much longer, at this point, nobody really knows). Even more importantly, the process not only continued; it *expanded*, until the entire planet was its victim, and as it expanded – then more so, still, after it could expand no longer – it *intensified*, becoming evermore concentrated within the contours of its total expansion.

From that perspective – whether anyone explicitly saw it this way, or not – World War One was really nothing besides a settling of scores to determine how exactly the last stage of Western imperial expansion would take place, which most consequentially meant, "Who on Earth will benefit most from the final consolidation of Western expansion?" I say "whether anyone explicitly saw it this way, or not", to overtly emphasize that you don't have to necessarily accept an explanation of World War One in terms of a deliberate plan to bring about the war, as I've explained it, to view the conflict primarily as the key formative stage in the culmination of Western conquest, the process which has most singularly defined the planet's history in the uniquely critical 20th-century-beyond era.

The main reason for emphasizing that fact is to point out: the way the long historical process of Western civilization had been going by the start of the 20th-century, Germany would've someday soon been forced to attempt to conquer England, if England hadn't gotten to it first. *That simply followed from the rules of the Western Great Power game.*[cccxliv] Long before the start of the 20th-century, history showed that Western Powers always competed against one another through violence organized towards the sole aim of greater conquest, whether one Power invaded another on "domestic" fronts or they went after each other overseas, in competition for conquest of what the West's projecting mindset always labeled as "barbaric" peoples, or "savages".

All throughout the 19th-century, as I've said over and over, the latter form of conquest – overseas military occupation of peoples indigenous to desired areas of imperial expansion – ever-increasingly became the main priority of Western States; and as it happened this phenomenon was entirely interdependent with the Western "Industrial Revolution". Thus, Western States during the 19th-century were far more concerned with using military *Power* to conquer what would eventually become known as the "Third World" than they were with conquering other European nations' domestic territories. This is precisely why the stretch between 1815 and 1914 in European Great Power history was so often referred to as the "Hundred Years' Peace"[cccxlv]: if you look at warfare as something that occurs only between Western Powers on their home turf, then "Hundred Years' Peace" is a somewhat accurate label. But if you truly want to understand Western history, which is an absolute necessity if you want to understand the history of globalization and the global civilization, I think you'd be well-advised to view Western overseas imperialism as *purely* warfare; you should view it as the quintessential form of Western warfare.

Why does that matter so much? First of all, there's an inextricable relationship between the contemporary dominant culture's view of itself and the view that Western conquest of the rest of the planet was indisputably justified; the notion that in the end, it has done as much good as it has harm for the conquered peoples.[cccxlvi] And there's no reason for people to think this unless they really do believe, consciously or unconsciously, that Westerners were and are more "civilized" than everyone else, by which people mean "less savage" – in an overall sense, *better*. On the other hand, once you view Western imperialism as nothing but warfare, and reciprocally all Western warfare as nothing but imperialism, the positively sick notion that the Western conquest of Earth was actually *beneficial* to its victims can only melt away.

Secondly and relatedly, one can hopefully see that because imperialism was only warfare, and because the West was so thoroughly, uncontrollably synonymous with imperialism (and thus with warfare) by the beginning of the 20th-century, once Western militarization had already reached what were more or less its expansive limits, the continuation of imperialism – an absolute necessity for the continuation of any potential form of Western civilization – could only possibly exist insofar as the imperialism turned in on itself. That is, there had to be a reconquest of the Western domestic populations. As I've tried to elucidate throughout this work as a whole, there are unique and inescapable sociohistorical effects when warfare is the fundamental system of politicoeconomic growth, and never has a human cultural unit been so completely dependent on anything for its very existence, as the West is on the growth of war-wealth (which includes wealth based on international trade). Inherently, this is a problem.

So far as I'm concerned, it's *the* problem. At the same time, it's the very definition of Western civilization. And in turn, the problem embodied in its most extreme form by Western civilization raises similar questions about the problem represented by all civilizations. For even though the West was the most absurdly destructive version of them all (before the global civilization, which it of course was largely responsible for creating), it still only became what it was in the first place because there had already long existed a pattern of increasingly successful conquest-imposed cultures in the immediate surroundings of the region (western Europe) that ultimately became the launching pad for Western civilization. The West developed such particularly devastating effects in the long-term precisely insofar as it perfected the destruction ("growth") inseparable from the violently-induced politicoeconomic stratification endemic to the praxis of civilizations in general.

None of this is to say, "civilizations are all evil", in-and-of-themselves. To highlight the real problems inherently produced by the establishment of some structure implies only a desire to assert the absolute necessity for coming up with a different way of doing things, *not* a desire to exhibit what most might consider my "pessimism". We need to get as far as possible from this pathological mindset rigidly pitting every thing mortally against every other thing – demanding that the individual must unequivocally "support" one extremely microscopic phenomenon or its supposed opposite – and which has been the result solely of our contemporary mass-produced propaganda-enforced culture, and not because it's an effective way to think useful thoughts.

Nevertheless, there are also many things inextricable from how civilizations have always sociohistorically existed that are, indeed, evil; or at least, they *encourage* evils. I believe I've successfully made this term (*'evil'*) correspond to sociohistorical reality, insofar as history – especially contemporary history – teaches that some human beings have the potential to completely destroy the lives of the vast majority of human beings, while they simultaneously have (at least nominal) freedom to choose *not* to pursue such great destruction. What else can you call those things that humans do, primarily defined by the deliberate encouragement of ever-greater destruction, besides evils? What else can you call that culture which has been founded solely on pursuing those activities ensuring the greatest possible destruction, if not Hell?

Perhaps you're still not convinced. Well – the production of World War One was just the start.

III

A World In Peaces: "The Peace" as the Ultimate Embodiment of Contemporary Grand Strategy

Let's return to Prouty for a moment, starting this time where his own story – that is, the historically significant portion of it – actually started, which, just like the Cold War and directly parallel to it, was smack in the middle of World War Two. The main virtue in sourcing Prouty is that his story is fairly ordinary within the context of a most extraordinary phenomenon. Moreover, he was there from the literal outset, at the time unknowingly in the midst of the true turning point between the two extremely different yet seamlessly interconnected systems of total global warfare. Like seemingly everything for the majority of the overarching "confrontation" between the United States and the Soviet Union, the story intertwining Prouty and the Cold War emerged from both of the contemporary world's most strategically critical geopolitical pivots – southwest and southeast Asia, the two vast, diverse areas Westerners typically gloss over with the labels "Near East" and "Far East". From near to far, the original imposition of contemporary global hegemony via the imperial shield of the U.S. military would take place largely in these two subregions.

As a pilot in the Army's Air Transport Command, the original, non-independent precursor to the U.S. Air Force, Prouty was ordered to duty in July 1941 and ended up in Cairo and Tehran during the meetings between "the principals" in November 1943. A pilot of rare talent at a time when there still weren't many, he was given the remarkable task of transporting top-level U.S. delegates to and from such conferences. As such, Prouty had knowledge of certain kinds of historical facts that were, for a great deal of the second half of the 20th-century, knowable to very few individuals who weren't actually witnesses to their being made (knowable only to individuals at or working close to the highest levels of *Power*) – that is, until they were published as parts of Prouty's testimony. In turn, from my perspective, his overall worldview is the best proof of the facts he reports: this worldview could only have been formed in relation to facts Prouty would've had to have experienced first-hand, whether directly, concerning the operations he participated in personally, or indirectly, concerning operations detailed in the documents he reviewed for his assigned intelligence analyses.

For instance, Prouty claims as indisputable fact that at Cairo, where FDR and Churchill met with Chiang Kai-shek, the purpose wasn't only to formulate battle strategies against the Axis Powers, but also, just as significantly, to formulate grand strategy for what Prouty refers to as "a follow-on period of warfare in eastern Asia", in anticipation of victory over Japan. "Few historians seem to recall", Prouty notes, that Chiang's wife Mei-ling was also a participant in the conference: his wife Mei-ling, the sister of T.V. Soong – at the time, *the planet's wealthiest man* – whose representatives were advisors to the future generalissimo of Taiwan.[cccxlvii] However, the author places even greater emphasis on the fact that his chauffeuring of the Chinese delegation wasn't limited to Cairo. He also flew the Chinese delegates to the Tehran conference; thus, they would meet with Josef Stalin, even though this completely defies the notion inculcated by the contemporary dominant culture that Stalin and Mao (supposedly one of Chiang's greatest domestic threats at the time) naturally must've been such close allies, because "Capitalism" and "Communism" are automatically presumed to have always behaved, without exception, as the fiercest enemies. Unless Chiang and Stalin were at each other's throats? Prouty: "During the sometimes heated exchanges between Roosevelt and Churchill…*plans were made by all four conferees for a period of continuing warfare in Indochina, Korea, and Indonesia under the guise of that Cold War "cover story""*[cccxlviii] (emphasis added). "All four conferees": Chiang, Churchill, Roosevelt…*and* Stalin. Also, as Prouty repeatedly emphasizes throughout both of his texts, "cover story" is spy jargon for "lie".

Even before those conferences, in October 1943, Prouty had flown a team of petroleum experts led by General C.R. Smith, a Texas oilman and the founder of American Airlines, to Saudi Arabia. Lest any confusion arise concerning what Smith was doing on that trip, Prouty says FDR himself sent the team to southwest Asia to confer with individuals acting on behalf of California Standard Oil – the Rockefeller-controlled California Standard Oil. The results of the expedition, of course, have played no small role in all subsequent history. In response to the geologists' salivations, Roosevelt ordered that a 50,000-barrel-per-day refinery be built with the greatest possible haste. It was operational by the end of 1945: "Thus began the modern petroleum era in the midst of war."cccxlix

In September 1944, almost a year after those first conferences wherein the long-term post-World War Two order was already being planned (yet still a year before World War Two was officially over), Prouty flew two U.S. military higher-ups to Aleppo, Syria. Prouty and the crew he transported met with counterparts from the U.K., who told them "750 U.S. Air crewmen POWs" were "secretly en route [by train] to Syria from Romania via the Balkans and Turkey." The next day, when Prouty returned to Syria after arranging for thirty transport aircraft in Cairo, Prouty and the other pilots "…met the freight train from Bucharest…Among the 750 American POWs there were perhaps a hundred Nazi intelligence agents, along with scores of Nazi-sympathetic Balkan agents." Given that the Allies and Axis Powers were of course still ostensibly at war with one another, the "assets" were "…hidden in this shipment by the OSS to get them out of the way of the Soviet army that had marched into Romania on September 1."cccl Therefore, in what was perhaps a totally unique moment up to that point in human history, the future major war was being explicitly fought before the present major war came to a close.

Prouty mentions still one more, final step in this initiating sequence covertly signaling the beginning of the "postwar" order – meaning the order based on a perpetual nuclear arms race, so in that sense actually a "permanent war" order – which happened shortly following Japan's surrender (September 2nd, 1945). Since use of the atomic bombs meant the Allies no longer needed to invade Japan, there happened to be an enormous stockpile of unused war material sitting on the island of Okinawa. According to Prouty, "[a]lmost immediately" after Japan surrendered, the stockpile got reloaded onto U.S. Navy ships. Prouty, who was "on Okinawa at that time…asked the harbormaster if all that new materiel was being returned to the [U.S.]." The harbormaster replied, " 'Hell, no! They ain't never goin' to see it again. One-half of this stuff, enough to equip and support at least a hundred and fifty thousand men, is going to Korea, and the other half is going to Indochina.'" As Prouty so astutely notes in summing up, "In 1945, none of us had any idea that the first battles of the Cold War were going to be fought by U.S. military units in those regions beginning in 1950 and 1965…*Who selected* Syngman

Rhee and Ho Chi Minh to be our new allies as early as mid-1945?"[cccli] [Emphasis my own.] Which itself, I think, brings up another excellent point: the U.S. Government quietly made a "friend" out of Ho Chi Minh in 1945 before it loudly turned him into an "enemy" as early as 1954 – and all the while, it's commonly but erroneously thought that the U.S.'s "war" (postmodern colonial occupation) in Vietnam didn't begin until some point well into the 1960s.

Thus, not only did the hegemons' strategy exist before World War Two was over: there were, in fact, already significant tactical movements being undertaken towards implementation of that strategy. That is, the Cold War wasn't mainly a period of rupture concerning its historical relationship to World War Two; it was predominately a period of continuity, particularly at the level of greatest *Power*. (Or perhaps it's better to say its short historical aspect was predominately a continuation, its long historical aspect predominately a rupture.) The alliances may have ostensibly flipped, but to make the alliances the main subject of consideration when trying to understand warfare misses the point, and so often even does violence to the pursuit of real knowledge on the subject. The important thing to try to figure out is "Who's *really* at war with who?" Who honestly wins, when a war happens, and who loses? If we ask this question, and if, in answering it, we can unpack the propaganda – the 'psychological warfare' – from our minds, we can then see the true story: and it's quite at odds with the propaganda, to say the least.

Prouty fought in the real war, and he was one of the only individuals who did so to give a widely available, truthful* account of it. Certainly, he was the *highest-ranking* individual to ever give such an account. It may seem too bizarre, or at least not as important in the "grand scheme" of things, to treat with such seriousness – such seriousness that I'm building around it much of my understanding concerning so crucial a chunk of contemporary history. The reader might charge that to treat a single man's statements as being so uniquely significant violates the unwritten laws of historiography.

This would only be fair criticism, however, if either or both of two possible hypothetical conditions could be met: (1) if the facts provided by Prouty's record didn't fit into a broader sociohistorical context; (2) if the types of actions undertaken in the specific structure Prouty inhabited weren't as generally consequential as I consider them

---

* Truthful in terms of what the author's intent in producing the account seems to have been.

to be. As the present text aims to show, neither of these conditions can be met: therefore, I believe we should consider Prouty's books to be among the handful of most valuable sources for understanding the contemporary world.

What seems most expected indeed appears to have been the most important thing going on – the "Intellectuals" in the contemporary dominant culture should've known: the real war was, as always, going on between the elites and everyone else, represented at its most extreme points by the archetypal dynamic of masters vs. slaves. The novel aspect about this eternal conflict as it has existed since the start of the Cold War is that the elites, whether they're called "Capitalist", "Communist", or anything else, are for the first time in history fully *globalized*, which has provided a completely unique opportunity for synchronization of elite interests across all boundaries – and in turn, a unique opportunity for subjugation of everyone and everything else, a process, as always, afflicting the original targets of Western colonialism worst of all. The real war, in the contemporary world, has been mainly between the global hegemons and the "Third World". Everything else is made to fit between these boundaries.

Shouldn't that have always been obvious? Isn't it completely in line with how civilizations have always been? When was this supposed to have changed?

Where was the entire overt campaign of the Cold War fought? Not within the domestic territories of either of the Superpowers. And no matter the circumstances, whether the U.S. or the S.U. was the controlling force (although it was almost always the former) in whatever recently "decolonized" nation was being subjected to yet more imperial intervention by way of "proxy wars", the end results were always the same: the beneficiaries were those homegrown elites who collaborated with the occupier along with the recipients of their largesse, and the sufferers were everyone else. The Cold War, as was always more or less known by the wisest and hence most-silenced individuals in the global civilization, was a way for constant conquest to continue in a setting of "public opinion" generally but only vaguely hostile to the undertakings of imperial aggression.

Why, then, didn't the United States simply conquer the Soviet Union? Essentially, *it had* – simply by virtue of the Soviet Union's being forced to assume the identity of second Superpower. Leaving aside all received opinion, because it's always so heavily steeped in pure propaganda (and is especially so in the current era): if we view the history from a totally unbiased perspective, the Soviet Union was infinitely more valuable to the United States as an "Enemy" than it could've been as a "Friend". And in terms of the elites in the S.U., i.e. the Communist Party – which comprised more or less the same proportion of the population as did "the upper class" in the "Capitalist" U.S. – the U.S. was, likewise, eminently valuable for them as a perpetual target of governmental invective, required to justify the constantly expanding military spending inextricable from the most minimal functioning of a Superpower economy. In the "long" run, elites attached to the U.S.-led bloc would clearly be the "victors". But the Soviet elites had plenty of fun playing their role, as well, so long as it was able to persist.

*   *   *

If you want to truly understand why a major war was fought, especially in the context of the late modern and contemporary worlds, where the means of organized violence have become so totally concentrated that individuals in charge of choosing when to go to war have essentially perfected their abilities at influencing military outcomes, you can't look at only, or even mainly, how the war started. Most of all you have to look at how it "ended" – you have to understand what was accomplished by "The Peace". In this sense, "The Peace" becomes the best evidence as to why the war was fought, the quintessential representation of the aggressor's grand strategy.

As confirmed by a thorough, broad-sweeping study of Western and then global history over the past century-and-a-half or so, the trend of war during this time shows an evermore-rapidly increasing, industrially-based explosion in military spending, combined with an ultimately total centralization of control. All other economic growth during this time, and all other growth in governmental *Power* – both of which have been just as great as the military centralization – have emanated from this one starting point.

If there were no wars, and thus no military structure, there could be no contemporary politicoeconomic system. Do you think the hegemons don't know that? Do you think they don't design and implement policies accordingly?

At the same time, the contemporary public (and most of all, the public in the "First World") would find the State's actions morally unacceptable to the extreme, if those speaking on its behalf were to openly proclaim the real reasons why the State goes to war. But – again – the State must go to war, or the State won't exist. So everything the State says about war must be a fiction, which only truly becomes a lie if the person spreading the fiction positively knows it to be false. And regarding war – as with anything else, but especially regarding war – people can only become skilled at spotting carefully-crafted lies if they know what the truth really is. Therefore, lies can be told about war incessantly and almost everyone can wholeheartedly believe the lies (they can even be downright offended if someone calls them lies), since almost no one in the contemporary dominant culture understands what war actually is. And this is because so few individuals inhabiting the culture know any information at all relevant to contemporary warfare that's not based mostly on fictions.

Thankfully, we don't have that problem presently, because we've seen what war really is from a politicoeconomic perspective: organized violent competition forced by ruling classes upon populations living under State conquest, primarily benefiting the elite factions comprising those classes, followed by the hierarchically-ranked recipients of their largesse. We've also seen what war's main psychological function is, in this case specifically concerning the 20th-century-beyond era: as an ideological phenomenon, it provides the primary source of cultural order upon which all other functioning of globalization is ultimately based, however directly or indirectly. From both of these perspectives, it's natural that the history of the world wars constituted the central factor shaping the global civilization's gestation.

Thus, "how these wars ended" was in the initial establishment of the global civilization under the auspices of a U.S.-led hegemony. Most fundamentally, then, that's why the wars were fought. But as I've only started to show, just like the U.K. and the U.S. central governments established hegemony over the rest of the contemporary nations – which was so easy for those governments to do because they played such a formative role in the very creation of those nations – the former two entities were in the end themselves subject to the hegemony of an unofficial but almost incomprehensibly *Powerful* global ruling class. For once, the commonly used language in the contemporary world actually provides the ideal label for this entity: it's *literally* acts as what's commonly referred to with the term "shadow government". It's an institutionalized shadow government.

The contemporary shadow government represents the fully conscious realization of the Anglo-American conquest syndrome and thereby of the global hegemons: our narrative's main albeit mainly anonymous subjects. Along those lines, and inseparable from the context of the overall text, I believe this particular shadow government is best understood as the absolutely indispensable control mechanism for facilitating the very existence of such a maximally-expanded and maximally-intensifying version of the traditional Western cultural pyramid. In the contemporary stage of evolution for the now globalized *Power*-structure, the major problem for the hegemons – that warfare was/is more starkly essential to the system's very existence than ever before, precisely at a moment when the public viewed/views itself as being most morally opposed to the imperial reality – could only be solved with a tool as potent as an *officially-instituted* shadow government.[ccclii]

As I've said, one doesn't necessarily need to believe that the contemporary hegemons deliberately plan the exact scenarios of whatever particular wars their subordinate States end up in, to accept the undeniable fact that imperial warfare is the indispensable activity around which all Western history, and especially contemporary Western/globalized history, has been organized. But now I'm going to assert that even more disturbing fact: based on the *actual record* of the contemporary sociohistorical process, you must believe that the hegemons during this era have deliberately if quite broadly planned, many years in advance, the instigation of and, in turn (and more importantly) that they've deliberately planned "The Peace" following whatever particular war they've ended up in, ever since the wars of 1898-99. It happened with World War One, it happened again with World War Two, and, immediately proceeding the latter, it happened another time in the form of the Cold War, which, as I've said, marked the official establishment of the global civilization following the half-century of gestation during the years 1898-1945. Finally, the whole process transitioned seamlessly into the "Wars on Drugs and Terror" the U.S. is still "fighting" to this day. Moreover, although seeing this reality certainly requires an expansion of one's mental collection of empirical facts, it requires even more so an adjustment of one's philosophical attitude towards the nature of *Power* – and it's not necessarily even a more antagonistic approach that's called for, so much as a greater commitment to maintaining a long historical perspective in the formulation of one's political beliefs.

The particular, global civilization that would emerge unofficially with the detonation of atomic bombs in combat (in August 1945), and officially with the U.S.'s explicit transformation into a national security State (starting in July 1947), first became a realistic possibility, and in retrospect, only became a realistic possibility, as a result of the discussions following World War One, usually referred to as the "Paris Peace Talks". An especially bizarre episode in human history, it would nonetheless, in all its bizarreness, set the tone for the rest of the contemporary era. Ultimately, through the central control system of international finance – the U.S. branch of which was represented as usual by the leading financiers on Wall Street, epitomized by the House of Morgan – the Anglo-American hegemons would be setting the precise stage for World War Two in the key nations driving that later conflict, as they closely managed the outcomes of major international events every step along the way throughout the interwar era. Thus, as we've also seen in many others cases, we can most clearly see in this instance how international finance is above all else a *geostrategic* entity.

Primarily, the hegemonic sector set the stage by aggressively shaping broader elite responses ("opinion") concerning such events: not just by shaping discourse, but additionally, even more directly, by helping bring into being the particular phenomena that human beings were compelled to observe and consider due to the sheer spectacle of organizational force – by orchestrating the installation of dictators, financially fostering mass movements, etc. At all times, they craftily ensured the concealment of their role in determining the trends of global affairs, even as they seemed to possess reach in every key sector of humanity's politicoeconomic and cultural life; and once the elites as a whole were brought on board, the hegemons turned fully towards molding the masses. Here we see, illustrated in a most gruesome fashion, the reason why the leading international investing class, as it existed around the turn of the 20th-century, constitutes such a uniquely archetypal embodiment of the overall contemporary Anglo-American hegemony. The United States and its less boisterous partner, the United Kingdom, have held the decisive share of *Power* in the contemporary world, while within these nations certain financiers along with their ilk have held the decisive share of *Power* ever since the crucial first phase of globalization's development. The system they were so instrumental in setting up is the system we're all plagued by now.

But I must reemphasize as always: the reason why the system has been so uniquely "successful" – which in civilizational terms, remember, only means that it's the best at capturing and distributing energy for human exploitation, and in State terms means that it's the best at making war – is because the hegemons set up a system that the "good citizens" in the imperial "homeland" have themselves most greatly benefited from. And based on how history has gone since the event-clusters of this critical period between the end of World War One and the "end" of World War Two, I don't think we can come to any other conclusion about the system the hegemons set up: *things were/are always planned surrounding precisely this reality.* To an extent impossible with regard to events in any other past age, the major event-clusters comprising human history in the contemporary era are the products of a more or less unified hegemonic strategy, the main goal of which is nothing besides punishing those whose behaviors threaten the system, and rewarding those whose behaviors support it (with all sorts of unavoidable inconsistencies mixed in, of course). This strategy is what meticulously shapes the broadest contours of the global civilization.

It has always been the strategy; it has essentially never changed throughout its entire existence, even as the appearance of its external effects undergoes perpetual transformation. What kind of strategy is it? Who are the hegemons? In a financially-monopolized world, quite unsurprisingly, the strategy takes the form of an investment. The 20th-century-beyond era has been little more than one great big global industrialized investment for the ruling financial (-petroleum) class. Everything else has followed accordingly.

So characteristically of the contemporary world – this contemporary world the investors created – the most overwhelmingly destructive fact is at the same time the most nonchalant. In the globalized capitalist system, the truth is that human event-clusters can for the most part be the products of precise, secret planning, without things even having to be designed at every step of the way according to an explicit, *single* grand plan. The system only had to be set up in the first place, one plan at a time, and then maintained in shifting ways as time progressed, changing along with the rhythm of the global hegemons' infighting about other, at each moment less systemically vital matters. In this sense, "the" plan is the perpetuation of the global civilization itself. Moreover, because its history has shown how things on the surface change with such unique rapidity in a context of globalization, it seems quite certain that the system *couldn't* be (besides the fact that I'm arguing that it isn't) the result of a single overarching plan that has existed the entire time in the same untarnished form. Most notably, this latter alternative scenario would imply basically a singular lineage of planners responsible for *every* major decision, throughout all of history since the lead-up to World War One.

To elaborate on what I noted a couple of pages back, I believe the most significant difference between the two possible views is a philosophical one, and in particular has to do with one's general attitude towards the phenomenon of the social structure. Throughout this text, I've made clear my unequivocal philosophical adherence to viewing every individual human phenomenon in terms of its relation to some or another holistically encompassing cultural system, which latter is held in place by many varying levels of practically innumerable but somehow ultimately interlocking frameworks of human interaction, both occupational and otherwise – social structures. Concerning what's most germane to the immediate subject-at-hand, this view implies that no matter *who*, in the end, is most in control of the global civilization, it's always the holistic system's reproduction that matters above all else.

This points to what has really been going on throughout the 20th-century-beyond era – exactly what I've been arguing all along: the globalized version of a Western-originated industrial civilization has emerged, matured, and is now falling, all under the aegis of an Anglo-American-style financial-petroleum hegemony, no matter who specifically, in any given instance, has had "final say" in permitting the actions required to maintain this hegemony. Once the goal of perpetuating the Anglo-American hegemony was fully established in its first contemporary form by the end of World War One, there never needed to be another "grand plan" in place, but instead millions of little plans, doing whatever it took to continually reproduce the starting point of the Anglo-American-dependent hegemony. The hegemony is simply a systemic fact; not primarily significant insofar as it's connected to particular individuals, but insofar as particular individuals carry out the will of the *'hegemonic currency'*, by maintaining the environmental conditions necessary for the particular type of "success" associated with that currency's preeminence ("the almighty dollar").[cccliii]

Hegemonic success has primarily been achieved by the ever-increasingly conscious realization of the once largely tacit synchronization of major institutional activities, always existent in every civilization. In the contemporary global civilization, the synchronization of interests takes place in the form of a constantly-reproduced operational alignment of substrategies between (from most significant to least significant) (1) financiers/industrialists and energy corporations, the most important of which by far are represented by the petroleum industry; (2) mass media conglomerates; (3) arms manufacturers/operators; and (4) black market criminal syndicates centered around the illegal narcotics trade (see BOOK TWO of part 3). In other words, all the elements most significant to the U.S. Dollar's global hegemony.

The most *Powerful* and thus most influential synchronization of such activities has taken place on a totally globalized level by functionaries that necessarily transcend all conventionally-conceived politicoeconomic boundaries, in conscious service of a perpetually reigning hegemony held together by the interconnection between the always military-centered activities of the United States and the United Kingdom – an interconnection that must be painstakingly mired in obfuscation by the "First World" priesthoods. Basically, we can say that nothing important has ever really changed except for the particular makeup of the hegemons at any given time: the patterns are too overwhelmingly repetitive to ignore the fact that they're patterns.

One of the greatest obstacles towards seeing this as the only explanation for what has gone on in the past almost-a-century involves the near-universal failure of individuals inhabiting the contemporary dominant culture to appreciate how, if a nation is plugged into a single global economy – which essentially all nations have been to a perpetually-increasing degree since the beginning of industrialization – there's no real possibility of uniqueness for that nation's central social structure. (In this same vein, additionally, trading with the "Enemy" essentially becomes a necessity.) All nations, insofar as contemporary national States are synonymous with "types of entities that compose the membership of the UN", came to possess at least highly similar if not identical *'governing machines'* during the 20th-century. The conclusions of World War One and World War Two were the key moments initiating this state-of-affairs.

Throughout the 20th-century, all nations, by necessity of their entanglement within the single global capitalist economy – whether any nation was perceived to be a part of this economy or, alternatively, was perceived to be engaged in contemporary warfare "against" it – came to adopt a State-imposed strategy close to either one of two extremes on a common political spectrum, extremes which weren't very different from one another to begin with and would become less and less different as time went on.[ccliv] The crucial point of reference in this regard, both in terms of the history immediately before it and that immediately following, is of course the Cold War, wherein the entire planet ended up being split up into just three groups of nations. The first two groups of nations were represented by what were typically called in the United States the "First World" and the "Second World" nations, referring respectively to the capitalist so-called "Democracies", on the one hand, and the so-called "Communist" dictatorships on the other, with the U.S. being the leading nation in the "First World" and the S.U. the leading nation in the "Second".

It's quite a vivid representation of the 20th-century-beyond era as a whole, but especially the middle (period six – 1947-1991) and late (period seven – 1995-?) phases, to see just how much violence we must do to our language in order to explain contemporary history. Because the fact is, there was no real democracy whatsoever in the "Democracies", and no actual communism to be had in the "Communist" nations, if we contrast the history with the typical meanings of these words in individuals' minds. Thus, at least in the present text, we must adopt a label for the two "opposed" governing systems that's truly reflective of reality: we will use 'global fascism',[ccclv] in reference to both the capitalist "Democracies" and the "Communist" dictatorships.

There were the most comprehensively encompassing institutional command structures in history running industrialized military economies in both blocs, in two admittedly distinct cultural forms – although the two cultural forms were deliberately designed to serve essentially one common, "metacultural" purpose. Thus, the "warfare" between the U.S. and the S.U. wasn't just cultural but *sub*cultural, by which I mean it went on between two different entities within the same broadest cultural environment.

The purpose of this was to maintain one global civilization, in the specific form of a global financial-petroleum Empire.

In order for there to be a global Empire in the particular sociohistorical context, a context where the U.S. would necessarily be home base for everything, there couldn't be the appearance of just one State running the show single-handed. The sociohistorical process had reached a point where the planet had to be divided into two "Blocs" comprised of two leading States (and their respective allies) which, while supposedly at war, were unified at a higher level in the sense that together, they would ensure the continuing existence of a global *Power*-structure in an age when people would find its realistically-described existence so morally unacceptable, the system itself might not long survive if it were widely understood. For although organized violence is one part of the indispensable starting point for all civilizations, there's also that other, equally crucial component, which is what we can call 'organized morality', the basis for every religion. If the violent reality presents itself as too obviously contradictory to the imagined moral order presented by the civilization's central official ideology, or religion,[ccclvi] the entire combined politicoeconomic/ideological complex that is the civilization itself will break down.

Hence all the "SECRECY" since the start of the Cold War – which we can't even call true 'secrecy', because it's in actuality an official function of the State (whatever secrecy truly is, it's not that) – deliberately designed to minimize the potential for people in both blocs could never meaningfully discover the fact that, from the broadest perspective, the war wasn't between the two blocs at all. It was between the globally synchronized hegemons, and everyone else: even if the latter group was largely unaware of it.

Most of all, the war would be waged against the peoples in the third group of nations, which I haven't mentioned yet; these nations comprised what would be called the "Third World", an appellation so often employed with denigrating intentions. We're merely using it here since it's the best way to confront the Cold War on its own terms. As usual in the present text, the quotation marks are intended to remind at all times how dependent the label is on a specific sociohistorical context.

What also must be remembered at all times is how the "Third World" nations, universally, had been victims of Western imperialism in one way or another right up until the granting of each new nation's "Independence". Therefore, the "Third World" nations were in their very establishment completely overwhelmed by "First World" and/or "Second World" *Power*. By design, participation in one or the other main networks comprising the global economy (but usually the "First") was made to be an absolute prerequisite for nationhood of any kind. The "Third World" nations, too, then, were forced into a situation wherein they had essentially three choices, none of them very different from the others. They could become similar to (1) the capitalist "Democracies"; or (2) the "Communist" dictatorships; or (3) some mix of (1) and (2).

This all really started to take hold with the end of World War Two, as I've said; but in its earliest, crudest origins, it seems to already have been the roughly-conceived strategy immediately following World War One, at the latest. Indisputably, the investors – which group, as should go without saying, also included all "informal" representatives of the investors – were the individuals most responsible for what occurred in the meetings to set up the postwar order, an event-cluster sequence that took place in the first half of 1919 (the Paris Peace Talks). For a moment, without even bringing into our discussion the existence of a shadow government, it'll suffice simply to allude to the general goings-on making up the visible, public face of this utterly weird phenomenon, in order to properly illustrate the meetings' lethal hostility to anything remotely democratic. Ultimately, however, we'll also be able to perceive the obvious hand of a global shadow government operating for the eventual sole benefit of Anglo-American hegemony, cutting its teeth on what were, at the time, far and away the most globally consequential political summits in humanity's history.

Why was it such a strange historical occurrence? It was one of the only instances when the hegemony openly stood in its proper domain, right at the center stage of international affairs, with its true implications on full display. Foremost, the public activity of the meetings was most notably characterized by the victorious Powers' drawing up of what they deemed the juridical boundaries *for basically the entire planet*. This is the main thing we need to know in order to understand what the essential purpose of World War One was: to institute globally-encompassing international boundaries in the precise way desired by the leading representatives of the U.K. and U.S. States. In fact, that purpose alone, by creating the juridical framework State militaries across the whole world would defend and/or attack, made it at least theoretically possible that every polity on the planet would eventually become part of a single intercity cultural system (a single civilization).

Above all, the boundaries were drawn up under the guidance of England, the State that, in the context, was doing the most to further the Anglo-American hegemons' cause. In terms of effects, the plan would go far beyond what were the existing boundaries of our two leading nations, determining the fate of the whole planet for the rest of globalization's infancy. It continues, in turn, to shape the globe during what has been far and away its most consequential era. (The fact that this era is so uniquely important and has happened in about 67 years so far is the best imaginable evidence of what I mean by the concept of a long-historically accelerating speed of events during the civilizations stage of human cultural evolution.) No representatives of the colonial areas were allowed any sort of meaningful participation, although it was those peoples' fates that had been and would continue to be altered most drastically, and despite the fact that direct involvement of the colonized peoples in determining their own futures had been one of Wilson's promises in his Fourteen Points – which, it turned out, were just like campaign promises: they were intended to never be fulfilled. Thus, the leaders of the West devised (not for the last time)* an all-encompassing framework deciding how the rest of the world would have to live, indefinitely. Never had such an ambitious geographical scheme been officially attempted, let alone diplomatically accomplished; and even today, concerning many of the specific boundaries established in the years immediately following World War One, the plan implemented by the Paris Peace Talks remains law. In terms of less consciously available phenomena, the plan's "invisible", structural effects are present in everything shaping the now deteriorating[ccclvii] global politicoeconomic framework.

Therefore, even more so than those most unimaginably oppressed sectors of Western domestic populations, it was individuals in the "Third World" who ended up the world wars' greatest victims of all, and that officially began with the Peace Talks (a label

---

* As we'll see, the establishment of the post-World War Two order encapsulated by the beginnings of the Cold War would mark the last big nail in the coffin of possible "Third World" independence.

which, in retrospect, stands as a rare example of black comedy). For instance, the boundaries with the greatest long-term significance in the contemporary world are unquestionably those that were drawn up for the area today commonly called the "Middle East" or "Near East" (southwest Asia). Of all the places where new national boundaries were basically created wholesale amidst discussions between only those at the top levels of Western governments, mainly during this half-year period in 1919, no change was so suddenly transformative as the one in southwest Asia: and yet, simultaneously, no change has persisted for so many years in such nearly "pristine" form.

Why – it's as if this was one of the reasons why World War One was fought, in the first place!

Here's more or less exactly what I mean by "how wars end in the contemporary world" being the best possible gauge of why those wars are fought in the first place: the war ended with the German domestic front in shambles, "Communism" in Russia, English *Power* in the "Middle East", and monopoly conditions in strategic U.S. industries. To return to the hegemonic "overworld"ccclviii ultimately in charge of Anglo-American policy, I must once more reiterate, no matter your particular perspective on whether it's a "good" thing or a "bad" thing, it remains indisputable that the elite global financiers were, for quite some time leading up to World War One, in decisive control of the politicoeconomic affairs of both the United Kindgom and the United States. And these two nations, while not technically, *publicly* responsible for inciting the war's immediate sparks, were absolutely most responsible for covertly setting up the exact scenario wherein war would take place under the conditions most favorable for themselves.

Let's attempt to sum up what we know so far about the narrative on the surface, in order to then make the soundest possible speculation concerning "what happened in the interwar years". The two leading nations' general policymaking actions, individually and as a pair, had trended in only one direction for over a decade leading up to the war: the ideal sociohistorical setting for militarily crushing all potential for the German Empire to be a feasible global rival to the Anglo-American hegemony that was rapidly being established. Knowing the overall trend of events on the one hand, and on the other, the dominant control over U.K.-U.S. policymaking generally exhibited by the global financial elite, we must ask: had the uncontested controllers of U.K.-U.S. policy, and especially "foreign" policy, allowed such policies to go in a direction that could prove detrimental to their own positions? That is, was the overworld making decisions that would be good for the "national interests", at the expense of their own interests? Of course, as we've already seen, World War One certainly benefited the financiers and their favored corporations, along with all the "trickle-down" beneficiaries of this financial-corporate alliance, namely the "good citizens" in the emerging global empire, to the complete exclusion of virtually everyone else and everything else on the planet. So, finally, did those individuals who ultimately had the actual ability to bolster or veto specific actions taken by the two most *Powerful* States in the world *intend* for things to work out to their greatest advantage, or did events always just materialize that way on their own?

As you can see, the question isn't even "Who benefited?", anymore, because the answer to that question is beyond all doubt. The question can only be, "Were those benefiting conscious of how it was, exactly, that they were benefiting?" Obviously, almost no one besides those at the top levels (i.e. the deepest levels) possibly could've been. But concerning such unique individuals: isn't the latter question, when you think about it for more than a second – putting it in the context of everything else in the narrative – quite silly? Anyway, more abstractly, how could a human-made system as gargantuan as globalization have emerged and existed as it has for any considerable amount of time, if no one at all *intentionally* designed it and maintained it in that way, at any phase along the path?

Additionally, we also know that even though we can clearly recognize the two nations that have benefited most from globalization, it's still, by definition, not any single nation or couple of nations, which is/are ultimately controlling globalization – a system with its earliest official origins in the Paris Peace Talks concluding World War One (which also essentially marked the beginning of World War Two) – but rather a global market. It's certainly not a "free" market, and no such thing has ever truly existed in practice. But it's just as certainly capitalism, precisely insofar as capitalism has only ever existed in reality by way of State intervention. What's the primary mechanism of ever-increasing State intervention into the economy, which has always most definitively embodied capitalism in all its various forms? Have I really not yet made this perfectly clear?

War: as ever in the history of civilizations, war has represented the quintessential command structure for the economy in the global civilization, just as economics has been the number-one variable driving success in war. The globalized market has thus been, to be more accurate, a global militarized market.

War has always been the key determinative factor shaping the politicoeconomic system buttressing the ideological pyramid: the latter being the central psychologically-based structure holding every civilization together. What makes 20th-century-beyond history seem strange in this sense is how unprecedentedly pronounced has been humanity's adherence to this singularly consequential truth: above all because, compared to the enormous population of the contemporary dominant culture as a whole, it's necessary for a relatively very few individuals to be aware of this fact. If any substantial proportion of the system's population ever come to know that this is "how things work", the system could very well collapse on account of losing all its "moral capital".

Thus, as warfare in the contemporary world has become an evermore explicitly integral organizing principle shaping civilization as a whole throughout the 20th-century-beyond era, the mainstream in the "First World" – one part of humanity who could conceivably start to change things in this regard, to begin with by "renouncing their sins", so to speak – have become ever-increasingly repressed concerning how exactly our politicoeconomic system works. The thing making the global civilization seem strangest of all is that, to an extent completely unparalleled by all other periods in human history, this "natural" state of the civilization *is by deliberate design*. This is not only possible but also, within the context of the system, wholly necessary, mainly because, as I've said all along, the long historical process in the 20th-century-beyond period has been happening at a far faster rate than any other sociohistorical process throughout the entire existence of humanity, which most centrally indicates an exponential expansion to the already unsurpassed significance represented by the three interlocking cultural spheres revolving around capture-and-use of agricultural life-support.

On this basis, to begin speculating, we can say that whether anyone responsible for originally implementing the policy of global fascism stated it in these explicit terms or not, the ultimate practical purpose of World War One was to initiate the first phase in a viable long-term scenario for deliberately-imposed industrial State oppression, which has been servicing the politicoeconomic system's absurd "internal expansion" (implosion)[ccclix] ever since. In other words, it was a time for unprecedentedly broad-sweeping "revolutions from the top": the reactionary elements all over the world, no matter the extent to which their actions were consciously synchronized, or not (but from my perspective, the synchronization must've been in at least one sense extremely conscious) became uncharacteristically proactive in one fell swoop. The group I've referred to as the Anglo-American hegemons won out, and thus, according to the rules of the contemporary Great Power game, it was their global State capitalist system that was implemented in the postwar period. – The winners made the losers their slaves. – This was most clearly revealed, to sum up, insofar as World War One ended with the U.S. as essentially the sole creditor in the world amongst the Great Powers, which along with the U.K. would soon have the sole potential to control the decisive share of global oil production for decades to come, and, literally enforcing it all, the logistical potential to monopolize global arms manufacturing.

But for the budding global system to be most successful from a "public opinion" standpoint – really the only thing that mattered to the hegemons – the fact of a revolution from the top had to be hidden from the individuals in the imperial homeland. The English and the Americans wouldn't be as acquiescent to fascism as the Germans, the Italians, and the Russians, because the U.K. and U.S. States had long used the language of democracy as their noble purpose for imperial expansion, and also, interconnectively, because the U.K. and the U.S. were far more prosperous nations at the time in per capita terms. All this of course remains a critical dynamic in global affairs: such deceptive manipulation of public opinion is still something quite pervasive in the existent world, to say the least where it's very well prominently illustrated, in the sense that it constitutes a constantly enacted official policy, that all U.S. official positions (i.e., U.S. State propaganda) concerning the purposes of U.S. military engagements are designed primarily "for domestic consumption".

The thing that's less widely known, but still quite true, is that all this started long before the Cold War – during the lead-up to World War One; it expanded through the war itself, and exploded in its aftermath, which includes World War Two. In this vein, then, why would any individuals at the present late date continue, in their interpretations of contemporary history to take even the least bit seriously the U.S. Government's dominant narratives of its own actions as presented during the world wars, and the intermezzo that separated them? And yet, practically all conventional scholars of contemporary history do precisely that: whether unconsciously or consciously, they base their constructions of history on the propagandized version, using it as a starting point, at least, if not as an exclusive frame of reference. In turn, the myth of the U.S. as the world's savior from "Totalitarianism" triumphantly marches onward.

It has long been perfectly clear: the propagandized version of the World Wars, portrayed most representatively by the dominant narrative of U.S. history during that era – i.e., the "grand narrative" of itself the *Power*-structure tacitly refers to in all its official actions – is not only quite often beside the point, and thus at best can have *no* valuable impact at all on one's understanding of history, but is in fact almost always much worse. Typically, the propaganda transmits a representation of historical fact that's actually positively detrimental to one's understanding of contemporary history; it destroys even the *possibility* for cultivating a meaningful understanding of the contemporary world. Once again, I unfortunately have to add – this is exactly the point.

The history of the global civilization's gestation – the "testing phase" of globalization – is by no means easy to write about, and I realize it's difficult to read. Yet we must confront what really happened if we're to truly understand the world it spawned. While the establishment-approved mindset would immediately label him a "conspiracy theorist", I consider Antony C. Sutton's thesis to be the only reasonable starting point for any analysis of what was really going on in Western history during the so-called "interwar" period, which label itself conceals that there was a war going on the entire time. It was a war between the Anglo-American hegemons and all the domestic populations under their dominion; only the latter, much more numerous side was barely aware that it was fighting a war at all, and certainly had no idea who it was fighting against.[ccclx]

Sutton's thesis on this matter in particular, for readers unaware of it, is stated largely in three shocking books: *Wall Street and the Bolshevik Revolution, Wall Street and FDR,* and *Wall Street and the Rise of Hitler*. As mention of the titles already implies, Sutton's thesis revolves around a leading group of financiers with unparalleled ability to manage the politics of early 20th-century industrialization, who were all ultimately attached to the operational nexus they and their predecessors had long nurtured between London, Wall Street, and Washington. In sum, the same sector of individuals was ultimately in decisive control of the emergences of the Soviet Union, FDR, and Hitler – perhaps the three greatest symptoms of the particular event-cluster sequences leading to World War Two and from there to the Cold War. Sutton's work, the product of outstanding, bold research, is unequivocally some of the most valuable tangible evidence illustrating in action one most crucial segment of the Anglo-American hegemony, during one of the most critical phases throughout all human history. From my own perspective, I believe that this sector, because of what it was able to make happen structurally – the one connecting the highest levels of high finance to the highest levels of Western governments – was in fact *the* major flashpoint connecting the Anglo-American hegemony at all times to the event-cluster sequences ending World War One and those leading up to, comprising, and officially concluding World War Two. All of these sequences collectively pointed in only one direction: towards a fully-established Anglo-American hegemony over a globalized civilization/globalized interstate system following World War Two.[ccclxi]

It might all seem too absurd to even possibly be real. But just always ask yourself, in conceptual terms: to achieve the goal of unsurpassable *Power* – the implicit aim driving forward all modern Western civilization, but only a truly realizable possibility once there existed the imaginable, strived-for form of a global civilization – what *wouldn't* those with self-consciously imperial motives do?

*　　　*　　　*

At the same time, of course, one seriously errs – as in, misses the point completely – if one thinks the Anglo-American hegemons, or any group, would've truly aimed to exercise such ruthlessly autocratic management over world affairs in order to further anything remotely resembling an ideological principle as such is conventionally understood. This is an historically naïve view imposed mainly by the style of wartime propaganda itself. The aim for such total control in reality only has to do with *politicoeconomic order*, i.e., the broadly predictable functioning of the war-trade competition, without which (as has been the constant theme of the present work as a whole) no civilization could exist. Creation and perpetuation of the emergent globalized rigged contest between the two forms of fascism, a process beginning immediately after World War One ended and the constant theme all throughout the Cold War, was considered by the hegemons to be the supremely necessary global chain-of-events for keeping the existing financial-industrial war-trade competition in place, which was the necessary prerequisite for perpetuating the closest thing to the version of the cultural *Power*-pyramid existing at that time. Therefore, the hegemons imposed their desired politicoeconomic order – because they had the politicoeconomic ability to do so in the context, and because there also was, fortuitously for imaginative hegemons, massive but unformed public clamor for some kind of governmental "change". Motive, means, and opportunity.

If you're wondering, "How could any human beings do something so amoral?", then the notion of *a*morality should be applied to the situation most literally, by which I mean that morality never played a role except insofar as it was the costume incessantly worn by complexly concealed State warmongering. As always, the language of morality was invariably invoked to justify the constantly expanding preparation for more total warfare, which was absolutely necessary for the near-term survival of the social structure, no matter how damaging it might prove to be in the long run. Indeed, the whole point really is that hegemons run their systems to accomplish nothing besides what ultimately prove to be the shortest-term "solutions" possible, and this is how hegemons always run what are literally, it turns out, *their* systems. In the end the civilization-State-complex can only be a vast ideologically-situated habitation precisely reflecting the symptomology of its hegemons' rule over their conquests.

That is the problem.

In a cultural sense, the politicoeconomic problem is reflected most significantly in the problem of group-imposed morality. Most simply, this problem can be viewed as the situation human beings find themselves in whenever what makes the individual a "good member" of whatever dominant group reigns in the individual's locale is precisely what's most self-destructive for that individual. Few things in humanity's history are as crucial as this: the very problem with group-imposed morality – its ability to rapidly and unstoppably proliferate throughout a human population – is, at the same time, the source of its greatest success.

Clearly, wars provide the best (worst) examples of this phenomenon, and the best examples of all surround the world wars, especially World War Two. The last real gasp of European nationalism seemed as if it might take down the entire global system – but just like in the aftermath of World War One, global financial-corporate capitalism again survived intact; and this second time it would reemerge more triumphantly than ever during the earliest phase of the Cold War. The phenomenon most immediately responsible for starting the world down this path of no return in favor of globalized State capitalism is actually what's remembered today as contemporary capitalism's greatest failing, the Great Depression whose beginning was most memorably marked in the United States on October 29, 1929 with the run on the New York Stock Exchange. The panic then spread all around the world, shattering the economy of any nation substantially plugged into the emergent global capitalist market, run by the Anglo-American hegemons under the heading of an "informal" financial web entangling the total Western economy with four dominant institutional entities. These four entities were the U.K.'s Bank of England, the U.S.'s Federal Reserve, the Bank of France, and the system's "apex", the Bank for International Settlements located in Switzerland.[ccclxii]

Quite tragically for the rest of history, the German Weimar Republic was a part of this politicoeconomic system, a nation which had only become a (nominal) "Constitutional Democracy" following the "Revolution" of November 1918, marking the true end of German involvement in World War One, and thus interchangeably the explicit beginning of the Anglo-American hegemons' success in their plot to crush Germany. A completely unstable "Republic" dominated by transnational corporations with interlocking directorships in the U.K. and U.S. would be putty in hegemonic hands. This sort of nation was set up in Germany from 1919 onwards, owing primarily to the Paris Peace Talks in accompaniment with the subsequent arrangements designed to enforce the agreements reached in the talks, referring here most namely to the Dawes plan of 1924, which would restructure Germany's economy along the lines prescribed by Anglo-American banking (above all involving the formation of cartels).

As I've said, even if we accept the official accounts of events, when we look at the names of the individuals most influential in formulating the Paris agreements and the other agreements these gave rise to, it's indisputable that the Anglo-American financial-corporate elite was the milieu most responsible for drawing up and in particular for enforcing them. Remarkably, but by no means surprisingly, conventional historical scholars writing on the relevant sequences typically don't seem to find this detail to be the least bit curious, even though, as – again – even conventional accounting of events can attest, much of the fate of more or less the entire planet would eventually be decided based on the course of those first six months in 1919.[ccclxiii] Individuals standing in for financial houses and corporations might've been writing and implementing all of these agreements for the nominal aggrandizement of State *Power*: but remember, in every Western country at the time, State *Power* was the merest veil of public legitimacy for the deep state represented by the transnational financial-corporate overlords. So the consolidation of Anglo-American *Power* initially brought on by the enforcement of the 1919 meetings was primarily the consolidation of those global financial-corporate interests invested in the contemporaneous Anglo-American war-trade hegemony.

For instance, it's indisputable that Charles Dawes, the American ostensibly responsible for negotiating the above-mentioned 1924 plan that restructured Germany's entire economy – and, relatedly, a future Vice President/Nobel Peace Prize winner – was a financier linked inextricably to the House of Morgan. No matter how you look at it, globally-minded central bankers operating from London and Wall Street benefited from the arrangement in a manner that couldn't have been paralleled by any other group.[ccclxiv] Of course, this sector was among the few key links in the nexus that had all along been working to crush Germany.

As it turns out, the plot was to crush Russia, as well. Unlike the mistake earlier hegemons had made with Germany, these interwar hegemons were nipping Russia in the bud before it even got started. In a late, most sinister European manifestation of the timeless British diplomatic-military game called "balance-of-power", the number one item on the Anglo-American agenda – albeit the item necessarily concealed via endlessly convoluted compartments of intrigue – was to ensure the lethal division of Germany and Russia. The plan called for installation of a "Right-wing" authoritarian regime in Germany and a "Left-wing" authoritarian regime in Russia. Each nation would have no choice, the reasoning went, but to go for the throat of the other. Whichever side ultimately looked like it could be the bigger threat, the U.K.-U.S. would swoop in and support the weaker opponent.[ccclxv]

Here's a rare monument to the vital necessity for obliterating all conventional notions of "Left versus Right". As the conventional thinking would have it, in the 20th-century-beyond era, politics was largely an ideological struggle between the "Left", the "Right", and the "Center", on both international and national levels. Little else I can think of is more poisonous to a proper historical understanding of the contemporary world than the attribution of conventional ideological principles to individuals who are or have been truly *Powerful* in contemporary government, an error epitomized by the conventionally-imagined "Left-Right" spectrum and its conjoined twin, electoral politics.

On an international level, as the conventional perspective would hold, the Nazis and Fascists, in Germany and Italy, respectively, represent the "far-Right", the Communist Party, of course, represents the "far-Left", and the U.K. and the U.S. represent the "Center". From the standpoint of the Anglo-American hegemons, I don't think this could've been an accident, and we'll eventually (in *BOOK TWO*) explore some ideas as to why that would be, and what it might mean.

For a moment, let's imagine it was a total accident. The notion of a "Left-Right" spectrum on which one can accurately place the motives driving these unbelievably rapid, simultaneous national politicoeconomic transformations, is still at best only superficially relevant to the actual holistic change itself, and at worst militates ruthlessly against gaining any useful perspective at all on contemporary history. To begin, it plainly ignores all of the broadest and hence most determinative sociohistorical contexts: not just concerning the particular context when all of these contemporary conceptions were first taking hold (the 1920s and 1930s) but concerning all the rest of history, both before and after. It would be one thing if there were many other examples throughout history of imperial politicoeconomic systems operating purely, or even mainly, towards ideological ends; but there haven't been any such examples that I can recall, at least no examples relevant to the experience of Western civilization, considering how in the long run, the "Western-style" of politicoeconomic system was wholly characterized by endlessly expanding military commitments. The only assigned place ideology has in an imperial system, still a large and indispensable one, is to serve as *broad-sweeping* cultural support for military mobilization, i.e., to inflate a noble purpose. Indeed, this is precisely what we find the exploding ideologies of the '20s and '30s to have been if we engage with the relevant sociohistorical reality in a manner that goes even the least bit beyond the conventional way of looking at it – foremost, by viewing it not as anomalous, but quite contrarily, as being deeply woven into interconnected long and short historical processes.

If we abandon the uniquely toxic "Left-Right" model as a part our own perspective, while at the same time recognizing its tremendous currency throughout the contemporary dominant culture, it becomes easy to see that amongst all the nations, the major differences between the politicoeconomic systems emergent in the 1920s and 30s were *only* in the realm of the cultural, and even more exactly, in the realm of the *sub*cultural. That is, the ideological differences between and within the Western nations in the interwar years mattered exclusively on cultural grounds, so that's where each ideology made its greatest impact on behalf of its respective nation or nations. Considering all such nations as a group, then: at any given time, each nation's dominant ideology appeared to be violently at odds with its international "opposites", not to mention its opponents within its own nation; but in fact it's precisely in this way that every ideology did its equal part in supporting the evolution of the whole international politicoeconomic system. And this was "necessary" because in the end, all the nations had to be perfectly welded into a single universal (globalized) system built around corporate capital, the most advanced and hence the extinctive stage in the history of "private" wealth.

Up until that point (and, we can now see, through that point, as well), industrialization had been doing nothing but evermore-rapidly narrowing the possibilities for every politicoeconomic system it took control of: reflecting how, when industrialization spread to a juridically-bounded space, it always soon enough grabbed full *Power* over the local politicoeconomic system and always on behalf of a foreign entity in some substantial way. By the beginning of the 20th-century, as I've said, it had become clear that there were just two acceptable versions of capitalism for international Powers: they were represented by the Anglo-American industrial system, on the one hand, and the German industrial system on the other. All the major political conflict in the world subsequently became coordinated around the dispute between all the leading groups (factions) in charge of these two most similar, most hyperspecializing systems; the first round would be settled by "the masses" via World War One. It appears that ultimately, the planet was really only big enough for one global industrialized capitalist system,[ccclxvi] a state-of-affairs established by the world wars, coming to maturity during the Cold War, and culminating and declining with period seven, peak globalization. Thus, from the perspective of the interwar years, the overarching purpose behind World War One – that is, for its true aggressors, the Anglo-American hegemons – had basically been to spread the early 20th-century, Anglo-American version of industrialization into as many places as the postwar agreements would allow. Overtly, although all the rhetorical warfare sought to camouflage the bluntness of the motive, this mainly meant Germany; covertly, it ended up meaning Russia, as well. Again, the key to the Anglo-American strategy was that these two nations had to be pitted against one another for the plan to succeed.

Before we go forward I must just reiterate, that while I call it an "Anglo-American" strategy, it's really more proper to say it was a global strategy, seeking *Power*-consolidation *through the vehicle of* an Anglo-American hegemony: an order whose official actions were being increasingly relegated to the purview of the United States Government. While dependent on the U.S. and U.K. most of all, it could (can) only work so long as *all* governments remained primarily concerned with participating in the Anglo-American orchestrated, globalized capitalist market, rather than with supporting the needs of their national populations. Therefore, the very nature of a successful Anglo-American hegemony required that all other nations plugged into the Anglo-American system be essentially ruled as fiefdoms by whatever local ruler happened to be under the Empire's good graces for whatever reason at a given moment. The goal only called for supporting the United States above all other nations because the investors realized this strategy was the best for total monopolization – and, thereby, maximum stabilization – of *Power*, not for any reasons that could appropriately be called "nationalistic". Nationalism as such had nothing to do with it. The only "ism" it had to do with was *capitalism*; but a capitalism whose workings have absolutely nothing to do with any "free market" ideology except insofar as the latter serves as cover when necessary. Nonetheless, all major mass movements, the primary vehicles for contemporary "isms" in general, could somehow be covertly brought into line to serve the purposes of a perpetually expanding money supply, i.e., a globally omnipotent pyramid scheme, where total production of total resources fed a cycle of total debt.

The only way a perpetually expanding money supply could exist was for there to be a singularly *central* financial economy based on a single currency; and the only way such a globally centralized financial field could successfully exist in the sociohistorical circumstances first established throughout the 1920s was for the monopolized financial conditions to be inextricably tied to a monopoly on petroleum. The fulfillment of both of these requirements, in turn, had to be based on a monopoly of organized violence, most fatefully including the arms manufacturers.[ccclxvii] A holistic structural shift like this one, so carefully synchronized on such an unprecedentedly global scale, brought into fruition in such a short time, can't just occur by happenstance. I believe it was, rather, the next installment in the original strategy explicitly set in motion by the wars of 1898 and 1899, carried along through World War One. Clearly, it almost certainly wasn't the precisely laid-out plan the entire time, down to the last detail, but instead was enacted step by step, a state-of-affairs made possible by the capacity of a single tiny sector to create at each particular historical moment more immediate, more broad-sweeping changes on a global scale than the rest of humanity combined, in reaction to specific developments as they unfolded. Each event-cluster was then planned in reference to the results of the immediately preceding one; in other words, the tactics were planned in reaction to the state of the grand strategy's effects at any given time. And it was always surprisingly easy for the tactical maneuvers to accomplish their aims, because essentially all that had to happen, at this point in the process, was "new money/resources get invested here; earlier investments get pulled out there". But, as history closed in on the middle of the 20th-century, it became increasingly apparent to the system's controllers that this simplest methodology could only continue "indefinitely" if the total global financial economy, the total global petroleum-based production/distribution system, and the total global interstate military system were brought into as complete synchronization with one another as was possible. So that's what the grand strategy was trying to achieve, however consciously or unconsciously. And that's what happened.

Thus, the specific nature of the plan's "interwar" phase – the investment towards getting Germany and Russia into a war with each other – probably started to be designed around 1923. Its implementation officially began with the Great Depression emergent in 1929, and ultimately came to fruition with the Bretton Woods agreements of 1944, followed by the simultaneous conclusion to World War Two and implicit origin of the Cold War embodied in the detonation of the atomic bombs over Hiroshima and Nagasaki in August, 1945 – these acts of war being acts of enforcement for the Bretton Woods' "contract".

As long as the system needing war for its very existence is in place, war will always be inevitable:[ccclxviii] civilizations exist and grow, thus warfare does the same in parallel (and/or vice versa). And even if one has his or her doubts about this truth in general, still, concerning the particular case of World War Two, no one can disagree that, given the way World War One was concluded combined with the precise civilizational circumstances of the next two decades, World War Two was in that way absolutely inevitable, no matter one's perspective on precisely *why*.

From my perspective, the specific reason why it was inevitable – "why World War Two was fought" – must again be explained by judging how the war was ended, i.e., who became the most *Powerful*, over what kind of politicoeconomic system, as a direct result of the war's outcome. In this vein, the war turned out as it did, quite simply, because of exactly how the controllers of the system of advanced industrialized total warfare had sent the world to war, in the first place: if the war *wasn't* going to end up like that, the controllers wouldn't have started the war. Much more so even than the system of warfare leading up to and culminating with World War One, that which was built up in the interwar period and came to fruition with World War Two had been subject to the tightest controls in human history, meaning the system reflected a greater ability than ever before for human influence to produce its desired impact on immediate military outcomes.

To briefly mention just a couple of examples, during World War Two there were a very few industrial facilities of such strategic vitality to Germany's ability to wage the war, that if the Allies had decided to destroy any one of these facilities, the war would've been over essentially right away. Moreover, evidence suggests that certain individuals with an ability to influence the decision as to which overall course would be pursued in the war were well aware of the significance to Germany of those targets in question and thus, by ensuring that those strategically indispensable areas were protected, they were at the very least tacitly choosing to keep the war going.[ccclxix] Similar signs of a "hidden" agenda existed concerning the Japanese: the U.S. high command chose to ignore its potential for bringing an end to the war by way of Japanese surrender for almost a year.[ccclxx] These are simply facts. The only reasonable question, then, isn't even, "Did the Allies' controllers send their nations to war for purposes other than destroying the Germans and the Japanese as quickly as possible?", because we know the answer is "Yes" – yet, if we adhered to the conventional contemporary way of viewing warfare in general and in particular World War Two, the answer "No" would seem so obvious as to make the question appear wholly insane. Therefore, this contradiction alone renders virtually all conventional philosophical perspectives (as distinguished from empirical facts) on why World War Two was fought largely if not completely erroneous; and in my opinion, the only reasonable question is, "If the Allies' controllers didn't fight World War Two for the purpose of crushing Germany and Japan as quickly as possible, what was the real purpose "they" were fighting for?"

As far as I'm concerned, there was just one overarching purpose that matters: World War Two was fought to prepare the conditions for the Cold War. One must wonder then, if contemporary wars aren't fought in order to bring about peace, but in fact seem to be fought for precisely the opposite reason – so there can be more war – *what else* does the contemporary dominant culture not know about itself?

For one thing, it turned out that the best way one capitalist State could be a friend to another was to pretend to be its enemy. States need war to survive; industrialized capitalist States need it most of all. All the States that were a part of the Great Power system in the 1920s and 1930s were industrialized capitalist States.

Yes, including the Soviet Union: what basically no one understands, but what's absolutely essential to address if one wants to understand contemporary history, is that the Soviet Union was fundamentally a capitalist State, if we judge what is or is not capitalistic according strictly to what capitalism has actually been in the 20th-century-beyond era.[ccclxxi] By the 1930s, for further growth within the global *financial-corporate* economy – the very definition of 20th-century capitalism – to be possible, it was becoming quite clear that a State was really only permitted one form: some variation on fascism, which means oligopoly control over a totally militarized politico-industrial system.[ccclxxii] It would be strange, how few people realize this, were it not for the fact that the continuation of the system demands that only a tiny number of marginalized individuals view the world in such a fashion.

The most definitive aspect of a totally militarized, global capitalist economy is how singularizing it is. Even if the same tiny sector (the emergent global hegemons, who were defending no "principle" besides ever-expanding profit) *weren't* ultimately in control of every nation's affairs in the 1930s, the presence of even one totally militarized State within the developing global economic system would've required total militarization to eventually emerge in every other country that was a part of the system, in order for all those other nations to stay competitive. Thus, whether or not the U.S. Government, the Bolsheviks, and the Nazis were all controlled at some level by a single sector of humanity, the mere emergence of the Bolsheviks and the Nazis within a single global system would've in any case still demanded that the U.S. adopt a totally militarized government in response.

The only other option, which would've been so much better for humanity as to not even qualify here for fair comparison, was to destroy the entire capitalist economy altogether by implementing completely decentralized/ecologically-harmonious cultural conditions. However, this had no chance of succeeding within the scope of the real-world context, because the perpetuation of the existing politicoeconomic conditions had been the whole point, in the first place, of the entire mess that was the emergence of the global civilization. Therefore, no matter what your perspective on the matter is, one has to admit that, at least concerning *politicoeconomic* totalitarianism within the scope of the contemporary interwar era (the 1920s and '30s), once it found some way of succeeding in one country, it was basically inevitable that it would succeed elsewhere, as well. Either a homegrown totalitarian response would've necessarily emerged in any competing country contesting the original totalitarian regime, or, where no homegrown response was forthcoming, the original totalitarian regime would've conquered the competing country, anyway (I think this can be considered the essential kernel of truth embedded within the original Cold War propagandized doctrine of the "domino theory"). Finally, it should go without saying that all of these outcomes were "necessary" only insofar as militarized competition at the intra- or interstate level is the natural state-of-affairs for all civilizations, and especially for Western civilization; but because this has always been the case, similar outcomes have been and will remain necessary so long as systems exist that are organized the way civilizations historically have been.

Full politicoeconomic totalitarianism broke out within the heartland of every Great Power in the first half of the 1930s, after it had emerged in Italy and Russia during the previous decade. Clearly, for *culturally* nationalistic reasons, the totalitarian regimes had to brand themselves uniquely in every individual country. But all of the governmental transformations were based on the same essential premise.[ccclxxiii]

Italy and Russia were chosen as the "test cases", which is why they were the first to make the transformation. They were also given the most completely totalitarian politicoeconomic systems, one (Italy) to represent a "Right-wing" cultural movement and the other one (Russia) to represent a "Left-wing" cultural movement. I believe Germany was chosen as the other test case first, but because of Hitler's failed attempt at a coup d'etat (the "Beer Hall Putsch") in November 1923, pressure had to be taken off of Germany for long enough to get the plan back on the right track. So, Germany's economy was restructured under the Dawes plan in 1924 in order to create a short-term appearance of stable prosperity that would temporarily stem the tide of *real* communism – complete political decentralization of humanity (localism), the only scenario I can imagine that might've been able to avoid total capture by industrial capitalism, and for a brief moment in early post-World War One Germany, a somewhat realistic possibility[ccclxxiv] – and by the end of 1925 Mussolini established himself as "Duce" of Italy.

It was obvious that the single, totally encompassing national corporate-political system would have the hardest time overtly establishing itself in the United Kingdom and the United States, and especially the latter, because these nations had for so long been accustomed to such enormous growth, and hence such relatively greater liberty, that effective monopolization of corporate *Power* was an extremely tenuous project from a mass ideological perspective. As I've said, that had been more or less the main factor originally prompting the Anglo-American fear of a rising Germany. The investors were playing the "long" game (it has still ended up being quite short, from a temporal perspective): they were creating the perfect "Enemies" capable of sparking transformation to the Anglo-American politicoeconomic system, insofar as this system would have no choice but to effect totalitarian change when confronted with totalitarian competitors. The same thing had happened as a result of World War One, only it hadn't gone far enough to satisfy the investors, even if, in terms of the experiential knowledge gained, it had been successful beyond their wildest dreams.[ccclxxv]

Basically, the hallmark of the totalitarian politicoeconomic system was complete synchronization – or, as close to complete synchronization as was possible – of industrial (economic) and State (political) *Power*. The most relevant and in turn most significant question we can then ask is, "Why was such deliberately tight synchronization of industrial and State *Power* the most pressing concern for Western politicoeconomic systems during the interwar era?" For our present purposes, we can narrow down our answer to one major point.

To begin, certainly by the start of the 20th-century the absolute size of the total global economy was growing so rapidly that it was becoming increasingly difficult for the existing hegemonic order to control it as it had done throughout essentially the entire existence of 19th-century industrialization. Indeed, the success of the hegemons' monopolization over humanity's politicoeconomic affairs during this earlier period is what had allowed the Western-dominated international economy to grow at such an unprecedented and unprecedentedly constant pace in the initial era of international industrialization.

The British Empire was the premier entity for general politicoeconomic monopolization all throughout the 1800s: England controlled (1) the world's finances through the City of London, thereby possessing decisive influence over international banking; (2) the world's oceans with its navy, thereby possessing decisive military influence over international shipping; and (3) decisive influence over the world's strategic raw materials with its unparalleled colonial possessions. All of these geostrategic advantages, additionally, were *mutually reinforcing*. Within the framework of long and short historical processes I've argued for all throughout this text, a situation had emerged at an exponential rate, from the beginning of the "British Century" to the end, where short historical process (the affairs of any one sociohistorical entity) and long historical process (the affairs of humanity as a whole) were "melding" to an extent never before possible. Clearly, the grand proximate cause was the unstoppable spread of industrialization – of course, a Western- and more specifically British-catalyzed phenomenon. Whatever internationally minded group had been decisively controlling *all* Western politics throughout the first phase of industrialism, and doing so "informally" by totally co-opting the unique centralization afforded by the emergent global politicoeconomic system under the aegis of a British hegemony – only *it* can explain the origins of the group responsible for initially creating the global situation started by the wars of 1898-9, and completed by the foundation of the post-World War Two order.[ccclxxvi] Although, no matter who in particular ended up in control of it, we know it was in any case a global situation defined in terms of a reconsolidated, Anglo-*American* hegemony: reconsolidated as a result of the hegemons' setting up the perfect conditions for two great victories in two great wars, which in combination pre-emptively destroyed the possibility that any other States, especially Germany, Japan, and Russia, might establish some substitutive hegemony over the international industrial system.

Based on the longstanding sociohistorical nature of interstate politics, as well as the more recently established sociohistorical nature of late 19th-century industrialized Great Power politics, the Anglo-American/global hegemons had to have been primarily concerned with the rising of a competitor for hegemony over the global system that *they* had been most responsible for manipulating into existence. The hegemons couldn't have taken too kindly to even the mere thought of this. Their primary concern must've been the inherent conflict between globalization and economic nationalism, which is why they initially feared the Germans most of all. The two types of system – globalization and economic nationalism – can't exist simultaneously: but this had never been an acutely noticeable problem until right before the turn of the 20th-century (what I've called the inception of the contemporary world), because until then the state of international industrial expansion had only appeared in its simplest, least obtrusive form.

More deeply, the main contention was really between the "older money" financiers and the monopolist corporate *Powers* they themselves had built up.[ccclxxvii] With the emergence of Germany, the original global hegemons must've realized the potential threat they might face in all the places where they had, by necessity, created corporations managed under as centralized control as was possible. Moreover, the potential breakdown of the system itself would be a near-certainty if the financiers and their corporations remained antagonistic towards one another. This strong possibility forewarned of the most dangerous threat of all: truly communistic human settlements. Thus, the hegemons decided to come together and consolidate their rule, rewarding those especially adherent corporate monopolies with favorable long-term shares in the global plan.

This is why the long-term strategy *had* to be international synchronization of policy at the highest levels, under the direction of a single numerically-miniscule, monetarily-omnipotent sector. Real competition, competition with the ultimate aim of total annihilation, could no longer be permitted in any strategically indispensable sphere, because such would've sooner or later guaranteed the self-destruction of the global system itself. What all of this amounts to is that the hegemons in every Great Power were finally, fully coming to their senses concerning that most crucial fact: the real competition was between the hegemons and everyone else. Two individuals competing for the same hegemony *could* sometimes have fundamentally identical, achievable-in-common interests ("I against my brother, my brothers and I against my cousins..."), so long as the interests were solely related to avoiding the system's complete collapse. Beyond that, they could go right on fighting each other; albeit through layers and layers of deception, so no one's ever really sure who's fighting whom, which is the way things are by strictest design.

The strangest thing about contemporary history, then, is that the competing factions must cooperate so extensively in order to ultimately continue competing with one another. This elementary contradiction, I believe, embodies pure insanity, and it does so at the very highest (deepest) levels of the contemporary system. At every level of the structure below (above) the most *Powerful* level, the insanity explodes evermore potently, yielding a chain-reaction much like the workings of the most insane weapons of all – nuclear and thermonuclear bombs, which the hegemons also created, in order to set up the conditions for one of the most insane wars of all. Yet, quite tellingly about Western civilization, and thus by extension civilizations as they've generally existed throughout history, the most insane wars and weapons of all are also the most logical conclusions to everything preceding them for over six millennia, in the long evolution of the war-trade competition.

Sooner or later, a civilization would have to *self-consciously* destroy itself.

Hence we come to the main reason why, in the two decades leading up to World War Two, and the 1930s in particular, there was so much pressure for all the leading nations plugged into the international system of Western origins and Western control to totally interlink the policies of national corporations and national States. As I've said, "totally interlinked policies of corporations and States" is essentially the very definition of fascism, to the extent that this process couldn't occur in the exact way desired by those bringing it about – politicoeconomically stratified to the utmost extreme – without complete militarization of all the States imposing corporatist rule. From this perspective, the most important underlying reason behind adoption of policies combining corporations and States, specifically referring to how they were imposed by way of wholesale transformation all throughout the Western-dominated international system in the '20s and '30s, was actually, on an even broader scale, to ultimately combine all *nations* into a system for the existing hegemony's continuation that was workable on a global scale. The process of transformation was selected first by the global hegemons, who were willing to institute any "policy" necessary to make their vision materialize, including covertly building up the most absurdly ambitious dictators in history (save for themselves).

Again, it may sound too fantastic to be true, that the same sector ultimately ruling the United Kingdom and the United States was ultimately responsible for supporting Hitler and Stalin. But think for a moment about the record of the leading Allied nations in the postwar world, which is at this point confirmed in such thoroughly heinous detail as to be beyond all possible doubt:[ccclxxviii] granted that Hitler and Stalin ruled over two of the most evil regimes that have ever existed, is it really possible, nevertheless, to say they were unequivocally "more" evil than basically every regime the U.S. and U.K. have supported since? And besides whether or not it's actually possible – if it were possible, would it be *necessary*? Doesn't "ranking" in such a fashion, at best, only serve the purpose of saying, "that person's evil is unacceptable, this person's evil seems not *quite* so bad, so it's acceptable"? In fact, that's precisely the primary (albeit often unconscious) exemplary purpose Hitler and Stalin are used for in contemporary mainstream discourse, which is worse than never discussing them at all. Shouldn't all evil, or all willful amorality, be completely unacceptable? I would've hoped the answer was extremely obvious; but if you pay close attention to the contemporary dominant culture and how it affects its inhabitants, you'll soon realize how tragically unapparent it is to virtually everyone.

BOOK TWO – **Flawed or Fraud?** A Philosophy of Contemporary History, Narrated Historically

The narrative as I've presented it to you thus far – the narrative intended to exhibit that lived narrative explicitly responsible for forging globalization – argues for an understanding of formative 20th-century history which, contrasted with conventional perspectives, can only be considered outrageous. I would welcome such a characterization. At the same time, however, the historical analyst shouldn't construct perspectives purely for the purpose of provoking outrage, if his or her work is to be considered indispensable to historical understanding. In that respect, the most important question about everything I've been discussing remains: how does what happened in the first half of the 20th-century matter to what happened in the second half, and beyond? What impact has the lived narrative from the contemporary world's gestation stage had on the lived narrative comprising the contemporary world's explicit existence – that existence constituting the world we still live in?

A lived narrative is a special kind of process (I equate it with the unfolding-of-human-consciousness shaped by a sequence of culturally formative event-clusters), but it's a process all the same. More accurately, it's a path-dependent process, meaning that along every step of the way, the process's *beginning* is the most determinative factor of all in shaping how the process becomes manifest. I'm arguing that the lived narrative most responsible for shaping the contemporary world revolves around the event-cluster sequences spanning the wars of 1898-99, the world wars, the Cold War, and the phase referred to by the U.S. Military as its own reign of "full spectrum dominance". Therefore, from a long historical perspective, I'm arguing that at every step along the path between 1898-1899 and the present, the deliberate perpetuation of original Anglo-American alliance's structure at the 20th-century's turn is what's played out most forcefully, again and again.

Yet we must simultaneously recognize, from a short historical perspective, the peculiarities of the specific kinds of functions the processually-unfolding social structure is meant to fulfill, at different points along its chronological continuum. Only from the longest perspective does the defined holistic process have one beginning and one end. For instance, the end of World War Two could've been the end of the entire process, in terms of what was started in 1898-99 – however, the structure was reconsolidated unto its Cold War form, and so it lived to see another period. Likewise, the end of the Cold War could've been the end of the process. But the structure was reconsolidated once again; in turn, it would live to see yet another period.

Obviously, "a historical process" is in-and-of-itself not something immediately tangible, and so its reality can only be posited, sought out, and argued for. Its reality resides in *the description of* what's tangible: it's truly real to the extent that the description captures what it describes. So far as we know, when the strategy for the Cold War was first decided upon and its implementation began, no one responsible for ensuring that the original process of a globally industrializing conquest syndrome remained in place said out loud, "We're reconsolidating the Anglo-American hegemony begun in 1898-99 and put fully into place via the two world wars." And of course, even if someone did say it out loud, that wouldn't be, on its own, proof that the same process had been continuing the entire time and was being pushed forward still further through the establishment of the national security State. We would still have to show *in what way* there was a process started in the world of the Anglo-American wars of 1898-99, which was somehow still playing out through the bipolar world divided by the "Iron Curtain".

So: how should we posit, seek out, and argue for the existence of a particular historical process? How do we write a historical narrative – how do we make our ideas of history concrete? And more specifically, can we write a historical narrative that seeks to explain "the whole" of history during some period of time*? In the case of the 20th-century-beyond era of human beings on planet Earth – the contemporary world, including its gestation stage – I've approached the problem by equating the whole process with the establishment of a particular civilization. Since I've argued that the most unique and hence most defining characteristic of contemporary history has been the emergence of a

---

* What I've called a metanarrative, in homage to Hayden White.

potential for, realization, and exhaustion of the sole global civilization in humanity's history, nothing else seems to me a more proper subject for the contemporary metanarrative. Moreover, I hope my particular metanarrative may serve as well to provide a model for individuals constructing metanarratives of their own. In other words, not only do I believe that my narrative serves well as a representation of *holistic human history*, meaning a representation of the total existence of humanity, in this case concerning how it has happened since the monumentally consequential wars of 1898-99. I also believe, owing to the special subject matter of contemporary history, that the narrative is particularly well-qualified to translate across real historical boundaries, in turn providing a basis for some more general historical methods.

By this, I'm not intending to make a point about how "good" I think my history is, but rather, a point about what I consider to be, most concretely, historical reality, and specifically with regard to humans, sociohistorical reality. The point is about why I've chosen the subject matter I've chosen as the grounds for telling the story of all human beings during the defined era. Only at the level of the whole culture – and thus, in the context of the civilizational history, only at the level of the civilization itself – can we truly envision *humanity-in-action*.

Concerning individuals in the existent world, we can make things the most concrete: this is because all individuals in the existent world share a singular culture as their background. This world is a world insofar as it's hyperspecialized, and thus in one sense every hyperspecialization seems from "first-hand" perspective to be a world unto itself. But in the broadest, most consequential sense, we can see through the same phenomenon that nothing requires the starting-point of a unitary cultural world more than globalized hyperspecialization. So even if your sole context exists at the level of the numerically smallest communities in the total global population, every existent human being nonetheless inhabits what is the only completely singularized cultural environment in the planet's history.

That is, it's absolutely certain that there's some dimension of cultural reality commonly affecting every single individual on the planet right now. And in that case, there must be something providing the basis for this comprehensive singularization of all existent humanity's cultural situation; everything must spring from a common source.

Moreover, while there was never a globally singularized cultural world during previous eras of human history, at the same time, because we can now directly see what it means for all human beings to share one cultural world, our direct knowledge of *the fact that this world exists* provides the ideal empirical reference point for developing a framework for understanding all cultural worlds: a framework for understanding human reality. What does everything have to be like, for every thing to exist? This is what I'm always trying to find out. In the end there really can be only one answer; and any atomic answer we might find, if it's true, will necessarily be situated within the macrocosmic answer.

What can you say about fully-fledged contemporary history, which hasn't already been said about the history of its gestation phase? The story is old: and it gets older all the time: and it gets older *faster*. Only in this way can we understand the history of the present – by acknowledging how, stitched within every second, there's simultaneously our own history and the culmination to the histories of all prior humanity.

There was apparently only one feasible conclusion to World War Two: for the war to never end. We live in the world of nuclear weapons and their much more terrifying thermonuclear offspring – in the world of a totally mobilized global military machine; a planetary digital cash supply; a communications network that, seemingly with our implicit consent, records essentially every trace of our collective existence. But what does it all mean? Can we answer that? Is it a question we even know how to ask?

Let me start off by saying that we're only so unsure about contemporary history because – and here's something that's an absolutely uncontestable fact – States in the global civilization deliberately obfuscate their most significant actions from their publics. Most of all, and most relevantly in the present text, States obfuscate their actions related to warfare and trade. This in itself is entirely expected when considered in light of all prior interstate competition, something in exact accordance with the very nature of such competition. Whether States are competing more in the sphere of trade or more in the sphere of warfare in a given context, the nature of violent competition necessitates that competing entities – competing organizations – conceal their actions from their opponents. And in reality, a contemporary State's opponent is its public, even more so than other States.

That's because, while the hegemons are players in the competition, they're players of a special kind. *Players at a higher level*: they're not athletes; they're the owners, the administrative officials, and the referees. They're not soldiers – not even generals – they're the overarching reason why the wars are fought, the ones who the militaries actually belong to. Along those lines, "the public sector" is ultimately just what happens collectively to the most significant private sectors once the holistic system has passed some extreme threshold of complexity. The State has changed in ever-increasingly fluctuating ways all throughout the history of civilizations, though the one thing you can always say about any State is that it never emerged in the first place mainly because it had to, but mainly because it could. Nonetheless, once they're established, States create structural conditions that holistic cultural systems come to depend upon for their existence. But there's no State separate from the system it perpetuates, in the same way that there's no such system that, once it has been so perpetuated, can exist separately from the State.

Therefore, we must study the civilization and the State in conjunction: they happen in reality as intertwining systems – "civilization-State-complexes" – that exist amongst other such intertwining systems, which altogether come to form totalized civilizations, and from there, totalized intercivilizational structures, or in special cases like the Roman Empire and the global civilization, universalized structures. Studying things at this topical level is most appropriate because civilization-State-complexes are ends-unto-themselves: as a whole, the complex exists to perpetuate its own existence, which requires the maintenance of many specific interdependent conditions. The most critical question in the first place is "whether or not" a human culture is a civilization-State-complex, not "what kind" of civilization-State-complex that culture is. "What kind" is indeed the next most important question, but I ask whether or not first, since the similarities between civilization-State-complexes are, overall, more significant for understanding them than the differences.

What difference does all that make to our immediate discussion? Imagine a world where the Western civilization-State-complexes of national industrial imperialism, the characteristic conquest syndrome of the late modern period (1861-1945), never ended.

And not just a world where they never ended: a world where they evolved; they grew and grew.

In a way we don't have to imagine it, because it's our world. But in an even more characteristic way we do, because it seems so unlike the world as we typically live in it. Why is our world like this? Civilizational worlds always were to some degree. Never, though, was the situation so pronounced as it has been since the end of World War Two. The great secret to the contemporary misunderstanding of history is that only in the past couple-of-centuries or so have *Power*-structures been mostly reluctant to hide their zeal for conquest; and only during the contemporary world has this been the outright norm. Much more so than historical process, humanity itself is the thing that has changed.

There's a hypothesis much adhered-to by some contemporary historical scholars – including some of those whose writings I consider most valuable – which basically asserts that when the "Democracies"/ "Republics" in history that became Empires were still in their relatively insulated forms, insofar as they hadn't yet seen their phases of great expansion – they hadn't yet become Empires, even if they were already imperial – they could afford to give certain large swathes of their citizenries civil liberties. As they expanded, and so became Empires, the civil liberties gradually disappeared, for the most part.[ccclxxix] If proven correct, this hypothesis would reveal another of those incredibly important cultural states-of-affairs growing directly out of a State's main mechanism for producing wealth, among the most significant indicators of what kind of civilization-State-complex will exist in a given context. As I've noted, along those lines, the simplest way of looking at things sociohistorically is that, in the days before industrialization, "Democracies"/ "Republics" tended to grow out of primarily mercantile States, and "Monarchies"/ "Principalities" tended to grow out of primarily agricultural States.[ccclxxx]

This was the norm for most of the history of civilizations before industrialization. I say "most", and not "all", because there did sometimes emerge the right circumstances for States that were equally significant as both agricultural and mercantile agglomerations: and these invariably became the wealthiest States in their contexts. The best examples in the Classical world were Carthage and even more so Rome, which explains how they built vast interregional empires, and how the latter State became the center of the Classical world's universalized culmination. However, it was the initial representatives of Western national States that would constitute the very best examples of this phenomenon in history. And there were no greater such States than England and France, the two States that, by dominating western Europe in the interperiodic phase separating the early modern period's end and the late modern period's beginning (1776-1865), turned out to be the hugest catalysts of nationalism in human history. Of course, their ultimate emergence as leading models for the nationalization process wasn't the result solely of their direct dominance over affairs in the "Old World": even more so, in fact, it stemmed from the comparatively indirect dominance they were wielding over "Old World" social structures through their historical place as some of the original conquerors in North America.

Starting from this early modern, "New World" baseline, the formative 19th-century European industrialized nations unleashed history's second greatest surge in human energy usage, the greatest being that sustained by the global civilization.[ccclxxxi] I don't mean "greatest" from a specific quantitative perspective. I mean it *qualitatively*, although clearly my qualitative judgments have some certain quantitative basis. The important thing to know here is, compared to all prior history, the energy used by humanity in the 19th-century was "much, much more"; and in the global civilization (1947-) compared to all prior history, the difference has been "far more, even, than that". And before mass industrialization, too, it had already been gradually rising for many centuries.

Steadily, history had been getting faster and faster, and then it really accelerated – and then it finally exploded. Of course, from one perspective, the reason why humanity was using more and more, and much more, and much, much more, etc., energy, was because the number of individuals constituting humanity at any given time was always similarly skyrocketing. But in per capita terms, as well, individuals throughout the past couple of centuries have used evermore-rapidly increasing quantities of energy. Moreover, because the processes have been so tightly interlinked within the context of industrialization, it's extremely difficult to distinguish between their respective manifestations in reality. Almost certainly, the unique real-time surface visibility of industrialization, due to its being so rapid a sociohistorical process, is itself what most immediately gave rise to the contemporary concept of "economic growth".

I say "humanity" was using increasing quantities of energy; however, this can't be considered accurate without the greatest qualification. Like all past examples of economic growth in civilizations, but to a degree that only fossil fuels have been able to permit, industrialization has always been subject to intense stratification. Or it's better to say that, in the past couple of centuries or so, the intense stratification forever existent in all prior civilizations was subjected to industrialization.

Now, as I said, the posited generalization mentioned above implies that when "Democracies"/ "Republics" turned into Empires, the civil liberties they once offered to their citizenries generally became more restricted. Professor Peter Dale Scott, whose work I have the utmost respect for – without which I couldn't have written the present text – calls this "the dialectic of open societies".[ccclxxxii] The "dialectic" may very well describe earlier civilizations, although I don't think so. But more to the point, when scholars bring up this proposed general social process it's invariably in order to suggest a connection with the contemporary United States, contrasting the current, "new" United States' Empire to the nation during its pre-World War Two years of independence. And in my opinion, it doesn't apply in this case, at least not in any way that's critical to our understanding of U.S. history.

To refer to what existed in the United States before 1945 in terms of some domestically-inclined golden age of "civil liberties" that has been sorely lost can only ignore the indispensable processes that gave rise to a contemporary United States. The late modern U.S., my designation for the State as it existed in the period spanning 1865 to 1945, was wholly the reflection of a process made largely by foreign actors: already a truly global process, not something we can rightly restrict to the U.S.'s own juridical boundaries. Moreover, by the middle of period five (1898-99), the United States was terrorizing populations throughout the world just like every other Great Power. And even if that weren't true, what do you make of the nation that by 1865 had already expanded from the original thirteen states hovering around the Atlantic Seaboard to California, having in the most recent decades spread weaponized mass destruction to what remained of the continent's indigenous cultures (which granted wasn't much)?[ccclxxxiii] Do you, like the conquerors driven by "Manifest Destiny", themselves, consider Indians' civil liberties irrelevant?[ccclxxxiv] And although explicit slavery was repealed, did sharecropping and Jim

Crow laws constitute a more just system for blacks in the southern United States? In fact the system was just as crushing,[ccclxxxv] only now one could feel one was justified in blaming them – and not the inhumane social structure – for their own misery.

The U.S. Government evolved into the center of such a devastatingly successful conquest syndrome for the exact reason that, from the very start, it possessed such lethally ideal conditions for the *selective* spreading of "civil liberties" based on the severe stratification of wealth. A switch to a different process was never made, just an exponentially-increasing growth of the original one. States founded on polities manufacturing goods for a well-developed international market – such as late medieval Florence, or the modern European national States, or the United States in its various forms preceding the later contemporary world – fostered heightened *domestic* civil liberties in comparison to purely agricultural States because they originated with central mechanisms for sustaining economic growth that were separate from *though interdependent with* their security apparatuses. But even from the very beginning in these States, there was always a simultaneous, irreparable trend towards greater overall politicoeconomic exploitation, albeit on a different level from solely military functions. This is just what happens when States evolve.

It would be difficult to overestimate the significance of the italicized portion in the descriptor "separate from *though interdependent with* the security apparatuses". In terms of how things play out in sociohistorical reality, which should be our only frame of reference to begin with when conceptualizing humanity – that is, before we explicitly introduce our own perspectives – merchant States always emerged within broader contexts ("politicoeconomic systems") where agricultural "Monarchies"/"Principalities" already existed. You therefore can't reduce the merchant State purely to a trading function, because merchants can't trade when/where there's no demand for it.

In the first place, as you'll recall, such demand in the original precursor to the contemporary civilization (medieval Western civilization) solely arose on account of the "surpluses" accruing to the warlords, i.e., the nobilities. 'Surpluses' is within quotation marks because the quantities can't rightly be considered surpluses: as, for quite a long stretch of history, relatively few individuals in the polities producing the "surpluses" were adequately provided for in terms of life-support. The life-support the nobility controlled in the form of agricultural wealth "belonged" to them insofar as it was coerced – stolen – from the overwhelming majority of individuals living in the polities under noble rule. So, at the beginning of Western civilization's lived narrative, those populations subject to the rule of Western aristocrats worked primarily to feed the nobilities rather than themselves. The nobles were paid first; these sums were deemed "tribute", or "taxes". It's considered impolite to refer to the payments with the term that actually best describes them, which is "loot", or "booty".

Only that amount of life-support beyond what was taxed went to the peasants. Invariably, the myth would arise that the payments were for "protection", which corresponded to reality insofar as the nobles, indeed, had an incentive to protect what belonged to them: the peasants – and more specifically, their labor-product. There were always other nobles from neighboring territories who also wanted the peasants' tribute, just as the first nobles always wanted *their* neighbors' tribute, too. Trade networks expanded when and to the extent that nobles were receiving so much tribute from their peasants, they had no need for even more life-support.[ccclxxxvi] Because they were nobles, they couldn't ask the peasants for less tribute; this would annul one of the system's most characteristic features, and human cultural systems typically do everything they can to avoid consciously destroying themselves. Instead, they established connections with the closest trading centers, a very few of which still existed in western Europe after the fall of Rome, and exchanged the "surpluses" for rare luxury products that could only be found in faraway lands.

Aside from the facilitation of a growing demand for luxuries, and besides religion, there had been one other phenomenon essential to the workings of the system: arms, which in civilizations require metallurgists, and in the medieval period included, most significantly, ironworkers.[ccclxxxvii] The necessities for making iron – not just the metal ore, but also charcoal, for instance – are found in sufficient quantities in a limited number of places geographically, and this must've been one of the greatest ecological limiting factors determining the success of the various noble clans prior to the widespread return of intercivilizational trade to the territory becoming Western civilization. Without the existence of limiting factors such as these, it would be difficult to see how the most

Powerful among them so rapidly became such a numerically minimal sector of the population.

In some locales the nobility had originally descended from the Carolingians (Charlemagne's gang); others descended from different originally Germanic factions, still others descended from Vikings. But all in all, by the 11th-century CE or so, there were only around five major groupings of nobilities squabbling bloodily amongst themselves *for essentially all of western Europe*. Moreover, they were starting to move their conquests farther into north-central Europe, and beyond that to the northeast.[ccclxxxviii] The point is, long before Europeans started to colonize all over the planet, the nobilities had colonized the initial base-of-operations. Western civilization was run from the start by what were in no uncertain terms foreign ruling elites: and this dynamic would never change, even if the elites and their subjects eventually came to technically inhabit the same nations.[ccclxxxix]

The early Western national State, then, was nothing at all besides this originary dynamic of foreign elites ruling over local subjects taken to a new level of holistic complexity. As I've already suggested, what most greatly characterized the polities rightly considered the original modern nations of Europe was the process whereby certain agriculturally-based "Monarchies" were ever-increasingly taking on the trading functions conventionally dominated by "Democracies" / "Republics". However, although on the surface this may make it seem that the "Monarchies" were the ones holding the greatest share of *Power*, what was really happening was that additional, originally foreign entities were being incorporated into the structures of the newly nationalizing civilization-State-complexes.

Once Columbus stumbled upon the Western hemisphere, da Gama forged a trade route to the "Far East", and Magellan circumnavigated the globe, the traditional Western nobility couldn't help becoming completely captivated by the fact that the Earth was a round and hence finite space, meaning they now perceived the quintessential fact of their existence – competing for territory – to truly be a zero-sum game.[cccxc] For the rest of history, the evolution of the Western conquest syndrome would ensure that this became a self-fulfilling prophecy.

Fatefully, the nobles were far from being able to complete the interhemispheric conquest project on their own. International traders would gain so much prominence so quickly, if not in status then at least in wealth they were now already becoming more or less equal partners with the landed military elites, a most notable sign of the early modern world's explicit appearance. The nation would be a nation insofar as it competed in the now properly international domain, waging conflict at sea as much as on land. In their initial overseas colonization of the planet, the logistical shortcomings of traditional landed governing elites were made up for at first by the original "Democratic"/ "Republican" Italian city-States, and lately more dominant entities like those found in what's today the Netherlands. Columbus himself, of course, was Genoese, and the massive influxes of "New World" precious metals allowed Genoa's bankers, for a brief moment, to eclipse what had been until that time the biggest banking milieus in Western history, first the Florentines (such as the Medici) and then the south Germans, most notably the Fuggers.[cccxci]

After awhile, the newly implanted sectors responsible for the "Democratic"/ "Republican" influences would take over the old "Monarchies" altogether. This was the process that would lead England, and ultimately to a lesser extent France, to be the two most rapacious Powers in the modern periods of European history. The secret to their unmatched levels of success was the unity achieved between agricultural and mercantile factions amidst the rise of both Powers, in comparison with all the other States in western Europe during the relevant context – a phenomenon made possible by the fact that in such a relatively great number of cases, agriculturalists and merchants in these nations were found to be the same individuals.[cccxcii] Yet this was something achieved only at those phases when both Powers rose; and when the primarily mercantile factions eventually ripened, they struck (cf. English Revolutions of the 17th-century, French Revolution of 1789). Now we're brought to the question of the American Revolution.

The Revolution was a primarily foreign-orchestrated affair, and things couldn't really have been otherwise: the most successful colonists necessarily depended on international markets for their wealth, so that's where their *Power*-base lay.[cccxciii] The winners were, as ever in the history hereby spawned, the financiers, and maybe you'll find it as interesting as I do that the greatest constant in all three early modern

Revolutions (English Glorious Revolution of 1689, French Revolution of 1789, American Revolution of 1776) was that, at the end of each, central banks were established in the affected nations. Ever since, war always precedes – then proceeds from – central banks.

Thus, from the time of the early modern period (starting in 1521), when, from the hegemonic perspective, the world was now officially finite, to the beginning of the late modern period (1865), the trend the entire time was for merchants, the traditional founders of "Democracies"/ "Republics", to assume ever-greater control over "Monarchies"/ "Principalities", which had conventionally been linked to landed agricultural war-machines. The process didn't work nearly as well the other way around: "Democracies"/ "Republics" being taken over by "Monarchies"/ "Principalities" quickly became enterprises relegated to the past, perhaps best exemplified by the prompt falling to the international wayside of the Medici's Florentine duchy. Although the clichéd wisdom suggests the opposite, democracy and the modern nation were irreconcilable entities from the start; there was no gradual loss of "openness", but a foundation built on its very antithesis. Where a fully-fledged nation successfully existed, it could only be because democracy in the truest sense had been successfully quashed.

If not a story of spreading democracy, what epitomized the diffusion of the Western-originated nation? It must be said first off that we should consider the nationalization of the planet, in the sense of dividing the planet into the juridically-defined subunits of national States, to be *the* dominant social process of the past half-millennium, a process that ultimately became globally totalized. What it was, which explains how it was able to be the dominant social process shaping the most consequential span in humanity's history, was the all-historical reconsolidation of the traditional "Old World" conquest syndrome as it had evolved in Western civilization up to that point, at a time when the syndrome had become so fast and in turn so widespread that it was making the form of the city-State largely obsolete.

Here we see what the culturally-caused increase in the speed-of-events is really all about: the transference of conquest syndromes to ever-greater heights. When we want to measure the speed-of-events, then – qualitatively, as I've suggested we must – the best single indicator is the broadest geographic scale of the characteristic syndrome during a given period. Indeed, this itself is what's most responsible for setting those boundaries defining any individual period.

Prior to the medieval period, two major kinds of conquest syndromes had emerged within the central intercivilizational zone: land and sea.[cccxciv] Both were originally dominant in individualized city-States, but at the latest levels of complexity in the ancient and Classical worlds, imperial combinations of city-States eventually emerged that had reach both on land and at sea. Thus, ancient and Classical history centrally reflected a process of the original spread of individualized land or sea conquest syndromes ever farther westward from the initial jumping-off point of southwest Asia, concluding with the archetypal versions of dual-faced land-sea syndromes. The medieval period was about the mass coming together of different combinations of land and sea States – all collectively participating in the construction of an explicitly singularized form of "Old World" conquest syndrome. In any territory surrounding the Mediterranean, no matter what civilization you were in, if you started inland you would invariably find monotheistic, foreign landed elites ruling over subject peasantries of all the various locales. As you went towards the coasts, you'd find sea-based trading elites who provided the main means of politicoeconomic connection welding together all the landed civilization-State-complexes throughout the intercivilizational structure.[cccxcv]

The total politicoeconomic system created by the interstate combinations of land and sea Powers spread ever farther westward as well, until it too ended up in locales that were ideal for polities equally apt at playing the land game and the sea game. The resultant, early modern conquest syndrome, the internationalizing version of the medieval conquest syndrome, was now able to transcend the Western and Eastern hemispheres, thereby sustaining capitalism in its originary form. The late modern conquest syndrome was the fully industrialized version of that first interhemispheric conquest syndrome. The contemporary conquest syndromes, those unique to the global civilization, still haven't been explained in full.

If the dominant fact of the post-World War Two order is that it's really a continuation of the pre-World War Two order, then we should be able to find endless traces of the world that produced the A-bomb in the world produced by it. And we can. But we have to dig through the surface. We need to be able to perceive what's invisible, so we can bring ourselves to a point where the global civilization will reveal itself. The invisible becomes visible roughly parallel to the unconscious becoming conscious. For human beings, the process of the invisible becoming visible happens through symbolic representation. Accordingly, symbolic representation can serve to present the unconscious framework of reality to the conscious human mind.

As individual human beings collectively add to all humanity's potential for representing reality through symbols, they add to the collective potential for realizing the unconscious. In the contemporary world, human beings have practically infinite such means for representing reality. However, as a whole, humanity seems less able than ever to make the invisible realities visible. This is incomparably problematic – it's the invisible realities that are destroying both us, and – even worse – our Earthly environment.

The problem is not as insoluble as it at first seems, although interestingly this is only because we live in the global civilization, which itself seems to be the most insoluble problem there is. In the global civilization, the invisible realities are only superficially invisible. They're invisible to the extent that humans make them invisible. Humans make visible things invisible, in this sense, through ignorance.

Many existent historians seem to frown upon using present history as our starting point for understanding the past. But I believe that attitude is merely a reaction against the seemingly innumerable wrongheaded examples of "reading the present into the past"; and I feel it would be an enormous error, in that reaction, to prejudicially impose an arbitrary ban on all such interpretation. What we need to do, instead, is find out *in what sense* the present can be accurately traced backwards chronologically. If this couldn't be done at all – if it wasn't already being done to some extent in more or less every work of history – I don't see how historical scholarship of any kind could be constructed. A human being can't help but bring an understanding of his or her present world to bear upon his or her interpretation of worlds in the past: we can only understand other humans' histories because we experience one of our own first-hand. This should be seen not as a detriment, but as the greatest advantage, in the understanding of history. Although it only can be if we know how to properly accentuate that particular advantage.

Whatever else is true about time, there's at least one manner in which it can go only in one "direction": its passage in the context of the material planet directly perceived by human beings. Once a process on Earth starts, the measure of time itself in relation to the unfolding of the process (the chronology) can become part of, or even the basis for, one's representation of the process's progression. If processes didn't have beginnings and endings that could be verbally described by human beings through measurements of time, this wouldn't be true; but they do, so it is.

In the immediate present, the sociohistorical reality of the existent world, there's a civilization that was born dead. It's the global civilization. As soon as it started, it was essentially a guarantee that it would at some point collapse. As it continued, it became absolutely clear that the civilization had never had any purpose nobler than perpetuation of the underlying conditions in place: the conditions conducive to a global civilization, meaning global wealth stratification imposed by a concomitant stratification of knowledge, held in place (enforced) by the constant structural exercise of and threat of more violence.

However, when the global civilization was first established, through the intertwined holistic transformation of the U.S. Government and the U.S. Government's holistic transformation of the planet, it was almost impossible for the general state-of-affairs to be completely clear to human observers: except in two sectoral cases where individuals would've felt the state-of-affairs directly. On the one hand, an individual at the very top of the cultural pyramid could directly experience the state-of-affairs, someone socially internal to the *Power*-structure itself – a status which is, necessarily, always enjoyed by a mere sliver of any total human population – or, rather oppositely, one could directly experience the *Power*-structure if one was completely outside of it, being made to serve as the dirt beneath the pyramid's base. And even in these two separate cases, individuals almost universally perceived just the *effects* of the pyramid: not the cause, not the total pyramid itself.

Power-structures have always behaved like this, which, above all, is how they succeed – the greatest extremes of the stratification of wealth set the tone for everything else. What's so strange and uniquely awful about the contemporary world is, this exact state-of-affairs has been so deliberately implemented, by such an unusually conscious design.

That makes the abstract concept of "a process of State-driven civilizational evolution" something most concrete: the evolution of the stratification of wealth through the stratification of knowledge, held in place by the distribution of violence – ultimately, in total combination, the evolution of organized destruction. The three interlocking cultural spheres, among all the numerous striking reasons for their dominance, altogether embody the key adaptive mechanism for civilizations and their associated contexts (intercivilizational structures and civilization-State-complexes) *because they're most directly responsible for violently implementing and hence maintaining the stratification of wealth through the stratification of knowledge.*

Of course, the dual destructive stratifications that have forever been definitive of civilizations constitute the problem we started out with. But as I explained at the beginning, we had to address the problem in its exact sociohistorical context, or else we couldn't address the problem at all. Now we've finally gotten to the exact sociohistorical context, which could only happen once we reconstructed it whole from the ground up.

There's never been such a literal exhibition of violently-imposed stratification of wealth through the stratification of knowledge – appearing in the world as the whole structure of global organized mass destruction – than the "need to know basis" guiding the compartmentalization (stratification) of contemporary governmental activities, accomplished by the use of methods like clearance levels, and secrecy oaths with legally-binding confidentiality agreements. Nothing has been more resonant of the global civilization's tone throughout its duration. The *Power*-structure tries so desperately hard to hide the hand of grand strategy (geostrategic foresight), but what could possibly be a more apt indicator of a totally-encompassing design, and specifically one of modern Western origins, than the unrelenting hypercompartmentalization of an entire global social structure? What else does this and everything I've already described point to besides divide-and-conquer and balance-of-power, updated for the "Space Age"? What's better at revealing the hegemonic plan than precisely that phenomenon attempting to hide every significant thing contemporary governments do, and most of all everything related to governmental planning?

Since everything in the global civilization started from such an insurmountably complex baseline, at this point all the managers of the *Power*-structure have to do is perpetuate demographic conditions – which sounds so innocent; mundane. However, this isn't the basis for just advertising and public relations; it's the basis for the entire global system of State-imposed violence. The latter succeeds *because* the former (and everything like it) sounds so innocent. But these two phenomena in particular are, in fact, the same thing: and no, I don't mean they're "like" the same thing. In the contemporary world, the greatest warriors don't fight out in the open for control of our physical selves. They fight from behind closed doors for our "hearts and minds". And COIN (counterinsurgency doctrine) isn't just for the explicit field of physical warfare. Actually, what defines COIN itself most of all is that it's the physical warfare subset of the much larger strategy in place, which is a psychological strategy that never stops moving, a strategy based entirely on the "methodologies" of what's called in the contemporary world 'psychological warfare', which originally evolved directly out of the traditional practice of propaganda. Physical warfare in the global civilization is in this sense nothing more than a hyperspecialized battlefield within a much larger conflict, albeit one with unprecedented direct value for the *Power*-structure.

Why did propaganda start to become known as "psychological warfare"? As Americans were so averse to the very word "propaganda" itself, higher-ups in the U.S. war-machine came up with the term as a euphemism during World War Two. At least at the time when propaganda was turning into "psychological warfare", the latter label made the practice seem like something much more dignified – something of the utmost solemnity. In turn, it could command the greatest permission for official "SECRECY" on the part of the public.

Because the main motive driving the contemporary *Power*-structure is its insatiable demand for resources, the managers of the *Power*-structure, whether they realize it or not, are shaped by greed more so than any other characteristic, and in turn they tend to put themselves in awkward positions by going overboard – "getting greedy". They overplay their hands. In relation to propaganda and the contemporary world, this had occurred in World War One in a most notable fashion, specifically involving the Allies' managers. The effects this seemingly small detail would have on all subsequent history are incalculable: the detail is the main thing connecting the world before the nuclearization of humanity to the world after.

Throughout the history of civilizations, there has been an evolution of two moralities: one for elites, and another for the masses. All of humanity's history thus far comes down to this problem. At certain intervals, the problem intensifies until it reaches some level of maximum capacity, at which point human consciousness reacts on a massive scale. The contemporary world is the story of such intensification taken to its greatest possible extreme.

Starting surrounding the circumstances of World War One, the problem manifested itself to the elite factions essentially like this: "How can the whole world be fooled?" No elites had ever faced this problem before, because no elites had ever had to fool more or less "all of the people, all of the time". Why did they have to, now? *The world had gotten too small.* Humanity itself had never faced this problem.

Of course, the problem most likely didn't manifest itself explicitly in the terms of "How can the whole world be fooled?" – at least not to very many individuals. Instead, I think what had started to become clear to the emergent global hegemonic sector, around the first couple of decades of the 20th-century, was that the industrialized human universe of Western origins had gotten so big in relation to the planet Earth that sooner or later all the individuals in the world would have to live under the rule of a single State, in order for the existing status quo to continue. But at the same time, if the single State were to present itself to the masses *as* a single State – that would also mean the existing status quo couldn't continue: the existing status quo had been built, almost entirely, around *inter*state conflict. The solution at the highest levels was to implement a "shield" of an interstate system, which would conceal the existence in the background of the tacit singular arrangement going on at a higher level of *Power*. This strategy started to become officially implemented with the formation of the U.S. national security State in 1947 and all its attendant creations, which collectively marked the explicit inception of the global civilization.

It doesn't matter whether you believe this was what was (and is) actually going on. The important thing, rather, is that you accept that it was *logistically possible* – because there was only one way it could've been: and this one way also explains how we can know empirically that we're living in the culturally fastest period in humanity's history, providing the ultimate basis for chronologically connecting the present globalized history to all history prior. It was logistically possible because, in the global civilization, humanity as a whole has assumed the ability to totally mobilize the planet's total resources, which is also precisely what has made our culture the fastest culture in history.

Once that happened, anything became possible.

Whatever else is true about what's really going on in the contemporary world, I consider the total mobilization of total resources to be the absolute greatest tragedy – insofar as I think it's the tragedy that gives rise to all others. At the same time, it's the only logical starting point for studying our world, because in a world of never-ending efforts to conceal the truth, it's something that absolutely can't be concealed: it's known beyond all reasonable doubt that, physically, we've long been pushing the planet to its breaking point.[cccxcvi] And at this point it has been so well known for many years now – even as no one's doing anything about it, and appears very likely that no one ever will.

My own particular proposal on the matter is that the total mobilization of all the planet's most irreplaceable resources doesn't happen by accident: it has to be intentional. Let's get back to the transformation of propaganda into "psychological warfare". Believe it or not, this was perhaps the key thread in executing the plot to use all the resources. I hope the reader will bear with me; even in its simplest state, it's a complicated argument. Quite naturally so: what we're trying to understand here is nothing less complex than the contemporary world.

No matter how you look at it, the world before nuclearization transformed into the world afterward through the central mechanism of the U.S. Government. And as we've seen, immediately upon the establishment of the Cold War world, the U.S. Government – in accordance with its transformation into a permanent national security State – would be used as the headquarters for an institutionalized global shadow government. Certain problems would arise on account of the shadow government's having to reside within this particular center. As it so often does, the *Power*-structure would turn these problems into distinct advantages.[cccxcvii]

Propaganda would be the shadow government's main purpose amidst its exercising authority from within the institutional context of the burgeoning U.S. national security machine. This itself directly gave rise to use of the label "psychological warfare". In a rare moment for philology, we couldn't possibly have better confirmation of the real-world transition between word-usages, transforming what had always just been good-old-fashioned, publicly-despised propaganda into something demanding the highest respect, as it was relabeled to convey an association with that noblest human practice, military conflict. An operative in the "Intelligence" field who was summarizing the history of U.S. propaganda efforts up to the middle of the 20th-century – assuming no better authorities on this matter could've existed than individuals internal to the highest levels of the official *Power*-structure around that time – wrote, "The very term "psychological warfare" was intentionally dreamed-up to conceal…Forgetting that America had used propaganda in every national emergency, we confused ourselves, and weakened our psychological efforts to avoid arousing the national aversion to propaganda."cccxcviii

What was that "national aversion to propaganda" all about? In his excellent introduction to Edward Bernays' *Propaganda*, Mark Crispin Miller points to the national backlash against what the public rightly perceived as its having been badly duped during World War One. The managers of deception, the American propaganda committee, called everything the enemy said "propaganda". This backfired, giving the label itself, until then a fairly neutral term, a permanently derogatory connotation. Realizing that they'd been thoroughly oversaturated with disinformation by their own State as well, Americans during the interwar years, for whatever reason, took issue with their own government doing the exact same thing it so self-righteously castigated other States for.cccxcix

This was no small problem. On account of this state-of-affairs, the government found it nearly impossible to stimulate the necessary public legitimacy to allow the United States to join in on World War Two. Well – impossible, of course, until Pearl Harbor happened. I don't wish to discuss the details of Pearl Harbor. Well-informed individuals are at this point sufficiently aware as to what occurred: the highest echelons of U.S. Government at the time knew it was going to happen, and did everything in their *Power* to allow it to happen, precisely because such a dramatic attack was "necessary" to rouse the national group feeling.[cd] That's the most significant thing we need to know about Pearl Harbor; it illustrates a (geostrategic) mindset in which all contemporary notions of conventional morality break down.

In the aftermath of the war that Pearl Harbor allowed, the same mindset was taking over just about everything on the planet. At the highest levels of social control, importance seemed to be attributed solely to the masses' perceptions of reality – not to reality itself. Actually, the truly perverse thing about the mindset was that it seemed to believe that human perception itself *was* the only reality.

"Seemed to" – at the highest level, the mindset couldn't have truly believed that. Otherwise, the *Power*-structure wouldn't have spent so much time trying to manipulate reality in addition to manipulating humanity's perceptions of it. In fact, the manipulation of our perceptions was being accomplished in the first place by the manipulation of reality.

You see, at one point, as our author wrote, "psychological warfare" was nothing besides the refashioning of the word 'propaganda'. But things didn't stay that way: "psychological warfare" took on a life of its own. What those internal to the *Power*-structure had realized, by the earliest days of the Cold War, was that, for propaganda to be truly successful in such an unprecedentedly complex stage of human culture as that reflecting the latest phases of industrialization, warfare and propaganda had to be totally *synchronized*. The technological means of war had to be used to create an all-encompassing propagandized environment.[cdi]

This sounds like the most extreme possible extreme: and in a sense it is – in the sense that the global civilization is the most extreme possible example of the most extreme form of cultural unit in humanity's history. But then what else have civilizations been throughout their history, besides all-encompassing propagandized environments? The civilization is self-reproducing – indeed, it's self-proliferating. The global civilization is merely this made completely self-conscious. *It's the manifestation of a syndrome*, a syndrome of conquest. Simply by existing, the civilization propagandizes itself. That's why civilizations are so successful, and in being so successful, are so uniquely destructive.

Propaganda in the contemporary world finally merged fully with reality, once and for all. That's what psychological warfare is, out of the quotations: as a living breathing concept. It's a most horrible thing – perhaps the very worst thing there is. But if you want to change our world, you must know it.

Because it is our world.

I

Psywar-Trade Competition: The Mind of the Group

'Propaganda' in the contemporary meaning of the word, the meaning that birthed psychological warfare, can only be understood in relation to individuals like Edward Bernays. A nephew of Sigmund Freud, Bernays consciously saw himself as transposing Freud's psychoanalytic theories[cdii] onto the terrain of what he called "group psychology", a term perfectly reflective of the conventional academic context of the day. What was "group psychology"?

We'll get to what it was, exactly, soon enough. For now, it'll help lay ground for things to come if I mention that Bernays considered it the province of, among others, Gustav Le Bon (from a more "scientific" perspective), and Walter Lippmann (from a more metaphysical perspective); and basically, he viewed it as premised on the fact that, besides the human mind at the level of the individual, there was also a "mind of the group".[cdiii] From this initial premise, Bernays wrote, the thought "naturally arose", whether, if one could grasp the essential characteristics of the collective mindset, the masses could be tightly "regimented" without their knowing it?[cdiv] So whatever the "group psychology" turns out to be exactly, we know it's the thing that the *Power*-structure thought it necessary to exercise influence over most greatly in order to keep the masses nice and pliable for hegemonic goals.

But how do we know Bernays spoke on behalf of the *Power*-structure – the *real* one, which stands in the shadows behind the one we all see? To begin, Bernays was among the few decisive individuals charged with running the Committee on Public Information, the U.S. Government's censorship and propaganda regime during World War One: the episode most singularly responsible for introducing official propaganda councils into the upper echelons of Western national governments,[cdv] where they would forever stay. The other decisive individuals, noted by Bernays himself in *Propaganda*, were George Creel and the above-mentioned Lippmann, two men who wrote two other remarkably influential "treatises" (war doctrines) on the contemporary "science" of propaganda, respectively *How We Advertised America* (1919) and *Public Opinion* (1921). At least, texts of this nature would be considered so eminently notable by the main catalyst of what we'll call *'the psywar environment'*, the cultural world shaped entirely by the globalization conquest syndrome.

That catalyst was the U.S. Government's psychological warfare sector, an occupational milieu exploding onto the stage of global affairs in the middle of the 20th-century. Early in 1951, the national security State officially instituted a Psychological Strategy Board, which seems to have constituted the experimental installation of a Committee on Public Information – a device the American public had once accepted during a time of war – in a historical context that, aside from the rhetoric, the total re-mobilization of military machinery, and the "police action" in Korea, was still nominally supposed to embody "Peace". A reading list for the Psychological Strategy Board, put together in August, 1952, cites Lippmann, for one, as a writer "...of interest for general background reading on propaganda and public opinion."[cdvi]

To be completely accurate, the PSB was not at this time fully installed within the U.S. Government. Technically, the Board itself would never be so installed. Officially it only existed from early 1951 until late 1953, during which time its explicitly-stated objective was merely to "explore" the "potential" machinery that "might" at some point go into a fully-fledged psywar committee.[cdvii] In this sense, the PSB was more like a "blue-ribbon commission", rather than a true institution. At the end of its trial phase, the Board decided that the functions it was considering consolidating within a single organization would work most effectively if left within existing governmental departments. If psychological warfare was as high a priority for the new global imperial headquarters as I've suggested, why wasn't it given its own autonomous unit?

Here we'll see a perfect example of one of the shadow government's neat tricks, which it came up with, at the latest, by the time the Cold War was just getting up-and-running. Indeed, it seems appropriate to say that this trick *was*, in no small part, what got the Cold War up-and-running. To appreciate the trick's value, it must be pointed out that, in history before the global civilization, all of humanity's various *Power*-structures never really got their new strategies right on the first try. The best State-building strategies during this span of time, consisting of the whole history of civilizations until 116 years ago, were the best almost always insofar as they were the products of what was basically public experimentation after the fact: evolution as opposed to revolution (even as revolutions were, at the same time, the most determinative shapers of evolutionary contexts).

Yet human history is also quintessentially shaped by the fact that technological advances don't accrue solely to those individuals who initially invest in them: and this does much to explain the constantly, dynamically increasing speed-of-events in civilizations. When present sociohistorical processes get faster, it's in large part because they're gaining from work done by past cultures – in other words, cultures are benefiting from work they didn't have to do:

(1) Culture A discovers a technology, and does so in a context that, at its broadest level, is a violently-imposed structure of wealth stratification;

(2) Because culture A discovers the technology in this context, it's used primarily to make a profit for those individuals initially controlling it; and because it's used in that way, culture A ultimately spreads the technology to another culture – culture B – as an inadvertent consequence of the need, for cultural survival within a structure of wealth stratification achieved through violence, to always grow;

(3) Because, to start, culture B was a materially less complex culture than culture A, culture B gets the technology essentially "free of charge"; and because the context is one of violently-imposed wealth stratification, culture B focuses most of its energy-inputs on increasing the ability to violently exploit wealth within the existing system, instead of forging an entirely new one. In the end, culture B becomes a more complex – and more stratified – culture than culture A. The process continues spreading whenever/wherever possible. As more work can always be done with less direct investment by *presently existing* humans, history thereby gets faster. As it gets faster, the social structure tends to become more stratified.

Like I said, this was how everything worked throughout most of the history of civilizations until about 116 years ago, at which point the underlying pattern didn't really change; it just began to take on a sociohistorically unique form – one which would only be fully realizable within a system that could singularize the entire planet in its strangling embrace. Our present couldn't exist without the exact past just outlined having played itself out over and over again, which isn't to say that history repeated itself, but that a similar structure was always being taken, evermore-quickly, to new heights. My argument is that such a structure started to reach its highest heights at that point 116 years ago: the highest heights because we live on a finite planet, and so there could be no civilization more expansive than one distributed over the entire globe.

There couldn't be a more *expansive* civilization; but there could be, and would be, one that was more *intensive*. That is, by definition, the global civilization could only itself appear and subsequently evolve once there was in place the holistic logistical structure capable of sustaining one civilization for Earth as a whole. Thus, as it happened, the global civilization was a system that originated at a level of full expansion in relation to the entire planet, and so it could only ever evolve insofar as it was intensifying. A human-made system intensifies when the system already in place grows, not by being spread over ever-greater physical space, but by "filling out" within its expansive boundaries. In the global civilization, the system achieves this in its being taken to ever-greater *psychological* extremes. The system that started out as the violent exploitation of humanity spreading across geography became the basis for a system still characterized by constantly growing exploitative motion, but motion which was now mental first, reflected in geography secondarily.[cdviii]

The technology would no longer transfer from one culture to another, since now, there was only one real culture left on the planet: the culture of globalized industrialization. It's true that the latter is nothing more than the pure cultural (ideological) expression of the politicoeconomic system permitting its existence, but that doesn't make it any less of a singular culture. It just means the culture's most distinguishing characteristic is its complete interchangeability with the politicoeconomic system of which it's the expression, a state-of-affairs that has only occurred and could've only occurred in the context of globalized industrialization.

Thus, in the global civilization, technologies could transfer solely within a universally shared system. This means that technology transfers would occur between different social niches within the same cultural environment, not across cultural dividing-lines. For the first time ever, every institution everywhere across the planet had the potential to be completely translatable with all other institutions, because they were all being born (or reborn) out of an identical context, a context of total industrial mobilization of total resources, facilitated by the total monetization of ever-increasing war-fueled debt.

The point of bringing all this up now is – what's the ultimate technology? In a context of technology-for-profit held in place by organized violence, the ultimate technology is the State's governing structure itself, because it's precisely what holds in place the system of organized violence securing the whole technology-for-profit regime. In what sense is State government a technology? As I've said, technology is 'human knowledge and understanding allowing for the production and use of a given tool'. A tool is simply any deliberately manipulated complex of materials that a human can reliably recurrently use to get what he or she intends to get by using it. In defining terms here, we shouldn't be any more specific than that: a 'tool' only refers to the way human beings repeatedly *use* certain manufactured materials, in order to produce explicit desired effects.

State government may be a most special kind of organization, but still, just like any such phenomenon, it always constitutes the use of human beings as tools. Thus, government, like any human organizational phenomenon, is technological because it's dependent upon systematized knowledge concerning the use of manufactured materials (human beings as employees of the State) in order to produce desired effects (enforced policies). 116 years ago, when globalization started, two massive irrepressible processes were happening in this regard: and they couldn't long exist in a common context. On the one hand, for the first time in history, because of the until then unheard of life-support capacities of industrialization, a realistic potential was emerging that humanity might at some point be able to provide adequately for the life-support needs of all human beings on the planet. On the other hand, for the first time in the history of civilizations, there existed a realistic potential that at some point in the near future one State might be able to conquer and rule over all of the planet's human beings. Tragically, since the stratification of wealth had always been consolidated through the stratification of knowledge, only the highest sectors of the social structure were aware of the state-of-affairs, and hence only they were aware of the contradiction. The idealized potential for one State to rule over all of the human beings on the planet – or as close as humanity could get to actualizing this scenario – won out with ease. The beginning of the global civilization's establishment, via the emergence of the U.S. national security State, was the initial explicit institutional outcome of that victory.

Officially starting with the Cold War-implemented global conditions, an entire civilization was, for the first and only time ever, being built from the ground up according to a predetermined strategy – but this possibility existed solely because of all prior evolution based on all prior technological transfers, so the predetermined strategy was still being built along the lines of all prior civilizational history. Therefore, to refer again to the "neat trick" before I explain it, I must make clear that whenever it was used, it was the direct expression of a *Power*-structure that always knew exactly what it wanted, laying the groundwork for implementation of its already selected policy.

So when the Psychological Strategy Board, for instance, wasn't *explicitly* implemented, that didn't mean its general framework would be left unimplemented. Instead, the "spirit" of a Psychological Strategy Board was going to be installed into the U.S. Government under different letters – within an existing institution – thereby allowing it to thrive while also obfuscating the very fact that it existed. Think that's far-fetched? Well, it certainly happened in at least one other case, and this one case would allow the launching and perpetuation of essentially the ugliest institutional phenomenon known to the entire body of existent historical scholarship.[cdix] Not only that, but the institution was also apparently directly related to the Psychological Strategy Board. The two were part and parcel of the same completely unpublicized and for that reason immeasurably valued organizational force within the U.S. Government.[cdx]

Remember in the second section of the present narrative, when I said, "It wasn't even CIA itself that was initially running the global shadow government from within the U.S. State, but the still much tinier sliver within CIA responsible for covert operations"? The neat trick paved the road for this very sliver: the Office of Policy Coordination

(OPC), which (just barely) officially existed from 1948-52 – but which in spirit surely has been most instrumental in managing the global shadow government operating inside the United States Government ever since the former first came into *Power*, albeit doing so in a thousand different explicitly-labeled forms.[cdxi] It doesn't matter what particularized form the phenomenon appears in because, in accordance with the path-dependence driving the largest-scale sociohistorical processes, the main point is that the phenomenon (officially-sanctioned "Peacetime" covert operations) only had to be deliberately introduced into the world once. After that, it "took on a life of its own". And once a system takes on a life of its own, it lasts as long as it can (as I've said, "until it becomes energetically impossible").

Moreover, when they were introduced for the first time into their environment – the new global civilization – such operations, the basic stuff of the new/old invention psychological warfare, were introduced from literally the uppermost echelons of the dominant culture, the conquest-imposed elite ruling class. The individuals chosen to do the dirty work were mainly to be found in the New York Social Register: they went to Ivy League schools; they were from Greenwich, Connecticut.[cdxii] In no uncertain terms, they were an elite within the elite. (And once *this* sliver initiated something, the thing could really be kept going for as long as was desired.) What else did you expect a global shadow government to look like, in a context of advanced capitalist elitism? What could possibly be a more explicit, more deliberately carried-out enactment of the concept of stratification of wealth through the stratification of knowledge, imposed through the selective distribution of violence? Only those who "register" on an interhuman level – socially – can be willing tools of the *Power*-structure. In this vein, the most important knowledge really is who you know.

But practically all individuals living within a *Power*-structure's domain are *un*willing, or at least un*witting*, tools of the *Power*-structure. All individuals are born subject to (cultural) conditions they didn't create, and for individuals born into *Power*-structures, which is to say a dynamically increasing proportion of human beings throughout the past five-plus millennia, this almost always involves being violently exploited in some way. And specifically concerning the world of the 20th-century-beyond era, unless you're one of the few oldest individuals on the planet, you were born into the conditions of a *Power*-structure that, if not fully globalized, was definitely already fully globalizing. So whatever other superficial distinguishing characteristics there were that made them passionately hate each other, more or less all individuals since right before the start of the 20th-century have been the exact same type of human, if for no other reason than that they were born tools of the same *Power*-structure.

The petroleum geologist Colin Campbell has made this exact same point, if in different words, and so, essentially, has the sociologist William Catton. Campbell calls us contemporaries "petroleum man",[cdxiii] and Catton calls human beings since the beginning of industrialization *Homo colossus*.[cdxiv] Whatever feature you emphasize, though, specifically petroleum-fed industrialization or industrialization in general, it seems to me that the main thing about human beings born into the contemporary era is that they're part of an urbanization which, because of the onset of a most advanced phase of industrial capitalism, became truly global, and hence something universalizing in its relation to all human beings on the planet at once. While based on something truly horrific, it has still been proof in real time beyond the capabilities of any possible argument to deny it, that every human being, no matter how particularly malicious or harmonious, is one equal part of the same humanity – an entity that itself is a part of the same environment as all other things on Earth. Even in humanity's moment of thickest darkness we can find a cause for true faith.

But before we can learn to have any faith in humanity, we must honestly face the realities behind the human misery caused by humans. For, just as much as the cause for real faith, these other realities are built upon the fact that all humans comprise the same environment. Most notably, the runaway human-caused human misery in the existent world stems historically from humanity's long-term transition to a politicoeconomic system built wholly on global trading for profit.

As civilizations evolved, it became clearer and clearer, in the sense that it became ever-increasingly actualized, that the real mechanics of civilizational history took place *in the realm of long-distance transport*, manifesting most strikingly amidst the war-trade competition: control transport and hence the lines of supply, and you can control war; control war, and you can control the civilization. Because this was how every individual civilization evolved, it was how urbanized humanity as a whole evolved, in the long run.

As I've reiterated time and again throughout this text, in so many different contexts, international trade was always something that expanded most quickly to the extent that it was synchronized with international warfare – just as international warfare expanded most quickly to the extent that it was synchronized with international trade. Thus I've defined civilizations primarily through the concept of a war-trade environment: civilizations and their associated contexts (intercivilizational structures and civilization-State-complexes) are interlocking complex adaptive systems, integrated environments that whenever possible become more efficient at their underlying purpose – to facilitate ever-expanding conflict between elite factions over the mechanisms of war and trade. All other goals are subjugated by the constraints of this primary goal: precisely the state-of-affairs entailed in being subject to a conquest syndrome. If you want to properly study either war or trade as it has evolved in the past five-plus millennia, you must study both phenomena in conjunction with each other. To put it another way, in terms appropriate to the most recent, Western-dominated history, you can't study capitalism without studying the States it's interdependent with.

This is truest of all in the global civilization, and so, at this stage of maximum civilizational expansion and consequent maximum intensification, those things that are most expanded and most intensified are humanity's capabilities for making war and trade, capabilities which have evolved to such a degree at the literal expense of everything else there is. The psywar environment *is* a war-trade environment; or, better, a trade-war environment. It's a globally maximally intensifying trade-war environment that, because of "side effects" inhering from its own place in sociohistorical evolution – being the culmination to a long term growth of urbanized communal morality – must exist in a psychological climate that would be so horrified by the civilization's realities if it truly knew them, the system would more or less shut down due to lack of legitimacy.[cdxv] At the same time, these realities are so necessary to the system's constant functioning, and, in the contemporary world, certain aspects of reality can be documented so precisely, the realities can't be completely concealed. So, the system must exist "hidden in plain sight": we have to be culturally molded to look right at something and not see it for what it really is.

Now we can see fully why, as was discussed earlier, the shadow government in charge of the U.S.-centered national security machine deliberately manufactured the Korean War – and why it deliberately manufactures all other wars in the global civilization. Like Prouty said, the precisely designed conditions for such southeast Asian "warfare" (postmodern colonial occupation) had been cultivated since – at the latest – the end of World War Two, structured from the outset (well before the Cold War was ever a publicly acknowledged factor in U.S. political affairs) to fit nicely within the framework of a "Cold War "cover story"".[cdxvi] Hence, Korea and Vietnam were each arbitrarily divided into "North" and "South". In both cases, when the U.S. felt the time was right, the leading fascist Superpower labeled the civil-warring counterparts in each nation "Communist" (North) and "Capitalist" (South), and then "went to war" against the former. Of course, the "Communists" were nominally funded by the U.S.'s tacit junior partners, the Soviet Union and Mao's China, but it seems doubtful that there was any real reason for such funding besides the lending of additional credence to the cover story. The true gist is that the Cold War represented the original postmodern divide and conquer strategy.

As Prouty also argues, in terms of its importance to the aggressors – the Powers – the purpose of all physical warfare in the nuclear age is to perpetuate the highly-visible appearance of interstate conflict in as "controllable" scenarios as possible. In other words, the purpose of all physical warfare in the nuclear age is actually, from a larger perspective, *psychological* warfare (although it's based on what Prouty writes, this is my own phrasing). A conflict must be in place: an overt war. In my opinion, besides the main cultural purpose it serves of distraction – every war naturally absorbs massive quantities of public attention – there's the equally significant primary logistical purpose it serves, in providing what you might call a "main source" for the real, "covert" warfare taking place in strategic hot spots (most often, and most conveniently for the *Power*-structure, other areas within the geopolitical region where there's ongoing overt warfare). That is, the illegitimate wars require supplies that the covert warmakers can't get express authorization for from the aggressor governments, so they divert supplies from the legitimate war going on nearby.[cdxvii] If there's no legitimate war going on, there will quite simply be no legitimate supplies to divert.

I think that does much to explain the thing conventional scholars in the relevant fields seem to argue about *ad nauseum* in the contemporary world: why does the U.S. go to war where it does? "Why Vietnam?"[cdxviii] The better question is, why southeast Asia (for instance), at the particular time when the war took place?* Basically, once the warmakers have addressed some preliminary considerations of purely grand strategic relevance – a narrowing-down process guided by the main question, "Where do we generally need war right now?" – the real question for them is, "Why not?" The "U.S.", here meaning certain perfidiously symbiotic, global elite factions who use the U.S. Government as an imperial shield, has interests in certain regions, and it also needs to ostentatiously "make war" from time to time, and so it needs to make war on some nation or another in those regions. The right nation is selected based on more specific criteria within that initial broadest geostrategic schema, with the planners' main concern in this regard being what they can get away with (what kind of cover stories they can concoct, how the planned actions will fit in with off-the-books funding, etc.).[cdxix] Meanwhile, scholars earnestly scratch their heads and wonder just what cockamamie but, to be sure, ultimately "good intentioned" ideas are behind the Empire's latest war "blunder" (see essentially all mainstream "criticism" of the Iraq War). They sincerely ponder on what attractive alternative policies might be crafted, which the same *Powerful* individuals would assuredly approve of, if only they knew about them.

But by systemic necessity, there's no possibility of reasoning with groups that view war as the quintessential means for running an economic system, i.e., the highest echelon of publicly unaccounted for policymaking elites. They're *always* going to go to war, and they're always going to go to war pretty much whenever and wherever they want to, within only the vaguest of guidelines broadly set by the elites' own rules of "public opinion", which has become nothing more than one part of the game, albeit a most important part.

We have to change *what* we think about the wars in the contemporary world (we have to absorb the non-propagandized information); also, however – relatedly and even more importantly – we have to change *how* we think about wars in the contemporary world. In turn, inextricably, we have to change how we think about warfare throughout

---

* Depending on your analysis, any range between 1943 and 1975.

all of history. Although war has always had a primarily physical presence, it has at the same time always ended up having a primarily psychological *purpose* in its indispensable relationship with the human systems built around it. This is the most striking aspect of what I've argued for throughout the present text as war's ultimate, ever-present, rarely-spoken motive: the consolidation of *Power*.

While it's eminently painful to acknowledge, the simplest truth is that, fundamentally, *Power*-structures work[cdxx] – and in fact, they work better than anything else designed by humans. In other words, they're uniquely successful at what they set out to accomplish, which is the instatement and long-term, adaptive reinstatement of politicoeconomic relationships of conquest. *Power*-structures are successful at this in the long term to the extent that they master the use of selectively-distributed physical violence as the indispensable means for securing holistic psychological dominance. Since this is so singularly painful to recognize, we can't expect to morally evolve unless we confront its reality with the greatest force. For its factuality wouldn't be quite so disturbing if it weren't such a central factor in the ordering of all human affairs; and those in the contemporary world, most of all.

Perhaps I have to spell it out in completely unadulterated phrasing, for one to truly gather why the just-mentioned perpetual state-of-affairs is so disturbing: as a political mechanism, what I've labeled "the reason why *Power*-structures work" resembles nothing so much as the definition of terrorism. Aside from the use of war for explicitly economic functions, meaning either crude conquest (expansion) or the more uniquely contemporary form of military Keynesianism, we can consider the other essential function of war to be mainly political. The political function[cdxxi] of war, and in turn of the existence of the State-ruled war machine constituting the civilization-State-complex's *central organizing mechanism*, is at its core predicated solely upon terrorism. All State politics is, then, in one way or another – directly or indirectly – integrated with the logic of terrorism. And no phenomenon pervades everything else in the contemporary world like (corporate-) State politics, in all of its innumerable, diversely-manifested dimensions.

Primarily, this was what OPC was being set up to enforce, namely by invisibly infiltrating CIA and then using CIA to infiltrate everything else in order to exploit the most immediate access to the information supply held by history's most *Powerful* State.[cdxxii] OPC was set up in this way initially via the neat trick, which trick itself constitutes a perfect example of psychological warfare, in the form of disinformation. The very manner in which the institution came into existence epitomized its purpose: when institutions operate in such a fashion, they must always operate in such a fashion. By their very nature, they're never really there to do what they say they're there to do.

Let's imagine a scenario where an institution is there to do more or less what, in public, it says it's there to do. This isn't hard, because it was the normal way institutions acted throughout history: and if it weren't, institutions in the contemporary world that profit off of not being there to do what they say they're there to do couldn't be so successful. Except under extreme general circumstances, like those obtaining in the hydrocarbon age, official institutions can only profit in contexts where organizations are mostly honest, even if they're violently exploitative. For the most part, the State openly asserts its right to do whatever it can to impose its will.

We can imagine the "absolute monarchs" of early modern Europe (1492-1776), for instance. Although their *Power*, which was the result of the combination of landed wealth and military success (two phenomena that in reality can't be separated), may have been couched in the language of morality, the utilization of such language didn't in-and-of-itself have to constitute a lie. European monarchs and their supporters may have primarily operated according to a distinct ideology, but ideology is ideology precisely when it's not a lie: when someone, however misguided he or she may be, is a "true believer". From a present-day perspective, a monarch's self-conception that he possessed divinely-granted dominion over everything else in his realm was at best silly and at worst massively lethal, yet within the mindset of the context kings really could believe they were superior to everyone and everything else and in a certain way be right, and thus they could easily assume that this was why they had come to *Power* in the first place. In this sense, the ideology constituted a tragedy, but not quite a fraud.

So, in an ideological sense, the institutional presence of the monarchy itself wasn't a lie. The beliefs behind the ideology constituted what Roy Rappaport calls "Ultimate Sacred Postulates", which by definition can't be falsified, which is exactly why they're uniquely apt as central elements of culturally-specific belief systems.[cdxxiii] In other words, knowing the facts may lead us to view the king's assertion that he's the sole representative of God on Earth as a sort of fraud, but it wouldn't have been explicitly a fraud unless the king didn't really believe himself to be more *Powerful* than the Pope, which, in terms of the real-world context, was the whole purpose behind the cultural belief that the king was the sole representative of God on Earth. In this sense, even though it's beyond any possible doubt, that no king was truly the representative of God on Earth, there was a certain unreflective way in which this made sense *within the context of the cultural environment*, and all the milieus behind all the monarchies exploited it in the era when kings were first starting to challenge the Papacy. By always speaking primarily according to metaphorical generalities – focusing attention mostly on purely symbolic phenomena – the *Power*-structure could always at least implicitly associate military prowess with God's will, thus perpetuating a common belief in the king's connection with the Christian God. This was a successful strategy, first of all, to the extent that no one could disprove the claims made, and secondly, so long as the king's establishment could support his claims with material benefits and annihilate his detractors with force, the number of individuals who even wished to disprove the claims could likely be kept sufficiently minimal. As such, neither the concept of "king" nor the concept of "God" within the civilization ultimately made any sense without each other, which proved to be the key ideological state-of-affairs Western monarchs (and Popes) could exploit to gain moral support for military/political/religious goals.

From this perspective, everything related to the State and its ideological cultivation is kept largely outside the realm of outright fraud so long as individuals speak mostly according to fictions: that is, so long as they stay within the boundaries of the imagined order, which to the extent that it's really the imagined order, can't be a lie, because it's what individuals truly imagine. The State is so exceptional a social phenomenon on account of its being able to coordinate (centralize) the *Power* to manage so many seemingly disparate, indispensable organized mass activities within one entity. It can do this precisely because the imagined order seems completely impossible without the State.

The interesting thing is that the imagined order, insofar as it's based on the real one, and it must be based on the real one as closely as possible for it to successfully serve its purpose, *is* completely impossible without the State – just not for the reasons people typically think. As I said, once States take hold of politicoeconomic systems, there are no States without those systems, and no such systems without their States. This is what makes States so dangerous to everything that surrounds them, which is to say everything within the total domain of a *Power*-structure: everything else comes to depend on them, even though they're the central sources of all the worst problems in the areas they affect.

That last point may sound ideologically biased and overly critical, but I wouldn't be forced to come to such a conclusion were it not for the actual history of the 20th-century-beyond era in particular, with the conclusion becoming all the truer the further into time one goes. Of course, again, if one wishes to accurately focus blame on the State, one must always be sure to keep in mind as well – the State administrative structure was primed to be so uniquely dangerous in the contemporary context because its components could be so easily instrumentalized by anyone who knew how to work them, while it was also fairly feasible to keep the number of individuals with such knowledge extremely small. No State reflects anything in-and-of-itself: predominately through great acts of terroristic violence and regularized interstate wars, a State is foremost the reflection of the politicoeconomic goals driving whatever the central conquest class happens to be at a given historical moment.[cdxxiv]

Once industrialization really started to take hold, as everything in general became both more monetized and in parallel more corporatized, the most enormous energy-time supplies in human history would be set into motion and filtered mainly through the financially-dominated State in one way or another, a state-of-affairs that only worsened as time went on. The greatest human investments of all time went towards investment: the sector that did the least actual work got the most pay, and more and more pay as time went on; and this has much less to do with individuals being greedy (although that absolutely plays its role), and much more to do with its being what needs to happen for the system as it appears to survive.

These were the precise sociohistorical origins of our world. Therefore, it's only appropriate to criticize the contemporary State if it's done as a subsidiary branch of a larger criticism regarding capitalism – capitalism is capitalism insofar as it's a creature of the State, and insofar as the State is a creature of it. As all the processes relevant to the forever-intensifying entwinement of capitalism and the State emerged in history, and as they emerged in the 20th-century-beyond era like never before, one thing expanded more than all others: the *lie*,[cdxxv] which manifested itself most viciously and sweepingly in the form of corporate fraud.[cdxxvi]

The State and business appeared more and more like each other all the time, until they finally simply merged once and for all with the institutionalization of the global shadow government:[cdxxvii] once more we see why it's actually trade above everything else that's to blame for the "runaway human-caused human misery" in our culture. The "postwar" reconsolidation of the traditional Western capitalist system via the United States, the primary means for establishing the global civilization, happened how it did (*via* the U.S.) because the all-supreme *Power* of the system lay in its potential to facilitate a globally-integrated trading regime. But it was a globally-integrated trading regime that would only be able to exist in the midst of a globally-divided war regime.

There were never greater collective efforts to build group feeling – public legitimacy – than those undertaken during the Cold War; and yet there were also never any that were, in the end, quite so phony. The efforts were mirror images, not just of each other, but equally of what Bernays was talking about in his quest for the manipulation of "group psychology". As we can now understand in context, group psychology is described over and over again by its masters as nothing more complicated than the "herd mentality",[cdxxviii] revealing the desire for literally the identical relationship that thousands and thousands of years of "Old World" State ancestry had inculcated as the ideal relationship between rulers and subjects. Except, because of the incomparably rotten structural conditions at the very foundation and because the hegemonic sector in the contemporary global world was so unprecedentedly self-aware in its actions, the re-imposition of the traditional State dynamic was (and had to be) predicated on an unprecedented level of *intentionality* in the elites' deception, i.e., an unprecedented level of fraudulence.

How are the total resources totally mobilized? What does total mobilization mean? It used to be widely stated during the Cold War that humanity as a whole had become "totally mobilized";[cdxxix] the aptness of this phrasing in describing the global civilization hasn't gone the way of the Soviet Union. In the first place, it can only be done with an economy that has undergone total cash monetization: indeed, the technical banking jargon for centralizing a cash polity's reserves was once, if it isn't still now, "mobilization" – as in "mobilization of funds".[cdxxx] Additionally, we must keep in mind that it has been solely the complete reign of industrialization over the planet that has permitted the total cash mobilization of the planet's strategic resources. Finally, in the cultural climate of exponentially-more-extreme wealth stratification the West was used to when its elites were setting up the global civilization, only totally mobilized war machines going full blast all over the planet could constantly support both ever-increasing industrialization and the concomitant perpetual monetization of everything. Truly we see, in real time, the meaning of "all or nothing".

As outrageous as this state-of-affairs may at first seem, when we consider all prior history of civilizations leading to the global civilization, a "totally mobilized" humanity is exactly the reality that should've been expected to eventually emerge. What makes everything so unusually insane amidst this fairly predictable background is that the *Power*-structure has been so successful at convincing us everything has changed. On the other hand, such success also becomes, in the end, the best imaginable proof that the system is a fraud: to truly constitute deception an action needs to be intentional, and the existence of such well-patterned confusion, on such a massively systematic scale, can only be the result of an intent to deceive – one which emanates above all from the highest ("unofficial") level of *Power*. Intentionality is indeed the true measure of morality – and *a*morality.

Contemporaries find morality such a difficult concept to understand because, more so than anything else, it can't be reduced to something material. Only experience itself truly teaches us morality; but this doesn't make morality something that's not real. Much more likely, it makes it the realest thing there is.

Before the appearance of the global civilization, wherein commentators like to believe in a contrived notion called "Objectivity", historical thinkers widely, consciously perceived the implicit connection between the practice of constructing historical knowledge and that of teaching morality.[cdxxxi] In this vein, as ordinary as they might seem in our contemporary world, I believe there are no actions more rife with amorality than those where individuals utilize their knowledge of real-world (historical) processes in order to selfishly exploit the continuation of those processes. For, as I said, as wrongheaded as any given ideology might be, as terrible as the consequences of that ideology might be, as terrible as its real-world consequences are, the ideologue remains outside the realm of lying so long as that individual really feels that his or her beliefs are right. But oftentimes, actual knowledge of real-world processes cancels out the individual's ability to "innocently" persist in believing whatever ideology he or she clings to, no matter what the individual tells him- or herself: the unbelief doesn't have to be put explicitly into words to be real.

Now I have to start saying outright what *I* really believe, which always naturally frightens the worker in empirical reality. The more I studied humanity and its history, the more I came to believe that the biggest change of all, in the age when nothing but the biggest changes in history were happening in every sphere of human life, was that empirical reality had never been so forcefully documented in its comprehensive entirety. The course of the 20th-century-beyond era was dictated primarily by the exponentially exploding combination of the communications and military spheres;[cdxxxii] in turn, the whole system, which throughout its evolution was never very stable ecologically, went completely haywire.

This is something I have to "believe" because it can never really be proven in the same sense as many of the other hypotheses I've presented throughout the text – for one thing, since there was only one 20th-century-beyond era on planet Earth, we'll never know what would've happened if that one aspect were different. The strangest thing about our thoughts as we typically have them is that, no matter how empirical is the focal point of any given thought, all of them collectively ultimately seem to be predicated upon beliefs that can't be reduced to any single determinate empirical proof. But we continue believing them because that allows us to discover so many other things we *can* prove. Eventually we might be able to prove some of those first things, but we may never get to prove any of them. Almost certainly, also, we will someday abandon some of these beliefs in favor of new ones. The point is, regardless of their provable "factuality", they allow us to operate in the world, and so they take on a kind of truth.

It seems clear then that there are at least two different kinds of truth. One is truth in the quite limited sense we're most accustomed to referencing in the contemporary world: truth as plain factuality. The other is what we can consider "moral truth", what Rappaport aptly refers to as "adaptive truth". This is what's involved when we innately sense that fictional stories, for instance, seem to contain the truest messages of all. Basically, a text is adaptively true, morally true, insofar as the lesson it teaches can make the world a more harmonious (symbiotic) place to live in than it would otherwise be.[cdxxxiii]

That is, regardless of their inherent factuality, statements can be (adaptively) true *within the contexts of texts*. Humanity's employment of this most rare tool can often typify the most humane imaginable qualities. But it's another one of those tools that just as easily can be abused, utilized with the greatest imaginable intent to harm.

Most simply, let's consider an adaptive truth to be a real expression of the general belief that it's beneficial for individual human beings to live harmoniously with other life on the planet; this constitutes one side of the spectrum of human traits. An adaptive untruth, then, on the other side of the spectrum, would be a real expression of the general belief that the individual human being has no responsibility to anything besides him or herself. In this sense, we can look at life lived within a State-ruled polity, throughout most of history prior to the contemporary world, as being somewhere in between (although typically closer to the untruth side), and moreover something that fluctuated according to the conjunctive fluctuations of many other variables.

For most of the history of civilizations, the State-ruled polity wasn't *explicitly* a fraud, to the extent that it spread the perception that it was beneficial for human beings to live harmoniously with other human beings. But simultaneously, it was *implicitly* a fraud insofar as, for the system to work as it did, so many other individuals – those who counted among the "them" group in the perpetual battle of us vs. them – had to be designated "unqualified" as human beings, which both wasn't reality and also embodied purely destruction: a lie told to reach an essentially malevolent goal. It could remain outside the territory of explicit fraud, though, so long as individuals really believed that the State's enemies weren't really human beings, a belief that most individuals could keep largely at the back of their minds anyway, spending little if any time seriously examining it because they were, naturally, focused mainly on "their own lives".

I believe this characterizes how the official abuse of communal morality in civilizations was manifested before the contemporary world, and epitomizes why it typically constituted a mainly *un*conscious fraud. Things were already starting to change rapidly in this regard with the initial wave of industrialization: but there wasn't yet an entire global culture built wholly on the inversion of the abuse, which would be a much worse fate. We know this because it's precisely what has happened in the contemporary world.

The inversion of the abuse says that everyone is in the community, but that we can only help the community by helping ourselves, which is so out of line with the spirit behind the simplest notions of morality that it makes the whole fraudulence of the sociohistorically evolved *Power*-structure seem like a tangible reality. But that's only if you know better, and almost no one does. Unfortunately, this has largely been because of the deliberate actions of the structure-builders themselves, and resultantly we've been "convinced" (brainwashed) into building our entire world around the fraud.

The overwhelming onslaught of mass confusion in the existent world stems from building our civilization top-down around the system's most audacious fraudulence. Perhaps civilizations were always like this, to such an outrageously acute degree, but I personally don't believe that could've been possible. Of course, as was just mentioned, the State was always implicitly a fraud insofar as it cultivated communal feelings in its citizens ultimately for the purposes of violent exploitation, towards the end of maintaining social dynamics of *Power*. However, if we use the contemporary all-encompassing fraud as our principal point of comparison, it's clear that past State fraudulence emanated mostly from States *at their origins*, and otherwise the fraudulence became largely compartmentalized. I believe States were successful in past stages of cultural evolution precisely because, for the most part, as they grew, they allowed more and more individuals to "buy in" to the State, meaning States typically grew when they could make life more attractive for certain additional demographic sectors. But this usually also meant that life would be made much less attractive for many more individuals somewhere else within the constraints of the system. Here's where the argument gets quite complicated.

When a State grew, and consequently, evolved, it was substantially in parallel to the State's skill at creating its own reality by furthering its outright physical conquest in certain "foreign" areas, which would in turn fuel the State-imposed conquest culture within the "domestic" environment, where the fraud could remain mostly implicit to most individuals. What might've had to have been imposed in the form of a lie if individuals knew more information could remain unfalsifiable, since, in the realm of "not (yet) enough information", it could be predicated on pure ideology, pure faith in the system. This was possible because States had frontiers they had to protect, which meant they had external enemies they had to keep at bay: in turn giving the State the central basis of legitimacy it needed in order to keep internal enemies at bay. So long as States had real external enemies – most namely, other States who really did want to conquer the first-mentioned States – individuals in *Power*, no matter how great was the benefit from conquest that always accrued first and foremost to themselves, could convince themselves that they were truly deserving of that greatest benefit because they kept their subjects safe from their enemies, which was true, albeit in the most technical possible sense. Official ideologies of kingship in particular and of the State in general were meant to forever cling as tightly as possible to this shred of technical truth, employing it as the basis for all other social order. The ruling class really believed it knew what was best for the masses it ruled over, and in this way, no matter how intrinsically despicable its actions were, so long as it remained within the mindset of the moment, it could always unconsciously deceive itself into believing that its actions in managing the *Power*-structure were morally sound. Having convinced even itself, it could easily convince everyone else.

In the contemporary world, there are in reality individuals – those in positions of greatest *Power* – who most certainly intend to deceive in the severest way. This accords with the fact that the State in the contemporary world, at those highest levels that are responsible ultimately to factions working in technically unofficial channels, deliberately creates or (what amounts to the same thing) deliberately sustains its own "Enemy". The argument I'm making here, which can't be proven because it's based on what people really believed, or can only be indirectly proven in the sense that certain facts resonate with the individual reader, is that the system succeeded in the past because, so long as it had a real enemy, even the managers of the *Power*-structure could believe the ideologies the *Power*-structure deliberately contrived. On the larger scale, cultures run by *Power*-structures absorbed their formative ideologies so unreflectively, only at rare intervals did it occur to individuals on a mass level that the existing order might not be moral, moments which were, as a result of their rarity, highly determinative for subsequent history when they happened.

I believe that the only way this strategic pattern could've ever possibly changed once and for all, and the way that it did change in terms of globalization's sociohistorical reality, would be if circumstances arose where one group was ultimately intentionally creating both opponents in humanity's most significant intergroup conflicts. At that point, no matter what any given (elite) individual told himself, he was explicitly perpetrating a fraud on the individuals over whom he proclaimed he had a responsibility to rule. Oh, consciously, even if he "knew everything", an individual might've very well thought he believed his own lies. But somewhere, unconsciously, every individual exposed to the explicit facts had to viscerally *feel* the system's inherent fraudulence.

Concerning the processes immediately leading to the global civilization, the conflict between the official morality and the unofficial one had never become more palpable, which is why the system would necessitate the spread of mass confusion for its very continuation. In relation to civilizations and States, the long historical distinction between the official morality and the unofficial one is this: the unofficial one is the one human beings typically feel physiologically in the form of conscience. Human beings living in the contemporary dominant culture who aren't murderers, for instance, don't just refrain from killing people because they're taught not to, but for the most part because, under normal circumstances, we're morally incapable of murder. This phenomenon has a well-known psychological basis, what's conventionally known as a "criminal threshold". The quite low criminal threshold prevailing in the contemporary dominant culture at large is no doubt mostly shaped by the fact that, due to the unprecedented level of State monopolization over violence in the contemporary dominant culture, human beings in general that are born into the culture are much less likely to commit murder or other serious violent acts. But that in itself can't be separated, at some level, from the fact that the overall urbanized human *morality* has evolved to the point where individuals find killing other individuals morally unacceptable under most circumstances. In other words, to some substantial extent, the State must've found it easier to monopolize violence over time because more and more individuals under their rule were becoming less and less prone to physical violence.

The main sphere of abnormal circumstances involves the military, in which case individuals in dominant cultures overwhelmingly find murder to be morally acceptable – even righteous – so long as there's a noble purpose. (In military contexts, of course, individuals inhabiting dominant cultures almost universally cease to call murder "murder".) Thus, historically, the strength of official morality has flourished insofar as violence in service of the State hasn't been seen as an end-unto-itself, but as a means to a greater end. I believe this is why the discussion is so complicated: knowing what we know in the contemporary world, *we* can see that the purposes behind State-building were never really noble, but solely had to do with constantly reconsolidating elite rule. But in terms of life within any given historical moment, I believe that, for so much of civilizational history until globalization, *perpetuating elite rule was really seen as being the direct equivalent of morality*.

That is, I think for the most part, people (including the elites) really didn't "know better", in the sense that general belief in the cultural pyramid was so unreflective, questions of conscience in relation to the State rarely arose. Not only was it tacitly assumed under most circumstances that the State wasn't abusing its *Power*; that wasn't even a consideration, except at certain moments where the State's will to dominate appeared unacceptably blatant. I think this is why the official morality was so successful at controlling the unofficial morality for so long, and I believe it's why the system evolved to the point where it led to the evolution of industrialization: primarily because of the ability of a tiny elite to make it "okay" for their miniscule milieu to be completely above the law, as they exercised this status in such a fashion that, in the near-term, it prevented much greater outbreaks of cultural disorder than might otherwise occur.

Yet this means that elites were never actually "in control" in the way they've always trained people to think about "control", in establishment-funded texts across all the different media forms, which until the early 20th-century meant virtually all texts with wider distribution than personal journals or letters. (As an aside: take note, how extremely rare it is for people to acknowledge the fact that the joint activity of reading-writing for intellectual stimulation has been a rich person's game throughout almost its entire existence). As I said awhile back (part 2, sec. 1), laws in civilizations – specifically, the laws enforced by States – are meant to minimize disorder rather than maximize order. This is relevant because we have to understand that a substantial level of cultural order, and interdependently, social order, had to be present in any precivilizational system before civilizations and States could emerge, which was exactly why such systems were able to sustain precivilizational levels of complexity. Such order lasted more or less until systems of that type started to conquer each other with primordial versions of militaries, directly sparking a much greater necessity for the realm of officialdom, which in turn led to a greater dependence on the official morality. So although it was certainly necessary for a great number of reasons, I suspect official morality became an indispensable part of the primordial civilizational *Power*-structures mainly as a way to *limit* as much as possible the disorder caused by (1) the structural conditions of conquest and later, and relatedly, a bit later on, (2) the ever-increasing number of human beings forced to live in ever-closer quarters, resultant from the advent of urbanization. At its inception and for a very long time afterwards, the State was the order that could be salvaged in a realm of great disorder.

But once industrialization got started, it wouldn't be long before even that most minimal act of maintaining stability was totally ravaged, along with the planet's natural resources and its sanity. The process that had its beginnings in the explicit origins of capitalism – the fueling of "Old World" culture with "New World" conquest – would be given the energy-time investments necessary to conquer literally everything. The elite factions and their hierarchical subordinates resultantly ate through what was still left of the moral structure like termites. Then they built a new one in its place, made to look just like the old one.[cdxxxiv] Except, since it was imposed in the most deliberately planned-out way imaginable, solely in accordance with what was most monetarily profitable, it lost every shred of mythological innocence.

Perhaps all elites always knew there was nothing truly noble in their actions: perhaps they were always doing nothing besides totally deceiving their masses; perpetrating grand frauds. But I believe fraudulence only became the outright norm as a result of industrialization and, even more especially, globalization. In this vein, there's a contemporary view of the State – one I happen to subscribe to – and what it can be compared to: proposed by, among others, the late Charles Tilly, one of the handful of most influential historical sociologists in the contemporary world (and one of the individuals I'm most indebted to for my own views on the State and its evolution). The quintessential model for what the State is, and what it has always been, is organized crime.[cdxxxv] The phenomenon the phrase "organized crime" serves as the label for just couldn't be seen as something definitively amoral until the contemporary world.

We don't really find that particular comparison being made until the 20th-century,[cdxxxvi] which is, I think, in the first place because the concept of organized crime *per se* is something that has only existed in the context of globalization, the dually-encompassing politicoeconomic-ideological environment. (Notions of criminals of course existed – just not notions of "organized crime" in a contemporary sense.) This makes it quite interesting, how there's so much idolization of gangsters in contemporary pop culture products, since the allure seems to derive mainly from the notion that gangsters are "enemies of the State", which imbues them with a romantic connotation of going against "society's" norms. Though based on the real-world histories of the contemporary world in general and organized crime's place in it in particular, the latter is actually *perfectly* emblematic of highly admired social norms dominant in the culture-at-large. And this is due to the totally unbridled domination of the contemporary State – but remember, the contemporary State insofar as it's the definitive manifestation of the corporate capitalist conquest syndrome. Above all, in the global civilization, everything unconscious became conscious, the implicit fraud became explicit, insofar as the State, which had always been "like" contemporary organized crime, became organized crime in actual fact.

Literally, this is what has happened: the rulers of the existent State and the rulers of organized crime even contain some of the same people – in many cases, this is true "at the highest levels"[cdxxxvii] – or at least people working in the exact same activities, which amounts to more or less the same thing. This shouldn't surprise the reader of the present text: what's a more unadulterated embodiment of "elite factions", after all, than mafia families? Also: nothing characterizes the perpetually ever-faster quest for *Power* more than a desire to be "the boss".

*   *   *

The worst thing about fraud is that it operates with the greatest possible *intent to harm*. This is why Dante, incorporating the moral philosophy of Aristotle, considered fraudulence the worst category of sins: the quality of humanity's intentionality is something unlike anything else on Earth, which I personally believe to be the most uniquely human thing there is.[cdxxxviii] The individual human being can "mean to" accomplish goals with the totality of his or her behavior[cdxxxix] to an extent absolutely impossible for any other organism on the planet. Fraud, then, amounts to the worst possible transgression against the moral responsibility inherent in simply being a human. Even the intent to physically maim another individual in itself isn't quite so amoral, because it's born mainly out of humanity's "animal" side rather than its more properly "human" side. Although the two are in the end not unrelated: fraud is at its very worst when it's connected to murder, insofar as the combination of murder and fraud holds the most terrifying potential for constant expansion.

To truly understand how no other combination surpasses this one in its potential for intentionally-caused harm, we can only consider it in its manifestations as an inextricable part of some *living system* – and this, for instance, is precisely what I mean when I say morality can only be learned through experience. We can usefully think of experience as being mainly "indirect" or mainly "direct". In terms of indirect experience, I believe the written narrative is the best for learning morality, and that the historical narrative can be the best kind of all in this regard. However, direct experience tends to be more effective for learning in general. Fortunately, direct experience can in certain cases also be embodied in the historical narrative form; I think this constitutes the most effective form of learning there is.

But how do we embody direct experience in the form of historical narrative? No non-first-person narrator is supposed to write him or herself into the story, least of all the historical narrator. Yet no matter what the historian believes him or herself to be doing, I don't think we can get around the fact that the historian *must* somehow involve his or her own life in the construction of the narrative. The historian is necessarily a human being, after all, and as I said, only this fact has allowed historians to understand how sociohistorical processes shape individuals' lives – this being the definitive aspect distinguishing the concept "human history" as prose form.

Every human being is a life: like all other lives, the beginning is birth and death is the end. Far in the background of any (typical) human life, providing the main context that gives the life meaning, there are historical events, the individuated processual actualization of parts of holistic cultures. The most significant of these events happening in any given time-place locale cluster together – I've called these, simply, event-clusters – and in so doing, not only constitute moments in systems within which individuals are embedded, but just as importantly, constitute much of the foundation upon which individuals build understandings of those systems.

For the historian to embody direct experience in a constructed narrative, he or she must build off of his or her position as an individual experiencing a present culture. The historian should use this experience as the primary means for narrativizing those event-clusters that comprise the central lived narrative (the lived metanarrative) defining the cultural background that shapes his or her own life. Whether or not the reader agrees that morality should have anything to do with the writing of history, the reader nonetheless now knows my belief on the matter, and in turn it should make sense that I believe *the making sense of the metanarrative going on in one's own life can be the basis for the greatest contribution to humanity's understanding of morality – or the worst conceivable affliction to the same*. Relatedly, I believe that every human being's moral responsibility is to do whatever he or she can in order to contribute to solving the problems he or she was born into. Consciously and joyously helping to perpetuate the problems one was born into is the height of amorality.

Now we can finally sufficiently see why the contemporary world is the most amoral era in human history, and thus, in my opinion, when history was at its worst. To sum up how we got to this point before we go forward: urbanized humanity, as a complex adaptive system, evolves, which process I've argued for as being interchangeable with the whole evolving process of human history during the past 5,000-plus years. Further, I've portrayed the evolution of urbanized humanity as being epitomized by the evolution of civilizations. The civilization, I've asserted, acts as one of three inextricable subsystems within the holistic system, the other two subsystems being the intercivilizational structure and the civilization-State-complex. The former represents the civilization's external context, and the latter its internal one. Insofar as they're all subsystems, each subsystem is interrelated with the others, and each is interrelated with the whole. The whole is the continuous reconsolidation of the subsystems within the systemic environment. This is what it means for something to be "more than the sum of its parts": all the parts have to work together and altogether they have to work with the environment.

I've equated the process of human history as a whole during the past 5,000 years with the process of urbanized humanity's evolution because, as I've said, I consider the process of humanity's growing cultural complexity to be the singularly definitive process for humanity's *total* natural evolution, insofar as it most closely reflects the temporally-unfolding spectrum of humanity's general ability to systematically create and destroy over geographical terrain. And the growth of urbanization has unequivocally been the greatest, fastest stage of evolving cultural complexity in humanity's history. The history of humanity started with the first explicit technological breakthrough, the use of complex language – thus starting humanity's metanarrative, insofar as humanity is a quintessentially technological phenomenon – evolving until the greatest (most consequential) technological complex in history was innovated, the global civilization. Thus we see that cities, and to an even greater degree city systems, are nothing more than the largest of tool-complexes.

In between the emergence of language on the one hand and the emergence of the global civilization on the other, there was the last interglacial transition, which, through its catalysis of mass migrations, overpopulation of fragile hunter-gatherer ecosystems, and the unprecedented spike of lethal interhuman conflict these almost certainly must've led to, gave rise to the emergence of settlements and the consequent emergence of agriculture. The emergence of successful agricultural settlements in many different locales all across the Fertile Crescent, around the same time, created the conditions of violent intergroup competition wherein the appearance of agricultural settlement systems would occur, a scenario that, after much growth, eventually led to the first cities. The appearance in some subregions of many cities within striking distance of each other finally led to the first civilizations, and most importantly of all, the appearance of this scenario in contiguous yet ecologically distinct subregions led to the first intercivilizational structure, comprising the total politicoeconomic system formed by the original civilizations revolving around the southwest Asian/northeast African/southeast European nexus. That intercivilizational dynamic would transfer from period to period via the archetypal civilizations transcending intercivilizational worlds – and so the nexus's first intercivilizational period represents the ultimate origins of contemporary globalized humanity.

The most extreme examples are the ones that have always set the tone for all other civilizational evolution, with "extreme" here referring above all to the capacity civilizations contain for organized destruction – a capacity epitomized by the State. Resultantly, the State itself eventually overtook civilizational evolution in its entirety. Once it did that, the stage would be set for a potential *total historical collapse of civilizations*, the stage where we find ourselves now. The sole question remaining is, will the evolution of *Power*, i.e., the evolution of organized destruction, destroy itself alone? Or will it destroy everything else as well, leaving no trace of Earth's existing life after it's done? The human beings on the planet now will determine this question's answer.

Of course, I already mentioned that in part 1, but so much else had to be explained before the question's unique urgency could truly be grasped. And this urgency, we can now see, resides here: morality in the existent world is just like morality in all other past ages, all across the planet; human beings are responsible for doing whatever they can to try to solve the problems they're born into. But the problems in the existent world are all the problems all historical humanity created and never bothered to solve. In fact, humanity seems to have always just made them worse.

Why can't we just put the problems off a little longer? Unfortunately, all human beings with the ability – the *Power* – to change things in the past have, sometimes consciously, unconsciously at others, acted according to this exact same impulse. Nothing has done more to contribute to the current state-of-affairs: where extinction not only seems conceivable, but in a certain sense, expected, because absolutely nothing from the past prepares us for what we have to do now. Humanity has never done it before as one entity. Done what? I hesitate to say: it'll sound childish, irrelevant.

We have to *care*. For something beside ourselves: perhaps for everything beside ourselves.

I know it's preposterous. Forgetting that for a moment though, what do I mean by "as one entity" humanity has never done it before? Let's consider humanity implicitly as having always been one, total thing, which we can now do retrospectively with the greatest accuracy – for we've seen from direct experience that it can be a total thing *explicitly*, as it is in the form of the global civilization. What does humanity as a total thing experientially teach us about humanity as a total thing conceptually?

In the existent world, even as human beings, at least theoretically, have a realistic potential to see themselves as one, global community, human beings in practice are clearly so divided amongst themselves in every imaginable way that simply bringing up the question of whether or not we can, to any substantial extent, "put all our differences aside" and do something useful would seem, under normal circumstances, more or less pointless. But we're not dealing with normal circumstances. The global civilization, especially at this latest stage (period seven), the existent world, is eminently swollen with potential for incomprehensible catastrophe. Here's something to gnaw on: the entire global politicoeconomic system, the largest ever in existence, and almost certainly the largest that will ever be in existence, is basically synonymous with humanity's extraction and utilization, *i.e., organized destruction*, of the planet's petroleum resources. Since petroleum can't be replenished, at least within the range of any timeline meaningful to the human beings using it (although possibly even not at all), it's what's known as a "nonrenewable" resource.

So, as a world, we've put all of our eggs in the petroleum basket, and on Earth there's ultimately only one supply of petroleum, the one that currently exists. On its own this is sheer insanity. But we haven't even gotten to just how limited is this limited resource.

Concerning the rate of petroleum extraction, there's a model that many commentators find questionable, many others swear by, originally propounded in 1956 by the petroleum geologist M. King Hubbert. At first, Hubbert applied the model to petroleum alone, since questions about humanity's uncontrollable rate of petroleum extraction were what prompted the research sparking Hubbert's construction of the model. But Hubbert would soon realized and eventually illustrate the model's relevance to humanity's depletion of many other critical resources, as well. (Heinberg) Considering the present rates of destruction in combination with projected global demographic trends, even according to the most "conservative" estimates, which aren't actually conservative since they're purposely designed to be overly optimistic, the world will run out of petroleum by about 2040.

What's the model? Basically, human beings deplete (destroy) certain resources according to an astonishingly regular pattern. The rate of extraction increases quite constantly until it reaches some maximum limit, at which point no matter how much effort (energy-time) is invested in extracting, the quantity of acquired resources can only steadily decrease. The more one continues to extract, the less return there will be on one's investment, until it simply becomes pointless to extract any longer because one would be investing more energy into the process than one gets out of it.[cdxl]

The model plotted on a graph reveals a bell-curve: a mathematical equivalent to the historian's concept of "rise and fall". No matter the resource to which it applies, no matter the place – it's always a bell-curve. This is why the state-of-affairs we find ourselves at now is typically referred to as "*peak* oil". As much as those individuals managing the *Power*-structure who know of its significance would like it to simply go away, it appears indisputable that we're now already at or perhaps even past the point where there will only be less and less return on our investment. In other words, the global economy is self-destructing in real time.[cdxli]

F. William Engdahl, a researcher who I'm greatly indebted to, and especially so on matters related to the contemporary history of petroleum (which is not very different from saying, "matters related to contemporary history"), seems to have the same reaction to "Hubbert's peak" that I initially had. Mass human behavior can't be so well-patterned that it will always, no matter what, spontaneously materialize in a fashion that can be represented with a bell-curve.[cdxlii]

Obviously, in general, I long ago passed the point where I find it difficult to accept that, in quite a diverse group of circumstances, human behavior on a massive scale can manifest with such striking regularity. But more specifically, here – I think the concept of Hubbert's peak in particular explains a great deal more than is normally expected. And the reason why shows what good instincts Engdahl has, in his viewing the idea of human beings behaving *en masse* in the shape of a bell curve as so unlikely: I don't think it would be possible if not for the specific long historical phenomenon Hubbert's peak perfectly exemplifies.

I believe Hubbert's peak defines long-term processes wherein humanity's main characteristic is its tendency towards ever-increasing demand. Now, before I say why I believe Hubbert's peak works specifically under these conditions, I must note – referring to such a characteristic as the characteristic of "humanity", as a whole, is necessarily problematic. But that's why I've gone to such great lengths to argue for exactly what I mean by "humanity" as being the most proper way in which we can say humanity has really been a whole, throughout all of its history. Indeed, it's the implicit argument of the entire text: humanity is always implicitly a whole, no matter the explicit circumstances, because all human beings, no matter how far apart from each other in space and time, have literally shared the one broadest holistic context of historically-unfolding planet Earth. No matter what, in the end, the same environmental context has supported and integrated us all. There's really only one geography. What's important about human history is humanity's total existence within the largest immediate existence, within the whole of the planet and all its other life. The process being played out so explicitly (consciously) at this latest stage of cultural complexity was being played out implicitly (unconsciously) at the earliest stage of cultural complexity.[cdxliii] Therefore, even though nowhere near all of the human beings have been responsible throughout history for the general tendency towards ever-increasing demand (a dynamic, not a linear, tendency), the whole of humanity is nonetheless obviously still affected most devastatingly when even just one tiny sector of the total population trends in this direction.

In fact, there's no real-world process that better embodies the characteristic of a phenomenon emanating from the smallest number of individuals but detrimentally affecting the greatest number, than the ever-increasing, ever-fulfilled demand of a tiny sector for vital resources. And what is this characteristic besides the definitive aspect of civilizations throughout their long historical evolution? It's the stratification of wealth through the stratification of knowledge, held in place by the structure of violence; the cultural pyramid, which is inextricable from the social structure and vies always to become or to continue acting as the historical sun.

In the contemporary world, where everything unconscious becomes conscious, this trait of ever-increasing demand, emanating from a cultural pyramid's topmost apex, reveals itself to be the linchpin of a phenomenon that resembles nothing so much as...*a pyramid scheme*. Implicitly, this is precisely what urbanized humanity has always been. But the mythologically-supported ideology, the clothing dressing up the brutal reality, was always a far more meaningful factor to the ruling class than it is now, something that I believe changed in parallel to the long historical evolution of cultural complexity, deteriorating most at those intervals witnessing the greatest bursts of sociohistorical speed.

The degradation of adaptive truth in the communal morality stemmed in the first place from the forever faster speed-of-events, insofar as this latter was simultaneously the reflection and cause of the changing pace of economic growth – which in civilizations has always been, more accurately, politicoeconomic growth, precisely because civilizations and States are driven by the fact that everyone has to pay up to people higher on the pyramid, i.e. people closer to the center of the *Power*-structure. The new thing that happened in the contemporary world was that, with globalized industrialization, the speed-of-events went into maximum overdrive, and resultantly the civilization and States became more or less *solely* about paying up to people higher on the pyramid. The *Power*-structure, and essentially only the *Power*-structure, received wealth-inputs more astonishing than any pre-contemporary could've ever imagined.

Virtually everyone seems to underestimate just how inherently, deliberately unjust *Power*-structures have been throughout their entire history, simply as a matter of course. The main point of every *Power*-structure, no matter when/where it appeared, was always to distribute the violence consolidating the wealth-distribution through knowledge-distribution system (i.e. the cultural pyramid). Thus, the *Power*-structure, instead of being an end-unto-itself, primarily exists to hold in place an even greater structure of *Power*, the cultural pyramid: the ultimate basis sustaining every civilizational ideology. On its own, without going into any detail more gruesome than that, this underlying state-of-affairs constitutes purest injustice: it awards cultural success mainly or in the worst cases solely to those individuals contributing to political coercion and economic exploitation, rather than those who contribute to whatever moral order there is. Political coercion and economic exploitation in civilizations are always based most materially on physical control over the production of wealth, and the individuals who exercise that control, in so doing, always – always always – exploit the publicly-created value (the value maintained by the legitimate moral order's existence) itself for private gain.

That is, the individuals who provide the greatest basis for producing wealth, not just the individuals who do the hardest physical labor but more generally all those who simply contribute to communal morality – the individuals who do what they say they'll do,[cdxliv] *who fulfill their obligations*, thereby creating an atmosphere of social trust – always in the long run end up getting ripped off one way or another, precisely because they make the communally beneficial choice to contribute. The question to be answered is merely "To what extent is it" ("it" being any given elite sector) "ripping the public off, at any given moment?" The private exploitation of the public works most of all based on nothing besides status, that psychological aspect of humanity fostered mainly by life in civilization-State-complexes, but which from the longest perspective started rapidly increasing in its significance alongside the inception of agricultural settlements. Status is the need to know who's dominant over whom, from the very top to the very bottom; the true source of everything explicitly cultural in civilizations: nothing more than the way everything looks on the surface.

At the same time as it has been so constantly ubiquitous throughout humanity's agricultural history, the inherent grave injustice has nevertheless taken on innumerable different shapes at different times, and as I've said it seems to have taken an ever-swifter turn towards total amorality since industrialization's onset. So, things do seem to "get worse" at certain times. Why is that?

Before I get into the reason why, let me say that in practice, what makes it so difficult to explain why the contemporary world is clearly much worse than the rest of history put together – at the same time as it's such a natural reflection of all prior civilizational history – is that we have to compare pre-global history's two worst politicoeconomic/cultural orders to understand how globalization emerged how it did. And the natural state of the existent world, and the history it grew out of, which is actually that history of the two worst cultures ever, makes us inclined to pit everything against everything else, in the sense that, whenever we juxtapose two things, it's demanded of us that we favor one over the other ("pick a side!"). One useful thing about Hell as a model, though, is that it allows us to unequivocally say everything in Hell is still in Hell: even as one sin is deeper down than another – more explicitly vital to the persistence of Hell's whole structure.

One of the systems was the ideal case of what we can call "noble patriarchy". The other was the ideal case of what we can call "financial patriarchy", which originally grew in parallel to noble patriarchy. Globalization is like a special case of financial patriarchy. This best puts into context why the broad trend of contemporary history was never about "civil liberties" that got diminished. Much more disturbingly, it was all about who generally qualified as "good children" to what kind of sadistic father. And the fathers only got more sadistic, and more deliberately sadistic, as the sociohistorical periods passed.

When we look back on the evolution of civilizations, we see that every period was like a testing ground for the next one: a time-place where the next great conquest syndrome "auditioned" for its future at the center stage. Others have made essentially this same point before, and they've done so specifically in reference to the European experience of mercantile marine militarists ("bourgeoisie", financial patriarchs) overtaking agricultural land-owning militarists ("aristocracy", noble patriarchs).[cdxlv] The most important thing to consider, though, isn't just what point a writer makes. This is certainly crucial; but it's even more crucial to consider what point the same writer makes *in relation to* what particular context. It matters what point the writer is really trying to make, implicitly, beyond the explicit, particular points made on the surface in the form of verbal sentences.

In this case, it's most significant to consider *how* and *why* patriarchies benefiting from their control over wealth gained ultimately by navy dominance eventually overtook patriarchies benefiting from their control over wealth gained by army dominance – and why, out of the situation of global naval dominance, there grew the most awe-striking conquest syndrome in history, that controlling the wealth gained by air and space dominance. This last-mentioned, by far most complex syndrome is one of the central bases for my characterizing globalization as "a special case of financial patriarchy".

I'll refer to the special case as *'criminal patriarchy'*. At our point in history, ruling elites (members of or associates of leading factions) act like nothing besides the contemporary definition of organized criminals, engaging particularly in a form of criminality known as "white-collar crime": corporate/financial crime. Foolishly, individuals in the contemporary dominant culture have long widely perceived this to be "not as bad" when contrasted with some other types of crimes, although this perception seems to be coming around somewhat owing to certain notable event-clusters of recent years. From my perspective, white-collar crime is the worst kind, for one thing because it harms on the greatest scale,[cdxlvi] in its greatest instances eroding trust at the level of whole cultures. "Blue-collar" crime, by comparison, typically "only" erodes the trust of individuals directly affected by a given crime. (In my view, then, essentially the exact opposite of the "broken windows" theory seems to be the case.)

How and why did the elite shift to outright criminality occur? The best model to use as a basis for our explanation is again the criminologist's: the most elegantly simple concept of a "criminogenic environment".[cdxlvii] But my example of the criminogenic environment is sure to be much larger than that considered by the typical criminologist.

So how and why did the archetype of the noble patriarch morph into that of the financial patriarch, and how did the latter in the end become the archetype of the criminal patriarch? These developments happened interconnectively with the combined exponential increases in distinct but inextricable fields: the planet's exponentially-increasing cash monetization of resources and exponentially-increasing urbanization – ultimately reaching the maximum level on each count – which together would define the globalization of the Western-originated conquest syndrome. That is, the criminogenic environment, the explicitly war-trade domain of the war-trade environment that is the civilization and its contexts, became the whole Earth; a chronologically communicable globe. The hegemons deliberately created the whole environment in which they could/would securely commit their crimes, crimes everyone else had to be legally restrained from committing in order for the hegemons to maintain their monopolies. This monopoly is what manifests culturally as the legitimate moral order. Thus did the hegemons make themselves into criminals who couldn't be prosecuted.

It may seem that it should be impossible for such an anomalous state-of-affairs to occur on such a relentlessly proliferated scale. But no matter how you look at it, by itself a global civilization is an anomalous state-of-affairs on the most relentlessly proliferated scale. Beyond that, the only question is – how do you look at a civilization on this most maximally intensified, maximally specialized scale? How do we interpret what we're looking at? Can we see what's being hidden in plain sight?

It's often helpful to try and look at things as simply as possible while simultaneously maintaining an appreciation for the fact that, whatever scenario you come up with, it must refer to a reality that's naturally of extreme complexity. This approach is most helpful of all when thinking about humanity's politicoeconomic side. As I was writing this book, I came up with a way to help me see what I was really looking at when I observed the contemporary world in any given situation: a kind of game I would play. I would prompt myself, "Imagine the state-of-affairs in Western civilization before the Cold War: and then imagine that these conditions continued once the Cold War started on a fully global, nuclear scale, evolving from there and in turn worsening at ever-faster rates as time passed."

In virtually all real-world situations, this was helpful in understanding the world we're still living in, concerning both how it's the same and how it's different.

As with most sociohistorical periods, the one the Cold War shaped (period six 1947-1991) could only be fully understood once it was demolished. Ours (period seven 1995 -?) is the sole one that could've been understood essentially the entire time, because it seems to have been built to self-destruct. In fact, it seems this quality was being built into the politicoeconomic system before the Cold War was even over; it just wouldn't be implemented in its completely individuated set of circumstances until after America "won". What seems clear about the world I was born into, is that when I was born into it it was already dead.

I was born in 1988, and it seems clear that from the outset of the '80s, beginning with the "Reagan Revolution", the plan of the global shadow government was nothing more than "loot the system".[cdxlviii] As much as it seems like this was always what was going on in Western civilization and the global civilization it spawned, outright institutional looting is in fact something unique: unequivocally, the fastest path to total destruction. The elites' intent to completely destroy the system they insisted they were protecting was something only *unconsciously* present in all prior manifestations of Western and global rule; it was never the literal main objective until the phase leading right up to and continuing through the existent world. Why not? For one thing, that would've been just too fraudulent to handle, even for the elite mindset. After all, even at earlier points in the contemporary world, when they were still manufacturing both sides of intergroup conflicts, the elites could still convince themselves they were doing "what was best" for the world, even as it happened to be what was worst. They could say to themselves, "It may be conflict, but it's conflict that creates order", although it seems obvious at this point that all they were doing was creating conflict that allowed themselves to profit off of *dis*order. In sum, they could convince themselves they were adhering to a doctrine of "the lesser of evils".

More critically, getting to the logistical capacity allowing the holistic politicoeconomic system to exist, true elites, as prudent stewards of Empire, have always at least unconsciously known that if they just plain loot their systems, the latter will soon enough be so corroded they won't be able to produce wealth anymore, thus destroying the basis for the thing the elites use wealth to create – what they love even more than wealth, status. The purpose of the State in sustaining the conquest syndrome seems, historically, to have been to solve that very problem: how can the elites loot the system at just such a pace that the system won't disintegrate? Although I of course can't be "inside their heads", it seems only logical that consciously systematically destroying something you claim to be protecting creates as complex a scenario as it gets, and so people wouldn't go to those lengths unless they absolutely "had" to: for instance, if the event-cluster sequences the hegemonic sector produced before it became aware of the planetary petroleum supply's true limitations had locked the hegemons into a scenario where the only remaining option was to consciously self-destruct. As inherently amoral as the entire system is, I still can't imagine the elites explicitly looting the *Power*-structure's institutional value unless they knew that their present course had long been the most unsustainable path possible; the path more or less leading to extinction. Since they no longer believed in anything at all besides their own profits – a result of the system's very nature – the hegemons did what you'd expect them to have done in such a dire situation, which was to see to their own interests; interests shared with literally no one else.

How do we know that this looting is what has happened? At first it seems to hide itself in the fact that it's all around us. The main preliminary question to be answered is, how self-aware do you think elites at the highest levels of *Power* are? I believe elites at the highest levels of *Power* must be the most self-aware individuals in existence, if only due to their occupational requisites. That is, they consider their job description to be the exercising of completely unrivaled control over the global civilization. With that said, what is the real nature of that "control" they exercise over this system they benefit from most?

Maybe you noticed above that I said only those who register socially, those who can count themselves among the elites, can be willing tools of the *Power*-structure. What I mean by it is most relevant here: the nature of the *Power*-structure is such that not even those who we'd typically think of as "in control" of the system can really control what it does – they can only choose to do the things that constitute the system's particular form of "control". Or, they can choose to not do those things, in which case they won't any longer find themselves parts of the hegemonic sector; and there will always be others willing to take their spots. Either way, the system, so long as it can continue being reproduced, never fundamentally changes except insofar as it worsens. If the "gods-on-Earth" were really godlike, they could change the system at will into anything they wanted. They're much closer to managers than gods.

Since the late Cold War, at the latest, the mechanisms have certainly been in place for the entire global system to be looted by the hegemonic sector, as it has been quite impressively throughout the past three-plus decades. Again, we find this exact state-of-affairs to be perfectly visible in some sense on the surface, albeit obfuscated in the entire remaining suffocating fog of useless information. In "The News", the corporate media machine tells us to our face that "the top 1% of wealth-earners own 52% of the wealth". But the fact is presented devoid of all historical context and resultantly seems to be a situation that fell from the sky, with no discernible human cause and in turn no remedy. It's of course left out that this should've been perfectly expected based on every major economic policy passed by the U.S. Government, affecting the entire planet, for over thirty years. And it absolutely can't be recognized that this state-of-affairs is precisely what the *Power*-structure means when it says – as it always does – it's "at war" – as it always is – to protect "our national security".

Once more we're struck with the usefulness of trying to look at things as simply as possible within an endlessly intricate context. If you want to know precisely what "national security" means, just think of a "security system". A security system, meaning the electronic alarm apparatus sold as a service to "Homeowners" in the contemporary dominant culture, has one objective, which is to protect a person (and his family) and his wealth. Well, this is exactly what the thing called "national security" is meant to do, only on the largest possible scale.

We can only recognize what's on the surface as a manifestation of the truth so long as we keep in mind that when it's on the surface it must be presented devoid of all temporal context longer than the prior few days, and that the propaganda squads cling to fictions as much as is possible. For example, you can't disprove "They hate us for our freedom". You can only try and prove that "they" hate "us" for other reasons.

But insofar as you're trying to prove that, you're somewhere unconsciously accepting that this line wasn't designed specifically to distract, whereas that's precisely what it was designed to do. Of course those truly responsible for running the *Power*-structure know "they" don't hate "us" for "our freedom": the real issue is, the "First World" system needs war to survive, and thus it needs the victims of war. Since the war machine exists simply to maintain its own existence – in reality, *it* doesn't need the "noble purpose" to go to war, the system's sense of morality does; the war machine *does* need the system's sense of morality – the greatest victims of "First World" warfare are the general populations in those countries that have committed no greater crime than being born in territories where desired resources happen to be located. So if there's really a "they" and an "us", and "they" really hate "us", the reason is because the system associated with "us" murders the individuals associated with "they" by the millions, in order to destroy their homes and steal their resources, so we can burn up as much oil as possible as quickly as possible, because the hegemons never had any more imaginative ideas. And when you think about it that's actually a better justification for hatred than most. More to the point, it's an excellent reason for the *Power*-structure to obfuscate the nature of its activities.

II

The self-regenerating geostrategic money machine

The specifically contemporary version of national security primarily creates a safe environment for protecting monetary wealth, which as we know isn't actual wealth. Rather, money is a tool used for instrumentalizing actual wealth: the best such tool in history. The technology ultimately used to create money – not the technology used to make currency, but rather the technology that makes debt valuable in the form of cash, within a holistic politicoeconomic system – is finance.

Since almost no one actually understands money, virtually everyone overlooks the fact that the very existence of a monetized economic system can't be some politically neutral state-of-affairs that falls into place on its own, but quite oppositely requires the most politically intentional maneuvers to constantly be taken, on behalf of highly specific kinds of interests. How especially true this is, then, in a totally monetized system, and one that comprises an entire planet holding over 7 billion human beings. To reiterate, the proper name for making one bank ultimately subordinate to the control of another, most *Powerful* bank – the latter being a central bank – is *'mobilization'*. For its existence to be possible, the central bank must be able to mobilize, i.e., utilize, the funds of its subordinate banks, which are typically, in the contemporary setting, all the banks within the central bank's national jurisdiction.

In a national setting, then, in order for the central bank to mobilize all the funds of its subordinate banks, there has to be a common national money supply, which means a common national debt. How does that happen? First of all we must acknowledge that it can only happen within the realities of an existing politicoeconomic system. And the only such real-world setting within which modern/contemporary central banks have ever existed is the one that has been dominated by the Western-originated international war system. According to an interesting pamphlet drawn up by the J.P. Morgan Company during World War One, for which it almost single-handedly managed the financing on the Allies' side, the national debt always soars highest during times of war, and they were in the best position to know.[cdxlix] I didn't need to consult that source to know this information, but as Walter Lippmann (the spokesman for the Morgan-managed *Power-structure's* view on "public opinion") said, "…until we know what others think they know, we cannot truly understand their acts".[cdl] So, not only is it true that World War One was made possible by the establishment of the Federal Reserve: just as importantly, the Federal Reserve was only made possible in the first place because of World War One. As a result of the Allies' victory, the United States was awarded the most hegemonic creditor status in human history – until the same status it would enjoy during and after World War Two – a status that, in a comprehensively financialized global arena, was tantamount to having sole say-so in public affairs. More generally, in the whole sociohistorical evolution of civilizations before the global civilization, this was as close to total monopoly control over humans' lives as could be achieved by other humans.

But monopoly control *in relation to other human life*, from a cultural perspective, is one thing. Control in relation to the whole living planet is quite another, and it happens to be the thing that matters most: the specifically ecological perspective. I believe the taking and perpetuating of monopolistic control over all other human beings, although in one sense the basis for an incomparable degree of cultural stability, is in another sense the phenomenon most responsible for driving what is, as has long since become totally obvious, complete ecological instability.

The key to understanding lies in the way the hegemonic sector must exercise its cultural monopoly. To begin, for the entire span from the earliest origins of World War One – the wars of 1898-99 – until the end of World War Two, on an international level, all across Western civilization, the ruling class (the hegemonic sector) was walking a tightrope. The entire system was breaking down before the hegemons' eyes.[cdli] Not because they didn't have essentially total social control, but because they *did*.[cdlii] As it turns out, total social control is quite a difficult thing to perpetually maintain: but difficult from a mainly ecological rather than a mainly politicoeconomic perspective; and in turn, from an eco-psychological perspective, the perspective most properly relevant to the conquest syndrome.

The span between the wars of 1898-99 and the official beginning of the Cold War in 1947 consisted of one of the greatest eco-psychological transitions so far in human history. Think of the conquest syndrome as a complex adaptive system that's both a part of and parallel to the much larger complex adaptive system of urbanized humanity. In this sense, the conquest syndrome, just like any evolving entity, seeks to stay alive, and it's in seeking to stay alive that the conquest syndrome adapts. This isn't a metaphor: the conquest syndrome literally fights to stay alive in the form of the hegemonic sector, which always fights to maintain its own interests. Thus, at the highest levels of the cultural pyramid, where the conquest syndrome always ultimately originates, the syndrome is completely interchangeable with the sector comprising the individuals who run it. So we can in fact observe parts of the adaptive process itself in the form of collective (organized) human action.

In part 1 of our journey, I made mention of the fact that throughout almost the entire history of civilizations, it was more or less impossible for elites (or anyone else) to know that all civilizations ultimately collapsed. I believe this was one of the things that changed most with the contemporary world. Or at least, I believe the *implications* of the fact (all civilizations collapse), if not the fact as I explicitly state it, were made conscious to the elites – made conscious roughly in this form: "we are simply parasites on everyone else, and sooner or later they're going to realize it". They felt their days were numbered – in other words, the conquest syndrome felt its days were numbered. This led to the states-of-affairs wherein industrialization in general and industrialization in the contemporary world (the global civilization) in particular were both quintessentially stories of the reactionaries becoming totally proactive for the first time ever. The defining characteristic of "proactive reactionaries" has had its greatest significance insofar as it has led to such rapidly proliferating long historical turning points: so many thresholds passed in so little time. Above all else, the contemporary world is the processual playing out of the passing of specifically cultural evolutionary thresholds.

This has unequaled significance in relation to all contemporary history because *once an evolutionary threshold is passed in the first place*, the new structural form reached with passage can and does subsequently progress unto the highest heights ("the logical extreme") that are energetically possible for that structure. In fact, such progression is possible *only* once some original threshold is passed. In the presently relevant case, when the deliberate imposition of a global conquest culture happened for the first time, by definition it happened in a world where there was not yet a global conquest culture. As such, it wasn't at all clear what was going on until the process leading ultimately to the establishment of a global conquest culture – the initial process of globalization in the second half of period five (1898-1945), which led to the structure of a global civilization in periods six (1947-1991) and seven (1995-?) – was fully established. And it couldn't have been completely clear what was going on until the global conquest culture itself, the global civilization, was fully established.

But these processes did become fully established; by 1919 in the first case and 1945 in the second, respectively when the "informal" Anglo-American alliance of the hegemonic sector initially started dictating terms to the rest of the planet, and when the U.S.-produced dual nuclear holocaust in Japan did the job of dictating terms to the rest of the planet on its own. In being fully established – and here's what truly makes the passing of those initial thresholds so immensely consequential – these processes, at first just the forging of new global paths, in the end created a fully individuated global entity: the urbanized globality, one planetary civilization. After that, the central process wouldn't change direction: it would simply grow evermore quickly until it reached a maximum point of acceleration, after which it could only start to collapse. During this time, as a result, all other human processes became trapped within the wholly singularized cultural environment of inevitable global collapse.

At the point when the individuated structure, having just become individuated, started growing, the fact of its existence gained the potential to become completely clear to individuals living in it. To understand what I mean by "completely clear", consider how I've equated the whole process of contemporary history with 'globalization', while at the same time only defining the process from 1947 through the present with 'the global civilization'. Human beings went from living in a globalizing but still pre-global world – a world where human beings were technically becoming globally connected by a single trade system, but where this process itself remained almost entirely beneath the surface – to a world where the now fully singular trade system, because it existed in the particular context of global industrialization, made the world an explicitly singular space. However, for exactly the reason that there's so much intrinsic unity constituting the existence of a global civilization, the hegemonic sector has done everything in its *Power* to prevent from being actualized "the potential" for the process of globalization "to become completely clear": total communal unification is simply unacceptable in a setting of private exploitation of public wealth, so cultural conflict must be deliberately instigated. Division must be consciously spread.

Notice, though, that it's primarily cultural conflict going on, not primarily politicoeconomic conflict – cultural division being spread, not mainly politicoeconomic division. Actually, it's *sub*cultural conflict; all war is between entities within the very same culture. In what sense is this true? Or even if it's true, what does it matter? For instance, does it mean there's no real conflict going on in the contemporary world, no real war?

Here's what I believe happened by 1945 at the latest: the hegemonic sector realized an all-important fact, and it would do everything in its *Power* to keep the fact to itself, for as long as it possibly could. The physical warfare system had reached an expansive limit, and as such it could no longer be allowed to evolve uncontrollably as it always had. There were essentially two options. Either warfare could be phased out altogether; or there could be a replacement for physical warfare that fulfilled the same psychological functions, within the new physical constraints.[cdliii]

This immediately gave rise to the *conscious* – intentional – implementation of the psychological warfare system, which was meant to be like a new kind of game that only the most "select" individuals could play. In fact Prouty emphasizes that the best way to think of what he calls "The Secret Team" is exactly what the label states: a "team", just like those that compete in professional sports.[cdliv] Think of things like "controlling a Power with a position on the UN Security Council" and/or "Power's possession of a nuclear weapon" as the membership fees necessary for becoming part of "the ownership" of one of the teams. Only those in the hegemonic sector who are most *Powerful* are fit to play the positions of owners, the ones who compete with each other in the sense that their respective teams compete with other owners' teams. But their bodies are never on the line. To them, war is truly just a game; albeit one more serious than anything else.

This reminds me of something else Lippmann said in the time immediately after the World War One "Peace Talks". First I must mention the context. All human beings, he has just asserted, operate "as if on a leash", solely within the ideological confines of their particular "social set", as Lippmann calls it.[cdlv] In my perspective, the "social set" is the fundamental unit of the cultural pyramid, the psychological counterpart to the material settlement hierarchy (social structure) forming the politicoeconomic system's central basis. "Our social set," he says, "consists of those who figure as people in the phrase 'people are saying'; they are the people whose approval matters most intimately to us."[cdlvi] In other words, they're those whose faces we can see most clearly when we picture "the herd".

Wherever there's the herd, there are always herd leaders. Lippmann calls them "the social leaders": he says they're "weighted with the ultimate eugenic responsibility."[cdlvii] Remember, this was long before World War Two, before the Nazis caused eugenics and ethnic cleansing to fall out of style with the Anglo-American oriented ruling class – in public discussion, anyway.[cdlviii]

Lippmann continues to remark that, uniquely, the social leaders are responsible not only for knowing the nature of their own sets; they also need "a persistent sense of [their] place in the hierarchy of sets." The social leaders are responsible for making sure every individual in the set knows his or her place in the world-at-large – the world structured psychologically by the "hierarchy of sets", which is more or less what I call the cultural pyramid, and which, Lippmann adds, "is bound together by the social leaders."[cdlix] Finally, he writes that a rare handful of sets are so significant to the culture as a whole, all the other sets ("subordinates") copy them; and what he says next is what directly relates to my pointing to the hegemonic sector as the container of the psywar teams' owners. At the very highest level, Lippmann says, there's a certain most important social set, the significance of which "comes from the fact that here at last the distinction between public and private affairs practically disappears. The private affairs of this set are public matters, and public matters are its private, often its family affairs." Above all, "its power in foreign affairs is always very great, and in wartime its prestige is enormously enhanced."[cdlx]

This is an essentially perfect reflection of my concept of "elite factions" that, collectively, constitute the hegemonic sector, the context containing the owners of the teams: for the *Power*-structure holding the global civilization in place to run "properly" – by which I simply mean for the system to work as it does – there has to be some highest point on the cultural pyramid where there's no distinction "between public and private affairs". Its individuals comprise what is by necessity the most "exclusive" social milieu on the planet, and since their private affairs, that is, their livelihoods, involve the factors with the greatest possible consequences for everything else in the system, they have the most absolute *Power* in decision-making. In the particular sociohistorical context of the contemporary world, this last fact happens to make their "set" the most *Powerful* social milieu in human history. Now we're face-to-face with that most troublesome word, "conspiracy". I've largely tried to avoid it. Not because I think it's impossible for "conspiracies" to be significant factors in shaping history, just that they're not relevant to certain discussions where the word is typically brought up, almost always purely as an *ad hominem* attack – "Your ideas are conspiracy theories, therefore you're crazy; therefore, your writing is irrelevant."[cdlxi]

From my perspective, though, there's nothing any "conspiracy theorist" could say that suggests a system more amoral than what's apparent simply by studying what's actually on the surface, so long as you study it from a long historical perspective. If we take issue with "conspiracy theory", then – at least concerning the most representative "bad" examples of "conspiracy theory" – it shouldn't necessarily be for the facts "conspiracy theorists" use. The facts easily discovered about contemporary politics from an overwhelming number of definitively conventional sources are just as horrifying and outrageous as those cited by the seemingly most far-fetched "conspiracy theorists". As with facts presented in all writings, we should only take issue with "conspiracy theorists" over their facts if the facts they cite are clearly either totally fabricated or deliberately framed in misleading ways.

We should take issue with individual "conspiracy theorists" based mainly on their *philosophies*, rather than their facts. For instance, what almost all mainstream "Left-wing" commentators say when they denounce "conspiracy theorists" is something along these lines: "You think that if we just get rid of a few bad apples, everything will be fine." Now, on the one hand, I'll assert as much as anyone else – we must set our sights on much more than "a few bad apples"; the system itself is the problem, and especially the *Power*-structure that the system revolves around. But in relation to whether or not there's a miniscule group making decisions in secret on a global scale, decisions primarily meant to perpetuate an all-encompassing environment of deception, I find the argument of "we can't just get rid of a few bad apples" to be completely beside the point. Indeed, the hegemonic sector must exist precisely *on account of* the comprehensive *Power*-structure it's responsible for managing, and that *Power*-structure is possible precisely insofar as it operates in the form of a top-down command hierarchy ultimately run by its smallest (topmost) milieu.

Thus, most specifically, if we're to take issue with any individual text on the grounds that it constitutes a "conspiracy theory", it should be because of its philosophy of the *Power*-structure. It should be about the extent to which the individual writer presents the "conspiracy" either as being detached from any real-world structural framework on the one hand, or as a symptom of the system as a whole, on the other. This is why I don't think the notion of "conspiracy" is very relevant to the present text, as I've been singularly focused on the system as a whole and its structural framework for our entire journey. However, in recognition of the typical mode of discourse in the existent world, I must explain why individuals that would likely be called "conspiracy theorists" by most contemporary commentators wrote some of my most important sources (although the vast majority of my sources come from "mainstream" writers).

First, I believe that the writer's philosophy of the *Power*-structure isn't just relevant to how one should judge the historical writings of a "conspiracy theorist". In fact, as every historian is always writing about the *Power*-structure whether he or she knows it or not, I believe it's the most determinative element shaping all historiographical writing, and in turn has the greatest significance for our understanding – or misunderstanding – of history. As this fact is largely overlooked, it almost always leads to historical misunderstanding. If you don't know that what you're looking at is a *Power*-structure, and/or if you don't know what a *Power*-structure is, then how can you ultimately understand the goings-on related to it?

If we consider what commentators pejoratively mean when they refer to "conspiracy theorists", they're usually focused on two authorial traits: (1) the writer attributes the worst social problems to the evil motivations of those individuals truly (and secretly) in *Power*; and, relatedly, (2) the writer attributes a seemingly limitless ability to manipulate events, i.e., "total control", to such individuals at the highest levels of *Power*. These two things are typically supposed by objectors to be completely incompatible with an ability to see things from a structural perspective. I agree that, concerning how the two characteristics usually manifest in reality, the writers who display these characteristics often fail to provide enough insight regarding how their arguments fit in with some bigger cultural picture. But there are still scenarios where even those seemingly most extreme ideas put forth by individuals viewing things out-of-context can be situated within a proper frame-of-reference.

Additionally, a structural perspective of humanity, if it's to be an accurate reflection of reality, can itself only be one of the key dimensions under consideration. Concerning what I've argued for, there are interlocking metaphysical and experiential aspects that must be incorporated. For instance, we can only construct concepts (metaphysical) of amorality and morality within the structural frameworks of texts – whatever the media format – and a narrativistic framework (experiential) best serves the specific subject matter.

Moreover, since everything written in a text, in order to appropriately reflect reality, must be considered and constructed within a holistic context,[cdlxii] and as this is true in a historical work more than any other kind, it's obviously never necessary for a historian to completely agree with every thing written in another text in order to utilize evidence from the text. If this were true, it would be practically impossible to usefully cite any other work as evidence – in which case we might as well consider all scholarship useless. Actually, it's precisely the job of the historian to give all evidence equal consideration to begin with, whether or not he or she believes him- or herself to be in complete agreement with every thing written in the text where the evidence is found.

That's to begin with. What one then must do in judging any piece of evidence is to evaluate the holistic context in which the evidence is presented: and this is exactly how, in a historical text, we start to determine the writer's philosophy of the *Power*-structure. Now, concerning what I mean by "philosophy of the *Power*-structure", it's not an option for a historian to *not* have a philosophy of the *Power*-structure – since *Power*-structures are always the ultimate frames-of-reference for historians, however unreflectively, the most one can say is that a given historian has an undeveloped philosophy of the *Power*-structure. My thinking on it is, since you must have such a philosophy no matter what, if you wish to study history properly, you're better off explicitly addressing that philosophy than you would be if you left it unexamined.

Civilizational history can in fact be *best* understood through development of a comprehensive philosophy of the *Power*-structure, which is precisely why I wrote the present text as I did. The *Power*-structure is a sociological constant necessary for devising any remotely useful definition of 'civilizations', both in terms of comparing different civilizations as well as comparing different eras within a single civilization's existence. As Pierre Bourdieu said – specifically in relation to sociology – "It is because there are constants that we can understand things."[cdlxiii]

The *Power*-structure isn't just any constant, but has been the ever-present constant evolving core driving the whole history of civilizations: always in the middle of everything. Since there's still a civilization in existence, and since, as I've argued, civilizations have been evolving at ever-faster rates throughout history, finalizing in the existent world's maximum sociohistorical velocity, we should expect nothing besides the most evolved *Power*-structure in human history – and that's exactly what there seems to be. Proceeding from this initial hunch, we then try to figure out exactly what the *Power*-structure entails by considering all of the best available historical evidence. Trying to understand the history of the global civilization is thus like doing history through archaeology. We have to keep looking at every single thing we know to be there beyond doubt, we have to look at an enormous past record of how those types of things emerge, and, knowing that there is in the end only one metanarrative, we have to try to establish the most realistic broad chronology by imagining the likeliest interconnections capable of joining together all known artifacts.

Based on how the ever-increasingly and finally totally Western-dominated history of capitalism had gone until 1898, how it went from 1898 to 1947, and how it is now, even as there's so much unknown in between 1947 and the immediately present historical moment, we can still say the most important – and by far the most tragic – thing about contemporary history, which is at the same time also the simplest. Western civilization, the civilization that spawned total planetary imperialism, didn't stop evolving, but kept evolving unto a global, nuclear scale, and did so primarily via the military hegemony of the United States. Everything we imagine about history from the Cold War onward must fit within the paradigm of that same old Western imperialism – but we must also keep in mind that this imperialism was now at a point where it was evolving into wholly new, maximally intensifying global circumstances. So many of those examples so often labeled "conspiracy" in the existent world are simply this process's being nakedly revealed, a revelation the system has always fought viciously to minimize, especially in its imperial heartland: the result being the lethal misunderstanding of its own history at every level of the dominant culture.

Looking beyond the propagandized understanding of history – with the establishment of the global civilization, the hegemonic sector's direction to its agents working closest to the spotlight must've been something along the lines of, "Set up the most complex imaginable legal system, and then corrupt it." Because this is exactly how the system in the present, most evolved phase seems to really work, in relation to the United States and its global behavior: the most *Powerful* individuals make the laws so that they and their cohorts can break them – for profit. The "War on Drugs" is perhaps the best example. Whose decision was it, ultimately, for the United States Government to do everything within its *Power* to provide logistical support for the global drug trade, while at the same time, facilitating drug law enforcement paramilitaries (police forces) with global reach alongside penal codes for narcotics offenses that would eventually yield the world's largest prison population? Whose decision ensured that these "policies" (war tactics) would be detrimental mainly to impoverished ethnic and cultural minorities, those sectors of the population *always* bearing Western imperialism's brunt?

Whose decisions, over and over again, allow such tragedies to be perpetuated to their greatest logical extreme? Whoever they are, they weren't elected, they hold positions of *Power* that the public can/will never know about, and they operate in ways that are, by design, directly opposed to the system's publicized goals. Moreover, they transcend all conventionally perceived boundaries of opposition – "Cops vs. Drug Lords", "Democrats vs. Republicans", "Intelligence Agents vs. Terrorists"; they exist throughout every presidential administration; they effortlessly float between jobs in business and jobs in government.

Again, you can call it "a conspiracy"; to a certain extent, it doesn't matter what word we use. On the other hand, as I said at the very beginning of this narrative, I believe 'conspiracy' is a word best befitting this phenomenon in its individual instances. Certainly, individual, hyperspecialized examples of what are, in light of how the existent dominant culture presents itself, complete contradictions to what the system legally intends to accomplish, can rightly be labeled conspiracies. What we're dealing with, instead, is something that's at once much larger, much more dangerous – and from a long historical perspective, much more ordinary. We're dealing with something legitimately sanctioned by the *Power*-structure, whereas the legal definition of conspiracy tacitly implies a normal crime, with normal potential to be prosecuted. In reality, we're dealing with what we've already seen in a thousand different ways to be the one fundamental purpose behind all civilization-State-complexes, that aspect most indispensable to their very survival throughout all civilizational history: geostrategy.

Let's forget for a second *what everyone says* about the global civilization: let's just focus on the material pattern, the archaeology of the dead culture as it still presently is in the existent world. In that case, we see the global geography filled with nothing besides industrialized nations, and those nations controlled by nothing besides militaries. And yet we see relatively few things that look like wars as conventionally understood, i.e., two States or coalitions of States fighting episodically.

But we do see something else involving these militaries, which looks exactly like another militaristic function essential to all prior civilizations: occupation, colonization's worst symptom. This is best thought of as perpetual war: perpetual conquest.[cdlxiv] In the global civilization it exists on the most ubiquitous possible scale. We'd do well here to recall what colonial occupation was all about in history before the global civilization. In all times earlier than the middle contemporary world (1947-1991), colonization invariably had to do with the conquest culture (the occupying civilization-State-complex) demanding forcibly something from its victims (the individuals living in the colonized territory), something the conquerors "needed" – in the sense that the "something" was a requirement for perpetuating the conquest culture.

Few things that look like full-blown wars, but an all-encompassing climate of never-ending warfare – some of the bloodiest examples of which the State itself, without a shred of shame, calls "Low Intensity Conflict".[cdlxv] Really, each militarized action is merely one particle of an overall intensity that's practically infinite, apportioned throughout constant rapid microstrikes all over the planet, always there to let the global population know who's boss: warfare taken to where there seems to be no limit, a constant posture of violence imposed by a single shape-shifting act of war distributed in every of the planetary system's molecular actions. *Every single thing competes for our hearts and minds*, and an indispensable part of this is the demonstration of force: the "stick", to the "carrot" that is the system's array of innumerable consumptive items awarded to its good citizens. In the end there's just a single population and a single *Power*-structure running it. To the system, the population – the whole population – is always nothing more than an insurgency lying in wait, subconsciously pregnant with some potential to disrupt the forever-tenuous yet never truly in danger until it runs out of resources status quo. Resultantly, the system runs ops on us, all of us, in every thing it does; a self-regenerating geostrategic machine pushed to the farthest brink of its capacity. It has worked insofar as only a part of it, and numerically (population-wise) a very small part of it, is intentionally fraudulent. But at the same time, the fraud couldn't possibly work without the comprehensive structural framework of the holistic system, which it parasitically penetrates towards the end of transmitting its globally totalized corporate-capitalist conquest syndrome. In turn, everything within the fraud's jurisdiction, which in a maximally intensified global civilization must be everything in humanity's planetary environment, becomes at the very least an indirect fraud, as well.[cdlxvi]

We can look at all history of civilizations prior to the global civilization as reflecting an implicit alliance between all States as they exist at the publicly visible level, which in modern history only started to become explicit with industrialization, and which only became a totally-encompassing cultural environment once the global civilization emerged and started evolving. The *Power*-structure present in every civilization in one form or another had invariably sustained flawed systems, to an extent varying along with each different civilization. But in history since the beginning of the modern world, the system didn't start to become mostly fraudulent until industrialization, and it didn't start to become totally fraudulent until globalization. We're now at what I believe to be the last phase of the process: the system won't tolerate any greater degree of fraudulence; and yet it has so totally maximized its potential for growth based on fraud, it possesses no other behavioral possibilities.

Before the global civilization, States were implicitly allied insofar as they all played the same war-trade game. Even two avowed "Enemy" States, which were enemies on the surface insofar as they competed for the same resources, had common interests in a deeper sense: they were both motivated by a desire to perpetuate the same war-trade environment. It's only in the holistic war-trade environment, after all – it's only in a totally urbanized ecosystem – that geostrategy works, just as the war-trade environment only works due to *geostrategic mindsets*. Civilizations and conquest syndromes are typically symbiotic with each other and parasitic in relation to everything else.

Thus, from the dual perspective of the civilization and the conquest syndrome, it doesn't matter, and has never mattered, what conquest syndrome you inject into the civilization, or what civilization you inject the conquest syndrome into – so long as the symbiotic relationship works to perpetuate the parasitic relationship of the civilization and the conquest syndrome in relation to the planet as a whole. From a material perspective, that is, and what better perspective to use to assess the last vestiges of the religion of materialism run amok, all a civilization needs in order to exist is a conquest syndrome that can operate it in the prevailing sociohistorical conditions.

In shifting the alliance between all States from implicit to explicit, the hegemonic sector found the best strategy in human history for perpetuating its own existence. It was too good at its job, in fact. It seems that the globalization conquest syndrome, in creating the presently dead but still existing civilization, evolved itself out of existence.

Let's revisit the notion that each stage of civilizational evolution is like an audition for the next stage. We know that after their start as the merchant traders of late medieval Europe, the financial patriarchs would become, via the Columbian conquest, equal partners with the noble patriarchs in the early modern world's hegemonic sector, with the former rapidly overtaking the latter throughout the period. This culminated with the combination of nationalism and industrialization – collectively, the bourgeoisie revolution – starting at the end of the 18th- and filling up the entire 19th-century. Then there's our world, which started in 1947. The transition in between the end of the bourgeoisie revolution and the beginning of the global civilization was a transition between different niches of dominance within globalizing Western capitalism. Two observers who cultivated some of the best holistic global historical perspectives in the late 20th-century explained the whole scenario essentially as the takeover of the nobility by the financial and industrial elites (end of 18th- through 19th-centuries), and the subsequent takeover of the original financial and industrial elites by the contemporary corporate elites.[cdlxvii] From my perspective, the corporate elites were auditioning for positions of dominance in the global civilization in the years spanning 1898 to 1947.

The individuals who pointed this out weren't, say, European Marxists, but Americans very much within the contemporary *Power*-structure's mainstream. Now we can see a perfect real-world example of how necessary it is for a writer to start off from an existing empirical basis in sociohistorical thinking, and *then* to depart to one's individualized analytic direction. No matter what our ideology is, in other words, we know there was only one process constituting human history – what really happened – and thus two or more individuals studying history must be able to see the same thing from different perspectives. The philosophies don't have to be identical for there to be many of the same facts; indeed, for there to be the real things we can rightly call "philosophies" and "facts" existing in the same world, the identical set of facts can never reproduce the exact same philosophy. However much overlap there is between the respective philosophies of two human beings, they'll always be at least a little bit different.

Interestingly, one of the individuals was a way ahead of his time forerunner of existent "world historians", someone quite aptly referred to as a "macrohistorian",[cdlxviii] Carroll Quigley. The other, even more interestingly, wasn't a historian at all, but a systems analyst and engineer, Buckminster Fuller. In the contexts I'm referring to, Quigley was writing about the global economy as of 1964, and Fuller was writing about it as of 1981. I don't care in the least how you classify the ideologies of these two men, and anyway I think there's very little significant difference between essentially all contemporary mainstream ideologies that could serve as categories. Actually, I find these two writers so striking because their backgrounds were almost identical in terms of how completely inside the establishment they seem to have been, considering at the same time how singularly focused they were on contemporary humanity as a phenomenon revolving entirely around a global war-trade politicoeconomic system. It's especially impressive, of course, concerning how relatively early were the dates of their economic pronouncements in the two relevant texts, suggesting that the writers truly were at the vanguard of establishment thought.

The two texts were at once treatises on humanity's cultural evolution and broadly sweeping "macrohistories" – metanarratives. Although most historians would certainly consider these texts purely "secondary sources", I disagree. In general, I feel that there's much unnecessary confusion related to what primary and secondary sources are. No text is in-and-of-itself a primary source or a secondary source. What makes a text "primary" or "secondary" is how the scholar chooses to use it: either as a direct record of the sociohistorical process one is writing about (primary); or as the useful perspective of another researcher on the same or a similar process (secondary).

However, I also feel that this by no means needs to be an "either/or" situation: a single source can be used both as a primary and secondary source in the scope of the same work; we can call a text being used in this way, simply, a "primary-secondary source". Only the unimaginative title is something I made up. Hyperspecialists of "intellectual history", in fact, mainly use sources in such fashion.[cdlxix] For a text to be utilized as a primary-secondary source, it needs to be used as a model analytical work and also, owing to its status as such a work, as a record of a certain chronologically-dependent mindset posited by the historian.

So Quigley's text, *Tragedy & Hope*, and Fuller's text, *Critical Path*, besides being analytical commentaries on humanity's cultural and in particular technological evolution, are also, as documents, records of a mindset directly relevant to the sociohistorical context the authors were situated within. Most of all, this is true on account of their personal backgrounds. Both were ideal examples of one of the most sociohistorically representative sectors of the dominant culture: that miniscule portion of the external *Power*-structure closest to the cultural pyramid's internal apex. Whether we like observing how they typically think or not, we must admit that the intellectual establishment contains the only individuals with both the experience *and* the capability to reveal how elites are actually thinking at a given historical moment. And elites – in the contemporary world, most of all – as a whole embody a quintessentially psychologically-based phenomenon, so we can best understand them through evidence of psychologically-based phenomena. We'd be remiss not to examine what they consciously and unconsciously reveal in the documentary record.

In the specific cases of Quigley and Fuller, we find the contemporary geostrategic mindset on full display; but it's the geostrategic mindset being viewed from a critical – although extremely non-confrontational – perspective. In each case, it's probably accurate to look at the very act of documenting the mindset in textual form as the most critical aspect, although Fuller's text is much more overtly critical than Quigley's. I think this can be explained at least in part by the specific eighteen or so years separating the writing of each text: what Quigley already saw in 1964 could be seen all the more clearly by the audience in 1981, which, in addition to the writer's own naturally distinct philosophical approach, was what led Fuller to be even bolder in his analysis.

Prior to total industrial warfare and thus the true origins of full mass industrialization, eighteen years were not many; although there were also great distinctions between different preindustrial eras. A much greater "amount of history" certainly happened in eighteen years within Western civilization around the year 1700, for instance, than during the same length of time in the West around the year 1400. But at the inception of the late modern world, the world of mass industrialized Powers (period five, 1865-1945), Western history became an exponentially-accelerating process; and once the global civilization emerged in full (period six, 1947-1991), the *whole planetary history* became an exponentially-accelerating process. Thus, although it obviously can't be directly quantified, eighteen years at this point within the global civilization (1964-81) was surely qualitatively comparable to around a couple of centuries in the early modern world (period four; 1492-1776), and comparable to at least half-a-millennium at any point prior.

Naturally, the logical focal point for making comparisons is the intercivilizational structure (or universal civilizational structure, depending on the era), and the typical length of time it takes to rise and fall. Fuller made his ominous pronouncements in 1981 (the book was published in 1983), by which time Quigley was already deceased. But despite the most unusual degree of sociohistorical process that happened in the eighteen years separating their analyses, and although ostensibly coming from entirely different scholarly fields – and Fuller wasn't even technically a scholar in the particularized sense of an officially-sanctioned academic – the two men wrote from an almost identical perspective, the main difference being that Fuller wrote from a standpoint much farther along the path to extinction.

What made their viewpoints almost identical? In my mind, there were three central factors: (1) as I already said, coming from the establishment themselves, they were privy to the ways in which other elites thought, which largely includes knowing the types of things they thought about; (2) they thought about the contemporary world in terms of its place within a long historical lineage of evolving cultural systems; and (3) they seemed to be certain that the contemporary civilization would soon collapse if drastic measures weren't taken. Each of these things is of course interrelated with the others.

They may not have used the label "complex adaptive system", but that's essentially what they saw all historical humanity as, and to differing extents each saw humanity, during its phase that I call the contemporary world, as a global complex adaptive system. And, since they saw humanity as a global complex adaptive system, and specifically as an imperial example of such a system, they could see that human beings realistically had, for the first time in history, only two choices: change the system, or soon enough, become extinct. Quigley implicitly suggested this and in one part of the massive text mentioned it outright, already in 1964 (the text was published in 1966).[cdlxx] Fuller's 1981 statement was straightforwardly based entirely on this premise, and he actually suggested his own solution to the problem. He said the system could be saved – but the transformation would have to be started immediately, and implemented by 1989. Fuller died in 1983, the same year the text was published, at the age of 94.[cdlxxi] Needless to say, the transformation he suggested wasn't implemented.

Most significantly, I believe they could so easily make this association between humanity as a global complex adaptive system and species' collapse, i.e., extinction, only because they were so close to the epicenter of officialdom – the point where the distinction between public and private ultimately disappears and a single social set rules the world. In other words, they *knew* what elites actually did, and how they seemed to think about their actions: knowing the contemporary elite mindset experientially, they could easily understand it. Understanding both it and the world, they could see the connections between officialdom and the world it runs with a clarity rarely possible in the global civilization.

Therefore, their perspectives were so similar in scope and makeup because they were looking at the identical thing from a vantage point largely the same, save for the separation of eighteen of the most exponentially accelerated sociohistorical years in human history. This surface disparity was however merely greater proof of much deeper similarities: history was so absurdly accelerated and had superficially changed so much solely due to the fact that human history in civilizations unfolds through complex adaptive systems. That is, things in general can only change so rapidly when certain special things stay more or less the same.

Essentially, then, between 1964, when Quigley saw humanity as being at a global crossroads, and 1981, when Fuller saw humanity headed for all-encompassing annihilation in a matter of not many decades, individual human beings alive throughout those years had at least the potential to see first-hand, if they viewed the world in a certain way, a civilization's self-destruction. Not only that, but the civilization in question was the only global civilization in human history. The "certain special things" alluded to above made this possible. These were the particular civilization's sociohistorically-determined adaptive mechanisms, what I call the repositories.

Indeed, Fuller called the introduction to his text "Twilight of the Power Structures", and it would be hard to find a more concise description of the present phase of human history. Individuals, even or especially individuals most inextricable from the establishment, have viewed the global civilization as a system inherently headed for self-destruction for at least five decades. In this light, the most unusual thing about the existent world isn't that the global civilization is collapsing, but the fact that it somehow still exists.

Maybe only Jean Baudrillard, the late 20th-century French theorist, came up with a phrase more fitting for current history, the title of an essay he published in 1983: "In the Shadow of the Silent Majorities". According to Baudrillard – obviously much more overtly a "critic" than the other two writers just mentioned – "the social" by the early '80s was already long dead, and "The only referent which still functions is that of the silent majority."[cdlxxii] In other words, in the "First World" of the global civilization, the only thing that still existed in terms of "community" was the voting mainstream, that entity that exists purely as a statistical entity; as "Opinion" which is constantly tracked, simultaneously directed through endless marketing polls. The world was no longer being properly represented via humanity's conceptualizations of it. There was now a world going through the latest version of the same old (imperial) motions, but a population – most namely, the "First World" mainstream and the elites everywhere else – completely cut off from that world, which as a replacement had some sort of imaginary world "simulated" to them through a gigantic complex of electronic media devices.[cdlxxiii]

Clearly this describes nothing besides public opinion/psywar taken to its greatest physical limits: the maximum capacity for any human ecosystem – hence, the outermost historical reaches for an eco-psychological syndrome. One of Baudrillard's analogies for what was the existing silent majority at the time he was writing is particularly apt, and actually fits the existent world all the more. He says "the mass" (the silent majority) resembles "those half-dead systems into which more energy is injected than is withdrawn."[cdlxxiv] I don't know whether or not he knew that this was literally what was going on in the global civilization – it was indeed quickly reaching the point, on a globally total level, where human beings would be investing more energy into their system, in the form of fossil fuels, than they got out of it. It seems unlikely that at the time, he would've known about the state-of-affairs explicitly in those terms, since relatively few individuals even in the existent world see this scenario clearly, and in our world it's happening much closer to the surface. But here is certainly a striking example of everything unconscious becoming conscious, of truth always finding a way to reveal itself however ubiquitous the deception and confusion in the world may be.

Over a decade before Baudrillard was writing, the United States, the most gargantuan Power in history, had reached its own peak in petroleum production. This meant that, no matter how much the oil industry invested in extraction within the geographical space of the contemporary United States, it would almost certainly never be able to produce more oil than had been pumped in the peak year (1970).[cdlxxv] October 1973 saw the emergence of the "Arab oil embargo"; in its wake, the global shadow government immediately (and quietly) linked the entire "First World" economy – demand – to OPEC – supply. Thus began what has been arguably the most insidious relationship between the U.S. and any of the monstrosities ("National States") it has created: America's support of Saudi Arabia.

Although at first glance it seems like the embargo was "terrible" for the American economy, we'd only be making a false comparison if we labeled it as such: we can't compare the resultant U.S. economy to that existing before what was, at the time, an unprecedentedly enormous price hike, because in general the global economy was starting to undergo a once-in-history transformation.[cdlxxvi] In this transformation, humanity began to be subjected to, for the first time in history, a *literally* (explicitly) singularized planetary economy,[cdlxxvii] in the form of a global State capitalist (fascist) market. We can only consider, then, what surely would've happened if the OECD-OPEC monopolistic automatic demand-supply machine hadn't been installed. The global civilization, as it had only just barely existed (between 1947 and 1973), would've collapsed.

So, for the hegemonic States leading the emergent global federation of nations, compared to total collapse of the status quo, the price hike was a far more favorable scenario – if you consider only what was preferable to the hegemonic nations, *and* only if you consider the most immediate short-term conditions. For the strategy to be implemented properly, the silent majorities of the "First World" nations had to be constantly convinced ("brainwashed") to consider *solely* what was favorable for themselves, and to only be concerned with the most immediate short-term conditions. Of course, this strategy had essentially already started to be implemented in the thick of the Cold War. But in the '80s it took on the most insidious "Individualist" form.

The strategy pursued would be one of cultivating systems in the imperial heartlands, especially the United States and United Kingdom, where as many individuals as possible could care solely for their own most unfettered instant gratification. The strategy was so good at what it was put in place to do because it barely needed to be consciously implemented, since the one premise it was built on was to play solely to humanity's most self-destructively alluring impulses. Clearly, it had to be consciously implemented from the very apex of the cultural pyramid, insofar as this translates to the top of the visible *Power*-structure. But besides that, there was next to no conscious coercion necessary, as falling prey to one's worst demons is the easiest thing for a human being to do. When it's not only sanctioned, not only encouraged, but actually *demanded* by the highest levels of officialdom – the sacred center – what real chances do the inherently self-absorbed inhabitants of dominant cultures have?

Yet, as is widely repeated in contemporary "serious discourse", "I was just following orders" isn't a legitimate justification for acting amorally.[cdlxxviii] To be sure, this moral axiom is never truly manifested in practice – but the concept itself is interesting and worthwhile. *Even* if someone is ordered to do something by a *Powerful* person, it states, one shouldn't consider that a free pass to ignore the moral responsibilities inherent in being a human.

The system itself would suffer a total breakdown if this rule of thought somehow started to be widely enforced in reality. People can say all they want about the Nuremberg Trials, etc., etc.; but essentially every single consequential action the existent State takes is ultimately premised on the notion that if someone *Powerful* orders you to do something, the normal rules of morality no longer apply. And this is really the same thing as saying the *Powerful* shouldn't be bound in any way by the normal rules of morality.

That's literally how the latest (and last, I predict) version of the cultural pyramid operates, via the hegemons' most prized possession, the global *Power*-structure. Not only can the *Powerful* do whatever they want: a decisive portion of the population morally sanctions practically every thing the *Powerful* do. How is this possible? It's simple; individuals don't really care what the *Power*-structure does, so long as they themselves are taken care of. And the far greater proportion of individuals who aren't taken care of, but are explicitly exploited – physically crushed and spiritually destroyed – don't have any say whatsoever in what the *Power*-structure does.

Individuals in the hegemonic sector know this, and if they didn't know it, the system couldn't "thrive" as it currently does,[cdlxxix] as it has throughout the contemporary world, and as past incarnations of *Power*-structures did throughout history. The inhuman fact is that the system can only continue to exist for as long as the "good citizens", the silent majorities of the Empires, are kept materially satisfied. This is how the hegemonic sector gets away with what it gets away with: it dispenses largesse. In the end, that's all civilizations have ever been about. Individuals who get rich off of the blood-drenched profits of war and trade exercise control over vast numbers of subordinates – "masses" – who emulate them, competing in a game reflective of the highest game played by the grand strategists. That goes on down the line of the pyramid, until you get to the designated dirt beneath, which the whole structure eternally stomps on.

The secret horror of civilizations was that civilization-State-complexes always lived off of their frontiers, no matter if they were originally founded upon "Monarchies"/ "Principalities", "Democracies"/ "Republics", or some combination of both. It could no longer remain a true secret, however, *once a civilization emerged with no physical frontiers*. This happened with the rise of the global civilization; but I don't think it was a surprise to the hegemons. I think they themselves saw it as the fundamental predicament with the potential to destroy their survival, and I think they've seen it as such for much longer than most people might think.[cdlxxx]

At the beginning of the 20th-century-beyond era (the wars of 1898-9), the international capitalist hegemons, for the first time ever a sector truly globalizing in nature, went about defining – and in doing so, inventing – their own frontiers. These have been more or less the same frontiers for the entire stretch since the end of World War One, with the modifications appearing almost entirely on the surface, never really in the internal structure. All we need to do to understand this is never lose track of the fact that the Cold War and the "Wars" sustaining drugs and terror have not just been departures from everything between the wars of 1898-9 and World War Two, but direct culminations as well. From a perspective keeping all prior history in mind, this is the most typical result we could've expected; so it's only difficult to accept when we compare the propagandized understanding of contemporary history perpetuated by the contemporary *Power*-structure to the actual details, which despite their honestly horrifying nature are nonetheless the actual details. The central event-cluster sequence of global industrialized warfare, in contributing to the perpetuation of the traditional Western imperial structure amidst new frontier-less circumstances, constantly changed the world surrounding the sequence, and thus the system unfolding through the sequence always had to adapt to the world it changed. Because the hegemons were so successful at influencing the changes that happened, and even more so at influencing humanity's understanding of the changes, nothing significant changed except insofar as there was an ever-faster growth rate unto ever-greater scales of destruction.

Aside from the obvious blunt physical destruction, an even worse destruction was happening mentally, related to humanity's understanding of its own world. This can be explained by the actions the imperial structure took in perpetuating itself, and the particular conditions these actions created. In sum, the *Power*-structure was constantly creating circumstances for itself where it became more and more difficult to tell the truth in public, and more and more necessary to create not just lies, but elaborate metanarratives of unalloyed deception. The tipping point was the start of the Cold War – that is, the "unofficial" start prior to the end of World War Two.

Not long before that, prior to the explicit start of World War One – during what I've framed as the lead-up to World War One, with the birth of the U.S. as an official Great Power, competing with all the rest in an implicit alliance with the British Empire – the shadow government didn't even really conceal its constant operating within the *Power*-structure's highest levels. U.S. government was almost unabashedly open in its corruption, which was feasible since people didn't yet see that form of corruption for what it was, at least not the way many Americans do today. In other words, essentially all people who could have any affect on the system thought it was completely normal for the corporations and business interests to have a say in everything the people did:[cdlxxxi] or at least, a silent majority thought so, which is really all that matters in a system of advanced industrialization. How is this different from today? It's true that today, most people in the contemporary dominant culture who think about it, which is to say a minority of those in the "mainstream" (which itself is a small minority of the global civilization), also probably think that corporations have a big say in what goes on in the government. But many of the same people probably also think that the government *could* control corporations – if it "wanted" to.

Neither is really true, in the sense that they're both beside the point. The point first of all, is: corporations don't simply "have a say" in the existent government; certain corporations *are* the government, and not a single corporation could exist without the concomitant existence of the State. Second, nothing has really been able to control corporations, historically. Their existences have merely been directed (to a large extent unconsciously) according to options constrained by ecology and culture, unfolding in adherence to systemic rules of a game that has been going on much longer than the history of corporations as such, a game brought to its long historical culmination in the contemporary world of global corporatism (fascism). What goes on in a government is always merely a symptom, albeit the main symptom, of the private interests most indispensable to the workings of the whole system, just like the leading private interests always reciprocally become a symptom of the government. These interests, and the government they sustain, are indispensable in a specifically geostrategic sense.

It doesn't matter what anyone does: whoever controls the geostrategic mechanisms, the repositories, controls the civilization. This is why, since they first emerged, civilizations have required States to survive – only the interstate system, the interstate *war-trade* system – can ultimately maintain the stable juridical division of territory necessary for keeping in business all leading geostrategic mechanisms within a civilization. To live in a State you must play by the State's rules, so the one-percent of individuals or whatever similarly tiny minority (the apex) administrates the geostrategic mechanisms of any given civilization-State-complex has forever had decisive influence over civilizational politicoeconomic systems. Within that one-percent, too, there's a similar hierarchy. Actually, the holistic hierarchy is nothing more than the reflection of the hierarchy within the apex.

On its own, this has been the greatest source of violence throughout civilizational history, as it has, directly or indirectly, led to all of the others. Everything else ultimately becomes coerced into a system where the ones who control the cultural repositories, the leading institutions representing the communications, life-support, and military spheres, get to decide all matters of life and death; who's inside the frontiers, and who's out in the cold. And the deciding factor is nothing nobler than who can rally the most/best troops, whether mainly through physical mobilization or psychological mobilization. Either way, both are inherently geared towards conquest for profit, which allows the most wealth to be concentrated within the tiniest sliver of the population and then replicates a similar albeit less intense pattern all the way down the pyramid. Not only are all civilizations "like" this, but in fact all civilizations are civilizations insofar as they *are* this.

The initial main difference between the world of civilizations sparked by capitalism (a world where companies, like aristocracies and organized religions, became the operational bases for Powers) and the world before was that, prior to capitalism, there had been meaningful limits, both ecological and moral, to the constantly-increasing rapidity of civilizational expansion built off of conflict-driven wealth systems. Once capitalism started, introducing a world where the bourgeoisie finally became more necessary to the overall system than the aristocracy or the clergy, those natural limits would steadily grow less and less meaningful until they finally seemed to disappear altogether with industrialization. But they only *seemed* to disappear altogether: as it turns out, contemporary humanity remains subject to the most narrowly defined conditions. In fact, civilizational constraints actually increase in parallel to humanity's technological "Progress" – which in civilizations can't mean actual progress in the sense of 'improvement', as such "Progress" typically gets organized almost exclusively around military affairs – and such constraints have increased with industrialization as never before. In other words, the faster is a civilization's technological progression, the less true choice there is in terms of how the overall system will operate, since such progression can only continuously maintain itself according to conditions of ever-increasing specificity. In the most extreme case of all, the global civilization, it seems that there's only one real choice: "Yes" to the system or "No" to the system. All of its more exact details had been selected for throughout all prior history. Consciously or unconsciously, all participants in the publicly visible political arena are merely fighting over what precisely "Yes" to the system should mean: in turn sustaining "Yes" to the system no matter what, which is the main point.

Whether emanating primarily from religious, noble, or financial elites, *Power* is the driving force behind all systemic evolutionary activity in civilizations; and, as a politicoeconomic phenomenon, we find *Power*, the status of "being the boss", to be, in the end, merely the fastest way to the most profit for the smallest group in a given sociohistorical context. – The least physical work for the greatest reward. – This has worked as a general organizing principle because at any given moment it has managed to sustain the most cultural order in the least amount of time. Precisely in this vein, capitalism ended up as the dominant fact of history first due to the modern traders' shattering all prior records for cultural acceleration, in their implicit competition with the nobility for cultural dominance; and due, second, to the constant shattering of new records achieved throughout the rest of history by all the successive trader niches that would gain dominance within the financial patriarchy.

Although the *Power*-structure is driven from the very top, it works precisely because the top stimulates a much more limited level of success for a great many more people below its own supreme level, which of course still necessarily constitutes a minority in the scope of the civilization's whole subject population. In our own world, this state-of-affairs seen out of context has misled most people in the contemporary dominant culture to think that things have become more or less equalized, or at least that they were that way until recently, i.e., the idea of the "American dream" that has abruptly disappeared. The reality is something completely different. In the wealthiest nation in history, where the production of wealth has been faster than anything ever possibly imagined in any other civilization, wealth production has for the entire time still been – indeed, it has been more than ever before – totally controlled by a percentage of the population so small, we'd hardly notice its existence, if it weren't for its decisive ability to influence more or less every significant international event-cluster defining the metanarrative.

This ability to make systemic things happen with the greatest speed is the definition of success when it comes to logistics; what the traders have always done best. Following the wisest commentators on the military's long historical role in shaping civilizational evolution,[cdlxxxii] we find logistical capacity to be the driving force behind success in geostrategic activities. The politicoeconomic ability to hierarchically organize human beings and materials for directed actions, which is always at least indirectly related to and at most the same exact thing as organized violence for profit, is in turn the material foundation of all high status, the most important "substance" making up the cultural pyramid. Ever since the emergence of agricultural settlement systems, and especially since the appearance of multiple interrelated civilizations, cultural elites have been tied up exclusively with the war-trade competition.

Fuller, who described himself as apolitical[cdlxxxiii] and worked for the U.S. Government and other governments around the world as a consultant for much of his life, mentioned at the very beginning of his introduction to *Critical Path*, "Twilight of the Power Structures", that the two greatest problems humanity faced were "tax-hungry government and profit-hungry business". Specifically, he thought these problems were most destructive insofar as "government and business" used coercive control over energy (namely hydrocarbon) sources as the singular method for making monetary profits.[cdlxxxiv] I believe this is why, as destructive as the initial history of Western civilization was under the rule of primarily noble patriarchies, nothing else in history compares to the destructiveness of the financial patriarchies who originally took the reigns in the overseas Empires in Columbus's wake, truly initiating the culture of capitalism. The evolution of the financial patriarchies was led by their spawning of economies that were more and more and more destructive at what was ultimately an exponentially increasing rate. Noble wealth could never grow so quickly by itself. Therein lay the potential and ultimately the realization for the Western financial hegemony's subjugation of everything there was, which ended up including the nobility.

Aside from the sun, which is the common source of energy for everything on the planet and thus ultimately for all other energy sources, we can divide energy sources utilized by human beings in civilizations before industrialization into four main groups: (1) organized muscle energy (humans and work animals); (2) food energy (agricultural products); (3) wind-water energy (either nautical or windmills); (4) plant and mineral energy (coal, wood, gunpowder, the tensile strength of metals). As usual in this text, I must note that all the categories were invariably interrelated with each other. Industrialization continued with all of these broad forms of energy and their systemic entanglement. What made it the greatest systemic transformation in the history of the planet was its ability to use its version of the interrelated categories to create and *maintain* an exponentially-increasing rate of civilizational evolution, and it did this above all through skyrocketing exploitation of (4) – especially petroleum.

In practice, the main difference between industrialization and all prior history is that, during the reign of industrialization, the traders became essentially autarkic on an eventually global scale, secured by their capacity to decisively control all the forms of energy. This is the material definition of total global *Power*. Moreover, this is basically the only process that has been taking place: nothing else matters. It's a system of conquest for the sake of cold profit and absolutely nothing else, the all-historical system at its most astonishingly efficient, though for that reason most inevitably extinctive stage. Through the intentional implementation of this industrial monopolization of all life and the entire planet, accomplished through the human tools organized by institutions (primarily the *Power*-structure and its facilitators), all other possible orders are almost instantly removed from the environment. Whether it "had" to happen like this or not, there's no denying that industrialization as it has really happened has been a long genocide, headed towards a species' suicide. It just didn't reach back to the domestic heartland of the dominant culture that wielded it as a weapon until its final stages – until the culture had no other choice but to cannibalize itself.

Industrialization, most significantly and simply manifested via the use of metal machinery powered by fossil fuels, theoretically could've become the greatest catalyst for the advancement of a just social structure ever discovered, or rather, the energy harnessed by industrialization could've been used towards such an end, by leading to other substitutive technologies negating the need for industrialization. Only "theoretically", as all that happened was the capitalist hegemonic sector remained in *Power* – because it was this sector that had ultimately driven the frenzy of industrialization in the first place – leading to what was basically a total monopoly of the international finance structure that originated explicitly surrounding the British Empire around 1815, but which from a longer perspective had started evolving in northern Italy in the late medieval period. And how had the earlier structure evolved? By financing Western civilization's never-ending, forever-growing system of interstate warfare and its inextricable counterpart in the ideological domain, the growth of the Catholic Church.[cdlxxxv]

Of course, though, the other spheres predated the international finance structure's emergence. When the structure first came onto the scene, then, energy was distributed fairly evenly between the spheres. Actually, at first, international finance benefited the other two spheres, and this is why it was able to persist and flourish. Like all forms of addiction, when the prevailing spheres in the late medieval world could quit finance they didn't want to; and when they very well may've wanted to, they couldn't. Once the system as a whole becomes financialized – fundamentally dependent upon the cash monetization of debt – you can't "unfinancialize" the same system, since everything else in the system has come to form around money. At that point the financiers have everyone exactly where they want them: although in the long run, they're ultimately just as constrained by the financialization of social structures as their subjects.

In the ancient world, long before cash, a similar underlying process happened, revolving around the State itself. Indeed, it happened in the very first civilization that we know of, in southern Mesopotamia. Hans Nissen points out that when States first came into existence in Sumer, it was most likely because they were necessary in order to settle the greatly increased quantity of intracommunal disputes inevitably arising when precivilizational populations saw their original moments of rapid growth – not in order to execute massive infrastructural "public works" projects, like the canals that appeared at a much later date. Irrigation of the kind requiring such complex logistical efforts wasn't necessary when the State first emerged; and, relatedly, it wasn't yet possible in the sociohistorical context.[cdlxxxvi]

When the sociohistorical situation urgently necessitated those efforts, they also, at that point, happened to be possible.[cdlxxxvii] "Real historical potential" can in this sense be seen to rest on two factors: whether an imagined scenario is logistically feasible; and whether the systemic necessity for the fulfillment of that scenario exists. If there's a "systemic necessity" for the fulfillment of a scenario, it means that the system needs that scenario to occur in order to ensure its own continued existence. At a certain point in the ancient history of southern Mesopotamia, after the civilization there had existed for many centuries, the many centuries of accumulated civilizational existence brought the culture to some periodic maximum in population for the particular politicoeconomic system.

Sometime during this height of growth for one of the originary ("pristine") civilizations, natural ecological patterns started substantially changing, as they perpetually do on Earth, regardless of human desires. The general combination involved less rainfall and overstrain on the land's ability to maintain continuous production of vital resources for an interurban system's population levels. *If* the existing system of resource production and distribution were to continue for the same demographic levels, then essentially the sole realistic imaginable scenario was for the population to rely upon the State's organizational capacity. This is to say nothing of the abilities of individual human beings – in fact, the point is that, in the most advanced stages of a conquest syndrome, the

State's main result is the stifling of individual human capabilities that might otherwise flourish. The most significant aspect is "If the *existing* system…were to continue". A State doesn't always have to constantly fight for its very existence; but by the time it must, it's able and willing to do so. And at that point, also, human beings have been culturally dependent on it for so long, their immediate livelihoods depend upon the State's prolongation. Throughout history, almost all individuals subject to the civilization can afford to concern themselves only or mainly with their own immediate needs, while individuals comprising the ruling class itself concern themselves almost exclusively with their own immediate desires. On a mass level, no one stops to reexamine.

Is that all everything comes down to? It certainly seems, from a long historical perspective, as if the myopic self-absorption encouraged by conquest syndromes – whether coercively or seductively – regularly drives States and in turn civilizations to propel themselves ever-faster towards self-destruction. As I've just suggested, the myopic self-absorption happens in two interconnected ways, which are inverses of one another: from the perspective of the conquerors on the one hand, and the perspective of the victims, on the other. Those two sides make up the two poles bounding the rest of the syndrome; the apex of the pyramid and the dirt beneath, the hegemons and the slaves.

It's hard to determine a *singular* "cause" of the self-absorbed myopia, but I of course believe we would do well to draw our attention to one essential feature of civilizations, whether ancient or contemporary: the use of exhibitions of strength in military affairs to determine who will administer official moral orders. When international finance finally became the hegemon over all human life with industrialization's onslaught, it had never evolved separately from the war-morality system, but had been superimposed upon it. Thus, industrialization as it happened didn't lead to a world where truly *anything* is possible: it merely represented the logistical capabilities of Western warfare taken to their greatest, fastest imaginable limits.[cdlxxxviii] In other words, even – no, especially – when the bourgeoisie finally took over once and for all by creating the conditions for and fulfillment of modern industrial corporations, they weren't creating a new system. They simply were, and saw themselves as, the new aristocracy.

But in their attempt at reconstructing the old world in completely new conditions, the hegemons put themselves one more level removed from the system they were running, in comparison to the relationship between the original aristocrats and their system. The critical difference was that aristocrats grew out of the system that they ran, whereas the industrial system grew out of the individuals running it. The war system – the purview of the aristocracy – originally grows out of the violent opposition naturally obtaining between agricultural settlement systems in civilizations, whereas the bourgeoisie elites have to intentionally create and sustain markets to survive as bourgeoisie elites.

Here we get to the brunt of everything we've discussed in the text thus far: since markets have to be intentionally created and cultivated, and the institutional controls over a holistic monetary system constitute market control at its most complex level, *there's no politically neutral money.*

*   *   *

As we've seen, cash economies are by nature expressions of an extremely specific form of politicoeconomic dominance, financial dominance. The very existence of a cash economy – and interchangeably, the existence of a form of money – indicates the success of some existing financial elite: as we've also seen, always a war-trade elite. The first bankers in Western civilization, most typically from northern Italy, became successful not just insofar as there was booming manufacturing and trade emanating from their home area, but equally insofar as there were warlords (aristocrats) all over Europe in constant need of cash advances, and thereby debt, to pay their armies; and also insofar as there was the Catholic Church, perhaps even more of a financially-fueled institution during the medieval period than the military.

With virtual immediacy, the initial financialization of a system makes it so that dependence on money becomes not at all a choice: as the financialized system evolves, money tends to become more and more systemically indistinguishable from life-support. Eventually, at the acute phases, every bit of life becomes translatable into a price; every single thing can be sold. The fastest path from any desire to its fulfillment becomes cash.

As a result, more and more desires can constantly be fulfilled – and fulfilled more quickly – regardless of the morality associated. If a desire exists, it can be monetized, and once monetized, it can be gratified as soon as the cash is ready in hand.

The industrialization of the totally financialized interstate war system took things to still much more audacious heights. Not only could a price be attached to more or less every thing in existence; in addition, there was an *exponentially*-increasing quantity of human-made things in the world, and an inextricably associated boom in the desire for these things, ultimately rooted in a tiny sector of the dominant culture. Moreover, all this utilization of resources revolves around the manufacture of war materials – most of all, arms. The word "arms" is more accurate than the word "weapons" in this context because, in a totally financialized, totally industrialized war system, every thing is or can be made into a weapon.

For the most part, to reiterate, arms in the totally financialized, totally industrialized war system are used more as weapons in a psychological sense than weapons in a physical sense. But aside from their terroristic purposes that we've already discussed, arms are, especially in the context of the global civilization, mainly economic rather than military weapons. In fact, this represents the entire idea behind the particular manner in which the contemporary *Power*-structure has implemented Keynesian theory.

Of course, it also represents the thinking behind the implementation of all fascist (corporatist) economies that began right before the contemporary world's official establishment. As Quigley pointed out almost fifty years ago, fascism, or corporatism, was nothing besides the conventional vested interests' use of practically unlimited military budgets to spend themselves out of the Depression.[cdlxxxix] In other words, as I've said, the system the reactionaries imposed when they became decidedly proactive. Regardless of the particularities defining any single national culture, this characteristic politicoeconomic system was the same in every single fascist nation, meaning every industrialized nation in the world since the 1920s, which at some point later in the 20th-century came to mean the entire planet.

Although Keynes surely knew precisely how the national States in his sociohistorical context intended to employ his methods, he himself nonetheless admitted that governments could use deficit spending on pretty much anything as a means to stimulate overall economic growth with that spending, as long as the spending fulfilled certain general conditions. Basically, whatever the spending was directed towards needed to be something requiring the greatest input of strategic materials, which would also be constantly destroyed – thus necessitating constantly recurring, constantly fulfilled demand. And it needed to be something that wouldn't be available on the "consumer market", while simultaneously supporting great numbers of "working class" manufacturing jobs: in turn, it would serve as a command engine guaranteeing the economies of scale and salaried market bases necessary to allow people to constantly buy more and more material conveniences with "disposable income"[cdxc] – hence buttressing that same consumer market. This last thing was essentially the key.

Whatever you can think of that fits these characteristics, there's only one system that can fulfill these conditions *and* the conditions demanded by the hegemonic sector: the appearance of a warfare system that a silent majority of the world supports. The silent majority must support the appearance because that's how the individuals that work for the *Power*-structure – the individuals who actually make the *Power*-structure happen – are able to perform their actions under influence of a feeling that they're doing the right thing, which is ultimately necessary, to some minimum degree, for the *Power*-structure to materialize. All the hegemonic sector is concerned with is making the *Power*-structure materialize, which means "projecting" the *Power*-structure on a perpetual basis. The hegemonic sector knows just how to present things such that individuals will fulfill the *Power*-structure's requirements while simultaneously believing they're primarily acting to defend their own interests.[cdxci] Indeed, this is what the contemporary hegemonic sector does best.

The saddest, most sickening part of our culture, the dead culture that just won't go away, is that it's there just because it can be – and it *knows* that's why it's there. No one who's remotely close to the true levers of control believes in anything at all besides the Power they work for: dominance is its own purpose. A self-reproducing geostrategic money machine, creating a demand for black market drug traffickers in one instance and the "supply" to violently contradict those criminals in the next, in the form of police forces as socially disturbing as the drug enterprises, in many cases filled with worse criminals than those in the underground economy. Our culture is most destructive of all insofar as its atrocities are so utterly pointless.

It's strange to view atrocities in this way, as all atrocities are basically pointless. It can potentially be quite dangerous, in fact, to call some atrocities more pointless than others, since this necessarily also implies that there are some atrocities with more of a point. There's at least one way I can think of, though, in which certain atrocities are indeed the most pointless – and I think acknowledging it should also counteract the notion that calling some atrocities the most pointless of all *necessarily* has to imply that the less pointless ones "aren't as bad".

The most pointless atrocities, those prevalent in the contemporary world to an extent impossible in all prior history, are the ones whose true meanings are most greatly obfuscated – and these are the most pointless because learning "the right lesson"[cdxcii] from them is almost out of the question. This frames the relevant perspective from which to view the issue of "what atrocities aren't as pointless?", such that we can avoid the mistake of thinking it's meant to indicate that other atrocities aren't as bad: the perspective of those individuals who must live in the atrocities' aftermath. Here we see how true it is that "laying blame" for humanity's sociohistorical problems should never be about chastising certain individuals. Simple chastisement is the last thing we ever want to associate with that most serious problem of figuring out which structures really are responsible for harmful sociohistorical phenomena: focusing solely or mostly on particular individuals easily distracts from the truly primary topic, human organization – the definitively structural, systemic phenomenon – the thing representing the greatest potential to harm.

What our culture is naturally best at is creating false dichotomies, so it's no surprise that a false dichotomy seems to constantly surround discussion of "conspiracies", one pitting "structuralists" against "individualists". On this question, "structuralists" versus "individualists" typically seems to represent a fight between the mainstream "Left" and the mainstream "Right". Rather than producing positively any useful insights, this opposition does a far better job of epitomizing what's so inherently problematic about virtually all contemporary mainstream discourse. The entire model of discussing everything in the contemporary world is wholly flawed – in relation to politics most of all, yielding essentially all contemporary political discussion overly complicated. The only way to avoid that trap of over-complication, as far as I can see, is to assume outright that this itself is part of the systemic design: in the globalized world, the system's visible structural activities, as they seem to happen, are intended to do nothing so much as spread confusion and division. That is, simply by knowing that an individual event-cluster sequence is "a war in the contemporary world", for instance, it's almost guaranteed that this episode's main meaning is "the elite factions fooling the masses".

Thus, if I'm correct, and the argument of "structuralists" versus "individualists" as it relates to "conspiracies" in the contemporary world is merely a false "Left-Right" dichotomy, we should abandon it immediately, since nothing related to civilizational politics can be accurately seen outside the context of the warfare system, and contemporary "warfare" is mainly about elites fooling the masses. Again, I'm arguing that what most people seem to call "conspiracies" in the contemporary world are, when not fabricated, simply nakedly revealed examples of how indispensable the self-reproducing geostrategic money machine is to contemporary human life. In other words, they're the system in its most normally functioning state. When they refer to real-world sociohistorical phenomena, the "conspiracies", which "Left" structuralists mainly see either as urban legends or else just as irrelevant from notions of the world working as a structural whole, and "Right" individualists seem to see as mysterious, anomalous forces completely incompatible with the world created by "our Founding Fathers", are simply the long-term evolution of Western civilization being presented in real time – and in plain sight.

Past humanities could so easily ascribe such sacred morality to their *Power-*structures *to the extent that they didn't see everything constituting the system at once.* Most of the time, under normal circumstances, there was never even the potential for them to see the big picture. This was essentially the meaning of the saying, "You can't fool all of the people all of the time…", the main point being, in typical circumstances, you didn't have to. As long as what the average individual saw was his or her one microscopic systemically circumscribed, microscopic niche under the tent, enough people were, enough of the time, kept from questioning the legitimacy of the whole damn circus.

Under normal circumstances in the contemporary world, on the other hand, many individuals have at least some minute potential to see the big picture. Technologically, information has become so potentially democratized in the world of globalization, the structure has to do everything in its *Power* to maintain the fraud, above all by "spoiling" the opportunity for democratization with overload and disinformation. Especially in the existent world, so much of what the fraud truly is, is simply out there in the open, ready to be assimilated into a broad understanding if only individuals capable of assimilating the broad understanding would absorb it. How strange is it for instance, that individuals write quite conventional-seeming books extensively, indisputably documenting the completely preposterous system that is the illegal drug trade, where the U.S. State vigorously sustains a gigantic global black market that unequivocally benefits professional sociopaths most of all, while also playing the morally-righteous enforcement arm for the system that publicly claims to counteract the same global black market? Yet even amongst individuals who know about it the best, very few have an adequately clear concept of the true implications, and so the problem never goes away; it just grows and grows. And at this point, no matter what, everyone, if they merely wish to be historically accurate, must admit that the U.S. Government supports the illegal drug market, since it's so well-known that unless the self-sustaining supply-demand relationship of a substance targeted for legal prohibition is totally eradicated (a wholly hypothetical scenario anyway), prohibition will have no greater effect than skyrocketing prices, thus ensuring the continued steady and likely increasing supply. Even if you can't accept that the State explicitly aids drug traffickers, then, you must admit that it does so implicitly with its criminalization policies that, in light of the vast quantities of easily available, irrefutable historical evidence can only be considered completely ludicrous – if the purpose truly is to destroy the illegal drug trade.

At this moment in history, though, we're also far past the point where it's possible for anyone substantially knowledgeable on the subject to deny that the State explicitly aids drug traffickers, suggesting that one of the key purposes of the policy regime of drug criminalization is to keep prices elevated: which would mean that the traffickers, at least to this extent, are in control of governmental policy. Concerning the U.S. State's explicit aid of illegal drug traffickers, the only reasonable point of disputation is the exact extent to which this State – the entity that incarcerates a greater number of individuals for drug offenses than any other such entity on the planet – has provided such aid. For instance, Alfred McCoy, without a doubt the best known and most widely respected individual in conventional academia to study the U.S. State's role in supporting some of the worst global offenders in the illicit drug business, focused mainly on CIA in his classic text *The Politics of Heroin*, first published in 1972 as *The Politics of Heroin in Southeast Asia*. McCoy found none other than OPC to have been the critical mechanism initially integrating the "Golden Triangle" opium supply into the global schema of U.S. covert operations.[cdxciii]

However, as indispensable as McCoy's work is, the author nonetheless seems to fall prey to hyperspecialization as concerns the implications of his analysis regarding what might be CIA's purpose in supporting the production and distribution of illegal narcotics. That is, he doesn't know enough about the field of covert operations/psychological warfare in general. On the other hand, his writing on such an unconventional topic from such a conventional perspective (the perspective of a contemporary officially-educated academic) provides us with a fine example of the falsity of that dichotomy set up between "Left" structuralists and "Right" individualists in relation to conspiracies".

Much of it has to do, in the first place, with what one takes "conspiracy" to mean. Any useful question about the role of "conspiracy" in contemporary life shouldn't have to do with the word in its actual legal definition: if by "a conspiracy" everyone simply meant, literally, 'conspiracy' – the secret organized plotting to break the law participated in by multiple individuals – there could be no legitimate question at all about whether or not this plays a significant role in global human affairs. In the existent world, we can consult the most mainstream sources and see that individuals running the planet constantly meet secretly and plan to break the law.[cdxciv] If you don't know this, you don't know anything about the history of our world.

Rather, the legitimate question about "conspiracy" has to do with whether or not the event-clusters making up the system's history inherently embody the perpetration of a gigantic fraud – including the question, most significantly, as to whether or not the U.S. Government is run by an entity external to the government itself. My position on the matter is that it's a non-issue, and its existence mainly reflects the way the *Power*-structure is so adept at perpetuating legitimate-seeming non-issues for stereotyped "Opponents" to argue over.[cdxcv] The greatest model for this is obviously the standard "debating" format on "Cable News", a phenomenon, by the way, that barely existed until a couple of decades ago, but which has somehow come to completely dominate the individual's "understanding" of "Politics": almost invariably meaning, in the existent world, "the business of elected officials".

The argument between "Left" structuralists and "Right" individualists in this case is, in the end, entirely premised on what couldn't be a bigger fallacy: the notion that the government's actions have ever been, are, or could ever be primarily determined by behavior widely visible to the public. In fact, it's partly inaccurate to even use the word 'government' as a label for those goings-on directly related to the U.S. State that its public can readily discover. In the explicitly political arena, government is what always occurred throughout history behind closed doors: the routine operating procedures of an enormous holistic administrative structure working nonstop. What the public is witnessing is indeed government; but again, not in the sense that the public is typically led to believe. The public sees the *effects* of government, whereas the establishment-approved mainstream discourse leads individuals to believe they're observing the causes.

In civilizations, politics – the human struggle to control other human beings – is *always* played out mostly beneath the surface of the wider public's awareness. It couldn't possibly work, otherwise. Nonetheless, the dominant contemporary understanding of politics in the United States displays a particular lack of critical information, and this is the main problem sustaining the failure of existent historical understanding. Moreover, this failure at understanding history emanates foremost from the official academic "Historians".

You may think that I criticize due to my envy of official academics, envy that you may automatically assume I must have, as I'm not one of them and yet I seem to try to be. But, if my own denunciation of that possible assumption means anything, I can assure you that I harbor no envy in relation to the distinguished official scholars, and even if I do have some unconscious envy I don't know about, I think it would still have absolutely nothing to do with my intentions here in criticizing official academia. I criticize official academics, rather, and official "Historians" most of all, because I want to salvage the useful contributions to knowledge they've actually made. Those contributions can only be salvaged, however, by incorporating them into the broadest possible perspective, which often means criticizing the broadest perspectives of individuals whose writings you cite as competent sources when it comes to empirical evidence.

This goes for "Left" structuralists as well as "Right" individualists. Here's the sum of my thinking on what sources are acceptable to use, and in what ways it's acceptable to use them: any source is acceptable as long as it's relevant to the discussion, and as long as in the writer's arguing for its relevance, a clear distinction is maintained between the evidence presented and the writer's own philosophy. (And, after that, of course, the source ultimately must be acceptable concerning its factuality relative to the historian's intentions in employing it.) Now, that's all fine for the author in terms of his or her thoughts in the midst of writing; but how does the writer translate this distinction into the reader's ability to perceive the distinction?

All I can do is offer the present text as an example, as this will explain what I mean in practice. As I've said, I believe all historians in general, and historians of conspiratorial behavior most of all, should be judged on their factual accounts primarily in terms of the philosophy of the *Power*-structure their work illustrates. Along these lines, before even judging one author's facts compared to others', the facts presented should be assessed in terms of their relevance to the author's overall argument, and this relevance is to be assessed, in turn, as relates to the author's philosophy of the *Power*-structure he or she is narrativizing.

If the historian's work shows an undeveloped philosophy of the *Power*-structure, we can typically only utilize the work's raw facts. Concerning historians in the existent world, the historian shows an undeveloped philosophy of the *Power*-structure when he or she puts together all the various pieces of evidence to create a picture mainly in accordance with the conventional individual's worldview in the contemporary dominant culture. This may seem too indeterminate to help us; but illustrating that a writer is doing this is much easier than you might think.

One of the most telling indicators that the writer has largely absorbed the conventional contemporary worldview is the unreflective acceptance of the dominant culture's own account of its military activities. Historians of the contemporary world are especially plagued by such unquestioning acceptance. It's truly difficult to find a single one who hasn't at least partially succumbed to this natural tendency of the civilizational individual.

For instance, McCoy, even as he's among the few most knowledgeable individuals in the scholarly community on the U.S.'s despicable drug policy, and in general among the finest historians I've come across, still starts from a premise that accepts as basic fact the notion that the U.S. State's main goal in fighting the Cold War was to destroy "Communism". McCoy considers that – the U.S. State's publicly stated premise for standing permanently in a totally mobilized military posture – to have been the key reason why OPC made the initial decision to fund the U.S.'s covert warfare in southeast Asia (subsequently transferring the strategy to other places) with proceeds from the illegal narcotics trade. Rabid anti-Communists would've done anything to crush the Soviet Union, and thus they started a process of doing so using the most amoral imaginable methods in those territories the United States was occupying.[cdxcvi]

While McCoy's facts are, in my evaluation, beyond reproach, his philosophy concerning the global *Power*-structure, for the reason just mentioned, has a tiny flaw. I understand what McCoy is trying to do, in his impressively detailed treatment of U.S. official involvement in the illicit drug trade: he's trying to make the most cautious case possible: because even that case is shocking, and all the more shocking for its empirical reliability. But one should only focus on "caution" when it comes to the rhetoric used to make an argument – one should never tailor his or her narrative of what was going to suit a prefabricated conception of what would sound more or less shocking. "Facts are facts." McCoy's own facts point to a qualitatively different reality than what McCoy seems to believe.

For instance, McCoy argues that, similarly to the argument about the U.S. intentionally targeting its own soldiers in Vietnam with the CIA/OPC-protected heroin supply from Laos, there's "little evidence and even less logic" to the theory that blacks in South Central Los Angeles were intentionally targeted with the Latin American-originated cocaine supply CIA allowed to be poured by the ton into the U.S., which at least indirectly helped spark the emergence of a market for crack.[cdxcvii] Here, McCoy is referring to what the heroic murdered journalist Gary Webb called the "dark alliance", in his remarkable text of the same name: the use of cocaine trafficking Nicaraguan exiles via Oliver North and company to illegally fund that nation's infamous "Contra war".[cdxcviii] I agree, there's little *direct* evidence; but where would you find such evidence, anyway? I doubt individuals who could pull off something so gut-wrenchingly disturbing – truly serious criminals – would ever let that kind of evidence come close to seeing daylight.

This wouldn't be so significant a detail, if there weren't, in actuality, a great deal of empirically-based evidence from so many other areas of historical life to suggest that an intentional targeting of the sort McCoy denies is all too logical from the standpoint of the *Power*-structure. McCoy seems to view the phenomenon of U.S. State protection of the drug trade to be tactical, rather than strategic – indispensable to individual covert operations, but not necessarily indispensable to an overall strategy's existence. Too few scholars of contemporary history really contemplate why things like covert operations exist at all, and what the meaning of their *holistic* existence is.

Covert operations have existed since *Power*-structures have existed. Contemporary covert operations are so unique, and so uniquely significant to the history they shape, due to the fact that, in the contemporary world, they represent an institutionalized part of human affairs – and, I assert, the one that's most generally consequential in the contemporary, most consequential phase of human history. As such, moreover, we can actually study covert operations as *historians*; a completely unique opportunity in human history. Resultantly, this makes such operations not entirely "covert". But remember, their point isn't to embody literal secrecy in the sense of complete physical unknowability: in the contemporary world, that never could be possible. Their point is to have true meanings that are almost impossibly difficult for the typical individual to assimilate into his or her general perspective of reality (worldview).

To put it another way, the *Power*-structure is much more concerned with hiding the causes of its actions than it is with hiding the effects. So, *if* we just pay attention to the effects, then to that extent we're looking at historical reality the way the *Power*-structure would like us to look at historical reality. Again, this criticism of the conventional approach to history has nothing to do with my believing that contemporary historians are intellectually inept; I don't believe that in the least. The criticism is necessary precisely because I believe that neglect of the minutest details can lead even a most capable contemporary historian such as McCoy to unreflectively accept certain incorrect assumptions, which end up skewing his or her entire historical perspective. And such a result should be entirely expected: the main intention behind contemporary covert operations is to skew humanity's understanding of its own presently-unfolding history.[cdxcix]

In the specific case of why the United States was maintaining a posture of permanent imperial mobilization during the Cold War, moreover, making the incorrect assumption had an especially detrimental *general* effect, since the geostrategic purpose is always the cause most intentionally obfuscated by contemporary covert operations, and the U.S.'s overarching purpose in facilitating the Cold War was the embodiment of purest geostrategy. McCoy came out with his first edition of his text in 1972, and although he has reissued it multiple times since (the latest edition was published in 2003), the work's "defeating Communism" angle was too intertwined with the structural foundation of the narrative to change anything fundamental in that regard, whether the author would've, or not.[d] Anyway, most crucially, in 1972, when the United States still appeared to be completely wrapped-up with destroying the Soviet Union, virtually none of the key documents most relevant to the real formulation of U.S. grand strategy were yet declassified.

Every historical phenomenon takes place in the context of everything, the totality of phenomena in their comprehensive combination at any given moment on planet Earth. With this in mind, the "documents most relevant" to how top U.S. national security establishment planners came up with and implemented Cold War grand strategy were those that had to do primarily with State propaganda – "psychological warfare" – and most namely, those documents related to the Psychological Strategy Board. Nothing had a higher systemic priority than psychological warfare in the precise global context wherein the Cold War first became institutionalized.

From such documents we see that the newest/oldest soldiers in human history, the psychological warriors, introduced into U.S. Government from the top-down *the very idea itself* of the Cold War as an existentially definitive showdown between the U.S. and the S.U.. In a May, 1952 report entitled "Preliminary Estimate of the Effectiveness of US Psychological Strategy", the author focuses from the beginning on what he presents as unvarnished truth: at the time of the document's production, America was far behind in the Cold War. Luckily, he knew "the reasons for our failure":

(a) Primarily we lack an overall strategic concept for psychological operations…to defeat Soviet Communism…by a counter-offensive on a global scale;

(b) We have not yet based our psychological strategy on a recognition…that, for the Kremlin, this is already an all-out war…

(c) The Cold War has now entered a new stage: …Communist psychological strategy has shifted. In this new phase…the Kremlin's psychological strategy is concentrating on the effort to isolate the United States as the main enemy of peace, while identifying the Soviet Union with the peaceful aspirations of the world…By the subtlety and persistence of their propaganda, the Communists are attaining some disturbing success in spreading the lie that America's main objective is not peace, but world domination…[di]

It may seem like the author really believes what's written, for instance that the author really believes America's "main objective" is peace rather than world domination. Why would he intentionally put on the pretenses of an ideology he didn't actually subscribe to in a document classified "TOP SECRET", which wouldn't be released for almost forty years? Under such a line of thought, the system as evidenced here would simply be flawed, rather than fraudulent.

However, such an interpretation would ignore the fact that every thing must happen in the context of a sociohistorically specific everything. Beyond that, the more factors we have that can narrow a phenomenon's immediate context, the clearer becomes our vision of the relationship between the phenomenon and its overall context. If we ignore the larger context, or simply take it for granted, we're liable to succumb to a grave misinterpretation of facts – frequently resultant from a single wrong or neglected detail.

Consulting Prouty, we see that in policy planning sessions, quite often – and one would imagine that it always happened, in the most systemically critical cases – the "intelligence" provided, supposedly meant to influence decision-making objectively, was in fact the deliberately-designed advertisement for a predetermined objective needing officialdom's rubber-stamp: something that was going to happen one way or another, because the system needed it to happen. The "intelligence" drawn up would then merely be a reflection of plans already in place – perhaps already in motion – and its distribution among members of the planning team was primarily a mechanism for conditioning the team as a whole to the psychological strategy already settled upon.[dii] What the writing of this particular intelligence estimate really means, therefore, is not what's actually written, although the two things are necessarily related. To understand this, we have to consider what the specific psychological strategy was. Continuing immediately from where we left off:

(d) …our existing strategic concept, summed up in the phrase "Peace Through Strength" is no longer adequate…*Particularly…in the under-developed areas of the Middle East and South and Southeast Asia*…it seems to be actually backfiring…where the Communists have been able to distort it into meaning "rearmament for war"; and as a slogan…the "Peace Through Strength" concept should be replaced by a new conception that might be titled "Peace, Prosperity, and Freedom Through World Partnership"…

(e) in this same context, we are made to appear to the peoples of many countries as engaged in an effort to mobilize them in our struggle against Soviet Communism; whereas…our psychological strategy must be to establish the truth that our sole aim is…full partnership with them in a common effort to actively defend their freedom and that of all humanity;[diii] (Emphasis in '(d)' my own.)

Aside from how eerily similar is the phrase "Peace Through Strength" to Orwell's "WAR IS PEACE", etc., especially concerning the fact that *1984* had been published so recently,[div] notice how the psychological strategy "must be to establish the truth". That is, the primary objective of the psychological strategy isn't to actually do something, but to convince people of something. And notice how absolutely unlimited the objective is: "full partnership with them in a common effort to actively defend their freedom *and that of all humanity*". So the objective of the psychological strategy was to convince people of something related to the U.S.'s role in relation to all humanity.

What went unsaid was the fact that the U.S. Government only *could* have a role in "defending freedom" when it came to "all humanity" insofar as the U.S. was politicoeconomic hegemon over the entire planet, and that it became such in the exact same way that every other hegemon in history gained hegemony "on its turf": by being war-trade champion. By having the *Power*-structure most well-suited for organizing death into wealth. The U.S. Government during the national security State's reign is simply the epicenter of this long historical constant, at a point when the constant exists on a globally-singular scale.

But in the moral climate present in the contemporary world, which exists not least of all owing to the rhetorical attractiveness of American *Power*, that's obviously the last possible thing on Earth that can be said outright. And no sector of humanity has ever been more aware of this fact than the individuals who must face it on a constant day-to-day basis for their entire lives, those comprising the hegemonic sector – the sliver of contemporary humanity totally transcending the most indispensable geostrategic spheres. Since our culture is a civilization, such a sliver must exist; and as I've argued that our civilization is the global civilization (the only one), it should seem natural that I believe the most logical theoretical position to explore in trying to understand contemporary history is to view it as a *Power*-structure run by a *globally*-influential hegemonic sector. In general, in the contemporary, most advanced phase of capitalism, I believe the 'sector' is the proper basic demographic unit to employ, as it best reflects the deliberate hyperspecialization of everything in the contemporary world.

Global hyperspecialization itself is the surest possible sign of the contemporary *Power*-structure, and we currently experience it in every single facet of our daily lives. So the hegemons can say as much as they want that they promote "Peace, Prosperity, and Freedom Through World Partnership" (or any more recent equivalent of that tagline); ultimately nothing can hide the fact that what they run is a *Power*-structure just like all the other *Power*-structures in human history, albeit one taken to the most extreme conceivable degree. Indeed, hegemonic propaganda makes acceptance of this point extremely easy: for instance, consider how *Power*-structure representatives so often call their dominion a "Superpower". What could that be in reference to besides what were traditionally called the "Great Powers",[dv] the original European players of the fully-fledged Western war-trade competition? And what was a "Great Power" besides the epitome of an Empire on a modern (and thus national) scale – 'Empire' being throughout history the *Power*-structure's most strikingly symptomatic label for itself?

In this case, I agree with the elite propaganda; our culture is in that category. That's relevant here because I think it's how we can best put covert operations into context – how we can see the causes behind the effects on the political surface, a sight that will unify the vast amount of evidence we do have in the existent world, but which has been blown into millions of scattered pieces by hypercompartmentalization, lies and propaganda, and general confusion. Covert operations and everything they bring with them are nothing besides so many indices of the global governing class's holistic behavior: such phenomena collectively comprise the global shadow government insofar as it exists primarily by instrumentalizing the publicly visible governing machines in all the many nations, all of which at this point, including the United States, are only subunits of the one whole system. This isn't "a conspiracy"; it's the long historical status quo finally experienced in real time, but experienced, unfortunately, by human beings completely disconnected from their world's reality.

I've developed this theoretical perspective based largely on a methodology constructed by McCoy that I believe is quite ingenious in its simplicity. When, in the late '60s/ early '70s, he was first studying the strange repressed world of simultaneous governmental policing against/support of drug traffickers, he naturally noticed that this was by no means a phenomena unique to the Cold War era.[dvi] In fact, the modern history of this two-faced policy started – where else? – in the West during the early modern period (the period of the archetypal version of capitalism proper), associated above all with – whom else? – the British Empire, in the early 17th-century. Most namely, the original practitioner of this perfidious sport was the East India Company.[dvii] In his excellent book, *The Business of Empire: the East India Company and Imperial Britain, 1756-1833*, the economic historian H.V. Bowen mentions opium just once in the entire narrative; though in that light, I find it extremely interesting, as well, how he argues that the Company's significance to the British economy far surpassed the significance apparently attributed to it by the implied consensus of contemporary scholarship.[dviii] Besides the intangibles Bowen mentions, in other words, the Company's import within the Empire's whole scope also could've owed to something tangible, yet obsessively repressed and obfuscated. It would be far from strange if the black market economy had been so uniquely significant to the official economy, especially in relation to a repository that embodied perhaps the quintessential example of an archetypal capitalist organizational structure. Actually, reviewing the present-day economy – which we know descends ultimately from archetypal capitalism – it would seem entirely expected.

McCoy, a southeast Asian specialist, began his research into the U.S. Government's sanctioning illegal drug traffickers by studying the history of European imperialism in Vietnam. The eminently reasonable assumption he tested, which seems to have been quite on the money, was that U.S. involvement in the illegal opium and heroin trade was at first mostly just continued the southeast Asian opium trade as it had existed under the British and French Empires. However, from the outset there was at least one main difference: what had been legal to buy and sell under governmental regulation was now, although still regulated by the government, criminally prohibited as a commercial commodity. Resultantly, the same official body's simultaneous support of this criminal activity had to be heavily camouflaged.[dix] Contemporary publics typically frown on such blatantly fraudulent behavior.

Thus, what makes McCoy's method unique isn't the fact that he posited a connection between two successively existing historical entities in the form of a sociohistorical process – indeed, that's the job of every historian. The uniqueness derives from his having theorized (and in my view, amply proved) that one can use historical method to combat contemporary State secrecy, by connecting phenomena now clouded in such secrecy to those preceding contexts wherein they were viewed as socially acceptable. For instance, we know generally that the United States, in assuming the identity of leading Superpower, originally took over the role most notably played by the British Empire. This is one of those things that's merely a matter of historical fact, not something having to do with how you look at history. Beyond that, adding my own perspective on the matter, since I view the Empire as the thing always at the center of the social construction of historical fact, we can look at the transition from Anglo to American Empire in the contemporary world – from English-dominated Western civilization to U.S.-dominated global civilization – as the most important possible element in the shaping of all contemporary historical fact.

I believe that all contemporary political secrecy ultimately revolves around, not "a conspiracy", but the continuation of an Anglo-style Empire, from an American base, in the global civilization. The reason "a conspiracy" is a non-issue in this sense, even though this description may be almost identical in every other way to how the notion of "a conspiracy" is used in contemporary discourse, is because it's not outside the law: in fact, in civilizations, this is simply how *the law itself* has always worked. Controllers of the law are elites who use the law as a weapon to preserve existing social order under their collective hegemony. The system has just never been quite this out-of-wack, as it has never had to happen so quickly on such a large scale before, while being so openly documented. There's nowhere for the system to hide *except* "plain sight". Resultantly, human beings have never been so deliberately misled about how the system works. Indeed, the *Power*-structure itself, the most visible aspect of which being the government we actually see – the cultural government – is nothing besides one big "cover" (lie).

III

Unmasking the fraud

As a mass phenomenon, the widely-held notion that the government should be there mainly to help people is something oddly new to the world since about the end of the 18th-century[dx] and especially since the beginning of the 20th, when government has never been so intentionally detrimental to the individuals it rules over. The government was always just there to rule the system – that's what people thought, if they thought about it at all – and that's what it did. Civilizational government, because it was always controlled by the State, i.e., the militarized repository's command center, was there to continuously secure the conditions for a system that had been unjust before the State even existed. Only normally, no one said it was "unjust": it was simply the way things were. All such matters, as items for discursive thought, remained almost fully out of the range of mass consciousness.

This worked because the *Power*-structure was always made to be ideologically inextricable from God: it was made to be sacred, which in a system made for destruction means "do not destroy" whatever the sacred thing is. Since it was sacred, there was a certain standard it had to uphold. It couldn't go beyond a certain threshold of perceivable amorality – or, better yet, the system's amorality had to be constrained as tightly as possible by the rationale of the system.[dxi] But so long as it stayed mostly within its constraints, the apex of the *Power*-structure could generally count on gaining sufficient moral acceptance from its subjects for as long as the civilization was energetically possible.

The reason why this worked for such a long time was because the speed-of-events was so *slow* compared to its rate in the days of capitalism – and so especially compared to that during industrialization, and most especially, the age of globalization. Basically, to use a schema familiar to evolutionary biologists and economists alike, the system worked because usually, in the phases of civilization prior to capitalism, beyond a certain level of growth it wasn't as *profitable* for the *Powerful* to intentionally harm the individuals under their domestic rule, as it was to intentionally invest in them. The *Powerful* always know what system works for them and how it works, if only as a purely unreflective, functional matter of occupation.

Beyond a State's least complex stage, in fact, under most historical circumstances prior to industrialization, it's essentially always more advantageous for the *Powerful* to invest in their State's own institutions than it would be for them to harm those institutions.[dxii] This has everything to do with warfare, the basic premise according to which any State emerges, consolidates itself, and grows.[dxiii] Warfare works in this way, first of all, because it provides the most orderly possible avenue for the system's main cause of disorder, amorality: the amoral parts of the system, like murder, theft, rape, etc., are momentarily turned into weapons for the good (the profit) of the internalized domestic community. Secondly, this simultaneously "exports" the potential disorder – as we've seen, the singular ruling doctrine guiding late 19th-century Western "social imperialism".[dxiv]

By making all the public rituals either explicitly or more often implicitly associated with the central organizing principle of warfare, the State essentially says, "This is the kind of disorder we will tolerate; all other disorder will be rooted out and punished to the fullest extent of the law." Throughout the vast majority of the temporal length of most civilizations, the State works because it's a swift hammer – but just as importantly, a predictable one.[dxv] At the relatively fragile and slow levels of economic growth, the explicitly political side of humanity typically can't afford too much audacity. At any given moment a situation might arise calling for all the support the State can get from its citizens, which means it also must usually refrain from behaving towards those citizens with intent to harm. In sum, investing resources in causing additional cultural disorder would be harmful to the State's objectives.

It seems to me that there were two key phases of history when this started to change: with the origins of cash (the origin of money as a commodity) early in the Classical world; and the emergence of mass industrialization at the end of the early modern world and all throughout the late modern world. In both of these cases, deeply flawed systems eventually became worst-case scenario systems – systems of fraud – as a result of transitions from primarily external warfare to primarily internal warfare. In both of these cases, the financialization of the military sphere was the key variable related to transformation.

Let me reemphasize that cash and industrialization were two innovations that, at their earliest points, were only *starting* to change the flawed systems they infiltrated into systems of outright fraudulence. At a certain ultimate point, in each case, the entire system itself became a fraud. No single historical development can be said to be the "cause" of the final transition to total fraud: rather, in each case, a quintessential symptomology ultimately emerged that was representative of the long historical evolution. Clearly, these symptomologies were the complex combinations of processes leading to the emergence of two State formations, the Roman Empire and the U.S. national security State.

Interestingly, the Roman Empire was a fraud in the sense that it tried to maintain the illusion that its transformed government was restoring the world to how it had traditionally worked, whereas the U.S. national security State was a fraud in the sense that it tried to maintain the illusion that its transformed government signaled a world that would be different from anything seen before. Essentially, the same thing happened in each case: governmental transformation represented the transition to a world where "domestic" territory and "foreign" territory had been totally combined into a single universalized system. But this doesn't mean that history "repeats itself". It means that States as individual systems and subsystems of civilizations, civilizations as individual systems and subsystems of intercivilizational structures, and systems of multiple civilizations all evolve according to the same general processes throughout time and over geography, which is why they can be considered "the same kind of systems" (urbanized systems). Politicoeconomic growth based on the cultural order of violent exploitation expands unto ever-greater heights. The war-trade wealth pie gets bigger throughout each intercivilizational period, with its potential maximum increasing also from period to period.

These structural similarities aren't only what allow us to properly understand the history of civilizations; they're what allows there to be a history of civilizations, in the first place. But they refer mainly to questions of complexity, which are questions primarily of material culture. Questions of psychological culture are quintessentially historical, as they collectively refer to the specific individuated cultural manifestation located in a certain finite geography, the thing that can only happen once.

The emergence of the symptomologies themselves called the Roman Empire and the U.S. national security State didn't represent completely unique historical developments insofar as they constituted transforming States within transforming civilizations: rather, what was truly singular in each case was *a cultural population's perception of itself as one community*.[dxvi] Clearly, this is a phenomenon that can exist in reality, in the first place, solely at the level of ideology. But the characteristically ideological phenomenon, nonetheless, ends up having a characteristically ubiquitous empirical impact on all material aspects of human life. Insofar as there was a particularly dominant material symptom of fraud common to both cases, it was irrepressible material excess, purest embodiment of the cultural self-perception of inherent superiority – although the self-perception of inherent superiority manifested in two historically distinct forms.

The most dangerous and lucrative thing that can happen in a warfare system is for the system's elites to discover a certain fact – the system doesn't really have to work like it says; it just has to look like it's working like it says. If there's a "dialectic" here shaping the evolution of human "societies", this is it: although the system works for as long as it can, at certain intervals in the meantime, certain parts of the population subject to the system start to question it. When such questioning hits a certain threshold, the *Power*-structure reacts,[dxvii] and – so long as the system's continued politicoeconomic growth is possible – it's able to avoid collapse, usually by a mass violent outburst followed by "reforms".

This is one of the best reasons explaining why "society" is the wrong model for what individuals (including virtually all sociologists) usually mean by "society", as well as why "dialectic" is the wrong model for the broadest process driving "society". Since human populations relate to the environments they live in, whether they're mostly harmful or mostly benign to those environments, as symptomologies, 'the culture' is the quintessential concept defining those populations, because the symptomology primarily transmits through the population at the level of culture proper, i.e., at the level of ideology. And, in turn, since human populations are so uniquely defined as cultural symptomologies of specific planetary environments, dialectic is the wrong model for how those populations behave.

The populations always behave as wholes to begin with – they constitute systems without having to be "manufactured" as the result of dialectic. The populations behave as a result of an evolutionary process irreducible to any single factor, and thus certainly not reducible to dialectic. Certain kinds of human *ideas* are created in the form of opposites ("thesis and antithesis"), not certain kinds of human populations. Such ideas then contribute to shaping those populations, and are successful at this to the extent that they're useful fictions – models of reality made by the human mind.[dxviii] Reality is real to the extent that humans imagine it accurately.[dxix]

Yet when referring to what dialectic is typically used as a model for in classical historical materialism (Marxism) – the sociohistorical process, which I say is truly evolutionary and not dialectic – it nonetheless can be partially explained in reference to the dialectic. The dialectic just doesn't explain how human populations *have to* evolve. Rather, it describes a major aspect of the main strategy via which human beings have evolved throughout civilizational history. Moreover, this evolutionary strategy behind civilizations seems to be one that's beneficial to the expansion of States, but detrimental to the long-term existence of human populations. That is, we always should've been fighting with everything we have the constant superimposition of dialectic onto human populations, not trying to rigidly adhere to it.

The thesis emerges, the antithesis emerges to oppose it, and their conflict results in a new scenario, the synthesis. On the surface, this is what has gone on in history. But Marx erred when he located this process in the antagonisms of economically-defined sectors: to the extent that it has occurred, it's what has gone on primarily between the organized antagonisms (wars) of culturally-defined "Enemies".

Even in explicitly capitalistic civilizations, the default human mindset isn't one geared towards economics. It's geared towards politics, but politics of a particular kind – *cultural* politics. Now, to some degree culture is always political, and politics is always cultural: both are shaped by history and thus inextricable from it, but at the same time also stand apart from it somehow. This is why, while the human historical always transmits at the level of the social, the social always transmits at the level of the cultural (ideological), which is to say every thing in a human culture must always be looked at as interconnected ultimately with everything else.

Thus, besides the fact that humans can't be mobilized on a massive scale towards State objectives purely for those particular economic purposes States always desire, as these purposes always defy the interests of the vast majority of individuals, it may be impossible to mobilize individuals – to control them – on purely economic grounds, period. Nothing, and certainly not Marxism, could've controlled human beings in such fashion without controlling the cultural. Practically anything can control human beings if it controls the cultural. If this weren't true, how could the theories of a 19th-century European political economist enthralled with the writings of the most reactionary State-worshipper[dxx] have resonated so strikingly, all over the 20th-century planet, with individuals who for the most part had no idea about Hegel, or the dialectic? Contemporary Marxism was always a cultural phenomenon, and a phenomenon of the contemporary dominant culture in particular. More than anything else, it represented the status quo's capture of the "Left-wing" subculture, creating a "Left" that had mass ideological currency while also being, simultaneously, conducive to the existing *Power*-structure's continuation.

Even if there were no actual evidence of it, I would suggest that if Marxism as a cultural movement hadn't served in the first place as the global capitalist establishment's idea of an acceptable "Left", the ideology never could've permeated the world as it did. Moreover, though, we also have substantial evidence showing that contemporary Marxism – specifically referring to the ideology conventionally considered the ideological basis for what was Soviet-style "Communism" as well as Western European-style "Democratic Socialism", in the days before the acceptable globalization ideology for both the "Left" and the "Right" simply became "Neoliberalism" – was originally funded by no milieu so much as the kingpins of Wall Street, that uniquely symbolic bastion of the global capitalist establishment. The best-known proponent of this fact was Antony Sutton, who I prominently referenced in our narrative's third chapter. But it's essential to mention, too – Sutton was greatly influenced in his argument by Carroll Quigley,[dxxi] who was closely associated with the very same establishment, and explicitly stated in *Tragedy & Hope* that certain most *Powerful* overworld players centered around

Wall Street's highest elements had long been funding notable Marxist intellectual products.[dxxii]

Clearly, as Sutton also pointed out, their helping to fund the "Russian Revolution" in 1917, their serving as patrons for myriad "Left" think tanks and publications, and all the rest, was only part of a grander strategy that also required sustaining the acceptable form of "Right", most fatefully including the Fascists and the Nazis. I know that, even as I've already primed the reader for this exact argument, every mention of it still evokes sheer absurdity, so much so that I'm afraid discussing it here may do nothing besides distract. But I believe ignorance of this background is perhaps the thing most singly responsible for skewing individuals' understandings of contemporary history, to the point where even the most unusually well-informed of scholars get duped. We mustn't avoid it.

Further, the argument only seems absurd if there's no reasonable *contextualizing* explanation offered regarding why on Earth capitalists would fund "Communists". Sutton himself had an unusually impressive philosophical grasp on the situation, which, aside from the fact that his work is demonstrably the product of impeccable research, is the reason I find so convincing his argument concerning the tiny Wall Street milieu surrounding the J.P. Morgan Company, and its part in the rise of the Bolsheviks, Hitler, and FDR. Although denigrated as a "conspiracy theorist", there's no denying that Sutton was a uniquely capable scholar – even if we're using the word in only its most conventional sense. The *Power*-structure itself would have to admit that: he was a researcher for the establishment-revered Hoover Institution until he was dropped for having the audacity to write about the long history of U.S. technological aid to the Soviet Union both before and after the Cold War, something which few if any mainstream scholars have ever addressed.[dxxiii]

How could the U.S. national security State have possibly come into existence when it did, how it did, without the existence of the Soviet Union? Could there have possibly been a more culturally convenient "external Enemy", which also had the politicoeconomic means to sufficiently terrify Americans into submitting under imperial mobilization? Here, we're faced with the identical scenario as that related to the U.S. State's double-edged policies in the "War on Drugs" and the "War on Terrorism"; or rather, in the "War on Drugs" and "War on Terrorism" era we're faced with the identical scenario as that which defined the Cold War, only the former represent the model behind the latter taken to an even greater extreme. Whether or not the U.S. actually supports outright the "Enemies" it brainwashes its subjects into lethal unceasing hatred for, at the very least, it nonetheless still allows those "Enemies" to profit by engaging them exactly how they require in order for them to perpetuate their own war-fueled existences.

Beyond that, we can only properly address the actual aid offered to the Soviet Union by the United States through a much broader perspective than would be used by typical contemporary historians. Noticing (1) the evolution of speed as it progressed throughout the periods, and (2) how directly connected certain periods are to the periods immediately before and immediately after them, it wouldn't be incorrect to say that we can go a long way towards understanding a certain period's sociohistorical speed by determining how direct is the connection between that period and those preceding and succeeding it. Obviously, the fastest periods in history have been those dominated by Western civilization and its eventual creation, the global civilization: periods four through seven. That there's a relationship between the directness of the succession from one period to the next and a period's sociohistorical speed is not based just on intuition; and the reasons why such a connection exists are perfectly explicable.

Let's return at last to my notion of urbanization as the materially-implemented relationship between conquest syndromes and their chronologically communicable spaces. The complex adaptive system of urbanized humanity is centrally formed by the social structure constituting the total interactions between all civilization-State-complexes, i.e., under normal "Old World"-originated historical circumstances, between the intercivilizational structure, all the civilizations in it, and all the States in those civilizations. A conquest syndrome's history is nothing besides the hegemony over that system playing itself out within its processually transforming chronologically communicable space.

How direct the connection is between one period and those before and after it, and relatedly how fast history moves in the particular period, revolves around *the interdependence of a conquest syndrome with its predecessors and successors.* Interdependence in this case rests upon the manner in which one period shifts into the next. Most significantly in this vein, if we periodize as I suggest, we'll notice that there was a most devastating and comprehensive collapse leading from the ancient world to the Classical world; a quite expansive collapse leading from the Classical world to the medieval world; and a long, drawn-out collapse of a Power long past its prime – the Byzantine Empire – leading from the medieval world to the early modern world.

But the key to the last turning point is that it wasn't catalyzed mainly by the death of the conquest syndrome from the fading period, but rather by the transposition of that conquest syndrome onto what would be, in the rising period, the first worldwide (interhemispheric) intercivilizational scale. This is precisely what I mean when I say that interdependence of conquest syndromes with past and future syndromes can be judged in terms of how "one period shifts into the next". All conquest syndromes are interdependent with those in their immediate past and future, to some substantial extent; what largely determines speed is *the degree* of interdependence.

Only via Western civilization have we seen anything resembling total interdependence between conquest syndromes, and only via the global civilization have we seen literally total interdependence between conquest syndromes. Total interdependence between the conquest syndromes in successive sociohistorical periods happens when there are individuals comprising the conquest syndrome in one period who also comprise the conquest syndrome in the next period. This happened with the transition from period five to six, when late modern Western civilization became global civilization, and with the transition from period six to seven, when the global civilization transformed from its first to its second manifestation.

That was impossible at any time prior, since the start of one period had never followed the end of the previous one in close enough succession. Here's the main reason why I consider it so important to view the start of globalization as the transition between the end of Western civilization and the beginning of global civilization: this was the first time in history where it was truly possible for hegemons to start implementing the precise conditions for a future conquest syndrome while still inhabiting the present one. And this is primarily what links every phase of contemporary history – the history of the rise and fall of globalization.

In effect, for the only time in history, the conquest syndrome became the whole civilization. That is, the hegemony became entirely interchangeable with the complete urbanized environment. However, while in practice this was and only could've been decided upon in contemporary history, it was a development that had been building for the entire history of capitalist culture, and by extension for the entire history of civilizations. Remember, globalization is the long-term culmination of the evolution of capitalism, just like the evolution of capitalism is the long-term culmination of the evolution of civilizations.

Again, capitalism wasn't created in the first place by Western civilization alone, and couldn't have been created in such a way. Capitalism was definitively created by interactions between all civilizations in a worldwide context, a process that became established for the first time as a result of the forging of the post-Columbian order. Western civilization was always a story, not of an end-unto-itself as Westerners as well as perhaps most of the West's critics like to think, but of conquest dependent upon the preceding context established by other, non-Western – but still *dominant*, i.e., conquest-imposed – cultures. To say that Westerners were the best conquerors in history automatically indicates that there were other conquerors in history.

Intriguingly, the form of "Islam" the West finds itself "fighting" at the present moment has its earliest ancestors – to the extent that this "Islam" has anything to do with the actual religious tradition – in the conquest syndrome that so fatefully spread, starting around the 8th-century, into the geography of what would become Western civilization. For early Muslim traders and warriors (intercivilizational competitors), the decision to spread their influence wasn't indicative of a deliberately invented plan so much as an unreflective strategic mindset geared towards transmitting the conquest syndrome one is a constituent of, always the most natural course to take for individuals constitutive of conquest syndromes. In the same way, the conquerors of the "New World" from Western civilization weren't really coming up with a new strategy when they first encroached upon the Americas, but were just making one easy decision, requiring barely any conscious thought on their behalf: to continue spreading their conquest syndrome. The new grand strategies would emerge later, and wouldn't fully form until much later. Although even those would still usually constitute the implementation of that same decision – "continue spreading the conquest syndrome" – except they constituted it at more complex phases of development. Both Quigley and the much earlier philosopher of history, my greatest scholarly influence, Giambattista Vico, said essentially this same thing, which I paraphrase as: human history follows regular paths across time and space, but this doesn't mean human beings have no free will – it means that when the same choices are made with this will, similar consequences will follow.[dxxiv] This is precisely why we can view every civilization as the same general kind of system as every other civilization.

I've held off on bringing up Vico until now, as I feel his influence in my thinking is so prevalent, I couldn't possibly express it with enough concision such that it wouldn't disrupt the textual flow. Therefore, I decided to save discussion of Vico for the end, when the reader can immediately see what I mean simply by my bringing up some of the philosopher's main ideas. A lifelong inhabitant of Naples and starting at the end of the 17th-century, a longtime professor of Rhetoric at the University of Naples, most scholars who focus on such matters consider Vico one of the earliest philosophers of history, along with the late 14th-century Islamic historian from Moorish Spain, Ibn Khaldun, to whose work I also owe a great deal of gratitude.[dxxv] (Besides that, they're both also considered some of the earliest social scientists.) Vico was also a lifelong hopeful to get the professorship of Law, which paid a much larger sum than Rhetoric and was a great deal more prestigious. This goal of his was repeatedly rejected and ultimately, never fulfilled.

It's thankful Vico never got the job: since he no longer had to worry primarily about that habit of thinking in a socially acceptable fashion necessarily associated with publicly prominent occupations, he was able to contemplate human history in as free a way as was at that time possible. Resultantly, he constructed one of the most original perspectives on human history ever devised. Vico's *New Science* was the first work ever to put forth a view on history shaped by a comprehensive theory of cultural evolution. Although he's usually considered someone whose work wouldn't be appreciated until long after his own time, I believe his writing had an influence far greater than is typically realized. Marx, for instance, referenced Vico at least once, in *Capital*, albeit just in a footnote;[dxxvi] but I think his theory of historical materialism was actually largely an attempt at synthesizing Vico's "theory of times" with Hegelian dialectic.

That theory of Vico's is based on an assertion, ultimately derived from the Classical-era Egyptian historian Manetho, that all past peoples ("nations") in all historical periods pass through three consecutive "ages": an age of gods, an age of heroes, and an age of men. Each represents a phase when a different institutional form – what I would call a different repository – is dominant in the polity. I don't think it's necessary to group history into these three different ages. Rather, it's more appropriate to simply say, as Vico also essentially does, that humanity's mass consciousness starts out at a primarily mythological baseline, and as history progresses, mass consciousness becomes evermore historical.[dxxvii]

The concept of "the Ages" is still useful because it's more or less true that all civilizations start out with religious (mythological) hierarchies as the dominant institutional form; move onto the warlords as the next dominant institutional form; and end up with the traders as the most complex, most historical institutional form. These three thresholds correspond to Vico's "gods, heroes, and men".[dxxviii] Most critically, there's never a point where all three things aren't existent in some form at the same time, which is one reason why the model of a dialectic going on between two sides, represented by two diametrically opposed economic classes – aristocrats and bourgeoisie – is a flawed portrayal of civilizational reality from my perspective.

The dialectic is flawed in this sense, for one thing, because oppositions such as aristocracy and bourgeoisie – intended to stand for higher and lower economic classes, which isn't even entirely accurate – are only one form of the competition that goes on (and not even the main one driving sociohistorical process in civilizations). Marx himself wrote about this extensively in as basic an example of his thought as *The Communist Manifesto*.[dxxix] However, he still insisted upon an ongoing dialectic between diametrically-opposed antagonistic economic classes as the main processual aspect of civilizational history. I agree that economic antagonism has been the underlying force of civilizational evolution; but it's also just as clearly almost never at the forefront of thought for any individuals in quite those terms, except for perhaps certain individuals in ruling classes.

Moreover, in reality, the antagonism never *mainly* took a form exemplified by aristocracy vs. bourgeoisie. It was always mainly combinations of factions that cut across those kinds of boundaries, fighting amongst themselves through setting whole populations against each other. The visible *Power*-structure itself, at the same time as it accidentally confirms the invisible *Power*-structure's existence, also makes it seem like something else altogether. As Baudrillard, who started out as a Marxist and ended up as a non-"Right" critic of Marxism, wrote, "[The masses] are given meaning; they want spectacle."[dxxx] The contemporary *Power*-structure is so sinister precisely because it knows how to "give the people what they want" in the most convincing imaginable package, wholly in ways advantageous to itself.

What Sutton argues, for instance, suggests that Marx, who was paid to write *The Communist Manifesto* in part by the wealthy pirate Jean Laffitte,[dxxxi] was actually being paid *via* Laffitte, by interests embodying what I would call the primordial manifestation of the global shadow government. (In contemporary intelligence parlance, Laffitte would in this case be called a "cut-out".[dxxxii]) This was as part of the European failed "Revolutions" of 1848, which Communists participated in along with many other members of "the working class".[dxxxiii] A great deal of confusion surrounds such event-cluster sequences typically labeled "Revolutions", and I believe much obfuscation clouding up many other areas of historical significance can be best confronted by addressing this overarching confusion.

If one is under an assumption that "Revolutions" are meant primarily to change a status quo of *Power*-structure relationships between rulers and ruled, then from this standpoint, all such sequences, and most especially the ones in the modern and contemporary worlds, have essentially been failures. But of course, such change is never the primary purpose: all "Revolutions" are invariably driven from the top-down. Such change, rather, has forever represented merely the *pretext* for "Revolutions", which is why they always fail from the standpoint of those masses responsible for their execution. From the standpoint of their true primary purpose, on the other hand – securing the hegemony of one agglomeration of factions over another – every "Revolution" succeeds smashingly.

One could hardly find a phenomenon better exemplifying Bernays' chillingly open admission that, for the global *Power*-structure's original psychological warriors – those responsible for conditioning the Western publics for World War One – the highest objective was to manipulate the masses into conforming to elite strategies in such a way that they would fail to realize they were being manipulated.[dxxxiv] This is what causes so much unnecessary confusion about "conspiracies": the thing most responsible for giving rise to "conspiracy theories" is also the thing most necessary to the system's general operability. Imagine the planet of the 19th-century, amidst the worldwide onslaught of industrialized Western national Empires – all attached in some way to the ubiquitous but simultaneously ever-tenuous hegemony of the British Empire. Now imagine the world that directly led up to the 19th-century, a world of ever-expanding Western overseas Empires, run almost entirely by trading companies.

If the primary purpose of the "Revolutions" in the modern world, which would ultimately carry early modern Western civilization into late modern Western civilization (during the late 18th-century and the 19th-century), was to fundamentally alter the status quo, then "revolutionaries" obviously should've targeted not just the aristocratic warlords profiting off of the continental European war system. Even more so, in fact, they should've targeted the bourgeoisie kingpins running European foreign holdings, as these were already much greater forces than the monarchies that had originally legitimated them. Clearly, the dominant merchant classes weren't targeted at all; quite contrarily they represented the main challengers to and ultimately the victors over traditional noble rule. This was what Marx was truly referencing when he discussed "aristocrats vs. bourgeoisie". What he didn't mention was that it was predominately land-based versus predominately sea-based *elites*, contested by both sides via sacrificed bodies of the masses. Naturally, the changes to Western-style State structures that came as a result of the "Revolutions" were such that the new State-formations reflected almost exclusively the desires of financial ("bourgeoisie"/ predominately sea-based) elites within the overall war-trade environment.

"Conspiracy" is a moot point, and in being so constitutes a far more beneficial term for those who use it to silence than for those who use it as an analytic tool in historical investigation. Acts of what might typically be called "conspiracy", either concerning how some writers use the term earnestly or how others use it to denigrate those writers, are usually just symptoms of the global civilization working exactly how it must to survive as a civilization. Sir Ronald Syme, one of the most respected Roman historians of the 20th-century and rumored to have been an English intelligence operative during World War Two, stated perfectly the reason why, in his 1939 classic about the rise of Augustus and the Roman Empire, *The Roman Revolution*. However, he wasn't talking about "conspiracy", which particular word didn't yet have the same meaning it does in current public discourse: he was talking about how, "whatever the form and name of government", at all times in civilizational history, "an oligarchy lurks behind the façade."[dxxxv] He just meant this assertion uncritically; matter-of-factly. "All governments are run by oligarchies." Even the ones called "Democracies" – even the ones called "Soviet Socialist Republics". It's just the way of the world. Nothing to get excited about.

If only the current public were equally accepting. Yet in this day-and-age, the public is strangely unreceptive to attitudes that unabashedly promote wealth-just-for-the-sake-of-wealth imposed by the State's murderous fist. Thankfully for itself, the hegemonic sector is more aware of this fact than is any other conscious entity, and illustrates the world to the public accordingly. Only after a lot of research could I finally accept that, in the existent world, the very presence of some contemporary version of a Western-style government in a territory shouldn't suggest that all governmental activity in that territory is intended mainly to deceive and distract. Rather, it should suggest that governmental activity in that territory is intended *solely* to deceive and distract: quite alarming, insofar as some contemporary version of a Western-style government inhabits every single square inch of the planet. The whole world around, governments do nothing besides defraud those people rigidly subject to their laws.

Since the global civilization has been so deliberately constructed into a holistic system of fraud, every public institution in the contemporary world is at the very least implicitly fraudulent. In many cases, and regarding the most *Powerful* institutions, all cases, the institutions are explicitly so. Implicitly or explicitly, all the institutions are meant to hide the fact that the State is the same thing it has always been: the conquest syndrome's central organ – the quintessential expression of oligarchy, the driving factor behind all civilizations. And the present State is this expression taken to its all-historical breaking point. If oligarchy was always the central mechanism of civilizational evolution – the conquest syndrome's nucleus – then so long as civilizations evolved, more wealth would forever be consolidated into fewer hands. This is exactly what happened throughout the history of civilizations. All else was subsidiary.

Naturally, the most wealth is consolidated in the fewest hands in the contemporary world, and above all in the existent world, the immediate present. That is, the oligarchy is most oligarchic in the world as it presently exists. To be sure, civilizations haven't evolved in one straight line – least unjust distribution-of-wealth at the earliest phase of civilizations and most unjust distribution-of-wealth at the latest, with only constant regular growth in between. Rather, there *tended* to be less unjust overall politicoeconomic systems amongst the civilizations at the earliest phases of the intercivilizational structure, and there tended to be more unjust overall systems amongst the civilizations of the latest phases, those of capitalism. In the phases in between, the process typically unfolded in dynamic cycles of growth, rising and falling from the short historical view but progressing overall geostrategically, from the long view. But I must also add here my belief that the long process has only "progressed" in relation to history thus far; and the nature of geostrategic growth leads me to believe that the evolution of civilizations must at some point peak long-historically, just like it does in individual cases.

We can thereby interpret the immediately present moment in the history of civilizations not just as the peak of the global civilization, but also, and even more importantly, as the epicenter of civilizational evolution's long historical peak. From the perspective constructed in the text as a whole, the entire process, starting with the very first interaction of civilizations, has been coterminous with the evolution of *Power*. And perhaps more than anything else, because of the precise circumstances under which they actually happened, the modern and contemporary "Revolutions" paved the way for the apparent culmination to this oligarchic progress.

I must emphasize to the reader doubly: in a given "Revolution", the "revolutionary feeling" wasn't created by the oligarchy – but that's exactly why it's possible for the "Revolution" to succeed in transferring the old hegemony over legitimate governmental administrative structures to the rising hegemons; the greatest result of any "Revolution", wherever/whenever it happened. The kind of elites running a government has to change if the government is to properly evolve in accordance with the preceding long-term shifts in the "private" sector, a requirement needing to be fulfilled for the civilization in general to continue to grow as it has been growing. Thus, mass uprisings against the present hegemons have to occur. But the most important thing for the reader to remember is that the particular civilization only continues to evolve insofar as *old structures are never truly wiped away.* Indeed, the civilization's old structural underpinnings are completely refitted so they can thrive in their new sociohistorical environment.

Turning now specifically to the "Revolutions" affecting modern Western civilization, the holistic sphere of interlocking cultural spheres – life-support, military, and communications – was reinterpreted then reapplied to an intercivilizational environment of evermore-total Western conquest, the practically inevitable ultimate result of Western civilizational evolution as especially driven by the Western State. Aside from everything we've seen of the precise conditions defining the past couple-of-centuries-plus: even if we had no other knowledge, simply by knowing that a similar national structure spread as a result of every "Revolution", we should've assumed that the same hegemonic sector, and in turn the same general oligarchy, was in this way taking control everywhere the similar national structure went. This is based on nothing besides all prior civilizational history: in every earlier example where an identical form of social structure spread to new territory, one will find that it's because the same conquest syndrome had extended its tentacles.

Concerning the modern and contemporary "Revolutions", what's most likely to stop people from realizing that, or even if they momentarily realize it, what's most likely to stop them from internalizing it as historical reality, is nothing besides nationalism, or any ideological equivalent of nationalism such as Marxism.[dxxxvi] Already in the early 18th-century, before fully-fledged nationalism even existed, Vico conceptualized the underlying phenomenon: he called it "the conceit of nations", the natural tendency of every individual living in a culture to automatically (unthinkingly) operate as if the culture is superior – the measure of everything else.[dxxxvii] In the terminology of contemporary scholarship, the word for this is 'ethnocentricity'. The typical individual in a civilization has so much unconsciously invested in the mythological understanding of his or her culture's history, certain facts, and certain ways of looking at facts, are practically impossible for the individual to assimilate into his or her worldview. The only way to change this is for the individual to completely change his or her worldview, which is far too costly a measure for almost everyone. It's akin to transforming oneself into another person. Very few human beings have the time and energy for that – and this is most basically what it means to be the victim of a conquest syndrome.

Now, if individuals believe that even "Revolutions" don't change things except to allow them to continue worsening, then transforming the world, at least initially, seems more or less hopeless. This is how I felt at first when I started to realize that, concerning all modern and contemporary "Revolutions" as they happened in reality, their greatest effects were to allow rising combinations of elite factions to wrest control of existing systems from incumbent combinations of elite factions. "Revolutions" were never the least bit revolutionary, since in reality, their main impetuses were civil wars within oligarchies.

This makes perfect sense insofar as the eventual maximum expansion and centralization of State *Power* was always the key result of any successful "Revolution", i.e., any instance where a fundamental transfer of *Power* between different repositories occurred. And in the actual sociohistorical context of Western history, which is the only thing we should be initially concerned with in our attempts to assess the politics of Western civilization, the maximally-centralized State was never a politically neutral shell that could be filled with any objectives one desired, but always primarily *a vehicle for official entry into the war-trade competition*, which is to say an institutional force for imperial mobilization. True elites, the owners of the largest centralized governments and real runners of *Power*-structures, owe their wealth entirely to Empires.

Whether or not he ignored it intentionally, Marx failed to properly emphasize the greatest fact in politics, the military, and the greatest fact in capitalist politics, the central bank. Control over the "means of production" in general isn't what capitalists use to rule, but control over the means of production *of destruction*, which is what the Communist Party used in order to rule over the Soviet Union, an Empire with the second most preposterously enormous military in history. In fact, *The Communist Manifesto* specifically urges a program of "industrial armies" and "central banks",[dxxxviii] the latter of which being, above all, what prompted Sutton to consider Marx an outright fraud. It really doesn't matter, though: whether or not Marx himself was intentionally committing fraud, his primary backers – if they were indeed industrial capitalists – were clearly using his work to commit a fraud, by drawing the "Left" to a position that would cause it to ultimately neutralize itself by engaging in the Great Power game. Anyway, what was "Socialism" in general, in its heyday, besides the reflection of a desire for more prudent governance over Western imperialism?

Moreover, Marx himself wouldn't have had to be acting fraudulently to accept the backing of capitalists. In fact, if he really believed what he wrote, it wouldn't have mattered who he accepted help from, because he expected his ideas to win. He could've accepted backing from capitalists while completely under the ideological impression that this was just an example of that self-destruction of capitalism he so famously theorized. What happened instead, of course, was that the capitalist hegemons would consolidate their total resources amongst themselves in a process starting around the end of that half-century in which Marx wrote, working towards one totally monopolized push – in which Marxism, at least the well-established thing that calls itself "Marxism", would indisputably play a vital part.

Ignoring all personal motives, let's just consider the Marxist "Revolutionary" program as Marx himself stated it, and as some Marxist "revolutionaries", at least, tried to implement the program throughout the 20th-century – because this is where the greatest contradictions lie: between the perceived goals of many Marxists and "Communists," and the changes that were made in history when certain groups amongst them took *Power*. If we understand 'revolutionary' to refer to the imagined nature of a great transformation in a culture's status quo *Power*-relationships, then no Marx-inspired "Revolution" could've been revolutionary. The status quo *Power*-relationships in the places where Marxism aimed its "Revolutions" wouldn't and couldn't be changed by the imposition of industrial military oligarchies, as the industrial military oligarchy was already the feature most essential to the *Power*-structure of Marxism's supposed competition. Marx made some very specific policy recommendations, so whether or not he knew that these recommendations weren't actually revolutionary, we know that what he advocated were institutions that at the time of writing, in one instance, had only so far emerged under the conditions of modern Western capitalism, and in the other instance, would in the very near future be the prime catalyst for the emergence of late modern capitalism. Again, the institutions were, respectively, central banks and industrial armies.

In every culture before global capitalism, earliest origins ca. 1898, there were frontiers. There was space outside the culture where the culture didn't have decisive influence, i.e., hegemony, the spirit of a conquest syndrome. What Marx recommended – to repeat, whether he knew he was recommending it or not – was simply "Proletariat" hegemony over the existing industrial politicoeconomic system, which he said he recommended so as to eventually bring about "a classless society".

Now, Marx advocated steps that he said would ultimately lead to this "classless society", which included transference of all private property to a State run by a proletariat dictatorship.[dxxxix] Facts like that led Sutton to advocate for the destruction in one's worldview of a "Left-Right" spectrum as a means for understanding politics, to be replaced with an "authoritarian-individualist" spectrum.[dxl] Marx may have been advocating authoritarianism to eventually do away with it, but the important point from a geostrategic perspective is that he was advocating authoritarianism. This could always be, in the end, subverted for oligarchic purposes after the "Revolution" took place, and that's pretty much exactly what always happened after the masses sacrificed their bodies. Thus, while Sutton may be typically viewed as "Right-wing" – branding him with a label warning all non-"Right-wing" individuals "STAY AWAY!" – he rejected such labels altogether with the strongest emphasis, and with his whole body of work made perhaps the best case of any writer I've come across for why those labels do nothing but deceive and distract.

Clearly, even in the explicit words of the founding father himself, any stage short of the final goal in the Marxist revolutionary program yields a government of ruthless authoritarianism. Therefore, capitalists could back a Marxist "Revolution", do what they could to ensure that it got up-and-running, and facilitate its existence within the Soviet Union, for instance, without there even being any contradiction: all they had to do was let the "Revolution" happen, fight the expansion of the "Communist" system to international dominance, and back the most Statist, authoritarian leaders within the Communist Party. More than anything else, this is what leads to confusion about what it means for the U.S. to have "supported" the Soviet Union. Throughout history, the best support one such entity – in this case, a State – could offer another was to *allow it to have a sphere of influence*. That is, the State can just agree to mostly leave the other State alone within its prescribed domain, allowing it to do what it does. Ignorance of this important truth is tantamount to a complete misunderstanding of State warfare, which itself is much the same thing as a complete misunderstanding of politics.

If one has the goal of being truly revolutionary, simply engaging in interstate warfare, or anything fundamentally resembling interstate warfare, is the best way to negate that goal. The ultimate purpose of interstate warfare, whether the practitioner is conscious of it or not, is to create *'reciprocal frontiers'* between the territory of the two warmakers. Warfare between two parties more or less automatically facilitates a psychological frontier based on the physical frontier between the two parties – "Enemies" – which must be sustained to sustain both cultures. Therefore, at least implicitly, each side of the conflict sustains the other.[dxli] Seen in this light, the tendency for hegemons of industrialized cultures to explicitly create their cultures' own "Enemies" is simply the all-historical unconscious fact of greatest significance being made conscious: the unavoidable bringing to the surface of civilizational evolution's deepest darkest secrets.

*   *   *

Once and for all, as clearly as I can express it, here's how I view the underlying logic driving forward the existence of all States: within the scope of a single civilization, except in special universalized cases, either an interstate system exists, meaning the civilization is internally divided into juridically-bounded subunits; or an intrastate system exists, in which the civilization is comprised of a single State internally organized into administratively-determined subunits. In the interstate system, the States exist primarily as competing war-trade hubs within the largest urbanized context (the intercivilizational structure or the civilization), whereas in the intrastate system, the State exists primarily as the ultimate expression of institutionalized monopoly over the war-trade activities of a juridically-bounded space, insofar as that space exists within an intercivilizational structure (or whatever the largest relevant context is). Within the special universalized cases, such as the Roman Empire and the global civilization, what happens, basically, is the turning of an interstate system into an intrastate system.

That is, the juridically-bounded territories of the old system become administratively-organized territories in the new universalized system. Only in first noting this commonality can we ultimately properly understand the greatest differences between the structure of the Roman Empire and that of the global civilization. And by understanding those differences, in turn, we can see how the logic that allows the State to continue existing is still always essentially the same, whether that State is an ancient city-State within an interstate network, an ancient centralized "Monarchy", the Classical "Democracy" or "Republic", the Western industrial capitalist "Nation", or the "Soviet Socialist Republic".

The State exists insofar as there's interstate war, and where there's interstate war there's necessarily interstate trade, which is ultimately just war in other clothes, on other terrain. War is what ensures every State its *'sovereignty'*.[dxlii] For two "Enemies" at interstate war to truly be "Enemies", their conquest syndromes have to be substantially interchangeable: each has to be able to just "cut off the head" of the other and replace, in the event that it conquers the other's territory. This means that such "Enemies" are always necessarily representatives of systems that have more similarities than differences. In this vein, two simultaneously existing State-run politicoeconomic systems in the same civilization are typically "different" to the extent that they can be complementary: again I return to the archetypal relationship between agricultural land-owning war-trade elites and mercantile seafaring war-trade elites. In this relationship, each depends upon there being exchangeability between the two major forms of war-trade wealth: the form earned from agricultural land and the form earned from producing and exchanging goods. In other words, both "noble" elites and "bourgeois" elites, which is to say, in either case, participants of the *oligarchy*, depend upon there being interchangeability between an official currency – cash, or monetary wealth – and actual wealth – life-support resources.[dxliii] Resultantly, neither can be truly "antagonistic" towards the other in-and-of-itself. In fact, due to the nature of the war-trade environment, competition is usually much fiercer within economic "classes" than it is between different ones. Once again, I reiterate that the normal course is for some noble elites and some bourgeois elites to come together, in order to fight other similar hybrid combinations. It's certainly typical for one side to have a greater emphasis on landed wealth and the other side to have a greater emphasis on mercantile wealth, but it's unusual for two sides to mobilize for war against one another unless there's some significant diversification of wealth-production within each opponent's domain.

With so much focus on England as the model for bourgeoisie "Nations" that supposedly overthrew their noble antagonists, Marx nonetheless failed to realize or avoided the fact that England's long-term aptitude for allowing capitalism to develop and spread within its boundaries came mainly as an effect of its success at striking a working balance – a *modus vivendi* – between aristocrats and merchants within a juridically-bounded space.[dxliv] When traders wanted to use noble-ruled land throughout history, they almost never tried to get rid of the aristocratic institutions in that territory, but instead took the much less costly route and paid the nobles off. This was one of the most reliable methods during the entire existence of civilizations for gaining a sphere of influence: paying off the existing party in charge. Nobles had a corresponding coequal interest in bourgeoisie success, given that all the things the nobles bought to keep up their lifestyles – without which, there would be no nobility at all – were ultimately provided at some point by trading elites. Ignoring individualized conflicts, neither the bourgeoisie nor the nobles could exist without the existence of a structure that contained both nobles and bourgeoisie. The question to be answered for anyone who thinks otherwise is why on Earth would the bourgeoisie elites destroy their best customers, and why would the nobles destroy their greatest sources of non-agricultural wealth?

The industrialization mindset, which has only existed for about two centuries in total, and in most places outside of western Europe and the U.S. for much less than a century, is the particular mindset accustomed to viewing "Progress" as human history's automatic course. It's next to impossible for an individual enthralled by an industrialized dominant culture – above all, most non-poor individuals living in the West at any point during the past couple of centuries or so – to see things any other way. Concerning such individuals, the only possibility for seeing things otherwise involves the complete transformation of one's state-of-mind; an unacceptably difficult task for virtually every individuals who ever inhabited the contemporary dominant culture.

The expectation of "Progress" assumes that "Freedom" simply grows in parallel to the passage of time: along with the procession of history comes a co-occurring increase in the justness of "the distribution of wealth". Of course, this is merely the experience of the 19th-century western European bourgeoisie superimposed onto the totality of history. Marx represented one of the greatest examples of a sharp mind that fell victim to "Progress's" ideal, believing the bourgeoisie to naturally be a step up from the nobility, in the same way as "the Proletariat" would be a step up from the bourgeoisie.

On the other hand, revolting against the dogma of "Progress", which reflects a righteous impulse, far too often leads to another misunderstanding of human history – one which may be worse, for it's a "half-truth", and as the early 20th-century German sociologist Franz Oppenheimer says (specifically regarding Marx's writings), half-truths "…are far more dangerous than total untruths, since their discovery is more difficult, and false conclusions from them are inevitable".[dxlv] The misunderstanding comes in the form of a belief that human history is necessarily fundamentally random, subject to no continuous evolution at all. Oppenheimer, another of my greatest influences, himself displayed susceptibility to the allure of "Progress" in what's undoubtedly his best-known work, *The State*, published in 1908 in Germany and in 1922 in the United States. Oppenheimer offers the soundest scientific approach towards the State ever written, more complete even than Charles Tilly's, despite the fact that Tilly wrote at the opposite end of the 20th-century; though I believe one can gain the best grasp on the State by reading both theorists in conjunction, keeping each writer's respective historical context at the forefront of one's mind. As regards *The State*, the specific timing of its publication allows it to serve as a perfect means for conducting a natural experiment. Since it was published right before the Western State would take its final turn towards total authoritarianism, Oppenheimer can't be charged with simply identifying a process made exceptionally striking by the war.

In fact, at the time of writing, the first decade of the 20th-century, Oppenheimer clearly expressed a belief that the condition of the State as it had existed for millennia – one he diagnosed personally – seemed to be disappearing. Based on his interpretation of what was happening in the U.S. Government of his contemporary, he theorized that the State's traditional form, wherein it had always been purely a vehicle for consolidating conquest, was ultimately giving way to what he labeled a "Freemen's Citizenship".[dxlvi] If we put this view in its proper sociohistorical context, it was probably most in-line with something typically believed by "Socialists" who advocated evolutionary rather than revolutionary programs: the belief that "Socialistic" policy regimes could be gradually implemented through electoral victories in "Democratic" central governments.

At that point, recall, the Germany Oppenheimer lived in had only recently adopted any electoral/parliamentary institutions at all, one of the changes effected by the Franco-Prussian war of 1871. In this era shortly before the outbreak of internationalized total warfare, and even for some time after, electoral institutions, which had almost universally been installed via "Revolutions", plausibly seemed to many Westerners like logical cures for what appeared by comparison to be the arbitrary brutality of "Monarchy". It would've been much more plausible, however, if "Revolution" truly reflected a destruction of *Power*'s foundation – as opposed to being merely an addition to that foundation; or at most, a reinterpretation.

"Revolutions" weren't revolutionary, and in turn, electoral institutions, at least in terms of how they existed in their distinctly late modern Western format, would prove incapable of changing the systems they overtook, since the State's fundamental pattern of "constant economic growth through the culturally-secured violent exploitation of a juridically-bounded and administratively-determined space" never changed. Indeed, the electoral systems would be used in large part for the purposes of propaganda – the purposes of culture – on behalf of the most extreme Powers of all: propaganda specifically aiming to conceal the fact that the fundamental pattern never transforms, only worsens. At the same time, the electoral system's other, interlocking primary purpose would be to serve as the main arena for the new psychological/culturally-based, unspeakable form of warfare associated with the nuclearization of humanity.

The form of government in the existent world, a failure in every other sense, is the greatest imaginable success from the standpoint of an oligarchy, an oligarchy that does everything it can to conceal its very existence, but which must exist insofar as the traditional form of State never went away. It's so successful because, from conventional points-of-view in the existent dominant culture, it's so remarkably confusing – so apparently chaotic: and yet, it represents nothing besides the playing out of a global civilization, which by necessity of the cultural complexity required for a civilization on a globally singularized scale, means it must be the most orderly imaginable politicoeconomic system that has ever existed. This suggests that the system, which seems so unbearably confusing on the surface, must at some level be very simple. Additionally, insofar as civilization-State-complexes always reflect nothing so much as the strategies oligarchs use to perpetuate their *Power* – which is essentially all "geostrategy" ultimately refers to – the level where the system is simplest must be at the apex of the apex of the cultural pyramid. Thus, insofar as this level is expressed in human group self-consciousness, there must be some individuals in the world who perfectly understand how the system works; otherwise the system, which is necessarily the direct result of some underlying strategic logic, would dis-integrate, in the word's most literal sense.

Since the simplest general explanation for what goes on in the global civilization is that it's the culmination of capitalism's evolution – and thereby, the culmination of the evolution of civilizations and their associated contexts – the simplest explanation concerning all of the things about the system that, if plainly stated, would seem so confusing to one of its typical subjects, is that things are as the *Powerful* desire them to be. At the highest levels, this requires individuals to set and work towards achieving long-term, broad-sweeping objectives for affairs affecting the whole globe. The notion that the *Powerful* don't or even can't implement complicated long-term strategies couldn't be more inappropriate for the scenario of the contemporary world, where the incomparably complex nature of the system does nothing less than *demand* that those who run it devise and execute intricate long-term objectives involving coordination between many seemingly disparate areas of human life. In this sense, the theorized motive behind every individual covertly-influenced action that might seem completely inexplicable on its own appears perfectly albeit appallingly rational if we keep two things in mind: (1) the underlying conditions of globalized urbanization, most namely the conditions necessary for a corporate industrial oligarchy, can't exist without the construction of long-range global geostrategy. And inseparably, (2) successful geostrategy in the contemporary world requires the constant total planetary mobilization of populations and resources.

With these things in mind, consider Oppenheimer's definition of the State, which, although written less than a decade prior to World War One, might as well have been written on a completely different planet from the one the war would leave in its wake. This juxtaposition, of course, is what makes the definition more than an elegantly simple theory and renders it the basis for a natural experiment:

> What, then, is the State as a sociological concept? The State, completely in its genesis, essentially and almost completely during the first stages of its existence, is a social institution, forced by a victorious group of men on a defeated group, with the sole purpose of regulating the dominion of the victorious group over the vanquished, and securing itself against revolt from within and attacks from abroad. Teleologically, this dominion had no other purpose than the economic exploitation of the vanquished by the victors.[dxlvii]

While writing in a European context that had seen a most unprecedented streak of almost a hundred years with barely much open warfare between European States on European territory – and himself not immune to the myth of "Progress" – Oppenheimer was still able to see the State for the thing it had always been: a sacred center primarily utilized for securing conquered territory. Presumably it was Oppenheimer's social evolutionary perspective that, while on the one hand providing the basis for so much of his theory that was dead-on, on the other hand also led him to believe that humanity was very possibly finally evolving out of its ancient civilizational habitus of conquest-for-profit, citing the abolition of explicit slavery and the greater spread of electoral institutions as examples, with the U.S. obviously serving as the contemporary inspiration for both.[dxlviii] After World War One happened, with World War Two clearly in the works, Oppenheimer astutely observed that these were just the last desperate attempts on behalf of those running a doomed system to hold onto their control.[dxlix] What he probably misjudged, and what almost all of even the most capable contemporary commenters seem to misjudge, is the unrelentingly ubiquitous extent of the damage this fatally-flawed system can do on its path to certain collapse.

Oppenheimer died in the midst of the Allies' predetermined road to victory in World War Two, so he would never get to witness the strategy of implementing a permanent global wartime economy in an era of supposed "Peace". Of course then I can't comment on what might've thought of this strategy. But what I see is the exact embodiment of Oppenheimer's definition, on the grandest conceivable scale: "…a social institution, forced by a victorious group of men on a defeated group, with the sole purpose of regulating the dominion of the victorious group over the vanquished, and securing itself against revolt from within and attacks from abroad." And even more importantly, I see something with absolutely "…no other purpose than the economic exploitation of the vanquished by the victors." To assign anything more profound to the purpose of the State than well-planned use of violence in consideration of what's good for the bottom line is already to misunderstand the history of the contemporary world.

The original long-range planning for the contemporary world occurred amidst the event-clusters of 1898-99, continuing through World War One and the interwar years. At every step along the way, the main purpose behind the strategizing was nothing besides setting up those conditions necessary for implementation of the next step, meaning the next war. When World War Two finally happened, regardless of any officially declared loyalties and oppositions, the best way to look at it is that, on a global scale, the "new guard" of the hegemonic sector – headed by the oligarchy – was making a seamless transition to its Cold War role by grabbing the reins from the "old guard".

As we've seen, it's absurd historically to take the belligerents' word for it when it comes to "what they're fighting for", and this has been taken to its utmost extreme with the conditions surrounding globalization. Truly, it's a painfully difficult thing to know not only "what they're fighting for" when contemporary wars happen, but even more basically who "they" are. The easiest way to approach this incredibly confusing territory is to start with Oppenheimer's definition of the State, specifically concerning the State's "…sole purpose of regulating the dominion of the victorious group over the vanquished, and securing itself against revolt from within and attacks from abroad." So we must ask, who are the "victorious" when contemporary wars happen, and who are the "vanquished"? Considering contemporary warfare while looking beyond officially declared alliances, it's easy to see that the real winners are always wealthy, and the real losers are always impoverished.

If we completely avoid the propaganda except insofar as it's accidental evidence of the true underlying conditions, we can see that no matter what contemporary war one considers, the winners are always the corporations and all other similar organizations integral to the war effort, and more precisely the individuals that defend these entities as their own interests. In the contemporary world, it's inaccurate to refer to this whole collectivity as the "military-industrial-complex" – unless one expands one's definition of the military to include more or less the entire contemporary dominant culture. The problem can then be rightly viewed for what it is, what could only rightly be called the "everything-industrial-complex", under the intrinsic hegemony of the all-encompassing global security State.

To do this, you have to drastically transform how you think of contemporary war; you have to think of every individual war as being also – and more significantly – a *battle*, within a war that started in 1898, never ended, and took place in a "theater" which in actuality was the entire globe and eventually expanded outside the planet. But even concerning the circumstances under which oligarchs took their fight into outer space, the goal was still always primarily the securing of a better vantage point for consolidating conquest on the planet itself: to look at the whole Earth as if through a microscope, to study how best to perpetuate oligarchic conditions. In reference to the Cold War, writing at the peak of the U.S. population's distaste for the Vietnam occupation, Prouty points out that wars are always won simply in terms of which side outlasts the other, which side can make the other side bow out first.[dl] Concerning the wars in the contemporary world leading up to and including the Cold War, the planners, emanating from a business sector that did essentially nothing besides quantitatively monitor the planet's resources in monetary terms, split the Earth's strategic resources in two different piles and stacked the deck against the side they needed to lose – the side that wasn't the United States. At the highest levels of contemporary *Power*, then, all overt military policy is necessarily unified. This doesn't mean that there's no actual competition going on between the people ultimately running the system, just that the competition doesn't go on at the level of direct conflict between State militaries. The overt wars are for the masses, to conform them to the system; and for the warriors (which in the contemporary world means bureaucrats even more than it does "soldiers" as traditionally conceived), to mobilize their support toward the desired ends.

In the past, other similar entities – Empires – faced this exact same problem. The Roman Republic was an Empire in all but name long before the rise of Augustus, the first Emperor. Once its militarized expansion had led it to conquer the entire Mediterranean from shore to shore by the end of the 2nd-century BCE, true military conflict ceased to have an effect on whether or not the Roman military would continue to have constantly increasing resources devoted to it, and the Roman military resultantly became just the culture's leading vested interest, and as such the quintessential real-world embodiment of the Empire's continued existence. Competition continued, but it was at the level of who got to control the essentially unchanging military Empire, not at the level of individual military conflicts. Competition continued within a context where the Roman military was already always the winner.

Prouty cites the late 19th-century French general and military theorist Ardant duPicq, who wrote an invaluable treatise called *Battle Studies*. In particular, he brings up duPicq's indispensable assertion that ancient battles were never "massive all-out confrontations" – sprawling, chaotic "melees" – but rather "hand to hand" clashes between the few men on opposite sides of the same perimeter, with the prime purpose of battle being to always renew this front line. The general's job was to make sure that he could engage the enemy with more well-equipped men than could the other side: more men moved to the front lines for as long as was possible, until the battle was decided.[dli] Within its own sphere, war was perfectly orderly. There were *rules*. It was a game. The chaos stemmed from the irrepressible expansion of the regime war imposed on everything else.

In the contemporary world, light-years past duPicq's time in a historical sense, I see from my perspective looking back that we can't limit the definition of "the perimeter" to mean solely that line immediately separating two opposing formations. Especially in the existent world of peak globalization, we see that it's not accurate to look at "the theater" merely as a field of two battling militaries: it's the total global environment. So now, the main perimeter isn't one between two skirmishing armies, a phenomenon that doesn't even really exist anymore in its traditional form, but between the civilization itself and its psychological frontiers. In a far deeper sense than all officially stated loyalties, the perpetual war is between the global security State on one side and everything that doesn't environmentally support it on the other.[dlii] This is what it really means for there to be permanent total mobilization. The "alliances" conform themselves to this preceding reality.

"Securing itself against revolts from within and attacks from abroad": remember, unlike any Empire in human history, including Rome, the global capitalist Empire has no real "abroad". It's the intrastate system made out of the interstate system from period six, which latter-mentioned system first started to appear at the end of globalization's first stage. The interstate system formed through the entire process of period six, which formation would set up the conditions for the final stage of contemporary history, period seven. An excellent Marxist sociologist, William Robinson, taking the Cold War to really be what it said it was on the surface, asserts that a globalized market didn't fully emerge until 1995 with the establishment of the World Trade Organization, which he also points to (in this case, I think, correctly) as the official introduction of the global State (what he calls the "transnational state").[dliii] In my definition of the global State, I've followed much of what Robinson says, although I disagree with his suggestion that we should "return to the historical materialist conception of the State."[dliv] I agree with Oppenheimer, who as long ago as 1908 saw precisely this aspect of Marx's theory to be its fatal flaw.[dlv]

Oppenheimer's criticism of Marx's theory of the State rests on Marx's portrayal of the State as the institutional outgrowth of the dominant economic class, whereas Oppenheimer – basically stating the inverse – sees the dominant class as the outgrowth of an original act of conquest consolidated via the emergence of the State.[dlvi] In this way, Oppenheimer brilliantly and succinctly distinguishes between political and economic means of obtaining resources, which distinction I've largely adopted: the economic means involve living off of one's own labor product, whereas the political means involve living off another individual's labor product, which one has stolen.[dlvii] Marx's view of all life as bluntly economic ignores this indispensable distinction; in my opinion this is again the result of Marx's *unreflective* reliance on the specifically 19th-century Western economic system as his sole frame-of-reference.

Vico, too, viewed the State as an institution that could only be rightly understood insofar as it had been born from the precise conditions necessary for sustaining violent domination by one group over another.[dlviii] Obviously, Marx himself did as well – the workers' reign was to be installed via a "Revolution" – but framed that as at most a secondary detail, insignificant to the grand scheme of things considering what he expected to ultimately be accomplished.[dlix] Of course Marxism in general, at least concerning how one dominant form of it existed in practice, was wholly dependent on the notion that you must take up arms against the existing *Power*-structure in order to (eventually) change it. I've already said that I think this is the best conceivable method for ensuring that the existing *Power*-structure won't change and will only worsen.

The hierarchy within urbanized humanity as a whole – conceptualizing 'urbanized humanity' as the holistic entity comprising the cultural pyramid/social structure/historical solar system – is just the cultural embodiment of the economic hierarchy established by the definitively political act of war, the war that always exists so long as an Empire does. Global civilization is a global war hierarchy. So long as that hierarchy is the core hierarchy shaping humanity, *Power* can only evolve according to the same underlying pattern, no matter what it presents itself as on the surface. Selling the "Cold War cover story", as Prouty called it, was the only way the global permanent war machine could be fully institutionalized in the real-world context.[dlx] Therefore, even (and in my opinion, especially) someone who thought of him or herself as a true capitalist could in theory quite logically support the existence of the Soviet Union. Without it the global war machine would've withered and died, with all the precisely laid-out plans for the global economy dying alongside it. Capitalism is nothing without the war machine, just as, at certain well-advanced stages of its evolution, the war machine is nothing without capitalism.

This is how the oligarchic mindset works: no global oligarch could've logically been against the installation of a Marxist system in Russia unless he or she personally had some way of profiting more, on behalf of the overarching American hegemony, with another kind of system. Considering this, we must always keep in mind that we're not talking about just any sociohistorical conditions when we talk about the context in which "Communism" took control of a substantial portion of the globe, but specifically those conditions that existed in the early 20th-century precursor to the contemporary dominant culture. In that vein, I'm left with no other conclusion but that the main strategic objective for the oligarchs after World War One was to create the perfect "Enemies" around which to mold their planned civilization, their global Empire. Thus, it must've been very rare for any oligarch to be sincerely internally opposed to the implementation of "Communism" via the Russian central government. What oligarchs would've been divided amongst themselves on was the direction that "Communism" would take; this was the truly important thing, and this was predominately what manifested at the level of human action.

Just like any other mainstream political ideology, which indeed Marxism represented in much of the world throughout most of the 20th-century, Marxism has two main aspects: what adherents believe, and how this translates into sociohistorical reality. "Adherents" of course come in a variety of degrees. What I'm concerned with are individuals who *thought of themselves as* "Marxists"; specifically, I think it's necessary to explore how such individuals felt about the Soviet Union. Often, especially today, individuals who were/are Marxists from a philosophical perspective disown the philosophy's relationship to the Soviet Union. Obviously, to paraphrase what was said so well in the film *Network* as long ago as 1976, it would be very surprising if they were actually discussing Marx's theories in the POLITBURO[dlxi] – to which I add, except insofar as the surface language of those theories was used for propaganda purposes. On the other hand, there's no denying the fact that Marx was used again and again as a "revolutionary" rallying point, and among the individuals worldwide calling themselves "Marxists", the number of those who looked favorably upon the Soviet Union was probably comparable to the number of those who viewed that nation with disdain. In any case, Marx's writings must've had some significant connection to the Soviet Union, even if it's not quite clear what this connection was.

Clearly, it would be much easier to simply ignore the problem and move onto something else, but I think it has great significance for our understanding of contemporary history, so it's something that must be reflected on – even if the reader disagrees with my interpretation, it's still necessary to think about the problem, and what a better interpretation might look like. To understand the issue I think we first of all have to separate in our minds three terms, which are used in so many different ways they might as well have no real meaning anymore: communism, Marxism, and socialism. I distinguish between 'communism' on the one hand and "Communism" on the other in the same way that I distinguish between all actual meanings of words and the meanings represented by the purely conventionalized use of those same words. This is wholly intertwined with the complete confusion laden throughout the issue of the Soviet Union and its relationship to Marxism. 'Communism' is an ideal indicating the preference for a certain kind of polity, whereas "Communism" was an actual cultural political phenomenon that, for a time, was foremost associated with the Soviet Union, an entity representing essentially the furthest imaginable thing from communism. Moreover, making matters even more confusing, "Communism" was the name given to the Soviet style of government mainly by its "Enemies", whereas the Soviets themselves mainly referred to it as "Socialism". Additionally, "Socialism" is different from 'socialism', again with the one being a material phenomenon and the other being an ideal. Making things more confusing still, "Socialism" was also the name for another mainstream ideology primarily associated with the "First World" European States.

It can only make sense to consider any of the ideals to be interchangeable with its correspondent political phenomenon to the extent that one ignores the fact that there's almost no fundamental difference, from one State to the next, in terms of the conditions under which any contemporary government operates. In this way, the identical thing that can be said of "Communism" and "Socialism" can also be said of most mainstream ideologies on the "Right", i.e., all the various forms of "Conservatism". This isn't confusing at all so long as we understand that *Power* has no governing ideology; it does simply whatever's most profitable.

That's why, even though all other contemporary systems have little true interchangeability with their eponymous ideals, "Capitalism" is still essentially capitalism, and "Fascism" was more or less still fascism. Yet, while "Capitalism" and "Fascism" were quintessential representations of capitalism/fascism in the 20th-century, the dominance of capitalism/fascism obviously went far beyond those public manifestations. If we're going to simply focus on being historically accurate, *all* governments in the global civilization were/are capitalist/fascist, and these things are interchangeable insofar as fascism is the globally industrialized reiteration of what capitalism had historically been.

"Fascism" and "Capitalism", insofar as these were the main cultural movements directly associated with capitalism/fascism, represented ideological support for industrialized total war mobilization, specifically the forms associated with the Axis powers during World War Two and the U.S. during the Cold War, respectively. Fascism represents the politicoeconomic system that was necessary to implement in order for the traditional capitalist system – the cultural system originally ruled by trader oligarchs and dominated worldwide by Westerners – to exist in a world of global industrialization. From this perspective, I'm arguing for a 20th-century history dominated by a force not much different from the form of "global fascism" that the international legal scholar Richard Falk posits as being emergent ca. 2003,[dlxii] and similarly the already-mentioned "transnational capitalist State" set forth by William Robinson, which the sociologist argues became officially institutionalized with the WTO in 1995.[dlxiii] The difference is that I argue for the latest, existent phase as the direct culmination of multiple, prior phases of global fascism held in place by the transnational capitalist hegemony, phases that humanity had necessarily already gone through before the emergence of the global civilization-State-complex; and from a broader perspective as the culmination of everything already implicitly building for about 6,000 years of urban evolution. Eventually, the oligarchy that always existed in one form or another to decisively control the evolution of everything else in civilizations would, if left uncontested, evolve until it had a monopoly over *global* affairs – and this would necessarily be the stage immediately preceding absolute collapse. The turns Falk and Robinson so rightly point to as key indices of transformation didn't represent the beginning of the global capitalist/fascist State, but the beginning of the end.

Since the very beginning of the contemporary world, there has been no point at which the whole planet wasn't the victim of complete conquest by one or another form of a Western-originated industrialization, whoever the particular conquerors happened to be at a given moment. *Aside from any officially declared loyalties*, there was no point at which the individuals truly controlling the Great Powers – the contestants in World War One, World War Two, and beyond – didn't see the planet primarily in terms of their jockeying amongst one another for turf in a globally finite arena. If the sociohistorically-evolved form of capitalism is indeed, as I suggest, the model we should rightly apply, then simply according to the logic of that most basic model, secretly divvying up the territory while maintaining a façade of open warfare should've been the most sensible option, assuming that one has no concern whatsoever for morality. (The oligarchs can't have a concern for morality, because their only concern is what works for their system. This is precisely what true morality isn't.)

In the early 20th-century, all it would've taken for the individuals truly running the Great Powers (the oligarchs) to recognize that fact would've been a recognition of the underlying pattern traditionally driving their own sector's sociohistorical behavior. Here's what had happened for about four centuries of international competition between Western Great Powers: individuals from the up-and-coming Powers would challenge the individuals in the present number-one spot, and the number-one spot would in turn fund challengers to the number-two spot. Obviously, Britain was the greatest player at this war-trade competition; in fact, the contemporary form of geopolitics, geostrategy, grand strategy – whatever you wish to call it – was explicitly introduced as part of the decadent British Empire's attempt at a pre-emptive strike aiming to postpone its own fall.[dlxiv] Only subsequently would such democratic luminaries as the Nazi party and Josef Stalin dutifully study the doctrine, mainly as a means of blocking the enemy who invented it. The point is that democracy and global grand strategy can't exist in the same environment. Anglo-American planners and all their globally-dispersed cohorts weren't only aware of this fact, but were (/are) more precisely obsessed with it.

Although the term 'geopolitics' is a uniquely contemporary one, I call the phenomenon itself the *contemporary* form geopolitics because it's really nothing besides the sociohistorical evolution of *Power* translated into a political doctrine. This is perhaps the main reason why, knowing about Sutton's research on Marx, I can't ignore the suspicion that Marxism's actual main purpose in history was above all to serve as a tool of grand strategy – just like, from an "opposite" perspective, the real main purpose in history behind promoting Adam Smith's "free market" ideology was geostrategic. Smith, of course, was an economist for the British East India Company, an organization that was among the originary historical instigators of using black market opium money to fund imperialism; one of the most blatantly despicable examples in history of directly profiting off of human misery, and like so many such examples originally an invention of the

British oligarchy. In Marx's case, if his writings were promoted to serve a strategic purpose, the scenario would've fundamentally been this: again, whatever Marx's intentions, his work (and especially *The Communist Manifesto*) would've been promoted around the time of the failed 1848 "Revolutions" in Germany, on account of its ability to serve two apparently contradictory purposes at once. Simultaneously, it made an impassioned argument that could ideologically mobilize a great mass of communist and socialist-minded individuals for "Revolution", which as it happened would also pre-emptively neutralize that mobilization's true revolutionary potential. This would've been intended to create a German bourgeois nation ready-made for competition with France, a creation which would eventually happen by other means, of course leading in turn to the Anglo-American alliance's destruction of Germany's Great Power potential through the episodes of 1898-1945.

As with all warfare in civilizations, then, the main point is rarely to completely destroy the entirety of "Enemy" territory; almost always, the main purpose is to destroy methodically, with the intention of capturing prime territory – especially the symbolic center.[dlxv] If one of the reasons why Marx's work was promoted in 1848 was to serve British purposes, it would've been in order to psychologically capture the communist and socialist cause without destroying it. Anything that can mobilize that many individuals, the theorized rationale would go, not only can but must be made useful to the prevailing hegemony somehow. How could it possibly be a bad thing, the oligarchs must've thought, to control the very individuals who consider us their opponents?

Anyway, whether that was the purpose of funding Marx to begin with, it was certainly the reasoning behind the Anglo-American establishment's infiltration of the mainstream "Left" at the beginning of the 20th-century. "Those individuals shouldn't be destroyed; they can be made to support our version of industrialization. In fact, we *need* them for our industrialization to ultimately continue." Even if the purpose in funding Bolshevism started out as the desire for a captive market, as Sutton largely suggests in earlier works,[dlxvi] the most indispensable aspect of the Soviet Union to the global system would undoubtedly soon become its role as the thing large swathes of the U.S. population feared most, in turn securing their support of endless U.S. military commitments, the aspect Sutton gives greater emphasis to later on.[dlxvii]

With that sort of thinking, conventional ideological beliefs can't be fulfilled via the conventionally-existing system. Indeed, that sort of thinking requires a system that ensures conventional ideological beliefs will always be perpetuated *while remaining* always unfulfilled. This is why the average individual in the global civilization is so ill-suited for seeing the reality of the situation: why would anyone support something financially with the outright intention of causing its failure?

Yet Quigley tells us that no less a Power than the J.P. Morgan Company and its attendant factions implemented this very strategy around the time of World War One, and not only that, but "…other financiers had talked about it and even attempted it earlier." Specifically, the factions wanted to infiltrate the "Left" in the United States at the time – not in order to destroy it, but to "keep an eye on it", and when necessary, to decisively influence the course of events it would take.[dlxviii] I mention this not to excoriate the "Left", insofar as this is by no means a state-of-affairs unique to the particular phenomenon. Indeed, there's no conceivable social sector comprising the contemporary dominant culture that's not somehow subject to this kind of neutralization. It's what real war in a context of globalization looks like, and the oligarchy has a monopoly on war.

Even if one honestly analyzes the system from the most conventional perspective, it's easy to see that warfare in the contemporary world, no matter what official Power was ostensibly causing it to take place, was an area of human life controlled by institutions ultimately working on behalf of the world's most monetarily wealthy individuals. Going deeper, I assert that these individuals were so monetarily wealthy precisely insofar as their institutions deliberately brought about overall conditions in the global civilization adhering as closely as possible to a rule of "control over monetary wealth = social control". In other words, they controlled warfare – and in turn, everything else – by financializing everything at a historical moment when "their people" were as close as was possible to possessing total control over the planet's financial institutions, its vital resources, and its war machines.

Thus, the nature of the monopoly's controllers when it started forming determined the particular surface appearance of the monopoly: the original global elites made the kind of world where late 19th-century Anglo-American-associated oligarchs could most easily "feel at home" and thrive. How could human beings knowingly set the world at war simply for their own gain? Probably even those oligarchs who considered themselves most "egalitarian" couldn't have passed up the opportunity to totally centralize Western imperial *Power*. It's not always possible to establish monopolies; the timing has to be just right. If one fails to do it when it seems to be possible, one may never get that opportunity again. And besides, if the group was going to go along with you or without you, you might as well go along with it. No reason to suffer for something you couldn't change. In other words, even the oligarchs, or in fact, especially the oligarchs, are subject to the herd mentality. They're the *Principes* (most literally – the first citizens) of the herd mentality.

Going deepest, since contemporary warfare has been totally monopolized precisely in accordance with its being *the* long historical culmination of warfare's evolution, I argue that every act of warfare in the global civilization must be definitively related in some way to the same global group of oligarchs competing amongst themselves – "competing", that is, under the umbrella of the monopoly. Competition at the apex of the apex, the level of the oligarchs, just doesn't look the same at all as it does at the mass level. At their level, it's a nice friendly game at the club.[dlxix] On the mass level, the nice friendly game translates into irrevocable mass hatreds, exponentially upward-spiraling violence, and populations suffering permanent psychological damage.

At the apex of the apex, the historical transition from noble patriarch to financial patriarch, and the subsequent historical evolution of financial patriarchy – culminating with the criminal patriarchy dominant in the middle and late stages of globalization (1947-1991, 1995-?) – both become matters of literal historical fact; Lippmann's concept of a social set where distinctions between the private and the public disappear embodied in real-life individuals. Recall my attribution of unparalleled significance to the fact that only in the contemporary world did it become possible for the individuals comprising the existing conquest syndrome to simultaneously start implementing the next one, which happened for the first time with the meta-event-cluster sequence spanning the Anglo-American colonial wars of 1898-99 to the U.S.'s atomic slaughter of Japan in August, 1945. Now the significance comes fully to light: since the periods shifted with such unprecedented speed, the conquest syndromes could be passed *directly* from one generation to the next, by word-of-mouth in the form of person-to-person occupational tutelage.[dlxx]

This means there has been the greatest possible opportunity for the most "sensitive" aspects of the global national security environment to be shared without a need for documentation. Most strikingly, the rules of the game itself don't have to be written down, since the players of today's game learn from individuals who helped invent yesterday's game, or at least individuals who learned from those individuals. Nothing could provide sounder assurance of continuity-of-policy from year to year. Consider the classification system for government documents: typically, individuals think of "TOP SECRET" as the highest classification, although there's at least one other known classification that's even higher, "ULTRA-SENSITIVE".[dlxxi] My argument is, whatever the highest *named* classification, there must be a level above that without a name, without any officially acknowledged presence. The individuals privy to that unspeakable classification don't write down the things they do – certainly not in public records, even those most deeply buried.

Yet that doesn't mean there's no formal regularity to their behavior. The laws of this level, in fact, need to be the most well-established and tightly maintained throughout the whole social structure in order for the system to work properly.[dlxxii] According to this postulated idea of a highest, unlabeled classification, everything below the apex in its working totality could be the *only* proof possible of the tinier apex's existence: and in my view, the real-world working totality appears to prove the existence of a highest, unnamed classification. This isn't nearly as controversial as it may superficially seem – we know, for example, how every single component of the system works according to some rigid occupational hierarchy, and that every hierarchy answers to a still higher hierarchy. What I'm saying is that at some point, the hierarchy of all the hierarchies must come to a spot where it ends, where the pyramid "closes"; and that all the "secrecy" (obfuscation) of the system is ultimately meant to hide the role of the apex, and thereby the system's true nature. We can't see the mountain peak because it's covered in clouds, but we must assume it's there due to the entire mountain visible beneath.

Now, it would be one thing to avoid making such working assumptions about a whole system if what we were dealing with was simply disorder. But it's not that, nor could it be. To form a structure, everything happening within the structure has to accord to some underlying order. Moreover, I've identified and described exactly what kind of structure, and in turn what kind of "order", it is: it's nothing besides the structure of a civilization; hence it's maintained by the kind of order historically prevalent in that sort of structure.

Since humanity's cultural worlds have to work as whole systems, and since the whole system in the contemporary world is a civilization, there are extremely specific conditions it must fulfill to maintain its existence, which I've tried to make clear with the entirety of the present text. One must develop accurate working assumptions about how such a system works in order to properly understand any of its individual aspects. It turns out that the oligarchy itself is the component most necessary to any civilization's existence as a civilization: if the existent world really exists in the form of a civilization, the safest possible working assumption is that it's ultimately ruled by an oligarchy. No one could imagine a better depiction of this than the establishment's outright obsession with "economic growth", depicted above all by the irrepressible doctrine of "infinite" growth, so transparent in its true purpose as a governing concept that it would be laughable, were it not destroying everything in existence. For one thing, besides the present economic system as idolatrized by "Economists", the only other phenomenon in the world requiring "infinite" economic growth just to survive is *a Ponzi scheme*, a.k.a. a pyramid scheme.[dlxxiii]

Resultantly, for the first time in history, the rulers of the system are what the criminologist William K. Black calls (in a discursive context that's only slightly different and in any case inextricably related) "control frauds". Black, who was also one of the U.S. Government's chief regulators responsible for resolving the S&L crisis of the 1980s, uses the term to refer to the type of corporate criminal that profits by intentionally running his company into the ground. As he dissects so brilliantly, the conventionally-sanctioned "Economists" of the time, and even for some time after – this only started to change slightly following the megaterrorist attack[dlxxiv] called the "2008 Financial Collapse" – fraud wasn't something one had to worry about in the case of the failing S&L's. "Market Discipline" guaranteed that CEOs wouldn't deliberately cheat their own companies, since, if they were perceived to be performing dishonestly, or even just poorly, as CEOs, this would be accurately reflected by "The Market's" responses.[dlxxv]

It's probably true that the majority of CEOs wouldn't deliberately cheat their own companies, although in my opinion that has far less to do with "The Market" than it does with the moral capacity of most human beings. But the whole point here is that CEOs intentionally running their companies into the ground aren't individuals behaving as CEOs *per se*, but *conmen* (sociopaths) utilizing the companies they premeditatedly destroy as nothing more than vehicles for fraud. "The Market" can't guide these men or women, since they don't care about the rules of "The Market", or anything else – because they're frauds. The real issue, then, is that "Economists" think criminality doesn't play a significant role in shaping U.S.-dominated global capitalism.

In that way, they're not at all different from the vast majority of officially-sanctioned "Scholars", or for that matter the vast majority of individuals inhabiting the contemporary dominant culture. Yet even without knowing much about the history of the specific culture, still, by an acquaintance with the much longer histories of civilizations in general and capitalism in particular, we should in the first place expect crime to play an unparalleled role in shaping the contemporary politicoeconomic system. Then, in a research of the relevant history aiming to reach a balance between breadth and depth, one should seek out as many signs as possible that this doesn't hold true. I've undertaken such an investigation. What I've learned is that this most definitive aspect of all State-ruled cultures – but most of all, the capitalist ones – manifests more strikingly in the contemporary world than it ever has before; and that within the contemporary world, it has become exponentially more pronounced as time has passed, in the existent world reaching its all historical peak.

Crime, which is to say, from the broadest relevant phenomenological perspective, amoral behavior, played an unparalleled role in shaping the evolution of civilizations insofar as it led foremost to the passing and enforcement of laws. This wasn't historically dialectic: the crimes and the laws weren't intrinsically opposites, but were only thought to be so by human beings. The *ideas*, then, appeared as dialectical pairs, whereas, in practice, crimes, laws, and the human beings affected by them formed altogether a complex adaptive system, a unified set of constantly interacting with one another regulatory functions that always strived above all to reproduce the whole set's equilibrium conditions. And at the moments when drastic environmental changes made reproducing those conditions impossible, it would always strive to reproduce whatever it could of the existing structure, in an overall "package" better suited to the new environment.

Out of the necessarily interconnected crimes and laws that they, in turn, were interconnected with, human beings built and maintained the most complex social structures in history. Conquest syndromes are so uniquely capable of spreading insofar as, almost automatically, their being absorbed convinces the absorber that the systems they hold in place are absolute necessities. They're successful at this to the extent that they can work while leaving the vast majority of things unsaid: most namely, all those things that would suggest the system's only purpose is to reproduce oligarchic conditions. Thus, the system's official ideology – the conquest syndrome's main outward vehicle – tries to leave unsaid all evidence that its systemically-encompassing actions are "absolute necessities" solely from the standpoint of reproducing a deliberately unjust social structure.

If we consider the origins of oligarchy to be more or less the origins of organized crime families, oligarchic behavior becomes much more understandable. We must keep in mind, though, that for much of history these families prospered by keeping (some minimum level of) order in addition to causing disorder. This isn't to endorse past oligarchies, but quite the contrary to explain why an inherently flawed system was nonetheless able to always succeed so prominently. By the time governments, the public faces of oligarchies, are well in place, the hegemonic war-trade hierarchy permits less immediate disorder than there would be if no such hegemony were in place.

However, this fact always simply postpones the disorder, and in that way makes for an eventual outbreak of disorder much worse than if all oligarchy had simply disappeared to begin with. Moreover, the sole reason why the initial establishment of hegemony is able to prevent further immediate disorder has to do with the fact that, when no hegemony is in place, it mainly indicates that different factions are still caught up in an ongoing process of fighting for hegemony. The only way elite factions stop fighting over a territory is when one of them wins – establishes hegemony. But after that, the elite factions typically must set their sights on fighting elite factions from outside their home turf. It's the nature of the system they control: kill for profit or be killed for profit. Always on to the next "Enemy".

At least during much of the precapitalist days, though, and even to some extent in the capitalist epoch, the oligarchs themselves frequently had to put their own bodies on the line to get glory: after all, kings were nothing but supreme warlords; they were often killed in battle. And as for traders, the same dynamic was in play on other terrain. The original trading elites had to go out to sea, making dangerous journeys in terrifyingly unknown foreign lands. This is what kept the system honest, to the degree that it was.

Implicitly, fraudulence is there from the beginning in conquest-imposed cultures, as I've said. But it doesn't proliferate immediately; it ebbs and flows for a while. It starts to proliferate, it seems, the moment that everything the elites do starts getting outsourced to others. The system slowly begins to separate itself from being purely associated with singular dynasties, and becomes an entity-unto-itself, ruled by the *office* of the monarchy. It's no longer the home base for a handful of unusually successful traders – it's the heart of the systemically irreplaceable logistical core of a trading empire.

Still, so long as there are frontiers, the fraudulence can remain mostly unconscious – beneath the surface. The vast majority of individuals are kept unawares of how the system actually works, and aren't concerned with it anyhow. They fear the "Enemy" beyond the gate and thereby trust the one inside it, who they see not as "Enemy", but as "Protector". Their concern is their work and wage, their daily bread, and their close circle of family and friends.

For all of those things – work, wage, daily bread, family and friends – almost entirely without realizing it, they depend upon the existence of the whole social structure and the politicoeconomic system sustaining it. This is made possible by the existence of the *Power*-structure, which exists exclusively through the centralization of war-trade control. Or, it's better to say, the *Power*-structure is the literal embodiment of that centralization.

For now, the only question that remains is why? But we must keep in mind that we need to ask and in turn answer this question in a precise context: the context of everything we've already seen along our journey. What does "Why?" really mean in that case?

How about, first, "Why are things the way they are?" As I've tried to show, there are many, many reasons, of many different kinds; and even more importantly, all of these reasons, insofar as they exist within a unified (planetary) historical field, necessarily must be interconnected.

For instance, consider the notion of 'evil'. I've argued that the phenomenon of evil does really exist as a driving force of human cultural evolution – but again, as *a* driving force, by no means the only one. Indeed, the very fact of the existence of 'evil' as a real concept acting in the world, as I've presented it, requires a most precisely configured set of sociohistorical conditions in order to effectively operate. Evil in fact is able to work best when it's what's most responsible for configuring the sociohistorical conditions. Resultantly, while 'good' may always have more or less the same definition throughout history, the quality and extent of evil always changes according to sociohistorical flux. That is, the good always manifests in actions undertaken with humble respect for one's environment; whereas disrespect for one's surroundings manifests in a million different ways, to a million different degrees.

Yet as an overarching principle, I still can't think of a better singular metric to use for judging all those innumerable ways and degrees than the level of intentionality used in acts of destruction. Therefore, in terms of "Why are things the way they are?", to the extent that we can narrow it down to one thing, that thing is the unrelentingly ever-increasing sociohistorical acceleration of intentionally-planned destruction. This one thing dominates in relation to everything else because it has a greater and more immediate ability than any other thing to affect the holistic planetary environment.

This thing isn't as abstract as I first make it seem: in reality, it's just the exact feature that has allowed military affairs to increasingly take hold over all other human cultural evolution since the origins of agriculture, but especially since the origin of ever-larger settlement systems. For the evolution of humanity surrounding the affairs of its militaries is in the most significant sense not an isolated fact, but the leading index of the whole history of *Power*: in the beginning and at the end, civilizations don't work without *Power*, and *Power* in civilizations doesn't work without the military, which is the fundamental reason why there are States.

Coming into existence to solve a specific problem, the State takes on a life of its own with virtual instantaneity in the form of the "private" interests it sustains. The more absolutely dominant those interests are within the context of everything else, the faster the sociohistorical process. It might simply be, actually, that great accelerations of the sociohistorical process in civilizations have been more or less synonymous with the most rapid increases in the proportion of planetary wealth-production dominated by vested interests. This works, I believe, to the extent that at any given moment, it's the fastest means of attaining holistic cultural order over the greatest space.

Putting everything in the previous few paragraphs together, in other words, if considered as separate entities, oligarchies and militaries have identical goals. But of course, considering everything we've seen on the rest of our journey, we can easily see how, in reality, oligarchies and militaries refer to two different aspects of the same (unitary) phenomenon – in turn, there's only one objective, which is the perpetuation of geostrategic entities, i.e., in terms both physical and psychological, *Power*-structures. This simultaneously serves the needs of oligarchies and militaries as wholes.

On an even broader level, what should be of even greatest concern – what makes the long historical nexus between oligarchies and militaries so uniquely crucial from a short historical perspective – things are the way they are insofar as the oligarchic military structure creates *a system the masses support*. Indeed, this is what it means in practice, and in the contemporary world, above all, to be "the fastest means of attaining holistic cultural order over the greatest space." The all-historical culmination of this phenomenon's evolution was the long/short historical melding definitive of 'globalization', epitomized by the once-and-for-all industrial capitalist transformation of the whole planet: the creation of what I call the psywar environment.

At that point, one might rightly say there ceased to be any truly military purpose in military affairs whatsoever; although, once a militarized system exists in the first place, the continuation of the system itself becomes the military's most natural purpose of all, so it's better to say that the traditional purpose of the military was taken to its greatest imaginable extreme. The deepest purpose of every military is to simply continue existing, so a system where the military *self-consciously* seeks to perpetuate its own existence to the exclusion of every other objective isn't a contradiction, but is rather the most logical thing in the world. Contradictions only arise when we start to compare the reality to what individuals in the cultures defined by warfare typically take to be the purpose of their warmaking: when we compare the historical to the fabulous.

This brings me to, secondly, "Why are things so hard to change?" To begin, in the contemporary world, our mythology is entirely interchangeable with our history, a problem impossibly compounded by the fact that the establishment treats the writing of "History" (the history of the *Power*-structure) as an indispensable area to be controlled by its psychological operators. Not solely in terms of direct influence on scholarship, but – what's of even higher significance – in the outright concoction of the *material* "Historians" write about.

Thus emerges yet another point of similarity between the era of the U.S. national security State and that of the Roman Empire: in my opinion, the most meaningful similarity of all. From the longest scale perspective, there are relatively few cultural contexts in history wherein human beings understand the past *primarily* in terms of written historical narratives. When historical writing emerges, it emerges as a reinterpretation of mythology, and is initially, in many ways, overtly inseparable from it. This is why, in the relevant imaginaries, historical writing manifests so definitively as "History": the latter is indeed the necessary starting point for understanding cultures where the prevailing representations of the past are historical narratives.

Such cultures are always the most advanced *Power*-structures in their respective sociohistorical contexts, making it so "History" seems to be the direct equivalent of history. But "History" is really only interchangeable with history from the internal perspective of those very highest levels of all-historical human organization. Yet, since the cultures with that perspective are, as historical entities, defined precisely by the unrivaled enormity of their social dominance, the misperception that "History" is the sole embodiment of history has an impact completely disproportionate to the temporal length of those moments where it appears most prominently. The most *Powerful* hierarchical structures humanity has ever known got that way by *stealing the history* of everything within their domains (chronologically communicable spaces). Essentially, this is how conquest syndromes self-replicate on the most complex scales. Self-replication is the sole aim of any conquest syndrome.

Therefore, stealing a whole sociohistorical period will bring more success than anything else a conquest syndrome can do. Of the past examples where conquest syndromes accomplished such grand historical larceny, the most audacious of all involved cases where conquest syndromes created whole sociohistorical periods essentially all on their own. Only industrialization has facilitated such audacious systemic fraud, and as it has happened – all we can concern ourselves with at first if we're to study reality – industrialization has represented a conquest syndrome of explicitly Western origins. At the same time, implicitly, as we've seen, industrialization was simply the last major phase of sociohistorically-evolved capitalism, the latter being a phenomenon wholly grown from an *inter*civilizational – and ultimately interhemispheric – structure.

That is, the world made the West, and then the West remade the world in its own image. To fully appreciate the naturally deliberate injustice of Western rule, we have to understand it as the worst-case scenario lying dormant in all prior historical evolution based on such injustice: a most extreme reflection of all preceding civilizational history, which, in its aspect of greatest impact, is the story of the evolution of warfare accomplished through humanity's most complex institutions, wherein the latter were ultimately made into mere vehicles for carrying out geostrategic design. In a system built for war, every thing is or can be made into a weapon, leading to the contemporary situation where every thing literally *was* made into a weapon (the psywar environment). Relatedly, everyone was made into a soldier fighting on behalf of one or another "cause". The system strives to continue existing, and is at war with everything that would hinder this existence. Meanwhile, every episode that the system says is war is really just a prop. Confusingly, this makes those props not really war in the superficial sense the system claims, but really war in the deepest sense: the militarized system fighting for its continued existence.

In that sense, if the main goal of warfare is merely to not die, as says duPicq,[dlxxvi] then individuals have a very good reason to not oppose the State. For opposing the existent State, especially in the form of an idea, is nothing less than an act of war –

according, at least, to the State. In the existent world, where everything unconscious is conscious, the State literally declares you "Enemy" if you give even the slightest signal of refusing to obey its omnipotent will. But this doesn't mean the State is strong. It, in fact, means that it's weak.

The final transformation of Western extremism from unconscious to conscious started to be accomplished through the industrialization of humanity, and from there, the out-of-control exponential increase in humanity's self-consciousness was accomplished through the total globalization of Western industrial capitalism. Essentially, this was all of humanity's past civilizational evolution coming back to haunt it. The lesson here must be that racial, ethnic, religious, or any other particularized demographic subdivisions never had anything essential to do with *originally* causing the insoluble problems of humanity's past. The culprits weren't traits unique to any race, religion, or otherwise, but traits all human beings throughout all of history have been susceptible to. These traits were aided and abetted mainly by the specificities shaping particular geographical domains, with certain geographies, at certain times, giving rise to *Power*-structures at certain times more readily than other locales, and among these, a still much smaller number being the most conducive of all to the building of *Power*-structures.

Within its chronologically-conditioned geography, any *Power*-structure must have a premise for its existence that the people can support, and this premise must be a fiction, because the empirical truth is that as a whole the people necessarily get much less than they put into it. By its very nature, according to its foremost intention, the *Power*-structure is the gravest injustice. In earlier times, the injustice was legitimated like this: the *Powerful* are naturally better. This would work for long stretches of civilizational history, but was eventually challenged in every context where it appeared.

One such challenge was Christianity; another was Islam; in another part of the world, at an earlier time, it had shown up as Taoism, and in yet another, Buddhism. According to the scholar and activist David Graeber in his excellent book *Debt: the First 5,000 Years*, these were long-term responses to the cash economies that had only so recently emerged in human history. Graeber rightly points out that, more than anything else, cash economies indicated expansive systems of far-flung (interregional) warfare.[dlxxvii] (Vico, too, connected the origins of money to the costs of warfare, almost 250 years ago, albeit for a different reason.[dlxxviii]) Thus, with the very invention of cash, occurring as it did situated wholly within a context of war, it was already prefigured that the monetarily wealthy could someday capture the military sphere.

Cash wasn't able to take over warfare completely until capitalism emerged. But it had already taken over religion by that time; and especially, the religions originally albeit unconsciously spawned as responses to the rapid social disintegration following from the very emergence of cash economies. Still, for a long time, this was mainly an implicit capture. Cash wasn't yet creating its own totalized environment.

Slowly, this started to change – though in some locales much more strikingly than in others. In the West, the explicit capture took place preeminently in the newest imperial hot spots: in the north Atlantic, where traders from all over flocked in search of wealth. One should never lose sight of the definitively *inter*national quality coloring mercantile dominance from the outset. I find it quite revealing, for instance, that the term "prime minister" originally referred to the individual elected by Italian merchants would elect to represent them as a collective, in their dealings whilst working in foreign communities.[dlxxix] From its very beginning, the prime minister should be seen as the spokesmen for a holding company of foreign interests in its *modus vivendi* with local nobility.

"Conspiracy theories" abound positing the U.S. national security State as little more than the resurgence of the British Empire on a totally globalized scale. The immense plausibility of this scenario truly makes one wonder how "conspiracy theory" became so synonymous with "lunatic". On the other hand, it's equally incorrect to view British Empire as a phenomenon aiming to reproduce English culture in order to fulfill a goal that could be rightly seen as "nationalistic", or attached to any other similar -ism. Capitalism is unique precisely insofar as it has *no ideological goals whatsoever*. It is purest *Power* – entirely politicoeconomic, entirely operational, no space at all for morality.

More than anything, this is what makes "conspiracy" a moot point. The thing I find most terrifying about the existing system is that, *even if* the individuals truly running it had the best possible intentions, the system couldn't be modified. All that's possible, at this point, is for its underlying structure to be adhered to or not adhered to. To the extent that there's an "invisible" cabal running the world, which to me is completely obvious, this still isn't "a conspiracy", but quite divergently represents a legal system itself, running exactly how it's meant to be based on over 6,000 continuous years of cultural evolution in agricultural settlement systems. What's so effective about the way the cabal operates is that its conspiratorial behavior typically aims just at not "messing with" history's general course of history – in other words, the cabal's behavior is aimed at not letting things change. This calls for the least possible direct intervention on its behalf at any given moment.

Nevertheless, since we live in an era where the whole point of everything seems to be to test what exactly Earth's physical limits are, the playing out of the whole systemic process happens on such a maximally-grown scale that "least possible direct intervention" still indicates the tightest constant management of human affairs ever achieved. To make such unprecedentedly complex designs as simple as possible, the cabal works by focusing its attention on recurrently facilitating the broadest conditions allowing for all other systemic behavior: this is how it minimizes the number of changes to the system's invisible social structure. What this means is that, no matter what, in the contemporary world, any thing that large numbers of individuals participated in was, due to that fact alone, likely one part of a grand strategy intending to accomplish nothing nobler than the status quo's perpetuation.

When I say there was "no space for morality" in capitalism, I mean that, concerning the overall strategy of the globalization culture, for instance – again, the only culture in history to be constructed according entirely with a predetermined strategy – moral considerations as the average contemporary individual would understand them were solely a factor insofar as they guided the fabrication of propaganda. Globalization only worked because all of the system's most representative aspects were designed according to intentions in stark violation of the general population's morality. In practice, the system's unique capacity for destruction owed to that singular aspect which received the greatest proportion of energy-time inputs: the ability to appear sufficiently moral while acting simultaneously with deliberate amorality.

To reiterate, as a measure of communal morality, the only thing I've found important here is the apparent level of concern *a culture as a whole* has for acting morally in particular sociohistorical contexts. The assumption here is that the greatest limiting factor for the morality of a whole population is the sort of morality built into the system-at-large, which I've argued is a factor inextricable from the culture's broadest politicoeconomic system. In other words, amorality, on the broadest level, is typically much more harmful when it appears as the lack of a positive attribute, rather than as the possession of a negative one.

However, certain human-made environments tend to give rise to particularly large populations of individuals possessing "negative" attributes, in this sense, which is to say, possessing the propensity for *anti*social behavior (behavior that counteracts, or *negates*, "the social"). Throughout history, such environments were primarily those constituting the logistical (geostrategic/sociohistorical) baseline conditions for the emergence of civilizations. For whatever reason, the area most conducive to antisocial behavior was the central intercivilizational zone; and the problem was always most overwhelming on the European side of the Eurasian continent.

Whether you agree with my interpretation or not, I've said that I think the reason never had to do mainly with any individual's choice at any given moment, but always was something dependent in the first place on the longest sociohistorical evolution; and above all on the chronologically specific geography of civilizations. The cabal knows this fact, so much so that it forms the basis for one of the closest things it has to a religion. It has mastered the dogma – the dogma appearing in the world in the form of contemporary geopolitics.

In fact, concerning the milieu where contemporary geopolitics originated – at the highest levels of the British oligarchy, at the beginning of the last century – there were always attached to it individuals viewing everything related to humanity in terms of the long sociohistorical evolution of civilizations, who focused primarily on geography. The most famous, of course, was Arnold Toynbee.[dlxxx] What goes unsaid in Toynbee's work, is that from the precise context whence he emerged, his kind of work, too (perhaps his kind of work above all), is a field of warfare, or what amounts to the same thing, it's *treated as* a field of warfare by those running the *Power*-structure.

In such a context, the goal of "objective truth" *per se* could never successfully be attained by conventional scholarship – but mainly because it was never ultimately what was being sought. The goal was always, consciously or unconsciously, Empire's perpetuation of itself, since that was the only goal civilizations themselves had ever known. Contemporary oligarchy felt (feels) that nothing else is possible, insofar as they saw themselves as the only ones conceivably capable of running things. Being subject to the herd mentality worse than everyone else, albeit in their own uniquely "superior" way, the oligarchs would rather die a sure death than live in the terror of uncertainty. Oligarchy works in the scope of everything else in civilizations on account of the oligarchs' *subjection of themselves* to the unreflective necessities of the in-group as a whole – that is, those things demanding to be fulfilled for the oligarchy itself to exist – where the requirements of perpetuating a specific set of conditions make the only real choice "Yes" or "No" to the system ('1' or '0'). When the structure is everything there is, the cabal itself simply becomes another part of the machine, even if it's the one that initiates all the other parts. All the insolubility of the system as a whole resides in this state where the lone individuals seeming to have the *Power* to transform the system become the individuals least capable of truly changing anything.

This may bring up one more – the last – question, "Why bother bringing any of this up?" Let the system collapse according to its own momentum. Clearly this would be so preferable that just by bringing it up, it must be apparent that I believe it to be impossible, or else I wouldn't have spent so much effort constructing the present text.

The contemporary regime invested so much wealth in stockpiling such incomprehensible quantities of destruction, I suspect that letting the system simply collapse on its own would lead to nothing less than the annihilation of all Earth's existing life. To take what's unfortunately at this point "just one" example, allowing the current system to dissipate without a plan for its controlled demolition would lead to a scenario where there's no mechanism of ecological control over the nuclear stockpile. In that case, I'm infinitely more troubled by thoughts of what could happen simply from the unmanaged volatility of these "resources" themselves, than I am by notions of their falling into the hands of any individual or group. Without the system that the arms support, they can do nothing of any value for anyone who might try to use them.

The life-support and communications spheres need to be totally transformed. This needs to happen in such a way that it will become retrospectively the beginning of a non-militarized humanity. That is, life-support and communications need to change according to that objective.

A non-militarized humanity would surely combine at least two fundamental cultural practices in its structural foundation: (1) permaculture and ecological agriculture; and (2) gift economy. Now, from a metaphysical perspective, I believe its mythological inquiries would be historical – as opposed to its historical inquiries being mythological, which is what yields "History". When I refer to "mythological" here, I'm talking about the cosmological, not the fantastic; I'm talking about the way cultures understand the origins of the worlds they simultaneously inhabit and create, indisputably a necessity for the existence of any human culture. Those responsible for running our own culture recognize this, although they do so in order to abuse the responsibility inherent in possessing the knowledge.

It can perhaps even be said that the hegemons of our culture recognize this better than any individuals in history, precisely concerning how they use control over "History" as the quintessential methodological basis for their psychological warfare. This is the most amoral possible thing, insofar as it's the worst example in history of individuals aiming to *perpetuate* the problems they're born into. The scale of sin is so grand it's automatically obvious how impossible it is for any individuals outside the hegemonic sector to commit it, which is to say, to intentionally perpetrate the crime. Certain such individuals actually create "Historical Events", out of thin air and sociohistorical process.

That perfectly effectuates the strategic goal of neutralizing contemporary humanity's potential for understanding its own history – the story of the ever-evolving sociohistorical process, as it exists in a totally unique yet for the same exact reason, totally familiar way in the contemporary world. However, while acknowledgement of such unimaginably vast amorality is no doubt of almost incomparable significance for the accurate construction of a history reflecting the lived narrative of globalization, far more significant, in the end, was that amorality representing the lack of a positive attribute, rather than that representing the possession of a negative one, such as could be found in the hegemonic sector. Whatever the sector's actions were, there was at least a substantial minority of individuals in the contemporary dominant culture *as a whole*, which still had theoretical freedom to choose the course of their lives to an extent never before approached by any other human beings in history. And it remains true that they chose to act as the vast majority of human beings throughout all prior history had chosen in situations of a similar kind but lesser degree. They chose to enhance their own interests and neglect those affecting everyone and everything else.

This is amoral insofar as it precludes moral choices from being made – amorality as the simple lack of moral contribution; precisely what it means when one's energy and time is "wasted". The existent world is this on the largest scale, at all-historically maximum hyperdrive. The wager the contemporary oligarchy makes, repeated infinitely, is that contemporary individuals, when given a choice between the two, almost universally tend towards making choices that enhance their own *wants* over making a choice that enhances another person's *needs*. Actually, individuals in the existent dominant culture don't even see themselves as making this choice: it's only barely a true choice; it's the self-actualization of totally unreflective human brain activity. You can't even call it thought, in the existent world. It's just the mechanics of human brain activity, happening. In this way, then, the materialist habit of looking at the world is only the industrialized mindset unreflectively describing the one thing it knows: itself.

How can those in a world of hydrocarbons see themselves in a world without? They can't: contemporary individuals who envision a world without hydrocarbons have already started to go to that other world. Looking at the existent dead world from somewhere between it and the one beyond, it seems as if all prior history had been "intended" (?) to do nothing besides bring us to this point. It's a point that will determine whether "civilized" humanity ever really had any bit of humanity worth speaking of, or if the great social experiment constituting human history was all for naught.

Tellingly of the whole, it's not a question of "What?" – as in, "What to do?" – it's a question of "How?": how do we actually accomplish the things we need to accomplish? In other words, we're dealing with a situation where, it's not at all that we have a lack of theoretical solutions – we're aware of what's good for us, and not only do we *know that* they're good for us, but in fact we *understand why* they're good for us – but a complete inability to even begin to conceive of practical ones. What kind of humanity would be logistically incapable of militarization? This is what we need to figure out.

Before I'm decried as Utopian for even raising the question, let it be known that the *Power*-structure itself has long considered this problem and even spread the rumor that it had solved it…with nuclear and thermonuclear weapons. As history clearly shows, all this did was remove one main aspect of warfare – straight-up conquest of land for profit, the lifeblood of all capitalist economies prior to the global civilization, not to mention the remainder of civilizational history – while leaving the other two intact. The nuclearization of humanity yielded an urbanization wholly dependent upon the two other vital (and interconnected) purposes of warfare: (1) sustaining cultural elites (founded upon oligarchies) and (2) terroristic control. Far from a system capable of controlling itself at will, nuclearized humanity "worked" solely insofar as the interconnection between these two remaining features of warfare was able to remake everything else in its own image at all times.

"9/11" was as pure an incarnation of this ontological fact as one could conceive delivered in a single event-cluster. It was nothing besides the global State using the entire living planet to rejuvenate itself for one last hurrah in one fell swoop, on a single day, in a scenario having no other purpose than the reconsolidation of its own immediate survival. This day has then essentially been lived again every single day since. Without even acknowledging the explicit connections between individuals "in both camps" – between the U.S. war machine and, for one, al-Qaeda – implicitly, it's absolutely indisputable that the only interests in the world served that day were those connected with these two entities, which is to say, if only indirectly in any given case, the interests of every thing constituting the dual politicoeconomic/ideological phenomenon of globalization.

As for the explicit connections, they could be found, as always in the contemporary world, in the unnamed interface between what Peter Dale Scott refers to as "Drugs, Oil, and War".[dlxxxi] But the reason for the unrivaled success of this particular nexus goes beyond all of these most systemically indispensable things individually: the nexus succeeds insofar as it constitutes purest logistics, which also happens to illustrate how trade – always an inherently militarized sphere in civilizations – invariably comes to dominate war, whenever the two are central parts of the same system. Nevertheless, in the end, we see that, like the individual who owns things that "end up owning him", trade's domination of war leads to a trade that dominates and overwhelms itself, by having irreversibly committed itself to a policy of hypermilitarization in a world where real war is no longer an option.

At the highest levels, contemporary "trade" was simply international finance, just like "war" in the contemporary world was represented by petroleum. But of course, the truly unique thing about the contemporary world was that even these highest-ranking sectors were simply parts of the machine, albeit the only ones that intentionally brought about precisely those statuses for themselves. That's because the finance-petroleum trade-war nexus deliberately created – and hence deliberately reproduced, year after year, day after day in all its most routine procedures – the machine, and this is the singular thing it cared about truly keeping "secret". Even this had to eventually come out sooner or later, though, because when the whole world works as a terribly efficient machine, the very fact that it is a machine can't honestly be hidden.

The question never should've been "How do we bring the current public face of the oligarchy to justice?" This is what every "Revolution" was built on, and why every "Revolution" failed to be revolutionary. Once you decide to play the same geostrategic game, and commit to that decision for even the smallest calculable fraction of time, the possibility for actual change is lost until the next time when such a possibility should emerge, at which point it will simply be decided again in that split-nanosecond, at which point the existing Power will always survive in an altered form. The revolutionary changes have to start long before the question of "Revolution" can be seriously asked – the existing Power always essentially survived so long as its challenger *even responded to the question*. The current public face of the oligarchy will be brought to justice when the system it benefits from no longer exists.

At this point, the necessary preceding revolutionary changes have already started to take place, which makes our situation different from every prior one precisely insofar as we've actually started to correctly identify the problems and solutions. The only question now is, will we be able to implement the solutions we know to be absolutely necessary? Or, will *Homo sapiens* succeed at destroying once and for all the imaginary possibility of "humanity", and perhaps even all the current life-support capacity of Earth? We'll get to the answers, but we had to discover how to ask the right questions first. Believe me, I know that the present text contains nothing but the very very beginning: the things I had to get out of my head before I could move forward. Welcome to the new world!

ⁱ Quoted in Alan E. Bernstein, *The Formation of Hell: Death and Retribution in the Ancient and Early Christian Worlds*, (London: UCL Press Limited, 1993), p. 113.

Part 1:

ⁱⁱ Göran Sonesson, *Pictorial concepts: Inquiries into the semiotic heritage and its relevance to the interpretation of the visible world*, (Bromley, England: Lund University Press, 1989), Chapter I. This reflects my interpretation of Sonesson's pictorial semiotic approach: it's the result of incorporating the basis of his general philosophy with my perspective as a whole.

ⁱⁱⁱ Giambattista Vico, trans. Thomas Goddard Bergin, and Max Harold Fisch, *The New Science of Giambattista Vico, Third Edition*, (Ithaca, New York: Cornell University Press, 1968; originally published 1744), p. 3: "...the philosophers have not yet contemplated His providence in respect of that part of it which is most proper to men...", what Vico calls "the civil world or world of nations".

^{iv} Jared Diamond's *Guns, Germs, and Steel: The Fate of Human Societies*, (New York, London: W.W. Norton & Company, 1999) convincingly illustrates the material (to use the term I use in developing my perspective in the present text, 'structural') geographical basis for cultural evolution with *Guns, Germs, and Steel*; R. Buckminster Fuller's *Critical Path*, (New York: St. Martin's Press, 1981) shows how, in State-ruled cultures, war is always the key technological basis for this evolution; and Jean Baudrillard builds much of his philosophy in *Simulacra and Simulation* (1981) and beyond (see Jean Baudrillard, translated by Sheila Faria Glaser, *Simulacra and Simulation*, (Ann Arbor, Michigan: The University of Michigan Press, 1994) and Jean Baudrillard, and Mark Poster (editor), *Selected Writings*, (Stanford, California: Stanford University Press, 1988)) on the brilliantly-put observation that human cultural systems can be viewed as entropic to an extent that parallels the quantity of information they produce; cf. *Simulation*, footnote on p. 86.

^v Richard Heinberg asserts *The Party's Over* (2005) and that we've reached *The End of Growth* (2011) (both published Gabriola Island, Canada: New Society Publishers); Dale Allen Pfeiffer frighteningly points out that advanced industrial agriculture is nothing so much as *Eating Fossil Fuels* (2006) (also Gabriola Island, Canada: New Society Publishers); and Vandana Shiva urges us to embrace *Soil, Not Oil* (2008)

(Brooklyn, New York: South End Press).

vi My philosophy on studying humanity is based mainly on my reading of Vico, as supported by Leon Pompa, *Vico: A Study of the New Science*, (Cambridge, United Kingdom: Cambridge University Press, 1990).

vii Jean Baudrillard, excerpt from *The System of Objects* (1968), in *Selected Writings*.

viii My understanding of 'systems', and most specifically on 'complex adaptive systems' in human historical contexts, is mainly influenced by Roy A. Rappaport, *Ritual and Religion in the Making of Humanity*, (Cambridge, United Kingdom: Cambridge University Press, 1999).

ix Heinberg's discussion of "climax ecosystems" in *Over*, pp. 16-21.

x Vico, *Science*, "Introduction".

xi Again, see Diamond's *Guns* as a whole for the relationship between geography and cultural evolution.

xii Baudrillard is right when he calls cultures "singularities", "Jean Baudrillard. Cultural Identity and Politics. 2002". http://www.youtube.com/watch?v=q3kgjjTE0dk, uploaded August 24, 2007 by egsvideo, http://www.egs.edu (accessed April 24, 2014).

xiii Deliberately a reference to Karl Polanyi, *The Great Transformation: The Political and Economic Origins of Our Time*, (Boston: Beacon Press, 2001).

xiv Diamond starts *Guns* at about 11,000 BCE, loc. 557, also cited below.

xv Charles Tilly, *Coercion, Capital, and European States, AD 990-1990*, (Oxford, United Kingdom: Basil Blackwell Ltd., 1990).

xvi William I. Robinson, "Social Theory and Globalization: The Rise of a Transnational State", *Theory and Society*, Vol. 30, no. 2 (Apr., 2001): 157-200.

xvii Thomas Schoonover, *Uncle Sam's War of 1898 and the Origins of Globalization*, (Lexington, Kentucky: University of Kentucky Press, 2003), makes the historical argument in favor of this dating most convincingly; see Martin Meredith, *Diamonds, Gold, and War: The British, the Boers, and the Making of South Africa*, (New York: PublicAffairs, 2007), for the basis behind my assertion that these two distinct event-clusters constitute, in a larger sense, one event-cluster-sequence, and in a much larger sense, one whole episode in the metanarrative of globalization.

xviii Robinson, p. 159, rightly says that there's a "centralization of command and control of the global economy in transnational capital", but fails to appreciate that precisely this is primarily a political and not primarily an economic centralization.

xix Franz Oppenheimer, translated by John M. Gitterman, *The State: Its History and Development Viewed Sociologically*, (Auburn, Alabama: Ludwig von Mises Institute, 2010; translation originally published New York: Vanguard Press, 1922), pp. 24-6, whose brilliantly simple distinction in this regard is followed, with minor contextual modification, throughout the present work.

xx L. Fletcher Prouty, *JFK: The CIA, Vietnam, and the Plot to Assassinate John F. Kennedy*, (New York: Skyhorse Publishing, 2009), final chapter, "Twenty-One – *Game Plan of the High Cabal*", especially in the last paragraph (on p. 345) where he says, "This is the way things are. Successful men plan ahead."

xxi For a mainstream popular account of a most striking manifestation of this phenomenon, see Thomas Frank, *What's the Matter with Kansas? How Conservatives Won the Heart of America*, (New York: Henry Holt and Company, 2005).

xxii Rappaport, "1 – Introduction".

xxiii Ibid., "3 – Self-Referential Messages", especially section "9. Ritual occurrence and the articulation of unlike systems".

xxiv Heinberg, *Over*, "1 – Energy, Nature and Society".

xxv William R. Catton, Jr. *Overshoot: The Ecological Basis of Revolutionary Change*, (Champaign, Illinois: University of Illinois Press, 1982).

xxvi Diamond, cf. loc. 1614; Richard A. Diehl, *The Olmecs: America's First Civilization*, (London: Thames & Hudson Ltd., 2004), pp. 11-2, also cited below; David Graeber, *Debt: The First 5,000 Years*, (Brooklyn, New York: Melville House Publishing, 2011), loc. 3895-908; J.H. Parry, *The Age of Reconnaissance: Discovery, Exploration and Settlement 1450 to 1650*, (Berkeley, California: University of California Press,

1981), "Chapter 1 – Attitudes and Motives", pp. 19-37.

xxvii Carroll Quigley, *The Evolution of Civilizations: An Introduction to Historical Analysis*, (Indianapolis: Liberty Press, 1979), p. 168, also cited below.

xxviii See David Stannard, *American Holocaust: Columbus and the Conquest of the New World*, (New York: Oxford University Press, 1992).

xxix Fuller calls this "ephemeralization", cf. p. 133; Virilio's entire oeuvre is based around this state-of-affairs, as encapsulated in *Speed and Politics: An Essay on Dromology*, (Los Angeles: Semiotext(e), 2006).

xxx Baudrillard's *Simulation* is a monument to the cultural effects of this political reality.

xxxi Uncomfortable with the "unscientific" (i.e., qualitative) implications of the term "civilizations", Joseph Tainter, in *The Collapse of Complex Societies*, (Cambridge, United Kingdom: Cambridge University Press, 1988), simply refers to all anthropologically-documented cultures as "complex societies". (p. 40) But all of what I call "civilizations" have nonetheless collapsed owing to scenarios described superbly by Tainter's theory.

xxxii Samuel Noah Kramer, *The Sumerians: Their History, Culture, and Character*, (Chicago: The University of Chicago Press, 1963), Kindle loc. 488; Hans J. Nissen, translated by Elizabeth Lutzeier and Kenneth J. Northcott, *The Early History of the Ancient Near East 9000-2000 B.C.* (Chicago: The Chicago University Press, 1988), p.14, pp. 196-7.

xxxiii White, *Form*, "1. The Value of Narrativity in the Representation of Reality"; Virilio makes a long essay formed around essentially this same metaphor with *War and Cinema: The Logistics of Perception*, (London: Verso, 1989).

xxxiv See Jean-Paul Sartre, *"What Is Literature?" and Other Essays*, (Cambridge, Massachusetts: Harvard University Press, 1988), pp. 80-103, for an excellent discussion about the changing relationship from historical period to historical period between writers and their respective establishments.

xxxv See Toby Wilkinson, *The Rise and Fall of Ancient Egypt*, (New York: Random House, 2010), on one of the original examples of this, as regards one of the earliest and most significant education-stratifiers in the history of civilizations – writing. Cf. loc. 926-38.

xxxvi Nicholas Humphrey, *The Mind Made Flesh: Essays From the Frontiers of Psychology and Evolution*, (New York: Oxford University Press, 2002), p. 1, referencing Arthur Conan Doyle's creation, Sherlock Holmes' famous quote that when you've "eliminated the impossible, whatever remains, *however improbable*, must be the truth".

xxxvii See Rappaport, "13 – Religion in Adaptation", on the primary significance of the existing order in limiting the possibilities for contemporaneous human imagination.

xxxviii Schoonover, loc. 617, especially as relates to the Panama Canal.

xxxix Fuller, cf. xx-xxiii.

xl Virilio, *Speed*, "Part 4: The State of Emergency".

xli Peter Dale Scott, *American War Machine: Deep Politics, the CIA Global Drug Connection, and the Road to Afghanistan*, (Lanham, Maryland: Rowman & Littlefield Publishers, Inc., 2010), "10 – Obama and Afghanistan", loc. 5362-89, 'The War Machine and the Drug-Corrupted Afghan War'.

xlii Richard Falk, *The Declining World Order: America's Imperial Geopolitics*, (New York: Routledge, 2004), pp. 5-12 on the Realist International Relations school.

xliii Baudrillard, *Simulation*, p. 173 in *Selected Writings*.

xliv Marjorie Cohn, and Kathleen Gilberd, *Rules of Disengagement: The Politics and Honor of Military Dissent*, (Sausalito, California: PoliPointPress, 2009), "One – Resisting Illegal Wars".

xlv Pierre Bourdieu, and Priscilla Parkhurst Ferguson (translator), *On Television*, (New York: The New Press, 1998), p. 45.

xlvi Tainter, p. 23, "…industrial societies may well contain overall more than 1,000,000 different kinds of social personalities (McGuire 1983: 115)".

xlvii Virilio, *Cinema*, p. 83: concerning the (at the time of writing, only just recently emerging) phenomenon of round-the-clock cable news, says "…this isn't really news footage any longer, but *the raw material of vision*, the most trustworthy kind possible".

[xlviii] Content and form in the sense meant by White; which from my perspective is also quite similar to Baudrillard's emphasis of "the medium" and "the message" – specifically in referencing McLuhan's assertion that "the medium is the message". Essentially, all of these are also the same thing, from different perspectives, as Vico's focus on "the true" being "precisely what is made", first stated in *On the Most Ancient Wisdom of the Italians*, also cited below. Every recorded human truth, because it's uniquely the product of a human being, also constitutes, in another aspect, a historical fact. Even the explicitly metaphysical has its inextricable empirical side.

[xlix] "Logistical" precisely in the sense meant by Virilio, *Cinema*; and concerning TV in this context, see pp. 56-8, the discussion of the variety-show style Reagan television extravaganza special, also known as 'Directive 75'.

[l] Baudrillard, *Simulation*, p. 170 in *Selected Writings*, on what he calls "fourth-order simulacra": "It bears no relation to any reality whatever: it is its own pure simulacrum."

[li] See two of Baudrillard's work from the early-to-mid-'80s, *In the Shadow of the Silent Majorities, or, The End of the Social and Other Essays,* (New York: Semiotext(e), 1983*)*, and *America* (London: Verso, 1988) – and then consider the states-of-affairs described as having evolved to one higher degree with the commercialization of the Internet, i.e., the planet's mass inextricability from the World Wide Web, as especially perpetuated with the ubiquitous spread of handheld computers.

[lii] White, *Form*, pp. 11-4, referencing Hegel.

[liii] This is made clear by John France, *The Crusades and the Expansion of Catholic Christendom, 1000-1714,* (New York: Routledge, 2005), cf. pp. 105-6.

[liv] Diehl, pp. 11-2.

[lv] Jonathan Mark Kenoyer, *Ancient Cities of the Indus Valley Civilization*, (New York: Oxford University Press, 1998)., pp. 39-45 on the geographical preconditions for civilizations, also referenced below.

[lvi] Quigley, *Civilizations*, "5 – Historical Change in Civilizations", cf. pp. 149-50.

[lvii] Carroll Quigley, *Tragedy & Hope: A History of the World in Our Time*, (San Pedro, California: GSG & Associates Publishers, 1998), pp. 83-6, relating these to Western civilization and Orthodox civilization, of which he thought the Soviet Union was the latest manifestation. In a way this was true, but in a larger sense, all other civilizations besides Western civilization officially died with the inception of the global civilization, insofar as globalization is a culture of such distinctly Western origins.

[lviii] See a similar chronological distinction also in Graeber, "Chapter Ten – The Middle Ages (600-1450 AD)"; and see Tamim Ansary, *Destiny Disrupted: A History of the World Through Islamic Eyes*, (New York: PublicAffairs, 2009), for a broad-sweeping popular history that views Muhammad's death as the symbolic birth of Arabic or Islamic civilization, cf. "3 – Birth of the Khalifate".

[lix] See the map on p. 1 in France, 'Three civilisations around a sea', which is also cited below, and which is indispensable to the perspective cultivated throughout Part 2 of the present text.

[lx] A similar element is very important in Quigley's theory of the "stages of growth" in *Civilizations*, wherein the "peripheral states" always end up as the most *Powerful* during the late stages of civilizations, cf. pp. 157-8.

[lxi] Paul Kennedy, *The Rise and Fall of the Great Powers*, (New York: Vintage Books, 1987), loc. 423.

[lxii] Rappaport, "2 – The ritual form", section "2. The logical entailments of the ritual form", loc. 543-59.

[lxiii] France repeatedly emphasizes this general theme of interdependence between monarchs and popes, cf. p. 100.

[lxiv] Tilly, pp. 152-60, 'Trajectories of Capitalized Coercion'; as discussed in Part 3 of the present text, Schoonover focuses centrally upon the notion of "social imperialism", cf. loc. 282, also cited below.

[lxv] Shiva, "Introduction – Triple Crisis, Triple Opportunity".

[lxvi] Tilly, pp. 11-5.

[lxvii] Rappaport, loc. 2609.

[lxviii] Baudrillard, *The Mirror of Production* (1973), p. 114 in *Selected Writings*.

[lxix] Dante Alighieri, and John Ciardi, *The Inferno*, (New York: Penguin Group, 1982), "Canto I – The Dark Wood of Error", pp. 27-33.

[lxx] See Dante Alighieri, translated by Aurelia Henry, *The Monarchy*, (Kindle edition, 2011; translation originally published 1904), loc. 781-93 where he states the purpose of the work.

[lxxi] R.W.B. Lewis, *Dante: A Life*, (New York: Penguin Books, 2001), "One – Dante the Florentine".

[lxxii] Graeber, loc. 4691-764.

[lxxiii] William Appleman Williams, *The Contours of American History*, (London: Verso, 2011), "*Introduction:* British Mercantilism as the Political Economy of English Backwardness".

[lxxiv] Sonesson, pp. 60-5 on indexicality, pp. 150-62 on iconicity, with both concepts discussed in relation to pictures; although, my usage of the terms indexical and iconic are really my own, as applied specifically to sociohistorical process.

[lxxv] Dante, *Inferno*, "Canto XI", pp. 103-9.

[lxxvi] Michael C. Ruppert, *Crossing the Rubicon: The Decline of the American Empire*, (Gabriola Island, Canada: New Society Publishers, 2004), pp. 558-9.

[lxxvii] See Kenneth S. Deffeyes, *When Oil Peaked*, (New York: Hill and Wang, 2010), "One – Bell-Shaped Curves"; and for a vigorously devastating piece of journalism analyzing the empirical condition of the state-of-affairs as it existed about ten years ago, see Ruppert, just cited.

[lxxviii] Heinberg, *Growth*, cf. "Introduction – The New Normal".

[lxxix] This is one of Robinson's central points.

[lxxx] W.R. Jones, "The Image of the Barbarian in Medieval Europe," *Comparative Studies in Society and History*, 13, no. 4 (1971): 381, which article I've used thanks to Francis Jennings, who cites it in *The Invasion of America*.

[lxxxi] Thomas Brown, and George Holmes (editor), *The Oxford Illustrated History of Medieval Europe*, (New York: Oxford University Press, 1988), chap. 1 "The Transformation of the Roman Mediterranean 400-900", p. 1.

[lxxxii] See, for instance, the excellent juxtaposition drawn between "Part I – Before Columbus" and "Part II – Pestilence and Genocide", in Stannard's *American Holocaust*.

[lxxxiii] Pfeiffer, "4 – Eating Fossil Fuels", especially loc. 314-56 on "food miles".

[lxxxiv] Diamond, cf. "Chapter 9 – Zebras, Unhappy Marriages, and the *Anna Karenina* Principle"; Stannard, "Chapter 4", cf. pp. 101-18.

[lxxxv] Richard A. Goldthwaite, *The Economy of Renaissance Florence*, (Baltimore: The Johns Hopkins University Press, 2009), "Chapter Two – The Shifting Geography of Commerce", cf. 'Northwestern Europe', loc. 2610-782.

[lxxxvi] Graeber, loc. 4456.

[lxxxvii] Ibid., loc. 3919.

[lxxxviii] Baudrillard, *Simulation*, p. 172 in *Selected Writings*, mentions something that parallels this, about how Disneyland is there to say "the adults are elsewhere", in turn referencing Foucault's assertion about prisons.

[lxxxix] See Lisa Marie Cacho, *Social Death: Racialized Rightlessness and the Criminalization of the Unprotected*, (New York: New York University Press, 2012), cf. pp. 3-8.

[xc] Pfeiffer.

[xci] Oppenheimer, "Chapter III – The Primitive Feudal State".

Part 2:

[xcii] Dante, *Inferno*. Why else would Hell be "geographically" structured like a late medieval Italian city-State and filled with Florentines and other Italians, with the sins worsening as one headed closer to the epicenter? Of course, this is the most natural thing for any writer to do – to structure the world one writes of just like the only world one is capable of referring to from first-hand experience.

[xciii] Goldthwaite, loc. 179, loc. 1315.

[xciv] Tilly, for instance on pp. 43-44. But the evolution of the national State as it has occurred through those centuries is one of the whole book's most important features.

[xcv] Ibid., p. 39-40, p. 45, for Europe's extreme geopolitical decentralization in the late medieval age, which only started to change around the end of the fifteenth century.

[xcvi] France, "1 – In the Beginning", and see extremely useful map of "Three Civilizations around a Sea" on p. 1.

[xcvii] Quigley, *Civilizations*, p. 168; the author, referencing, as he tells us, the early 20th-century historian James Henry Breasted, calls this zone the "Northwest Quadrant".

[xcviii] For instance, see France, p. 24, where, regarding the First Crusade, he says "it is now clear that Urban had Jerusalem in mind from the first". Although Jerusalem is of course located well inland, no invaders from the West could possibly conceive of coming to *Power* there without the naval footholds on the coast.

[xcix] This is a major theme in Abulafia, "Part Three – The Third Mediterranean, 600-1350", cf. pp. 241-6; and perhaps the major theme in France, where practically all the most important wars of the time can best be seen as possible combinations between all major groups on opposite sides of religious/cultural (and hence civilizational) divides.

[c] France, cf. pp. 18-21, where he first introduces the role of Byzantium in sparking the Crusade, and pp. 335-7, where he talks about the "New World" created, which in my view only emerged when it did on account of the fall of Byzantium. As the rest of the text attests, the Crusades in general were inextricably involved with the affairs of Byzantium, always at least in the all-important ideological sense.

[ci] Abulafia, p. 23.

[cii] Nissen, "Chapter Four – The Period of Early High Civilization (ca. 3200-2800 B.C.)", see especially p. 69, where he says that if there's any time that we can reasonably associate with the emergence of the Sumerians "with a high degree of probability", it's the beginning of this period he designates.

[ciii] Wilkinson, loc. 663; he puts forth 2950 B.C.E. as the date for the unification of Egypt (Upper and Lower).

[civ] Abulafia, pp. 73-9; pp. 89-94.

[cv] Ibid., pp. 22-6.

[cvi] Robert Drews, *The End of the Bronze Age: Changes in Warfare and the Catastrophe ca. 1200 B.C.*, (Princeton, New Jersey: Princeton University Press, 1993), "Chapter One – The Catastrophe and its Chronology".

[cvii] Goldthwaite, loc. 2746-82; Kennedy, "3 – Finance, Geography, and the Winning of Wars, 1660-1815".

[cviii] Goldthwaite, loc. 692-704.

[cix] Ibid., loc. 795.

[cx] I., loc. 802.

[cxi] I., loc. 2617.

[cxii] France, p. 204; Abulafia, "Part Three – The Third Mediterranean, 600-1350".

[cxiii] Kennedy, "1 – The Rise of the Western World".

[cxiv] France, pp. 97-104, although it's impossible to imagine the text as a whole without this idea; and see Fuller, pp. 67-71, on land States and sea States, where he also mentions the Crusades.

[cxv] Oppenheimer; Tilly.

[cxvi] Graeber, "Chapter Ten: The Middle Ages (600 AD to 1450 AD)".

[cxvii] Abulafia, pp. 252-7.

[cxviii] Fuller, pp. 32-7, on the importance of Arabic numerals and especially the concept of zero (cipher) transferring to the West from Indian civilization via Arabic civilization; Graeber, loc. 5845-57, also comments on the importance of the cipher, and adds to that double-entry book-keeping. See also Graeber, loc. 5311-5419 on the significance of the spread of medieval Indian banking practices to the West.

[cxix] Quigley doesn't explain the proper reason for it, in my opinion, but he nonetheless fairly accurately depicts the historical trajectory of the growth pattern, in both *The Evolution of Civilizations*, "5 – Historical Change in Civilizations", and *Tragedy and Hope*, pp. 3-12.

[cxx] France, p. 1, "Three Civilizations Around a Sea"; the part about the evolution of systematic destruction is based mainly on my reading of Tilly, *Coercion, Capital*, cf. especially "1 – Cities and States in World History", and most particularly 20-28, the section titled 'War Drives State Formation and Transformation'.

[cxxi] France, p. 253.

[cxxii] For my understanding of cultural complexity, I rely mainly on Tainter, *Collapse*, "2 – The nature of complex societies", which is so useful here precisely because, according to the purpose of the work, Tainter discusses it in the context of social collapse, most notably involving the collapse of what I define in the present text as civilization-State-complexes.

[cxxiii] With unique precision, Oppenheimer refers to this as "law of the agglomeration about existing nuclei of wealth" (p. 114).

[cxxiv] See Diamond for this term in relation to the very first example of such a process, as it would relate to the success of human settlement systems, concerning the first successful agricultural settlements, loc. 1861-73.

[cxxv] See Robinson for this phenomenon embodied in what he calls "the transnational state", which is much the same as what I call the global State, p. 161.

[cxxvi] Tilly, "3 – How War Made States, and Vice Versa".

[cxxvii] Goldthwaite, loc. 2596-608.

[cxxviii] Graeber, "Chapter Eleven: the Age of the Great Capitalist Empires (1450-1971 AD)"; Tilly, pp. 91-5.

[cxxix] Quigley, *Tragedy*, p. 324.

[cxxx] Arnold J. Toynbee, and D.C. Somervell, *A Study of History: Abridgement of Volumes I-VI*, (New York: Oxford University Press, 1974; originally published 1946), pp. 1-2.

[cxxxi] Goldthwaite, loc. 805, loc. 10033.

[cxxxii] Graeber, loc. 6511.

[cxxxiii] Goldthwaite, loc. 6734-982.

[cxxxiv] Ibid., loc. 5154-202.

[cxxxv] *I.*, loc. 5166.

[cxxxvi] *I.*, loc. 1442.

[cxxxvii] *I.*, loc. 1453.

[cxxxviii] *I.*, loc. 1478.

[cxxxix] *I.*, loc. 1429.

[cxl] Gregory Cochran, and Henry Harpending, *The 10,000 Year Explosion: How Civilization Accelerated Human Evolution*, (New York: Basic Books, 2010), point out that "Moderns showed up in Europe about 40,000 years ago…" (p. 25) and assert that "modern humans" may have been "able to *talk* the Neanderthals to death" (p. 26).

[cxli] White, "1 – The Value of Narrativity in the Representation of Reality".

[cxlii] Kramer, "Chapter Six – Education: The Sumerian School"; Quigley, *Civilizations*; Parry, *The Age of Reconnaissance*.

[cxliii] Vico, p. 63, 144.

[cxliv] See, for example, James Lovelock, *Gaia: A New Look at Life on Earth*, (New York: Oxford University Press, 1995).

[cxlv] This is Tainter's thesis; see "6 – Summary and Implications".

[cxlvi] William A. Green, "Periodizing World History," *History and Theory*, 34, no. 2 (May, 1995): p. 99. The differences all lie in the past couple of centuries or so, the span that the present text takes as its central focus. The last epoch-marker for Green is 1492, whereas this work has three periods that start in later centuries, and the most recent one – that of the existent world – starts in 1995.

[cxlvii] Cochran and Harpending, p. 31.

[cxlviii] Rappaport, referencing the renowned twentieth-century American anthropologist Leslie White, loc. 288.

[cxlix] See Diamond, "Chapter 5 – History's Haves and Have-Nots".

[cl] Diamond, loc. 1830-1901; Nissen, pp. 25-6.

[cli] Diamond, loc. 1745-80; Felipe Fernandez-Armesto, *Civilizations: Culture, Ambition, and the Transformation of Nature*, (New York: The Free Press, 2001), p. 175, quoting archaeologist Brian Fagan.

[clii] Diamond, loc. 1805-17.

[cliii] For instance see reference to the contemporary scholarly version of this theory in Anthony, loc. 2653-65.

[cliv] Nissen, pp. 39-42.

[clv] Ibid., pp. 18-21.

[clvi] See table in Diamond, loc. 1637-57; and see David W. Anthony, *The Horse, the Wheel, and Language: How Bronze-Age Riders from the Eurasian Steppes Shaped the Modern World*, (Princeton, New Jersey: Princeton University Press, 2007) on the groups that he argues were the original precursors to the Proto-Indo-Europeans, "Chapter Eight – First Farmers and Herders *The Pontic-Caspian Neolithic*".

[clvii] Kramer, loc. 461.

[clviii] Quigley, *Civilizations*, cf. p. 101.

[clix] Diamond, loc. 1879.

[clx] See Anthony, loc. 2675-87, on the immense significance of the original division between herders and farmers – especially for the precursors to the Proto-Indo-Europeans.

[clxi] Anthony, loc. 1524-36, on the first herders who left Anatolia around 6700-6500 BCE; and Nissen, pp. 42-3, on the first settlement systems.

[clxii] Nissen, pp. 36-7.

[clxiii] Oppenheimer, pp. 51-81, "(d) The Genesis of the State".

[clxiv] Oppenheimer, again see "(d) The Genesis of the State"; this general assumption also obtains in Tilly's work, and in Vico's as well; see "The Ideal Eternal History" in *The New Science*.

[clxv] Oppenheimer, pp. 58-61, he bases this idea primarily on the work of Ratzel; see also p. 33, "(c) People Preceding the State Herdsmen and Vikings", where he says that "Herdsmen…have developed a whole series of the elements of statehood…".

[clxvi] Kramer, loc. 1321-30; the same archetype shows up in another of the earliest civilizations, in the same intercivilizational zone, ancient Egypt – Wilkinson, loc. 712-85, "The imagery of early kingship was as enduring as it was violent."

[clxvii] Oppenheimer, pp. 42-5.

[clxviii] See Tilly, p. 68, for the case of modern and contemporary European and Euro-modeled States, where the more violence is concentrated in the State, the less physically violent the population as a whole tends to be. Of course, this is to say nothing of psychological violence.

[clxix] Oppenheimer, pp. 66-8.

[clxx] Quigley, *Civilizations*, pp. 211-3.

[clxxi] See Abulafia for this phenomenon in medieval Venice, pp. 250-6.

[clxxii] Nissen, p. 49.

[clxxiii] See Kenoyer for one possibility on the Eastern extremity, although at a much later date than we're concerned with here, p. 50 – Kenoyer's map has to do with the Indus Valley civilization in 2800 to 2600 B.C.E.. But the argument pursued here is that the most significant trade routes, the ones that constituted the intercivilizational structure, were the ones that were able to form over the longest time, so it's not as far out

of our range as one might at first think.

clxxiv Nissen, pp. 8-11.

clxxv Ibid., see p. 41, *Figure 11*, a very useful typological illustration of the different, increasingly complex levels of the earliest settlement systems.

clxxvi Tainter, pp. 26-8.

clxxvii Nissen, p. 55.

clxxviii Gwendolyn Leick, *Mesopotamia: The Invention of the City*, (New York: Penguin Books, 2001), loc. 922, outlines the Uruk period as spanning ca. 3800-3200 BCE; Kramer, loc. 571 says the Sumerians likely showed up sometime in the second half of the fourth millennium; which accords with Nissen, p. 69, also quoted above. The argument pursued in the present text assumes that the Sumerians represented the second phase of dominance in the southern Mesopotamian civilization, the first phase in which there was a full-blown intercivilizational structure, the latter emerging with the establishment of pharaonic Egypt.

clxxix Nissen, pp. 55-7.

clxxx Ibid., pp. 65-7.

clxxxi Based generally on my readings of the following authors cited in the present text: Leick; Kramer; Nissen; Anthony.

clxxxii Fredy Perlman, *Against His-story, Against Leviathan! an Essay*, (Detroit: Black and Red, 1983), p. 32, referencing Frederick Jackson Turner and Lewis Mumford in noting, "With the rise of the first Leviathan there is a virtual technological revolution in vessel production."

clxxxiii Kenoyer, pp. 39-45 on the major preconditions for the emergence of a civilization.

clxxxiv Virilio, p. 40, *Speed*, "...this political police schema, accepted until very recently by every ideology...".

clxxxv Oppenheimer, "Chapter I – Theories of the State"; but the whole work really must be understood from this perspective.

clxxxvi Ronald Syme, *The Roman Revolution*, (New York: Oxford University Press, 2002), p. 8.

clxxxvii Kramer, loc. 630-63.

clxxxviii Wilkinson, loc. 2919-31.

clxxxix Rappaport, loc. 309-26 on "the great inversion" that language, as an adaptive mechanism, represents.

cxc In *The New Science* this is one of Vico's "three principles of humanity" – and the one most significant to his thought – p. 97, 333; it's also central to Rappaport's text, and fittingly he was strongly inspired by Vico, cf. loc. 451-74.

cxci Rappaport, see "13. Religion in Adaptation", especially section "9. The Cybernetics of the Holy".

cxcii See again Tainter pp. 26-8, referenced above.

cxciii Rappaport, "...adaptive processes define (and bound) living systems", loc. 6032.

cxciv Ibid., loc. 620.

cxcv Rappaport, loc. 286-302; Anthony says (and reiterates) that Proto-Indo-European wasn't primarily an ethnic but a cultural category, significantly seeing such a category in terms of shared ritual and linguistic systems amongst social groups, cf. 6910.

cxcvi Rappaport, loc. 686.

cxcvii France, p. 24, on this phenomenon as it related to the 'Catholic core' during the Crusades.

cxcviii See Nissen, pp. 8-11, also cited above.

cxcix Leick, loc. 1078-181, citing Nissen, among others.

cc Kramer, who says that in Sumer there arose probably the very first "relatively high civilization", loc. 571, also wrote a book called *History Starts at Sumer*.

cci See Nissen, "One – Sources and Problems", on the potential (and often times the necessity) for using material sources even during periods where written sources are present.

ccii Tainter, p. 24.

cciii Obviously in homage to White's *Metahistory: The Historical Imagination in Nineteenth Century Europe*, (Baltimore: The Johns Hopkins University Press, 1975).

[cciv] Cochran and Harpending, p. 31, also cited above.

[ccv] Diamond begins *Guns* here – loc. 557, saying it's a good place for comparison of "historical developments on the different continents".

[ccvi] See Nissen, "Three – From Isolated Settlement to Town (ca. 6000-3200 BC)", through "Four – The Period of Early High Civilization (ca. 3200-2800 BC)".

[ccvii] Wilkinson, loc. 663.

[ccviii] Drews, p. 4.

[ccix] Ibid., p. 3.

[ccx] This is the main point addressed in Virilio, *War and Cinema*, which is subtitled *The Logistics of Perception*, and is in fact bluntly stated when Virilio says, "Cinema is war…", p. 39, citing Gustav Le Bon's assertion that "War touches not only the material life but also the thinking of nations".

[ccxi] For this perspective that sees metaphor in particular and tropes in general as the roots of all linguistic behavior, see Vico, pp. 129-32, which happens to be one of the main bases for White's *Metahistory*, cf. "Preface".

[ccxii] Stannard, "2".

[ccxiii] See Tilly, "2 – European Cities and States"; Kennedy, "The "European Miracle"", loc. 666-953.

[ccxiv] Nissen, pp. 18-24.

[ccxv] Ibid, pp. 6-7.

[ccxvi] Anthony, "Chapter Nine – Cows, Copper, and Chiefs", especially loc. 3061-112.

[ccxvii] Tainter, pp. 148-52.

[ccxviii] This is Diamond's main point in *Guns*, cf. "Prologue – Yali's Question".

[ccxix] James Mahoney, "Path Dependence in Historical Sociology," *Theory and Society*, 29, no. 4 (2000): 512.

[ccxx] Graeber, loc. 950-63.

[ccxxi] Anthony, loc. 473-85.

[ccxxii] Ibid., loc. 510.

[ccxxiii] *I.*, loc. 4955-99.

[ccxxiv] *I.*, "Chapter Five – Language and Place The Location of the Proto-Indo-European Homeland".

[ccxxv] *I.*, loc. 4115-41.

[ccxxvi] Oppenheimer, pp. 51-2.

[ccxxvii] Tilly, p. 14.

[ccxxviii] Ibid., pp. 132-3.

[ccxxix] Colin Wells, *Sailing from Byzantium: How a Lost Empire Shaped the World*, (New York: Bantam Dell, 2006), loc. 298-458; Mahmood Mamdani, *Good Muslim, Bad Muslim: America, the Cold War, and the Roots of Terror*, (New York: Doubleday, 2004), pp. 27-33.

[ccxxx] Vico, p. 64, 147 on "the nature of institutions"; see also Pompa, pp. 42-6.

[ccxxxi] Wells, loc. 515-88.

[ccxxxii] Tilly, cf. p. 128.

[ccxxxiii] France, loc. 246.

[ccxxxiv] Ibid., loc. 205.

[ccxxxv] *I.*, loc. 250.

[ccxxxvi] *I.*, loc. 144.

[ccxxxvii] All quotes in this paragraph from France, loc. 287.

[ccxxxviii] Ibid., loc. 225.

[ccxxxix] Fuller, p. 58.

[ccxl] Oppenheimer, "(d) The Primitive Feudal State of Higher Grade", pp. 105-19.

[ccxli] See Rappaport on the "performativeness" of rituals, loc. 1838-69.

[ccxlii] Heinberg, *Over*, pp. 29-30.

[ccxliii] Stannard, p. 268.

[ccxliv] Heinberg, *Over*, cf. p. 29.

[ccxlv] For instance, See Graeber, footnote 16 in "Chapter Twelve", loc. 10384, on how CIA uses the word "slavery" to refer to the relationship between undocumented workers in the U.S. and their employers.

[ccxlvi] Gore Vidal, *Dreaming War: Blood for Oil and the Cheney-Bush Junta*, (New York: Thunder's Mouth Press/Nation Books, 2002), pp. 157-8.

[ccxlvii] Douglas A. Blackmon, *Slavery by Another Name: The Re-Enslavement of Black Americans from the Civil War to World War Two*, (New York: Anchor Books, 2009), "Introduction *The Bricks We Stand On*".

[ccxlviii] Heinberg, *Over*, cf. p. 30, on "energy slaves".

[ccxlix] Vico, p. 63, 142.

[ccl] Polanyi, loc. 986-1189 on "*haute finance*".

[ccli] William W. Freckling, *The South vs. the South: How Anti-Confederate Southerners Shaped the Course of the Civil War*, (New York: Oxford University Press, 2001), loc. 540.

[cclii] Tilly, "3 – How War Made States, and Vice Versa".

[ccliii] Williams, pp. 107-8.

[ccliv] See Freckling, loc. 363-94.

[cclv] Ibid., see the map loc. 375.

[cclvi] Quigley, *Civilizations*, pp. 392-3.

[cclvii] Kevin Phillips, *The Cousins' Wars: Religion, Politics, and the Triumph of Anglo-America*, (New York: Basic Books, 1999), "1 – The Protestant Background of Anglo-American Expansion and the Cousins' Wars".

[cclviii] Quigley, *Tragedy*, pp. 44-6.

[cclix] Phillips, "Preface".

[cclx] Graeber, "Chapter Seven – Honor and Degradation *Or, On the Foundations of Contemporary Civilization*".

[cclxi] See Oppenheimer, loc. 925, and Vico, pp. 238-9, 636, on how nobles, in their earliest manifestations, take pride in being called "robbers".

[cclxii] Prouty, *JFK*, p. viii, quoting Leonard Lewin's highly controversial *Report from Iron Mountain on the Possibility and Desirability of Peace*.

[cclxiii] See David Graeber, ""Consumption"," *Current Anthropology*, 52, no. 4 (2011): 489-511, for an excellent essay questioning why "eating food" is the principle metaphor employed for labeling every single thing constituting what I would call "what contemporary humans do with their "disposable incomes"".

Part 3:

I

cclxiv Schoonover, loc. 235; Kennedy, Introduction.

cclxv Falk, p. 227; Robinson, pp. 158-59.

cclxvi See Schoonover, loc. 408.

cclxvii Georg Hegel, translated by J. Sibree, *Introduction to the Philosophy of History*, (Scotts Valley, California: IAP, 2009; translation originally published 1858), p. 40, also cited below.

cclxviii See Detlev J.K. Peukert, translated by Richard Deveson, *The Weimar Republic*, (New York: Hill and Wang, 1989). Peukert, in setting out to delimit the chronological range of Weimar, says that "To define a phenomenon is to specify its boundaries", p. 3.

cclxix See Russ Baker, *Family of Secrets: The Bush Dynasty, America's Invisible Government, and the Hidden History of the Last Fifty Years*, (New York: Bloomsbury Press, 2009), cf. p. 45.

cclxx See especially Sallust, translated by A.J. Woodman, *Catiline's War, The Jugurthine War, Histories*, (New York: Penguin Books, 2007), and specifically the first title, which is usually called, instead, *The Conspiracy of Catiline* (Naddeo, p. 25); for Roman historians' influence on all modern Western historians see Barbara Ann Naddeo, *Vico and Naples: The Urban Origins of Modern Social Theory*, (Ithaca, New York: Cornell University Press, 2011), especially "Chapter 2: Vico's Cosmopolitanism *Global Citizenship and Natural Law in Vico's Pedagogical Thought*", where the author points to Sallust as the main influence for one of Vico's earliest works; and for a full treatment of the influence generally, see Ernst Breisach, *Historiography: Ancient, Medieval, and Modern, Third Edition*, (Chicago: University of Chicago Press, 2007).

cclxxi Johnson, *Empire*; Scott, *American War Machine*, etc.; Michel Chossudovsky, *America's "War on Terrorism"*, (Pincourt, Canada: Center for Research on Globalization, 2005); Alfred W. McCoy, *The Politics of Heroin: CIA Complicity in the Global Drug Trade*, (Chicago: Lawrence Hill Books, 2003); Ruppert, *Rubicon*; Gary Webb, *Dark Alliance: The CIA, the Contras, and the Crack Cocaine Explosion*, (New York: Seven Stories Press, 1999).

cclxxii Tilly, p. 69.

cclxxiii Scott, *Machine*, cf. loc. 584-97.

cclxxiv See Henry Ford quote, for instance; in Graeber, loc. 7720.

cclxxv Thomas Pakenham, *The Scramble for Africa: White Man's Conquest of the Dark Continent from 1876 to 1912*, (New York: Avon Books, 1991), pp. 239-41.

cclxxvi Falk, pp. 2-6.

cclxxvii For an excellent popular narrative of colonial American history seen from the perspective of competing European Empires see Alan Taylor, *American Colonies: The Settling of North America*, (New York: Penguin Books, 2001).

cclxxviii Parry, pp. 19-22.

cclxxix See Vico, *New Science*, pp. 20-21; and White, *Form*, pp. 13-14.

cclxxx Ansary, pp. 1-3; Fuller, p. 71.

cclxxxi Colin Wells, *Sailing from Byzantium*, loc. 646.

cclxxxii Howard F. Stein, "The Indispensable Enemy and American-Soviet Relations," *Ethos*, 17, no. 4 (Dec., 1989): 480-503.

cclxxxiii See Sutton's *Western Technology and Soviet Economic Development* trilogy, and in particular the third volume, Antony C. Sutton, *Western Technology and Soviet Economic Development, 1945 to 1965*, (Stanford, California: Hoover Institution Press, 1973).

cclxxxiv Vladislav M. Zubok, *A Failed Empire: The Soviet Union in the Cold War from Stalin to Gorbachev*,

(Chapel Hill, North Carolina: The University of North Carolina Press, 2009), pp. 92-3.

[cclxxxv] F. William Engdahl, *A Century of War, Anglo-American Oil Politics and the New World Order*, (Concord, Massachusetts: Paul & Company Publishers Consortium, Inc., 1993), "Foreword".

[cclxxxvi] Prouty, *JFK*, p. 108.

[cclxxxvii] C. Wright Mills, *The Power Elite*, (New York: Oxford University Press, 2000; originally published 1956), pp. 4-8.

[cclxxxviii] Engdahl, *Gods of Money: Wall Street and the Death of the American Century*, (Wiesbaden, Germany: edition.engdahl, 2009), p. 202; see Gar Alperovitz, *The Decision to Use the Atomic Bomb*, (New York: Vintage Books, 1996), for the most widely-referenced scholarly contradiction to the officially-sanctioned history of Hiroshima and Nagasaki.

[cclxxxix] Engdahl, *Gods*, "Chapter Ten: Washington Drops the A-Bomb", pp. 197-209.

[ccxc] Matthew M. Aid, *The Secret Sentry: The Untold History of the National Security Agency*, (New York: Bloomsbury Press, 2009), "Prologue: The Origins of the American Cryptologic Effort Against Russia".

[ccxci] Tim Weiner, *Legacy of Ashes: The History of the CIA*, (New York: Anchor Books, 2008), p. 3, also cited below.

[ccxcii] For the basis of my J.P. Morgan comparison, see Sutton, *Wall Street and _____* trilogy; for the basis of my SS comparison, see in particular Antony C. Sutton, *Wall Street and the Rise of Hitler*, (San Pedro, California: GSG & Associates Publishers, 2002), especially "Chapter 7: Who Financed Adolf Hitler?", pp. 99-114.

[ccxciii] L. Fletcher Prouty, *The Secret Team: The CIA and Its Allies in Control of the United States and the World*, (New York: Skyhorse Publishing, 2011), p. 32.

[ccxciv] Scott's *Machine* is a masterful tracing of this evolution.

[ccxcv] Gregory Hooks, "The Rise of the Pentagon and U.S. State Building: The Defense Program as Industrial Policy," *The American Journal of Sociology*, 96, no. 2 (Sep., 1990): 358-404.

[ccxcvi] Engdahl, *Gods*, p. 4; also see footnote 4 on page 60.

[ccxcvii] Paul L. Atwood, *War and Empire: The American Way of Life*, (New York: Pluto Press, 2010), pp. 112-4.

[ccxcviii] Ibid., pp. 174-7; pp. 181-2.

[ccxcix] Prouty, *JFK*, p. 9; Chapter 3.

[ccc] Ibid, pp. xvi-xvii.

[ccci] Scott, *Machine*, loc. 332-46; loc. 723.

[cccii] Engdahl, *Gods*, 197.

[ccciii] Campbell Craig, *Glimmer of a New Leviathan: Total War in the Realism of Niebuhr, Morgenthau, and Waltz*, (New York: Columbia University Press, 2003), "Preface".

[ccciv] Prouty, *Team*, p. 1.

[cccv] Scott, *Machine*, loc. 747-61.

[cccvi] Weiner, p. 3; Prouty, *JFK*, p. 10.

[cccvii] Quigley, *Tragedy*, p. 919; Prouty, *Team*, pp. 121-2.

[cccviii] James H. Blount, *The American Occupation of the Philippines 1898-1912*, (New York: The Knickerbocker Press, 1912), "Preface".

[cccix] Quigley, 130-3, 136-7; for an outstanding (and exceptionally thorough) recently published narrative of the Rhodes-Milner milieu's role in sparking the Anglo-Boer war – and thereby, 20th-century South African history – see Meredith's *Diamonds, Gold, and War*.

[cccx] Schoonover, loc. 348-59, loc. 796-807.

[cccxi] Engdahl, *Gods*, pp. 34-8.

[cccxii] Polanyi, "Chapter One – The Hundred Years' Peace".

[cccxiii] Quigley, *Tragedy*, 68-9.

[cccxiv] Schoonover, "Chapter 4 – U.S. Domestic Developments and Social Imperialism 1850s to 1890s" as a whole; for the explicit definition, see loc. 1293.

cccxv Engdahl, *Century*, "Chapter One: The Three Pillars of the British Empire", especially pp. 8-12.

cccxvi Gabriel Kolko, *The Triumph of Conservatism: A Reinterpretation of American History, 1900-1916*, (New York: The Free Press, 1963), loc. 5034-43; Engdahl, *Gods*, pp. 40-1.

cccxvii Engdahl, *Gods*, pp. 35-7.

cccxviii Kolko, pp. 242-4, pp. 252-4.

cccxix Engdahl, *Gods*, pp. 53-4; for a concise day-by-day summary of the week leading up to the bill's passage, see Antony C. Sutton, *The Federal Reserve Conspiracy*, (San Diego: Dauphin Publications, 2014), "Chapter Nine: the Money Trust Cons Congress", pp. 61-75.

cccxx Atwood, pp. 115-6, p. 119.

cccxxi Engdahl, *Gods*, pp. 64-70.

cccxxii Meredith, p. 345, p. 392.

cccxxiii See Phillips, *The Cousins' Wars*.

cccxxiv Kennedy, "5 – The Coming of a Bipolar World and the Crisis of the "Middle Powers": Part One, 1885, 1918"; Tilly, "5 – Lineages of the National State".

cccxxv Quigley, *Tragedy*, p. 211.

cccxxvi Engdahl, *Century*, "Chapter Two – The Lines are Drawn: Germany and the Geopolitics of the Great War"; Quigley, p. 416, pp. 436-7

cccxxvii Engdahl, *Century*, pp. 45-7.

cccxxviii Quigley, *Tragedy,* pp. 466-75.

cccxxix Atwood, pp. 96-101.

cccxxx See Walter Lippmann, *Public Opinion*, (Kindle edition: Amazon Digital Services, Inc., 2012; originally published 1921).

cccxxxi Atwood, p. 110; Howard Zinn, *A People's History of the United States 1492-Present*, (New York: HarperCollins Publishers, 2003; originally published 1980), pp. 362-4.

cccxxxii Atwood, pp. 119-21; Zinn, pp. 366-71.

cccxxxiii See Zinn, "Chapter 13 – The Socialist Challenge".

cccxxxiv Based on Kolko, "Chapter Two – Competition and Decentralization: the Failure to Rationalize Industry".

cccxxxv Edward Bernays, *Propaganda*, (Brooklyn, New York: Ig Publishing, 2005; originally published 1928), pp. 83-4, pp. 90-4; Kolko, pp. 57-60.

cccxxxvi Kolko, pp. 26-30.

cccxxxvii Ibid., pp. 34-6.

cccxxxviii *I.*, p. 38.

cccxxxix *I.*, pp. 66-78.

cccxl Francis Neilson, *How Diplomats Make War*, (Auburn, Alabama: Ludwig Von Mises Institute, 2011; originally published New York: B.W. Huebsch, 1915), pp. 51-2; Sidney Bradshaw Fay, "New Light on the origins of the World War, I. Berlin and Vienna, to July 29," *The American Historical Review*, 25, no. 4 (July, 1920): 620-4.

cccxli Generally, see Lippmann and Bernays; and for a contemporaneous real-world example, see Meredith, p. 375.

cccxlii Matthew Frye Jacobson, "Imperial Amnesia: Teddy Roosevelt, the Philippines, and the Modern Art of Forgetting," *Radical History Review*, no. 73 (1999): p. 125; Kolko, "Chapter Eight – The Politics of 1912".

cccxliii Atwood, p. 105, pp. 107-9.

cccxliv See Ratzel, quoted in Virilio, "War is taking your frontiers to the enemy's territory", *Cinema*, p. 58.

cccxlv Polanyi, pp. 4-9.

cccxlvi See Parry p. 327, and also Pakenham, p. 689. Even those who are among the most useful conventional historians feel a compulsion to find some silver lining in imperialism – usually in the form of,

"Western imperialism is at least the very kindest form there is!"

[cccxlvii] Prouty, *JFK*, loc, 461-73.

[cccxlviii] Ibid., loc. 482.

[cccxlix] *I.*, loc. 473.

[cccl] *I.*, loc. 491.

[cccli] *I.*, loc. 951.

[ccclii] See Bernays, "Chapter One – Organizing Chaos", for a description of the gestating global hegemonic sector that runs along these lines.

[cccliii] Engdahl, *Gods*, "Chapter Eleven – Creating the Bretton Woods Dollar System".

[cccliv] Quigley, *Tragedy*, pp. 550-4.

[ccclv] See Falk for one view on the existent example of this phenomenon, "Chapter 12 – Will the Empire be Fascist?".

[ccclvi] See Rappaport for the basis underlying this (anthropological) view of religion.

[ccclvii] Falk, "Introduction" and "Chapter 11 – Human Rights and Civil Liberties".

[ccclviii] See Scott, *Machine*, for this highly accurate label; briefly explained loc. 300-312 and incorporated throughout the work.

[ccclix] See Baudrillard, *Simulation*; see *Majorities* p. 3, pp. 26-7, etc.. But besides these particular citations, I believe this notion of implosion is one of the most key points necessary for understanding Baudrillard's later works.

[ccclx] Sutton, *Wall Street* trilogy.

[ccclxi] Engdahl, *Gods*, pp. 218-22.

[ccclxii] Quigley, p. 310, pp. 324-5.

[ccclxiii] See Margaret MacMillan, *Paris 1919: Six Months that Changed the World*, (New York: Random House, 2003).

[ccclxiv] Quigley, p. 308.

[ccclxv] Engdahl, *Gods*, pp. 77-83, pp. 88-97; Antony C. Sutton, *Wall Street and the Bolshevik Revolution*, (Forest Row, United Kingdom: Clairview Books, 2013), "Chapter 11 – The Alliance of Bankers and Revolution", pp. 169-79.

[ccclxvi] For a similar view from a more emphatically structural perspective (rather than my own experiential one), see Pfeiffer, loc. 859-67, on Richard Duncan's "Olduvai Theory".

[ccclxvii] See H.C. Engelbrecht, and F.C. Hanighen, *Merchants of Death: A Study of the International Armament Industry*, (Auburn, Alabama: Ludwig von Mises Institute, 2011; originally published New York: Dodd, Mead and Company, 1934), especially "I. Consider the Armament Maker", and "XVII. Status Quo".

[ccclxviii] Ibid., loc. 225-38.

[ccclxix] Sutton, *Hitler*, cf. "Chapter Three – General Electric", especially pp. 39-42, 'A.E.G. Avoids the Bombs in World War II'.

[ccclxx] Alperovitz, cf. "Chapter Two – General Efforts to End the War".

[ccclxxi] For a philosophical approach to this problem, see the works of both Baudrillard and Virilio.

[ccclxxii] Quigley, *Tragedy*, p. 550.

[ccclxxiii] Sutton, *Hitler*, "Preface".

[ccclxxiv] See Peukert, pp. 21-3.

[ccclxxv] Engdahl, *Gods*, "Chapter Four – Morgan's Fed Finances a European War".

[ccclxxvi] For this entire paragraph thus far see Engdahl, *Century*, "Chapter One: The Three Pillars of the British Empire".

[ccclxxvii] Quigley, *Tragedy*, cf. pp. 532-3

[ccclxxviii] Atwood, cf. p. 177.

II

ccclxxix Kennedy, cf. loc. 8009-21; Scott (who references Kennedy here), *Machine*, loc. 4125-44; Chalmers Johnson, *Empire*, cf. p. 2; Scott also references Kevin Phillips in this regard (loc. 4144), and often cites a couple of his books that I haven't read – however, I've been greatly aided by another one of Phillips' books, *The Cousins' Wars*.

ccclxxx Tilly, pp. 45-54; but the theme runs all throughout the text.

ccclxxxi See Heinberg, *Over* and *Growth*; and Catton, *Overshoot* and *Bottleneck*.

ccclxxxii Peter Dale Scott, *The Road to 9/11: Wealth, Empire, and the Future of America*, (Berkeley, California: University of California Press, 2007), pp. 6-7.

ccclxxxiii See Stannard, *Holocaust*.

ccclxxxiv See Francis Jennings, *The Invasion of America: Indians, Colonialism, and the Cant of Conquest*, (Chapel Hill, North Carolina: The University of North Carolina Press, 1975), especially "Chapter 1 – Crusader Ideology – and an Alternative".

ccclxxxv Blackmon, "Introduction".

ccclxxxvi Quigley, *Tragedy*, p. 42.

ccclxxxvii France, pp. 332-3.

ccclxxxviii Ibid., "2 – The Papal Monarchy and the Invention of the Crusade".

ccclxxxix Vico, pp. 54-7, but also runs as a major theme throughout the text.

cccxc Prouty, *JFK*, pp. 2-3.

cccxci Goldthwaite, loc. 1087-99.

cccxcii Tilly, cf. p. 153, also cited below.

cccxciii Phillips, "4 – The British Empire and the Civil War in the Western Hemisphere, 1775-1783".

cccxciv Perlman, who made this the central focus of *Against His-story! Against Leviathan!*, cf. p. 74. He calls the land State a "worm" and the sea State an "octopus".

cccxcv See France, cf. pp. 103-5, and Abulafia, "Part Three: The Third Mediterranean, 600-1350", chapter "1. Mediterranean Troughs, 600-900", pp. 241-57.

cccxcvi See the works cited in the present text by Heinberg, Catton, and Pfeiffer.

cccxcvii Prouty, *Team*, p. 127, pp. 403-4.

cccxcviii "PSYWAR WWI + II", p. 4.

cccxcix Miller, pp. 13-5.

cd Engdahl, *Gods*, pp. 153-8.

cdi Lippmann, cf. pp. 7-10, the general idea runs all throughout the book; also, see document entitled "Psychological Warfare Research: A Long Range Program – Part One, Essential Background Information", produced under the auspices of the Human Resources Research Office, "operating under contract with" the U.S. Army, and finished in March 1953 (cover page, p. i), the month that Stalin died. See especially pp. 35-46, "Inventory of Modern Psychological Warfare Media and Techniques".

cdii Ron Chernow, book review for Larry Tye's *The Father of Spin: Edward L. Bernays and the Birth of Public Relations*, http://www.nytimes.com/books/98/08/16/reviews/980816.16chernot.html.

cdiii Bernays, p. 71.

cdiv Ibid..

cdv Engdahl, *Gods*, pp. 70-3.

cdvi "Psychological Strategy Board – Bibliography", document dated August 15, 1952.

cdvii "Preliminary/ U.S. Psychological Strategy".

cdviii See the works of Baudrillard starting with *Simulation* (1981).

cdix Scott, *Machine*, loc. 753-67.

[cdx] Well into the narrative told in "PSYWAR WWI + II", cited above, it becomes clear that it's being told from the perspective of OPC. For instance, the agency becomes the main topic of discussion in the last quarter or so of the document; on pp. 79-80, Frank Wisner's name is crossed out when it says who the author interviewed on certain of OPC's activities, and he was one of the main individuals involved in OPC; and consider the highly classified information that was redacted, cf. p. 67, p. 69, indicating the author's access to extremely sensitive material of contemporaneous significance. My assumption is that this is the perspective on the history of psychological warfare that OPC wanted transmitted to the PSB at large.

[cdxi] See this evolution, one essentially trending towards total privatization of operations, in Scott's *The Road to 9/11* and *American War Machine*.

[cdxii] Scott, *Machine*, loc. 358.

[cdxiii] Ruppert, pp. 22-6.

[cdxiv] Catton, *Overshoot*, p. 273.

[cdxv] See Graeber, "Henry Ford quote", loc. 7720.

[cdxvi] Prouty, *JFK*, p. xxviii.

[cdxvii] Prouty, *Team*, "Chapter 15: Logistics By Miracle".

[cdxviii] Seth Jacobs, *America's Miracle Man in Vietnam: Ngo Din Diem, Religion, Race, and U.S. Intervention in Southeast Asia, 1950-1957*, (Durham, North Carolina: Duke University Press, 2004), p. 20.

[cdxix] See MSP documents, etc.

[cdxx] See Tilly, "coercion *works*", p. 70.

[cdxxi] Oppenheimer, pp. 24-6, and all throughout the work.

[cdxxii] See Prouty, *Team* and *JFK*, especially the first chapter of each work.

[cdxxiii] Rappaport, loc. 3974-4157.

[cdxxiv] Oppenheimer, p. 14; also, the text is largely structured surrounding this idea.

[cdxxv] Rappaport, loc. 333-419.

[cdxxvi] See William K. Black, *The Best Way to Rob a Bank Is to Own One: How Corporate Executives and Politicians Looted the S&L Industry*, (Austin, Texas: University of Texas Press, 2005), "1. Theft By Deception: Control Fraud in the S&L Industry".

[cdxxvii] Fuller, LAWCAP ("lawyer capitalism"), cf. p. 114.

[cdxxviii] See Bernays; Lippmann.

[cdxxix] For this term, see, for example, Herbert Marcuse, *One-Dimensional Man: Studies in the Ideology of Advanced Industrial Society*, (New York: Routledge, 2007), cf. p. 21; and see Mills, *Elite*, for one of the earliest scholarly diagnoses of this phenomenon, if not yet the actual term.

[cdxxx] E.E. Agger, "The Federal Reserve System," *Political Science Quarterly*, 29, no. 2 (Jun., 1914): p. 266.

[cdxxxi] Oppenheimer, see online writings.

[cdxxxii] Virilio's *Cinema* constitutes an excellent example of *essaying* (attempting) a broad-sweeping description of this interconnection.

[cdxxxiii] Rappaport, loc. 6501-9.

[cdxxxiv] Baudrillard, *Simulation*, pp. 166-8, 174-7 in *Selected Writings*.

[cdxxxv] Charles Tilly, Peter Evans (editor), Dietrich Rueschemeyer (editor), and Theda Skocpol (editor), *Bringing the State Back In*, (Cambridge, United Kingdom: Cambridge University Press, 1985), "War Making and State Making as Organized Crime", pp. 169-86.

[cdxxxvi] See Albert Jay Nock, for example, *Our Enemy, the State*, (Auburn, Alabama: Ludwig von Mises Institute, 2010; originally published 1935) (loc. 1364, for instance), a work which was centrally influenced by Oppenheimer – thus providing a symptom of the explanation as to why social scholars on the "Left" in the U.S. never embraced Oppenheimer (Nock was considered a part of the "Old Right").

[cdxxxvii] See for instance Scott, in such works as *Deep Politics and the Death of JFK*, (Berkeley, California: University of California Press, 1996), *9/11*, and *Machine*; and McCoy, *Heroin*.

[cdxxxviii] Dante (skip for now).

cdxxxix See James H. Leuba, "On Three Types of Behavior: The Mechanical, the Coercitive (Magic) and the Anthropopathic (Including Religion)," *The American Journal of Psychology*, 20, no. 1 (1909): 107-119.

cdxl See Heinberg, *Over*, p. 1, pp. 95-118; for a work by a specialist devoted to the subject's current reality, see Kenneth Deffeyes, *When Oil Peaked*, and in particular for the present footnote, "One – Bell-Shaped Curves".

cdxli See Heinberg, *The End of Growth*; and Matthew R. Simmons, *Twilight in the Desert: The Coming Saudi Oil Shock and the World Economy*, (Hoboken, New Jersey: John Wiley and Sons, Inc., 2005), especially "6 – Oil Is not Just Another Commodity (A Primer on the Science of Producing Oil and Gas)".

cdxlii Engdahl, *Gods*, p. 351.

cdxliii Vico, p. 62, 134, "Things do not settle or endure out of their natural state."

cdxliv Rappaport, loc. 1014; also see Graeber and "baseline communism", loc. 1986.

cdxlv Friedrich Engels, and Karl Marx, *The Communist Manifesto*, (Kindle edition: Amazon Digital Services, Inc, 2006), of course, i.e. nobles vs. bourgeoisie (cf. loc. 30); but for more nuanced views see Vico, and for more contemporary, more nuanced views, see Quigley, *Tragedy*, and Fuller, *Path*. (See discussion below).

cdxlvi See Black, pp. 7-9.

cdxlvii Ibid., p. 5.

cdxlviii Cf. "Foreword" by Catherine Austin Fitts in Ruppert's *Rubicon* about her exposure of such looting, and on a massive scale, at HUD.

cdxlix *War Loans of the United States and the Third Liberty Loan*, (New York: Guaranty Trust Company, 1918), http://www.archive.org, cf. pp. 13-9 on history of U.S. debt escalation, major war by major war.

cdl Lippmann, p. 6.

cdli Quigley, 365-6.

cdlii Engdahl, *Gods*, "Chapter Five: Gold, Conflicting Goals and Rival Empires".

cdliii Prouty, *JFK*, pp. 5-7.

cdliv Prouty, *Team*, loc. 405.

cdlv Lippmann, p. 24.

cdlvi Ibid, p. 25.

cdlvii Ibid., p. 26.

cdlviii Ruppert, "Chapter 29: Biological Warfare".

cdlix Lippmann, p. 26.

cdlx Ibid., p. 27.

cdlxi Baker, pp. 492-3.

cdlxii Vico, "…philosophy undertakes to examine philology…", p. 6, 7; Pompa, "1 – The Structure of the 'Scienza Nuova'", especially pp. 3-5.

cdlxiii *La sociologie est un sport de combat*. Directed by Pierre Carles. France: C.P. Productions, V.F. Film Productions, 2001.

cdlxiv See Aimé Césaire, translated by Joan Pinkham, *Discourse on Colonialism*, (New York: Monthly Review Press, 2000), pp. 31-46, especially the comparisons between Nazism and its foremost historical predecessor – overseas colonization.

cdlxv Mamdani, pp. 95-100.

cdlxvi Baudrillard's simulacrum is a good start towards understanding this phenomenon, *Simulation*, here considering particularly his "four orders" of the simulacrum, p. 170 in *Selected Writings*.

cdlxvii See Quigley, *Tragedy*, pp. 38-62; and Fuller, pp. 114-6.

cdlxviii See quote by Dr. Peter Krogh on back cover of *T&H*.

cdlxix See Craig, *Glimmer*; and Naddeo, *Naples* for two diverse (both very notable) examples.

cdlxx Quigley, *Tragedy*, p. 865.

cdlxxi See back cover of *Critical Path*.

[cdlxxii] Baudrillard, *In the Shadow of the Silent Majorities*, p. 19.

[cdlxxiii] Ibid., pp. 20-1.

[cdlxxiv] Ibid., p. 22.

[cdlxxv] Heinberg, *Over*, p. 42.

[cdlxxvi] Simmons, p. 48.

[cdlxxvii] Robinson, 170-3.

[cdlxxviii] Cohn and Gilberd, pp. 2-3.

[cdlxxix] See U.S. planning documents.

[cdlxxx] See Lippmann's *Public Opinion*, for example, which is all about the "necessity" of maintaining peoples' mental frontiers: their cultural preconceptions – what he explicitly calls "stereotypes", cf. especially pp. 40-9.

[cdlxxxi] Kolko, "Chapter One – Monopolies and Mergers: Predictions and Promises".

[cdlxxxii] Including individuals as different from each other as Fuller (*Critical Path*), Prouty (*The Secret Team*), and Virilio (*Speed and Politics* and *War and Cinema* both give this central emphasis).

[cdlxxxiii] Fuller, p. 190.

[cdlxxxiv] Ibid., xvii-xviii.

[cdlxxxv] See Part 2 of the present text.

[cdlxxxvi] Nissen, pp. 58-60.

[cdlxxxvii] Ibid., p. 61, p. 73.

[cdlxxxviii] Baudrillard, excerpt from *Fatal Strategies* in *Selected Writings*, pp. 185-92; and of course this is the main idea behind all Virilio's work.

[cdlxxxix] Quigley, *Tragedy*, p. 550.

[cdxc] Ibid., p. 535, p. 547.

[cdxci] Bernays, p. 71.

[cdxcii] Mamdani, *Saviors and Survivors: Darfur, Politics, and the War on Terror*, (New York: Random House, 2009), p. 3.

[cdxciii] McCoy, pp. 166-8.

[cdxciv] Scott, *Machine*, loc. 348.

[cdxcv] Again, see Lippmann about the "necessity" of stereotypes, pp. 40-9.

[cdxcvi] McCoy, pp. 14-7.

[cdxcvii] Ibid., pp. 528-9.

[cdxcviii] Webb, *Dark Alliance*. This is the central argument of the text.

[cdxcix] Webb, p. 485; Baker, pp. 492-4.

[d] Note the ultimate conclusions reached in "9 – The CIA's Covert Wars", in the latest edition of McCoy's text, which after the first edition was, to fit the revised editions' more globally universal concerns, appropriately given the more general title of *The Politics of Heroin: CIA Complicity in the Global Drug Trade*. By the way: aside from this one detail the chapter is an essentially flawless example of historical writing. This is how big a difference a single detail can make, even in what are overall the most noteworthy contributions.

[di] "Preliminary Estimate", pp. 4-5.

[dii] Prouty, *Team*, "Chapter 13 – Communications: the Web of the World". This is also a major theme in the actual historical examples narrativized in *JFK*, with the secret influences at the highest levels of *Power* always staying at the forefront of the flow-of-events by forever ensuring their collective role as gatekeeper of information.

[diii] "Preliminary Estimate", pp. 5-6.

[div] George Orwell, *1984*, (New York: Penguin Books, 1977; originally published 1949), p. 4, p. 16. p. 27, etc..

[dv] Kennedy's *Great Powers* offers an excellent introduction to what are the empirical examples of Great

Powers in "1 – The Rise of the Western World".

[dvi] McCoy, "Introduction: A History of Heroin".

[dvii] Ibid., pp. 77-84.

[dviii] H.V. Bowen, *The Business of Empire: The East India Company and Imperial Britain, 1756-1833*, (Cambridge, United Kingdom: Cambridge University Press, 2006), pp. 22-9.

[dix] McCoy, pp. 127-46; and see mention of Nixon's characteristically colorful take on the ever-expanding U.S. illicit drug market, in the discussion of the Nixon administration's role in creating the Drug Enforcement Agency (DEA), pp. 391-9.

[dx] See Tilly's invaluable discussion of the changes in Western governments first associated with the French Revolution, pp. 107-26.

[dxi] See Vico, cf. p. 62, 132, "Legislation considers man as he is in order to put him to good uses in human society."

[dxii] Oppenheimer, pp. 229-35.

[dxiii] Tilly; for his own concise summary cf. especially *Coercion*, pp. 14-5.

[dxiv] Schoonover, loc. 1441-52, "exporting the unemployment".

[dxv] Vico, pp. 93-4, 321, 322.

[dxvi] Anthony, cf. especially "Chapter Seven – How to Reconstruct a Dead Culture", and also loc. 5855. This is perhaps the most general underlying theory tested (and in my view largely proven) in the work (*The Horse, the Wheel, and Language*) as a whole – that we can reconstruct the history of a chronologically-geographically situated population insofar as individuals in that population perceive themselves, to some extent, as *a* culture – even if that's not the exact term they use. I believe this is the essential basis for what I call humanity's lived metanarrative.

[dxvii] Vico; I consider this to be one of the key ideas behind the "theory of the times", see p. 167 below.

[dxviii] See Lippmann, p. 7; and of course this idea is indispensable in Baudrillard's work.

[dxix] Giambattista Vico, translated by L.M. Palmer, *On the Most Ancient Wisdom of the Italians: Unearthed from the Origins of the Latin Language*, (Ithaca, New York: Cornell University Press, 1988; originally published 1710), p. 46 – "The true is precisely what is made."

[dxx] Hegel, *Introduction*, p. 40, "The State is the Divine Idea as it exists on Earth."

[dxxi] See *Wall Street and the Bolshevik Revolution*, and for the Quigley influence see for instance beginning of *Wall Street and the Rise of Hitler*.

[dxxii] Quigley, *Tragedy*, p. 938.

[dxxiii] Sutton's *Soviet* technology series.

[dxxiv] Quigley, *Civilizations*, p. 161; Vico, p. 425, 1108.

[dxxv] Ibn Khaldun, and N.J. Dawood (editor), translated by Franz Rosenthal, *The Muqaddimah: An Introduction to History*, (Princeton, New Jersey: Princeton University Press, 2005), translation originally published 1958).

[dxxvi] See Bergin and Fisch in the introduction to their translation of *The Autobiography of Giambattista Vico*, (Ithaca, New York: Cornell University Press, 1963; translation originally published 1944), pp. 104-5.

[dxxvii] Vico; this is perhaps the most significant idea animating *The New Science*, 3rd ed.. Cf. especially his explicit statements of the "theory of times", first on p. 20, 31; see also Pompa, pp. 45-9; and for the similar views of a contemporary student of Vico, see White, *Form*, pp. 3-14.

[dxxviii] Vico, *Science*, cf. pp. 20-5.

[dxxix] For example, see Marx and Engels, *The Communist Manifesto*, part "III. Socialist and Communist Literature", where the authors discuss how the older classes such as the aristocrats and petty bourgeoisie have aligned themselves with various strands of socialist thought.

[dxxx] Baudrillard, *Majorities*, p. 10.

[dxxxi] Sutton, *Federal Reserve*, pp. 41-3; interestingly, see also Virilio, *Speed*, p. 66.

[dxxxii] Scott, *9/11*, p. 35-6.

[dxxxiii] Sutton, *Federal Reserve*, p. 33.

[dxxxiv] Bernays, "Chapter IV – The Psychology of Public Relations".

[dxxxv] Syme, p. 7; the entire text is a tribute to this sentiment.

[dxxxvi] Interestingly, see Bergin and Fisch for this same categorization in the same section ("F. In the Marxist Tradition") of the introduction to *Autobiography*, pp. 104-7.

[dxxxvii] Vico, p. 61, 125, 126.

[dxxxviii] Marx and Engels, loc. 308-17.

[dxxxix] Ibid., loc. 297-308.

[dxl] Sutton, *Bolshevik*, "Chapter 1 – The Actors on the Revolutionary Stage".

[dxli] See Stein, "Indispensable Enemy".

[dxlii] See Prouty, *JFK*, pp. 4-6.

[dxliii] Baudrillard was centrally focused on this point early in his career, especially in *For a Critique of the Political Economy of the Sign* (1972), *The Mirror of Production* (1973), and *Symbolic Exchange and Death* (1976). It never went away; he just went beyond it in later works.

[dxliv] Tilly, cf. p. 153.

[dxlv] Oppenheimer, pp. 25-6.

[dxlvi] Ibid., pp. 18-9.

[dxlvii] *I.*, p. 15.

[dxlviii] *I.*, pp. 16-8.

[dxlix] I. (?)

[dl] Prouty, *Team*, pp. 381-3.

[dli] Prouty, *Team*, pp. 379-80; Ardant du Picq, translated by John N. Greely, and Robert C. Cotton, *Battle Studies*, (Kindle edition: Amazon Digital Services, Inc., 2012; translation originally published 1921), loc. 626-36.

[dlii] See Nafeez Mossadeq Ahmed, *The War on Freedom: How and Why America Was Attacked, September 11th, 2001*, (Joshua Tree, California: Tree of Life Publications, 2002).

[dliii] Robinson, pp. 159-60.

[dliv] Ibid., p. 158.

[dlv] Oppenheimer, pp. 1-4.

[dlvi] Ibid., pp. 13-6.

[dlvii] *I.*, "Chapter II – The Genesis of the State". This indispensable distinction runs through the entire text.

[dlviii] Vico, see for instance pp. 53-6, where he begins the detailed introduction of his well-known theory on the origins of Rome, in which the plebs, at first, weren't at all like citizens, but were much closer to slaves.

[dlix] Marx and Engels, loc. 201, loc. 302.

[dlx] Prouty, *JFK*, pp. 7-9.

[dlxi] *Network*. Directed by Sidney Lumet, screenplay by Paddy Chayefsky. USA: MGM, United Artists, 1976.

[dlxii] Falk, pp. 232-6.

[dlxiii] Robinson, pp. 179-80.

[dlxiv] Engdahl, *Century*, 56-8.

[dlxv] Beatrice Heuser, *The Evolution of Strategy: Thinking War from Antiquity to the Present*, (Cambridge, United Kingdom: Cambridge University Press, 2010), p. 76.

[dlxvi] Sutton, *Bolshevik*, "Chapter XI – The Alliance of Bankers and Revolution".

[dlxvii] Antony C. Sutton, *America's Secret Establishment: An Introduction to the Order of Skull & Bones*, (Walterville, Oregon: Trine Day, 2002).

[dlxviii] Quigley, *Tragedy*, p. 938.

[dlxix] Baker, p. 339.

[dlxx] See Russ Baker's excellent book.

[dlxxi] Prouty, *JFK*, pp. 161-2.

[dlxxii] See Vico, (?).

[dlxxiii] Black, p. 48, "For a Ponzi, growth is life."

[dlxxiv] Falk, p. 2, p. 32.

[dlxxv] Black, pp. xiv-xvi, p. 16.

[dlxxvi] duPicq, loc. 546-87.

[dlxxvii] Graeber, loc. 4739-64.

[dlxxviii] Vico, pp. 16-8; also see p. 161, p. 163, where Vico theorizes that the emblems on coins directly derived from military ensigns.

[dlxxix] Goldthwaite, loc. 1762, "*primo ministro*".

[dlxxx] Toynbee, *History*.

[dlxxxi] Scott, *Machine*, loc. 487-508; also see his book of that title, which I haven't yet read.

Made in the USA
San Bernardino, CA
24 October 2017